The Age of Fragmentation

The field of economics has proliferated in complexity and importance since the Second World War. Alessandro Roncaglia recounts the history of the different approaches (marginalist, neoclassical, Keynesian, Austrian, monetarism, rational expectations, institutionalist, evolutionary, classical-Sraffian) and the different fields (micro, macro, money and finance, industrial and game theory, institutions, public finance, econometrics), illustrating the thought and personality of the most important contemporary economists (from Hayek to Sraffa, from Modigliani and Samuelson to Friedman, from Simon to Sen, and many others), focusing on the conceptual foundations of the different streams. At the same time he appraises critically the important debates and controversies in the field and concludes by discussing possible future directions for economic thought. This follow-up to *The Wealth of Ideas: A History of Economic Thought* is a readable introduction to the contemporary economics discourse, accessible to economics students and informed general readers, and an important complement for advanced students and economists active in specialized fields.

ALESSANDRO RONCAGLIA is Emeritus Professor of Economics at the Sapienza University of Rome, member of the Accademia Nazionale dei Lincei (since 2018 in its Presidency Council) and former President of the Italian Economists Society. His book *The Wealth of Ideas* (Cambridge, 2005) received the Blanqui Prize of the European Society for the History of Economic Thought. He also won the Guggenheim Prize in the History of Economic Thought for 2019.

The Age of Fragmentation

A History of Contemporary Economic Thought

Alessandro Roncaglia
Sapienza University of Rome

CAMBRIDGE
UNIVERSITY PRESS

University Printing House, Cambridge CB2 8BS, United Kingdom

One Liberty Plaza, 20th Floor, New York, NY 10006, USA

477 Williamstown Road, Port Melbourne, VIC 3207, Australia

314–321, 3rd Floor, Plot 3, Splendor Forum, Jasola District Centre, New Delhi – 110025, India

79 Anson Road, #06–04/06, Singapore 079906

Cambridge University Press is part of the University of Cambridge.

It furthers the University's mission by disseminating knowledge in the pursuit of education, learning, and research at the highest international levels of excellence.

www.cambridge.org
Information on this title: www.cambridge.org/9781108478441
DOI: 10.1017/9781108777766

English translation © Alessandro Roncaglia 2019

First published in English by Cambridge University Press 2019 as *The Age of Fragmentation: A History of Contemporary Economic Thought*
Originally published in Italian as *L'età della disgregazione. Storia del pensiero economico contemporaneo* by Editori Laterza © Gius. Laterza & Figli 2019

Printed in the United Kingdom by TJ International Ltd. Padstow Cornwall

A catalogue record for this publication is available from the British Library.

ISBN 978-1-108-47844-1 Hardback
ISBN 978-1-108-74581-9 Paperback

Contents

Acknowledgements   *page* ix

1   Introduction: A Non-linear Discourse   1

Part I   The Background   11

2   The Foundations: Classicals and Marginalists   13
    2.1 Introduction   13
    2.2 The Classical Approach   14
    2.3 Self-Interest and Felicific Calculus: Smith versus Bentham   21
    2.4 Karl Marx   22
    2.5 The Marginalist Approach   24

3   The Immediate Precursors   31
    3.1 Introduction   31
    3.2 Wicksell and the Swedish School   32
    3.3 Veblen and Institutionalism   35
    3.4 Weber: The Method, between Theory and History   37
    3.5 Schumpeter: From Statics to Dynamics   41
    3.6 Keynes on Probability and Uncertainty   48
    3.7 Keynes on Finance and Employment   52

Part II   The Giants of the Short Century   57

4   The Founder of Neo-liberalism: Friedrich von Hayek   59
    4.1 A General Portrait   59
    4.2 The Formative Years and Career   63
    4.3 Theory of the Trade Cycle and Theory of Capital   66
    4.4 Theory of Capital and the Debate with Kaldor   71
    4.5 Spontaneous Order and the Market as a Mechanism of Knowledge
        Diffusion   76
    4.6 Methodological Individualism, Political Individualism and
        Economic and Political Liberalism   78
    4.7 The Denationalization of Money   83

5   The Revolutionary: Piero Sraffa   88
    5.1 Early Contributions: Money and Banking   88

5.2 Friendship with Gramsci   91
5.3 Criticism of Marshallian Theory   93
5.4 Imperfect Competition and the Critique of the Representative Firm   95
5.5 Cambridge: Wittgenstein and Keynes   97
5.6 The Critical Edition of Ricardo's Writings   100
5.7 Production of Commodities by Means of Commodities   102
5.8 Critique of the Marginalist Approach   106
    Appendix   108

Part III   The Disgregation of the Mainstream   111

6   The New Microeconomics: General Equilibrium
     and Expected Utilities, Theory of Industrial Organization   113
     6.1 From One Shore of the Atlantic to the Other   113
     6.2 The New Foundations: Expected Utility Theory   115
     6.3 The Traditional Foundations: Walrasian General Equilibrium   119
     6.4 Samuelson's Marshallian–Walrasian Synthesis   126
     6.5 The Marshallian Microeconomics of the Chicago School:
         The Imperialism of Economics   129
     6.6 The New Theories of the Firm   133
     6.7 Game Theory and Industrial Organization Theory   139
     6.8 Other Micro-applications   144

7   The Macroeconomics of the Neoclassical Synthesis   146
     7.1 Macroeconomic Theory after Keynes   146
     7.2 The Neoclassical Synthesis   147
     7.3 The Phillips Curve   155
     7.4 Marshallian Varieties of the Neoclassical Synthesis   157
     7.5 Growth Theory   159
     7.6 Theories of Economic Development   164
         Appendix   171

8   The Myth of the Invisible Hand: Neo-liberal Streams   177
     8.1 The Origins of the Invisible Hand   177
     8.2 Ordoliberalism: From Eucken and Röpke to Merkel   181
     8.3 From the 'Old' to the 'New' Austrian School   186
     8.4 Hicks's Austrian Theory   192
     8.5 Friedman and the Chicago School   196
     8.6 Rational Expectations and Supply-Side Economics   203
     8.7 Public Choice   208
     8.8 Mont Pèlerin Society and the Web of Think Tanks   212
     8.9 The Washington Consensus and Expansionary Austerity   215

9   Applied Economics and Econometrics   218
     9.1 Theoretical Backgrounds of Applied Economics   218
     9.2 Input–Output Tables   220
     9.3 National Accounting   222
     9.4 The Naissance of Econometrics   226
     9.5 The Developments of Econometrics   228

Contents

9.6 The New Descriptive Statistics: The Search for Indicators 230
9.7 Market Regulation, Market Creation and Auctions 233
9.8 Between Theory and Applied Economics: The Economics
of Energy Sources 238
9.9 The Environment and the Economy 241

Part IV The Weakening of the Paradigm 245

10 Behavioural Economics and Bounded Rationality 247

10.1 Rejecting the Notion of *Homo Oeconomicus* 247
10.2 Rationality and Behavioural Paradoxes: Behavioural Economics 250
10.3 Experimental Economics 252
10.4 Herbert Simon 257
10.5 Kahneman and Tversky's Prospect Theory 260

11 From Efficient Financial Markets to the Theory of Crises 265

11.1 Introduction 265
11.2 Monetarism 266
11.3 Economic Policy: From Keynesianism to Monetarism 269
11.4 The Theory of Efficient Financial Markets: From
Modigliani–Miller to Fama 273
11.5 Financial Markets and Institutions 277
11.6 The Keynesian Theory of Financial Markets: Hyman Minsky 279
11.7 Money Manager Capitalism 283

Part V Is a New Paradigm Possible? 287

12 Post-Keynesian Macroeconomics 289

12.1 The Cambridge Tradition 289
12.2 The New Cambridge School 292
12.3 Michał Kalecki 294
12.4 Nicholas Kaldor 296
12.5 The Debate on Interpretation of Keynes 298
12.6 The Debate on the Theory of Capital and Critique of the
Marginalist Theory of Value 303
12.7 The Cambridge Theory of Distribution 308
12.8 The Sraffian Schools 310
12.9 Towards a Keynesian–Sraffian Synthesis? 316

13 Marxism, Evolutionism, Institutionalism 319

13.1 Introduction 319
13.2 Criticism of the Labour Theory of Value and Developments
in Marxism 321
13.3 Analyses of Change in the Economic and Social Structure:
Polanyi and Galbraith 326
13.4 Neo-institutionalism 331
13.5 Evolutionism and Institutionalism 335
13.6 Evolutionism, Institutionalism and Analysis
of Technical Change 340

13.7 Development Economics and Interactions with Cultural Evolution   343
13.8 Competition among Institutions   345

14 Ethics and the Problem of Power   **349**

14.1 Introduction   349
14.2 Utilitarianism and the Ethics of Consequences   352
14.3 Income Inequalities as an Ethical Issue   360
14.4 Welfare Economics   363
14.5 Equality of What? The Capabilities   367
14.6 Conservation, Revolution or Reforms   371
14.7 The Economists' Ethics   374

References   377
Index   419

Acknowledgements

In writing this book, I have been greatly helped by my experience, since 1979, as editorial collaborator, assistant editor, editor and finally director with legal responsibility for the journals *Moneta e Credito* and *BNL Quarterly Review* (since 2008, *PSL Quarterly Review*), in part but not only thanks to the work connected to the series of articles of 'Recollections of eminent economists'. Similarly, I have been greatly helped by my teaching activity, from 1973 to 2017, giving courses in introductory economics, macroeconomics, microeconomics, economic policy, international economics, monetary economics, growth economics, applied economics, development economics, history of economic thought, economic philosophies, economics of energy sources and crisis economics: you might say a bit of everything, as a general economist, following a tradition that many might consider obsolete, perhaps with reason, but which enriched my work, driving me to consider new issues and different viewpoints. Thus in writing this book I have been able to make use of my previous writings, from which I have drawn material, in particular from the final chapters of *The wealth of ideas* (2005) and the *Brief history of economic thought* (2017).

Thanks are due to Matteo Caravani, Marcella Corsi, Franco Donzelli, Giulio Guarini, Cristina Marcuzzo, Aldo Montesano, Pietro Rossi, and especially to Carlo D'Ippoliti and Mario Tonveronachi, for their most useful comments on previous drafts of this work; to Phil Good and Tom Ferguson for their encouragement and to the Institute for New Economic Thinking for financial support in preparing the English edition; to Graham Sells (Chapters 1–5 and 11–14) and Julia Hartviksen (Chapters 6–10) for revising my very poor English style; to Theresa Kornak for her careful editing; to Jim Diggins for a thorough indexing of the book and to Jayaval Radhakrishnan at Integra for coordinating the production process. My thanks are also due to my brother Gino, for his tranquil confidence in maintaining from the outset that I would be able to complete this book, and to Cristina for her unfailing support.

Finally, being well aware of the limits implicit in this attempt, I would like to thank in advance all the readers who will let me have their comments, criticisms and suggestions.

1 Introduction: A Non-linear Discourse

The idea of writing this book was dismissed as crazy by many of my friends. The book is here, now, but they may still be right, given the breadth and complexity of our field of enquiry: contemporary economic research, from the Second World War to the present. Consider the mass of economic journals (some thousands) and books (ditto) published yearly; consider the fact that economists active in the period under consideration by far outnumber the authors of economic writings of all the previous periods. Thus, although there are on average a thousand pages read behind every single page of this book, my ignorance remains pervasive and the account of each area of research will be scanty and simplified.

However, confronted with the fragmentation characterizing economic research today, in order to evaluate the present state of our science it may be useful to reconstruct its lines of development, inquiring into their interrelations and the underlying philosophies, or worldviews. My hope is that this will help explain why contrasting views abound in theoretical research. As Joseph Schumpeter (1954, p. 4) maintains, studying the (in our case, recent) history of economic thought may be useful to 'prevent a sense of lacking direction and meaning from spreading'.

The task is clearly a very difficult one, and we cannot expect it to lead to a univocal solution. 'There are more things in heaven and earth, Horatio, than in your philosophy': Hamlet's lesson holds in many research fields, including the economists' search to understand the functioning of human societies. It also holds for the search to reconstruct the history of any field of human culture, including the history of economic thought. Indeed, in this case it holds perhaps even more than for other fields, owing both to the intersections between worldviews, analytical developments and political passions, and to the continuous evolution in the economic and social structure of human societies.

As we shall see, the very definition of economics may take on different connotations;[1] above all, we are confronted with a multiplicity of worldviews logically preceding the multiplicity of theories. The different worldviews affect both the selection of the specific problems to be dealt with and the framing of the analysis. It is one thing is to study the evolution of technology, but quite another to consider the motivations behind human actions. It is one thing is to conceive economic theory as the way in which humans tackle the problem of scarcity, but again quite another to look at the set of economic relations from the point of view of the division of labour within a circular flow of production, distribution and consumption. In reconstructing the history of economic thought, different approaches (classical, marginalist, Keynesian and so on) inter-sect with different research fields (macroeconomics, the firm, public finance and so on).[2]

Within each approach, basic concepts and, in many instances, the theoretical schemes utilized for the analysis of different issues show significant affinities. Moreover, there are dialectical relationships of self-definition through opposition, between external and internal criticisms, theories and concept definitions shifting in response to difficulties emerging in analytical debate. Also, owing to the increasing specialization of researchers, over the past seventy years research in the field of economics has been characterized by far more fragmentation than hitherto, and increasing over time; this implies ever more frequently losing contact with the final goal of economics, namely interpretation of the economic reality confronting us and its evolution, which requires a multiplicity of competences on the part of the individual researcher.

All this means that recent developments in economic research cannot be illustrated by following the simple linear course of their development over time, nor by a catalogue of independent themes and theories. Often it will inevitably mean going back in time, as well as shifting from one approach or one field of research to another and back again. However,

---

[1] Economics, the term currently used today for our field of research, was introduced (by Marshall 1890) to mark a discontinuity with classical 'political economy', pointing to a stricter affinity with the 'hard sciences' such as physics or mathematics. However, as Alice in the Wonderland says, the meaning of the words is whatever we choose for them; thus, I shall use economics in a broad sense, possibly more akin to that of classical economists than to Samuelson's 1948 notion.

[2] Both 'research approach' and 'field/area of research' are aggregate notions, with bound-aries that are difficult if not impossible to define in a clear-cut way. Each economist may present more or less heterodox distinctive elements within his or her field of research; as for the research fields, it should suffice to recall the difficulty to define systems of classification for journal articles, like those appearing in the *Journal of Economic Literature*: commonly, more than one code is reported for each article; classification sets are never considered perfect, and are occasionally revised.

precisely as a reaction to the dangerous trend towards a fragmentation of economic research, we need to search for connections and lines of development and find justifications for them.

Obviously, the reconstruction proposed in this volume, though meditated at length and founded on a vast mass of material (the bibliography falls far short of accounting for all the books and articles consulted over more than half a century of study of our subject), may be criticized on many counts. In this Introduction I shall try to justify some of my choices, although there are bound to be disagreements, in particular on the weight attributed to authors, schools, approaches and research fields.[3]

As far as this latter aspect is concerned, let me point out immediately that in a book like this, focused on a survey of the troops and illustration/ interpretation of the different research approaches (hence, focused on concepts and ideas more than on models or individual economists), it may be useful to allot more space than usual to developments outside the mainstream, even independently of the partisan propensity of the author. In the long run, as a rule the more innovative heterodox thinkers may receive more attention while the orthodox thinkers dominating in a given historical period may recede to a secondary position.

In any case, I can well imagine that each reader will find the treatment of their specific research fields far too brief and simplified. Some may even view some topics bordering on other social sciences as external to the field of economics. The former criticism might indeed hold for the whole of the book, despite the need to select and simplify the material to be considered; the reader should also keep in mind that my objective is a reconstruction, albeit a concise one, and not representation on a reduced scale, as in the case of geographical maps. As far as the latter criticism is concerned, however, I hereby notify my dissent. Refusal to consider so many aspects of social life as an integral part of the issues tackled by economists obviously may simplify our research work, but it also implies a loss of depth that may turn out to be very dangerous, especially when we expect the results of our research to influence economic policy.

Quite often, those working within a given approach and tackling specific issues decide to ignore the multifaceted nature of economic research, or fail to perceive it. Whatever (often very little) is gained in

---

[3] Some studies (e.g. Kosnik 2015) offer data on the percentages of articles or pages published in the different research fields in a more or less extensive and more or less representative selection of journals. These data have a certain relevance for an understanding of what economists are doing; however, in a work like ours even considerable deviations between these proportions and the space allotted to the different research areas are – I feel – justified.

depth is more than offset by a loss in general vision and critical capability. Economic research thus risks getting lost in a meander of blind alleys. The danger is even more serious for those conceiving of research as a guide to action. Here, connections between different aspects of the most complex issue of how to pursue the common weal may be lost sight of. Also, the opposition between different theses may be perceived as a clash of a priori tenets, thus barring mutual understanding in the open debate between opinions based on contending approaches, the characteristics of which should be set out and discussed. Each economist engaged in a specific field of research may find it advantageous to consider that field from outside, thereby realizing that certain traditional axioms may actually be questionable.[4]

The historian of economic thought tries to build a bridge between the different approaches, by reconstructing their foundations and illustrating their internal evolution. Obviously, historians of thought are entitled to hold a personal opinion: as economists, they are part of the debate being illustrated to their readers. We are in any case confronted with a constraint: respect for the scientific criteria of the history of thought, which we may summarize as philological respect for text and context. The possibility of dissent remains open, indeed much wider than in the case of mathematical theorems; however, the debate may take place in an open way if the approach is to search for textual or contextual elements in support or refutation of each interpretative thesis. As Kula (1958, p. 234) writes: 'To understand the others: this is the historian's aim. It is not easy to have a more difficult task. It is difficult to have a more interesting one.'

* * *

Once we accept as a fact of life that there are different approaches to economic theory,[5] interpretative work needs to pay attention to an aspect quite often overlooked in current debate. As Schumpeter (and before him Max Weber) observed, theoretical models are grounded on a web of concepts; each concept, though retaining the same name, may differ even radically from one approach to another. The theoretician in his or

---

[4] Let us recall what John Stuart Mill wrote (in his essay 'Auguste Comte and positivism', 1865, quoted by D'Ippoliti, 2011, p. 106): 'A man's mind is as fatally narrowed, and his feelings towards the great ends of humanity as miserably stunned, by giving all his thoughts to the classification of a few insects or the resolution of a few equations, as to sharpening the points or putting on the heads of pins.' Mill may possibly appear too severe on the need for specialization present in every field of scientific research, though such a need is not denied: what is being criticized is the exclusive focus on a specific theme of research, without ever raising the eyes to observe what surrounds it.

[5] That is, when accepting a 'competitive' view of the history of thought, rejecting the 'cumulative' view that assumes continuous progress within the same basic view of the economy: cf. Roncaglia (2005), pp. 2 ff.

her work often pays scant attention to this aspect, assuming as given the approach dominating his or her research field. As a matter of fact, however, construction of such a web of concepts – and the associated choice, often only implicit, of a web of simplifying assumptions – constitute from the logical viewpoint the first, far from simple, step on the path of any research: the 'stage of conceptualization'. Building formal models and comparison with empirical reality are only the second and third steps: they, too, are quite complex, especially the third, but never so much as the first. In order to compare theories grounded on different approaches, it is crucial to consider first of all the first step, namely the web of concepts, and only subsequently to consider the strictly analytical issues. This is why in these pages greater attention is paid to concepts than to theoretical models; a few analytical elements are briefly illustrated in a couple of appendixes. Often, to make the going easier for readers who have not had a university education in economics, analytical issues are relegated to footnotes or bibliographical references.

We can begin by taking not one but two steps backwards. Part I of the book is devoted to recalling the premises of the recent economic debate. Chapter 2 offers an overview of the main approaches adopted in the history of economic thought: the classical one, with Adam Smith and David Ricardo (and, in some respects, Karl Marx); the marginalist one, with William Stanley Jevons, Carl Menger and Léon Walras.[6] We shall also recall the distinction between the monodimensional (felicific calculus) and the pluridimensional (passions and interests) notions of the motivations of human action. Chapter 3 considers the main protagonists in the period going from the end of the nineteenth century to the middle of the twentieth century: Knut Wicksell, Thorstein Veblen and Max Weber; John Maynard Keynes and Joseph Schumpeter. The latter two in particular had a notable influence in the period following the end of the Second World War, namely the period on which we focus attention, but died when this period had just begun.

Part II constitutes a bridge between the debates of the inter-war period and those of the subsequent period. It is devoted to two authors: Friedrich Hayek (Chapter 4) and Piero Sraffa (Chapter 5), who published important works both before and after the Second World War, and hence belong to the period we are considering. At the level of the conceptual foundations, these two scholars represent to the full the two main

---

[6] Labels such as classical, marginalist, mainstream and heterodox economics obviously constitute simplifications, and cannot be given clear-cut definitions. They are useful as general indications, but leave ample room for internal differences and difficulties of classification.

competing approaches active in the European culture of the 'short century', namely the period running from the beginning of the First World War to the fall of the Soviet Empire:[7] the conservative view, extolling the invisible hand of the market, and the revolutionary one bringing to the fore the distributive conflict between wages and profits. This explains why more space has been allotted to them rather than to other economists – such as Sir John Hicks, Milton Friedman or Paul A. Samuelson – whose contributions rest on already well-established basic conceptual foundations.

As to the period directly addressed in this book, the choice of the line of exposition constitutes a serious problem, open to different solutions, each with its negative implications. The solution adopted here highlights the cultural–analytical debate, devoting ample room – as noted earlier – to heterodox views (which in fact are such only in the decades considered here, but were not necessarily such in earlier periods and may turn out not to be such in the future). As we shall see, some chapters are devoted to research fields, others to schools or streams of thought, while still others combine these characteristics.

Thus in Part III we consider the development of the dominant research approaches – the so-called mainstream – in the main research areas (micro, macro, applied economics), together with the main neo-liberal streams, quite different from one another but sharing the thesis of the efficacy of the invisible hand of the market at the political-cultural level.[8]

Part IV is devoted to those fields of debate – the axiom of rational behaviour and its limits, finance and crises – that show clear-cut opposition between different research approaches, with the consequence that the analytical results, even when accepted as such, are given conflicting interpretations.

Part V is mainly devoted to heterodox research streams: post-Keynesians (Chapter 12), Marxists, institutional and evolutionary economists (Chapter 13); post-utilitarians and the capabilities theory (Chapter 14).

---

[7] The notion of the 'short century' was utilized by the British historian Eric Hobsbawm (1917–2012; 1994, p. 3), in opposition to the notion of the 'long century', the nineteenth century covering the period from the French Revolution in 1789 to the beginning of the First World War in 1914; it is now widely accepted. As a matter of fact, the fall of the Berlin Wall in 1989 and the fragmentation of the Soviet Union in the immediately subsequent years mark a cultural break, blurring the opposition between socialism and capitalism, market and planned economies. Thus, our book covers two historical periods (pre- and post-1989) significantly different on the political plane if not on the plane of economic theorizing.

[8] Once again, the term 'mainstream' is meant generically, pointing to the (internally quite varied) set of theories that dominated economics teaching in the period under consideration.

Apart from a few broad allusions, the possibility of convergence on the conceptual if not on the analytical level of these streams is left open.

* * *

In the post–Second World War scenario, the barycentre of the economic debate moved from the East to the West of the Atlantic: from Europe, winner or loser but in both cases in ruins, to the triumphant United States.

Precisely as a collateral product of war research, not widely known to the public at large but an important pillar to a newly emerging dominant economic culture, we have the developments in the theory of general economic equilibrium connected to game theory and expected utilities. The polyhedral von Neumann was at the centre of these developments, together with the network of economists and mathematicians grouped in various research centres, such as the Cowles Foundation and the Rand Corporation, and in the most important universities. Game theory and expected utilities imply a reconstruction of the microeconomic foundations of the marginalist approach, and find their place side by side with the old Marshallian tradition still holding out in major centres like Chicago and a number of minor universities.

Power relations at the political and cultural level, beyond the strictly economic sphere, led to Keynes's partial defeat at Bretton Woods when confronted with the US ideas for the reconstruction of the post-war international economic system. The same constellation was among the factors behind the rise of a new cultural hegemony, which absorbed and annihilated the main elements of novelty of Keynesian theory within a 'neoclassical synthesis' with the marginalist approach to value and distribution. The East Coast of the United States, particularly MIT with Paul Samuelson, Franco Modigliani and Robert Solow, contributed the essential elements of this hegemony, both at the level of pure theory and at the – also quite important – level of their incorporation into a well-structured textbook vulgate.

However, at the theoretical level the compromise between the marginalist and the Keynesian approaches is of necessity fragile: with rational expectations theory, the marginalist foundations tend to overcome the Keynesian residuals, also at the level of policy. Thus, also due to the evolution of the international economic situation (crisis of the Bretton Woods system, then the two oil crises of 1973–4 and 1979) and then of the political situation (with Margaret Thatcher's victory in Great Britain and Ronald Reagan's victory in the United States), neo-liberalism in its various versions took the lead over progressive liberalism, increasingly concentrated in the US universities of the East Coast.[9]

At the political level, but not on that of theoretical construction (although both extolled the invisible hand of the market), the neo-liberal positions of monetarists and rational expectation economists found an ally in a rejuvenated Austrian school that gave central importance to the problems of knowledge and uncertainty and of the time dimension. The new Austrian school was supported, albeit with some autonomy, by Hayek's research and his political-cultural initiatives, such as the foundation of the Mont Pèlerin Society. We cannot place ordoliberalism within this school, but it is in many respects connected with it; it developed in Germany and remains important there, as well as – albeit in a modified form – in the European Union's economic policy.

Econometrics was born well before the beginning of the Second World War; the foundation of the Econometric Society dates back to 1933. On the borderline between applied economics, statistics and probability theory, it developed rapidly in the post-war period, with the construction of large econometric models utilized for forecasting and policy purposes. Developments in econometrics gave rise to intense research activity and the construction of an a-theoretical economics that claims to deal with specific economic issues on the sole basis of statistical inference. Wassily Leontief's input–output models and linear programming, although in many respects connected to general equilibrium theory, are also considered as analytical tools for applied research. A recent development in applied research, closer to descriptive than to inferential statistics, consists in research aimed at building synthetic indexes for socio-economic phenomena: human development indexes, indexes of well-being, of economic freedom, of democracy. Such indexes allow us to quantify intrinsically qualitative variables, so as to enable use of them to study their impact on economic variables such as the rate of economic growth or per capita income. On the borderline between theoretical and applied economics we then have some research fields of great practical relevance, such as market regulation and auctions, the economics of energy sources (a field in which I did some work in the past) and environmental issues.

Mainstream economic theory has dominated for decades, but not without opposition. A fundamental battlefield lies in the theory of value. Devastating criticisms by marginalist economists of the labour

---

[9] In Italian I was able to differentiate between 'liberale', a political category, and 'liberista', an economic category focused on free trade and free entrepreneurship. The term 'neo-liberal' is utilized here, following current usage, to designate currents of thought better depicted as 'liberisti'.

theory of value upheld by the classical economists and Marx were already looming large by the end of the nineteenth century (and the Marxian approach, though surviving, has been deeply affected by them), to be followed in the second half of the twentieth century by equally devastating criticisms of the traditional marginalist theory of value and distribution. Consensus on the analytical results of these criticisms is not accompanied by corresponding consensus on their implications, due also to some misunderstandings which we shall try to clarify. Concerning these aspects there are in fact a variety of views within both the marginalist–neoclassical and the classical–post-Keynesian fields; moreover, the separation prevailing between research fields fosters widespread ignorance of these analytical findings and especially of their wide-ranging implications.

Gradually, from within the very new mainstream microeconomics based on expected utilities came to light the anomalies, mostly reabsorbed within the dominant approach but accompanied by the collateral development of alternative research lines. Such is the case of behavioural economics, which has as its starting point analysis of the cases (viewed as paradoxes, but as a matter of fact quite general) where the agent's behaviour does not follow the paradigm of rationality, identified with the maximization of expected utility. From here to the development of notions such as bounded rationality (Simon) is a short step. The emergence of behavioural economics was accompanied by the development of experimental and cognitive economics, with bioeconomics and other streams of research such as Daniel Kahneman and Amos Tversky's 'prospect theory', commonly embraced within, but not always fully compatible with, the mainstream.

Incredible as this might seem, not even the recent world financial crisis gave rise to a new interest in the foundational themes of the theory of value, also concerning the ability of market mechanisms to ensure optimal equilibrium conditions. Within the monetary field, the renewed debate was livelier, more or less parallel to debate on the theory of value: the mainstream thesis of efficient financial markets (reinforced by consideration of rational expectations) was opposed to Hyman Minsky's thesis of the intrinsic instability of market economies and the unavoidable return of crises of ever greater dimensions.

This latter idea fell within the stream of post-Keynesian macroeconomics, a wide field rich in internal differences which constitutes one of the pillars of a possible approach alternative to the mainstream one. The centre of these analyses was in Cambridge, UK, where Richard Kahn and Joan Robinson, Nicholas Kaldor and others were at work; here we find in transit such an anomalous character as Michał Kalecki, while an

Anglo-Italian school developed around Sraffa. The US post-Keynesians as well (Jan Kregel, Hyman P. Minsky, Sidney Weintraub), albeit with their specific ideas and their internal differentiations, had a reference point in Cambridge.

Another field concerns the study of institutions, and the focus on change: a field where Marxism had been active since its origins. Authors like Michael Polanyi and John Kenneth Galbraith constitute a link to more recent research. More directly connected to the marginalist approach, on the other hand, we have neo-institutionalism. Confronting it, partly innovating and partly connected to the Marshallian tradition, we have an evolutionary–institutional stream that presents itself as heterodox as compared to the dominant marginalist approach. On the borderline between growth theory and the analysis of economic-social institutions lies an extensive research area on development economics. Already briefly dealt with by Hayek, competition between different institutions came to the fore with increasing economic globalization.

Finally, an important current of researches concerns different aspects of ethics in the economic field, with the developments of utilitarianism and the ethics of consequences. The ethics debate is relevant to, among other things, the issue of income distribution, long at the centre of economic research, and welfare economics. On the borderline between economics and philosophy, Amartya Sen has provided important contributions, such as the notion of capabilities. We are confronted here with the non-neutrality of the economists' work, connected to the weighty and complex theme, all too often overlooked, of power in the broadest sense of the word: economic, political, social and cultural.

Paraphrasing Gramsci, we might conclude that within today's economic culture the US mainstream approach dominates but without necessarily retaining hegemony. Knowing how varied and complex the economic debate of the last few decades in the economic field has been may help us understand (and question) the more or less solid foundations of the different theoretical approaches, but also of economic policy choices, and hence in improving our ability to tackle the difficult situation confronting us, with the devastating crises and prolonged periods of stagnation it entails.

Part I

The Background

2 The Foundations: Classicals and Marginalists

2.1 Introduction

Consideration of economic issues has a long history, and an even longer prehistory. Here we shall take into account only some aspects of the less recent period, focusing attention on the conceptual foundations of the two main alternative approaches that intersect in the course of time. The first, the classical approach, dominated from the second half of the seventeenth century to the mid-nineteenth century (§2.2). The second, the marginalist approach, has dominated from the dawn of the twentieth century to our own time (§2.5). Before considering the marginalist approach, we shall in §2.3 recall the Smithian notion of self-interest and the Benthamite felicific calculus, both useful in evaluating the contemporary economic debate. We shall then go on in §2.4 to illustrate briefly some aspects of such a heterodox author as Karl Marx.

In Chapter 3 we shall consider some authors – Knut Wicksell together with Thorstein Veblen, Max Weber, Joseph Schumpeter and above all John Maynard Keynes – who are difficult to classify but who exert a direct influence on important streams of contemporary economic thought.[1]

The basic notions of the marginalist approach – the opposition between resource scarcity and human needs and desires, recourse to supply and demand in explaining prices – have been present in economic thinking since antiquity, though in a rudimentary form. It was only in the second half of the nineteenth century that the theoretical structure found reinforcement with the notions of marginal cost and utility, although some major problems remain open, as we shall soon see. The classical approach too, which began to develop in the second half of the seventeenth century, reached a solid theoretical structure with David Ricardo but presented

---

[1] For a more detailed account of the history of economic thought, the reader may refer to Roncaglia (2005a, 2016a).

13

serious analytical problems that would be overcome only in the second half of the twentieth century.

The vicissitudes of the two approaches thus intersect: albeit with alternating fortunes, both have been simultaneously present throughout the multicentennial history of economic science. However, it is common practice, and reasonably so, to consider them in sequence, starting with the contributions to the classical approach by authors such as William Petty, Adam Smith and David Ricardo, and going on with the protagonists of the so-called marginalist revolution: Carl Menger, William Stanley Jevons and Léon Walras.

2.2   The Classical Approach

William Petty's (1623–87) contribution is important on two counts. First, we should recall the introduction – under the name of Political Arithmetic or Political Anatomy – of a modern method of analysis, quantitative and objective, that recalls the scientific turn of Baco and Hobbes, but also of Galileo. Second, we should recall his contribution to the definition of the main concepts, from surplus to natural price.[2]

Let us consider the first element:

> The Method I take to do this, is not yet very usual; for instead of using only comparative and superlative words, and intellectual Arguments, I have taken the course (as a Specimen of the Political Arithmetick I have long aimed at) to express my self in Terms of *Number, Weight,* or *Measure*; to use only Arguments of Sense, and to consider only such Causes, as have visible Foundations in Nature; leaving those that depend upon the mutable Minds, Opinions, Appetites and Passions of particular Men, to the Consideration of others.[3]

The reference to the 'mutable Minds, Opinions, Appetites and Passions of particular Men' is, by opposition, aimed precisely at the tradition of scarcity and utility, demand and supply, prevailing in what we may call the prehistory of economic science.

Along the same line as Petty's we may then recall Adam Smith's (1723–90) distinction in *The wealth of nations* (1776, pp. 72–81) between natural and market prices: only natural prices constitute the theoretical variable object of analysis, whereas market prices are subject to the contingent effects of occasional vicissitudes influencing the demand for and supply of some commodities, as in the case of the death of the sovereign provoking an increase in the demand for black cloth.[4]

---

[2] On Petty, cf. Roncaglia (1977).   [3] Petty (1690), p. 244.
[4] Cf. Roncaglia (1990b) and (2005a), pp. 139–43.

According to the classical economists, demand for the various commodities depends mainly on consumption habits (gradually evolving in the course of time), and not on the pursuit of maximum utility on the part of the consumer. In essence, the classical authors approach the demand side as a separate area; in developing their theory of value they focus attention on the objective data of technology: from Petty's reference to physical costs, possibly summed up in labour alone or in the land–labour combination, to Richard Cantillon's (1697–1734) developments, which attempt to extract from the labour–land combination a land theory of value, up to the labour theory of value developed by David Ricardo (1772–1823), and then taken over, albeit with different implications, by Karl Marx (1818–83).[5]

According to the classical economists, equilibrium prices are not the prices corresponding to equality between demand and supply, but those allowing the economic system to reproduce itself over time. The balancing of supply and demand is a relatively vague notion, connected to actual market price movements; the latter is not a theoretical variable determined by a condition of equilibrium consisting of equality between demand and supply, as is generally the case within the marginalist approach. Among other things, in this second case it is necessary to consider demand and supply as respectively decreasing and increasing functions of price (in the mathematical sense of the term *function*). On the contrary, the notion of stable functional relations connecting market prices to the demand and supply of the different commodities is wholly extraneous to the classical approach of Smith, Ricardo and Marx.

The 'objectivism' of the classical approach implies a physical definition of the surplus and analysis of the network of exchanges and distributive relations that, given the technology, allow for the continuous functioning over time (the reproduction) of the economy. This does not necessarily mean following Petty (and especially Galileo)[6] in assuming the existence of laws written into the world that the scientist needs to discover, in the etymological sense of the word, i.e. to unearth them from the covering of contingent elements that hide them from immediate view. For instance, Adam Smith, forerunning methodological views that spread only in recent times, considered the 'laws' a creation of the scientist, 'mere inventions of the imagination, to connect together the otherwise disjointed and discordant phaenomena of nature'.[7]

---

[5] Cf. Cantillon (1755); Ricardo (1951–55); Marx (1867–94).
[6] 'This great book which is open in front of our eyes – I mean the Universe – ... is written in mathematical characters' (Galilei 1623, p. 121).
[7] Smith (1795), p. 105. Cf. Roncaglia (2005a), pp. 118–20.

As for the conceptual foundations, a major step ahead came with the transition from a generic notion of the surplus (or *overplus*) to a precise analytical notion. The generic notion is to be found, for instance, in the Bible, where it says that one has to give to the poor what exceeds one's needs, on the definition of which nothing is said. The analytical notion points to the excess of the quantities produced compared to the quantities of the different commodities used up as means of production and as means of subsistence for the workers employed in the production process. For instance, in an economic system that has as its sole product 500 tons of corn, obtained through the use of 200 tons of corn required to maintain the 400 workers employed in its cultivation and 180 tons of corn utilized as seed, the surplus comes to 120 tons of corn.

The analytical definition of the surplus is a systemic one, in the sense that it relates to the economic system as a whole. It can be utilized with reference to a single productive sector only if we assume that the sector produces the totality of the means of production and subsistence necessary for its own functioning, as we did earlier (and as Petty does in some examples) by referring to corn as seed and as the sole means of subsistence for the production of corn. The definition of the surplus is in any case a physical definition: the surplus consists of a set of commodities, each taken in a quantity equal to the difference between quantity produced and quantity utilized in the entire set of productive sectors of the economy. Only once the problem of value has been solved, by measuring the various commodities in terms of a common unit of measure, such as the labour directly or indirectly necessary to produce each of them, can we express the set of commodities constituting the surplus as a monodimensional magnitude; in this way the surplus corresponds to Marx's notion of plus-value. For the classical economists, who adopt the labour theory of value but are aware of its limits, the basic notion of the surplus is the physical and multidimensional one. Indeed, Smith's definition of the wealth of nations as 'all the necessaries and conveniences of life which it annually consumes' in proportion to the population (Smith 1776, p. 10) is itself a multidimensional physical notion; it is only when we go on to the modern notion of per capita income that the need for a measure of value arises, hence the necessity of a theory of relative prices.

We thus come to the view of the functioning of the economic system as a circular flow of production and consumption that has as reference the yearly sowing–cultivating–harvesting cycle typical of agriculture. The issue taken up by classical economists consists of the analysis of the conditions of reproduction, cycle after cycle, of an economic system based on the division of labour – hence analysis, in distinct steps, of production, distribution, circulation and accumulation of the product.

Within the classical framework, prices are indicators of (are derived from) the relative difficulty of production of the different commodities. The starting point for determining them, for all the classical economists, is given by their physical costs of production. The problem of value consists precisely in finding an analytical mechanism allowing us to move from the multidimensional notion of physical costs to the mono-dimensional notion of value.

It would be superfluous here to retrace the steps of this research. We will confine our attention to the main aspects. The difficulty arises over two circumstances. First, to determine the price of a commodity we need to know its cost of production, but this in turn depends on the prices of its means of production, which are in turn produced, so we have a vicious logical circle. Second, the determination of prices must respect the condition of the uniformity of the rate of profits in the different sectors given the assumption of free competition common to the classical economists.

For a long time the first difficulty was solved through the so-called labour theory of value, which meant reducing the value of the means of production to the quantities of labour directly or indirectly required for their production. However, this solution is not rigorous: it leads to violating the condition of uniformity of the profit rate, as production of the different commodities is commonly characterized by different proportions between fixed and circulating capital, different durability of fixed capital goods and different lengths of the production period. David Ricardo was well aware of this difficulty, to the extent that he considered the solution based on the labour theory of value as approximate and provisional.[8] It was only at the beginning of the twentieth century that authors such as Ladislaus Bortkiewicz and Vladimir Dmitriev addressed their research in the direction of a simultaneous determination of the whole system of prices and of the rate of profits.

Apparently this is the same direction taken by the theoreticians of general economic equilibrium as originally set out by Léon Walras; however, this latter approach is grounded on a different conceptual foundation, the subjective one of scarcity and desires, and implies a simultaneous determination of prices and quantities produced and demanded (which in equilibrium are required to be equal).

Within the classical framework, the solution finally came with Piero Sraffa (1960), who – as we shall see in Chapter 5 – isolated the problem of determining prices (and their relationship with the distributive variables, wage rate and profit rate) from the task of accounting for levels of production and employment, income distribution and technology.

---

[8] Cf. Ricardo [1817] 1951, vol. 1, pp. 30–43.

Relative prices and one of the two distributive variables are jointly determined, taking the second distributive variable and technology as given; in the absence of assumptions on returns, this implies taking production levels as given as well. However, for the entire golden age of the classical approach – from the mid-seventeenth century to the second half of the nineteenth century, from Petty to Ricardo and Marx and their immediate disciples – the issue of value remained a major unsolved problem.

Within the classical framework, the issue of value is considered central, but as a tool with which to tackle the real target of the analysis, namely study of the wealth of nations and the distribution of income, as well as wealth and power among the main social classes: landlords, capitalists and workers.[9] The division of labour takes on fundamental importance for both aspects: the growth of wealth stemming from technological progress and the formation of different classes and social strata.

As far as the first issue – the wealth of nations – is concerned, division of labour favours technological progress through various mechanisms of a dynamic kind ranging from reduction of production costs obtainable when the quantity produced increases ('increasing returns to scale') to the fact that, as stressed by Charles Babbage (1832), subdivision of the work process favours innovations. Intensifying the division of labour is thus considered the main element for growth of per capita income, and hence of the wealth of nations.[10]

As far as the second aspect is concerned, the division of labour raises the need to recognize the existence of a multiplicity of commodities, productive sectors and work activities – hence representation of the productive process as a circular flow of production, exchange and distribution (developed analytically around the mid-eighteenth century in the *Tableau économique*, 1758–59, by François Quesnay, 1694–1774). At the end of each productive process, each sector (and each productive unit) sells its product, except for the part required by itself in the next production period, thus obtaining the money necessary to acquire on the market both the means of production needed for continuing production and the means of subsistence for its workers. The part of the proceeds which remains once production expenses are paid constitutes the profit for the capitalist (or the rent for the landlord).

---

[9] Marx is an exception: as we shall see in the text that follows, his theory of value has a direct role for the interpretation of commodity fetishism and for demonstrating workers' exploitation.

[10] National accounting notions, such as those of per capita product or income, became common usage only in a relatively recent stage; however, using them to illustrate to today's readers the thought of the classical economists does not mean distorting interpretation of them.

Within the classical framework, the market is conceived as a web of repetitive flows that, period after period, allow the various sectors to sell their product to other sectors and obtain in exchange the means of production and subsistence necessary to continue the production process. Thus the market is not conceived as a point where supply and demand meet (a specific point in time and space, like the medieval fair or the stock exchange), as instead is the case within the marginalist approach. The classical economists conceive as natural prices – i.e. the prices determined by the theory – those that satisfy two conditions: first, the earnings of each productive sector are sufficient, period after period, to cover acquisition of the means of production and payment of wages to the workers; and second, a rate of profits equal for all sectors obtains (under the hypothesis of free competition; in the more general case in which there are barriers to entry we can have sector profit rates above the competitive rate).

Natural prices are thus of a twofold nature. On the one hand, they are the prices determined by the theory, which isolates the main factors, namely those operating in a systematic way (the relative difficulty of production of the various commodities and the influence of the distributive variables), from contingent and occasional factors affecting current prices (classical economists' market prices). On the other hand, natural prices are the prices that guarantee the continuous reproduction, period after period, of the economic system based on the division of labour, because each sector is able (insofar as it recovers production costs) and has an inducement to (insofar as it obtains a return equal to that of other sectors) to start a new production process. On the first count, natural prices have an interpretative aspect (as the best way to explain what happens in a capitalist economy, on the basis of objective data such as technology and income distribution). On the second count, natural prices have a normative role, insofar as they point to the conditions that must be satisfied, at least as far as exchange relations are concerned, to guarantee the regular functioning of the economy.

At least since Smith's times, in classical economists' minds the notion of the wealth of nations has expressed the degree of development of the economy and corresponded to what today we indicate as per capita income. In Smith's analysis, it depends on labour productivity and the share of productive workers over the total population; in turn, labour productivity, being the more important of the two variables, correlates with the dynamics of the division of labour, which thus constitutes a core element of the classical approach. Smith considers both its positive and its negative implications: increase in productivity, impoverishment of the quality of labour and what was later to be called alienation. Moreover, various authors, in particular Charles Babbage and Karl Marx, associate with the evolution of the division of labour both the process of mechanization and the evolution in the social structure.

The share of workers employed over the total population is linked to accumulation. In the initial stages of capitalist development the modern core of the economy expands, while the set of traditional activities contracts; we thus have a flow of workers from the traditional to the modern sectors of the economy. The expansion of the modern core of the economy (manufacturing industry, characterized by an increasing use of machinery) finds a limit in the accumulation of capital more than in the availability of workers, as the latter are easily drawn from the declining traditional sectors, and indeed more than in the expansion of demand, favoured by the reduction in the prices of products manufacturing sectors substitute for products of the traditional sector.

Say's law, according to which production creates its own demand, is interpreted in an empirical way by Smith and others, in the sense that progress in productivity is accompanied in the course of time (and with reference to the long period: Smith suggests a centuries-long trend) by an increase in production and not by a fall in employment. Ricardo, on the other hand, interprets Say's law in a more rigid way, as the impossibility of general overproduction crises. Thus Ricardo is able to link income distribution to growth through the assumption that profits are entirely invested while rents go into luxury consumption and wages go into necessary consumption; under certain simplifying assumptions, the profit rate and the rate of growth of the economy are equal.

In short, the main characteristics of the classical school, which was to be superseded by others with the marginalist revolution that began at the end of the nineteenth century, are the notion of surplus; the economy viewed as a circular flow of production, distribution, exchange, consumption and accumulation; the notion of the market as a web of repetitive exchange flows; the central importance attributed to the division of labour and its evolution over time (technical progress) in explaining the wealth of nations; a theory of distribution built on the opposition between the main social classes defined on the basis of their respective role in production (capitalists, workers, landlords); an objective theory of value wired to the difficulty of production and the conditions of reproduction over time in the flow of production; and growth linked to accumulation and hence to income distribution (profits).

2.3 Self-Interest and Felicific Calculus: Smith versus Bentham

Let us now consider an important aspect of the classical approach concerning the motivations for human action, often relegated to a secondary plane when focusing attention on the theory of value. This aspect was developed particularly by Adam Smith, in the context of the Scottish Enlightenment. In a few words, according to Smith the agent is driven by a complex set of passions and interests, among which self-interest dominates. This view is basically different from the marginalist view of the rational *homo oeconomicus* focused on maximizing his own utility under the constraint of his resources; on various counts this latter view draws on Bentham's felicific calculus, on which more in a while.

In *The wealth of nations* (1776) Smith opposes his old master Hutcheson, maintaining that humans are not driven by benevolence towards others but by their own self-interest. Some commentators at the beginning of the twentieth century saw in this thesis a contradiction with the *Theory of moral sentiments* (1759), in which Smith maintains an ethic of 'sympathy', in the etymological sense of the term, from the Greek 'to feel together'; namely, humans are motivated by the desire to be liked by others.

As a matter of fact, neither Smith nor his contemporaries, imbibed by Enlightenment culture, saw any contradiction between the two motivations for human actions. It was quite common at the time to consider human beings as driven by a complex set of motivations, bundled together in two categories: passions (not irrational, but a-rational: love, pride, envy and so on) and interests (rational, as in all cases in which material objectives – personal security, accumulation of wealth – are pursued in a consistent way). The philosopher studying these motivations and simultaneously forging a theory of ethics (namely, studying both how things go and how they should go) stresses within this complex set some dominant motivations. Thus Smith's self-interest is not to be interpreted as an absolute – as unconditional selfishness – but as a motivation dominant yet conditioned by a strong brake, the moral force of sympathy, or in other words the desire to receive the approval of others (or more precisely, in a formulation that Smith developed in his 1759 book and which in many respects antedates Kant's ethics, to obtain the approval of an invisible arbiter, our conscience, which evaluates our actions while taking into account the information we have).

On the other hand, a one-dimensional view of the human being, derived from seventeenth-century sensism (for instance, Hobbes's *De homine*, 1658), was proposed by Jeremy Bentham (1748–1832) with his felicific calculus. This consists of quantitative evaluation and algebraic summation of pleasures and pains stemming from each action or set of actions (where pleasures obviously have a positive sign and pains a negative sign). Good is whatever gives as a result of this algebraic summation a positive felicific magnitude; bad is whatever gives a negative result, thus reducing the amount of social happiness.

To Bentham's way of thinking, felicific calculus aimed at evaluating the social impact of individual choices and especially of governments' political choices, on which the London philosopher focused attention in his attempts to outline a rational penal code or an ideal prison. Bentham aimed to substitute traditional deontological ethics, within which criteria for ethical judgement are provided by some authority (in particular, by the religious authorities) or by tradition, with a consequential ethics, according to which ethical judgement depends on the consequences of actions, evaluated through felicific calculus.

As we shall see more clearly in §14.2, though sharing Bentham's consequential ethics, John Stuart Mill (1806–73) criticized the one-dimensional view of felicific calculus in his essay *Utilitarianism* (1861), stressing the qualitative differences between different kinds of pleasures and pains, which cannot be reduced to quantitative differences. Moreover, Mill makes a clear distinction between the ethical issue, in which we have to take into account the consequences of our actions though it is impossible to do so in a univocal way, and the issue of consumer's choices, which he saw as associated mainly with habits and social customs – a view substantially shared by the whole classical tradition.

2.4   Karl Marx

Marxism had enormous importance in the political life and the philosophical and social debate of the twentieth century; as far as economic theory is concerned, it can be considered as a modified and in some respects expanded version of the classical approach. After the fall of the Berlin Wall (1989) Marxism lost most of its political and cultural weight, at least in Western countries, accelerating a tendency already initiated with the rise of neo-liberalism.[11]

Karl Marx (1818–83) took over Ricardo's analytical structure: the notion of the surplus, economic development connected to the division of labour (mechanization) and accumulation; subdivision of society into

---

[11] The exception of China is actually more apparent than real, as the Chinese authorities' invocation of Marxism is mainly lip-service.

the classes of capitalists, workers and landlords; and labour theory of value for explanation of exchange ratios. Here we shall not consider Marx's political and philosophical views, where the differences with the classical approach are of considerable significance.

The labour theory of value was then extended into a theory of exploitation (and, correspondingly, the notion of the surplus was transformed into the notion of plus-value), with a distinction between labour (the activity of working) and labour power (the person of the worker). As is the case with every commodity, the value of labour power is given by its cost of reproduction, which is in this case the cost of the means of subsistence necessary to keep the worker alive and to ensure the survival of his progeny. If with the labour theory of value we express such means of subsistence in terms of the labour directly and indirectly necessary to produce them, and if this latter magnitude proves lesser than the quantity of labour usually performed by the worker, we have plus-labour. For instance, if eight hours are required to produce the daily means of subsistence and if the working time is ten hours a day, we have two hours of plus-labour. However, the attempts to solve the problem of transforming labour values into prices of production are unsuccessful, as various critics of Marxism were already pointing out at the end of the nineteenth century. Debate on this point continued into the post-war period.

Another aspect of Marx's theory with some relevance in recent economic debate concerns the distribution of income. Here Marx focuses attention on the conflict between capitalists and workers, attributing a secondary role to landlords. In this context he develops the notion of the reserve army of labour which, together with the unemployed, includes workers in the backward sectors of the economy, ready to move as soon as possible into the modern expanding capitalist sector. The expanding and contracting stages of the industrial reserve army account for the alternating vicissitudes of wages and profits. As we shall see, in the contemporary macroeconomic framework, with the so-called Phillips curve, this role is attributed to the unemployed alone. Also, in the marginalist approach unemployment is considered an indicator of the pressure of supply in the labour market, while in Marx's theory the industrial reserve army is, rather, an indicator of the bargaining power of the two social classes, and it is this latter that determines the path of income distribution. What can be explained is the movement of the distributive variables, while their level at any moment in time is not considered as resulting from equilibrium between supply of and demand for labour.

Less relevant for our purpose are the aspects of Marx's economic analysis more closely connected to his political ideas, and in particular the unavoidable breakdown of capitalism and the transition to a socialist society characterized by state ownership of means of production, and subsequently to a communist society in which humans would be freed from compulsory labour. These are the so-called laws of movement of capitalism: increasing industrial concentration (which in fact took place, at least in the decades following publication of Marx's writings), polarization of capitalists and proletariat (contradicted by the growing importance of the middle classes), and the tendency to a falling profit rate and increasing poverty for workers (which does not take into account the effects of technical progress).

In the second volume of *Capital*, finally, Marx developed a theory of simple and expanded reproduction schemes, in many respects forerunning Leontief's input–output tables, Sir Roy Harrod's model and Piero Sraffa's analysis of prices of production, all of which we shall discuss in the text that follows.

2.5   The Marginalist Approach

The subjective approach based on equilibrium between supply and demand (i.e. between available resources and the needs and desires of economic agents) did not emerge all of a sudden, with the publication between 1871 and 1873 of the main works of Jevons, Menger and Walras, respectively in English, German and French. Actually, it had a long tradition, having already appeared in classical antiquity and the Middle Ages: a tradition that slowly waxed stronger over time, with development of notions such as work interpreted as sacrifice (already present in the Bible), consumption seen as a source of utility (as early as Aristotle and Thomas Aquinas), intensive rent associated not with extension of cultivation to ever less fertile lands but to use on a given plot of land of ever greater quantities of means of production and labour (Turgot 1766; von Thünen 1826–50) and so on.

The marginalist approach can thus be considered an analytical refinement of the subjective approach already present in antiquity. In it, the value of goods is given by scarcity and utility; the market is conceived of not as a network of exchanges allowing the different sectors to recover the means of production with which to start a new cycle of production again, but as the point where demand and supply meet, as in the medieval fairs and then in the stock exchange; wages, profits and rents are considered remuneration for the productive contribution of the factors of production capital, labour and land; income distribution is thus analysed as a special case of the problem of price determination.

All these elements, long present, towards the middle of the nineteenth century were coordinated into a view of the functioning of the economy explicitly hailed as differing from the classical one, by authors such as Mountifort Longfield, John Rae, George Poulett Scrope and William Nassau Senior. There were also attempts to find a mediation between this approach and the classical one (as did for instance, at least to a certain extent, John Stuart Mill). Thus, all was ready for the so-called marginalist revolution.

Between 1871 and 1874, as anticipated earlier, appeared the main works by the leaders of the three streams in which we may subdivide the marginalist approach: the *Principles of political economy* (1871) by the recognized founder of the Austrian school, Carl Menger (1840–1921); the *Theory of political economy* (1871) by the British William Stanley Jevons (1835–82); and the *Elements of pure economics* (1874) by Léon Walras (1834–1910), the French founder of the so-called Lausanne school. The three streams show significant differences, which will be considered in the text that follows; however, they also present common basic characteristics, opposed to those characterizing the classical approach.

Common to them, first of all, is the return to the pre-classical paradigm of scarcity and utility. The problem taken up for consideration is that of balancing between scarce available resources and multiplicity of human needs and desires. Two elements were utilized to solve this problem. The first was methodological individualism, i.e. the idea that the individual constitutes the atom on which the theory is built. The second was the analytical notion of equilibrium between demand and supply; with this notion, the analytic requirement of equality between the two variables substitutes the generic classical references to a tendency to a balancing of the two magnitudes. In other words, the analysis starts with the decisions of a rational *homo oeconomicus* confronted with resource scarcity and aiming to maximize his or her utility, considered as a one-dimensional measurable magnitude. Only as a second step, once the equilibrium solution for the individual agent has been determined, does the analysis take into consideration the interrelations between different agents, each of which is supposed not to be influenced by the preferences of the others: a very restrictive assumption, as it denies the social character of the economic agent.

Thus, compared to the classical approach of the circular flow of production and consumption, here we have a view of the economy as a one-way road leading from scarce resources to the satisfaction of human needs and desires; an individualistic framework instead of an analysis based on the social classes of capitalists, workers and landlords; a subjective view of value instead of an objective one; systematic recourse to the condition of equilibrium between supply and demand to solve the analytical problem of price determination. Compared to the pre-classical subjective approach, we have two new analytical notions, marginal utility and marginal productivity: respectively, the additional utility deriving from consumption of an additional unit of a commodity, and the increment of production deriving from utilization of an additional dose of a factor of production.

Let us now consider characteristics and main developments of each of these streams.

Carl Menger, leader of the Austrian school, had an education in jurisprudence and a diffidence towards the use of mathematics in a social science like political economy. His 1871 volume opens with a long discussion on the notion of goods and the nature of needs; much more than the determination of economic equilibrium (referred to each individual, and only as the sum of individual equilibria to society as a whole), what is considered important is the specification and characterization of the elements concurring in its determination. This explains, among other things, his insistence on the limits of the forces leading towards equilibrium, particularly the limits to knowledge, and on the need to study the economic process in its evolution. The leading role of the market, in fact, consists in providing individual economic agents, especially but not only through prices, with synthetic information on the spectrum of elements influencing demand for and supply of each individual good. As we shall see in the text that follows, these themes were subsequently to be developed by Ludwig von Mises and Friedrich Hayek, and to constitute the elements characterizing the new Austrian school.

An important analytical contribution was then offered by one of Menger's pupils, Eugen von Böhm-Bawerk (1851–1914; 1899). He sought to build a more robust theoretical structure than Menger's, and to this end created a bridge with the general equilibrium theory developed by the Lausanne school. In his analytical building, the rate of interest is conceived of as a variable leading to equilibrium the two elements, the marginal productivity of capital and 'abstinence', i.e. the preference for immediate over future consumption. To measure the 'quantity of capital' utilized in the productive process, Böhm-Bawerk resorted to the notion of the average period of production: an average of all the time intervals in which the hours of labour directly and indirectly required to obtain a given final product are locked up. On this theory and its limits we shall be returning in various contexts, as it plays an important role in Hayek's theory, in his debate with Sraffa and in the debates in capital theory.

The second stream of the marginalist revolution is the one originated by the British economist Jevons: a graduate in sciences, well acquainted with mathematics, he took as his point of departure Bentham's utilitarianism, and hence the one-dimensional measurability of pleasures and pains. And yet, Jevons was not interested in interpersonal comparisons, but in clarifying the way a rational *homo oeconomicus* operates his choices.

To avoid Mill's criticisms, recalled earlier, Jevons took utility as an abstract relationship between a good and a person, not a property intrinsic to the good; for him (1871, pp. 92–3), 'The calculus of utility aims at supplying the ordinary wants of man at the least cost of labour.' Thus his notion of the motivation for human action departed from Smith's: no longer self-interest, but sheer material selfishness dominates the 'rationality' of the marginalist *homo oeconomicus*.

The archetype chosen by Jevons is Robinson Crusoe who, alone on his island, has to decide how much time to allot to rest or to work, and how much to each of the different activities which allow him to obtain the various consumption goods (hunting or fishing, for example) or the capital goods that enhance the efficacy of his work (tools, fences for his goats and so on). The solution to the problem utilizes differential calculus, and the assumptions of decreasing satisfaction for each consumption good, increasing sacrifice for work and decreasing returns for each kind of activity. In equilibrium, the marginal disutility of labour needs to be equal (obviously with an opposite sign) to the marginal utility of each consumption good (which Jevons calls 'final degree of utility'). For instance, in allotting his time to hunting, fishing and rest, Robinson Crusoe will choose in such a way that the last fraction of time allotted to each of the three activities has the same utility. The value of capital goods, too, is determined with a perspective evaluation, on the basis of their marginal productivity (namely the increased production yielded by an additional dose of capital) and of the marginal utility of the additional doses of consumption goods thus obtained. The economy as a whole is not directly the object of analysis; collective behaviour is obtained as the aggregation (sum) of individual behaviours, considered as independent from one another, with a questionable assumption that would, however, remain pivotal in subsequent developments of the marginalist approach.

The third stream of the marginalist approach is that of the Lausanne or general economic equilibrium school, originated by Walras. This stream would remain substantially extraneous to Anglo-Saxon culture up to the post-war period (with the exceptions of an Austrian version exported to London by Hayek at the beginning of the 1930s and of some of Hick's writings, in particular *Value and capital*, 1939) but, as we shall see, it would become synonymous with rigorous economic theory in contemporary economic debate. Walras borrowed from physics the notion of equilibrium between forces; equilibrium for the economic system as a whole is determined as the solution to a set of equations, increasingly complex as we proceed from a pure exchange system to a system with exchange and production, up to systems including accumulation and, finally, money. Here we shall limit our reference to the pure exchange system; the data of the problem consist in the number of commodities and economic agents, their preferences and their endowments of the different goods. Preferences are expressed as individual demand functions for the various commodities, which Walras derives from utility functions. For each individual there is a budget constraint, ensuring equality between the value of goods demanded on the whole and the resources available to the individual. The set of equations determines equilibrium values for prices and quantities of the various goods exchanged. According to Walras, a process of adjustment (*tâtonnement*) ensures stability of equilibrium. This was for him a crucial tenet, abandonment of which would leave his entire theoretical construct meaningless; however, his attempts failed and subsequent theoretical developments arrived at a negative conclusion.

Walras's successor to the Lausanne chair, Vilfredo Pareto (1848–1923), an engineer by training, brought forward the mathematical analysis of general economic equilibrium, following the logic of rational mechanics manuals. Instead of (measurable) marginal utility, he proposed the notion of 'ophelimity' – an ordinal notion conceived of as a means to get away from the utilitarian philosophical tradition. He also proposed the notion known as 'Pareto optimum' – a set of solutions to the economic variables such that no change from it may improve the situation of an individual agent without at the same time worsening the position of at least another agent – and demonstrated that competitive equilibrium corresponds to this optimum. However, Pareto did not succeed in demonstrating the existence, stability and uniqueness of the competitive equilibrium, and hence of any such optimum. Possibly it is precisely the growing consciousness of the limits of pure economic theory, the more evident the more rigorous it becomes, that gave a decisive push to a shift of Pareto's interests in the direction of sociology in the last stage of his research activity (the *Trattato di sociologia generale* was published in 1916).

We may possibly see as a fourth stream of the marginalist approach, although it only came twenty years after the first three, the one inaugurated by Alfred Marshall (1842–1924), whose *Principles of economics* (1890) dominated economics teaching for a long time, both directly and as a model for other textbooks. His target was a syncretic approach: the subjective theory of value and the notion of equilibrium between supply and demand were taken up from the founders of marginalism and their forerunners; attention to production and the distinction between increasing, constant and decreasing returns were taken up from the classical approach, and in particular John Stuart Mill.[12] On this basis Marshall proposed models of equilibrium for the firm and the industry, for the short and the long period. Translated (by Jacob Viner and Arthur Pigou) into the schemes of U-shaped average and marginal cost curves, these analytical models, dominant in elementary microeconomics textbooks to this very day, are widely utilized, notwithstanding their limits, in applying economic theory to the analysis of actual industrial economics issues. Wittingly or unwittingly, in the post-war period economic theory was imbibed with Marshallian culture, especially in the fields of application of the pure theory of value. Marshall dominated British economic culture through his pupils and his textbook, but also through the British Economic Association and the *Economic Journal*, both founded in 1890.

Two other characteristics of Marshall's thought exerting a strong influence on subsequent economic culture are the method of short causal chains, which would be taken up and modified by Keynes, and the attempt to incorporate elements of Darwinian evolutionary thought into economic analysis, subsequently taken up by the evolutionary stream.

The method of short causal chains corresponds to Marshall's diffidence towards general economic equilibrium (of which Marshall provided an – at the time – adequate presentation in an appendix to the *Principles*). General equilibrium may in fact be misleading when confronted with the complexities of the real world, from which it isolates only a few economic aspects for analysis. Thus Marshall prefers the method of partial equilibriums, i.e. determining equilibrium – for the short and the long period, for the firm and the industry – by considering demand for and supply of each commodity as independent from what is simultaneously taking place in the markets for other commodities.

Marshall also utilized an evolutionary notion of the firm, as from the fifth edition of the *Principles* (1905), so as to develop the notion of a life cycle of the firm. This notion is utilized to solve (or, better, to circumvent, as we shall see in §5.3 when considering Sraffa's criticisms) the problem of compatibility between the assumptions of perfect competition and of increasing returns to scale, which are very important in reality. Evolutionary Darwinism had a strong influence on the *Principles*, accompanying the static view inherited from the founders of the marginalist

---

[12] The term 'neoclassical economics' was originally (by Veblen) attributed to Marshall precisely because of his syncretic approach; subsequently it was utilized (for instance by Hicks and Stigler) to refer to marginalist theory in general; Samuelson described the subject of his textbook as a 'grand neoclassical synthesis' (Samuelson 1948a) as from the third edition, 1955. Cf. Aspromourgos (1986). Here we shall utilize the term for Hicks–Modigliani–Samuelson's macroeconomics (illustrated in Chapter 7).

approach and implicit in the notion of equilibrium between demand and supply. Thus, in a complex interplay of text and footnotes, statements and qualifications, we can find in Marshall's text both the view then developed by Pigou and Viner and bequeathed to the textbook vulgate, and the germs of an evolutionary view. Within this latter, the notion of equilibrium tends to acquire dynamic connotations, in the attempt to keep in account both the irreversibility characterizing the actual movements of firms and industries along demand and supply curves, and the margins of manoeuvre available to firms even under competitive conditions. It is an evolutionary view stemming more from Lamarck than from Darwin's original contribution: under the influence of the sociologist Herbert Spencer (1820–1903), Marshall sought to take into account the heredity of the characteristics acquired in life by an organism in response-adaptation to the environment it inhabits. This line of reasoning, with the connected view of competition as a process of selection of the best firms, exerts a strong influence over a heterodox stream of contemporary economic research, namely the evolutionary approach. Marshall's influence on subsequent economic thought is in any case remarkably extensive, while his writings on the quantity theory of money, on the trade cycle with the interaction between real and monetary phenomena, on monetary institutions, etc., are also rich in seeds taken up by successive generations of economists.

3 The Immediate Precursors

3.1   Introduction

In the preceding chapter we briefly illustrated the two main approaches to economics, classical and marginalist. As we have seen, such broad categories include a variety of internal positions, concurring to constitute the background of the contemporary debate. Thus, it may be useful to briefly consider some at least of the authors who offered original contributions in the first half of the twentieth century, while recalling on some points one or the other of the two great – classical and marginalist – traditions.

A variety of views is an ever present characteristic of economic writings; here the point needs stressing in opposition to recent attempts to refer especially in teaching to a 'single line of thinking' needing no comparison with different views.

In this chapter we shall focus on five authors with very different backgrounds, research interests and lines of analysis. The Swedish economist Knut Wicksell was an acute theoretician, who recognized the problems in value theory which came very much under debate more than half a century later, and who inaugurated a major stream of research on the theory of the trade cycle based on the influence exerted by monetary factors over real ones. The American Thorstein Veblen, a charismatic and anti-conformist figure, is considered the father of modern institutionalism. The German Max Weber, the founder of modern sociology, proposed original solutions for the method of social sciences, in particular concerning the opposition between subjective and objective views, between the a priori approach of abstract theory and historical empiricism; he is also known for his contributions on the origins and structure of capitalist society. The Austrian Joseph Schumpeter worked out his theory of development on the basis of a dialectical opposition between static equilibrium analysis and dynamic analysis of change. Finally, the British John Maynard Keynes found a way to bring the uncertainty characterizing human actions into economic analysis, with consequent in-depth revision of the role of money and finance in the theory of employment.[1]

Obviously, various other authors made important contributions, and will be referred to where useful in subsequent chapters. A further problem concerns the distinction between immediate forerunners and full-fledged protagonists of the period we focus attention on in this volume. Only fifteen years separate the birth of the youngest of the 'forerunners' from that of the two authors – Friedrich Hayek and Piero Sraffa – whom we shall be considering in the next two chapters. However, in the case of both Schumpeter and Keynes, their lives ended immediately after the Second World War, while both Hayek and Sraffa offered major original contributions both before and after the war. Any demarcation line has its limits: we need to utilize such lines with caution, to achieve a reasonably clear exposition, but without attributing excessive importance to them.

3.2   Wicksell and the Swedish School

Unlike the case of the majority of economists, in the case of the Swedish Knut Wicksell (1851–1926) teaching and research activity in the field of pure economic theory followed a stage of lively activity as a neo-Malthusian polemist, lecturer and journalist. Wicksell's fame among his contemporaries stems above all from his role as a radical opponent of prevailing ethics and from his repeated goading targeting traditional opinions on family, religion, fatherland and state authority. It was this that held him back in the early stages of his academic career, arousing widespread hostility and even landing him – by then fifty years old and a professor – in prison for offence against religion.[2]

For a long time his interests in economic issues focused on the population issue. Wicksell was a passionate neo-Malthusian, supporter of birth control, with intense activity as propagandist on the subject. His studies in economic theory were initially a collateral activity, taking a central position only when the thirty-six-year-old Wicksell obtained a grant in 1887. He was thus able to study in London, Strasbourg and Berlin, and to attend Carl Menger's lectures in Vienna. He obtained a temporary lectureship at Lund only in 1899, finally overcoming the hostility of

---

[1] For a broader treatment, let me refer to Roncaglia (2005a), from which I drew the material for this chapter.

[2] These aspects of his life dominate the fascinating biography by Gårdlund (1956). Wicksell constitutes a clear demonstration of the erroneousness of the thesis, typical of the Marxist tradition, of an opposition between a progressive classical approach and a conservative marginalist approach. In this Wicksell is no exception: we may recall the social reformism of Walras, a supporter of the nationalization of land, and of the British Fabians.

a conservative academic environment. Only in 1905 did he become a full professor, subsequent to fierce controversies. He died in Stockholm in 1926.

His main writings in pure economics are *Value, capital and rent* (1893) and Interest and prices (1898), an article titled 'Marginal productivity as the basis for distribution in economics' (1900) and the two volumes of *Lectures on political economy* (vol. 1, *Theory*, 1901, and vol. 2, *Money*, 1906, translated into English in 1934–5). The English edition of the *Lectures*, edited by Lionel Robbins, also includes the main articles published in the same period, including a 1919 critique of Cassel's theories and a paper on the theory of capital, 1923.[3] Other important contributions by the Swedish economist, not considered here, concern the theory of public finance.

Wicksell made two major contributions to economic theory. First, in the 1893 *Value, capital and rent*, he developed a marginalist theory of distribution between capital, land and labour based on their marginal productivities. In this work, as in the first volume of the *Lectures*, Wicksell utilized Böhm-Bawerk's theory of the average period of production, briefly considered in the preceding chapter. However, having accepted it initially, Wicksell distanced himself from it while seeking to expand it so as to take into account the heterogeneity of the means of production. In essence, he oscillates between an aggregate and a disaggregated notion of capital, adopting the latter when identifying capital with the entire temporal structure of direct and indirect labour flows required to obtain a given product.[4]

---

[3] Gustav Cassel (1866–1945), a professor at Stockholm, a typical university 'baron', Wicksell's adversary and staunch conservative, is mainly known for his simplified version of the Walrasian theory, the *Theory of social economy*, published in German in 1918 and in English in 1923. It is the mediation of this work that is to be thanked for the spread of Walrasian ideas in German and Anglo-Saxon culture (Jaffé's translation of Walras's text, *Elements of pure economics*, appeared only in 1954). Cassel is also known for his contributions to international economics, such as PPP (purchasing power parity) theory, according to which under free circulation of commodities exchange rates tend to a level such as to guarantee the parity of purchasing power in the various countries, given the level of internal prices (that is, ten dollars acquire the same quantities of commodities in Italy, Germany or France or in any other country: if this were not true, there would arise a flow of commodities from the countries with lower prices towards the countries with higher prices; the consequent disequilibrium in balances of trade would lead to readjustment of the exchange rates). This theory has been the subject of extensive discussion at the theoretical level, and contradicted by a mass of empirical analyses on the subject, which rather appear to confirm the typically Keynesian thesis that financial flows dominate over commercial flows in the determination of exchange rates, giving rise to persistent deviations from purchasing power parities.

[4] For an illustration and critique of Wicksell's theory of capital, cf. Garegnani (1960), pp. 123–85.

Second, in the framework of the monetary theory illustrated in his 1898 essay and developed in the second volume of the *Lectures*, Wicksell formulated a distinction between the monetary and natural interest rate. The latter is determined by the 'real' variables which concur in determining the equilibrium of the economic system; it thus turns out to be equal to the marginal productivity of 'capital', as indicated by the marginal theory of distribution. The monetary rate of interest is instead determined on the money markets, with a certain autonomy with respect to the natural rate.

The relationship between money and natural interest rates is then utilized in explaining the cyclical oscillations of the economy and the inflationary or deflationary pressures on the general level of prices. When the monetary rate of interest is below the natural rate, entrepreneurs find it expedient to take loans in order to invest, thus generating an inflationary pressure. On the other hand, when the monetary rate of interest is above the natural rate, investments are discouraged and a deflationary pressure develops.[5] We thus have cumulative disequilibrium processes, which contribute to accounting for the trade cycle and inflation.

This theory, only outlined here, is part of a stream of monetary explanations of the cycle and of inflation that seek to reconcile two contradictory elements: on the one hand, a marginalist theory of value and distribution within which equilibrium values for prices and income distribution are determined; on the other, recognition of the fact, evident to any empirical economist, that deviations from full employment equilibrium do take place and that monetary variables do influence real variables. Wicksell's approach was subsequently taken up and developed by a number of economists, including Hayek.

The so-called Swedish school (Erik Lindhal, 1891–1960; Gunnar Myrdal, 1898–1987, Nobel Prize in 1974; Bertil Ohlin, 1899–1979) from the late 1920s took on various aspects of Wicksell's theory, but in particular proposed, in opposition to Keynes's analysis, the analytical tool of sequential or period analysis, based on the distinction between ex ante and ex post and on the sequential stages of production and market exchange, already present in the Austrian tradition and taken up in Britain by Hicks (1973).[6]

---

[5] In his theory of such cumulative – inflationary and deflationary – processes, Wicksell assumes that there are no changes in production techniques; as a consequence, neither income distribution, nor production levels or relative prices are allowed to change, and disequilibrium can only manifest itself in variations in monetary variables, namely the price level. On this point, and on the ambiguities of Wicksell's definition of the natural interest rate, cf. Donzelli (1988), pp. 67–71.

[6] Keynes (1973, vol. 14, pp. 184–5; cf. Kregel 1976, p. 223) rejects this technique 'owing to my failure to establish any definite unit of time'. In other words, sequential analysis needs to establish the boundaries of successive time periods in a sufficiently objective way (for

3.3   Veblen and Institutionalism

Thorstein Veblen (1857–1929), the son of Norwegian peasants who migrated to the United States, is considered the founder of US institutionalism. His university studies took him away from the community of origin but he did not adapt to the academic world. Nevertheless, he had an important role and, although many now see him more as a sociologist than an economist, for years he was the editor of the *Journal of Political Economy*, founded in 1892, and at the time the leading economics journal in the United States (together with the *Quarterly Journal of Economics*, founded in 1886); he was also among the promoters of the American Economic Association, and one of his pupils, Wesley Mitchell, was the founder of the National Bureau of Economic Research.

The theory of the leisure class (1899) is the title of his first and most famous book. Written in far from plain language, with a well-structured but difficult personal terminology,[7] the book is still a classic of its kind. Other writings followed, including *The theory of business enterprise* (1904), where Veblen points out the relevance of the distinction between industrial and financial capital, and *The place of science in modern civilization* (1919).

Veblen's research concerns institutions and economic customs, with a historical-evolutionary view deriving more from the German historical school than from Darwin's influence. He was a radical critic of capitalist society and, more generally, of a social system in which the main objective of agents is to excel over others through 'conspicuous consumption' (made possible by uneven distribution and at the same time contributing to its persistence). He studied the way social customs evolve from primitive to modern societies while keeping intact a social structure based on inequalities. He also studied the way educational institutions, and in particular the universities, help to perpetuate the affluent society.[8]

According to Veblen, the consumer is mainly driven by social habits and customs, not by rational utility maximization. Rather, as in the case of conspicuous consumption, other motivations may arise, such as the desire to excel over others, or for social upgrading.

---

instance, in the alternation between the working week and the final day of the market, as in the Marshallian–Hicksian model of the fish market: Marshall 1890; Hicks 1939). As a matter of fact, not only do productive processes differ in the time they require, but it is also impossible to encapsulate in a univocally defined sequential scheme the actual decisions of entrepreneurs and financial operators, and the timing of revising expectations and adopting new decisions.

[7] For instance, as Tsuru (1993, p. 61) notes, Veblen contrasts 'industry' (i.e. 'making things') with 'business' ('making money').

[8] For extensive illustration of his life, thought and influence cf. Diggins (1999).

By conspicuous consumption Veblen means consumption not necessary for subsistence but for differentiation from the others. The very
uselessness of such consumption is thus necessary to its very purpose.
Leisure is a manifestation of affluent consumption; indeed, it is its original
manifestation in primitive societies. The powerful person need not dirty
his or her hands with productive labour, and is nevertheless able to
consume in excess of his or her needs. A show of affluence is necessary
to retain power both by imposing a social model and, within society, by
asserting the elevated position of the person who can enjoy conspicuous
consumption. The latter changes in form but remains unchanged in
essence in subsequent stages of human history. In it we can also see the
original subordination of women: even when women participate in conspicuous consumption, in their case it is essentially vicarious consumption, through which the head of the family manifests his position of power.

Of course, Veblen's theoretical construction opposes the marginalist
one based on consumer sovereignty and considering consumption as
satisfaction of the agent's needs and desires. Not only the view of the
functioning of the economic and social system, but also the very tools of
analysis are different: the notion of equilibrium between supply and
demand is absent, while research focuses on social customs and their
evolution, culture (in the sense of the dominant mentality), and, especially, power relations, which appear more closely connected to culture
than to political or strictly economical life.

Veblen's successors retained his methodological approach, but showed
a less critical view of society. An important role in the birth of the
American Economic Association (in 1885) was played by Richard Ely
(1854–1943), founder of an institutional school at the University of
Wisconsin. Another leading figure in the Wisconsin school was John
Commons (1862–1945). US institutionalism was also strengthened in
the period immediately preceding the Second World War by the influx of
Austrian and German scholars escaping from Nazism. This, for example,
gave rise to the New School for Social Research in New York.[9]

Study of the institutions and the social structure, with even radical
differences from one country to another, was opposed to abstract theory
and the 'Ricardian vice', consisting in applying pure theory to reality
without the necessary caution. Today the contributions by institutional
economists are often classified as external to the field of economics, or at

---

[9] Tsuru (1993, p. 71) distinguishes, after the generation of the founder Veblen, a second
generation of institutionalists including Wesley Mitchell, John Commons and John
Maurice Clark, and a third generation including Galbraith, Clarence Ayers and Gunnar
Myrdal; within this latter group we may also include Tsuru himself.

the most on the borderline between economics, sociology and history. However, they are rich in prompts for economic analysis, occasionally resurfacing in other heterodox streams of research.

3.4   Weber: The Method, between Theory and History

The so-called historical school, present especially in Germany and continental Europe, saw ample diffusion in the second half of the nineteenth century. In this respect it may be useful to distinguish between the 'old' historical school, flourishing around the mid-nineteenth century (Wilhelm Roscher, 1817–94; Bruno Hildebrand, 1812–78; Karl Knies, 1821–98) and the 'new' historical school led by Gustav von Schmoller (1837–1917), having developed and grown around the *Verein für Socialpolitik* (Association for Social Policy) founded in 1872.

Exponents of the old historical school maintained the importance of statistical analysis for capturing the characteristics of a continuously changing society and stressed the historically relative nature of 'economic laws'. Commonly utilized in economic theory as if they were endowed with general validity, these 'laws' do not in fact take into account the specificity of individual countries and the organic relationship connecting economic and social development with other aspects of social life. The new historical school is more radical; in an oft-cited debate on method (*Methodenstreit*), Schmoller frontally opposed marginalist theory (in Menger's Austrian variety), criticizing its abstract nature. In the context of this debate, Max Weber developed an autonomous position, which has had an important and persistent influence on method of research in the field of social sciences.

Max Weber (1864–1920), professor of political economy at Freiburg and then at Heidelberg, Vienna and Munich, also worked on strictly economic issues.[10] His main work is *Economy and Society*, posthumously published in 1922; also well known is his essay 'Protestant ethic and the spirit of capitalism' (1904–5), later included in a collection of studies on the sociology of religion (1920–21). Common to these writings is the inquiry into the factors accounting for the origins and assertion of specific economic behaviour: a theme on the borderline between sociology and political economy, today commonly attributed to the field of economic sociology. The essays on method, originally published between 1903 and 1917, were collected in a book published posthumously (Weber 1922b).

---

[10] In fact, it is the view of the economic science which changed, from then to now, inducing today's mainstream to exclude researchers such as Veblen and Weber from the field of economics, even in the history of economic thought.

As mentioned earlier, the leader of the Austrian stream of marginalist theory, Menger, was involved in a fierce dispute with the leader of the new German historical school, Schmoller. The latter maintained the impossibility of grounding 'economic laws' on a priori postulates or on a basis which is considered insufficient in statistically recognized empiric regularities. Hence the need for a prior stage of capillary, wide-ranging collection of statistical data on all aspects of economic life – precisely the task assigned to the *Verein*. Menger, following in this the idealistic reaction to positivism, maintained instead that the a priori on which economic analysis relies can be derived from introspection. This is, for instance, what happens with respect to the norms of behaviour of the rational economic agent, considered as axioms the true foundation of which is (should be) evident to everybody. On the basis of such axioms we can build a deductive science, while empirical knowledge is always by necessity provisional and incomplete; thus, though useful in understanding reality, empirical knowledge cannot provide the foundations for building a theoretical-deductive system.[11]

It would be simplistic to consider Weber's an intermediate position between these two extremes.[12] It is, rather, an original position that rejects the a priori contents drawn from psychological introspection, but at the same time shares 'the need for a rational interpretation of human actions' (Rossi 2007, p. 12) and rejects the a-theoretical empiricism of the new historical school as well as Comte's positivist sociology assuming the existence of a natural order (or natural laws) in human societies.

Weber drew from the culture of his epoch the method of understanding (*Verstehen*), which in his opinion cannot be limited to introspective intuition but implies serious comparison with reality, including empirical verification of its results. Sufficient foundations for elaborating economic and social theories may be found by observing the real world, which allows for the building of a system of 'ideal types', i.e. categories that are abstracted from factual historical evolution. Such foundations are not a priori, eternal and unchangeable, but related to their historical context and evolve together with it.

Hence Weber's methodological position recognizes the validity of theoretical-deductive analysis, but tempers it by recognizing the role of historical-empirical research and by paying attention to the institutions and their evolution. Moreover, the social sciences are objective insofar as

---

[11] On the various streams of thought at the time and on the role attributed to introspection for knowledge, cf. Stuart Hughes (1958).

[12] We may recall in this respect that in his methodological essays Weber criticizes Roscher's and Knies's historicism: they consider economic development as organically connected to all the other aspects of the life of individual peoples.

they avoid any contamination with value judgements: the researcher's values may lead his or her research towards one problem rather than another or towards the selection of some elements rather than others within the infinite complexity of the real world, but should not determine the answers. Finally, historical–social sciences have as objects of their study not general laws but specific situations, endowed with an individuality; within these sciences, causality is not to be interpreted as necessity but as objective possibility: the multiplicity of causal relations stands in the way of deterministic explanations.[13]

The debate on method offers the opportunity to mention some developments now considered external to economics, but originally seen as a usual part of the research work of economists. Max Weber, today considered a most eminent sociologist and the founder of modern sociology, actually held a chair in economics, and was in many respects closer to the theoreticians of the Austrian school than to the exponents of the new historical school.[14]

Weber is considered 'the Marx of the bourgeoisie': his work, like Marx's, offers an interpretation of the capitalistic mode of production and its evolution. However, unlike Marx, Weber maintained that in the historical process of development the dominant causal link is not the one going from the material conditions of reproduction of the economy to the sphere of institutions and culture, but rather the one going in the opposite direction.

We should stress in this respect that, just as Marx is not a pure materialist, so Weber is not a pure idealist: both recognize that the material conditions of life and the productive organization of society, on the one hand, and culture and political and juridical institutions, on the other, are connected by a complex set of interrelations. The element of opposition between the two is a matter of the choice of the main causal link for the purposes of theory construction: from the social and productive structure to culture and institutions, as Marx maintains, or vice versa, as Weber holds.

The latter locates in the evolution of capitalism a gigantic process of rationalization not only of economic activity but of the whole of society: a formal rationality, driving the choice of the most adequate means for the attainment of selected ends. It is this characteristic which distinguishes modern capitalism from the ancient version, based as it was on 'material'

---

[13] Cf. Rossi (2007), p. 56.

[14] According to Weber, abstract economic theory (identified with Menger's theory) 'provides a systematically organized set of concepts (and rules) that do not reproduce the historical economic forms, but that are indispensable for their analysis' (Rossi 2007, p. 24).

rationality, driven by evaluation postulates stemming from tradition or from religious authorities. Correspondingly, Weber distinguishes the 'legal-rational' power typical of modern societies from the 'traditional' and 'charismatic' powers also present in modern societies but dominating in ancient societies.[15] This constitutes the background for his forecast of the development of modern capitalist societies in the direction of a progressive bureaucratization of the state and the productive process, with the growth of middle strata of functionaries and technicians. It is a forecast that focuses on the middle classes, thus opposed to the Marxian vision of a process of proletarianization.

On the origins of capitalism, too, Weber follows a different road from Marx, maintaining that a crucial role is played by the affirmation, with Protestantism, of a specific culture (the 'spirit of capitalism') favourable to concrete engagement in society (against the asceticism of medieval Catholicism or of Counter-Reformation).[16]

Other important contributions concern the sociology of religions and urban sociology. In both cases Weber enquires into the elements that allow for social cohesion, going beyond the solidarity internal to the parental group typical of primitive societies. Thus, the 'religions of redemption' favour the brotherhood of the faithful. Also important is the distinction between adaptation to the world and mystical practice characterizing different religious traditions: as a rule, mystical practices imply indifference towards worldly issues, and so towards the prevailing political and social institutions as well; adaptation to the world may imply (as in the case of the Confucian doctrine), but not necessarily, a-critical acceptance of the existing social order.

Finally, let us recall the two conferences held in 1919, *Politik als Beruf* and *Wissenschaft als Beruf* (Weber 1919). In the essay on politics, Weber

---

[15] Weber stresses that the law, in a modern capitalist society, should be addressed in a formal-rational way so as to guarantee the computability of results, namely to make it easier to forecast them.

[16] In the wake of Weber, cf. Tawney (1926). On Marx's ideas on the transition from feudalism to capitalism, cf. Dobb (1946); the issue has given rise to lively controversies in the Marxist field: cf. Dobb *et al.* (1954), Brenner (1978) and the bibliography quoted there. For a position analogous to Weber's in stressing the importance of culture for the evolution of political and economic institutions, but different with respect to the identification of the driving force (not Protestantism, but Scholastic thought), cf. Schumpeter (1954, pp. 97–102) and, more recently, Chafuen (1986). An important critical illustration of Weber's and Tawney's theses is due to Viner (1978, pp. 151–92), who stresses that before Weber various authors had associated the naissance of capitalism with Protestantism, pointing in particular to the role attributed to the direct study of the Holy Writings by the faithful (in contrast to the hierarchical structure of the Catholic Church), hence to individual instruction and thinking. Weber's distinctive thesis is considered to be the importance he attributed to the doctrine of predestination and to the idea that success in business constitutes a sign of election.

distinguishes between political involvement in the sense of devotion to a cause (which is, or should be, typical of any citizen) and the profession of the politician, in general a full-time paid job, which implies adopting an ethic of responsibility rather than an ethic of belief, thus open to compromises on the means to be adopted to attain the ends.[17]

3.5   Schumpeter: From Statics to Dynamics

Joseph Alois Schumpeter (1883–1950), by birth a citizen of the Austro-Hungarian Empire, a student in Vienna and Austrian minister of finances in the immediate aftermath of the First World War, moved to the United States (to Harvard University) in 1932. He is known mainly for his thesis that the process of economic development is driven by a sequence of innovations realized by entrepreneurs with the purchasing power provided to them by bankers. The fascination of this idea stems at least in part from its twofold political implications: it brings to the fore the personalities of the entrepreneur and the banker, protagonists of the development process, while it opposes Keynesian active policies and considers crises a necessary ill stimulating the vitality of capitalism. Moreover, the view of a dynamics endogenous to the economy and society, and of the decadence of capitalism, appears to place Schumpeter alongside Marx in opposition to the traditional economic equilibrium theories.

Together with his scientific work, Schumpeter took on important didactic work. Among his pupils at Harvard are a number of the major economists of the twentieth century, from Wassily Leontief to Paul A. Samuelson, from Paul M. Sweezy and Richard Goodwin to Hyman Minsky, and from Shigeto Tsuru to Sylos Labini.

In his first volume published in 1908 Schumpeter was already taking a view that he maintained in the writings of his maturity, as well, 'methodological liberalism'. In Schumpeter's own words (1908, p. 156, italics added): it is 'advantageous not to set the methodological assumptions once and for all our purposes, but to adapt them to each objective and, once such specific assumptions appear adequate to the purpose, *to be as liberal as possible*'.

Schumpeter (1908, p. 3) starts from the statement that 'all sciences are nothing but … forms of representation' of reality, and criticizes the idea 'that the formulation of exact "laws" is possible' (p. 12): a methodological position similar to that of Keynes, who conceives theories and formalized models as tools for orientation within reality, and radically different from

---

[17] For an in-depth treatment of the different aspects of Weber's thought, only hinted at here, cf. Rossi (2007).

the position, widespread at the time, according to which mathematical laws express the intrinsic essence of things, so that the theoretician's task is to 'uncover' such laws from the accidental phenomena enshrouding them.

From the viewpoint of methodological liberalism, Schumpeter criticized as sterile the debate on method still under way in those years between those who (like Menger) considered economics an exact science and those who (like Schmoller) saw it as closer to the historical-social sciences: 'the historical school and the abstract one are not in contrast and ... the only difference between them is their attention for different issues' (Schumpeter 1908, p. 22) or, perhaps better, in different aspects of the same reality – an extremely complex reality that cannot be reduced entirely to one problem or another.

A corollary of methodological liberalism is a cautious attitude towards methodological individualism, i.e. the method of analysis which starts from the individual – from his or her preferences and endowments – and which is at the root of marginalist economic theory. Schumpeter (1908, p. 83) stresses the distinction between individualistic science and political individualism (liberalism), stating that 'there is no particularly close relationship between' the two and that 'from theory in itself we can draw arguments neither in favour nor against political individualism'. In this he follows the separation, advocated by Weber as well, between theoretical propositions that fall in the field of science and value judgements that fall within the field of politics.

The distinction between economic liberalism and political liberalism is analogous: the former is identified with 'the theory that the best way of promoting economic development and general welfare is to remove fetters from the private-enterprise economy and to leave it alone', while political liberalism is identified with 'sponsorship of parliamentary government, freedom to vote and extension of the right to vote, freedom of the press, divorce of secular from spiritual government, trial by jury, and so on' (Schumpeter 1954, p. 394).

In his 1908 book, Schumpeter follows the marginalist tradition, according to which the value of economic goods is expressed by demand for them relative to their scarcity. However, he rejects Jevons's utilitarianism, based on the identification of value with the (subjective) measure of the ability of goods to satisfy such needs. In what appears as an *ante litteram* critique of revealed preference theory (illustrated in Chapter 6), Schumpeter states: 'psychological deduction is simply a tautology. If we say that somebody is prepared to pay something more than somebody else because he values it more, with this we do not give an explanation, since it is precisely from his evaluation that we infer the fact that he offers to pay a higher price' (Schumpeter 1954, p. 64). As a consequence, according to Schumpeter the so-called principle of decreasing marginal utility 'in economics ... is not a law ... but a basic assumption for the generalization of given scientific facts. As such this assumption is in principle arbitrary' (p. 71). Similarly, 'the *homo oeconomicus* – the hedonistic computer – ... is a construction the hypothetical character of which is now known' (pp. 80–81).

Schumpeter considers the theory of prices to be 'the core of pure economics' (Schumpeter 1954, p. 106). However, his illustration of this theory is not without defects and does not offer novel analytical contributions. What is interesting, rather, is the interpretation he gives of this theory. In his opinion, the point of arrival of the theory of economic equilibrium is what he calls 'the method of variations'. In fact, 'we can never explain an *actual* state of equilibrium of the economy' (p. 361), but only what consequences change in one of the data has on equilibrium: 'This is the only reason for which such laws have been constructed' (p. 360). This method – what is nowadays called comparative statics analysis – may be used only in a very limited ambit, with respect to infinitesimal changes: 'rigorously speaking, our system excludes any change whatsoever' (p. 375). However, economic equilibrium theory is useful because with it light can be shed on a particular aspect of economic realities subject to continuous change: habit, repetitiveness, the myriad of mechanical actions of everyday life.

We should add that comparative static analysis is possible only when we are confronted with stable equilibriums, and Schumpeter is well aware of the fact; otherwise, a change in the data may lead the economy in any direction whatsoever, rather than towards the new equilibrium. Schumpeter returns to the requirement of stability in one of his last pages: 'we equate the proof of an equilibrium tendency to a proof of the *stability* of the equilibrium solution' (Schumpeter 1954, p. 1002 n.; cf. also further, p. 1009 n., where he recalls his pupil Samuelson according to whom 'the problem of stability cannot be posed at all without the use of a specific dynamic schema, i.e. without specification of the manner in which the system reacts to deviations from equilibrium').

The main point of differentiation between Schumpeter and traditional marginalist theory concerns the theory of interest. Schumpeter criticizes the theory developed by his professor Böhm-Bawerk, who 'defines interest as the premium of present goods over future goods' (Schumpeter 1908, p. 329), and against this theory takes a dynamic approach: 'The essential phenomenon is the interest deriving from credit which serves for the creation of new industries, new forms of organization, new techniques, new consumption goods' (p. 335). In the static system, according to Schumpeter, the money market plays a secondary, passive role, while it becomes an active player only within the process of economic development.

This thesis is developed in the *Theory of economic development* (1912). In this book, the dichotomy between statics and dynamics is substituted with a dichotomy between theory of circular flow and theory of development. The circular flow corresponds to the stationary state, in which the economy reproduces itself, period after period, without structural change; in this context Schumpeter admits the possibility of only purely quantitative growth, from which changes in production technologies and consumers' tastes are excluded by definition.

By contrast, development is characterized by change. The role of active agent in the process of change is attributed to the producer, while consumers follow passively and 'are educated by him if necessary' (Schumpeter 1912, p. 65). Having recalled that 'to produce means to combine materials and forces within our reach' (p. 65), Schumpeter notes that 'development in our sense is then defined by the carrying out of new combinations' (p. 66), namely 'the introduction of a new good', ' the introduction of a new method of production', 'the opening of a new market', 'the conquest of a new source of supply of raw materials or half-manufactured goods' and 'the carrying out of the new organization of any industry, like the creation of a new monopoly position ... or its destruction' (p. 66).

The introduction of new productive combinations is the work of the entrepreneurs, who are such only insofar as they make innovative choices. That of the entrepreneur is a key category: as the originator of change, the entrepreneur generates capitalist development (while within the classical approach it is the process of development that generates the drive to change); his motivation is not that of the *homo oeconomicus*, but rather 'the dream and the will to found a private kingdom ... the joy of creating, of getting things done, or simply of exercising one's energy and ingenuity' (Schumpeter 1912, p. 93).

Alongside the entrepreneur, Schumpeter extols the role of the banker, considered equally necessary. In conformity to traditional marginalist theory, to which Schumpeter adheres, in equilibrium there are no unused resources on which entrepreneur-innovators can rely. Thus entrepreneurs can accomplish their innovations only if they have at their disposal some purchasing power with which they are able to draw from consumers and old firms the resources needed to start new productive processes. This purchasing power is created ex novo by the banks: thus, the innovative and executive capacity of entrepreneurs needs to be accompanied by the ability of the bankers to correctly evaluate the potentialities of new initiatives. Bankers too, like entrepreneurs, have to accept the challenge of uncertainty (and the consequent risks of losses and failures) that accompanies anything that is new.

Entrepreneurs set on innovation apply to bankers who, if they decide to finance the innovation, agree to the loan and thus create the means of payment with which the entrepreneurs can enter the markets for productive resources. By assumption, in equilibrium all available productive resources are already utilized; as a consequence, the additional demand cannot be satisfied with an increase in supply. Thus, there is an increase in prices, which automatically reduces the purchasing power of consumers and traditional firms. The inflationary process allows new firms, financed by banks with newly created means of payment, to draw productive resources from their traditional uses.

This is a theory of 'forced saving', implicit in the idea that the economy tends to full employment. This theory is common to various analyses of the Austrian school, such as Hayek's trade cycle theory discussed in the text that follows. Also the monetarist theories of crowding out of private investments by public expenditure, formulated in the 1950s and 1960s in response to Keynesian policies, are but variants of the theory of forced saving.

The trade cycle is connected to the process of development. The phases of expansion take place when the innovation is imitated by a swarm of new firms attracted by the temporary profits realized by the entrepreneur-innovator. The phases of recession arrive when repayment of the loans provokes a decrease in bank deposits, or in other words in fiduciary money supply (a credit deflation). Moreover, firms pay the banks back thanks to sale in the market of products obtained with the new productive combinations; this exerts a downward pressure on the demand for, and the prices of, the old products, which leads to bankruptcy for firms that have remained anchored to old production technologies, and especially those most directly hit by competition from the new products. Thus, those who fail to keep up by adapting to the innovation are expelled from the market.

If innovations were uniformly distributed over time, taking place now in one sector of the economy, now in another, the phases of expansion and recession would concern different sectors in different periods of time, while development would on average follow a regular path for the economy as a whole. However, according to Schumpeter the development process is discontinuous. In fact, innovation implies a break in the traditional way of proceeding; in other words, the barrier represented by the forces of tradition must be overcome, and this is all the more easily done the more widespread the change is within the economy. Thus innovations appear grouped in swarms. Schumpeter's trade cycle theory, like Marx's, is thus characterized by the endogenous nature – that is, internal to the theory – of the relationship between cycle and development. Within both theories, the situation at the end of a cycle must be different from the situation at the beginning, because of technical change which plays an essential part in the cyclical movement of the economy.

Schumpeter's theory of development remains substantially unchanged in the ponderous work on *Business cycles* (1939), with some additions: we find analysis of market forms other than perfect competition and the simultaneous presence of short, long and very long period cycles. The fifty-year cycle is connected to epoch-making innovations that affect the whole of the productive system: the steam engine, railways with the transport revolution, electricity or information technology in our own times.

In *Capitalism, socialism and democracy* (1942) Schumpeter maintains that capitalism cannot survive and is destined to be supplanted by socialism. However, unlike Marx, Schumpeter does not consider this as a triumphant march of human progress but rather as an advance on the road to decadence.[18]

Schumpeter's thesis had already taken shape before the Great Crisis,[19] and has nothing to do with the stagnation theories based on the dissolution of investment opportunities, which, after Keynes, were taken up and developed by Hansen (1938); rather, it looks back to Weber's (1904–5) view of capitalism as an all-embracing rationalization process affecting both productive activity and culture. According to Schumpeter, there is a contradiction inherent to capitalistic development: economic stability requires incessant development, but this creates growing difficulties for political stability. Beyond a certain point, such difficulties make the breakdown of capitalism inevitable.

The core of Schumpeter's argument is the connection between economic development and the destruction of the politico-social

---

[18] Schumpeter (1946, pp. 103–8) summarizes the theses of his 1942 book and proposes that 'free men' react to the tendencies present in society, which risk leading to the 'decomposition' of society and the victory of 'centralized and authoritarian statism', with a 'moral reform' drawing on the corporative principles of the encyclical *Quadragesimo Anno* of Pope Pius XI.

[19] The central thesis of the 1942 book had already been foreshadowed in Schumpeter (1928, pp. 385–6): 'Capitalism, whilst economically stable, and even gaining in stability, creates, by rationalizing the human mind, a mentality and a style of life incompatible with its own fundamental conditions, motives and social institutions, and will be changed, although not by economic necessity and probably even at some sacrifice of economic welfare, into an order of things which it will be merely matter of taste and terminology to call Socialism or not.'

foundations of capitalism. The connection has two aspects: on the positive side, growth of an opposition to capitalism associated with the spread of a rationalistic way of thinking and the swelling ranks of intellectuals; on the negative side, the weakening of capitalism's protective strata, consisting mainly in the ranks of small and medium entrepreneurs, faced with the growth of the big bureaucratized firms. The former aspect concerns what the Marxist tradition considers the superstructure of capitalistic societies, the latter the structure; the two aspects interact in the process of social transformation.[20]

Bureaucratization of the economy hinders both the innovative action of entrepreneurs and the 'creative destruction', i.e. bankruptcy of slow-moving firms, which frees resources for the innovating firms and functions as continuous natural selection of the ranks of firm owners and managers. Bureaucratization is the result of changes in dominant market forms through a process of industrial concentration which implies, among other things, transformation of the activity of technological innovation into routine. (Much the same was already being argued by Karl Renner and Rudolf Hilferding, leading representatives of Austrian socialism and Schumpeter's companions at Vienna University.)

The Schumpeterian theory of market forms stands out distinctly from the traditional marginalist theory, given its intrinsically dynamic character. Against 'the traditional [static] conception of the *modus operandi* of competition', which leads to the so-called law of the one price, Schumpeter (1942, pp. 84–5) opposed

the competition from the new commodity, the new technology, the new source of supply, the new type of organization (the largest-scale unit of control for instance) – competition which commands a decisive cost or quality advantage and which strikes not at the margins of the profits and the outputs of the existing firms but at their foundations and their very lives. This kind of competition is as much more effective than the other as a bombardment is in comparison with forcing a door ... It acts not only when in being but also when it is merely an ever-present threat.

Competition, we see, is associated with freedom of entry into the market for new innovative firms. This means attributing little importance to the barriers to competition stemming from market differentiation, upon which Chamberlin (1933) insists. It also foreshadows a radical critique

---

[20] Schumpeter follows Weber in rejecting Marxian materialism, according to which the evolution of the superstructure is determined mainly by what happens within the structure of human societies; the causal relation is not, however, inverted, but leaves room for recognizing a complex interdependence between the two aspects.

of anti-monopolistic policies based on the number of firms active in the market.

The process of industrial concentration also generates drastic change in the social structure: 'The perfectly bureaucratized giant industrial unit not only ousts the small or medium-sized firm and "expropriates" its owners, but in the end it also ousts the entrepreneur and expropriates the bourgeoisie as a class which in the process stands to lose not only its income but also what is infinitely more important, its function' (Schumpeter 1942, p. 134).

Economic and social transformations are accompanied by equally radical changes in culture and ideology: 'capitalism creates a critical frame of mind which, after having destroyed the moral authority of so many institutions, in the end turns against its own; the bourgeois finds to his amazement that the rationalist attitude does not stop at the credentials of kings and popes but goes on to attack private property and the whole scheme of bourgeois values' (Schumpeter 1942, p. 143). Intellectuals favour the spread of critical attitudes towards capitalist society, and in particular an attitude of rejection towards the heroic role of the entrepreneur and that basic institution of capitalism which is private property; hence the 'decomposition' (p. 156) of capitalistic society.

3.6   Keynes on Probability and Uncertainty

John Maynard Keynes (1883–1946) was born in Cambridge, the son of a lecturer and head administrator of that university and of one of the first women graduating there, the first to be elected mayor of that city. He attended secondary school at Eton and university at Cambridge, where he studied mathematics and classical humanities. After a brief spell at the India Office, he went back to Cambridge as a fellow of King's college – a position he was to retain for the rest of his life; he also became an economics lecturer at the university. He participated in the cultural life of his country at the highest levels: as a member of the elitist secret society of the Apostles (together with George Moore, Bertrand Russell and Lytton Strachey) and as a member of the London Bloomsbury circle (together with Virginia Woolf). Both before and after the First World War he worked for the Treasury; after the war, he was a member of the English delegation to the peace conference (but resigned, in opposition to the rigidity of the reparations imposed on Germany); during the Second World War he played a leading role in the Bretton Woods conference, which produced the blueprint for the post-war international monetary system (even if his boldest proposals were not accepted). He was for decades the editor of the *Economic Journal*, at the time the most prestigious journal in the field of economic research. Publication of his works, in particular of the *General theory* (1936), was hailed as a major event and gave rise to fierce debates.[21]

Subsequent to his death, especially in the first decades, references to Keynes in economics debates were continuous; however, in most cases Keynes's original thought was misunderstood or surreptitiously adapted in such a way as to consider it as internal to the marginalist tradition. Because of this, in illustrating his work we shall focus attention on the innovative elements differentiating him radically both from the previous marginalist tradition and from the subsequent neoclassical synthesis, discussed in Chapter 7.

We may begin by stressing that Keynes's education was as a mathematician and philosopher; his first original contribution concerns probability theory (or in other terms his view of uncertainty, which took on a decisive role in his subsequent economic theories).[22] Moreover, this contribution corresponds to his views on the world and the nature and requirements of analytical enquiry.

The *Treatise on probability* was born as fellowship dissertation in 1908; it was then revised and finally published in 1921. It is thus a much thought over work, whose theses Keynes never explicitly disowned, repeatedly recalling them, even if often only implicitly.

What is important from our viewpoint is not the mathematical treatment, but Keynes's vision. In this respect, Keynes developed his approach in opposition to the previous lines: classical probability theory (Bernoulli, Laplace) and frequentist theory.

Classical probability theory was born as a study of games (dice, cards, roulette) for which it is possible to rigorously specify the set of possible events (the 'space of events'). We also need to distinguish between elementary events (like drawing a single card), generally characterized by equal probability, and complex events consisting in the contemporaneous occurrence (union) of elementary events (for instance, drawing two or more cards). Probability theory is assigned the task of deducing from the equal probability of elementary events the probability of complex events (for instance, 7 or 3 as the sum of rolling two dice). According to this approach, probability is defined as the ratio of favourable cases (those in which the event takes place) to the number of all cases, considered as having equal probability on the basis of the principle of indifference

---

[21] For an accurate biography of Keynes, cf. Skidelsky (1983, 1992, 2000). For synthetic expositions of his ideas, cf. Roncaglia (2005a, chapter 14) and Skidelsky (2010). For a more in-depth interpretation of his theory of employment, cf. Tonveronachi (1983).

[22] On Keynes's probability theory, cf. Roncaglia (2009a).

(or principle of sufficient reason) that applies when there is no reason to consider one elementary event more probable than any other.

Frequentist theory, instead, has an empirical-inductive foundation, rather than a logical-deductive one. It abstracts regularities from a long series, at the limit an infinite one, of repetitions of the same event. The probability of an event is defined, within this approach, as the limit to which the relative frequency of the event tends in a series of random observations, statistically independent of one another, of a given variable (for instance, measurement of the weight of conscripts or even earlier, in the field of physical sciences, measurement of the results of an experiment repeated a number of times in ideal laboratory conditions).

Keynes remarks that in both instances the field of application of probability theory is limited to a restricted set of events, rigorously speaking to a void set. In fact, all 'regular' games are such only in theory (dice may be loaded, or in any case not perfectly regular: cases that cannot be identified a priori); statistical series cannot have infinite length and, especially in the case of social phenomena, it is impossible to assume the stationary nature of the phenomenon under consideration, ruling out change over time. In substance, Keynes harks back to Hume's scepticism with respect both to deductive reasoning, difficult to apply to the real world even in accurately limited frameworks, and to inductive reasoning, i.e. the possibility of inferring from a limited series of observations, no matter how extensive, a scientific law endowed with general validity. For the great mass of human vicissitudes we need to develop a different approach, based on the fact that uncertainty, although always there, shows different features from one situation to another.

Keynes avoids the simplistic dichotomy between risk and uncertainty proposed by Knight in a work published in the same year but independently (Knight 1921). According to this dichotomy, risk is a matter of quantifiable probabilities, and is thus subject to mathematical analysis, in fact corresponding to those cases in which the classical or frequentist approaches may hold; uncertainty, which cannot be measured, includes all the rest.[23]

[23] Frank Knight (1885–1972) was, together with Henry Simons (1899–1946) and Jacob Viner (1892–1970), an exponent of the 'old' Chicago school, active in the inter-war period, better kept distinct from the 'new' Chicago school dominated by Milton Friedman, illustrated in Chapter 8. The main purpose of Knight's book is to explain/ justify profits (net of interests) as a non-systematic component of firms' income, connected to uncertainty, and more precisely to non-expected changes in the conditions which concur to define a competitive equilibrium. A divergence is thus created between selling prices and costs, which can be either positive or negative (and Knight 1921, p. 365, maintains that firms as a whole generally obtain a negative result). This theory

Knight's work had a wide circulation and great influence, so much so that the Knightian dichotomy is occasionally attributed to Keynes himself, even by his pupils and followers (in particular by those who stress the role of what is called 'fundamental uncertainty'), with disastrous consequences for interpretation of Keynes's thought. If we confine ourselves to the simple dichotomy, theoretical analysis of the cases in which uncertainty is present is impossible: we are led to assume away uncertainty, which is precisely what exponents of the neoclassical synthesis do in their reconstructions of Keynes's analysis. Keynes, instead, considers full knowledge and perfect uncertainty as the extremes, never to be perfectly realized in practice; the set of human activities is located between these extremes, which means that the activities cannot be considered without taking into account the greater or lesser degree of uncertainty surrounding them.

What Keynes's contribution proposes is precisely a logicist theory of probability, not limited to the extreme cases but applicable to the whole range of human events. This requires two further steps.

First, we need to clarify that the evaluation of probabilities is not an objective property of the phenomenon under consideration, but a logical relationship connecting available knowledge to a proposition specifying an event. This evaluation is achieved by an agent, working in specific conditions of knowledge of the relevant circumstances; the available information may vary from person to person and in the course of time for the same person. However, this does not mean that Keynes's theory is a subjective one, since it is assumed that the agents work out their probability evaluations while objectively taking into account the information at their disposal, striving not to be influenced by their preferences for outcomes.[24]

A thoroughly subjective theory, declaredly based on introspection for the evaluation of probabilities, was proposed by Ramsey (1931). Unlike

---

was utilized by Knight in defence of free initiative and entrepreneurship (since entrepreneurs bear the responsibility for taking risks, necessary for the development of economic activity).

[24] However, it may be worth noting that there is not much difference between Keynes's position and the subsequent one taken by one of the founders of the subjective approach to probability, Bruno De Finetti (1906–85). De Finetti (1974, p. 7; quoted by Galavotti 2005, p. 218) stresses that the evaluation of probability depends on two components, one objective (information at our disposal), the other subjective (our opinion on unknown circumstances, based on what we know). The difference seems to consist in the fact that de Finetti focuses his attention on the de facto evaluations made by the agents, while Keynes, in accordance with Moore's ethics of individual responsibility, appears to distinguish between 'rational' and 'irrational' beliefs, thus pointing to an ideal agent (in some respects analogous to Smith's invisible arbiter) who utilizes available information in the best possible way: probability is objective in the sense that it does not depend on our preferences (Keynes 1921, p. 4).

Keynes, Ramsey assumes the measurability of subjective probabilities, through some psychological method (such as a 'psycho-galvanometer'), for all states of the world, which he assumes to be identifiable. To this end he refers to Wittgenstein (1921), thus aiming to reconstruct an axiomatic system representing coherent probability evaluations for each individual. As we shall see, it is to Ramsey and de Finetti that Savage explicitly looks in his axiomatic construction of expected utility theory.

Second, we need to introduce a new dimension in probability evaluation: the 'weight of the argument', namely the degree of confidence of the agent in his or her evaluation of the event. The weight of the argument may differ from person to person (some have more information than others: there is the professional meteorologist and the person who simply looks at the sky in order to decide whether to take her umbrella with her) and may change over time for the same person (for instance, after looking at the sky I may also read the weather forecast on the internet).

In taking her decisions, the agent considers both her own evaluation of the circumstances and the greater or lesser degree of confidence in her own evaluation; in a sense, the degree of confidence is a measure of uncertainty, which is never totally absent but is never absolute. As mentioned earlier, we should not think of a quantifiable measure;[25] it is, however, possible to distinguish among situations characterized by types of uncertainty so different as to require separate treatment. For instance, as we shall see, it is better not to consider decisions concerning investments and decisions on current production levels on the same analytical level.[26]

3.7   Keynes on Finance and Employment

Thus, Keynes avoids relying on general equilibrium theory, which places on the same analytical plane phenomena implying structurally different conditions of uncertainty. In doing so Keynes is following a Cambridge tradition: his professor Marshall also favours short causal chains rather than omni-comprehensive consideration of cause and effect interrelations keeping all the variables of the economy together in interminable chains.

---

[25] For an attempt to find a measure of the degree of confidence and an analysis of related issues, cf. Gärdenfors and Sahlin (1982).

[26] With his 'theory of groups', proposed in the *Treatise on probability*, Keynes points precisely to the expediency to provide separate treatments for the probability evaluations of different sets of events (for instance, dice or roulette, the expected productivity of investment projects in new productive plants, the path of monetary variables in the immediate future, the possible outcome of a marriage), and hence for the construction of theories aiming to interpret them.

Keynes thus prefers to rely on distinct analytical blocks, distinguishing between fields characterized by different decisional conditions: investment decisions (requiring evaluations over a long-period horizon, and hence structurally somewhat uncertain) from those on production levels, and real-economy decisions from finance decision, the latter being characterized by a very short time horizon.[27]

The Keynesian theory consists of three analytical blocks, to be considered in a logical sequence: the mechanism for determination of the interest rate (liquidity preference), that for determining investment levels, and for determining income and employment (the multiplier).

The three blocks are characterized, as anticipated earlier, by structurally different kinds of uncertainty.[28] In the first case we are concerned with financial agents taking decisions on the allocation of wealth among more or less liquid assets, on the basis of their expectations on interest rate movements in the immediate future. In any given instant in time the set of interest rates is determined by the confrontation between agents who expect an increase in interest rates and those who expect a fall; today's interest rates are thus determined on the expectations of tomorrow's interest rates, and hence of the path followed by the economy and by monetary policy. Speculative expectations dominate the scene, while the elements indicated by traditional theory – the preference for present over future consumption (determining supply of loanable funds) and the marginal productivity of capital (determining their demand) – appear to be irrelevant.[29] Demand for money for transaction purposes, connected to income, is also irrelevant in comparison to choices concerning the allocation of wealth, which can be revised every day, or indeed at every hour or minute (as professional operators in financial markets do all the time: relatively few, but certainly those who decide over the greatest share of wealth), while the demand path of income and hence the transactions demand for money is relatively stable over time. The expectations of financial agents are relatively unstable and continuously being modified;

---

[27] Here we are referring to the *General theory* (Keynes 1936), in which Keynes seeks to demonstrate the possibility, indeed the likelihood, of equilibriums characterized by under-employment of the available labour force. His previous work, the voluminous *Treatise on money* (Keynes 1930), aimed instead at demonstrating the instability of production and employment levels. Cf. Tonveronachi (1983).

[28] The same subdivision in analytical blocks and the same logical sequence between them may be deduced from an interpretation of Keynes's thought focusing on chapter 17 of the *General theory* and the notion of liquidity. Cf. Tonveronachi (1992).

[29] Hicks (1939, p. 164) maintains that in such a way Keynes leaves the rate of interest 'hanging by its own bootstraps'; Kahn (1954) replies that there is no logical circularity in Keynes's theory and stresses its main point, the instability of liquidity preference, which means that demand for money cannot be considered a stable function of interest rates (as instead does Hicks in his IS-LL scheme discussed in Chapter 7).

as a consequence, the financial markets are unstable, and transmit their instability to the other sectors of the economy.

Another element to stress in the Keynesian treatment of financial markets is the distinction between the notion of liquidity as a tool allowing for immediate reaction to any turn of events, and so as a guarantee against uncertainty, and the notion of money as a tool for exchange. Liquidity may be provided, under different market conditions and regulations, not only by circulating money and current account bank deposits, but also by other financial assets; for instance, by bonds that banks may offer as a guaranty for obtaining immediate loans from central banks. Liquidity is the relevant notion in analysis of the financial markets (i.e. concerning what is – not quite precisely – called speculative demand for money), while the traditional notion of money is the one relevant to what we call transactions demand for money.

Decisions concerning investment levels are taken by considering expected returns on plants and machinery over the time-span of their active life (or at least over a time-span sufficient to recoup investment costs). As a consequence, the uncertainty surrounding these decisions is high and, though they concern years-long intervals of time, they may change abruptly and considerably when the prospects for the economy change; as a matter of fact, taking into account the importance of monetary and fiscal policy, or of regulations and industrial policy, the political climate, too, is very important. Like financial operators, entrepreneurs taking decisions do not look back but forward, to the future. Interest rates, i.e. the cost of loans and their greater or less abundant availability, enter into their evaluations, though the main element is represented by expectations regarding sale prospects and the conditions contributing to the determination of the product price net of taxes. In fact, among the main variables influencing the level of investments what matters more is not the current level of profits but the degree of unused productive capacity: if it is high, as happens in periods of stagnation, entrepreneurs know that production can be increased by increasing capacity utilization, with no need for new investments aiming at expanding productive capacity.

Finally, entrepreneurs' decisions on production and employment levels depend on what Keynes calls the principle of effective demand. With it, Keynes takes the point of view of the entrepreneur, estimating income from the sale of the product (growing as the quantity produced increases, but at a decreasing pace) and production costs (also increasing with the quantity produced, but at an increasing rate).[30] The point of intersection of the two

---

[30] The assumption of increasing marginal costs is not essential to Keynes's theory; he was ready to abandon it when confronted with Dunlop's (1938) and Tarshis's (1939)

curves (representing entrepreneurial expectations of proceeds and costs for different employment levels) is the 'point of effective demand', which corresponds to the level of production that entrepreneurs will choose. Up to that point, proceeds are greater than costs, while from that point the contrary occurs. Expectations of costs obviously depend on technology, the prices of the means of production and the wage rate, but also on elements such as industrial conflicts or the tax burden, which can vary over time in consequence of political vicissitudes. Expectations of demand depend on the general conditions of the economy, but also on the competitors' strategies, the easiness of access to foreign markets and so on, and hence once more on variables not limited to the strictly economic field.[31]

Keynes stresses that within his theory the rate of interest no longer has the function of bringing into equality demand for and supply of loanable funds (in this case, in the simplest model of an economy with no public sector and no relations with foreign countries, savings and investments). This role is, instead, attributed to changes in the level of income, which bring savings to equate investments. In the real sector of the economy, investments are considered the less stable component of aggregate demand, whilst consumption (and hence savings) is more strictly connected to income.

Moreover, unemployment drives money wages down, but not necessarily real wages. The fall in labour costs may, in fact, bring about a fall in money prices; the worsening of expectations induced by deflation may contribute to further depressing investments and production levels. Thus the self-regulation mechanism (unemployment causes falling real wages, and this stimulates demand for labour) that should automatically drive the market economy towards full employment falls to pieces.

Keynes thus takes a favourable view of policies supporting demand (the monetary and fiscal expansionary policies commonly associated with his name). In the absence of such policies, the social malaise generated by widespread and persistent unemployment may constitute a risk for the stability of the political institutions and of the market economy itself.[32]

---

empirical criticisms. Actually, the abandonment of the assumption (in view of sizeable empirical evidence) reinforced the Keynesian critique of the thesis of an automatic tendency towards full employment equilibrium.

[31] Rather than into a model of macroeconomic equilibrium (as Hick's IS-LL model), Keynes's ideas may be translated (as Kregel 1976, 1980b does) into models considering a sequence of different assumptions for short- and long-run expectations, static and shifting. Cf. also Tonveronachi (1983) and Roncaglia and Tonveronachi (2014).

[32] Cf. Keynes (1931). In maintaining this thesis, Keynes had in mind both Soviet communism and the rise to power of fascism in Italy; the subsequent rise to power of Nazism in Germany only reinforced his belief.

Distrust of automatic equilibrating mechanisms in the market economy is accompanied by the fear that economic instability may have negative effects on economic activity and employment. Thus, even more than to monetary and fiscal policies supporting demand, Keynes attributes importance to the rules of the game, which should be chosen both to favour stability – hence to reduce uncertainty – and to stimulate economic activity.

In this respect we may recall the proposals Keynes advanced during the Bretton Woods 1944 conference, convened to draw up the rules of the international economy for the post-war period. There Keynes favoured policies to re-launch international trade after the stagnation of the inter-war period, so as to stimulate growth in the world economy; at the same time, he favoured stable exchange rates and direct foreign investment, but opposed short- and very short-run speculative financial flows. He was also favourable to measures, like the institution of the International Monetary Fund and the World Bank, that could avoid the need for restrictive policies on the part of countries with negative trade balances. In fact, he proposed mechanisms aimed at ensuring symmetry in the adoption of expansionary and deflationary policies, so as to prevent the weight of adjustment from falling mainly on the countries with negative trade balances: in the absence of adequate rules of the game, countries with positive trade balances may continue to accumulate foreign financial assets, while countries with negative trade balances are compelled to intervene, adopting restrictive measures before exhausting their foreign reserves.

The negative effects of the absence of adequate rules of the game have been felt in the last few decades, and particularly keenly within the euro area, where the strong pressure to adopt restrictive fiscal policies in countries with a high level of public debt is not balanced by a parallel pressure to adopt expansionary policies in countries like Germany with fairly sound public accounts and a very positive trade balance. This contributes to economic stagnation and, as Keynes foresaw, to the emergence of populist and nationalist political factions. Keynes's ideas thus appear decidedly relevant to today's conditions and are continually being recalled in the current policy debate.

Part II

The Giants of the Short Century

4 The Founder of Neo-liberalism: Friedrich von Hayek

4.1 A General Portrait

The opposition between Western and Soviet countries characterized nearly the whole of the twentieth century, but grew more and more acute on conclusion of the Second World War, when US production of the atomic bomb was followed by development of the bomb by the Soviet Union, on top of which came the Korean War. After the Second World War, which many experienced as a war in defence of freedom and individual liberties against Nazi and fascist dictatorships, the debate on economic systems – market versus planned economy – which continued a debate already under way in the inter-war decades, took on ideological overtones as a clash between the Western democracies and Stalinist dictatorship.

Popper's 1945 book *The open society and its enemies* belongs to this debate. In it, Popper criticizes the holistic view of society, according to which the whole is superior to the individual, attributed to Plato and Aristotle, Hegel and Marx. Here and in what follows it will be useful to distinguish between political liberalism and economic liberalism: a distinction in some respects analogous but not identical to the one between classical liberalism and neo-liberalism: we shall be returning to these themes both in this chapter and in Chapter 8.

Political liberalism has to do with individual freedom and economic liberalism with laissez-faire, i.e. with the freedom of action of agents, particularly of firms, in the fields of the economy and finance. Distinguishing between the two, it is possible to choose the former as end while subordinating to it the latter, or vice versa. For instance, Keynes follows the first route when maintaining that a certain measure of public intervention in the economy may be necessary to preserve an adequate level of employment and to keep inequalities in income distribution within acceptable limits. In this way we can avoid social conflicts which might jeopardize the very survival of democratic institutions.

Symmetrically, economic liberalism may be considered as a vital end to be pursued even at the cost of accepting violations of political freedom, as was the case in Pinochet's Chile.

However, in the climate of the 1940s and 1950s, political and economic liberalism tended to be on the same side, opposing communist dictatorships. Thus, along much the same line as Popper's book we find Hayek's *The road to serfdom* (1944), concentrating political fire on the planned economy and more generally on any form of state intervention in the economy. Hayek's theoretical researches on the trade cycle in the 1920s and 1930s corroborate his opposition to the mixed economy (a market economy with a significant presence of the state in the economy, a presence growing in the early decades of the post-war period); this opposition was then confirmed in the decided cultural policy pursued by Hayek.[1]

Both planning and public intervention are considered inefficient for driving a developed market economy, as Hayek and others had already maintained in the inter-war debate. Still more important, the power of the central planner and of the state authorities in a mixed economy are held inevitably to lead to a disequilibrium of forces between state and citizen, and so at least potentially to a situation of oppression for the great mass of the population. This latter argument retains at least in part its validity even if we deny the other pillar of economic liberalism, namely the self-regulatory ability of market economies.

The opposition between the two positions – attributing priority to political or to economic freedom – concerns two aspects. First, those maintaining the priority of economic freedom (the neo-liberals) tend to attribute scant importance to market failures and great weight to the automatic equilibrating mechanisms of the market; in this way, they downplay Keynes's fears of a shift in public opinion in countries with persistent economic difficulties towards populist, nationalist or in any case authoritarian ideas. Second, neo-liberals, by attributing major importance to the concentration of power in the hands of state authorities, tend to downplay the risk of concentrations not simply of income but also of power within the private economy and finance, or the

---

[1] With the caution that is necessary when using labels, always reductive, Hayek may be defined as a liberal, certainly not a conservative: a label he himself emphatically rejected. See the Postscript 'Why I am not a conservative' in *The constitution of liberty* (Hayek 1960, pp. 397–411). Hayek cannot be defined an economic liberal tout court, considering his criticisms of pure laissez faire; cf. for instance Hayek (1944, p. 89); Hayek (1948, pp. 109–11). Caldwell (2011, pp. 312–6 and p. 329) recalls that the term neo-liberalism was coined in the 1930s in order to distinguish from laissez-faire the liberalism of the supporters of the importance of the state for creating the institutions in which the market and competition may flourish.

disequilibrium in bargaining power among social classes, and in particular but not only between workers and capitalists.[2]

Hayek's contributions as an economist and social scientist concern both these aspects, with a clear view of the link between them. As a matter of fact, freedom of action in the economic field is considered a corollary of individual freedom: 'Freedom will prevail only if it is accepted as a general principle whose application to particular instances [such as the economic field] requires no justification' (Hayek 1973, p. 61). As we shall see, the choice of side in the theoretical battlefield was accompanied by a politico-cultural engagement in divulgation and organization that was to have considerable – albeit largely indirect – influence in the vicissitudes of the last fifty years.

Given the nature of this work, we shall focus mainly, but not exclusively, on more strictly economic issues. Thus, after some biographical details, we shall consider Hayek's early contributions in the field of trade cycle and employment theory. These contributions pursued two objectives, critical and constructive. On the one hand, Hayek criticized what he called under-consumption theories, including Keynes's theory stressing the need for public intervention in support of global demand in the presence of unemployment. On the other hand, Hayek re-proposed in a more complete form – integrating monetary phenomena and the issue of relative prices – the thesis already held by the first marginalist theoreticians of the self-regulating capacity of the market, though in the framework of cyclical oscillations. In this context, Hayek adds, public intervention would only have counter-productive effects, accentuating disequilibria.

These contributions, in particular *Prices and production* (Hayek 1931), are the object of Sraffa's (1932) 'Keynesian' criticisms; Hayek himself appears to have been to some extent aware of the capital theory difficulties which, though not emerging in the debate with Sraffa, ex post appear to us as connected to it.[3]

---

[2] Hayek favoured anti-trust legislation, but over time his worries about monopoly seem to have melted, possibly in parallel with the transition intervening in Chicago in the two decades following the conclusion of the Second World War, as indicated for instance by changed opinion on patents, first condemned and then defended. Cf. van Horn and Klaes (2011).

[3] In fact, Wicksell, of whose *Lectures* (1901–6) Robbins edited the English translation, published in 1932, already perceived the problems concerning the aggregate notion of capital utilized in the aggregate production function and in the traditional marginalist theory of capital and distribution (when the profit rate – namely the 'price' of the 'factor of production' capital – changes, capital per worker may move in the opposite direction to that foreseen by the theory: the so-called capital reversal manifested in real and monetary Wicksell effects). On these themes cf. §§ 5.8 and 12.6.

Hayek's researches on the theory of capital concluded, after another ten years' work, with a large volume published in 1941, to be discussed in §4.4. In this book, as in the previous writings, the analytical work revolves around the notion of equilibrium, common – albeit in different forms – to the whole marginalist tradition. In this case, too, the Cambridge criticisms (this time by Nicholas Kaldor, a former colleague of Hayek's at the London School of Economics, before moving to Cambridge and to Keynes's camp) appear to be destructive. Hayek, already aware of the limits of his analysis, repeatedly stressed in his book, abandoned that research field, never to return to it.

The research field on which Hayek now focused concerned the formation of a spontaneous order in a society as the outcome of individual actions; in this context he developed the view, characteristic of the Austrian school, of a process of knowledge adaptation and diffusion through the market. The theory of the process of knowledge acquisition is worked out at the conceptual level, not through formal theoretical models; thus, at least at first sight, it does not appear to need to be anchored in a demonstration of the existence of a unique and stable equilibrium. This theory will be considered in §4.5.

Hayek's political and economic liberalism, constituting as already mentioned the core of his thought (it will be considered in §4.6), is characterized mainly by its faith in the self-regulating ability of the market and the thesis that a totally laissez-faire economy tends to grow more than an economy where the state plays an active role, and so by radical opposition to Keynesianism, including its domesticated variants, such as the neoclassical synthesis illustrated in Chapter 7. Hayek is thus a supporter of a radical economic liberalism, at the level of the conceptual representation of the economy even before approaching theoretical models; this support was also actuated through a web of associations and think tanks, such as the Mont Pèlerin Society, founded in 1947. As we shall see, together with other streams of neo-liberal thought (Friedman and the monetarist school, the new Austrian school, ordoliberalism) up to the counter-revolution (as compared to the Keynesian revolution) of rational expectations, Hayek's thought exerted great influence on many developments, notably in the field of politics, up to the austerity policies imposed by Germany within the European Union. The concluding section of the chapter (§4.7) is devoted to Hayek's specific proposal as a radical economic liberal, namely the denationalization of money – once again a topical subject nowadays, with the circulation of crypto-currencies like the bitcoins, and so well worth looking into.

4.2   The Formative Years and Career

Friedrich von Hayek (1899–1992, Nobel Prize in 1974) is possibly better known for his economic liberalism than for his theoretical contributions in the field of economics.[4] In the 1930s, however, he appeared to many as the best theoretical champion of the continental school, the natural opponent to the Cambridge school for those who did not share the policy implications of Keynesian theory.

He was born in Vienna, then the capital of the Austro-Hungarian Empire, to a well-to-do family with academic traditions (his maternal grandfather was a renowned professor of civil law, his paternal grandfather was interested in natural history and biology; his father was a doctor with an interest in botany; both brothers became professors, one of anatomy, the other of chemistry). His beginnings as a secondary school student are unimpressive: he was flunked in Latin, Greek and mathematics and obliged to repeat the year. But his interests ranged over various fields, and an academic career appeared a natural outcome for him.

After military training, in March 1917 he was sent to the Italian front, in the artillery, for months on the banks of Piave. He fell ill with the terrible Spanish flu that killed thousands all over Europe, and then, during the retreat, contracted malaria as well.

Hayek registered as a student at Vienna University, at first taking an interest in psychology. During a stay in Zurich, in winter 1919–20 (a terrible winter in a Vienna exhausted by the military defeat), he attended lectures on canon law, worked in a research laboratory on the anatomy of the brain and attended the lecture course by Moritz Schlick (1882–1936, a physicist and philosopher and a leading exponent of logical positivism and founder of the Vienna Circle). In Vienna, when Hayek came back from Zurich, the economics chair was held by Othmar Spann, an adversary of individualism, liberalism and democracy as well as positivism and an organizer of student meetings in the forest, whose ideas would become reference for the Nazis, but who from Hayek's point of view had the great merit of putting into his hands a copy of Menger's *Principles*.

Hayek himself said that it was this book that turned his interests towards economics. He thus set out for Munich to study with Max Weber, who unfortunately died before Hayek could attend his lectures.

---

[4] Hayek's writings are numerous. His autobiography (Hayek 1994) is a precious source, but on many points is to be taken with caution. An – affectionate and clear – overview of his contributions was provided by his friend Fritz Machlup (1976). Here I mainly rely on Caldwell's (2004) intellectual biography, a rigorous and amply documented work from which, however, I dissent as far as the evaluation of Hayek's theoretical contribution is concerned.

In his final year at university, Hayek found his point of reference in Friedrich von Wieser, just back to teaching after a spell in the government. Opinions differ over Wieser's influence on Hayek; the latter recalled Wieser with affection in an obituary (Hayek 1926).[5] More important was Ludwig von Mises, to whom Hayek turned in search of a job, with a letter of presentation by Wieser, being admitted to the famous *Privatseminar* (also known as *Miseskreis*), a small debating group meeting every two weeks under Mises's direction.[6]

Shortly after graduating, Hayek spent a year in the United States, where he attended lectures at Columbia University in New York and worked as research assistant collecting data on the trade cycle.

Back in Vienna in the summer of 1924, he got married in 1926 and from 1927 held the post of the first director of the newly born Austrian institute for the study of conjuncture.[7] He began publishing some works in German, on monetary theory and the theory of the trade cycle. Among his readers there was Lionel Robbins, newly appointed – only thirty years old – to the economics chair at the London School of Economics.[8] This was a turning point: Robbins invited Hayek to give some lectures in London, with the aim of countering the rising star of Keynesian theory with the continental tradition, more conservative in policy. Hayek's lectures, at the beginning of 1931, proved a great success; thus, with Robbins's support,[9] in autumn 1931 Hayek moved to the London School of Economics appointed to the economics chair entitled to Tooke.

---

[5] Cf. Caldwell (2004), pp. 142–3.

[6] Mises, a supporter of an all-out economic liberalism, will be discussed in §8.3, when considering the new Austrian school which emerged in the post-war years in the United States under his influence more than that of Hayek.

[7] The Österreichische Konjunkturforschungsinstitut was founded on Mises's initiative, aiming, in study of the trade cycle, to propose an integration between theory and empirical analysis in opposition to the purely empiricist approach of the National Bureau of Economic Research in New York, focused on finding regularities in the path followed by the economy. Initially the Institute was staffed only by Hayek and two employees, but soon grew thanks to a grant from the Rockefeller Foundation.

[8] Lionel Robbins (1898–1984) dominated the London School of Economics (where he had been professor since 1929) in the central decades of the century; a supporter of Hayek against Keynes, he was a leading figure in the policy debates of the period; as from 1960 he served as chairman of the *Financial Times*; his best-known work is *Nature and significance of economic science* (1932), with his often quoted definition of economics ('economics is the science which studies human behaviour as a relationship between ends and scarce means which have alternative uses': ibid., p. 14); he is also the author of important works in the history of economic thought.

[9] But also, curiously, with the support of William Beveridge (1879–1963), collaborator of Sidney and Beatrice Webb, founders of the London School of Economics (LSE), and member of the group of Fabian socialists, from 1919 to 1937 director of the LSE. Not well versed in economic theory, Beveridge was at the time hostile to Keynes (while in subsequent years he became a supporter of Keynesian policies together with the welfare state,

In these conferences Hayek frontally attacked under-consumption theories and proposed a different theory of the trade cycle, anchored on the traditional marginalist theory of value. The conferences led to a book, *Prices and production* (Hayek 1931), followed by two articles in *Economica* (the journal of the London School) (Hayek 1931–2), critically reviewing the recently published *Treatise on money* by Keynes (1930). The first of the two articles provoked a fierce reaction from Keynes (1931), followed by a reply by Hayek. Subsequently, apparently at Keynes's request, Sraffa (1932) published a strongly critical review of *Prices and production*, again followed by Hayek's reply (1932) and Sraffa's counter-reply; this controversy is illustrated in the text that follows.

Hayek remained at the London School of Economics up to the end of the Second World War, continuing his theoretical work but also participating in the policy debates. Like Robbins, he was also a refined historian of economic thought.[10]

After the Second World War, Hayek moved to Chicago, in 1950, and returned to Europe (to Freiburg in Germany, then to Salzburg in Austria) in 1962. The move to the States and the years preceding it marked a shift in his interests, from pure theory to what we might call theory of economic and political systems, a field in which he had already been working previously but which now took on a central position. *The road to serfdom* (Hayek 1944), translated into more than twenty languages plus a summarized version published by the *Reader's Digest*, sold more than a million copies; it is but the best known of these works.

---

the birth of which he contributed to with the famous Beveridge Report of 1942 and his 1944 book *Full employment in a free society*), and probably he did not perceive that Hayek's arrival reinforced Robbins's position, with the result that LSE shifted towards conservative economic orthodoxy. Hayek's critique of the welfare state is set out in *The constitution of liberty*, Part III (Hayek 1960, pp. 253–394); as part of that critique Hayek (pp. 391–4) stresses the risks of public financing of research in the field of the social sciences and the positive role of the private foundations, afterwards so important in the development of US mainstream economics (cf. Mirowski and Plehwe 2009; Mirowski 2011; van Horn et al. 2011).

[10] For a collection of his writings on the history of economic thought and economic history, see Hayek (1991). Particular mention deserves his critical edition (Hayek 1951; new ed., ed. by S. Peart, 2015) of the correspondence between John Stuart Mill and Elisabeth Taylor, protagonists of a long love story that began when Ms Taylor was already married; the two got married only after her first husband had died, a few years before her death. In these vicissitudes Hayek probably saw a parallel with his own experience: on returning from his stay in the United States in the 1920s he found that his girlfriend had already gotten married in the meantime; when, subsequently, she was widowed, Hayek embarked upon a stormy legal battle to obtain divorce from his first wife; he obtained it only by moving to the States, and was thus able to marry his first girlfriend in a second marriage.

In the post-war years Hayek went back to a research stream already explored in the 1930s, concerning the role of the market in the diffusion of information; however, he focused his researches and his activities (among other things with the foundation of the Mont Pèlerin Society in 1947) largely in the direction of supporting neo-liberalism.

Hayek received the Nobel Prize in economics in 1974; he died in Freiburg in March 1992. A provisional bibliography of his writings (in Gray 1984) includes 18 books, 25 pamphlets, 16 edited or prefaced books and 235 articles.[11] An edition of his writings, originally planned in nineteen volumes, has been under publication for many years.[12]

4.3   Theory of the Trade Cycle and Theory of Capital

In his first years after graduation, during his stay in the United States and at the Institute of Conjuncture in Vienna, Hayek worked on analysis of the trade cycle.

In this area, the positivistic culture of the time inspired researches like those conducted by Wesley Mitchell (1874–1948) at the NBER (National Bureau of Economic Research) in New York, with a prevalently empirical orientation seeking 'economic barometers' that could be used to forecast the short-period evolution of the economy.

Hayek, who shared the position adopted by Menger in the 'battle on methods', considered this stream of research too a-theoretical: a point in method to which we shall be returning in the text that follows. Moreover, faced with the attacks on the marginal theory of equilibrium, considered too abstract and unable to take into account the economic oscillations continuously taking place in the real world, Hayek sought to show how the basic theoretical principles may be usefully applied to this issue as well.[13]

Simultaneously, Hayek intended to criticize the theoretical foundations of the Keynesian interventionist policies proposed as a remedy to

[11]   Hayek – like his adversary Sraffa – was an economist with a rare and deep culture. In this respect, the Vienna of the 1920s was a unique melting pot: the ethologist Konrad Lorenz was a playmate; the philosopher Ludwig Wittgenstein was a relative and a comrade-in-arms in the final year of the First World War; the physicist Erwin Schrödinger was a family friend, and we might go on.

[12]   Edited by W. W. Bartley III, then by Bruce Caldwell, *The collected works of F. A. Hayek* is being published by University of Chicago Press. Nineteen volumes are planned, plus an out-of-the-series volume with a long and lively biographical interview with Hayek (Hayek 1994). Many of his writings have been translated into various languages.

[13]   Hayek (1937, p. 243 n.) maintains that the economic theorist does not need the notion of ideal types (proposed by Weber, but Hayek does not cite him) since the logical construction is a general one, but has to utilize them when applying the theory to the explanation of specific social processes.

unemployment (Britain had been going through crisis since 1926). In this respect, he set out to show that an increase in consumption, which, according to Keynesian theory (or to under-consumption theories, to which Hayek more generically refers) should be stimulated in order to counter unemployment, led rather to an increase in unemployment; analogous results (a positive one according to Keynesian theory, a negative one according to both traditional marginalist theory and Hayek) would derive from a redistribution of income in favour of wages.

To illustrate Hayek's theoretical contributions in his early writings we may focus attention on *Prices and production* (1931), a slim but packed volume that originated from the lessons held at the London School of Economics. In it, Hayek presents a theory, gradually worked out in a series of previous works, combining the marginalist foundations of a real equilibrium of relative prices and quantities with analysis of short-period fluctuations connected to essentially monetary phenomena, their adjustment processes and the reaction to policy interventions.

As far as the marginalist foundations are concerned, Hayek draws on the notion of the average period of production proposed by Böhm-Bawerk. It consists in this: for each product let us consider the quantities of labour directly and indirectly required to obtain it; the average period of production corresponds to the average length of immobilization of the various quantities of labour. For instance, if producing a table takes ten hours of work, applied in the course of a year, plus ten hours of work applied one year previously in order to obtain wood, nails, etc., plus another ten hours of work applied two years previously in order to obtain the iron with which to produce the nails etc., we have thirty hours of work on the whole needed for an average period of production of two years.

On this notion Hayek then applies the Wicksellian mechanism of the relationship between natural and monetary interest rates, together with the theory of forced savings proposed by Mises in 1912 and also utilized by Schumpeter (1912) in his theory of the trade cycle.[14] In other words, recalling that the natural rate of interest corresponds to the return on investments, while the monetary rate of interest is the one paid on loans, entrepreneurs invest only if the real rate of interest is higher than the monetary one; thus the oscillations of the two rates account for the fluctuations of investments and the cyclical path of the economy. The theory of forced savings comes into play when demand for investment goods exceeds productive capacity; we then have an increase in prices,

---

[14] Schumpeter (1954, p. 887), recalling Hayek, attributes to Wicksell the theory of forced savings, while referring to Bentham and especially to Thornton (1802) as precursors; Hayek himself (1931, pp. 18–19) also refers to Malthus.

which reduces the purchasing power of families, and hence their consumption, freeing productive resources that can be transferred from the sector of consumption goods to the sector of investment goods (precisely the point of the forced savings theory).

The novelty introduced by Hayek is consideration of relative prices through a two-sector model: a sector producing consumption goods and a sector producing investment goods. The movements of the relative price of these two groups of goods mark the various stages of the cycle, in a series of cause-and-effect relations that respect the basic elements of traditional marginalist theory.

In a few words, the mechanism introduced by Hayek works in the following way. When the natural rate of interest is higher than the monetary one, firms are induced to request bank loans to embark on investment expenditures higher than the equilibrium ones. Since the starting situation is – by the very definition of equilibrium – characterized by full resource utilization, additional investments imply an increase in prices, due to excess demand financed by bank loans. Inflation takes purchasing power away from consumers, while entrepreneurs benefit from it, because of the interval of time between the moment the means of production are bought and the moment in which the product is sold. Furthermore, the additional demand for investment goods generates an increase in their prices relatively to consumption goods. This in turn corresponds to an increase in the real wage rate, which makes it advantageous to lengthen the average period of production, i.e. recourse to production methods characterized by substitution of labour with machinery corresponding to greater quantities of indirect labour used in previous years.

These elements combine to constitute the ascending stage of the trade cycle. However, the increased incomes of the productive factors are transformed into a greater demand for consumption goods; the relative prices of these goods increase, and the real wage falls. This makes it advantageous to shorten the average period of production, utilizing less machinery and more labour; durable capital goods lose value.[15] Hence the descending stage of the cycle. Confronted with this sequence of causes and effects, policies of support for demand for consumption goods such as those proposed by under-consumption theories prove counterproductive. According to Hayek, indeed, such policies would accentuate the increase in the prices of consumption goods and the consequent loss

[15] Hayek also took up this thesis in subsequent writings (the last on the topic being published in 1942); in them he termed as 'Ricardo effect' the variations in the average period of production (or in the structure of periods of production) induced by variations in the real wage; this effect corresponds to the substitution between capital and labour in the neoclassical models based on an aggregate notion of capital.

of value of durable capital goods characterizing the falling stage of the cycle. In any case, more or less rapidly the capital accumulated in the ascending stage of the cycle (corresponding to forced savings) will be economically destroyed in the descending stage, so that the economy returns to its original equilibrium. What Schumpeter calls 'creative destruction' in his theory of the cycle (Schumpeter 1912) is in fact an essential component of the process bringing the economy to an optimal equilibrium, characterized by the absence of both unemployment and inflationary pressures.

Hayek's theory was conceived as a step forward, advancing from Wicksell's: Hayek's analysis also considers changes in techniques, in income distribution, in relative and in monetary prices. It thus appears as the most advanced alternative to the Keynesian research program: an alternative which also has the merit of being founded on the continental theory of value (albeit more in the Austrian variety than in the Walrasian one),[16] not well known in the Britain dominated by Marshall but which appeared more rigorous to Robbins and his colleagues.

Hence Sraffa's reaction, possibly prompted by Keynes himself: in the Cambridge environment, it was Sraffa who presented, though in a critical way, the continental theory in the Walrasian–Paretian version in his 1928–30 lectures on the theory of value. In an extensive review of *Prices and production* published in 1932 in the *Economic Journal*, Sraffa attacked the foundations of Hayek's analytical construction.

The criticisms of the non sequiturs present in Hayek's book are various. The main criticism concerns the inexistence of a central element in Hayek's construction such as the natural rate of interest. In a world in which the structure of relative prices changes over time, we have as many natural rates of interest as there are commodities (and, for each commodity, as many as the intervals of time taken into account).

Furthermore, according to Sraffa, Hayek does not fully understand the difference between a monetary and a barter economy, attributing to money only the role of means of exchange, thus excluding from his analysis the role of elements such as debt and credit or contracts denominated in money, including wage contracts. As a consequence, monetary factors are simply superimposed on real factors, and any hypothesis on the former influencing the latter clashes with the theory of value

---

[16] With his theory of capital Böhm-Bawerk tried to create a synthesis of the Austrian and the Walrasian approaches, abandoning Menger's position hostile to the use of mathematics in economics. While in *Prices and production* Hayek utilizes Böhm-Bawerk's theory of capital (though through the intermediation of Wicksell), in some respects Hayek's position in his maturity, after the failures encountered with his theory of the cycle, implies a return to Menger's ideas.

developed with reference to a real economy, with its simultaneous determination of equilibrium prices and quantities, techniques and distributive variables.[17]

Moreover, according to the theory of forced savings utilized by Hayek, an inflationary stage may correspond to an accumulation of capital quicker than is justified by the basic parameters of the economy, but then the system automatically switches back to its long run equilibrium through a deflationary process. In criticizing this thesis, Sraffa stresses that return to a state of monetary equilibrium does not reproduce the starting conditions identically, since the inflationary process influences income distribution.[18]

Hayek's reaction (1932) was inadequate. As a matter of fact, the import of Sraffa's critique is a more general one. It concerns the impossibility of reconciling the two constitutive elements of Hayek's theory: on the one hand, the influence of monetary over real factors in the framework of the trade cycle; on the other hand, acceptance of the marginalist theory of value to explain the 'real' equilibrium, which implies a clear-cut dichotomy between monetary and real factors.

Hayek (1932, p. 238) stresses: 'I have been assuming that the body of existing pure economic theory demonstrates that, so long as we neglect monetary factors, there is an inherent tendency towards an equilibrium in the economic system': the myth of the invisible hand of the market that – though Hayek might have found it impossible to understand – Sraffa rejected (as Keynes does in the *General theory*). Hence Hayek's charge against Sraffa's position as 'an extreme theoretical nihilism' (p. 238). Once he has assumed a tendency to equilibrium, in order to explain the economic cycles we find in the real world, the Austrian economist sees no other possibility than recourse to monetary factors.

---

[17] Keynes's support for Sraffa on this point when confronted with Hayek's reaction is meaningful. The latter concludes his reply stating that Sraffa 'has understood Mr. Keynes's theory even less than he has my own' (Hayek 1932, p. 249); Keynes, taking advantage of his position as editor of the *Economic Journal*, adds a sharp footnote: 'With Professor Hayek's permission I should like to say that, to the best of my comprehension, Mr. Sraffa has understood my theory accurately' (ibid.).

[18] Here Sraffa draws on an argument developed in his degree dissertation, Sraffa 1920. Vaughn (1994, p. 49) maintains that with his analysis of the trade cycle Hayek develops 'a theory of genuine disequilibrium processes' because 'even the correction of errors would not return the system to the previously achieved equilibrium': which is precisely the criticism raised by Sraffa! In the absence of a theory explaining equilibrium (and a stable equilibrium), disequilibrium processes remain hanging in the air, and in fact Hayek, after his second unfruitful attempt with the 1941 book, no longer attempted to build a well-structured theory of the trade cycle (or of disequilibrium processes), limiting himself to a few odd remarks that appear to be *obiter dicta*.

However, Sraffa is not a nihilist: despite Hayek's conviction (apparently followed in this by today's mainstream economists), the marginalist theory of value and distribution is not the only possible theory and, as Sraffa remarks in his answer to Robertson (Sraffa 1930, p. 93), if a theory 'cannot be interpreted in a way which makes it logically self-consistent and, at the same time, reconciles it with the facts it sets out to explain . . . I think . . . that it should be discarded'. In other words, if the marginalist theory cannot explain the trade cycle in a coherent way, we should proceed by building a different theory, as at the time – along different but not necessarily divergent routes – both Keynes and Sraffa were doing.

When, with the publication of Sraffa's 1960 book, recourse to the average period of production came in for definitive criticism, Hayek's approach lost even the initial appearance of solidity. However, some pointers in Hayek's works, concerning period analysis and the problem of intertemporal consistency, may be considered as contributing to the origin of modern research streams focused on the sequential analysis of disequilibrium, temporary equilibrium and general intertemporal equilibrium: certainly no mean accomplishment.[19] Hayek himself tried to proceed in this direction in the ten subsequent years, focusing on the pure theory of capital, as we shall now see.

The debate with Sraffa was preceded by a debate with Keynes, originating with the extensive and severely critical review of the *Treatise on money* written by Hayek immediately after its publication, which came in for an equally severe reply by Keynes. Neither economist, however, sought to understand the other's theoretical structure; we thus have a debate of the deaf, hardly very useful for theoretical progress. Consequently each of the two sides rapidly lost interest in pursuing the debate; in particular Keynes, who had begun writing the *General theory* within a framework rather different from that of the *Treatise on money*, refrained from replying to Hayek's second article.

4.4 Theory of Capital and the Debate with Kaldor

Alongside the other research streams considered in the text that follows, Hayek went on to work on the themes taken up in *Prices and production* in a few articles published in the 1930s and in the early 1940s, culminating in a book, *The pure theory of capital*, 1941, to which he attributed great importance at the time, seeing it as crowning his research on the topic.

---

[19] In particular we may trace to Hayek the analysis of intertemporal equilibrium, to Hicks (1939) that of temporary equilibrium, to Lindahl and other exponents of the Swedish school the sequential analysis of disequilibrium. Cf. Donzelli (1988).

In subsequent years, these themes were abandoned. Hayek did not even deal with them at any great length in his *Autobiography*, and generally his example is followed by interpreters of his thought. Yet, these are important works, which aim to contribute to the transition from an aggregate notion of capital, implicit in the average period of production, to a disaggregated notion, and from the analysis of stationary equilibrium to that of temporary and sequential equilibriums then developed respectively by Hicks and by the Swedish school, and subsequently by the new Austrian school, or to that of intertemporal equilibriums then developed by French and Anglo-Saxon theoreticians in the post-war period (Arrow and Debreu in particular).[20] Possibly the pressure to abandon this stream of research came from the shift towards the politically more important theme of comparison between capitalism and socialism and towards the themes of knowledge and the role of the market in its diffusion, which characterize the Austrian school in comparison with other streams of the marginalist approach; or the pressure may have come from realizing the limits of his theoretical construct, stressed in an article by another Cambridge economist, Kaldor, earlier on a colleague of Hayek at the London School of Economics.

Let us look into the issue. Hayek's basic thesis, in his 1941 book, is the same as in his 1931 book: it is dearth not of consumption, but of capital, which provokes crisis and unemployment, so that the only adequate policy consists in stimulating savings, or in other words the creation of new capital. This is, in today's terminology, a supply-side policy: in an economic system where by assumption the tendency to full employment operates, growth depends on accumulation.

The new book is declaredly motivated by the need to ground these theses on a solid theoretical foundation. In the introduction to the book, Hayek explicitly recognizes the limits of his previous attempt and the need to solve the more complex issues of the theory of value before going back

---

[20] Donzelli (1988, p. 21) stresses that we owe to Hayek the first precise formulation of the notion of equilibrium as a set of all plans of action rationally chosen by the agents and capable of being executed, namely compatible among themselves and with the external circumstances characterizing the economy. Hayek (1937, p. 44, quoted by Donzelli 1988, p. 22) adds that the equilibrium must be stable (a need explicitly recognized by Schumpeter, as we saw earlier, and by all the authors of the first two generations of marginalist economists): 'It is only with this assertion ['the supposed existence of a tendency towards equilibrium'] that economics ceases to be an exercise in pure logic and becomes an empirical science.' Indeed, as already stressed by Schumpeter and as Hayek states at the beginning of 'Economics and knowledge' (1937, p. 33), 'formal equilibrium analysis in economics' essentially consists in tautologies; further on (p. 43), he speaks of an 'admittedly fictitious state of equilibrium' and reaffirms that 'the only justification for this is the supposed existence of a tendency towards equilibrium'. On the impossibility of demonstrating uniqueness and stability of equilibrium cf. §§6.3 and 12.6.

to the themes tackled in *Prices and production*, even if in the general opinion the latter are considered more pressing. Hayek also explicitly indicates in the aggregate notion of capital connected to the average period of production the main limitation of his previous analysis; in a footnote (Hayek 1941, p. 296) he recalls Wicksell, attributing him with the merit of having been 'the only author who, to my knowledge, has clearly seen that the traditional way of treating a quantitatively determined stock of capital as a datum is illegitimate'. Thus, Hayek abandons the notion of the average period of production, which constituted an attempt to define a quantitative measure of the capitalist intensity of production processes.

At the centre of analysis we still have the notion of equilibrium and the requirement that it be a stable equilibrium. Compared with an 'instantaneous' notion of competitive equilibrium connected to a process of virtual adjustment taking place in logical time (typical of authors like Walras and Pareto), Hayek initially preferred that (attributable to authors like Marshall and Wicksell) of a 'stationary' competitive equilibrium; however, in the 1941 book he recognizes the limits of this construct and (more or less simultaneously with Hicks 1939 and Lindhal 1939) chooses the direction of a concatenated succession of instantaneous equilibriums.[21]

After a long and careful analysis of the basic concepts, the modus operandi of the theory remains analogous, in its structure, to that adopted in the 1931 book: the different stages of the cycle follow one another connected by a chain of cause-and-effect links, set in motion by the variations in the relative prices of consumption and capital goods that induce first a lengthening and then a shortening of the period of production (or in other words, in terms of the most common marginalist theory, first an increase and then a decrease in the capital intensity of productive processes). The difference lies in the fact that now the length of the periods of production is moving in the opposite direction.[22] Assuming that money wages and interest rates remain unchanged during the cycle, in the 1941 book Hayek starts with an increase in the demand for consumption goods (activated by any external cause, for instance an

---

[21] After illustrating this transition, Donzelli (1988, pp. 36–7) suggests that it is the abstract nature of the solution of instantaneous equilibriums that led Hayek to change direction in his research, towards the study of the 'real processes of diffusion of knowledge, coordination of individual plans, and so on', eventually arriving at a theory of spontaneous order (considered in §4.5).

[22] The point is not explicitly made by Hayek, who makes no clear comparison between his 1931 and 1941 analyses, but is stressed by Kaldor in his critique. Kaldor (1942, p. 381) remarks: 'The presence of so many contradictory arguments is not accidental: it is due to the desire to demonstrate, at all costs, that the scarcity of capital is the great cause of economic crises and a direct cause of unemployment.'

expansion of credit). The prices of these goods increase, and real wages decrease. Thus, it becomes expedient to shorten the production process, which reduces the demand for capital goods, with a fall in their prices that sets into motion a process running in the opposite direction. Once again, it is the excess of demand for consumption goods that originates a descending stage of the cycle.

Kaldor's (1942) criticisms – left unanswered by Hayek – concern various aspects of this construction, including the scant importance of the so-called 'Ricardo effect' (which, as Kaldor remarks, is to be attributed more to Wicksell than to Ricardo), according to which an increase in the demand for consumption goods leads to a decrease in the demand for investment goods. From a Keynesian viewpoint, such as that adopted by Kaldor, it is reasonable to assume on the contrary that an expansion in the demand for consumption goods stimulates the demand for investment goods: changes in the capitalistic intensity of productive processes take place, if at all, more slowly and with much less intensity.[23] 'New technical inventions are constantly occurring, and since they are mainly of a labour-saving character, they create a trend of constant deepening … which probably swamps any cyclical fluctuation between "deepening" and "enshallowing"' (Kaldor 1942, p. 380).

On this latter point, the criticisms of the average period of production (and the marginalist theory of value) advanced by Sraffa in his 1960 book, and confirmed in the subsequent capital theory debates, definitively established that changes in real wages are not automatically followed by correlated variations in the capital intensity of production processes. We shall return to this in the next chapter and in §12.6.

Long as it took to write, the book does not reach clear and solid results. Hayek himself appears unsatisfied with his results and the subsequent elaborations of neo-Austrian theoreticians in the field of capital theory. In his *Autobiography* (1994, p. 96), to the question, 'Wouldn't you say in retrospect that capital theory in the Austrian sense ended up with *Pure theory of capital?*' he answers: 'I'd say very largely. No one has done what I hoped would be done by others.' Dissatisfaction with the results obtained was already being expressed in the year following publication of the book in an article on 'The Ricardo effect' (Hayek 1942, p. 251): 'I am fully aware that all this is not very satisfactory and that a clear picture

---

[23] While Hayek implicitly utilizes the notion of capital as a scarce factor of production, common to all streams of the traditional marginalist theory of value and distribution, Kaldor saw it as obvious that the endowment of capital goods may be increased through investment. Hence a different approach to the objectives of the entrepreneurs: 'the relevant consideration is not the maximum profit on a given sum of capital, but the maximum profit on a given rate of output' (Kaldor 1942, p. 369).

of the precise process by which competition brings about this result ['that a rise in wages will encourage capitalists to substitute machinery for labour', p. 220: what Hayek calls the Ricardo effect] would be very desirable. But I am not sure whether this is possible.' According to Hayek, the problem is that 'we are dealing with a position of disequilibrium in which developments depend on the precise order in which the various changes follow one another in time'; as a matter of fact, it is the direct relationship between wage rate and capitalistic intensity of production processes, hence the inverse relationship between wage rate and employment, that is devoid of foundations. Clearly the issue then gets further complicated when Hayek (1941, pp. 306 ff.) tries to take into account technological change as well. Indeed, the complications tend to obscure the basic difficulties.

However, dissatisfaction did not suffice to bring Hayek to abandon the central theses of the traditional marginalist theory of value and distribution and the belief in an automatic tendency of a competitive labour market towards full employment. This tenet is still reaffirmed in his Nobel lecture in 1974, and in a work originally published in 1978 (Hayek 1999b, p. 213).

At least in part, the difficulties met by Hayek stem from the fact that the objectives he set himself were too vast. Indeed, his treatment of equilibrium is accompanied by attempts to tackle issues concerning change (including unforeseen changes, such as innovations), involving recourse to the analysis of input and output flows intersecting with analysis of instantaneous equilibriums, and recognition of the need for disaggregated treatment of value is accompanied by the quest for monodimensional values or functions allowing for determination of the rate of interest based on the opposed forces of 'capital' productivity and intertemporal preferences of consumers-savers. The book contains many interesting elements – especially at the level of the formulation of the relevant concepts – for various research fields: sequential analysis, intertemporal equilibriums analysis, and the implications of adhering to a marginalist theory of value and distribution for analysis of the trade cycle. It is thus a pity that all this has been abandoned: various of these elements were taken up in successive treatments of neo-Austrian capital theory, occasionally without indication, and as a rule without the awareness, which Hayek himself came to after publication of the volume, of the limits of the proposed solutions.[24]

---

[24] Hicks (1973) refers to Hayek's *Theory of capital* only once, and generically, in the introduction to his *Capital and time* (discussed in §8.4). We shall be returning to the models of intertemporal equilibrium in §6.3; and to the capital theory debate in §12.6.

4.5   Spontaneous Order and the Market as a Mechanism of Knowledge Diffusion

Having abandoned the fields of trade cycle and capital theory, Hayek focused his attention on the coordination mechanisms of the decisions of independent agents, gradually substituting the notion of equilibrium with that of spontaneous order, in the sense of 'qualitative relational structure' compatible with disequilibrium situations.[25] To the question of whether it is possible to define 'Hayek's problem', Hayek himself (1994, pp. 153–4) answered: 'the formation of complex orders'.

Hayek's thesis is that the coordination should not be imposed from above, through a centralized planning process, but can arise spontaneously, in a market economy, thanks to the invisible hand of competition.[26] Hayek noted the various obstacles to the emersion of this spontaneous order, and in particular the fact that knowledge is dispersed among many agents.[27] He maintained, however, that a market economy is superior to a planned economy precisely because the necessary information is transmitted in the former case in compressed form through prices,[28] and is thus available much more easily than in the latter case.[29]

---

[25] Donzelli (1988), pp. 42–3.

[26] Hayek cites Ferguson and Smith in this respect. Donzelli (1988, pp. 37 ff.) stresses that the notion of 'spontaneous order', present in embryonic form in Hayek's early writings, comes to the fore, finally substituting the traditional notion of equilibrium, at the end of the debates in capital theory (after Hayek 1941). With this notion Hayek refers to 'a structure of relations or a system of inter-individual connections presenting a relative stability or persistence' (Donzelli 1988, p. 38).

[27] 'The knowledge of the circumstances of which we must make use never exists in concentrated or integrated form, but solely as the dispersed bits of incomplete and frequently contradictory knowledge which all the separate individuals possess. The economic problem of society is thus not merely a problem of how to allocate "given" resources ... it is a problem of the utilization of knowledge not given to anyone in its totality' (Hayek 1945, pp. 519–20).

[28] Through the price system, 'in abbreviated form, by a kind of symbol, only the most essential information is passed on only to those concerned' (Hayek 1945, p. 527).

[29] The viability of a planned economy had been demonstrated by Enrico Barone as early as 1908 within the framework of a general economic equilibrium theory. Ludwig von Mises (1920), instead, maintained the impossibility, in the absence of a market, of computing the price system on which planning should rely; in this respect, Mises failed to take into account the answer already provided by Barone. Hayek (1935, 1940; reprinted in Hayek 1949), instead, insisted on the impossibility of obtaining the necessary information in practice. Oskar Lange (1904–65) answered them with an oft-cited article (Lange 1936–7), proposing a trial-and-error approach to planning which embodies elements of a 'socialist market'. Hayek (1940) replied that in a socialist market, in which the prices are modified by the planner, the adjustment process would fail because it could not proceed at the required speed. A different answer came from the British Marxist Maurice Dobb (1900–76), who in various writings (e.g. Dobb 1955) maintained the superiority of a planned economy not in the field of the allocation of resources but in that of ex ante coordination of investments.

Moreover, as from the 1937 essay 'Economics and knowledge' (an essay that Hayek [1994], p. 79, considers 'the most original contribution I have made to the theory of economics'), and with increasingly accurate exposition in subsequent writings, Hayek conceived of knowledge as a process of discovery and diffusion of information. In this respect he recalled and developed some ideas already present *in nuce* in the Austrian tradition of Menger and Mises, proposing a view of the functioning of the economy departing from that of traditional marginalism. In particular, the act of choice by the economic agent is seen as an experiment in conditions of uncertainty, the result of which modifies initial knowledge and expectations in a continuous process.

The formation of social institutions does not follow 'laws of evolution', but a process of selection within which the best institutions prevail. This is not a Darwinian process, referring to the selection of the individuals on the basis of their innate characteristics, but refers to institutions and customs connected to culture (Hayek 1973, p. 23); the same is true of rules and laws (p. 99).[30]

Other aspects to be recalled are tacit knowledge and customs ensuring a certain degree of stability in the behaviour of individuals.[31] The spontaneous social order may thus favour adaptation to continuously changing conditions, and even change in unknown directions. In this respect, according to Hayek the signals arriving from prices and their changes indicate to agents the directions to move in, without thereby imposing a condition of equilibrium between demand and supply.[32]

Elements of this kind are also prominent in Hayek's political writings. He maintains that economic liberalism is superior not only to centralized planning but also to mixed economies (as in the case of Roosevelt's New Deal) implying an active intervention of the state in economic life. It is thanks to these writings, especially the widely circulated *The road to serfdom* (1944), that Hayek achieved a prominent public image as one of the most famous political scientists of the twentieth century.

For our purposes, we may note two elements in this stream of contributions. First, though in works explicitly addressing not specialists but the public at large, Hayek retains the main elements of the Austrian school and its founder Menger: uncertainty, and economic activity as

---

[30] Rules are defined as 'a propensity or disposition to act or not to act in a certain manner, which will manifest itself in what we call a practice or custom' (Hayek 1973, p. 75).

[31] As for the notion of tacit knowledge, Caldwell (2004, p. 294 n.) points out Hayek's debt towards his friend Michael Polanyi.

[32] As a matter of fact, Hayek's thesis requires the (quite unrealistic) assumption of static conditions. Suffice it to recall the Schumpeterian view of technical progress – 'creative destruction' – that destroys tacit knowledge and habits.

quest for the power stemming from knowledge. Within this view, the analytical notion of equilibrium as equality between supply and demand is diluted in the notion of a spontaneous order, and the characterization of the economic agent may turn out to be far more complex than the monodimensional one of Benthamite utilitarianism leading to the notion of *homo oeconomicus*.[33]

Second, in the political writings the thesis of a spontaneous order emerging from the functioning of the market appears transformed from an analytical result that the theorist seeks to demonstrate to a simple assumption or postulate. It is assumed, without demonstration, that the institutions emerging from this process are optimal; it is assumed, without demonstration, that the process of institution selection is not distorted by an uneven distribution of knowledge, which in turn renders the distribution of power asymmetric, and so a possible source of manipulation of knowledge. In fact, Hayek reasons as if the results which he hopes to obtain, but does not reach, in his theoretical works – the tendency to an optimal equilibrium – had been obtained and could be transferred from economics to the field of political theory: an undoubtedly able rhetorical exercise, but totally devoid of analytic foundations.

4.6   Methodological Individualism, Political Individualism and Economic and Political Liberalism

An important aspect of Hayek's thought is his opposition to what he calls 'scientism', namely the pretence of the social sciences to take their place at the same level as the natural sciences, and hence 'constructivist rationalism', i.e. the idea that it could be possible and useful to build from above the social institutions, to be directed, again from above, according to the precepts dictated by some impersonal and objective reason: an idea unavoidably generating authoritarian tendencies.[34] *Taxis* (*made order*) is opposed to *kosmos* (*grown order*).[35]

Methodological individualism – the idea that the functioning of the economic system is to be explained starting from the choices of the individuals composing it –[36] was already to be seen in Menger and constituted a dominant tradition within the marginalist approach in all

---

[33] Hayek (1973, pp. 22, 69) explicitly criticizes Benthamite utilitarianism and approvingly quotes Hume: 'Though men be much more governed by interest, yet even interest itself, and all human affairs, are entirely governed by *opinion*.'

[34] Cf. Hayek (1942–4) and Hayek (1973), vol. 1, pp. 8 ff. The theme is also taken up in the Nobel lecture, 11 December 1974, available at www.nobelprize.org/nobel-prizes/economic_sciences/laureate/1974/hayek_lecture.html.

[35] Hayek (1973), p. 37.   [36] Cf. e.g. Hayek (1948), p. 69.

its variants. In Hayek's view, as in Popper's (1945) and indeed that of many other authors sharing their approach, this is not only a methodological rule, but a true political dogma, because of the connection implicitly or explicitly made between holism on the one hand (the idea that social aggregates may be studied autonomously from the behaviour of the individuals composing them) and political organicism on the other hand (the state, or the community, is 'more' than the individuals composing it) on which dictatorial regimes such as Nazism or Stalinist communism are grounded.[37]

However, it is possible to share Hayek's criticism of totalitarianism and its cultural roots without having to accept the identification between political individualism, i.e. the defence of individual freedom in the political as in the economic fields, and methodological individualism.[38]

The main reason for Hayek's adhesion to methodological individualism is in fact different, being philosophical in nature. In order to understand this point we need briefly to recall the cultural climate of the *Methodenstreit* and the climate prevailing in subsequent decades, up to the period of Hayek's first writings. In that period, the debate on method did not simply concern economics: it was the consequence of a frontal clash between positivism and neo-idealism, and among other things between the idea that knowledge stems from confrontation with empirical reality (and that theories constitute an abstraction, or rationalization, of the data collected) and the idea that, in the field of the human if not the natural sciences, knowledge stems from an *Einleitung*, i.e. from a process of inner reflection (as maintained for instance by Dilthey) that alone can provide 'true' axioms – such by direct acquisition – on which the deductive reasoning at the basis of theory construction can rely.[39] In economics, this is the nature of the axioms of rational behaviour, preference ordering, decreasing marginal utility (or ophelimity), increasing sacrifice of labour, all considered true precisely because derived from personal introspection.[40] Eventually, a methodological veer came in the 1950s, when it was recognized that human behaviour does not conform to the axioms of marginalist tradition (Chapter 10).

---

[37] Hayek, like Popper, recalls the medieval opposition between nominalism and realism; both, however, fail to recall the intermediate position proposed by Abelard, who held that the universal term was born to designate (and communicate) an effective aspect of reality; hence cannot be considered a simple *flatus vocis*. Cf. Roncaglia (2016a), p. 19.

[38] This distinction is clearly set out by another exponent of Austrian economic culture, Schumpeter (cf. §3.5).

[39] For an illustration of this comparison, and of the dominant role it had in the period under consideration, cf. Stuart Hughes (1958).

[40] On these themes cf. the essay on 'Scientism and the study of society' (Hayek 1942–4).

Individual behaviour thus expresses itself through actions stemming from rationally chosen action plans. According to methodological individualism, economic theory must consider the action plans of all the agents. Hence the central role of the Hayekian notion of equilibrium, consisting in the set of action plans that are compatible with each other and with the given conditions in which economic activity takes place (technology, resource endowments for each individual agent). Because of the cognitive limits of economic agents, realistically it is not possible for ex ante planning to ensure coordination of individual action plans. Coordination is entrusted to the market, which works as an adjustment mechanism ensuring equilibrium.

A typical characteristic of Menger's, and indeed Hayek's, view is that subjective knowledge is included among the variables affected by the adjustment processes induced by the working of the market, alongside prices and produced and exchanged quantities. Indeed Hayek, while becoming aware of the unsolved problems in the theory of value and distribution he himself adopts, attributed growing importance to the role of the market as an instrument of diffusion of information and adjustment of individual knowledge. Moreover, Hayek recalls, in its normal functioning the market embodies significant elements of tacit knowledge.

These are suggestive ideas, which fascinated many contemporary economists and were taken up in particular by the new Austrian school (§8.3). Yet, the proposal of notions, however interesting they might be, needs to find support in demonstration of their analytical fruitfulness, and so in a theory of value, distribution and employment that demonstrates the equilibrating efficacy of the market mechanisms. In sum, Hayek describes elements constituting a possible adjustment process towards an optimal market equilibrium, or towards a spontaneous order of society, but does not demonstrate the logical necessity of an optimal outcome for these adjustment processes. Thus, the main issue of the political controversy remains open with regard to the possibility of non-optimal situations in the economy and society, and as a consequence the expediency of an active role of the state in the economy.

Indeed, Hayek devoted the first decades of his long activity to the quest for a demonstration of the existence of such automatic adjustment processes in the market economy. However, after the controversies with Sraffa and Kaldor he did not return to these issues; the self-regulating power of the competitive market became an axiom, as did the basically competitive nature of capitalism, to the point of wholly ignoring the literature – discussed in the text that follows – on managerial capitalism

(Berle and Means, Marris), the affluent society and the industrial state (Galbraith), and on oligopoly (Bain, Sylos Labini).

In defending free enterprise, Hayek produced an important series of texts (including Hayek 1960, 1973) presenting his researches on the institutional set-up best suited to guaranteeing individual freedoms and a competitive market. Freedom requires that compulsion be substituted by the rule of law, which needs to be abstract and impartial, certain, known to all and equally applicable to all, universal: 'government by rules' and not 'government by orders' (Hayek 1948, p. 18).[41] These writings are interesting on many counts; here we shall briefly consider two of them.

The first aspect concerns the distinction between political and economic liberalism, between defence of individual freedoms and defence of free private initiative in the economic field. The connection between the two elements is not automatic. For instance, John Stuart Mill considered it impossible to isolate the defence of individual freedoms from the development of an equitable society as far as income and power distribution are concerned – as after him did the authors who associated active liberties (of opinion, vote, speech, etc.) with passive liberties (from hunger, misery, unemployment, etc.), and subordinated laissez-faire to the latter. Even without choosing passive liberties as objectives, Keynes – as we saw – considered the survival of the democratic institutions and the free market far from certain in a situation of widespread dissatisfaction arising when the economy takes a negative turn; more generally, the need to balance individual economic freedom and social justice through active state intervention was repeatedly stressed (among others, by liberal socialists such as Carlo Rosselli and the supporters of the welfare state).

On the contrary, Hayek, and many others with him, considers state intervention in the economy risky for individual freedoms because of the concentration of power that it implies. When the state (in principle, a proletarian dictatorship; in practice, an oligarchic *nomenklatura*) controls production, we are faced with one single employer. Since every citizen needs to work to earn a living, there is total dependency on those who control job allocation. In the mixed economy the influence of the public employer is not so strong, but it is still there and may even condition the way election campaigns are fought.

The second aspect is of great relevance today, concerning the freedom of movement of capital and goods among the various countries; this sets

---

[41] Hayek implicitly assumes that the rules and their interpretation be neutral with respect to the interests of the different social strata or groups; when this condition is not satisfied, the rules themselves constitute government coercion on all the citizens.

states competing in reducing fiscal pressure, environmental controls or regulations on safety in the workplace. Lower taxes and reduced regulations attract investments and productive capacity, with the creation of new jobs, at the expense of countries maintaining a more extended welfare state and more stringent environmental or work safety regulations. In other words, competition among states helps restrain public intervention in the economy; as a corollary, Hayek was favourable to state federations, such as the euro area today, because of the competition between states rigidly connected by a single currency and a single market.[42] Under these conditions a national monetary policy becomes impossible, but it also becomes very difficult, Hayek remarked, to tax any mobile asset transferable to another country, or to adopt more restrictive rules than those adopted in other countries on the environment or work safety.[43] Hayek was therefore favourable to federations between states and to fixed exchange rates.

Analogous results may be obtained, even in the absence of federal unions, through all the interventions that favour international mobility of goods, capital and financial assets. Hayek (1999b, p. 222) saw controls on international capital movements as 'the most serious menace not only to the functioning of the international economy, but also to personal freedom', so much so, in fact, that such interventions should in his opinion be explicitly forbidden in the constitutions of democratic countries. As a matter of fact, Hayek foresaw what has been happening in the last few decades: globalization leading to a substantial shift of power in favour of business, undermining state attempts to regulate private

---

[42] In 1977 Hayek (1999b, p. 133) declared that he considers 'utopian' the 'scheme of introducing a new European currency', while he declared himself favourable to economic unification; his opposition to a unified currency is explained by the fact that this would be a legal currency, which, because of the extent of its use, would render the consequences of (in his view unavoidable) mistakes in monetary policy very heavy.

[43] 'As has been shown by experience in existing federations, even such legislation as the restriction of child labor or of working hours becomes difficult to carry out for the individual state' (Hayek 1948, p. 260), while 'the diversity of conditions and the different stages of economic development reached by the various parts of the federation will raise serious obstacles to federal legislation' (Hayek 1948, p. 263); 'much of the interference with economic life to which we have become accustomed will be altogether impracticable under a federal organization' (Hayek 1948, p. 265).

Hayek is in favour of a system of proportional taxation of incomes: the liberal requirement of the equality of the starting points for all members of society must leave room for reward for merits and individual effort. Cf. Hayek (2011, p. 177), and especially *The constitution of liberty* (Hayek 1960, chapter 20). He does, however, respond favourably to the idea of a safety net at the level of social security, provided it does not imply redistributive policies or the compulsion to adopt a public insurance scheme (Hayek 1960, chapter 19). 'There is all the difference in the world between treating people equally and attempting to make them equal' (Hayek 1948, p. 16).

activity. This is an important theme, on which Hayek (and the Mont Pèlerin Society, which he created: cf. §8.8) have had a by no means insignificant influence, but all too little attention has been paid to it.

In conclusion, we may once again distinguish between appreciation of the conceptual representation of the market economy proposed by Hayek and the limits of his analytical construct. The success of Hayek's political writings may perhaps be explained, apart from his affinity to the cultural climate of the Cold War period and subsequently to the neo-liberal upturn of the 1970s and 1980s, with the suggestion of so many aspects of his conceptual representation, helped by his choice – followed by many – to leave aside the most controversial aspects of his economic theory while presenting his political views on the role of the market. As for the elements of Hayek's vision that attract most attention in contemporary debate – like the role of acquisition of knowledge by economic agents confronted with the market's responses to their actions – inclusion of them in a coherent theoretical system represents a challenge to be tackled on new grounds rather than a result left as a bequest by the Austrian economist.

4.7   The Denationalization of Money

One of Hayek's more striking proposals was abolition of the state monopoly on the creation of money, to be substituted with a system of private monies issued by banks and corporations in competition among themselves. This proposal has again become topical in recent years, with the spread of crypto-currencies like bitcoins; its interest for us also lies in the fact that it relies on the Austrian economist's set of economic analyses and brings out their intrinsic limits.

Hayek had taken an interest in monetary theory since his early years, but as a substantially secondary topic compared with his analyses first of the trade cycle and capital theory, and then of spontaneous order. His writings on the topic are collected in two volumes (Hayek 1999a, 1999b); what concerns us here is above all a substantial essay on *The denationalization of money*, originally published in 1978 as a pamphlet by the Institute of Economic Affairs in London (now in Hayek 1999b, pp. 128–229).

In other contributions, mentioned only en passant here, as in his works on the trade cycle and capital theory, 'Hayek was not prepared to separate value theory from monetary theory', as Kresge remarked (in Hayek 1999a, p. 12). In contrast with what is traditionally the case in the marginalist approach, money is not considered simply as a veil, neutral with respect to determination of the 'real' equilibrium of prices and quantities.[44] Indeed, Hayek repeatedly insisted on the distorting effects that variations in the quantity of money may have on relative prices, and all the more after the controversies on cycle and capital made it clear that it is impossible to refer to an aggregate quantity of capital and that the rate of interest has a complex influence on the choice of the techniques of production. Hayek stressed that in 1923 he had already recognized what Keynes maintains in the *Tract on monetary reform*, namely the need to distinguish between stabilization of the exchange rates and stabilization of internal prices; moreover, like Keynes in the *Treatise on money*, he repeatedly criticized the notion of general price level.[45] Hayek also rejected the thesis that it was possible to determine a priori the correct quantity of money to be circulated, as well as the thesis, characteristic of monetarism, that monetary policy could and should target 'a particular predetermined volume of circulation' (Hayek 1999b, p. 184): it is the market that indicates the road to be followed. In general, his thesis is that economic disequilibrium is caused by errors in monetary and fiscal policy, while a well-organized monetary system operates as support for a competitive economy that in a full laissez-faire regime is capable of optimal self-regulation.

From these theoretical positions other ideas follow: his defence of the gold standard in the initial stage of his research,[46] then the plans for an international currency based on a basket of commodities,[47] for which he drew on others' ideas, and the proposal for the denationalization of money and competition between private currencies, which saw him this time as the original proponent.[48]

According to Hayek, the right of seignorage attributed to the state constitutes a dangerous element allowing expropriation of private wealth through the inflation induced by monetary expansion. As a remedy, one

[44]   In a brief article of 1933 (reprinted in Hayek 1999a, pp. 228–31), the Austrian economist distinguishes between the theoretical function of the notion of 'neutral money', pointing to its limited ambit of validity, and the use of such an assumption in (the theory of) monetary policy, which is rejected.

[45]   On the difference between stabilization of internal prices and exchange rates, and indeed in criticism of the notion of a general price level, as a matter of fact both Keynes and Hayek were preceded by Sraffa (1920), who probably discussed the topic with Keynes in August 1921. Cf. §5.1.

[46]   See the first four writings reprinted in Hayek (1999a); the Austrian economist appears confident in the adjustment mechanisms originally described by Hume and attributes to the abandonment of the gold standard a primary role in the Great Depression of the 1930s.

[47]   Cf. Hayek (1943), reprinted in Hayek (1999b), pp. 106–14. The article preceded by one year the Bretton Woods conference; it thus belongs to a stage in which a debate was starting on how to reconstruct the international monetary system at the end of the war.

[48]   Hayek (1999b, p. 230) triumphantly states: 'I had opened a possibility which in two thousand years no single economist had ever studied.'

might well begin with independence of the central banks from the political authorities. But an even more radical remedy, that might allow for definitive defeat of inflation, consists in eliminating the state monopoly in issue of currency.

Introducing 'private' monies, in competition among themselves, would give rise to a selection process in which the worst currencies – namely those less stable in value – would disappear. While, according to 'Gresham's law', bad money chases away good money, here the opposite would hold. There would no longer be a fixed exchange rate between the different currencies, which would induce agents to treasure the best currencies: all agents would try to get rid of those currencies that tend to lose value more rapidly. Monetary stability and the reduction in the power of the state would favour private initiative and economic activity. An active monetary policy – according to Hayek a source of systematically negative consequences – would be rendered impossible. The need for a legal tender, namely a reference currency for contracts (a currency the creditor could not refuse as means of payment for his credits), is considered a false issue: creditors are damaged by anchorage to a legal currency in the case of inflation (or hyperinflation, as in Germany in the years after the end of the First World War), while the parties to a contract would be able to choose by common agreement a private currency to refer to. Moreover, in the presence of private monies in competition among themselves, market reactions to wage increases caused by the monopoly power of trade unions would make it clear that the latter are to be attributed with responsibility for unemployment (Hayek 1999b, p. 199).

It may be useful to point out some of the limits of this thesis – limits which underlie the whole of Hayek's economic philosophy. For the scheme to work properly, a perfect economic system is required: driven by competition, and so with no concentrations of power; characterized by absolute respect for norms; and competition not giving rise to instability. Let us consider these three aspects one by one.

Competition can prevail in the absence of a tendency to concentration, which requires unit costs of production to increase when the dimensions of the firm increase. However, this condition is not satisfied in general. In particular, in the case of private monies, those having wider circulation benefit far more than those having more limited circulation; in other words, scale economies are very strong, both in managing the currency and in ensuring it wide circulation. The more it circulates, the more the currency is known and accepted as a means of payment, measure of value and reserve of value. The less utilized currencies rapidly lose ground to the more utilized ones; this kind of process of concentration was foreseen by Hayek himself, although he does not seem to have seen it clashing with the basic assumption of competition.[49]

As for the second aspect, Hayek does not rule out the possibility of illegal behaviour – cooked accounts, use of fake news, and so on. But he relies on the press for the necessary control, which in modern economies is attributed to public agencies endowed with ample intervention powers (as with bank surveillance, now commonly entrusted to central banks or special agencies).[50] This is clearly an unsatisfactory solution, for three reasons. First, specialized technical knowledge is required for this task, and journalists are not selected on this basis. Second, conflicts of interest are likely (in many countries banks control or condition the major press publishing and broadcasting companies), as well as processes of concentration among information providers. Third, private monies, especially in the absence of serious controls, facilitate criminal organizations. For instance, today bitcoins are both the preferred private money and the money most used for recycling dirty gains by suppliers of illicit drugs, arms, human organs, and by tax evaders. In sum, Hayek's philosophy is that the public sector is prey to bad behaviour, while nothing really bad can come from the private sector; the real world appears to be at least a bit more complex.

The third aspect concerns Hayek's systematic misunderstanding of the Keynesian theory of finance.[51] As we saw earlier (§§3.6 and 3.7), according to Keynes the stock of financial assets is held on the basis of uncertain expectations of their returns, dominated in the very short period by variations in their prices; speculative decisions to buy or sell financial assets, based on very short-term perspectives, dominate over the demand of money for current transaction purposes.[52] Speculative activities, especially in the absence of adequate controlling agencies, are dominated by

---

[49] Hayek (1999b, p. 156) relies on competition to limit the dimensions of each issuer of private money; however, this is a simple petition of principle.

[50] 'So long as the press properly exercised its supervisory function and warned the public in time of any derelict of duty on the part of some issuers, such a system may satisfactorily serve for a long time' (Hayek 1999b, p. 224).

[51] The misunderstanding is probably due to the fact that Keynes deals with the themes of money and finance without connecting them to the theory of value, as Hayek instead deems necessary. Hence Hayek's (1999b, p. 115) harsh judgement of 'Keynes, a man of great intellect but limited knowledge of economic theory'.

[52] Hayek (1999b, p. 166) holds that for each private issuer 'the public preparedness to hold its currency, and therefore its business, depends on maintaining the currency value'; however, this is not true of speculative financial activity, for which demanding or offering a currency does not depend on its record of average stability in the long run, but on expectations regarding its very short-run oscillations, which may through mechanisms of self-fulfilling expectations (that Soros, 2008, calls *reflexivity*) lead to breakdown of the underlying equilibriums.

the biggest operators. As experience shows, oscillations in value determined by speculation may be quite marked, with correspondingly ample gains and losses; the bankruptcy of big operators may lead to systemic crises. Instability increases uncertainty, which depresses economic activity; the proportions of gains in the financial sector attract qualified workers and resources away from the real sector of the economy, with a slowing down of technical progress.[53]

Hayek's faith in the stability of the economy relies on three elements: the marginalist theory of value, which implies automatic adjustment to full employment in a competitive economy, in which a reduction of the wage rate engenders a reduction in the capital intensity of production processes; his theory of the emersion of a spontaneous order from individual actions and his view of the price system as a mechanism of information transmission; the strength of competition relative to the trends of concentration in income, wealth and power. His two-decade-long work on the first theme has turned out to be void of positive results. The same can be said of his thesis on spontaneous order: nothing, apart from apodictic statements stemming from his a priori preference for a free market, can ensure that a myriad of individual actions will not generate instability or suboptimal choices.[54] The third element, faith in competition, appears not to stand up to the test of hard facts, in the absence of a strong state adopting serious anti-trust policies. Hayek's ideas and theories nevertheless retain a central importance, both for the development of a wide-ranging system of concepts (a 'vision', in Schumpeter's meaning of the term), and for the enormous influence which in various ways they exert on contemporary political life: on the growth of a neo-liberal culture, on institutional transformation, and on the policy choices of the public authorities and private centres of power.

---

[53] Once again, we may look to the experience with bitcoins for evidence of the instability of the main private currency in circulation today. On bitcoins, cf. Böhme *et al.* (2015).

[54] As far as the theory of capital is concerned, as already noticed Hayek appears far more aware of the limits of his theses than his followers in the neo-Austrian school. However this caution does not extend to the politically central thesis of the invisible hand of the market, namely the efficacy of the market in creating a spontaneous order, reaffirmed again and again (for instance Hayek 1973, p. 114, states that there has been a 'demonstration by the economists that the market produced a spontaneous order').

5   The Revolutionary: Piero Sraffa

5.1   Early Contributions: Money and Banking

Piero Sraffa (1898–1983) is recognized as one of the leading intellectuals of the twentieth century, not only for his strictly economic contributions, but also for his influence on other major figures, from Antonio Gramsci to Ludwig Wittgenstein.[1]

In the field of economic sciences, Sraffa's cultural project was extremely ambitious: to shunt the car of economic science in a direction opposite to that indicated by Jevons, one of the protagonists of the marginalist approach. With his writings, in fact, Sraffa aimed to expose the weak points of the marginalist approach as developed by William Stanley Jevons, Carl Menger, Léon Walras, Alfred Marshall, and at the same time to re-propose the classical approach of Adam Smith, David Ricardo and, in certain respects, Karl Marx. Thus, Sraffa represents the pillar of a line of research alternative to the one proposed by Hayek, discussed in the previous chapter. For a better understanding of its nature and impact, it may be useful to follow the gradual development of this cultural project, from the early writings on money and banking to the edition of Ricardo's works and the slim but packed volume *Production of commodities by means of commodities* (1960).

The degree dissertation *L'inflazione monetaria in Italia durante e dopo la guerra* (Monetary inflation in Italy during and after the war), discussed with Luigi Einaudi,[2] also constituted his first publication (Sraffa 1920).

---

[1] In what follows I shall use, with some small changes, the chapter devoted to Sraffa in Roncaglia (2016a). For a more extensive treatment, cf. Roncaglia (2009b).

[2] Luigi Einaudi (1874–1961), a pragmatic liberal, professor of public finance at Turin from 1902, a member of the Senate since 1919, withdrew from public life under fascism and spent the final stages of the Second World War in exile in Switzerland; he then became Governor of the Bank of Italy in 1945, minister for the budget in 1947, and finally President of the Italian Republic (1948–55): see Faucci (1986). Here we confine our attention to two aspects: his policy – a very drastic one, and crowned with success – of stabilization of the internal value of the lira in 1947–8; his controversy with Croce on the

Rapid increase in prices is associated with expansion in the circulation of money, in line with the dominant tradition of the quantity theory of money. However, Sraffa's empirical analysis departs pragmatically from it to consider the various trends of different price indexes, the significance of which is connected to the different viewpoints of the various groups of protagonists of economic life, and in particular the social classes of workers and entrepreneurs. Implicit in this position is the idea that a general price index (a crucial notion not only for the quantity theory of money, but more generally for all theories that conceive of money simply as a veil, with no influence on real variables) is misleading precisely in that it obscures the central role of social conflicts in economic life.[3] This point is worth stressing because it is precisely the non-univocal nature of the concept of the general price level (and thus of its inverse, the purchasing power of money) that underlies Keynes's criticism of the quantity theory of money in the opening chapters of his *Treatise of money* (Keynes 1930).

The most significant original contribution offered by Sraffa's thesis, however, lies in the distinction between stabilization of the internal and the external value of money, or in other words between stabilization of the average level of domestic prices and stabilization of the exchange rate. The two things coincide, according to the traditional theory of the gold standard; however, at least in principle they should be kept separate. The distinction becomes essential when considering both short-run problems and inconvertible paper money systems, and was thus of crucial importance for the policy choices of the time.[4] Moreover, it is also linked up with the development of Keynesian theory: we may recall, in fact, that Keynes does not use it in *Indian currency and finance* (1913), but does

---

relationship between economic and political liberalism. On this latter issue cf. Croce and Einaudi (1957); the writings by Croce to which we refer date from 1927, those by Einaudi date from 1928 and 1931. Einaudi and Croce agreed that economic liberalism cannot be an absolute tenet, unlike political liberalism, but only a practical rule. However, Einaudi stressed the instrumental role of economic liberalism in favouring the diffusion of economic power (which would otherwise be concentrated in the hands of the state, or the political elite). The fact remains that no one could call him- or herself a liberal if he or she was solely interested in the most widespread laissez-faire in the economic arena. Despite holding conservative views, Einaudi thus opened the way to the development of a reformist or socialist liberalism, as represented by Piero Gobetti, Carlo and Nello Rosselli and the political movement 'Justice and freedom' (*Giustizia e libertà*). Sraffa, as a student at the top high school in Turin and a cousin of the Rosselli brothers, entered into this cultural climate and, though oriented towards Gramsci's Marxism, remained on very good terms with many protagonists of the democratic streams of anti-fascism.

[3] In a similar direction ran, a few years later, one of the critiques that Sraffa (1932) levelled at Hayek, illustrated in the preceding chapter.

[4] Cf. De Cecco (1993) and Ciocca and Rinaldi (1997).

bring it into his *Tract on monetary reform* (1923), having in the meantime (in August 1921) met Sraffa.[5]

Sraffa's early publications again address monetary issues, with an article of 1922 in the *Economic Journal* on the crisis of the Banca Italiana di Sconto in 1922, and one on the bank crisis in Italy – again in 1922 – in the *Manchester Guardian Supplement on the Reconstruction in Europe*. The two articles reveal a thorough command of the institutional and technical aspects of banking (probably thanks at least in part to the practical experience the young Sraffa had acquired in a provincial branch of a bank immediately after graduating) and a strikingly well-informed approach and awareness of the interests at stake.[6]

The first of these two articles (Sraffa 1922a) reconstructs the vicissitudes of the Banca Italiana di Sconto from its birth at the end of 1914 to its bankruptcy in December 1921. Sraffa concludes with some pessimistic remarks on the risks involved in direct relations between banks and enterprises, on the inevitability of such relations given the backwardness of Italy's financial markets and on the difficulty of bringing about any change in the situation, due in the first place to a lack of real will at the political level.[7] The second article (Sraffa 1922b) highlights the weakness of Italy's three leading commercial banks (Banca Commerciale, Credito Italiano and Banca di Roma), casting serious doubts on the correctness of their official accounts and of the institutional expedient (resorting to a 'Consorzio per sovvenzioni sui valori industriali') adopted to side-step the law setting limits to the support issuing banks could give to commercial banks.[8]

Monetary issues subsequently re-emerge among Sraffa's interests. A brief, biting attack on an article in *Popolo d'Italia* on the movements of the exchange rate of the lira was published in Piero Gobetti's (1901–26) *Rivoluzione liberale* in 1923; two important letters on the revaluation of the lira were published by Angelo Tasca (1892–1960) in *Stato operaio* in 1927; from 1928 to 1930, then, Sraffa gave courses at

---

[5] Among other things Sraffa was the editor of the Italian edition of the *Tract*, published in 1925 under the title *La riforma monetaria* by the Fratelli Treves publishers in Milan. Keynes and Sraffa meet in Cambridge in August 1921: at the time Sraffa was staying in London for a few months, attending courses at the London School of Economics.

[6] Sraffa's father, Angelo, a well-known professor of commercial law and sometime rector of Bocconi University, certainly had authoritative inside knowledge of the games played by the industrial and financial Italian elite.

[7] Explicit in this sense is the conclusion of the article: 'But even if these laws were not futile in themselves, what could be their use as long as the Government is prepared to be the first to break them so soon as it is blackmailed by a band of gunmen or a group of bold financiers?' (Sraffa 1922a, p. 197).

[8] Publication of this article drew a harsh reaction from Mussolini: cf. Roncaglia (1984) and Naldi (1998).

Cambridge University on the Italian and German financial systems, along with his more celebrated lectures on the theory of value. The 1932 controversy with Hayek, to which we shall return, also concerns problems in monetary theory.

Apart from their intrinsic value, Sraffa's early publications attest to his personality as an all-round economist, whose predominant interest in pure theory is accompanied by a thorough knowledge of the institutional details and exemplary analyses of specific real-world issues. Moreover, they show that Sraffa adhered to the idea that monetary and financial vicissitudes have an impact on the real economy: a central idea for Keynes, which Sraffa was also to recall in his most theoretical work, with the reference to the influence of the interest rate over the rate of profits.[9]

5.2   Friendship with Gramsci

In May 1919, at the University of Turin, Sraffa met Antonio Gramsci (1891–1937). They were introduced by Umberto Cosmo (1868–1944), who had been Sraffa's teacher of Italian literature at upper secondary school, and Gramsci's teacher at the university. In 1919 Gramsci founded *L'ordine nuovo* (The new order); Sraffa collaborated with some translations from German and three short articles sent from London on the occasion of his visit there in 1921. And 1921 also saw the foundation of the Italian Communist Party in Livorno; Gramsci became the party secretary in 1924. Sraffa never joined the party, fully maintaining his independence of views, while keeping up close intellectual relations with his friend.

An example of this is offered by an important letter from Sraffa that Gramsci published (unsigned, initialled S.) in the April 1924 issue of *L'ordine nuovo* with his reply (Gramsci and Sraffa 1924). In his letter Sraffa stressed the function served by the bourgeois forces of opposition in the struggle against fascism and the importance of democratic institutions for the social and political development of the proletariat. In Sraffa's opinion, in the situation of the time, characterized by the rise of a fascist dictatorship, the working class was absent from the political scene. The unions and the Communist Party were incapable of organizing political action, while the workers were compelled to face their problems as individuals, rather than as organized groups. 'The main issue, taking first place over any other, is one of "freedom" and "order": the others will come later, but for now they can be of no interest to the workers. Now is

[9] Sraffa (1960), p. 33.

the time for the democratic forces of opposition, and I think we must let them act and possibly help them' (p. 4).

In his answer, Gramsci rejected Sraffa's suggestions, maintaining that they would lead to liquidation of the Communist Party, subjected as it would have been to the strategy of the bourgeois forces of opposition, and criticized his friend for 'having so far failed to rid himself of the ideological residue of his liberal-democratic intellectual background, namely normative and Kantian, not Marxist and dialectical' (Gramsci and Sraffa 1924, p. 4). We should keep in mind, though, that Gramsci's position necessarily mirrors that taken by Amadeo Bordiga, then secretary of the Communist Party: a party in which the principle of centralist leadership prevailed, to the exclusion of any dissent from the official party line.

Indeed, the very fact that Sraffa's letter was published, probably after heart-searching discussions between the two friends, amounts to a recognition of the importance of the problems discussed in it and of the political ideas proposed by the young economist. Gramsci drew attention to these ideas, displaying greater openness towards them, in a letter reserved for comrades closer to his position, and thus less subservient to the Bordiga orthodoxy.[10]

The episode suggests that Sraffa played some role in the development of Gramsci's political thinking, away from Bordiga's line, at least away from the idea of the total opposition of the Communist Party to all the other political forces for the sake of the Bolshevik Revolution. Years later, Gramsci's political reflections appear close to the position Sraffa took up as early as 1924, when Gramsci in turn proposed a pact among the anti-fascist political forces for reconstruction of a democratic Italy after the hoped-for fall of the fascist regime. Indeed, in this respect we may consider significant the fact that, apparently in their last meeting in March 1937, it was to Sraffa that Gramsci entrusted a verbal message for the comrades still enjoying freedom, and one that he attached great importance to – the watchword for the constituent assembly, which summed up the proposal mentioned earlier.

Along with this fundamental point in the political debate, we must also recall the help Sraffa gave Gramsci after his arrest in 1926. It is he who took pains to get books and magazines to his friend in prison; he who explored the possible paths to freedom (on the binding condition, that Gramsci insisted on, and which Sraffa endorsed, that no concessions be made to the fascist regime, such as a petition for pardon would imply). Finally, it was he who ensured a connection with communist leaders in exile and gave Gramsci further food for thought (through the latter's

[10] Cf. Togliatti (1962), pp. 242 ff.

sister-in-law, Tatiana Schucht) in the reflections that eventually took shape in the *Prison notebooks* (Gramsci 1975).[11]

5.3 Criticism of Marshallian Theory

Thus, in the years following graduation Sraffa's interests ranged from politics to questions of applied economics, and in particular monetary economics. His interest in theoretical issues probably developed after beginning his academic career, in November 1923, as lecturer at the University of Perugia.

The fruits of Sraffa's reflections – a radical critique of the Marshallian theory of the equilibrium of the firm and the industry – are set out in a long article published in Italian in 1925, *Sulle relazioni fra costo e quantità prodotta* (On the relations between cost and quantity produced). Five years had passed since publication of the eighth edition of Marshall's *Principles of economics*, and one year since his death.

Sraffa's article falls within a debate on the 'laws of returns' sparked off by a paper by John Harold Clapham (1873–1946) published in 1922 in the *Economic Journal*. The point in question is of vital importance for the Marshallian theoretical construction and more generally for the theories of value based on equilibrium between demand and supply. Within this approach, in particular within the Marshallian method of partial equilibriums, a decisive role is played by construction of a supply curve for each product, expressing production costs as a function of the quantity produced, both for the individual firm and for the industry as a whole.

Marshallian theory singles out three cases accounting for all eventualities: constant, increasing or decreasing returns, according to whether the average unit cost remains constant, decreases or increases when the quantity produced increases. Clapham, a professor of economic history, tackled the problem of the concrete application of these theoretical categories, and came to a provocative conclusion: the theoretical apparatus under consideration is sterile, as the three categories of constant, increasing and decreasing costs are 'empty economic boxes' (this was also the title of his article), impossible to fill with concrete examples of real industries.

Clapham's article provoked immediate response, with an article in the following issue of the *Economic Journal* by Arthur Cecil Pigou, champion of a line of Marshallian orthodoxy that leads to the 'geometrical method' of demand and supply curves for the firm and the industry, for the short

---

[11] Some documentation on these activities can now be found in a posthumously published volume of letters from Sraffa to Tatiana (Sraffa 1991). Cf. also De Vivo (2017).

and the long period. This construct does not fully correspond to Marshall's view of the world; in fact, walking a tightrope through manifold ambiguities and corrections of direction, in subsequent editions of his *Principles* Marshall attempted to reconcile an evolutionary, and thus intrinsically dynamic, conception with an analytical apparatus based on the requirement of equilibrium between supply and demand, and thus necessarily static. Greater fidelity to Marshall's ideas was shown by Dennis Robertson (1890–1963), who raised further doubts about Pigou's analytical apparatus in a contribution to the debate (Robertson 1924).

In the following years the debate went on in the *Economic Journal*, with contributions by, among others, Allyn Young, Arthur Cecil Pigou, Lionel Robbins, Gerald Shove, Joseph Schumpeter and Roy Harrod.[12]

With his 1925 article, Sraffa joined in the debate Clapham had begun by arguing that the problem of the 'empty boxes' is not a matter of how to apply the categories of constant, increasing and decreasing returns to real situations, but rather the existence of insurmountable theoretical difficulties within the theory of firm and industry equilibrium. Underlying all this, Sraffa pointed out, there is a conceptual confusion: in classical political economy the 'law' of decreasing returns is associated with the problem of rent (specifically, with the theory of distribution), while the 'law' of increasing returns is associated with the division of labour, or in other words general economic progress (i.e. with the theory of production). Marshall and other neoclassical economists tried to put these two 'laws' on the same plane, co-ordinating them in a single 'law of non-proportional returns'. However, this means transposing increasing and decreasing returns to an ambit different from the original ones, which makes it difficult to apply the justifications originally used to account for the variations in costs following from the variations in the quantities produced in the new ambit. Sraffa illustrated these difficulties analysing the literature on the subject.

In particular, Sraffa stressed that decreasing returns are connected to changes in the proportions of factors of production, while increasing returns stem from expanding production and increasing division of labour.

---

[12] Allyn Young (1876–1929) was the author, in 1928, of an important contribution on 'Increasing returns and economic progress', but his influence on the development of economic thought is often indirect; for instance, the celebrated books by Knight (1921) and Chamberlin (1933) originated as doctorate dissertations under his supervision. Gerald Shove (1887–1947), one of Marshall's pupils, published few pages but was nevertheless an influential member of the 'Cambridge school'. On Robbins, Pigou, Schumpeter and Harrod cf. respectively §§4.2, 7.2, 3.5 and 7.5.

The former case – decreasing returns – occurs when a factor of production is scarce. Now, unless we identify the industry with all the firms using a scarce factor, variations in average cost associated with increased production in the industry under consideration will be of the same order of magnitude as variations in costs – hence in prices – simultaneously experienced by other industries using the same factor of production. The *ceteris paribus* assumption that underlies partial equilibrium analysis is thus violated. For instance, if an increased production of apples induces an increase in land rents (which in itself is dubious, as cultivation of apples is but one of the many uses of agricultural land), rents on land where pears are cultivated should rise too, and the price of pears should rise as well; the increase in the price of apples leads to a decrease in their demand, but at the same time, as apples and pears are substitutable goods, the increase in the price of pears leads to an increase in the demand for apples: the net effect may be positive or negative, i.e. the demand for apples may either rise or fall.

As for increasing returns, they cannot concern individual firms: if as they grow they become more efficient, firms would go on expanding until they reach a size incompatible with the assumption of competition. Nor can increasing returns be found in various industries at the same time; otherwise the *ceteris paribus* clause would be breached once again. Marshall, well aware of this, developed the category of economies of production external to the individual firm but internal to the industry; generalizing such a category might have ensured consistency between increasing returns, the assumption of competition and the partial equilibrium method. However, Sraffa considered such a generalization to be wholly unrealistic, adopted not to adhere to observed reality but to solve an otherwise insoluble theoretical difficulty. In conclusion, the theoretical construction of the Marshallian tradition cannot comply with the requirement of logical consistency except by recourse to unrealistic ad hoc assumptions, which obviously constitute inadequate foundations for a theory designed for general interpretative application.

5.4 Imperfect Competition and the Critique of the Representative Firm

Sraffa's 1925 Italian paper attracted the interest of Edgeworth, co-editor – together with Keynes – of the *Economic Journal*. On the suggestion of the former of the two co-editors, the latter asked Sraffa for an article for their review, and the young Italian economist was ready and happy to accept their offer.

The English paper (Sraffa 1926) is much shorter than the Italian one, and correspondingly much poorer in collateral elements of notable importance; the first half of the article consists in a summary of the main points in the Italian article, while the second half develops an original line of research. The idea is that, as a consequence of the imperfections present in all markets in the real world, within every industry each firm is confronted with a specific, negatively sloped demand curve, even when many firms are simultaneously present in the industry. There is thus a crucial difference with respect to the traditional theory of competition, according to which each firm should face a horizontal demand curve. The theory propounded by Sraffa is thus a theory of imperfect competition, and has the advantage of being compatible also with the cases of constant or increasing returns, while among other things it takes over various real-world elements suggested here and there in Marshall's work. However, Sraffa was already stressing the limits of this approach in the closing lines of his article. He remarked, in fact, 'that in the foregoing the disturbing influence exercised by the competition of new firms attracted to an industry the conditions of which permit of high monopolist profits has been neglected'. Basically, this means neglecting competition in the classical sense of the term, consisting in the shifting of capital from one sector to another in pursuit of the maximum returns.

In the following years the theory of imperfect competition constituted a flourishing field of research. Sraffa, however, though originating this line of research (subsequently developed along partially different lines by Chamberlin [1933] and Joan Robinson [1933], and influential still today), soon abandoned it. As we have seen, it is based on a notion of competition – the one on which the marginalist approach focuses attention, connected to the presence of many firms in the same industry – that is quite different from the notion developed by the classical economists, concerning the free movement of capital among the various sectors of the economy. It is in fact the conclusion to Sraffa's 1926 paper that paves the way for the modern non-neoclassical theory of non-competitive market forms, and in particular Paolo Sylos Labini's 1956 theory of oligopoly, based on the presence of obstacles to the entry of new firms into the economic sector under consideration. The classical notion of competition, furthermore, constitutes the basis for the line of research that Sraffa was already developing in a first draft (discussed with Keynes in 1928) of his 1960 book *Production of commodities by means of commodities*.

Sraffa's radical departure from the traditional framework of the theory of the firm and the industry was then evidenced in his contributions to the symposium on 'Increasing returns and the representative firm' published in the *Economic Journal* in March 1930. Here Sraffa's criticism is levelled against a version of the Marshallian theory more faithful to Marshall's own original framework than Pigou's, namely the evolutionary version Robertson presents in his contribution to the symposium (Robertson 1930), based on the concept of the firm's 'life cycle' which Marshall employs in an attempt to make increasing returns compatible with the firm's competitive equilibrium. Like a biological organism, the firm goes through successive stages of development, maturity and decline; the 'representative' firm is half-way through the process of development and thus at a stage of increasing returns to scale. As Marshall himself points out, a concept of this type, that sees the expansion of firms depending on the 'life cycle' of entrepreneurial capacities, may be plausible in the case of directly family-run concerns, but cannot apply to modern joint stock companies.

Thus biological analogies prove a false exit to the blind alley Marshallian analysis gets into, hemmed in by the contradiction between increasing returns and competitive equilibrium. Sraffa has an easy task in pointing out the *deus ex machina* nature of the biological metaphors that Robertson uses in Marshall's wake, which cannot fill in the gaps in logical consistency intrinsic to these analytic structures: 'At the critical points of his argument the firms and the industry drop out of the scene, and their place is taken by the trees and the forest, the bones and the skeleton, the water-drops and the wave – indeed all the kingdoms of nature are drawn upon to contribute to the wealth of his metaphors' (Sraffa 1930, p. 91). The conclusion to these brief contributions is a clear-cut break with the then mainstream views: 'Marshall's theory ... cannot be interpreted in a way which makes it logically self-consistent and, at the same time, reconciles it with the facts it sets out to explain'; thus, 'I think ... that [it] should be discarded' (Sraffa 1930, p. 93).

5.5 Cambridge: Wittgenstein and Keynes

The 1926 paper published in the *Economic Journal* had considerable impact, especially in Cambridge. Keynes was thus able to offer Sraffa a job as lecturer at the university. Sraffa decided to move to England, where he lived from 1927 until his death on 3 September 1983.

After a year spent settling down in Cambridge, for three years Sraffa lectured on the German and Italian financial systems and the theory of value. This latter course had a great impact: Sraffa discussed the theories of the classical economists – Ricardo in particular – and the general economic equilibrium theories of Walras and Pareto – little of which was known in the rather provincial England of the time – as well as advancing his own criticisms of the Cambridge (Marshall–Pigou) tradition, and in particular the theory of the firm.

In the quiet Cambridge environment, Sraffa developed his research along three lines connected in one great cultural design: work on the critical edition of Ricardo's writings, entrusted to him by the Royal Society at the initiative of Keynes in 1930; research in the field of the theory of value, which would lead after thirty years' labour to *Production of commodities by means of commodities*; and a collateral interest in the development of Keynesian theory, particularly in the early 1930s. Moreover, in Cambridge Sraffa made the acquaintance of the Austrian philosopher Ludwig Wittgenstein (1889–1951), who became a friend of his and on whom Sraffa was to have a significant influence.

Sraffa met Wittgenstein in 1929. The Austrian philosopher had just arrived in Cambridge, called there by Bertrand Russell, who had organized publication of the *Tractatus logico-philosophicus* (1921) a few years before. When they were both in Cambridge, Wittgenstein and Sraffa generally spent one afternoon every week together, talking not so much about economics and philosophy directly but ranging over a great variety of topics, from gardening to detective stories. These conversations had a crucial influence on the Austrian philosopher, and on the transition from the logical atomism of the *Tractatus* to the mature positions set out in the *Philosophical investigations*, published posthumously in 1953.[13]

Between Wittgenstein's initial and final positions there is a clear change, long thought out. With drastic simplification, let us focus attention on some aspects that are of more direct interest to us. The *Tractatus* argues that there is a correspondence between the world and the elements that constitute it (the 'facts') on the one hand, and our representation of the world (whose constituent elements are the 'thoughts', expressed in 'propositions') on the other. On this basis Wittgenstein argues that it is possible to build a logical, axiomatic set of propositions, each describing a 'fact' while together they describe the world, or rather, if not all the world, all that can be described in a rational form. On that for which no rational description can be provided (sentiments, religious beliefs, aesthetic judgements, etc.), says Wittgenstein, 'one must be silent'.

However, in the *Philosophical investigations* Wittgenstein abandons the idea of language as 'mirroring' the world, and the idea of the 'unspeakable'. Discussions with Sraffa seem to play a role in this. There is an

---

[13] Sen (2003, in particular p. 1242) suggests that Gramsci's ideas on the importance of social conventions in language may have influenced Wittgenstein through Sraffa, leading the Austrian philosopher towards what he calls an 'anthropological way' to address the philosophical issues he tackles.

anecdote that Wittgenstein himself told his pupils. One day, as they were travelling together on the train between Cambridge and London, 'Sraffa made a gesture, familiar to Neapolitans and meaning something like disgust or contempt, of brushing the underneath of his chin with an outward sweep of the finger tips of one hand'. The gesture can acquire a specific meaning only from the context in which it is performed; thus it contradicts Wittgenstein's idea that every proposition has to have a precise place in the axiomatic order of rational language, independently of the context in which it may be employed.[14]

Following this critique, in the *Philosophical investigations* Wittgenstein developed a new theory of language, and of the relations between it and the world it should describe. There is not just one type of language, Wittgenstein (1953, p. 21) asserts, 'but there are *countless* kinds: countless different types of use of what we call "symbols", "words", "sentences". And this multiplicity is not something fixed, given once for all; but new types of language, new language-games, as we may say, come into existence, and others become obsolete and get forgotten.' In general, Wittgenstein goes on, 'the meaning of a word is its use in the language' (p. 33). However, words do not correspond to simple elements of reality, and these simple elements cannot be defined; nor is it possible to produce a general theory of language.

Wittgenstein demonstrates these theses with a series of examples of 'language games' – namely, theoretical models that focus attention on particular aspects of the real language, presenting them as the general language of a group of people. From these examples we may conclude that 'there is not . . . any unique analysis of propositions into their intrinsically unanalysable elements. What sort of analysis will be useful and provide a real clarification depends on the circumstances, on just what is problematic about the propositions under consideration' (Quinton 1968, pp. 12–13).

We have no textual evidence to maintain that Sraffa agreed with the point of arrival of Wittgenstein's reflections. We only know that the Austrian philosopher's initial position drew criticisms from the Italian economist, and that these criticisms played a crucial role in Wittgenstein's subsequent thinking. Perhaps we may perceive Sraffa's political interests

---

[14] According to Malcolm (1958, p. 69), who relates the anecdote, the object of the discussion is Wittgenstein's idea 'that a proposition and that which it describes must have the same "logical form", the same "logical multiplicity"'; according to von Wright, as Malcolm reports in a footnote, the object of the discussion is the idea that each proposition should have a 'grammar'. In a conversation with the present author (21 December 1972), Sraffa confirmed the anecdote, telling me that von Wright was right.

behind his opposition to an a priori theory of language and his preference for a theory open to recognizing the role of social factors (the environment in which the 'linguistic game' takes place). We may also perceive here a methodological choice: rejection of all-embracing theories that pretend to describe any and all aspects of the world, starting from its elementary constituting elements; instead, the choice of flexibility in theoretical constructions, aiming in each case at the specific problem under consideration.

After Gramsci and Wittgenstein, a third protagonist of twentieth-century culture to have fecund exchange with Sraffa was John Maynard Keynes, who was fifteen years older. Four episodes are worth recalling in this respect; we have already taken a glance at some of them: the likely influence on Keynes of the distinction between stabilization of money in relation to the level of domestic prices and in relation to the exchange rate proposed by Sraffa in his graduate thesis; his participation in the 'Cambridge Circus' and more generally in the debates that stimulated Keynes's transition from the *Treatise on money* to the *General theory*; and his critical intervention (Sraffa 1932) on Hayek's theory, from which Keynes derived the theory of own interest rates that is at the centre of the analysis in chapter 17 of the *General theory*.

The fourth episode is recalled by Sraffa himself in his Preface to *Production of commodities by means of commodities*. Sraffa (1960, p. vi) recalls that 'when in 1928 Lord Keynes read a draft of the opening propositions of this paper, he recommended that, if constant returns were *not* to be assumed, an emphatic warning to that effect should be given'. Keynes is the only economist to be thanked in the Preface. (Sraffa's thanks also went to three mathematicians – Frank Ramsey, Alister Watson and Abram Besicovitch – and, in the Italian edition, to Raffaele Mattioli, a banker who long played a leading role in the Banca Commerciale Italiana as well as being a very close friend of Sraffa's and *magna pars* in the preparation of the Italian edition of the book.) The point Keynes intervenes on is of fundamental importance, as the absence of an assumption on returns constitutes a crucially distinctive feature of Sraffa's book, implying among other things abandonment of the marginalist notion of equilibrium as equality between supply and demand.

5.6   The Critical Edition of Ricardo's Writings

The difficulties economists like Robertson (in the 1930 symposium) and Hayek (in the 1932 controversy) had in understanding just what Sraffa was aiming at, and more generally speaking the widespread idea of Sraffa as a critical but not reconstructive spirit, reveal the extent to which the marginalist approach encroached on the classical tradition in the first half of the twentieth century. Hence the need for rediscovery of the classical approach, which Sraffa pursued with his critical edition of Ricardo's works: Sraffa's long-celebrated philological rigour is not an end in itself, but the tool for a critical enquiry into the very foundations of political economy.

Sraffa began work on Ricardo's writings in 1930, and went on with it for over a quarter of a century, alongside his theoretical work that was to lead to *Production of commodities by means of commodities*. Finally, between 1951 and 1955 the ten volumes of the *Works and correspondence of David Ricardo* appeared, followed in 1973 by a volume of indexes.

Sraffa's philological rigour played a decisive role in the rediscovery of the classical economists' framework, after a century of oblivion and misleading interpretations. Let us recall that when Sraffa began his work the most commonly accepted interpretations were those of Marshall (1890, appendix i), according to whom Ricardo is a somewhat imprecise and unilateral precursor of modern theory (since he takes account of the cost of production, i.e. supply, but not of demand, in the determination of prices), and of Jevons (in the Preface to the second edition of the *Theory of political economy*), who considers Ricardo responsible for perniciously diverting economics from the path of true science.[15] From either interpretation, no reason emerges to waste time on Ricardo's works. At most, one might recall his theory of rent as forerunner of the principle of decreasing marginal productivity, or his theory of money, or his theory of international trade based on the principle of comparative costs.

Sraffa's critical edition of Ricardo's *Works and correspondence* is unanimously recognized as a model of philological rigour. It was above all for this that Sraffa was awarded the gold medal of the Swedish Academy of Sciences in 1961: an honour that, among the economists, was also conferred upon Keynes and Myrdal, and which may be considered as anticipating the Nobel Prize in economics, awarded only beginning in 1969. The writings published in this edition, together with the apparatus of notes and, above all, Sraffa's introduction to the first volume restored

---

[15] In a subtler way, Jacob Hollander (1904, 1910) speaks of a gradual retreat on the part of Ricardo from the labour theory of value towards a theory of prices based on costs of production, hence in a direction open to the marginalist developments connected to the principle of decreasing marginal productivity, in turn considered as a development of the 'Ricardian' theory of differential rent. In his Introduction to Ricardo's *Principles*, Sraffa (1951) provides a destructive criticism of both this interpretation and that given by Marshall.

Ricardo – and through him the whole classical approach to political economy – to a central position in economic theory.

Sraffa stresses in particular the importance of the notion of the surplus, and of the conception of the economic system as a circular flow of production and consumption. The size of the surplus (the Smithian problem of the wealth of nations), its distribution among the various social classes (the problem on which Ricardo focused attention in his *Principles*) and its utilization in unproductive consumption or accumulation constitute the issues upon which the classical economists focus their analyses. Division of labour, surplus and the circular flow of production and consumption are thus the elements that characterize classical political economy: 'in striking contrast – as Sraffa 1960, p. 93, points out – with the view presented by modern theory, of a one-way avenue that leads from "Factors of production" to "Consumption goods"'.

5.7   Production of Commodities by Means of Commodities

The analytic representation Ricardo offers has a weak point in the assumption (the limits of which he himself recognizes) that relative prices are proportional to the quantity of labour directly or indirectly required for the production of the various commodities. In *Production of commodities by means of commodities* Sraffa comes up with a solution to the problem framed in terms of the classical conception.

There is therefore a close link between the critical edition of Ricardo's writings and the theoretical research Sraffa himself was engaged in. In the 1930s and 1940s work proceeded on the two fronts in parallel; in the latter half of the 1950s, once the work on Ricardo was completed (apart from the indexes), Sraffa concentrated on preparing for publication his more strictly analytic contribution, published almost simultaneously in English and Italian in 1960.

In analogy with the line of enquiry followed, according to his own interpretation, by the classical economists, Sraffa put at the centre of his analysis an economic system based on the division of labour. In this system, the product of each sector does not correspond to its requirements for means of production (inclusive of the means of subsistence for the workers employed in the sector). Each sector taken in isolation is not able to continue its activity, but needs to be in contact with other sectors in the economy to obtain from them its own means of production, in exchange for part at least of its product. We thus have the network of exchanges that characterizes the economies based on the inter-industry division of labour. As Sraffa shows, the problem of quantitative determination of the exchange ratios that become established among the various sectors is to be tackled, in a capitalistic economy, simultaneously with the problem of income distribution between the social classes of workers, capitalists and landlords. The intersection between these two problems constitutes what in the classical tradition is called the problem of value.

In this respect it is worth considering the specific meaning that the concept of value implicitly assumes within Sraffian analysis. Value does not stand for the measure of the importance that a certain good has for man (as is the case, for instance, within marginalist theory, where value is connected to utility); nor does it take on ethical elements as in the notion of the just price; nor indeed a quality of optimality, as the result of the maximization of some target function under constraints. The value of the commodities reflects the relationship that interconnects sectors and social classes within the economy. Moreover, Sraffa's analysis suggests an implicit reference to a specific mode of production, capitalism. In fact, it is based on assumptions (the 'law of the one price'; division into the social classes of workers, capitalists and landowners; a uniform rate of profits) that reflect its fundamental characteristics. In particular, the last of these assumptions – the equality of the rate of profits in all sectors of the economy – expresses in the simplest possible analytic terms a central aspect of capitalism: connection among the different parts into which the economic system falls (a necessary connection, as as we saw no sector can subsist in isolation from the others) is ensured by the market not only for exchange of products, but also for the partition of profit flows among the different sectors. In other words, the internal unity of a capitalistic system is guaranteed both by the productive interdependence connecting the different sectors and by the free flow of capital from one sector to another in pursuit of the most profitable use.

In the Preface to *Production of commodities by means of commodities* Sraffa stresses that his analysis of the relations connecting prices and distributive variables does not require the assumption of constant returns to scale. This, as we shall better see in the text that follows, is crucial for an understanding of the meaning that Sraffa attributes to the relations he analyses, in particular to the notion of prices of production.[16] However, in the Preface Sraffa also stressed that, 'as a temporary working hypothesis', 'anyone accustomed to think in terms of the equilibrium of demand and supply may be inclined ... to suppose that the argument rests on a tacit

---

[16] It also agrees with the criticisms Sraffa levels in his 1925 and 1926 articles at the Marshallian attempts to utilize 'laws of returns to scale', namely functional relations connecting cost and quantity produced, in the determination of equilibrium prices and quantities.

assumption of constant returns in all industries' (Sraffa 1960, p. v). Thanks to the assumption of constant returns, in fact, Sraffa's analysis of the relationship between relative prices and income distribution may be seen as part of a marginalist model of general economic equilibrium, in which the initial endowments of productive factors are given in such a way as to be compatible with the final demand of economic subjects. It is precisely in this way, thanks to the possibility of translating it into a particular case of marginalist analysis, that Sraffa's analysis may serve as the foundation for an internal criticism of logical inconsistency of the traditional marginalist theories of value and distribution. As a matter of fact, however, in Sraffa's book nothing is said of the relationship between demand and supply for each commodity: the assumption that equilibrium prices correspond to the equality between supply and demand, which characterizes marginalist economic theory, is absent from Sraffa's exposition.[17]

Let us now see the line of enquiry followed in *Production of commodities by means of commodities*.

When commodities are at one and the same time products and means of production, the price of one commodity cannot be determined independently of the others, nor the complex of relative prices independently of the distribution of income between profits and wages. One must therefore consider the system as a whole, with all the interrelations running between the various productive sectors, simultaneously tackling income distribution and determination of relative prices.

To begin with, Sraffa (1960, p. 3) shows that in a system of production for mere subsistence, 'which produces just enough to maintain itself', and where 'commodities are produced by separate industries and are exchanged for one another at the market held after the harvest' (i.e. at the end of the production period), 'there is a unique set of exchange values which if adopted by the market restores the original distribution of the products and makes it possible for the process to be repeated; such values spring directly from the methods of production'.

If the economic system under consideration is able to produce a surplus, also 'the distribution of the surplus must be determined through the same mechanism and at the same time as are the prices of commodities' (Sraffa 1960, p. 6). If the wage can exceed subsistence level, relative prices and one or other of the two distributive variables – wage or rate of profits – are jointly determined, once the technology and

---

[17] On this point, and more generally on the interpretation of Sraffa's works and the debate it originated, cf. Roncaglia (2009b).

the other distributive variable are known; the higher the wage is, the lower will be the rate of profits.[18]

Sraffa (1960, pp. 12–13) then goes on to analyse 'the key to the movement of relative prices consequent upon a change in the wage'. As the classical economists and Marx already knew, it 'lies in the inequality of the proportions in which labour and means of production are employed in the various industries'. Indeed, 'if the proportion were the same in all industries no price-changes could ensue', while 'it is impossible for prices to remain unchanged when there is inequality of "proportions"'.

Sraffa (1960, pp. 18–33) also constructed a particular analytical tool, the 'Standard commodity', thanks to which he is able to solve the Ricardian problem of an invariable measure of value, after having aptly redefined it. Ricardo attributes two meanings to the notion of a standard measure of value, which must not be confused: that of having invariable value (in relation to the complex of the means of production necessary to obtain it) when changes occur in the distribution of income between wages and profits, the technology remaining unaltered; and that of having invariable value in relation to the changes the technology goes through in the course of time (cultivation of ever less fertile lands on the one hand, and technological progress on the other).

Having made the distinction between the two problems clear in his Introduction to Ricardo's *Writings* (Sraffa 1951, pp. xl–xlvii), in *Production of commodities by means of commodities* Sraffa goes on to show how the former can be solved only in terms of the 'Standard commodity'. This is a composite commodity (i.e. a set of commodities taken in particular proportions) so determined that the aggregate of its means of production has the same composition as it has. In other words, in the Standard system – the abstract economic system the product of which consists in a certain quantity of Standard commodity – also the aggregate means of production correspond to a certain quantity of Standard commodity. Thus, with the standard system (and under the assumption that wages are included in the costs of production) it is possible to determine the rate of profits, just as in the 'corn model' that Sraffa attributes to Ricardo, as a ratio between two physically homogeneous quantities: the surplus, i.e. the quantity of Standard commodity given by the difference between product and means of production, and the means of production advanced by the capitalists.

Coming to the second problem – namely invariance in the face of changes in technology – measurement in terms of labour embodied

---

[18] The system of equations corresponding to this case is given in the Appendix.

clearly retains significance as a broad indicator of the difficulty of production.

With the distinction he draws between the two problems Sraffa offers a precise indication of the limits circumscribing any analytical solution to the question of the standard measure of value, and by so doing he implicitly points out the impossibility of establishing a scientific basis for any metaphysical notion of labour as absolute value: that is, as a substance embodied in the commodities which characterizes univocally the difficulty of production. Proceeding along this road, Sraffa perhaps might have hoped to stimulate a reinterpretation of Marx by freeing him from the residual Hegelian elements.

The analysis of prices of production is completed with the case of joint products and, within this category, fixed capital goods and scarce or non-reproducible means of production such as land. The book closes with a chapter on the choice between economically alternative methods of production in relation to variations in the rate of profits, and with four appendices including the 'References to the literature', where Sraffa explicitly associates his analysis with that of the classical economists.

5.8   Critique of the Marginalist Approach

While advancing a theory of production prices within the framework of the classical conception of the functioning of an economic system, Sraffa's book also offers the tools for a radical critique of the foundations of the marginalist theory of value and distribution. In this respect we can concentrate on two chapters: one on the average period of production and the final chapter on the choice of techniques.

Preliminarily, however, there is a serious misunderstanding we need to clear away from the path: namely, the interpretation of Sraffa's contribution as a general equilibrium analysis conducted under the assumption of constant returns to scale, in which it would have been possible to explain prices by focusing attention on production costs – the supply side – and dropping the demand side, and thus the subjective element of consumers' preferences.

Sraffa rejects explicitly and repeatedly – three times, in the Preface to his book – the idea that his analysis would require the assumption of constant returns. 'No question arises as to the variation or constancy of returns. The investigation is concerned exclusively with such properties of an economic system as do not depend on changes in the scale of production or in the proportions of "factors"' (Sraffa 1960, p. v). Sraffa then goes on immediately to stress that 'This standpoint, which is that of the old classical economists ..., has been submerged and forgotten since the advent of the "marginal" method.'

Between the classical and the marginalist approaches there are basic differences (summed up by Sraffa 1960, p. 93, by contrasting the 'circular flow' of the former with the 'one-way avenue' of the latter as an illustration of the functioning of the economy). We can, however, with an apparent but not substantive ambiguity, admit that the analytical results reached with regard to prices of production may be transposed into the conceptual picture of the marginalist approach, so as to serve as the foundation for an internal criticism of logical inconsistency of the marginalist theory of value and distribution. Thus Sraffa recognizes, as recalled earlier, that for readers brought up within the marginalist tradition the assumption of constant returns to scale may be helpful. With respect to these readers, indeed, the most important aspects of Sraffa's analysis are those concerning critique of the traditional marginalist approach, and with this assumption in mind we can read Sraffa's results as criticisms of logical inconsistency internal to the marginalist analytical structure.

The results in Sraffa's book that can be directly used as the foundation for a criticism of the marginalist theories of value and distribution concern the average period of production and the choice of techniques. The concept of the average period of production was propounded by a leading representative of the Austrian school, Böhm-Bawerk (1889), as a measure of the capital intensity of production, interpreting capital as 'waiting time', between the moment labour is employed (directly or indirectly) in production and the moment the product is obtained. Sraffa shows that, depending as it does on the rate of profits (see the Appendix that follows), the average period of production cannot be used to measure the quantity of the factor of production capital in the ambit of an explanation of the rate of profits taken as the price of this factor (cf. also Garegnani 1960).

With regard to the problem of the choice between alternative techniques of production when the rate of profits changes, Sraffa (1960, pp. 81–7) points out the possibility of a 'reswitching of techniques'; in other words, a given technique that proves the most advantageous for a given rate of profits may be superseded by another technique when we raise the rate of profits, but may once again be preferable when the rate of profits rises still higher. This implies that, however the capital intensity of the two techniques (or in other words the ratio between the quantities utilized of the two 'factors of production', capital and labour) is measured, the general rule that the marginalist theory of value rests on remains contradicted. Such a rule takes the distributive variables, wage rate and rate of profits, as prices of the corresponding factors of production determined by the 'law' of demand and supply, so that the quantity of capital employed in production should diminish (and the quantity of labour increase) as the rate of profits rises (and the wage consequently falls). With the 'reswitching of techniques', if this happens when one technique gives way to another with a rising rate of profits, the contrary occurs when the economy from the second technology turns back to the first as the rate of profits rises yet higher.

Sraffa's critique undermines the very foundations of the idea – crucial to marginalist macroeconomic theory – that a competitive labour market in a closed economy would automatically tend towards full employment equilibrium since the decline in real wages which should result from unemployment would prompt an increase in the labour/capital ratio and hence, given the endowment of capital, an increase in the quantity of labour employed.

Taking an overall view of Sraffa's work, we can see it as the sum of three parts: reconstruction of the real nature of the classical approach with his edition of Ricardo's works; critique of marginalist theory, whether in the Marshallian version or in Hayek's macroeconomic version, or as based on a theory of capital as a factor of production; and, finally, an analysis of value and distribution that is both analytically consistent and rooted in the classical conception of the functioning of the economic system. As far as this latter element is concerned, we may add (a point on which we shall return later, in §12.9) that various elements lead us to think that this re-proposal of the classical theory should be developed so as to take the Keynesian contribution into account.

Appendix

Let us consider Sraffa's price equations:

$$(A_a\, p_a + B_a\, p_b + \ldots + N_a\, p_n)\, (1 + r) + L_a\, w = A\, p_a$$
$$(A_b\, p_a + B_b\, p_b + \ldots + N_b\, p_n)\, (1 + r) + L_b\, w = B\, p_b$$
$$\ldots\ldots\ldots\ldots$$
$$\ldots\ldots\ldots\ldots$$
$$(A_n\, p_a + B_n\, p_b + \ldots + N_n\, p_n)\, (1 + r)\, + L_n\, w = N\, p_n$$

where A_a, B_a, $\ldots$, N_a, L_a represent the quantities of the commodities a, b, $\ldots$, n and of labour required for producing a quantity A of the commodity a; $\ldots$; A_n, B_n, $\ldots$, N_n, L_n are the quantities of the commodities a, b, $\ldots$, n and of labour required for producing a quantity N of the commodity n; r is the rate of profits, w the wage rate; $p_a, p_b, \ldots, p_n$ are the prices of the commodities. The equations are n, as many as the commodities, and allow us to determine $n - 1$ relative prices and one of the two distributive variables, wage rate or rate of profits, given the other.[19]

The technique of production is given; within the classical approach, it is the result of historical evolution and not of an a-temporal choice between alternative techniques. Production levels are given, so that – as Sraffa points out explicitly – the problem of whether there are constant, increasing or decreasing returns to scale does not arise. Thus, the equations cannot be interpreted as half of a general economic equilibrium system.

The system of equations reproduced above is utilized by Sraffa in various directions. As not all the quantities of the means of production have to be strictly positive, it is possible to distinguish between basic commodities, directly or indirectly necessary for the production of all commodities in the system, and non-basic commodities, either not utilized in production at all (but appearing only as products) or utilized only in their own production and/or in the production of other non-basics. Moreover, the system of equations that concerns the case in which each sector produces a single commodity can be extended to the case of joint production. In this way it is also possible to consider the case of fixed capital goods, which, once utilized in the productive process, may emerge from it as joint products, thus permitting rigorous determination of amortization (always under the assumption of a given and unchanging technology: in the real world, the main problem in determining amortization concerns technical obsolescence resulting from technical progress).

As for the critique of the marginalist theory of value and distribution, the system of equations is utilized, as recalled earlier, to demonstrate the impossibility of utilizing notions of capital that imply measuring it in value or indirect measures such as the average period of production in order to define well-behaved demand curves for capital, namely monotonically increasing when the wage rate increases, thus in such a way as to guarantee convergence towards full employment equilibrium.

Let us consider the average period of production. We should bear in mind that the series of the dated quantities of labour relative to the production of a given commodity, for instance commodity a, is obtained by reducing the means of production directly or indirectly employed in the production of the commodity a to the quantities of labour and means

---

[19] The Hawkins–Simon (1949) conditions, necessary for a solution for this system of equations to have non-negative values, correspond to the assumption that the system be able to produce a surplus, that is, that the quantities of the various commodities used up as means of production are (equal or) inferior to the quantities produced.

of production required for producing them, and subsequently proceeding in the same way with their means of production and so on, going back in time (which is a logical time, not historical: the technology does not change). We thus have

$$L_{a0} \; w + L_{a1} \; w(1 + r) + \ldots + L_{aj} \; w(1 + r)^j + \ldots = A \, p_a$$

where L_{aj} indicates the quantity of labour required j periods before the conclusion of the productive process for commodity a (and similar equations for commodities $b, \ldots, n$). The series is of infinite length if in the system there is at least one basic commodity. Sraffa (1960, pp. 37–8) demonstrates that as soon as two commodities differ for at least three terms in the series, when the rate of profits increases, the relative price of one of the two commodities in terms of the other may vary in an irregular way, increasing at first and then decreasing, then increasing once again. These oscillations show 'the impossibility of aggregating the "periods" belonging to the several quantities of labour into a single magnitude which could be regarded as representing the quantity of capital' (p. 38) within the framework of the marginalist theory of distribution.

As we can see, Sraffa's critiques (referring to the average period of production and, as we have just seen, concerning the reswitching of techniques) concern not only the aggregate production function, but more generally the notion of capital as a 'factor of production'.

Part III

The Disgregation of the Mainstream

6 The New Microeconomics: General Equilibrium and Expected Utilities, Theory of Industrial Organization

6.1 From One Shore of the Atlantic to the Other

The field assigned to this chapter is enormous. Rather than providing a broad and incomplete synthesis of the field, only the main areas of research will be discussed in order to highlight some key, basic elements.

Following the end of the Second World War, the centre of economic culture shifted from Europe, where both winners and losers were widely exhausted by the war effort, to the United States. Many Europeans sought an escape from poverty and racial and political persecutions during the war in the United States. The wealth of a winner of the war, who had not been hit by destruction within its own territory, constituted another important advantage; the Fulbright grant program, for instance, with its origins in this period, continues to finance studies in US universities for many young European economists or visiting professorships. Moreover, research activity was favoured (and somehow oriented) by funding provided by a wide web of foundations (such as the Cowles Foundation and the Rand Corporation) as well as by military programs begun in war-time and carried on during the Cold War.

Only recently has this latter aspect received the attention it deserves, being the object of in-depth research (Mirowski 2002, Van Horn et al. 2011; cf. §8.8). Together with a more pragmatic orientation towards a practical use of research results, the very immediate problems raised by the Cold War help explain some differences between the economic culture dominant in Europe and the economic culture that gradually spread from the United States, dominating on a global scale, though with a thousand variants and never in a complete way.

The most innovative research thus concerns decision analysis, which soon moves from parametric to strategic analysis: with the first, the individual, in making choices, takes prices as given, without any concern for the price-determining behaviour of others; with the second, the individual keeps the foreseeable reactions of others to their choices in mind.

The importance attributed to the notion of the economic agent's rationality thus allows us to delimit the field of possible choices, constituting both the basic pillar and the feeble point of the theoretical building. At the same time, we have a push to bring all aspects of human life within the compass of economic science, with what is called the imperialism of economics. The conceptual framework of the marginalist approach (rational *homo oeconomicus* tackling the issue of the optimal allocation of scarce resources) obtains a position of absolute dominance, putting an end to a long stage of coexistence and confrontation between different approaches.[1]

Because of the axiomatic way in which it is defined, the emerging, dominant notion of rationality allows to derive from consumers' order of preferences the usual ordinal utility functions, which from Pareto onwards dominate within the marginalist approach.[2] This is therefore the starting point in the next section for our attempt to reconstruct the path of recent microeconomic research, a more complex undertaking due to the exponential growth of research interest in this field, both in universities and in research centres. The trend towards a professionalization of economics, which had its roots in Marshall's times, affirms itself, imposing to economic research scientific criteria typical of the stages that Kuhn (1962) calls 'normal science': consistency with some basic axioms uncritically accepted, increasing closure towards whatever does not fall within this sphere. Hence, though in the presence of discordant voices, the growing importance of what is defined mainstream: a dominant approach bringing together the appeal to the marginalist tradition, the idolatry for mathematical models based on a monodimensional view of the economic agent, the predilection for liberalism in policy choices (though this latter preference is not shared by the exponents of the neoclassical synthesis, discussed in Chapter 7).

However, the mainstream is not a monolithic field: alongside the theory of expected utility (§6.2), we must distinguish between a research stream aiming at constructing an axiomatic general economic equilibrium model

---

[1] As Mirowski (2006, p. 348) stresses, 'there was no dominant orthodoxy in economics in America prior to World War II'. In the context of a situation characterized by a variety of approaches, the Great Depression scales down the institutionalist school in favour of a nascent macroeconomics of Keynesian derivation. Mirowski stresses the importance of the rising discipline of Operational Research, and the symbiosis between the rising neoclassical theory and the professionalization of the philosophy of science in the United States; out of this situation in the second post-war period emerges a neoclassical orthodoxy around three centres in competition: Chicago, the Cowles Foundation and MIT. We shall return to these themes later in this and in subsequent chapters.

[2] Quite different would have been, for instance, the implications of a reference to the good sense of the *pater familias*.

(discussed in §6.3), Samuelson's Marshallian–Walrasian synthesis (§6.4), the Marshallian microeconomics of the Chicago school and the trend to extend the method of constrained maximization to all aspects of human life (§6.5). Partly internal and partly external to the mainstream, new theories of the firm also emerged, in particular, the oligopoly theory by Bain and Sylos Labini (§6.6), the development of game theory and the related developments in the theory of industrial organization (§6.7). Finally (§6.8), in concluding, some developments: the principal–agent problem and that of asymmetric information will also be discussed.

6.2 The New Foundations: Expected Utility Theory

Here, two key points should be emphasized: generically, the adoption of the issue of individual decisions as the starting point of economic research; and more specifically, von Neumann's role. The first aspect can likely be connected to the military interest for a scientific formulation of decisions. The latter point pertains to the genius of the US mathematician of Hungarian origins and also to his varied activities as a consultant during and after the war (including his part in the Manhattan Project for the development of the atomic bomb and in ideating the first computers).

Born in Budapest, John von Neumann (1903–57) emigrated to the United States in the early 1930s. In 1933, he became the youngest member of the Institute for Advanced Study in Princeton, where his colleagues included Albert Einstein. He subsequently became the author of a well-known model of balanced growth (von Neumann 1937), and in 1940 began work with Oskar Morgenstern (1902–77)[3] to develop their *Theory of games and economic behaviour* (1944), which ultimately had a profound impact on the development of economic research in the United States.

This work has an axiomatic structure; together with the preferences of each individual for any possible event, the probabilities of the events are assumed as given. Given the axioms (the postulate of rationality and the absence of contradictions), the theory consists in a set of logically necessary relations.

Von Neumann and Morgenstern (1944, p. 17) consider utility to be a natural phenomenon, capable of objective measurement, drawing this assumption from pre-Paretian marginalist tradition: 'Even if utilities look very unnumerical today, the history of the experience of the theory of heat may repeat itself, as it happened, though in different forms and ways, for

---

[3] Morgenstern had migrated from Wien to Princeton for political reasons in 1938.

the theory of light, colours and radio waves.'[4] Moreover, von Neumann
and Morgenstern (1944, p. 18) assume that a unique measure of probability exists, defined for all events.

As for this second aspect, the frequentist theory of probability is preferred to the subjective one; in any case, they note, 'the two concepts
(probability and preference) can be axiomatized together' (von Neumann
and Morgenstern 1944, p. 19). What is thus considered is probabilistic
risk, not uncertainty.[5] The subjective approach to probability is subsequently introduced in a model of expected utilities à la von Neumann-
Morgenstern by Savage (1954).[6]

The main novel elements in von Neumann and Morgenstern compared
to the previous marginalist tradition relate to the game theory and most
notably, to the notion of expected utility, which constitutes an extension
of the problem of consumer choice among different uses of scarce
resources. With it, it is recognized that each act of choice may not have
a guaranteed unique outcome but rather a multiplicity of possible outcomes; the utility expected from an act of choice corresponds to the
average utility of the different outcomes, weighted with their respective
probabilities.

The axiomatic framing of the theory, in itself, does not make any
assumptions about the stability of utility functions and probabilities
over time; the assumption of stability, however, appears implicit in the

---

[4] Such a confidence re-emerges recently in neuroeconomics studies; however, the actual
results of these researches appear to lead in an opposite direction, for instance with the
separation between long- and short-run problems, hence among other things between the
demand for durables and non-durables, and other such 'anomalies' (cf. §10.3).
[5] As we saw, Knight (1921) opposes this notion of risk to that of uncertainty.
[6] de Finetti's (1930, 1931, 1937) and Ramsey's (1931) subjective probability theory
indicates the implications of a given set of probability evaluations effected by the
agent. Ramsey (but not de Finetti) assumes it to include all the possible states of the
world: 'We shall suppose that our subject has certain beliefs about everything'
(Ramsey 1931, p. 32). What is considered here is probabilistic risk; in other terms,
the theory indicates the implications of a given set of probability evaluations effected
by the agent. This – as Ramsey (1931, p. 28) stresses – leaves open the issue of 'how
far we shall act on those beliefs'. This latter is the problem that Keynes tries to
tackle with his notion of degree of confidence (cf. §3.6); according to Ramsey, who
draws on the methodological approach of the first Wittgenstein, the issue should be
abandoned and the analysis must focus on constructing a rigorous axiomatic model
of all that can be known in its entirety. As Wittgenstein (1921, p. 151) says, 'What
we cannot speak about we must pass over in silence.' On Sraffa's criticism of the
bipartition of the world – into what can be the object of logical representation in
a fully axiomatized system and what we cannot analyse scientifically – cf. §5.5.
Keynes (1921) propounds a more articulate position with his theory of groups
(cf. Roncaglia 2009a, p. 498) and by stressing the fact that there are substantial
differences among the degrees of confidence that can be obtained for probability
evaluations in different areas of the real world.

various hints to the use of the theory as an interpretation of the real world and as a guide to action.[7]

In order to analyse expected utilities, von Neumann and Morgenstern (1944, pp. 26 ff.) introduced a system of postulates that in substance correspond to completeness, continuity and transitivity (if I prefer A to B and B to C, I must also prefer A to C) both of preferences and of the probabilities attributed to various choices; furthermore, each preference relationship is considered independent from all other events (absence of external effects). Both utilities and probabilities are considered measurable (numerable).[8] The set of axioms ensures that probabilities and utilities (hence, expected utilities) mirror the properties of mathematical expectations. Hence, assuming that the agent has complete information, we can determine the choices (the solutions of the system) corresponding to a rational behaviour, namely a behaviour maximizing expected utility.[9]

Von Neumann's and Morgenstern's analysis concerns (in succession) zero-sum games between two persons, three persons, n persons, in which the gains of the one correspond to the losses of the other; the possibility of coalitions; non-zero-sum games, in which the sum of gains and losses is different from zero. In all of these cases, each agent has an initial endowment of commodities and may proceed to exchanges in order to improve their position; the solutions derived from the analysis thus correspond to market equilibriums (monopoly, duopoly, polipoly, competition) for the case of pure exchange.

---

[7] As we shall see in §6.5, the hypothesis of stability over time of individual preferences constitutes a central element for the Chicago school of Friedman and Stigler, while it is rejected by Hayek.

[8] The assumption of a regular (complete, transitive and continuous) ordering of preferences, that respects the independence axiom, by itself implies ordinal utility functions (defined less any increasing transformation); von Neumann and Morgenstern (1944) derive cardinal utility functions (namely defined less a linear increasing transformation) from a regular ordering of preferences thanks to the utilization of an arithmetic average of utilities weighted with probabilities of outcomes (I owe this remark to Aldo Montesano). The preference ordering may be obtained (p. 18, note) by asking the individual agents; such observations are considered to be reproducible (p. 24: this implies – though it is not said – that individual preference systems are stable over time).

[9] Within decision theory, developed first by von Neumann and Morgenstern, it is also necessary to assume that probabilities are independent of the consequently chosen action (the so-called postulate of probabilistic independence). This excludes the possibility of considering cases of self-fulfilling expectations, common in the field of financial markets but also present elsewhere (as Soros teaches us, deciding to speculate on a fall of the lira or the pound influences the probability evaluations of other financial operators, which renders the fall of these currencies more likely). Richard Jeffrey (1965) proposes a notion of *conditional expected utility* that avoids the need for this axiom; however, his proposal has been neglected in successive developments of economic theory as of inferential statistics. Cf. also Machina's analysis (1983) of the violations of the postulate and the proposal of a 'generalized expected utility'.

The approach of game theory, in which each agent aims to take into account the possible reactions of other agents in developing their strategy, is not a novelty: it has already been considered by various economists, among them Cournot and Bertrand in the nineteenth century and Hotelling in the twentieth century. It constitutes in any case an important change in perspective, representing a shift from the analysis of the isolated economic agent (Robinson Crusoe representing the archetype of the *homo oeconomicus* in Jevons's theory) to the analysis of the agent's choices vis-à-vis other agents, and from here to the analysis of general equilibrium in an economy where agents interact with each other. In the case of perfect competition, this does not involve differences relative to Walras's analysis and that of his successors; in such cases each agent is too small to influence the market with their choice, hence provoking the reactions of other agents. However, von Neumann and Morgenstern attribute great importance to the role of coalitions, namely to games in which the possibility of cooperation exists. They suggest that coalitions may assume non-insignificant dimensions, thereby provoking the reactions of other agents.

A controversial aspect of von Neumann's and Morgenstern's analysis, to which we shall return later, is the notion of rationality, which may be interpreted in a descriptive or in a normative sense.[10] The 'paradoxes' indicated by Allais, Ellsberg and various others, illustrated in §10.2, lead us to deny the descriptive validity of such a notion. Nonetheless, this notion raises perplexities and criticisms even in the normative interpretation (Chapter 14). This notwithstanding, expected utility theory constitutes the main reference for the pure theory of the economic agent's behaviour, from its formulation up to the present day.

Following von Neumann and Morgenstern (1944), an important contribution is provided by Savage with his *Foundations of statistics* (1954). Savage takes on the notion of expected utility and offers an axiomatic approach, by integrating it explicitly with the subjective probability approach proposed by de Finetti and Ramsey. The *Foundations* are since then considered as the basis of modern inferential statistics, but also imply an important shift in the conceptual foundations of expected utility theory, since, as hinted earlier, von Neumann and Morgenstern (1944, p. 19) adhere to the 'perfectly well founded interpretation of probability as frequency in long runs'.[11]

[10] On the notion of rationality, cf. Montesano (2005).
[11] In the second edition, 1953, when they are already aware of the line of analysis followed by Savage, the authors add a specific footnote: 'If one objects to the frequency interpretation of probability, then the two concepts (probability and preference) can be axiomatized together. This too leads to a satisfactory concept of utility.' Things,

Among the axioms adopted by Savage for his theory, wide debate concerns the so-called *sure-thing principle*. According to this axiom, the choice between two alternatives should not be influenced by those elements that have the same value in the two alternatives. As we shall see in §10.2), this axiom is contradicted by the so-called 'Allais paradox': an experiment of choice submitted by Allais to a number of colleagues, among them Savage himself, who provides (at least initially) an answer contradicting his axiom. Another aspect of Savage's theory is that the outcomes to which probabilities are attributed must be complete descriptions of the 'world' or 'totality of events' to which before him refers Ramsey, in order to avoid a theory 'vulnerable to counterexamples directed against the transitivity and additivity of values' (Gärdenfors and Sahlin 1988, p. 99); however, as Sraffa's criticisms to Wittgenstein and the abandonment of the initial position on the side of the latter show (cf. §5.5), this position is unsustainable.[12]

Compared to von Neumann's and Morgenstern's approach, which also emphasizes the choices of rational agents, the analysis of general economic equilibrium focuses on the issue of interdependent markets. Furthermore, starting with Nash's contributions (illustrated in the text that follows), subsequent analyses concerning strategic interaction between individuals focus on non-cooperative game theory.

6.3   The Traditional Foundations: Walrasian General Equilibrium

As hinted earlier, use of game theory implies a strategic view of the behaviour of the economic agent, who makes decisions in consideration of other agents' reactions. Thus, the research stream developed by von Neumann and Morgenstern introduces an important element of novelty in the stream of general economic equilibrium analyses, that in the

---

however, are different when one tries to provide an operational interpretation of the theory, as Samuelson does with his theory of revealed preferences briefly discussed below: while the frequentist interpretation allows us to consider the probabilities as objective data, independent from the preferences of the economic agent, in the case of revealed preferences a 'declaration of vote' (a series of choices actuated by an economic agent) may 'reveal' a preference ordering but does not allow at the same time to distinguish between utility and probability evaluations within each of the chosen alternatives. If then we accept the Keynesian approach to probability, that recognizes it to be difficult in many instances to attribute a numerical value to probabilities, the whole axiomatic castle of von Neumann–Morgenstern–Savage is deprived of its foundations.

[12] Obviously, these critiques could have been considered secondary if the Savage model were intended not as an attempt at interpreting the functioning of the economy but as a contribution to a simple (partial) operation of logical 'cleaning' of the personal opinions of each one of us.

Walrasian original formulation is limited to considering parametric behaviour: a choice justified by the assumption of perfect competition. In this case, each agent is too small compared to the overall dimensions of the market for their choices to have an impact on prices.

Within the marginalist tradition, the stream of general economic equilibrium originates, as recalled earlier, with Walras in Lausanne, with a book published in French. This stream drew attention in the Italian context, with Pareto, and later in Sweden with Cassel, but not in the Anglo-Saxon culture. Walras's book was translated into English, edited by Jaffé, only in 1954, but remains largely extraneous to university teaching, dominated by the Marshallian approach. In the United States, while John Bates Clark (1847–1938) and later, his son John Maurice Clark (1884–1963) at Columbia University, or Jacob Viner (1892–1970) at the University of Chicago, follow Marshall, and while in various other universities institutionalism prevails, only Irving Fisher (1867–1947) at Yale and a few others adopt the Walrasian approach. In any case, general economic equilibrium theory flourished in the United States, and thence (and from Maurice Allais's and Gerard Debreu's France) spread all over the world. The main influences were found elsewhere, however, particularly at the research centre the Cowles Foundation, which was very active in the 1940s and 1950s as a result of various grants for military research.[13]

The war years led to the blossoming of a new line of analysis, operational research and, in parallel, the development of Leontief's input–output analysis (discussed in §9.2). Interaction between operational research and economic analysis is essential, for instance in planning air strikes and determining where to bomb in order to produce the maximum possible damage, even indirectly, to the enemy. In the Cold War years, military interest for the developments of mathematical economics continued: conspicuous grants were introduced, accompanied by rules aiming to favour the interaction of researchers within the system but not with those who remained outside of it. The most abstract results of the related research were public, but were preceded by an underground diffusion that facilitated their acceptance and contributed to the development of a circle of elite insiders.[14]

The first research institution to constitute a pole of attraction for this kind of activity was the Cowles Foundation. From it originated important contributions to the development of new econometrics techniques.

---

[13] The Cowles Foundation (initially Cowles Commission for Research in Economics), founded by Alfred Cowles in 1932, operated in Chicago from 1939 to 1955, when it moved to Yale University and took on the new denomination.

[14] Cf. Mirowski (2002).

Linear methods of operational research were also developed. Research also developed to include the analysis of optimal solutions for problems with a multiplicity of agents and resources, leading to the analysis of general economic equilibrium. This research constitutes a search for solutions of real world issues, which drive the selection of simplifying assumptions.

On the other side of the Atlantic, in France, the mathematical school of Bourbaki[15] introduced a well-structured research on the axiomatization of mathematics. This approach stimulates Gerard Debreu's (1959) pure theory of general economic equilibrium.[16] The slim volume, a classic by this point, follows the principles of the Bourbaki group and utilizes set theory to analyse the properties of a model that is assumed to provide a stylized representation of a competitive market economy in an axiomatic form.

By competition, it is meant that each agent takes prices as given (namely agents are price takers) while there is no freedom of entry, as the number of firms is also taken as given. In this respect, the axiomatic theory of general economic equilibrium differs both from the classical tradition, which identifies competition with freedom of entry of new firms, and from Walras (whose approach considers price takers agents and freedom of entry) as well as from Pareto (whose approach recognizes freedom of entry, but does not assume price takers as agents).

Obviously, axiomatization differs in mathematics and economics. Indeed, the names designating the variables refer to an empirical reality, so one can ask questions about the correspondence between the axioms of the theory and the basic characteristics of the real world to which implicitly the names of the variables point. The rather widespread thesis, according to which what matters for the axiomatic theory of general economic equilibrium is only logical internal consistency, and not also its ability to represent in a schematic form the basic aspects of the real world, is unacceptable.

When the theorists on the two sides of the Atlantic did meet (also thanks to the Cowles Foundation), the line of analysis of general economic equilibrium emerged as the 'true' pure economic theory, compared to which the various Marshallian streams of research or aggregate growth theory appear as low profile simplifications. (Samuelson jokes on

---

[15] Nicholas Bourbaki is the pseudonym of a group of mathematicians active since 1935, with the objective to provide an axiomatic and systematic treatment of the different fields of mathematics.

[16] Gerard Debreu (1921–2004, Nobel Prize in 1983) was at the beginning of the 1950s a colleague of Arrow at the Cowles Commission in Chicago, then remained in the United States as professor, first at Yale and then at Berkeley.

the existence of a 'highbrow' economics, the one with a multiplicity of agents and commodities, and a 'lowbrow' economics, made up of aggregative models with a single commodity and a single representative agent, as in the growth model of his friend Solow [1956]; Frank Hahn replies, with a joke that may have cost him the Nobel Prize, that there are only highbrow and lowbrow economists.)

Kenneth Arrow's (1921–2017, Nobel Prize together with John Hicks in 1972) contributions to this line of research explain the name of Arrow–Debreu model for the axiomatic formulation of general economic equilibrium (see for instance Arrow and Debreu, 1954).[17] Great importance for its diffusion is to be attributed to the text by Arrow and Hahn (1971),[18] widely utilized as a reference in specialized research and in advanced microeconomics courses. A presentation of general economic equilibrium theory based on calculus is that proposed by MasColell (1985), also co-author of an advanced microeconomics manual (MasColell et al. 1995) illustrating consumer and producer theory as a premise for treating choice under conditions of uncertainty and asymmetric information, to arrive finally at the general economic equilibrium model; it soon becomes the new reference text for advanced microeconomic courses.

---

[17] Arrow's papers are collected in six volumes (Arrow 1983–5). For an illustration of his contributions to general economic equilibrium theory, cf. Duffie and Sonnenschein (1989). The demonstration of existence of (at least) an equilibrium for the model of general economic equilibrium, published by Arrow and Debreu in 1954, is presented to an Econometric Society meeting in 1952; on the same occasion an analogous demonstration was presented by Lionel McKenzie, also published in 1954. The demonstration requires convexity and continuity of preferences and production sets; furthermore, it requires that consumer endowments be internal to consumption sets. These assumptions imply the absence of fixed costs, making the U-shaped average costs curve of the Marshallian theory of the firm impossible (Duffie and Sonnenschein 1989, p. 572) – hence the importance of subsequent research aimed at allowing for local discontinuities, even if not in the aggregate, in particular when assuming the presence of a continuum of agents having infinitesimal dimension (cf. for instance Aumann 1966). Increasing returns to scale relative to the economic system as a whole are anyhow excluded.

[18] Frank Hahn (1925–2013), born in Germany but with Czech origins, naturalized English, studied at the London School of Economics and taught at Cambridge since 1960 (with an interval at the LSE, from 1967 to 1973) until his retirement in 1992. His inaugural lecture as professor in Cambridge ('On the notion of equilibrium in economics', Hahn 1973) proposes a notion of equilibrium that constitutes an original mediation between the Austrian, the Marshallian and the Arrow–Debreu schools: 'An economy is in equilibrium when it generates messages which do not cause agents to change the theories they hold or the policies which they pursue' (Hahn 1973, p. 25). Thus defined, equilibrium does not necessarily imply equality between demand and supply: too restrictive an assumption, that according to Hahn constitutes one of the limits of the Chicago school; moreover, Hahn rejects the Walrasian *tâtonnement* centred on the role of the auctioneer and the exclusion of out-of-equilibrium exchanges, another assumption that he considers too restrictive.

Let us now recall, in synthesis, some aspects of this research program and of its most recent lines of development.

The axiomatic formulation of general economic equilibrium theory has an analytical nucleus consisting of a few, key assumptions. There is a certain number of economic agents and a certain number of commodities. The initial endowments of economic agents and their preferences are considered as given. Preferences are assumed to be convex (which is equivalent, in the new context, to the postulate of decreasing marginal utility) and especially to be independent from each other.[19] Some rules of the game are also considered as given: essentially, a unique price for each commodity. On the basis of such data, the problem consists in determining the set of exchange ratios that stem from the interaction of the agents, when they try to improve their position through exchange.

Debreu (1959) extends the general equilibrium model to consider 'dated goods' (a bushel of corn available at a given instant in time is a different good from a bushel of corn available at a different instant in time) and 'contingent goods' (a same good, for instance an umbrella, is considered as a different good according to the 'state of nature', rain or fine weather). Debreu's model also considers productive processes, which transform the originally available goods into other goods; this means including the production sets in the problem's data (generally assumed to be convex, in fact restating the decreasing marginal productivity postulate). At a conceptual level, we also need to attribute to agents an additional role: that of coordinating productive processes, searching gain opportunities through buying means of production and selling the products obtained in the productive process.

Rigorously defined, this is a purely formal problem: determine whether, and under what conditions, there are solutions. Therefore, the problem of uniqueness and stability of the solutions is not considered. An interpretation is superimposed on the formal problem, in fact already implicit in the choice of terminology (economic agents, goods, preferences): namely, the theory is presented as a representation of the mechanisms of a competitive market. However, no explicit hypothesis is made as far as the institutional set-up is concerned. As we shall see in the text that follows, this interpretation opens the way to considering further issues, by extending the original scheme through a redefinition, always a purely formal one, of the basic concepts and/or the introduction of further assumptions.

---

[19] We should notice that this latter is a very strong assumption, that denies the social character of economic agents: an aspect which we shall come back to in the text that follows.

For instance, it is possible to consider contingent markets as markets for insurance certificates concerning different events, revealing the average probability distribution expected by the market. This requires the assumption that the set of all states of nature be completely specified, with each state of nature precisely defined, and with a probability function univocally defined for all possible states of nature.

In intertemporal general economic equilibrium models with contingent markets, exchange and production decisions are adopted in an initial instant of time, even when they refer to future times. Thus, these models differ from temporary general equilibrium models representing the economy in a given instant (or period of time), open to considering the future through the influence that agents' expectations (considered as exogenously given), relative to incomes, prices and quantities in subsequent periods, exert on current choices. Finally, sequential equilibrium models consider a succession of temporary equilibriums, in each of which exchange and production decisions are taken; opportune hypotheses may ensure the correspondence between sequential and intertemporal equilibriums.

However, consideration of the theory as interpreting the functioning of a competitive market economy is not argued through an analysis of the concepts, such as those of economic agent and commodity, that are defined only implicitly and, more importantly, in a very rigid and reductive way. The same is true for the postulates, such as that of convexity of preferences (and, in the expanded model, of production sets), perfect certainty (or, in the case of contingent markets, of purely probabilistic risk) and perfect knowledge, or complete definition of individual preferences over all commodities (and, in intertemporal models with contingent markets, for all moments in time and all states of the world). Often some postulates are not even mentioned. It is assumed that it is possible to univocally define each individual good (goods differing even slightly; for instance Chilean grapes collected two days or a week ago, must be considered different goods: the number of goods is wholly irrelevant for the theory, and we can go as far as to assume a continuum of goods)[20] and that it be equally possible to univocally define the states of the world

[20] This means that for each good the quantities demanded and supplied must be infinitesimal, departing from the assumption of perfect competition (unless we assume an infinite number of agents, each of them with an infinitesimal demand relative to the – also infinitesimal – dimensions of the markets). Furthermore, when the number of goods, states of nature and dates considered increases, the computational difficulty of agents increases exponentially: an aspect on which Radner (1968) relies for stressing the limits of the pure model of general economic equilibrium and the presence of a demand for liquidity (that rigorously speaking should be excluded from these models) even in the absence of uncertainty.

(an aspect on which the philosophical debate reaches opposite conclusions: cf. Wittgenstein [1953], totally ignored notwithstanding the importance that in those very years his contribution has in the cultural debate).

The results of these works are important, but cannot be considered to be the crowning achievement of the research program of general economic equilibrium originated by Walras. Indeed, results concerning the demonstration of the existence of solutions for the model of general economic equilibrium and its internal coherence (Wald 1936; Arrow and Debreu 1954; Debreu 1959) are accompanied by negative results as far as uniqueness and stability of equilibrium are concerned.[21] Reframing the problem in terms of decision theory, as done by von Neumann and Morgenstern, overlooks these aspects, as well as limits of the assumption of convexity of preferences, especially evident when it is extended to production sets.[22] These limits are ignored in mainstream presentations of economics, reflected in Samuelson's (1947) canonical *Foundations of economic analysis*.

Another negative result concerns the impossibility of extending the consistency of choices from the individual to the society. In *Social choice and individual values*, Kenneth Arrow (1951a) proposes the 'impossibility theorem', according to which there is no decisional procedure such as to simultaneously respect two requirements: first, to guarantee transitivity of social choices among three or more alternatives (if A is preferred to B and B is preferred to C, A is also preferred to C); second, to satisfy some conditions of 'democracy' expressed in formal terms: for instance, if one of the alternatives rises in the ranking of one individual, while the rankings of all other individuals remain unchanged, that alternative cannot decrease in the social ranking. In other words, even by starting from individual preference rankings that are complete and transitive, it is impossible to reach a complete and transitive social ranking of preferences.

---

[21] Dealing with stability obviously requires assumptions on how the system behaves out of equilibrium: for instance, if for a certain commodity supply exceeds demand, its price decreases. Stability may be guaranteed only under very restrictive assumptions, as shown in a definitive way by the contributions of Sonnenschein (1972), Debreu (1974) and Mantel (1974); for a survey, cf. Hahn (1982b). In general, little can be said on the dynamic adjustment processes (*tâtonnement*), that can follow the more diverse trajectories.

[22] Let us recall that increasing returns are incompatible with the assumption of perfect competition. Attempts, in recent years, to introduce local non-convexities in production sets in the context of general economic equilibrium analysis correspond more to the search for underdeveloped research fields in which to work than to a real understanding of the relevance of this limit in the analysis. For a survey of the results in various fields of research on general economic equilibrium models, cf. Mas-Colell *et al.* 1995.

6.4   Samuelson's Marshallian–Walrasian Synthesis

The true popularizer of the general economic equilibrium stream in the United States is Paul Samuelson (1915–2009), with his *Foundations of economic analysis* published in 1947, followed in 1948 by his foundational textbook, *Economics*. Based at MIT (Massachusetts Institute of Technology) since 1940, which eventually became one of the top economics research and education centres in the world, Samuelson received the Nobel Prize in 1970. He is undoubtedly a key founder of a new, emerging marginalist tradition – a fusion of the Marshallian theory of the firm, appeals to general economic equilibrium as method of analysis, neoclassical synthesis in macroeconomics, aggregate growth theory – that becomes the core of the modern mainstream.

Intelligent and witty, a hard worker, Samuelson was a natural leader, and built a diversified, motivated and meritocratic group at MIT. Samuelson's move from Harvard to MIT in 1940 and a failed move to Chicago in 1946 mark episodes in the history of US universities: in the first case, anti-Semitism of the then-president of Harvard, along with a missed promotion notwithstanding Schumpeter's threat of resignation (Samuelson had been one of his pupils), shaped the course of Samuelson's career. In the second case, a counter-offer from MIT rescued Friedman and his colleagues, leaving room a little later for Stigler's appointment. This also was amenable to the Cowles Foundation's (which was very interested in Samuelson and his work) move away from Chicago.[23]

At the time, Samuelson has already authored various publications in main journals.[24] One of his first writings (Samuelson 1938) still remains a fundamental reference point for the marginalist theory of the consumer. In it, Samuelson proposes an 'operational' version of this theory, turning upside down the traditional logical sequence by which consumers' choices are deduced from their preferences, that are not directly observable. In his case, the point of departure consists in consumer's choices; from them, thanks to some assumptions (in particular, the so-called feeble axiom of revealed preferences: if I prefer x to y when both are possible, I cannot prefer y to x) that express in formal terms the notion of the consumer's rational behaviour, it is possible to deduce the consumer's preference ranking.[25]

---

[23]   On these vicissitudes cf. Backhouse (2014a), Maes (2014), Weintraub (2014) and more generally Backhouse (2017). On the history of MIT cf. also Chenier (2014), Garcia Duarte (2014), Svorenčik (2014) and Thomas (2014).

[24]   In the more than seventy years of his research activity, Samuelson is persistently a prolific author. His writings are collected in seven weighty volumes (Samuelson 1966–2011).

[25]   Samuelson himself does not discuss the field of application of his theory. Sen (1973) maintains that the change in viewpoint does not substantially change the a priori

The principle Samuelson aimed to establish is that economics *can* become an exact science, on the model of physics. This must derive from the use of mathematics, or, more precisely, of differential calculus, commonly utilized in mechanics to study the movement of bodies and their equilibrium. He contended that this can be utilized in economics in terms of solving constrained maximum and minimum problems. These principles of formal theoretical rigour were imposed in subsequent decades in US universities, leaving behind the original flaw of Samuelson's line of analysis, namely adoption of postulates that have very little to do with the real world but that are essential for constructing the Samuelsonian theoretical edifice. These are the postulates of the utilitarian *homo oeconomicus* (endowed with individual preference sets that are independent from the preference sets of all other individuals) and convexity of consumer preferences with respect to changes in the quantities consumed of the various goods and of production techniques with respect to changes in the quantities utilized of the various means of production. This means, among other things, to exclude by assumption increasing returns to scale, so important in the real world, both in consumption (for instance, acquired customs and the importance of imitation in the formation of lifestyles), and in production (for instance, learning by doing, 'law of quadratic and cubic proportions', and so on).[26]

Samuelson (1947) begins with a definition of equilibrium systems and of comparative statics (meaningful only, as one of Samuelson's professors, Schumpeter, noted, if stability and uniqueness of equilibrium are guaranteed),[27] then proceeds to an illustration of the theory of

character of consumer theory: necessarily, 'the ratio of observations to potential choices [is] equal to zero', and 'comparisons have to be made within a fairly short time to avoid taste change' (ibid., pp. 56–7). Sen (1973, p. 131) concludes with a general critique to the marginalist theory of the consumer, recalling 'a problem of interdependence of different people's choices which discredits individualistic rational calculus'.

[26] We shall come back to these issues again and again in the text that follows.

[27] Within the theory of economic equilibrium, stability implies that a deviation from the position of equilibrium sets in action mechanisms that bring the economy back to such a position; often the term stability designates what with greater precision may be defined stationary, namely persistence over time of the conditions determining equilibrium. In the theory of revealed preferences (Samuelson 1938) the stationary of preferences is an assumption implicit in the fact that in the real world choices are necessarily taken in a sequence. This is, however, an unrealistic assumption. As noted by Sen (1982,'Introduction'), in the short period preference for variety induces me to choose fish today and meat tomorrow without this implying that I am not rational, while in the long run we cannot exclude changes in customs and tastes. In his original presentation of the theory of revealed preferences, Samuelson (1938) avoids the assumption of stability by recourse to an axiomatic presentation: choices are taken 'at the same time'. However, when meant in a purely axiomatic sense, his is not a theory of consumer behaviour, but a simple definition of rational behaviour, that in fact may be made compatible with any sequence of consumer choices.

maximizing behaviour. Subsequently he considers the theory of cost and production, then that of consumers' equilibrium. The second part of the *Foundations* is devoted to demonstrating the stability of equilibrium, and then to providing some elements of economic dynamics. Some mathematical appendixes conclude the volume.

The strong point in Samuelson's theory is its (apparent) rigour, that should have allowed leaving behind the ideological clashes (Samuelson did not ascribe to right-wing supporters of the Cold War but rather preferred to isolate his work from politics). There are two main weaknesses in the book. The first is the scant attention to the stage of conceptualization, which allows Samuelson to adopt a representation of the economy that ignores the complexities (multiplicity of passions and interests) of the economic agent transformed into a monodimensional maximizer, the uncertainties surrounding every aspect of real life (and, as Keynes stresses, with different kinds of uncertainty for the different fields of action), and the importance of increasing returns to scale. The second weakness concerns the insufficiency of the demonstration of stability of equilibrium: as it becomes clear first with Sraffa's critiques to marginalist capital theory and then with the theoretical work within the very theory of general economic equilibrium, stability and uniqueness of equilibrium can be demonstrated only under rather restrictive hypotheses.

Let us consider this second element. In a new edition, dated 1983, Samuelson's 1947 text is reprinted with no substantive changes, except for the addition of new material at the end. Here we find, within a treatment of input–output systems, some references to Sraffa's analysis and the capital theory critiques to be illustrated further on. Such references, however, imply a misleading presentation of Sraffa's analysis and a reductive evaluation of the bearing of its critiques of the marginalist theory of value and distribution. Indeed, Samuelson, by assimilating Sraffa's analysis to Leontief's, erroneously interprets it as a general economic equilibrium model in which the assumption of constant returns to scale (explicitly excluded by Sraffa in his 1960 book) allows determining relative prices while ignoring the side of demand. Furthermore, as far as the critique is concerned, Samuelson reduces it (following in this Joan Robinson's presentation of 1953, hence preceding publication of Sraffa's book) to a critique of the aggregate notion of capital utilized in aggregate production functions (as the so-called Cobb–Douglas ones, on which Solow's growth theory illustrated in §7.5 and the Appendix to Chapter 7 relies: 'the *simpliste* J. B. Clark parable', as Samuelson 1947, p. 568 of the 1983 edition, calls it): a critique considered valid concerning the issue of aggregation – an issue of which the MIT theorists declare to be well aware – and not to the traditional marginalist theory of value and distribution. Therefore, it is considered not applicable to the 'general' marginalist model. Thus, we are led to forget the fact that Sraffa's critique concerns not only and not so much the aggregate notion of capital, but also and especially the impossibility of demonstrating the existence of an inverse relation between real wage and employment, which is essential for the marginalist mechanism of re-adjustment to full employment equilibrium remaining the pillar of mainstream macroeconomics. Hence, the separation, hinted at earlier, between a 'lowbrow theory' in which the aggregate production function is utilized, for its simplicity and especially for obtaining definite results that otherwise could not be reached, and a 'highbrow theory', that of general economic equilibrium, endowed with internal consistency but not able to produce definite results, and within which the simple parables obtainable with the aggregate production function do not hold.[28] Various among Samuelson's contributions, even among the best-known ones, rely on the aggregate notion of capital: e.g. the so-called HOS theorem (Heckscher–Ohlin–Samuelson: cf. Samuelson 1948b) that explains international trade on the basis of the different endowments of factors of production – capital, land, labour – in various countries and based on the assumption of decreasing marginal productivity for each one of these factors.

A systematizer more than an innovator, Samuelson was nonetheless one of the most influential economists in the theoretical field following the Second World War. His very numerous contributions range over a variety of fields; his activity in teaching and in the formation of a wide-ranging, widely shared theoretical corpus confer to him an undoubtedly dominant position in contemporary economic culture.[29]

6.5 The Marshallian Microeconomics of the Chicago School: The Imperialism of Economics

The microeconomics of the Chicago School owes much to the Marshallian tradition, through the influence of a series of lectures on price theory held by Jacob Viner (1892–1970) for many years. Marshall's *Principles* (1890) are in fact the reference text for Viner's course; he utilizes it on the basis of

---

[28] The 'empirical' use of the aggregate production function too has been the object of various perplexities; according to Simon (1979b, p. 469), 'The data say no more than that the value of product is approximately equal to the wage bill plus the cost of capital services'; when in the Cobb–Douglas (the most commonly utilized kind of production function) the sum of capital and labour coefficients are set equal to one (as it is necessary to do, according to Euler's theorem, for ensuring equality between income and the sum of wages and profits), we are in front of an accounting identity, hence to a tautology. Cf. also Sylos Labini (1995).

[29] On the role of his textbook cf. Giraud (2014).

his own interpretation, based on the four couples of average and marginal cost curves: for the firm and the industry, the long and the short run (Viner 1931). This is the interpretation of Marshall's theory adopted in nearly all economics textbooks for the subsequent half century and beyond; but it is also an analytical structure object of Sraffa's (1925, 1926) destructive criticisms, so destructive that Marshall's own immediate pupils, such as Dennis Robertson, were induced to adopt the alternative evolutionary interpretation of Marshall.[30]

Viner's move to Princeton in 1946, and Simons's dramatic death in the following year, mark the transition from the 'first Chicago school' (Knight, Simons, Viner) to the 'second' (Friedman and colleagues).[31] The main lecture course in price theory – which remains the pillar for the instruction of the young – was inherited by Friedman, who after a few years produced a textbook (Friedman 1962), as an integration of the more elementary and uncritical textbook published by Stigler (1946). Friedman's text is dominated by the analysis of supply-and-demand equilibrium in an isolated market; equilibrium of the firm follows, still utilizing U-shaped cost curves (in the wide bibliography of the text there is no reference to Sraffa's two articles, 1925 and 1926, nor to the 1920s and 1930s debate on empty economic boxes, though it involves the most important economists of the time and was published in the most important economics journal of the time, the *Economic Journal*), then the labour market the equilibrium of which is determined by the equality between real wage and labour marginal productivity, assumed to be decreasing, to conclude with an analysis of income distribution (inclusive of wage differentials). This takes on in toto the marginalist tradition. Friedman's textbook is considered advanced,

---

[30] Cf. §5.3, and Roncaglia (2005a), chapter 13. Sraffa's critiques originate a wide debate. We may thus assume that they are known to Friedman and Stigler, who, however, prefer to ignore them: perhaps too easy a method to go around the difficulties. In fact Stigler (1941, p. 71) quotes in a footnote Sraffa (1926) and the ensuing debate, but adding: 'This recent discussion is too detailed and wide-ranging to permit consideration in the present study'; in the two subsequent pages it is recalled that Sraffa shows how the partial equilibriums method is, rigorously speaking, applicable only to the case of economies of scale external to the firm but internal to the industry, a case that Sraffa considers as wholly unrealistic; Stigler goes on focusing on external economies in general, giving no more attention to Sraffa's critiques. Let us note in passing that also Samuelson's text (1948a) skips over Sraffa's critiques, even if he himself considers them again and again in various of his subsequent writings.

[31] On the dramatic circumstances of Simons's death cf. van Horn (2014). With Viner, Chicago loses a high-ranking historian of economic thought, with a drastic fall in level in that area. To quote only two examples in this respect, let us recall Stigler (1951) attributing to Smith the thesis of the invisible hand of the market, a most serious error for a historian of economic thought (on the limits of Smith's liberism cf. Viner 1927; on the 'invisible hand', Rothschild 1994), and Becker (1974, p. 813) recalling Seneca, instead of Aristotle, with respect to the social nature of man.

referring to Stigler's text as an introduction; in both cases we are confronted with conventional manuals, already at the time falling behind the debates on the theory of the firm or on the theory of capital and distribution, the results of which are wholly ignored.

The assumptions required to obtain the equilibriums of the consumer and the producer (decreasing marginal utility and marginal productivity) are adopted without any discussion. This explains but certainly does not justify the belief in the existence of a unique 'true' economic theory, based on the faith in the invisible hand of the market, which characterizes the Chicago school. For the students, the absence of a critical formation constitutes an advantage: the techniques of supply-and-demand analysis, applied a thousand times over on a multiplicity of issues, guarantee a compact image of economics and a strong support for the ideology of the market as an invisible hand, driving in an unfailing path towards equilibrium.

On this basis, uncritically assumed, different developments evolve: in the microeconomics field, it is these developments that constitute the Chicago school's original contribution. The unifying element consists in adhesion to a rigid view (maximizing a monodimensional magnitude, interpretable as expected utility) of the rationality of the economic agent who tackles in the most diverse fields always the same problem: that indicated in the celebrated definition of economics by Lionel Robbins (1932, p. 20), 'economics is the science which studies human behaviour as a relationship between ends and scarce means which have alternative uses'.

George Stigler[32] began work on this method, followed by (and in collaboration with) his pupil Gary Becker.[33] The method adopted consists in bringing back any problem to the traditional analytical techniques of a rational agent's choices: there is, in his opinion, only one theory of human behaviour, the theory of utility maximization. Thus, for instance, the uncertainty deriving from the dispersion of the prices of a same good in the market is rendered endogenous, as depending on the investment choices in the acquisition of new information, decided on with the usual criterion of maximizing their expected returns (Stigler 1961). The unrealism of the assumptions necessary for the reasoning appears not to constitute a problem, as it is usual for Chicago economists sharing with Friedman (1953, pp. 3–43) the methodological criterion – which we shall

---

[32] George Stigler (1911–1991, Nobel Prize in 1982) obtained his PhD in Chicago under Knight; during the war collaborates to the Manhattan project; from 1947 to 1958 teaches at Columbia University, then at Chicago; among the founders of the Mont Pèlerin Society, is its president from 1976 to 1978. A collection of his writings in Italian, representative of his scientific production, is Stigler (1994).

[33] Gary Becker (1930–2014, Nobel Prize in 1992), PhD at Chicago, was with Columbia University from 1957 to 1968, then at Chicago.

return to in §8.5 – of considering irrelevant the unrealism of the assumptions to focus exclusively on the forecasting capacity of the theories.[34]

Stigler and Becker published *De gustibus non est disputandum* in 1977, an article in which they maintain the thesis of stability (or more precisely stationarity) of consumers' preferences, showing how on the basis of such an assumption (and of the traditional analytical techniques of rational choice) it is possible to explain 'phenomena widely believed to be inconsistent with the stability of tastes: addiction, habitual behaviour, advertising, fashion' (p. 89). The stability of preferences concerns the abstract notion of 'commodities', those that agents consider in their evaluation of the satisfaction derived from consumption (namely, in their utility functions); such 'commodities' are not bought and sold directly, but are composed of the usual consumption goods taken in given proportions.[35]

This approach was developed by Becker in a series of writings which apply the traditional techniques of rational choice to issues ranging from drug addiction to advertising, from marriage to begging, from discrimination to crime, from democracy to human capital, with admirable inventiveness but always with very unrealistic assumptions.[36]

The introduction of new arguments in the utility function was brought on by Akerlof (b. 1940, Nobel Prize in 2001; cf. Akerlof 1980), who added the element of reputation, aiming to incorporate recognition of social influences on the behaviour of the individual. In doing so, he aimed to explain the actual behaviour of the workers that leads to a positive rate of involuntary unemployment. In an analogous way, more recently, Akerlof and Kranton (2000) propose embodying the identity of the agent (gender, religion, nationality and so on: in general, the

---

[34] Considering information as a commodity, Stigler distances himself from the tradition of the Austrian school (Menger, Hayek), for which it is the market that through prices and their changes in the course of the process of adjustment between supply and demand provides economic agents with information. Stigler's approach differs also from that of MIT economists (Akerlof, Stiglitz) who focus attention on informational asymmetries, considered as a datum of the problem and the cause of market imperfections.

[35] This specific notion of 'commodity' is taken from a previous article by Michael and Becker (1973), in which we may perceive an echo of the notion of demand for characteristics proposed by Lancaster (1966, 1971), according to which consumers should not demand the commodity for itself, but as endowed with 'characteristics' (for instance vitamins, calories, etc.) that constitute the means for the satisfaction of consumers' wants and desires. In this way Lancaster intends to provide an objective basis for utility functions (*utilitas* rather than *complacibilitas*, in the suggestive terminology of the late Middle Ages). The thesis of stationary preferences is decidedly turned down by Hayek (cf. Caldwell 2004, p. 282; Gray, 1984, pp. 47–55, stresses the wide differences between Hayek's and Becker's approaches).

[36] The most important among these articles are collected in Becker (1996); in Italian, a collection of essays representative of Becker's scientific production is in Becker (1998).

self-consciousness of the agent) within the traditional model of rational behaviour, including identity as an argument in a generalized utility function, with the aim of tackling issues such as gender and social exclusion. Choices implying adhesion to or refusal of identity imply positive or negative effects both for the agent and externality for other agents. The idea here is to account for behaviours that appear contrary to self-interest. Externalities, in the sense of interactions among different economic agents, are dealt with by the tool of game theory; multiple equilibriums may result, depending on the parameters' values.[37]

In this way, however, the problem of social influences on the set of individual preferences is circumvented: each individual's preference sets remain unchanged, while interdependency commonly implies an adaptation – positive or negative – of the preference sets of each individual to those of the others, hence the collapse of the very foundations of the theory of consumer behaviour, in the expected utility variety as in that of the Marshallian tradition adopted in Chicago. Reputation, identity and belonging are phenomena that may be included only artificially in such theories. Ultimately, however, they illustrate their limits, stemming from assuming as data the individual preference sets.

6.6 The New Theories of the Firm

General economic equilibrium theory considers relations among independent economic agents and tries to show how, under certain assumptions, equilibrium solutions may be reached. A problem thus arises: why should the firm exist?

Let us recall that while within the market legally independent agents enter into relation with each other, within each firm an organizational set-up prevails based on 'command', that is, on hierarchy and on centralization of decisions and control over their execution. What is it then that determines the boundary between these two different forms of organization of economic life, market and command?

---

[37] Akerlof and Kranton (2000, p. 719) assume that identity is definable in an univocal and measurable way; this is necessary in order to consider 'gains or losses in identity' engendering gains or losses in utility. This conflicts with Mill's critique to Bentham (cf. §2.2) concerning the incommensurability of the different human sentiments: a point the importance of which is stressed by Sen's thesis (cf. §14.5) on the multiplicity of human belongings; indeed, when considered as a whole, the examples illustrated by Akerlof and Kranton go in the same direction, from the rituals of mutilation to gender dominance in some employments, from the sense of belonging to the university or school from which one comes to group links. In fact, what Akerlof and Kranton propose is a return to Bentham's felicific calculus.

Within the neoclassical tradition, the most widely accepted answer may be traced to an article published in 1937 by the American Ronald Coase (1910–2013, Nobel Prize in 1991), whose ideas have been taken up and developed by others over the past twenty years.[38] Coase stresses that market transactions have a cost for participants: it is necessary to collect information, and search for a counter-party ready to exchange and negotiate over prices and other conditions. All this implies time and expense. In the absence of the organizational structure of the firm, each worker would have to bargain to acquire a variety of inputs – the semifinished products and raw materials she herself uses, her working tools, engineering services, and so on – and then to bargain for the sale of their product, which in general will only be semi-finished or part of the final product. The firm allows for simplification, replacing the bargaining over all aspects of the productive process with an organization based on command (that is, on a hierarchical decision-making structure) and thus drastically reducing the number of necessary transactions. When the size of the firm grows, its internal organization becomes more and more complex and therefore less and less efficient; once a certain point is passed – corresponding to the optimal size of the firm – the costs of expanding relations based on command become higher than the costs of recourse to exchange, that is, to the market.[39]

A quite different answer to the question concerning why the firm exists is provided by radical economists looking to economic power relations. For instance, Stephen Marglin (1974) maintains that the superiority of the firm – in particular, of the large firm – as a form of organization of production is based on technological choices (mass production of standardized goods). An alternative line of technological development would have been possible, however, based on flexible production; such an alternative would have favoured organizational forms more similar to artisan shops than to large-size modern manufacturing. According to Marglin, the technological line of mass-scale production of standardized goods, thus the big corporation, prevails; this is mainly because this approach favours the appropriation of the surplus on the part of the dominant classes, thanks to control over the productive process made possible by

---

[38] We shall consider in §13.4 Coase's thesis according to which in the absence of transaction costs externality problems may be solved by fully specifying property rights (for instance, establishing whether it is the firm that has a right to pollute so that it should be compensated for renouncing this right, or the firm has a duty to compensate those damaged by its pollution), thus favouring the birth of ad hoc markets.

[39] Simon rejects the clear-cut opposition between firms based on command and the market, stressing the complexity of the internal organizational structure of the firm.

the organizational form of command and by division of labour within the firm.

Marglin's ideas are criticized by historian David Landes (1986). The latter re-proposes Smith's original answer: the modern firm prevails over artisan shops because it allows cost reductions, by exploiting (static and dynamic) economies of scale obtainable through the division of labour in the productive process and through the consequent introduction of machinery. It should be noted, however, that according to Smith's line of argument, firms do not have an optimal size: their growth takes place in time, in the course of a dynamic process which cannot be interpreted by the static analysis of traditional theory.

Growth in firm size, which brings big corporations to the fore, leads to another problem: who controls the firms? Public companies have top managers who are in general not the proprietors and are often very numerous.

American economists Adolf Berle (1895–1971) and Gardiner Means (1896–1988), in a book published in 1932, point to a new form of society, *managerial capitalism*, which they suggest is characterized by the public company and the separation between owners and managers. In an initial stage of the process of industrialization, *competitive capitalism*, small firms directly managed by their owners prevail. Subsequently, with the rise of big firms organized as public companies, ownership is subdivided among many small shareholders; the managers of the firm acquire sufficient autonomy to become the real protagonists of economic life, assuming responsibility for all decisions relative not only to the current life of the firms but also to strategic long-period choices.

Many economists (among them William Baumol, 1922–2017, in a book published in 1959), sharing Berle's and Means' ideas, infer from them a change in the objectives of the firm. More precisely, the objective of profit maximization prevails in the stage of competitive capitalism, when firms are directly managed by their owners; in the stage of managerial capitalism other objectives prevail, especially sales maximization, which better corresponds to the interests of the firm's managers.

Obviously, the managers have to consider the risk of being replaced, at the shareholders' annual meeting. This may happen when many shareholders, dissatisfied with the management of the company and in particular with their dividends and the share price, sell their shares on the stock market; in this case, the firm's takeover by a new group is favoured, as this new group can more easily acquire a sufficient number of shares to gain a majority in shareholders' meetings. It is on this constraint on managers' freedom of action that the 'theory of managerial capitalism' is based, as developed by Robin Marris in a book published in 1964.

The ponderous work by Chandler (1990) reconstructs the history of major manufacturing corporations in the United States, Germany and Great Britain since the last decades of the nineteenth century up to mid-twentieth century; apart from providing a wealth of ground material, the book reconstructs the changes that continuously take place in the market forms of the various sectors and in the firms' decision-making processes; managerial capitalism is thus examined in detail in its actual development.

An aspect stressed by Leibenstein (1966) concerns the so-called X-inefficiency, namely the wide variety in efficiency (productivity) among firms utilizing analogous techniques and analogous quantities of capital and labour. Inefficiencies, relative to the optimal use of the selected technology, may be due to the management's inability, a lack of motivation among workers (for instance, absenteeism) and an inferior quality of productive inputs. The actual importance of this issue, stressed by Leibenstein and confirmed by other researchers, points to the limit of the assumption of given techniques of production, commonly adopted in theories of the firm as well as in general equilibrium theory, and to the relevance of studies on the organization of the firm (such as those by Cyert, Simon and many others), on the sociology of labour and on actual market forms.

Another stream of research concerns the market power of large firms. The Italian Paolo Sylos Labini (1920–2005) and the American Joe Bain (1912–93), in two books both published in 1956, develop a theory of oligopoly (focusing attention respectively on the cases of concentrated and differentiated oligopoly), considered – in particular by Sylos Labini – as the common market form, compared to which pure competition and monopoly constitute two polar limit cases. In the case of oligopoly, the firms present in the market are partially protected from competition of potential entrants by a 'barrier to entry', the study of which is the subject of the theory. Such a barrier is not insurmountable (in which case there would be monopoly, while the case of a non-existing barrier corresponds to perfect competition). Its size, hence the difficulty to overcome it, depends on a series of factors discussed in the writings of Bain and Sylos Labini and in subsequent literature on the subject. For instance, in the case of concentrated oligopoly, the size of the barrier to entry depends on the minimal technologically optimal size of the plant, and in general, on economies of scale, which require the new firm to enter the market with a rather sizeable minimum production, so to make it difficult to find a market outlet at current prices; in the case of differentiated oligopoly, it depends on advertising expenses necessary to impose the new trademark on the market. Defended by these barriers, firms already active in the market may enjoy profits well above the competitive level and a certain freedom of action, though within the limits determined by the risk of new competitors entering the sector.[40]

Theories of the behaviour of the large firm which display noticeable similarities to those of Marris, Bain and Sylos Labini are developed by some Keynesian economists. Let us recall in particular Austrian Josef Steindl (1952), American Alfred Eichner (1976) and Englishman Adrian Wood (1975). These economists take over the Keynesian view according to which investment decisions by firms constitute the *primum mobile* in the evolution of the economy. Once the level of investments to be realized is decided, firms must decide how to finance them; for a number of reasons, they prefer to use internal sources (profits not distributed as dividends to shareholders) rather than debt or the emission of new shares.[41] Therefore, according to the post-Keynesian theory of the firm, entrepreneurs set product prices so as to obtain a profit margin sufficient to finance the desired level of investments.

Quite naturally this theory may refer only to firms endowed with some market power, which are able to autonomously set their product prices. In doing so, they are not rigidly constrained by competition with other firms. Even in the case of oligopolistic firms, however, it is to be doubted whether prices may be set freely, so as to generate an amount of profits sufficient to finance any amount of investments the firms desire to enact. We may thus interpret Keynesian theories of the firm as concerning utilization of margins of choice which top managers enjoy in the presence of strong elements of uncertainty and of oligopolistic conditions.

A development of the theories of market forms based on barriers to entry is the contestable markets theory developed by Baumol and others (1982). Perfectly contestable markets are those for which there is no cost

---

[40] This theory is reformulated by Modigliani (1958) in static terms compatible with traditional neoclassical analysis, with a neoclassical synthesis parallel to that realized by himself concerning Keynes's theory. It is in this form, rather than in the original one, which implies dynamic elements (for instance the rate of growth of the market influences the size of the barrier to entry; price-elasticities increase when the interval of time taken as reference expands), that oligopoly theory enters textbooks and the mainstream view of industrial organization theory.

[41] The Modigliani–Miller theorem, according to which under conditions of perfect competition and perfect knowledge the different sources of financing are equivalent (cf. Modigliani and Miller 1958; we shall come back to this theorem in §11.4) is considered inapplicable, explicitly or implicitly, by these economists, who in general consider as prevailing non-competitive market conditions and imperfect knowledge.

of entry or exit. In such markets, no firm can enjoy extra-profits. Indeed, any opportunity for extra-profits, even temporary ones, immediately attracts new firms into the market. An absence of exit costs allows new firms to avoid any risk, for instance due to reactions of firms already present in the market: if market conditions change and the extra-profits turn negative, the new firm can immediately exit without having to bear any cost (with what is commonly called a 'hit and run' strategy). Exit costs derive mainly from the existence of fixed capital goods which cannot be re-utilized once the activity for which they had been acquired is abandoned: the so-called 'sunk costs'. This element constitutes the main novelty of contestable markets theory relative to the theory of market forms based on barriers to entry.

Completion of this quick survey of the modern debate on the theories of the firm requires at least recalling evolutionary theories, which we shall come back to in Chapter 13. These theories have been proposed to explain in particular the behaviour of the firm and the industry in the process of technological change. In the approach proposed by Americans Richard Nelson (b. 1930) and Sidney Winter (b. 1935) in a book published in 1982, the industry structure at any moment in time is considered as the result not of a process of maximization (of profits or sales), but of an evolutionary process. Some firms may grow more rapidly than others, while some go bankrupt; the industry evolves over time as the result of the vicissitudes of firms within it. As in biology, recourse is proposed to mathematical stochastic models, which are able to allow for the random element always present in economic events, but also for the different probabilities of events. The 'genes' of firms – which determine their identities, transfer the main behavioural features from one to the other and undergo 'mutations' over time – consist of 'routines': standard procedures adopted by the firm in production, product commercialization, financial management and so on. In a market economy, the routines which prevail, and thus determine the dominant features of firms, are those which ensure success, namely those which ensure profit maximization in the long term.[42]

Finally, the law and economics stream, inclusive of those who study laws regulating markets, particularly anti-trust laws, reflects further engagement with these questions. This is in fact a heterogeneous stream, consisting of different positions, connected, as we will see, to the different economic approaches.

---

[42] In his Nobel lecture, Simon (1979c, p. 508) remarked that Nelson's and Winter's theory, as Marris's and others, explicitly or implicitly embodies his notions of bounded rationality and satisficing behaviour. This will be discussed further in §10.4.

6.7 Game Theory and Industrial Organization Theory

Most commonly, the element of superiority in game theory is demonstrated by the fact that it allows for the analysis of strategic behaviour, in which the agent tries to consider the reactions of others to her choices. The difference, compared to the analysis of parametric behaviour, is irrelevant in the case of perfect competition, where each agent is too small to influence the situation and the behaviour of other agents with her own behaviour; this is also unimportant in the case of monopoly, when there is a single agent in the market. Thus the difference becomes relevant when we deal with the case of oligopoly; it is precisely with respect to the new oligopoly theories (Bain and Sylos Labini, but the reference term is in fact Modigliani's 1958 model) that game theory encounters a season of growing utilization in the field of microeconomics, expanding to cover a wide variety of issues.

As hinted earlier, Sylos Labini's and Bain's oligopoly theories are based on barriers to entry: firms already present in the market (incumbent firms) are able to enjoy profits above the competitive level thanks to the fact that new potential entrants are penalized by the costs of entry into the market. In the case of concentrated oligopoly, on which we focus attention here, the barrier of entry consists in technological discontinuities and in economies of scale that allow large plants to produce at lesser costs than small plants. Thus, a new firm entering with a large plant, necessary for not having costs higher than those of the incumbents, would provoke a sizeable increase in the quantity produced overall, which in turn would translate into a decrease in product prices. This requires, however, the assumption (the so-called 'Sylos Labini postulate') that large firms already present in the market leave their quantities produced unchanged, even if in so doing they would earn less than by 'accommodating' the new firm by reducing the quantities they produce in order to support the product prices. Game theory allows us to evaluate the solidity of such an assumption, by considering the valuations of the new entrant on the reactions of the incumbent firms. Thus, it can be shown that, once the entry has taken place, the incumbent has the convenience to adopt an accommodating behaviour; the new entrant, knowing this, may decide in favour of entry; product prices are subjected to a downward pressure until, entry after entry, the competitive level is reached.

These results bring us in the direction of the traditional marginalist theory of the firm, according to which competition and monopoly are the two cases to be considered, while oligopoly is unstable and tends towards one or the other of the two extremes (the tendency towards monopoly taking place through the formation of coalitions).

The first studies originate a series of further writings. The incumbent firms may find it convenient to systematically maintain a non-accommodating behaviour any time there is a new entry, notwithstanding the costs implicit in this behaviour in terms of lower profits, in order to preserve a reputation such as to discourage new entries. In a series of repeated games, when the last turn arrives, reputation does not matter any longer; but if the new entrants know this, they may enter at the penultimate turn, and with backward induction we discover that a hard reputation will never be believed: a non-credible threat. In the case of an infinite succession of plays, however, or even with an indefinite number of plays (which is in fact the case Sylos Labini has in mind, thus considering his to be not a postulate but a common behaviour), non-accommodating behaviour is once again convenient. Thus, at the end of a long debate it seems that we are back where we started from, even if – as game theorists maintain – with an increased consciousness of the implications of the analysis.[43] In any case, game theory allows for a more general treatment, compared to which the cases treated by the traditional Marshallian theory appear as particular cases, rather than as different issues.

The theory of industrial organization thus has an impressive development, to the point of acquiring the status of a substantially autonomous research field, with various applicative branches. The two volumes of the *Handbook of industrial organization* (edited by Schmalensee and Willig, 1989) and the manuals by Tirole (1988) and Krouse (1990) offer a picture of the early developments in this area, concerning issues such as the factors determining the organization of the firm and the market, the behaviour of agents in the market, methods and results of empirical analysis and international comparisons. Subsequent developments go on to analysis of specific issues, with no substantial novelty; more interesting is instead the development of the analytical tools of game theory.

Use of game theory, introduced as we saw by von Neumann and Morgenstern (1944), constitutes a methodological revolution: 'language, concepts, and techniques of non-cooperative game theory have become central to the discipline' (Kreps 1990, p. 1). In various cases, with or without game theory, the results of the analysis do not change; but in

---

[43] A group of empirical analyses of the issue, collected in Geroski and Schwalbach (1991), does not bring to univocal results, though stressing the relatively modest role played by the new entrants relative to the competition already existing among incumbents, and especially the importance of the institutional environment, for the vicissitudes of specific markets.

other cases the results are different and as a rule appear more rigorous in the definition in the assumptions necessary for arriving at them.

The technical aspects of game theory are enough to keep many researchers occupied. Two techniques of analysis are important to note: representation of games in strategic or normal form, and in extended form. In the first case, and considering only two players, a rectangle represents the outcomes of the possible choices of the two players in a series of cells, with the lines corresponding to the choices of the first player and the columns to the choices of the second; within each cell, a pair of numbers represents the outcome of each pair of choices for the two players. Both static (with simultaneous moves) and dynamic games (sequential moves) can be represented in strategic or in extended form.

A Nash equilibrium is the outcome (pair of choices) whereby each player cannot improve their situation, given the choice of the other player.[44] Each game can have various Nash equilibriums, or none; moreover, as we shall see later when considering the so-called prisoner's dilemma, the equilibrium may be a non-optimal one (in Pareto's meaning: there may exist a better situation for at least one of the players without a worsening in the situation of somebody else).

Nash equilibriums concern non-cooperative games. In the case of cooperative games, in which two or more players can form coalitions, the notion of *core* is used: a set of payoffs for the players such that no coalition can improve the outcome for all its components.

Games in extended form are sequential in nature: each player moves when they know the move of the preceding player, but also knowing all the series of outcomes of each successive possible move. Each choice is called a 'node'. Each game expressed in extended form has a counterpart in a game expressed in strategic form, while the opposite is not true: any game expressed in strategic form may correspond to various games expressed in extended form. In the case of imperfect competition, games in extended form may be solved with backward induction. Beginning with the choice of the player effecting the last move (the most convenient for the player), we consider which implications this has for the preceding player, and so on.

Game theory deals step by step with increasingly complex problems. For instance, in an extended form game, we may assume that each player has to move without knowing the move of the previous player; in other terms, we may adopt different hypotheses on the information set available

---

[44] John Nash (1928–2015, mathematician, Nobel Prize in economics in 1994) is known to the public at large because of the movie *A beautiful mind*, an account of his life. In economics, his fame is due to the 'Nash theorem' presented in a brief article of 1950. His main essays are collected in Nash (1996); a wider collection, enriched by biographical and autobiographical elements, is Nash (2002).

to each agent. Through the introduction of 'choices of nature' we may introduce elements of uncertainty; if this is probabilistic in nature, the solution of the game may be sought out through the tools of expected utility theory.

Game theory is based on utilitarian grounds: we assume that each player aims at their best possible result, and that their occasional altruistic choices do not affect the maximizing decisions of the other, utilitarian and selfish, agents.

In the case of multi-step games, we may utilize analyses based on backward induction, in which the choices available in the last move of the game affect the choices in previous moves. Alternatively, we may use forward induction, in which the players' choices in the first moves offer indications on the likely successive moves of the agents. Backward induction presupposes a precise, even if probabilistic knowledge of the outcomes of all moves in the game; we can thus understand why forward induction is found to be applied in a greater number of actual cases, such as for studying conventions and social norms and their evolution. Concepts such as subgame perfection have been developed for the case of backward induction, in the framework of the so-called refinements literature (originated by Selten 1975), aiming to reduce the number of equilibriums to be considered.[45]

The refinements literature dominated in the 1980s; in the 1990s, attention focused on repeated games and on the evolution of the behaviour of agents, also through the techniques of experimental economics and computer simulations (tournaments).

When considering repeated games with the same agents, and cases in which Nash equilibriums do not correspond to globally optimal situations (as in the prisoner's dilemma),[46] cooperative behaviour may emerge. It is quite difficult to treat this kind of case mathematically; we may study various strategies of signalling and of answers to selfish behaviour, and one gets lost in a host of possible outcomes.[47] The fields

---

[45] Within this literature particular attention is given to the paper by Harsanyi and Selten (1988).

[46] The prisoner's game is an often quoted case: two persons accused of a crime are interrogated separately; each is promised pardon if one confesses while the other does not confess or a reduction in the sentence if the other confesses; in the absence of proofs, the prisoner who does not confess is penalized lightly if the other too does not confess, but heavily if the other confesses. Each of the two prisoners finds it convenient to confess, whatever is the choice of the other; as a consequence the optimal position, in which no one confesses and the penalty is light, is not chosen while the rational choice implies confession and a discount in the full penalty. Cooperation consists in both refusing to confess, in the hope that the other adopt the same behaviour.

[47] Kreps (1990, pp. 95 ff., quoted in Caldwell 2004, p. 334) comments: 'Too many equilibria and no way to choose'; in these conditions, an able theoretician may deduce

of experimental economics or of computer tournaments, to which we will return below, originate from the empirical study of this kind of problem; the results of these studies indicate in general that the behaviour of actual agents, open to the possibility of cooperation, is far more complex than that of the rational and selfish *homo oeconomicus*. This explains a return of interest, within game theory, for the possibility of spontaneous coalitions among players (corresponding to implicit collusion in anti-trust theory).

Game theory requires the rules of the game to be specified with absolute precision: results change with even small variations of these rules. Existence of multiple solutions for each game, together with the possibility of multiplying the cases of possible games at will by changes in the rules, provides a very wide field for applications (and publications) for researchers in the field; this, in the current situation of academic competition ('publish or perish') greatly favours this field of research. Results are, however, extremely fragmented: far from arriving at a general theory of economic behaviour, small fragments of theory may be multiplied at will, each of them dealing with extremely specific and abstract cases, connected to the unavoidable starting assumptions. Finally, the rules of the game are assumed as given, while in the real world they may change over time.

Limited rationality, agreed-upon changes in the rules, repeated games with adaptation of agents' mentality have introduced new fields of research, still now expanding. Thus, the so-called 'evolutionary turn in game theory' (Sugden 2001) appears to offer a way out of the problem of the multiplicity of equilibriums, through the introduction of processes of dynamic selection. Already, Schelling (1960) introduces the notion of prominence (salience, in subsequent literature) that allows convergence of individual expectations towards specific equilibriums ('focal points'). There is the need in all cases to introduce specific ad hoc assumptions; Binmore (1987) thus maintains the need to refer to empirical theories to understand agents' reasoning. Sugden (2001) remarks that in this sense, the 'evolutionary turn' does not solve the analytical problem of the multiplicity of equilibriums; the conclusion we may reach is that 'historical contingencies are important' (Sugden 2001, p. 124), and that we need 'major changes to the superstructure of the theory' (p. 128).[48]

---

the desired results (i.e. corresponding to what happens in the real world) through an opportune specification of the game.

[48] Sugden (1991) provides a useful discussion of the notion of rationality and the problems that arise from its use in game theory; in this case as well his conclusion is that 'the foundations of rational choice theory . . . are less secure than we thought' (ibid., p. 783).

Apart from this somewhat nihilist conclusion, we may observe that the new fields of research on game theory trespass into research areas discussed in the text that follows: institutionalism for rule changes, evolutionism for agents' adaptation, the philosophical debate on utilitarianism for the agents' motivations and so on.

6.8   Other Micro-applications

Beginning in the 1970s, within the theory of general economic equilibrium, a stream of research developed focused on the specification of circumstances that hinder or render impossible the optimal functioning of the market. Thus, the impossibility of fully specifying all aspects of an agreement gives rise to the so-called principal–agent problem, namely the possibility that the person who accepts a task (the agent) utilizes the margins of freedom of action available to them in their own interest rather than in the interest of the person assigning the task (the principal). A wide literature discusses the problem of designing incentive sets, so as to induce the agent to consider the interests of the principal as their own.[49]

The principal–agent problem is but a species of a wider genus, the search on the effects of imperfections in agents' knowledge. A vast literature – the so-called contract theory – deals with informational asymmetries, namely the different availability of information for different agents. In the field of finance, for instance, informational asymmetries are utilized in justifying the stability of the relations between the bank and the firm obtaining the financing. The different availability of information for the seller and the buyer of a good is at the centre of the lemon market theory proposed by George Akerlof in 1970: a mechanism of adverse selection, in which – with a generalization of Gresham's law – the bad commodity chases the good commodity away from the market.[50]

We may remark that, notwithstanding repeated appeals to general equilibrium methodology, quite often the models utilized in the analysis

---

[49] Among the first works on this issue let us recall Ross (1973); for an illustration of the results reached by this stream of research cf. Mas-Colell *et al.* (1995, pp. 477–510), a work so much 'at the frontier' when it was published as to turn out to be, more than twenty years later, far from antiquated; in general, reference to this text may provide a survey of the state of the art in the field of microeconomics, hence for other aspects briefly hinted at below in this section. Two proponents of this stream of research, Oliver Hart and Bengt Holmstrom, received the Nobel Prize in 2016.

[50] Akerlof's (1970) example is that of a seller of used cars: the buyer cannot evaluate with precision the state of the car offered for sale, and it is likely that if the price requested is the average one for a car of that age, the specific car offered for sale is of a quality inferior to the average. The cases in which this theory is applicable are very numerous: from the selection among requests for credit cards to insurance applications, up to the selection of workers on hire.

of principal–agent, asymmetric or imperfect information problems fall within the field of partial equilibrium analysis. Without simplifications, it is practically impossible to obtain meaningful results. Use of very simplified models for dealing with specific issues, with the introduction of ad hoc assumptions, is in fact the most practised road followed by research over the past thirty years.

These streams of research aim to provide rigorous microfoundations to the treatment of actual issues, originally dealt with in frameworks differing from general equilibrium, with the principal aim to explain the existence of unemployment without having to criticize the basic mechanisms in the traditional marginalist theory of value and distribution.[51] The outcome, however, is quite different: in trying to avoid an empty indefiniteness of results, one is compelled to adopt ad hoc assumptions. The most common conclusions bring us back to partial equilibrium analysis, or to the assumption of a one-commodity world: analytical rigour and/or realism are in any case sacrificed.

Conclusively, the stream of research of general economic equilibrium does not overcome its basic limits: it remains an abstract exercise end in itself. Indeed, recalling this approach is quite often a purely nominal tribute, an argumentative rhetoric to enhance the value of simplified models with a small theoretical content. Thus, both teaching and research in the field of general economic equilibrium theory are losing ground, with a significant fall both in the space allotted to this subject in degree and doctorate courses and in the share of publications in this field of research.

---

[51] This field of research has been named, somewhat misleadingly, new Keynesian economics; indeed, it is but a variant of the neoclassical synthesis illustrated in the Chapter 7, that aims to embody within the marginalist tradition some of Keynes's theses.

7 The Macroeconomics of the Neoclassical Synthesis

7.1 Macroeconomic Theory after Keynes

In the context of the varied debate on the macroeconomic themes of income, employment and money, many economists refer to Keynes's teachings, building upon or rejecting his work. In this respect, we may distinguish three main groups. The first is composed of neoclassical synthesis economists, dominant for more than three decades after the end of the Second World War: they are characterized by the adoption of Keynesian elements – particularly in what concerns policy – within the edifice of the marginalist tradition. The second group consists of monetarists and rational expectation economists, characterized by the more or less radical rejection of Keynesian theory, considered to be in contradiction with the analytical structure of the traditional marginalist theory of value and distribution. They maintain that the market works well both in the long and in the short run. Finally, post-Keynesian economists propose, in antithesis to the other two groups, the distinctive elements of Keynes's original thought, such as uncertainty and the role of effective demand, and maintain that the market incurs crises and periods of stagnation, thus requiring a systematic public intervention for an active management of the economy.

In this chapter, we will focus on the first group, with which macroeconomic theory has been identified for decades. In the next chapter, we shall discuss monetarism and the rational expectations school, the Austrian school and ordoliberalism, which constitute all-out rejection of Keynesian theories and policies. Post-Keynesian macroeconomics will be discussed in Chapter 12. Other aspects usually included in macroeconomic manuals will be discussed elsewhere; for instance, the theory of financial markets will be taken up in Chapter 11.

In the following pages, we will thus consider the development of the neoclassical synthesis, from the IS-LL model (also known as IS-LM model) proposed by Hicks to its development by Modigliani (§7.2). We

146

will then turn to the debate connected to the trade-off between unemployment and inflation (the so-called Phillips curve, §7.3). These theories are often presented as simplified (one-commodity, one representative agent) versions of general economic equilibrium theory; namely, they are connected to the simultaneous determination of equilibrium in various markets (for commodities, labour, financial assets, money). According to marginalist theory, equilibrium implies an equality of supply and demand, hence full utilization of available resources (labour included); hence, a group of theories attribute unemployment to the non-competitive character of the labour market; the bargaining power of trade unions hinders the real wage from falling down to the level corresponding to full employment equilibrium. Another group of theories, discussed in §7.4, interpret Keynes's thought as concerning the presence of obstacles different from the bargaining power of the workers hindering markets from reaching full employment, or as concerning the analysis of disequilibrium situations. We thus have models grounded on a variety of hypotheses on the limits to perfect competition set by informational asymmetries, frictions and rigidities of various kinds. In §7.5 we will then consider the theory of economic growth originated by Solow's model. Finally, in §7.6 we will consider the theory of economic development: an important and very wide field, rich in problems and research streams. In these two sections, we will also consider, for reasons of continuity, some contributions (such as Harrod's model in §7.5, structuralist theories or Kaldor's stylized facts in §7.6) external to the field of the neoclassical synthesis. An appendix provides a synthetic presentation of the main models discussed in the text.

As with the previous chapter, this chapter covers a wide field; we will only scratch the surface of the issues at hand, and point to key stages of the theories' development.

7.2 The Neoclassical Synthesis

Already before the Second World War, confronted with the experience of the Great Depression of the 1930s, many economists were inclined to lend an ear to Keynes's ideas on the opportunity of public investments in support of demand for countering unemployment; at the same time, they did not want to drop the marginalist theory of value and distribution that constituted the pillar of professional economics training. The idea of a public budget balanced on the average of a trade cycle (rather than annually) was already accepted at the time by many US economists; what appeared contradictory to the foundations of the accepted theory was the idea of persistent unemployment. In order to reconcile these two elements Keynes's theory is reinterpreted by its insertion into a marginalist framework; on the other side, ad hoc assumptions, such as the downward rigidity of wages, were introduced in the nucleus of the marginalist theory of value, thus opening the way to the possibility of unemployment in the context of the marginalist theory.

John Hicks (1904–1989, Nobel Prize in 1972) pioneered this approach. In an article dated 1937, Hicks proposes the so-called IS-LL scheme, which translates Keynesian theory into the more traditional terms of a simplified general equilibrium model, with three markets: goods, money and financial assets (in fact, a unique good and a unique financial asset). We may focus attention on the first two markets since, when they reach equilibrium, automatically – given their interrelations – equilibrium is also reached in the third market.

The market for goods is in equilibrium when supply, namely production, is equal to aggregate demand. In the simplified assumption of an economy with no external trade, no public expenditure or taxes, aggregate demand corresponds to demand for consumption and investment; aggregate supply, namely national product, that corresponds to national income, is equal to the sum of consumption and savings (by definition, equal to the part of income that is not consumed). The condition of equilibrium, namely the equality of aggregate supply and demand, is verified when savings, that are an increasing function of income, are equal to investments, considered a decreasing function of the interest rate.

The market for money is in equilibrium when supply and demand for money are equal. According to the assumption of exogenous money, money supply is determined by monetary authorities. These directly control the supply of legal currency and, indirectly, the quantity of money created by the banks (through constraints on banks' activities, for instance, by setting legal reserve coefficients). Demand for money is equal to the sum of two components: transactional demand for money, that is an increasing function of income, and speculative demand for money. Keynes focuses attention on the latter, considering the choice on the form, money or financial assets, in which wealth is held; this is considered a decreasing function of the interest rate. Hicks instead proposes a compromise between Keynes's monetary theory, characterized by the speculative demand for money, and the traditional theory that grounds the determination of the interest rate on demand and supply of loans (loanable funds theory). This is a hybrid compromise, however, which distorts the Keynesian theory focused on financial choices concerning the allocation of the stock of wealth in the short term, influenced in a decisive way more by expectations than by level and changes of the interest rate; moreover, the Hicksian reformulation of the speculative demand for money assimilates the Keynesian notion of liquidity to that of money, losing sight of the qualitative distinction between the transactional demand for money and the demand for liquidity.[1]

Given the supply of money, the system of equations determines the equilibrium level of the rate of interest and of income, hence employment, which in this model (as in Keynes's model) does not necessarily correspond to full employment. In Hicks's model, this is a consequence of the missed explicit consideration of the labour market, where demand and supply of labour are balanced.

Franco Modigliani (1918–2003, Nobel Prize in 1985, emigrated from Italy to the United States – as did various other Italian, Austrian and German economists – to escape racial persecutions) elaborates on Hicks's work. In a 1944 article, taken up and developed in another article in 1963, Modigliani extends the IS-LL scheme explicitly by also considering the labour market.

As for the other markets, in the labour market as well changes in prices tend to ensure equilibrium between supply and demand. In our case, the price that changes is the wage. In a competitive labour market, in the presence of unemployment, the money wage decreases. This sets in motion two different adjustment mechanisms. The first is the one taken into account by traditional marginalist theory: the fall in the money wage corresponds to a fall in the real wage, and this brings the economy back towards full employment. Within the traditional marginalist theory of value, it is assumed that the value of the marginal product of labour is decreasing: firms increase employment up to the point at which such value, namely the proceeds that the firm earns from the employment of an additional worker, reaches the wage level, corresponding to the cost of the additional worker; the downward pressure on the wage ends only when equilibrium between demand and supply of labour is reached, namely at full employment. The second mechanism of automatic adjustment – the so-called 'Pigou effect' included in Modigliani's model – is based on the increase in the real value of monetary balances held by families when the reduction of the money wage induces a reduction in

---

[1] Keynes's reaction to the article by Hicks, overall not a negative one (cf. Keynes 1973, vol. 14, pp. 71–84), is connected to the fact that – like Keynes – Hicks considers savings as explained by income, and stresses the limits of monetary policies (through the notion of the 'liquidity trap'): not necessarily an increase in the supply of money engenders the desired effects on the rate of interest and on investments. However, misunderstandings and shifts, and especially the insertion in a general equilibrium context, are more important and more dangerous that the openings present in Hicks's model, as it becomes apparent with its extension by Modigliani.

prices rather than in the real wage; this implies an increase in the families' wealth in real terms, which in turn induces an increase in consumption, and also in aggregate demand and employment.

To get the Keynesian result, namely the possibility of a state of persistent unemployment, we have to introduce an obstacle to the free functioning of the labour market. Such an obstacle was found by Modigliani in the non-competitive nature of this market, due to the bargaining power of the trade unions determining the downward rigidity of the wage rate.

In this way, the Keynesian theory appears as a particular case of the marginalist theory: that case in which full employment equilibrium cannot be reached, due to the fact that the labour market is not competitive. We thus have the neoclassical synthesis, namely a synthesis between the marginalist theory of value and the Keynesian theory of employment, or better, as already hinted, a particular case of the marginalist theory based on ad hoc assumptions, while the Keynesian theory is modified in essential respects, such as the role of uncertainty and expectations. In the 1950s, this approach took hold in the United States and then in the rest of the world, thanks to Hansen's work (1949, 1953); in the second half of the twentieth century, the neoclassical synthesis dominated macroeconomics teaching in universities all over the world.

The neoclassical synthesis reabsorbs the Keynesian thesis of the possibility of underemployment equilibriums within the traditional marginalist approach. This opens the way to recognizing the usefulness of public intervention in the economy; more precisely, unemployment can be fought by means of expansionary fiscal and monetary policies, in addition to labour market reforms aiming at rendering wages more reactive to unemployment.

Increases or decreases in public expenditure and/or in taxes and changes in the money supply may be utilized, more generally, in order to regulate the pace of the economy, avoiding or reducing cyclical oscillations (with the so-called 'fine tuning' policies).

So-called functional finance, namely the use of monetary and fiscal levers for the control of aggregate demand, was developed only after Keynes's death, in particular by Abba Lerner (1905–82), an enthusiastic Keynesian. Lerner adds other policy tools, in particular ingenious anti-inflationary schemes, to monetary and fiscal policies, following Weintraub's and Wallich's 1971 TIP (*tax-augmented incomes policy*: an incentive-based incomes policy with higher fiscal rates on the increments of money wages; cf. Lerner and Colander 1980).

In Keynes's theory, fiscal policy affects income and employment through the immediate reaction of consumption to the initial increase in income that sets in motion the mechanism of the multiplier. Modigliani (with Brumberg 1954) and Friedman (1957), however, maintain that consumption depends mainly on long-period income and on wealth, while it is relatively insensitive to short-period changes in income, such as those induced by Keynesian fiscal policies. More precisely, Modigliani and Brumberg (1954) propose a life-cycle theory of income, consumption and savings: in the central part of an individual's life, he or she works and earns an income (that may increase with career developments); savings in this stage (possibly forced savings, in the case of compulsory social security contributions) serve to guarantee an unchanged standard of life in old age. According to Friedman (1957), instead, economic agents take their decisions on consumption on the basis of their permanent income, equal to the probabilistic estimate of the incomes that will be obtained over the life course. In both cases, recalling theses originally propounded by Pigou, the influence of wealth on consumption is stressed.[2]

Let us recall, then, the extension of the neoclassical synthesis to the field of monetary theory. In this respect, the key reference is to James Tobin's (1918–2002, Nobel Prize in 1981) contributions. Tobin refers to general equilibrium theory in explaining the demand for money in the framework of a portfolio choice among different assets on the side of a rational agent in the presence of risk. In this case, the money supply may change, at least within certain limits (depending on profitability evaluations on the side of the banks) when the demand for loans changes.[3]

Among Tobin's contributions, well known to the public at large and still the object of heated debate, is the so-called Tobin Tax. Tobin originally proposed the Tobin Tax in 1972, after the fall of the international monetary system based on fixed exchange rates, in the form of a tax on foreign currency financial transactions, with the aim of hindering currency speculation. Variants of the Tobin Tax were subsequently proposed and extended to all forms of financial transactions, more specifically to those concerning derivatives. Also well known in the context of monetary and financial theory is 'Tobin's q', defined as the ratio between the market value of a firm (the valuation of its share capital on the stock

---

[2] These theses result in a blossoming of empirical investigations, in addition to theoretical work. The article by Baranzini (2005) on Modigliani's theory fifty years after its publication offers a wide bibliography.

[3] Cf. Tobin (1958, 1969), and more generally the essays collected in the three volumes of *Essays* (Tobin 1971–85). In passing, let us note that only the assumption of a unique representative agent allows us to utilize a theory referring to the behaviour of the individual financial agent with reference to the economic system as a whole; in referring to the real world we should consider the different types of financial agents. Furthermore, once more, the notion of liquidity is assimilated to that of money, while Keynes distinguishes them.

exchange) and the replacement value of its physical capital assets, introduced by Kaldor ('Kaldor's v', 1966), then taken up by Tobin (1969). According to this theory, the optimal investment strategy for a firm relies on the comparison between the value at which an additional unit of its capital (a share) can be sold and the investment cost necessary for acquiring a new unit of physical capital (a new unit of productive capacity).

The large-scale econometric models to be discussed in §9.5, proposed by Klein and others, are based on the theoretical framework provided by the neoclassical synthesis and reinforce its impact with the contribution they give to policy choices by providing a criterion for quantifying interventions.

Lucas (1976) criticizes these models because their utilization in the evaluation of alternative policy scenarios is based on the unacceptable assumption that their parameters remain unchanged in different scenarios. Lucas's critique reintroduces the need for microeconomic foundations for macroeconomics, an obvious consequence of methodological individualism.

To circumvent this critique and to carry on econometric evaluations of fiscal and monetary policy choices, some central banks, among them the European Central Bank (ECB), make recourse to DSGE (dynamic stochastic general equilibrium) models, which consider economic agents' preferences (as a matter of fact reduced to that of a unique representative agent) and insert them in a dynamic context, as in the overlapping generations models proposed by Samuelson referenced in the text that follows.

These models, however, fare badly in front of the 2007–8 world crisis, when it is possible to verify that results obtained from them depend on unavoidably simplified assumptions: linearity in reaction functions, recourse to aggregate production functions and to 'representative agents', normal probability distributions for events, and hence overall a very restrictive interpretation of the notions of general equilibrium, dynamics and uncertainty. The situation worsens (but the test of confrontation with reality is eliminated from the scene) when from the econometric models, composed of more than a hundred equations, we go on to the theoretical models, in which as a rule the representative agent is unique and the aggregate production function refers to the whole economy: the appellative of DSGE is in this case a fake (the real cycle models discussed in the next chapter are of this kind).

What has been called 'hydraulic Keynesism' (since it is based on the analysis of income and expenditure flows, cf. Coddington 1983), looks for a compatibility between Keynes's theories and his interventionist policy stance on the one side and the traditional marginalist theory of value and distribution relying on the notion of equilibrium between supply and demand on the other. Don Patinkin (1956) follows in the same direction, though with a partially different approach.[4] Instead of focusing attention on macroeconomic flows, he looks for a more direct link with general equilibrium analysis, interpreting Keynes's approach as an analysis of disequilibrium. Thus, for policy choices the problem becomes relevant concerning lags of adjustment to full employment equilibrium, when the system is subject to exogenous shocks.[5]

We may consider a development of the macroeconomic theory of the neoclassical synthesis also a set of models aiming to represent the working of open economies. In the so-called Mundell–Fleming model (Fleming 1962; Mundell 1963) and in subsequent versions and illustrations in macroeconomics manuals, Hicks's IS-LL model is expanded to include equations for imports (connected to income and to competitiveness of national products relative to foreign ones, expressed by the exchange rate and by the level of internal prices, while the level of foreign prices is assumed as given), for exports (which depend on world income, considered as given, and on competitiveness), for capital flows (connected to the difference between internal and external interest rates, given the exchange rate; as a development, expectations of movements of the exchange rate may also be considered) and, finally, for the condition of equilibrium of the balance of payments. The model is then utilized for analysis of the effects of fiscal and monetary policies; the

---

[4] Don Patinkin (1922–95), graduate of the University of Chicago, was a professor at the Hebrew University in Jerusalem. Patinkin (1974) goes back to the interpretation of Keynes's theory as disequilibrium analysis dealing with the 'liquidity trap', namely the existence of a limit below which monetary policy cannot bring the interest rate, in which case the weight of stabilization policies for income and employment falls entirely on fiscal policy.

[5] Hahn (1965) criticizes Patinkin's approach, stressing that the introduction of monetary balances in the utility function does not solve the problem: the equilibrium may not exist, or may correspond to a situation in which the price of money is nil. In other terms, it is not possible to have money playing a role in general economic equilibrium models. Patinkin's model has a central role in Roy Weintraub's (1977) reconstruction of researches on microeconomic foundations of macroeconomics. Though recalling Hahn's criticism, Weintraub (1977, p. 4) considers the problem of stability as solved while – following Samuelson – considering it as decisive, as logically prior to comparative static analyses. (In considering decisive the stability issue, Samuelson is preceded by his master, Schumpeter, and as a matter of fact, explicitly or implicitly, by all the founding fathers of the marginalist approach, in particular by Walras.) However, it is precisely in those years that Mantel and others clarify in a definitive way the impossibility of demonstrating the stability of general economic equilibrium models in the absence of additional assumptions that limit the field of application of the analysis (cf. §6.3). Weintraub (1977, p. 18) too, anyhow, concludes that 'Keynesian macroeconomics cannot be derived from any simple Walrasian microsystem'.

literature on this issue, that considers a number of variants of the basic model (distinguishing for instance between fixed and variable exchange rates) is very wide.[6]

The monetarist reaction to the neoclassical synthesis will be illustrated in the next chapter. It grows in importance at the beginning of the 1970s, with the inflationary pressure accompanying the 1974–5 and 1979–80 oil crises; behind the theoretical differences, which exist but which Friedman himself (1971) considers unimportant, the real clash concerns policy.[7] While 'Keynesians' are favourable to active monetary and fiscal policies for countering unemployment, monetarists criticize public intervention as useless, nay damaging, insomuch as it is a source of inflation.

It is interesting to note that in this attempt at a compromise between two radically different approaches – the Keynesian or the marginalist one – the neoclassical synthesis is doomed to lose: confronted with the fundamentalists of the marginalist approach and to their appeals to methodological individualism and the logic of market equilibrating mechanisms based on supply and demand, the appeals to market imperfections are doomed to appear as ad hoc justifications in support of interventionist policies trying to regulate the path of the economy that contradict the very nature of the market economy. As we shall see in the next chapter, this is the line followed by monetarists, rational expectations theoreticians, new classicals, and new Austrian economists. The outcome of the attempt at a compromise, at the end, is that of obscuring the basic defects of the marginalist approach: the unsolved problems of its theory of value and distribution (cf. §12.4), its unrealism connected to the missed recognition of Keynesian uncertainty and of its

---

[6] Robert Mundell (b. 1932, Nobel Prize in 1999) is also known for his analysis of optimal monetary areas (Mundell 1961), to be utilized later in support of the naissance of the euro but also, more recently, in criticizing its rules.

[7] Modigliani (1977), in his presidential address at the American Economic Association, agrees with Friedman both on the analytical affinities between monetarists and neoclassical synthesis Keynesians and on the opposition on policy, and defends in particular the positive role of discretionary stabilization policies. In fact, part of the debate focuses on a different evaluation of the reaction coefficients of investments and demand for money to variations of interest rates: the neoclassical synthesis Keynesians consider feeble the first ones and high the second ones, while monetarists would hold the opposite view. (Modigliani takes on an intermediate position, attributing relevance to monetary policy but considering it practically irrelevant in the case of the 'liquidity trap', when entrepreneurial expectations are so pessimistic as not to invest even in the presence of abundant liquidity and low interest rates.) Another empirical debate concerns the factual validity of the 'Ricardian theorem of debt equivalence' (Barro 1974), according to which public expenditure financed through debt does not induce an increase in private demand, due to the need to set aside resources with which to pay the expected increase in taxes that the state will have to introduce in the future in order to reimburse the debt.

fundamental role for an understanding of the functioning of financial markets.[8]

The lasting dominance of the neoclassical synthesis in the macroeconomic debate and in particular in university textbooks, like the dominance of the neo-liberal approach in subsequent decades, cannot be explained by their analytical robustness; the theoretical debate does not take place in a perfect void, but – as we shall see in Chapter 8 – is sensitive to ideologies and to political, financial and economic powers.

7.3   The Phillips Curve

Direct policy intervention aimed at reducing unemployment may favour an increase in money wages, in turn engendering inflation. This effect may be explained in terms of the relative bargaining power of workers and employers, as Marx suggests, or in terms of the traditional demand-and-supply mechanism in the labour market. More precisely, assuming a labour market in equilibrium when money wages do not vary (a point christened by Friedman (1968) 'natural rate of unemployment', that may be greater than zero in the presence of market frictions and rigidities), it appears reasonable to assume that a positive shift from the equilibrium point (a reduction in the unemployment rate) generates an increase in money wages: the speedier the shift, the greater it will be, and vice versa in the case of a negative shift.

The trade-off between unemployment and rate of growth of money wages is empirically noted in a widely cited 1958 article by the New Zealand economist A. W. Phillips (1914–75), whose research looks at the path of English money wages from 1861 to 1957. The decreasing curve representing such an inverse relationship (the so-called Phillips curve) constitutes, for the neoclassical synthesis economists, the set of possible policy choices: fiscal or monetary policy interventions may reduce unemployment but at the cost of simultaneously inducing an increase in money wages and hence in prices.

---

[8] The failure of the neoclassical synthesis, which in order to save Keynes's policy message deprives it of its theoretical foundations and its basic vision, has an important though relatively little known antecedent: Dugald Stewart's attempt, as Adam Smith's biographer, to rescue the Scottish philosopher from the discredit into which he risked falling in front of the conservative reaction to the excesses of the French Revolution. To this purpose Stewart separates two intrinsically connected aspects of Smith's thought, his liberal-progressive view of man and society on the one hand, and the free trade theses derived from this view on the other hand. Stewart is thus able to stress these latter ones, opportunely hiding under the carpet Smith's politically progressive theses, apparent in his support both for the French Revolution and for the independence struggles of the English colonies in North America. Cf. Roncaglia (2005a), pp. 149–54.

Phillips's article thus opens a series of debates. First, in the field of policy, the Phillips curve allows locating an important limit to Keynesian expansionary policies, since they generate inflation.[9] Given the importance of this fact, Phillips's article is followed by many empirical studies dedicated to different periods and different countries.[10] Some studies consider the path of prices instead of, or in addition to, that of money wages. After the 1973–4 oil crisis, there was an evident reduction of the significance of Phillips's curve estimates, due to the inflationary explosion induced by the sudden increase of oil prices.

Second, following a trend already present in the original Phillips article, the shift of the curve when considering the years of growth and those of decrease of unemployment separately is taken into account (Lipsey 1960): wage changes are quicker in the second case, compared to the first case.

Third, the original Phillips curve focuses attention on the relation between unemployment and the growth rate of money wages, thus ignoring the effect of wages on prices and consequently that of prices on wages. The validity of the Phillips curve is thus initially limited to the short term (Phelps 1967; Friedman 1968), and then ultimately denied for the short term as well (by the rational expectations school: Lucas 1972, 1976).[11]

Finally, the so-called NAIRU (non-accelerating inflation rate of unemployment) models oppose a curve representing wage demands as a function of the rate of unemployment to a curve (in the simplest case, a straight line parallel to the abscissa) representing the mark-up of prices over costs desired by firms, namely the margin (generally considered constant) that firms desire to add to costs in setting prices. There are

---

[9] This aspect is stressed by Samuelson and Solow (1960), the first ones to christen 'Phillips curve' the inverse relation between unemployment and rate of growth of wages (or of prices) at the centre of the debate.

[10] Let us recall here two studies (Sylos Labini 1972; Modigliani and Tarantelli 1976) concerning Italy: after the 'hot Autumn' of 1968, these propose, with good results, to integrate the simple mechanism of the Phillips curve (interpreted by Sylos Labini not as a neoclassical relationship between demand and supply in the labour market, but in the Smithian–Marxian sense of changes in the bargaining power of trade unions and employers), with indicators of the strength and intensity of trade unions aggressiveness expressed by hours of strike or by the share of workers renewing the wage contract in anticipation of the renewal date.

[11] Edmund Phelps, b. 1933, Nobel Prize in 2006 for his contributions to the microeconomic foundations of macroeconomics, provides important contributions on different aspects of macroeconomics, among other things considering search models in markets with imperfect information (Phelps et al. 1970), and utilizes the notion of hysteresis (the influence of past values of a variable on its current value) in order to explain how a short run increase in unemployment may induce an increase in the equilibrium rate of unemployment. In a 1990 essay he surveys the main macroeconomic research streams (but ignoring the post-Keynesians) stressing the originality of his 'structuralist' approach.

many variants of this basic model; correspondingly, it receives various interpretations, implying its insertion in the monetarist framework (substantially identifying NAIRU with the natural rate of unemployment), in the new-Keynesian one (that in its policy implications turns out to converge with the marginalist approach: not surprisingly, given its basic affinity in what concerns the competitive long-run equilibrium), or in the post-Keynesian one (as an explanation of inflation related to distributive conflicts).[12]

7.4 Marshallian Varieties of the Neoclassical Synthesis

Let us briefly recall here the three lines of research we may consider as variants of the neoclassical synthesis. The first one was originated by Robert Clower (1926–2011) and by Axel Leijonhufvud (b. 1933), who interpret Keynes's as a disequilibrium theory, as Patinkin had already done. They differentiate from the latter in that they maintain that the microfoundations of macroeconomics are to be found not in the Walrasian but rather in the Marshallian line of research, by considering the issues of information diffusion and of intertemporal coordination of real economies. In particular, Clower and Leijonhufvud stress that Keynes avoids the Walrasian auctioneer mechanism, hence the assumption of absence of exchange before equilibrium is reached.

Economic agents are price makers and not price takers (it is they, and not the market, that set prices). In this situation, in the presence of disequilibrium between supply and demand, exchanges are limited to the 'short side', namely to the lesser of the two magnitudes. In the Keynesian setting, when effective demand is inferior to potential supply, producer-sellers do not succeed in selling the whole of their product in the market. This provokes a fall in their income, hence a reduced demand on their side as well. Out of equilibrium, the quantities adjust (downward) quicker than prices.[13]

---

[12] For a presentation of macroeconomics assigning a central role to NAIRU, cf. Carlin and Soskice (1990); for a post-Keynesian/Marxist interpretation, cf. Rowthorn (1977); for a survey of the debate on NAIRU, Stockhammer (2008); for a recent survey also covering the debate on rational expectations and NAIRU, but overlooking heterodox streams, cf. Gordon (2011).

[13] Cf. Clower (1965); Leijonhufvud (1968). Subsequently, the models by Barro and Grossman (1971) and Malinvaud (1977) recast this line of research in terms of Walrasian schemes in which money prices and wages are fixed and exchanges may take place at non-equilibrium prices. The result is the possibility of a 'rationing' of demand or of supply, hence a 'classical' (as a matter of fact, neoclassical) unemployment caused by the downward rigidity of wages or a Keynesian unemployment induced by insufficient effective demand.

A second line of research is that of the so-called overlapping generations models, originated by Samuelson (1958a).[14] In these models, in
which it is common to consider a single commodity and a single representative agent, each generation lives for two periods; the younger generation, in the first period of life, produces and saves so as to be able to
consume in the second period (retirement) as well. In each moment, there
is a young and an old generation in the economy. The share of savings on
income depends on the rate of population growth and on the ratio
between the consumption desired for the first and the second period of
life. The rate of interest, which constitutes a prize for saving, brings in
equilibrium demand for and supply of savings, guaranteeing the continuous equilibrium of the system.

The third line of research is the so-called 'new Keynesian economics',
whose main exponent is Joseph Stiglitz (b. 1943, Nobel Prize in 2001).
Proponents of new Keynesian macroeconomics try to locate in different
kinds of 'market failures' the origins of unemployment; in other terms,
they try to provide microeconomic reasons for the rigidities that at
a macro level cause unemployment.[15]

A first group of contributions (Fischer 1977; Phelps and Taylor 1977;
Taylor 1980) assume rigidity of money wages, explained by recourse to
long-term wage contracts.[16] As it is obvious, the downward rigidity of the
wage halts the traditional marginalist mechanism of adjustment to full
employment equilibrium based on the fall of wages in the presence of
unemployment. Yet, Keynes (1936, chapter 19) explicitly excludes this
justification from his analysis, though – incredibly – it has been attributed
to him more than once.

The models based on efficiency wages explain why employers offer
wages higher than the equilibrium ones, by recalling their desire to retain
the most efficient workers or (the so-called shirking model) to ensure the
loyalty of their employees, difficult to control in all the aspects of their
activity (cf. for instance Shapiro and Stiglitz 1984).

---

[14] Malinvaud (1987) stresses that in fact the first to propose an overlapping generations
model is Maurice Allais (1947, Appendix 2, pp. 640–755). Since Allais was certainly not
unknown at the time (cf. §10.2, for his part in the debate on rationality and expected
utility), the story is a clear example of the importance of language barriers in the history of
economic thought.

[15] Cf. the essays collected in Stiglitz (2002), in which Stiglitz considers various kinds of
rigidities: imperfect information, price rigidity, non-competitive markets.

[16] Phelps and Taylor also assume a certain measure of price rigidity, parallel to that of
wages: both variables are set a period in advance. The papers quoted utilize models with
rational expectations; the first two articles focus attention on the existence, this notwithstanding, of real effects of monetary policies.

We then have the insider–outsider models (cf. for instance Lindbeck and Snower 1988), in which workers in employment have a margin of market power that they utilize for obtaining higher wages, at the detriment of higher unemployment levels: thus, this is a variant of the Modigliani model in which unemployment stems from a too high level of wages and their downward rigidity.

The so-called search models (see for instance Pissarides 1985) utilize the complexity of the employment search on the side of workers, and workers' search on the side of firms, in explaining the oscillations of the unemployment rate around its 'normal' level.[17]

Another group of contributions concerns price rigidities. We thus have models based on menu costs (cf. for instance Mankiw 1985), namely the costs of price adjustment on the side of firms, due to which the adjustment to demand takes place through changes in production and hence employment levels (thus assuming, without providing a rationale for this, that it is simpler for firms to modify the produced quantities rather than to modify the prices).

Finally, Akerlof (2007) refers to exogenously given behavioural norms, different from utility maximization, in explaining both the downward rigidity of nominal wages and other characteristics of Keynesian macro-economics, rejected in the debate following the rise of the neoclassical synthesis: dependence of consumption on current income (rejected by the theories of the life cycle or of permanent income: cf. §8.5), relevance of profits realized by the firms for investment decisions (denied by the Modigliani–Miller theorem: cf. §11.4), dependence of inflation on unemployment (denied for the long run with the notion of the natural rate of unemployment, and for the short period as well with the rational expectations theory), efficacy of monetary and fiscal policies (denied with the rational expectations and intertemporal inconsistency theories: cf. §8.6).

The success of this line of research is quite difficult to understand: with the aim of reproducing the results of Keynesian analysis concerning the possibility of persistent involuntary unemployment inside the marginalist tradition, ad hoc assumptions, often of doubtful plausibility, are inserted in the insecure theoretical foundations of models with a single representative agent and a single commodity, with a compromise that does not save either analytical consistency or realism.

7.5   Growth Theory

The history of modern growth theory begins shortly after publication of Keynes's *General theory*, with a celebrated article by Roy Harrod

---

[17] Christopher Pissarides, b. 1948, receives the Nobel Prize in 2010.

(1900–1978) published in 1939. Harrod utilizes the Keynesian approach to define an equilibrium rate of growth, the 'warranted rate of growth' that corresponds to equality between the growth rate of productive capacity and the growth rate of aggregate demand, thus characterizing an equilibrium path between demand and supply.[18]

Harrod's model, illustrated in the appendix to this chapter, is quite simple, as it is based on three equations: the first defines savings as a function of income; the second takes on the so-called accelerator theory (Aftalion 1913), determining investments on the basis of the increase in income and the capital/output ratio; the third reproduces the Keynesian condition of equilibrium, namely the equality between savings and investment. By substituting within the third equation the expressions for savings and investment given by the first two equations, we obtain the warranted rate of growth of income, equal to the ratio between propensity to save and the capital/income ratio.[19]

An analogous model, but with a somewhat different interpretation, was proposed in 1946 by the US economist (of Russian-Polish origins) Evsey Domar (1914–98). Domar focuses attention on the twin role of investments, simultaneously a source of growth of productive capacity and a stimulus to aggregate demand. His aim is to determine a growth rate for investments ensuring the balancing between these two roles. The result, though based on different analysis, is analogous to Harrod's.

Notwithstanding formal similarity between the Harrod–Domar model, the ensuing debate originated from a problem raised by Harrod in the final part of his article. This is the so-called knife-edge problem, concerning the instability of the actual growth rate as soon as it is different from the warranted rate. Harrod recalls that if actual growth, determined by aggregate demand, is higher than the warranted one, productive capacity needs to recover some lost ground; this implies an increase in investment, hence in aggregate demand, in the subsequent period, which provokes a further increase in the rate of growth. Alternatively, if actual growth is inferior to that corresponding to the warranted rate, investments will be reduced and the consequent decrease in aggregate demand will provoke a further decrease in growth.

---

[18] Thirlwall (2018, p. 28) remarks that the notions of natural and warranted rates of growth are already implicit in Keynes's *Galton lecture* at the Eugenics Society (Keynes 1937).

[19] An interesting debate concerns the interpretation of this rate of growth. Kregel (1980, pp. 104–5) stresses that it may be considered as 'a purely "notional" or reference concept' or as 'actually prevailing equilibrium', and that in Harrod's writings both notions appear, while only the first one should be used in post-Keynesian theory. Asimakopulos (1986, 1991, pp. 151–65) supports the second notion, both as an interpretation of Harrod and as the foundation for building a theory of the trade cycle.

This instability may give rise to cyclical oscillations of the economy, if coupled with a system of 'roofs' and 'pavements'. The 'roof' is provided by full employment; the absence of a 'pavement' endowed with sufficiently valid justifications re-proposes the Keynesian theme of the possibility of persistent unemployment. A continuous increase in unemployment can then take place when the actual rate of growth corresponds to the warranted one, but the latter is less than the 'natural' rate of growth, equal to the rate of growth of productivity plus the rate of growth of population.

There is wide debate on the possibility of persisting differences between natural and warranted growth rates and the existence of equilibrating mechanisms. In this vein, an important survey article by Hahn and Matthews (1964) suggests that we may reduce the multiplicity of contributions to three approaches. First, we have the classical (more precisely, Malthusian) approach, according to which adjustment takes place through the rate of growth of population, which decreases when the increase in unemployment induces a reduction in the wage rate. We then have Kaldor's (1956) approach, based on an adjustment in the propensity to save, induced by a change in the distribution of income: when unemployment increases, the wage rate falls and, since the workers' propensity to save is inferior to that of the capitalists, the average propensity to save increases, which corresponds to an increase in the warranted rate of growth. Finally we have the neoclassical approach (Solow 1956), based on an adjustment in the capital/income ratio: the decrease in the wage brought forth by the increase in unemployment induces firms to adopt techniques with a higher labour intensity, since labour is the factor of production the price of which is decreased; thus the capital-income ratio falls; once again, this corresponds to an increase in the warranted rate of growth.[20]

However, these equilibrating mechanisms are not without their defects. For instance, it is doubtful that in today's conditions, population growth should depend on the level of wages, according to an inverse relation, as required by the classical approach.[21] Kaldor's theory requires the increase in unemployment to induce a change in distribution in favour of profits, while in crisis or depression these latter may

---

[20] There is then the possibility of considering the natural rate as endogenous, namely dependent on the actual growth rate, through the presence of increasing static and dynamic returns of various kinds; in this case the appellative 'natural' appears inappropriate. Cf. Thirlwall and Leon-Ledesma (2000).

[21] A Malthusian mechanism may be re-proposed by considering migration as a function of wage differentials among countries, thus for each country with a migratory balance increasing with the wage rate.

decrease more than wages. Finally, Sraffa's (1960) critique and the ensuing debate (cf. §12.4) show that the capital-income ratio is not necessarily an increasing function of the wage. We thus come back to Harrod's original, typically Keynesian thesis: growth in a capitalist economy is intrinsically unstable.

The neoclassical theory of growth hinted at earlier was originally proposed in an article by Solow (1956) and simultaneously in a paper by Australian Trevor Swan (1918–89; cf. Swan 1956). This approach consists of adding a neoclassical aggregate production function to Harrod's model, in which the level of income is a function of the quantities of capital and labour employed in the production process. Following the neoclassical tradition, this function relies on the following constraints: income grows (continuously) when the quantities employed of labour and/or capital increase, but with decreasing increments (first derivative positive, second derivative negative, with respect to each of the two factors of production, in conformity to the assumption of decreasing marginal productivities). The growth of capital is determined by investments, the growth of labour by the (exogenous) growth of population. Savings and investments are equal, and remain equal over time. Supply of labour also grows at the same pace as the demand for labour. In this case, however, the causal link between savings and investments turns out to be the opposite of that in Keynesian theory, since it is investments that depend on savings, which in turn depend on income, according to a marginal propensity to save that remains constant over time. The real wage is equal to the marginal productivity of labour, and the rate of interest is equal to the marginal productivity of capital. In this way, the assumption of competitive markets ensures full employment equilibrium (demand for and supply of labour grow in equilibrium); this means that – as suggested earlier – the warranted rate of growth is equal to the natural rate. Furthermore, it is assumed that there are no increasing or decreasing returns, so that the product may be allocated without residuals to the two social classes, capitalists and workers.[22] Technical progress may be easily introduced as exogenous (namely not embodied in new machinery or in increased workers' experience).[23]

---

[22] It is the logical necessity of exhausting the product in the distribution between wages and profits that imposes the wholly unrealistic assumption of constant returns; this need is already stressed by Flux (1894); cf. also Stigler (1941).

[23] Cf. Solow (1957). Solow's 1956 model is synthesized in the appendix to this chapter. At MIT abundant theoretical work accompanies and follows Solow's article: cf. Boianovsky and Hoover (2014).

Notwithstanding its shaky foundations, concerning reliance on the neoclassical production function, Solow's theory stimulates various lines of research.[24]

First, Solow's original model, based on an aggregate production function in which the capital/labour ratio is a continuous and increasing function of the wage, is expanded to consider different aspects, such as the introduction of taxes, the presence of two or more sectors or an economy open to exchange with the rest of the world, without changes in the original approach.

Second, a rich and varied stream of empirical research aimed to determine the relative contributions of capital, labour and technical progress to the economic growth of different countries; the best known among these efforts is the research by Denison (1967). The contribution of technical progress is not determined directly, but residually, identifying it with that part of the increase in income that is not explained by the increase in the factors of production. Thus, some prefer to call this a 'residuum' (which may derive for instance from an improvement in 'human capital' due to investments in education and professional training) rather than technical progress; neoclassical tradition speaks in this context of 'total factor productivity'.[25]

To identify technical progress with the 'residuum', namely the part of the increase in income not justified by the increase in the quantities of capital and labour utilized in production, means rejecting what in empirical analyses appears as the most relevant part of economic growth. Some attempts at reducing the dimensions of the 'residuum' consist in considering the accumulation of 'human capital' together with that of physical capital, as in Lucas's 1988 model. A new stream of research (the so-called 'new theories of growth') was developed by Romer (1986), who extends Solow's basic model by considering technical progress as endogenous, namely connected to income growth, through introduction of increasing returns to scale or of learning by doing mechanisms that allow for a 'reinforcement' of human capital for given physical inputs of labour.[26] Other models, such as the 'neo-Schumpeterian' model by Aghion and

---

[24] Cf. Solow (2000) for a survey, and Pasinetti (2000) for a critique. Robert Solow (b. 1924) received the Nobel Prize, in 1987, precisely for his contribution to growth theory. On that occasion, Solow (1988, p. 311) indicated with clarity the objectives of his contribution: 'Growth theory was invented to provide a systematic way to talk about and to compare equilibrium paths for the economy.'

[25] Denison (1967) shows among other things that 'Solow's residuum', namely that part of the growth of income not explained by the quantitative increase of the factors of production capital and labour and commonly but simplistically identified with technical progress, is in a not small part explained by labour moving from one productive sector to another.

[26] Learning by doing phenomena manifest themselves when unit production costs decrease as experience is acquired, namely in proportion to the cumulated quantity of product. The object of an article by Arrow (1962, in which, to be precise, increasing returns are generated not by cumulated income but by cumulative investments), though playing an analogous role

Howitt (1992, 1998), introduce an intermediate commodity produced under monopoly conditions (so as to keep into account the property rights on inventions, as reified in patents) that embody a new technology, in the attempt to consider embodied technical progress.

This stream of research meets with an enormous fortune, notwithstanding its shaky foundations, which goes beyond the use of aggregate production functions and the assumption of a unique representative agent: as is known, increasing returns are incompatible with a competitive equilibrium of individual productive units, except in the case of economies of scale external to individual firms but internal to the industry (namely to the economy as a whole, in the one-commodity world formalized in endogenous growth models; see also Sraffa, 1925, 1926).

Pasinetti (1981) developed a disaggregated model of growth that is more faithful to the Keynesian approach of Harrod's model and theoretically more robust, not being limited to the case of a one-commodity world (or even worse, to a one-firm, one representative agent world). Leaving aside the normative interpretations proposed by Pasinetti himself, the model shows that only by fluke actual employment growth may correspond to that of labour supply, exogenously determined by demographic factors; moreover, a technical change different from one sector to another implies a continuous change in relative prices as unavoidable part of a capitalist development process. Thirwall (1979) proposes another post-Keynesian growth model, which considers growth as constrained by equilibrium in the balance of payments. We will return to these models in Chapter 12.

7.6   Theories of Economic Development

Within the traditional marginalist approach, hence of growth models à la Solow, it is evident that economic growth stems from the increase in the endowments of the productive factors, capital and labour, or from technical progress increasing their productivity. As we saw in the preceding section, this basis may be enriched by looking within these three elements. Thus, as far as labour is concerned, alongside quantitative growth, there is an 'empowerment' of labour abilities through education, namely through investment in human capital; as far as capital is concerned, we may take into account the subsequent generations of machinery embodying better technology (the so-called vintage capital models); as for technical

in the context of our present discussion, they should not be confused with the link between rate of growth of product and rate of growth of labour productivity (a dynamic form of increasing returns to scale, commonly explained by the fact that the new productive capacity embodies the latest technological innovations) christened 'Verdoorn's law' (cf. Verdoorn 1949) and utilized in Kaldor's (1957, 1961) growth models.

progress, stemming from investment in research and development, we may consider various forms of increasing returns to scale.

What does not change, within the marginalist framework, is the idea that growth can only stem from the supply side, as the equilibrating power of the market ensures the continuous balancing of demand to the level of supply corresponding to full utilization of the factors of production. This is the main point of distinction between marginalist and non-marginalist theories of economic growth.

A case in which the importance of market equilibrating mechanisms is evident is the mainstream explanation of the differences in levels of development among various countries (pointing to a different endowment of factors of production and/or to use of inferior technologies), together with the thesis of an unavoidable disappearance of such disequilibria. Indeed, in a competitive world market, the diffusion of the best technologies is automatically ensured (among others, by the multinational firms, that is, by foreign direct investments of firms from more advanced countries into countries with inferior technologies); moreover, international commercial flows exploit the comparative advantages of different countries due to greater or lesser endowments of the factors of production, while differentials in their prices connected to their relative scarcities induce migratory flows ensuring their most efficient distribution. Hence, this results in a set of policy recipes aiming at favouring the development of underdeveloped countries through an increased fluidity of international markets both of commodities and of factors of production.

This policy orientation has been prominent only since the 1970s. In the period following the Second World War, Marshall Plan aid in Europe constituted financial support to countries in ruins after the war, and also offered a Keynesian-type support to demand; in this second direction, there was also support for US spending on the war in Korea. The Cold War also contributed to Western powers' inclination towards the development of market economies worldwide, with selective policies of financial aid. In the first decades after the end of the Second World War, there was a formation of a progressive assertion of an economic theory of development based on public intervention, stemming from more developed countries, *in primis* the United States, as well as on the side of international institutions: United Nations, International Monetary Fund, World Bank and its affiliate for aid to development, the International Development Association (IDA).

Aid to developing countries is often considered as a moral obligation following colonial exploitation that gradually drew to a close in the first decades after the end of the Second World War. The remnants of the colonial system and the persistent power differential – military, economic, technological – led a number of economists, especially in developing countries, to speak of 'neo-colonialism' (Fanon 1961). This is a wide litera-ture (especially in France, where the Algerian issue gives rise to harsh political clashes), mostly poor in technical-analytical content, but often rich in ideas and in applied analyses connecting economic, political and social themes.

Dependency theorists (cf. for instance Furtado [1964] and Amin [1974]) consider the centre-periphery relationship in the world economy (between developed and developing countries) in terms of an unequal development within which the second group of countries is addressed to produce raw materials with low added value.

In the literature 'on the side of developing countries' we find also high-level scientific analyses, which give rise to important research streams. Let us recall here Prebish's and Singer's theses on the tendency towards a worsening of the exchange ratio between raw materials, mainly exported by developing countries, and industrial products, exported by developed countries.[27] Apart from simply pointing out the power gap, this tendency is explained with the different market forms prevailing in the primary and in manufacturing sectors: competition in the first case, oligopoly in the second, thus with a different mechanism of price formation in the two markets. Prebish's and Singer's thesis is presented as an essentially empirical idea, in the framework of a more general, 'structuralist' inter-pretation of the development issue in Third World countries and in particular in Latin America, which gives rise to a wide debate.[28]

Prebish, through the centres he organized and directed within the United Nations (first CEPAL or ECLAC, Economic Commission for Latin America and the Caribbean, then UNCTAD, United Nations Conference on Trade and Development), also supported a policy for 'late-comer' countries based on import substitution, hence on bilateral or multilateral agreements guaranteeing equilibrium between imports and exports and favouring industrialization in backward countries or, in the absence of such agreements, on the imposition of constraints on international trade unilaterally adopted by developing countries (the so-called import substitution policies). Two pillars of the NIEO (new inter-national economic order), central in the debates in the 1960s and 1970s, are the quest for policies of control over the activities of multinational (or transnational) firms and the attempt on the side of a UN commission, the

---

[27] Cf. Prebish (1950) and Singer (1950) and, for a presentation of the debate of the period in the wider framework of the history of the theories of economic development, Furtado (1970).

[28] This is a decades-long debate; cf. for instance Grilli and Yang (1988); for an illustration of the debate on this issue and more generally on modern theories of development cf. Grilli (2005).

UNCTC (United Nations Center on Transnational Corporations) to formulate a code of rules for these firms. These policies, however, were discarded in the 1980s and 1990s in front of the neo-liberal reaction of the leading classes of developed countries, discussed in the next chapter.[29]

Recently, there has been a return of attention to the debate on multi-nationals, on a number of issues: their success in drastically reducing their tax charges, with sporadic attempts at closing some roads of fiscal elusion; the growing importance of delocalization of productive phases leading to the so-called global value chains, which imply a growing interrelation between the productive systems of the various countries; and the related attempts at revising the statistics on international trade in terms of value added (hinted at in §9.2). The lobbying power of big transnational corporations, considered an irrelevant element in anti-trust proceedings, remains largely ignored by economists.

Theories of economic dualism concern not only the opposition between developed and Third World countries, but also between more and less developed areas within various countries.

Among the analyses of economic dualism, let us recall the model of dualistic development proposed by Lewis (1954). This is a classical-type model: paralleling the first stage of the process of industrialization of today's developed countries, in underdeveloped countries the constraints to growth stem from the pace of capital accumulation in the modern sector of the economy. At the same time, the availability of labour may be considered unlimited, owing to the wide areas of hidden unemployment in the 'primitive' sectors of agriculture and traditional handicraft.

This debate plays an important role in Italy, with its dualism between North and South. On the neoclassical side (cf. for instance Lutz 1958) it is maintained that re-equilibrium may come about through automatic market adjustment mechanisms, in particular from a greater flexibility of the labour market, with a differentiation of the wage rate between the two areas that should compensate the profitability gap, and favour labour migration and a growth of investments in areas that are lagging. On the Keynesian side (Spaventa 1959), it is maintained that dualism is a structural problem, to be studied in its dynamics while considering the market forms prevailing in the two sectors; in the absence of active policies of support for demand and industrialization, lagging-behind areas would be simply losing population without any re-equilibrium.

Among the research on economic development, a series of empirically oriented analyses, supported by theoretical motivations, leads to some generalizations ('laws', or 'stylized facts' in Kaldor's terminology, that

---

[29] On this story cf. Bair (2009).

seems to take up Weber's methodology of 'ideal types'). These are more or less systematic and persistent regularities, that once located, may receive a theoretical explanation but are not deduced from a general model of the working of an economic system; rather, they may be utilized as assumptions in the construction of 'realistic' models.[30]

Among the best established, let us recall 'Engel's law' (from Ernst Engel, 1821–96, director of the Prussian statistical institute) according to which the share of alimentary consumption in the total family expenditure decreases when income grows. 'Wagner's law' (from Adolph Wagner, 1835–1917, professor at Berlin University for decades) refers to the continuous growth in the share of the public sector and in the role of the state in the economy. In the same direction, but extended to all services, private and public, goes 'Baumol's law' (Baumol and Bowen 1966) according to which the sectors characterized by low productivity growth register an increase in their relative prices and in their share of employment.[31]

In the period after the Second World War, and before 'Baumol's law', let us recall 'Kuznets' law':[32] In the course of the process of development, inequalities in income distribution increase in the first stage – the stage of industrialization, which requires capital accumulation, hence a high share of savings on income, favoured by the concentration of national income in a few hands – and then a decrease in a subsequent stage, when the growth of industrial employment re-equilibrates bargaining power between workers and employers.[33]

Another interpretation of the path of market economies, connecting statistical analysis with analysis of cultural and institutional evolution, is that by Walt Rostow (1916–2003), who distinguishes four stages common to the path eventually followed by all countries: preconditions for take-off, take-off, transition to maturity and mass consumption stage (Rostow 1960). Opposing Marx's historical materialism, which focuses attention on economic structure, Rostow proposes an integrated theory of

---

[30] On 'economic laws' and their meaning cf. the fascinating lectures by Kindleberger (1989).

[31] However, the IT revolution modifies the situation in many branches of services (even if not in theatre representation and in music plays, taken as examples by Baumol: a Mozart's quartet requires today the same number of players and about the same time of play as when it was composed).

[32] Simon Kuznets (1901–85, born in Russia and emigrated to the United States in 1922, Nobel Prize in 1971) focuses his research on the collection and use of statistical data for theoretically interpreting long-run economic evolution. For a synthetic illustration of his method and his results, cf. Kuznets (1965); for his 'law', cf. Kuznets (1955).

[33] Among the many studies on the topic, the most interesting ones are those pointing to the reasons why individual countries shift away from Kuznets's curve: active fiscal redistributive policies (in particular concerning inheritance) and, most important, diffusion of free public education. Cf. Boggio and Seravalli (2003), pp. 29 ff.

development, within which economic, political, social and cultural changes interact.

Other regularities are connected to the presence of increasing static and dynamic returns to scale. As mentioned earlier, the so-called 'Verdoorn's law' (1949) concerns the link between rate of growth of income and rate of growth of productivity (technical progress); it thus constitutes a dynamic variety of increasing returns to scale. Arrow's 1962 'learning by doing' concerns the reduction in unit production costs that takes place while experience is acquired, and is thus proportional to cumulated gross investments.

Trying to give a systemic form to these regularities, Kaldor (1961) points to six 'stylized facts', namely empirical regularities valid not in the short but in the medium to long run, not deducible from traditional marginalist theory, but largely contradicting it, which may be utilized for constructing models until the economy does not diverge from these norms. Let us summarize these stylized facts: (1) rate of growth stable over a multiyear average, rather than with a decreasing tendency as it should happen as a consequence of the postulate of decreasing returns; (2) increase in the capital/labour ratio, independently from the chosen measure of capital; (3) stable profit rate; (4) sufficient constancy, on average, of the capital/product ratio; (5) correlation between share of profits and share of investments on income, hence wages growing in proportion to productivity; and (6) meaningful differences in growth rates of national product and labour productivity in different countries. Obviously, decades after their enunciation part of these stylized facts appear contradictory to what may be considered as a change of 'regime' in the world economy, with the abandonment of the Bretton Woods system and the rise of neo-liberal policies; in particular, the average rate of growth of income decreases, while the average rate of profits increases. With all necessary cautions, the method of stylized facts appears still defendable.

World productivity growth, though distributed in an uneven way among different countries, has a positive value for humanity as a whole: as Drèze and Sen (1990) show with wide-ranging research, after the Second World War famines no longer derive from an absolute scarcity of food, but from its uneven geographic and class-based distribution. This contention is important, and contradicts the often re-emerging Malthusian pessimism; it stresses the need for active policies for tackling the dramatic issues of poverty and famines, to be considered more as distributive problems (both at the local and global levels) than as problems of scarcity.

Gradually, in the course of the decades, there is a shift from debate on macroeconomic development policies to debate on policies related to specific issues, concerning among other things income distribution, the organization of education, health assistance and the use of natural resources, micro-finance and the role of the small firms, gender issues, the constraints posed by technical progress, property rights and the administration of the law and so on.

These are always choices connected to a basic underlying theoretical structure. For instance, the World Bank went through a stage in which, under the impulse of Hollis Chenery (1918–94, vice president of the Bank from 1972 to 1982), it developed the most reliable and wide-ranging database on developing countries, published yearly since 1978 in the *World Development Reports*, accompanying it with analyses of actual development issues open to a variety of theoretical approaches;[34] more recently, the Bank showed an increasing discrimination in favour of policies aiming at expanding the role of the market in the economy, in conformity to the so-called Washington consensus view discussed in §8.9.

The efficacy of public policies is favoured by attention to the incentives to an active behaviour of relevant agents. Various authors insist on these aspects, such as Banerjee and Duflo (2011), who follow a microeconomic approach focusing attention on specific issues, including the search for measures favouring scholastic frequency on the side of the pupils and the presence at school of the teachers, to forms of social control on the side of the families.

In conclusion, we may stress the importance of a line of analysis to which we will return in the final chapter: the shift from a monodimensional to

---

[34] For the setting up of his research, Chenery, who also addresses Southern Italy issues (Chenery [1955], where he maintains the opportunity to rely not on automatic market mechanisms based on price adjustments, but on a reasoned investment program in less developed areas), is compared to Kuznets and to Moses Abramovitz (1912–2000, who supports the catching-up thesis with which he explains the development of Western Europe in the quarter century following the conclusion of the Second World War, recalling the principle of decreasing marginal productivity, and studies the trade cycle, in particular the role of inventories; cf. Abramovitz 1989): cf. Dorfman (1991), p. 586; Syrquin (2018) illustrates Kuznets's and Chenery's contributions to the foundations of a quantitative approach to development economics. Among the main scholars concerned with the issue of developing countries let us then recall Irma Adelman (1930–2017; among her contributions cf. Adelman [1961] and the autobiography, Adelman [1988]), the first to construct a CGE (computable general equilibrium) model and among the first to develop the technique of social accounting matrixes; Gunnar Myrdal (1898–1987), exponent of the Swedish school, Nobel Prize in 1974, author of a wide study on poverty in Asia (Myrdal 1968); Ragnar Nurkse (1907–59; cf. Nurkse 1953), critical of central planning and supporter of balanced growth; Paul Rosenstein-Rodan (1902–85), who also deals with Italian economic dualism; Paul Streeten (b. 1917; cf. Streeten [1972] and the autobiography, Streeten [1986]); Thandika Mkandawire (b. 1940; cf. Mkandawire [2001] and the bio-bibliographical interview with Meagher [2019]). On Albert Hirschman see §13.7; here we should anyhow recall his theses in favour of unbalanced development (Hirschman 1958).

a multidimensional measure of the degree of development reached by an economic system. The notion of *capabilities*, proposed by Sen (1992), stresses the importance of elements different from per capita income for measuring the situation of individuals and that of social aggregates. Hence, a stimulus for the search of wide-ranging development policies, which considers the most appropriate policies from the point of view of stimulus to spreading education, a bettering of health conditions, etc.

Research on issues concerning less developed countries constitutes a separate branch of economic research; the approaches that prevail, however, in the basic branches of economic theory systematically influence, directly or indirectly, the lines of analysis in this field of research as well. Often, it is difficult to evaluate the degree to which specific contributions depend on the adhesion to the one or the other among general approaches; in many instances of applied research, the link more often concerns the way in which the results are presented, rather than their substantive content; here, however, as in other fields, a stronger and more explicit connection among the various sectors of economic research cannot but have positive effects.

Appendix

Marginalist/neoclassical theory considers full employment as a stable equilibrium, under competitive labour market conditions.

In its simplest version, we may consider as given the supply of labour, while the demand for it, N, is a decreasing function of the real wage rate: an increase (reduction) in the real wage renders more (less) convenient the use of the factor of production labour, and hence favours in the choice among the available production techniques those with greater intensity of capital (greater intensity of labour). When there is unemployment, in a competitive labour market, the excess supply of labour induces a reduction in the real wage, and this engenders an increase in the demand for labour.

Let us elaborate on this.[35] If by X we denote real income, by N employment, by W the money wage, by P the price level, by M the money supply, by k the inverse of the velocity of circulation of money (the so-called Cambridge k), with 'the first derivative' and with 'the second derivative', we may write down the simple 'Pigou pre-Keynes' model, which represents in synthesis mainstream pre-Keynes economic theory:[36]

---

[35] Cf. Roncaglia and Tonveronachi (1985).   [36] Cf. for instance Pigou (1933).

$$X = X(N), \text{ with } X' > 0, \ X'' < 0 \tag{1}$$

$$W/P = X'(N) \tag{2}$$

$$M = k\,P\,X \tag{3}$$

In this model, equation 1 is the neoclassical production function, in which a decreasing marginal productivity of labour is assumed; equation 2 expresses the equilibrium condition for the labour market, with a wage rate equal to the marginal productivity of labour; the money supply, exogenously given, determines the level of money income ($P\,X$) through an equation derived from the quantity theory of money, assuming as given the velocity of circulation of money (equation 3). The money wage is also considered as exogenously given; as a consequence, it allows us to determine the decomposition of money income into price and quantity elements, hence employment. We may summarize the three equations into a single one:

$$M/W = k\,X(N)\,/\,X'(N) \tag{4}$$

We thus have a positive relationship between the stock of money expressed in terms of money wage and the level of employment. Thanks to the properties of the neoclassical production function, in particular the assumption of decreasing returns, flexibility of the money wage in the presence of unemployment is sufficient to ensure the tendency towards full employment equilibrium, given the supply of money. Alternatively, if the money wage displays downward rigidity (namely, if it does not decrease notwithstanding the presence of unemployment), full employment may be reached, given the money wage, through an expansion in the money supply that determines an increase in prices, hence a reduction of the real wage.[37]

After publication of Keynes's *General Theory*, neoclassical theory embodies some formal elements of Keynesian theory while maintaining substantially unchanged the re-equilibrating mechanism based on the downward flexibility of the wage in the presence of unemployment. We may illustrate this by reference to two models: the first one represents Pigou's macroeconomic theory in his writings after 1936, and the second

---

[37] In synthesis, the assumption of a given money supply and the quantity equation stop the fall in money wages from wholly translating itself into a fall of prices, thus guaranteeing a reduction of the real wages. In neo-Keynesian models the representation of money and financial markets is more sophisticated than this; in order to obtain the tendency towards full employment, then, recourse is made to the flexibility of the interest rate and/or to the 'real wealth' (or 'Pigou') effect.

one represents the neoclassical synthesis in Modigliani's (1944, 1963) version.

Let us denote by I investments, S savings, i the interest rate, V the velocity of circulation of money; let us measure I, S and X in wage units (so that WX corresponds to nominal income), as Keynes does in the *General theory*. We may then represent as follows Pigou's macroeconomic theory post-1936:[38]

$$I = I(i) \text{ with } I' < 0 \tag{5}$$

$$S = S(i, X) \text{ with } S'_i > 0 \text{ and } S'_x > 0 \tag{6}$$

$$I = S \tag{7}$$

$$WX = MV(i) \text{ with } V' > 0 \tag{8}$$

$$X = X(N) \text{ with } X' > 0, X'' < 0 \tag{9}$$

Equations 5–7 may then be synthesized in the well-known IS function:

$$i = i(X) \text{ with } i' < 0 \tag{10}$$

and from equations 8 and 10 we get

$$M/W = X/V(i(X)) \tag{11}$$

thus obtaining once again a positive relation between the stock of money expressed in wage units and the level of production; equation 9 then provides the link between income and employment. Once again, tendency to full employment equilibrium is ensured by flexibility of the ratio between the stock of money and the money wage, hence by the flexibility of the money wage (given the stock of money) in the presence of unemployment, that is, by competition in the labour market, or by an expansionary monetary policy that given the money wage induces a reduction in the real wage through an increase in the price level.

Modigliani's (1944, 1963) neoclassical synthesis may then be illustrated with relatively modest simplifications[39] through the following model:

$$S = S(i, X) \text{ with } S'_i > 0 \text{ and } S'_x > 0 \tag{12}$$

$$I = I(i, X) \text{ with } I'_i < 0 \text{ and } I'_x > 0 \tag{13}$$

$$I = S \tag{14}$$

---

[38] Cf. Pigou (1950).
[39] Here we do not consider the influence of wealth over consumption, considered by Modigliani.

$$X = X(N) \text{ with } X' > 0, X'' \leq 0 \tag{15}$$

$$X'(N) = W/P \tag{16}$$

$$W = a\, W_0 + (1 - a)\, X'(N)P, \tag{17}$$

where $a = 1$ if $N < N^f$, and $a = 0$ if $N = N^f$, with N^f designating the full employment level;

$$Md = P\, L(i, X) \text{ with } L'_i < 0 \text{ and } L'_X > 0 \tag{18}$$

$$Md = M \tag{19}$$

Let us leave aside for the moment the equation for the money wage (or better, considering in it $a = 0$). The system 12–19 may then be synthesized in three equations: IS, LL, and the real wage as a function of employment:

$$i = i(X) \text{ with } i' < 0 \tag{20}$$

$$M/P = L(i, X) \text{ with } L'_i < 0 \text{ and } L'_X > 0 \tag{21}$$

$$W/P = X'(N) \text{ with } X'' \leq 0 \tag{22}$$

In turn, these three equations may be synthesized in a unique expression:

$$M/W = L\big(i(X), X\big)/X'(N) \text{ with } dX/d(M/W) > 0 \tag{23}$$

This confirms the main characteristic of the previous models: employment turns out to be an increasing function of the money supply, given the money wage, and a decreasing function of the money wage, given the supply of money; the downward flexibility of the money wage in the presence of unemployment, ensured by competition in the labour market, implies the tendency towards full employment equilibrium; in the presence of downward money wage rigidity (namely with $a \neq 0$), the needed reduction of the real wage may be ensured by expansionary monetary policy, through an increase in prices.

The complications that may be introduced in the basic model (for instance, introducing also wealth together with income as an explanatory variable for consumption) do not modify this characteristic.

Let us now look at Harrod's growth model:

$$S = s\, Y \tag{24}$$

$$I = k\, \Delta\, Y \tag{25}$$

$$S = I \tag{26}$$

from which we get the formula for the warranted rate of growth g_w (= $\Delta Y/Y$):

$$g_w = s/k \tag{27}$$

Let g_n be the natural growth rate, by definition implying continuous full utilization of the available labour force and the full exploitation of technological progress; we get:

$$g_n = n + \pi \tag{28}$$

where n indicates the rate of growth of population (or more precisely of the labour-force) and π the rate of growth of productivity.

The condition of equality between natural and warranted rates of growth then implies:

$$s/k = n + \pi \tag{29}$$

Let us consider productivity growth as exogenous; possible adjustment mechanisms between the natural and warranted rates of growth need refer to one of the other variables. Thus, if $g_n > g_w$, unemployment grows and puts a downward pressure on the wage: this may put a brake on population growth, reducing n ('Malthusian theory'); alternatively, since workers save a lesser share of their income than the capitalists, the decrease in wages implies an increase in s, the average propensity to save for the whole population ('Kaldor's theory'); finally, according to the traditional mechanism of the marginalist theory of distribution, the reduction of the wage induces a shift to techniques with a higher labour intensity, hence a reduction of the capital/labour ratio k.

Solow (1956) follows this latter approach by introducing into Harrod's model a neoclassical production function:

$$Y = f(K, L), \text{ with } f'_i > 0, f''_i < 0, i = K, L \tag{30}$$

or more precisely, utilizing a Cobb–Douglas function,

$$Y = A K^\alpha L^\beta, \text{ with } \alpha + \beta = 1 \tag{31}$$

This latter condition ($\alpha + \beta = 1$) corresponds to the assumption of constant returns to scale, needed (by Euler's theorem) for the sum of wages and profits to equal income. Together with the savings function $S = s\,Y$ and the equilibrium condition $I = S$, already utilized in Harrod's model (equations 24 and 26), Solow utilizes an equation describing the (exogenous) growth of labour over time at an exponential rate n,

$$L_t = L_0 \, e^{nt} \tag{32}$$

Solow is thus able to determine the condition that guarantees a growth of income over time such as to ensure persistent equality between demand for and supply of labour:

$$s \, f(k, 1) \; = s \, A \, k^{\alpha} = nk \tag{33}$$

where $k = K/L$ is the capital/labour ratio, and the exponential rate of growth n is the same for both income and employment.

As Solow illustrates, this model ensures both the convergence of the natural and the warranted rates of growth, through the flexibility of the capital/labour ratio, and the convergence among economic systems at different levels of development, as a consequence of the assumption of decreasing marginal productivity of the two factors of production, capital and labour.

Solow's model is enriched by introducing exogenous technical progress, by making A an increasing function of time (in equations 31 and 33); then, by considering investments in human capital, translated into a quantitative growth of the labour input, and by endogenous technical progress. In all these cases, the tendency to full employment equilibrium holds: growth depends on 'supply side' factors that determine technical progress and the increase in the factors of production capital and labour.

8 The Myth of the Invisible Hand: Neo-liberal Streams

8.1 The Origins of the Invisible Hand

The myth of the invisible hand of the market is commonly attributed to Adam Smith. It suggests that markets, if left free to operate, will automatically bring the economy to its optimal equilibrium position characterized by full employment and a 'just' distribution of income (to each factor of production according to its contribution to national income). This is, however, a serious error in the history of economic thought. Indeed, Smith speaks only thrice in the whole of its writings of an 'invisible hand': on one occasion it is a joke about the ignorance of primitive people attributing thunder and lightning to Jupiter's hand; on another occasion, the reference is a statement, typical of the Enlightenment period, concerning the possibility (not necessity) of the unintended positive outcomes of human action (the rich, devoted to luxury consumption, generate employment for thousands of people: a traditional theme in eighteenth-century literature); finally, in the only case in which the expression is utilized in the *Wealth of nations*, it concerns the nationalism of the entrepreneur who prefers to invest in his or her home country rather than in a foreign one: thus, a case in which the competitive market assumption of a level playing field is violated.[1]

The origin of the attribution of the invisible hand thesis to Smith can be found in a 1951 article by a proponent of the Chicago school, George Stigler (1911–91, Nobel Prize in 1982). In fact, Stigler reads Smith through the lenses of his time, and of his specific theoretical position: that of the traditional marginalist theory of value and distribution, for which the thesis of self-regulating capacity of the free market is a fundamental pillar.

---

[1] Smith (1795), p. 49; Smith (1759), p. 184; Smith (1776), p. 456. On the 'invisible hand' in Smith, cf. Rothschild (1994) and Gilibert (1998).

As we saw in Chapter 2, according to the marginalist theory, the self-regulating mechanism is provided by competition, which brings prices to the level at which demand equals supply; in particular, wage flexibility (full competition in the labour market) guarantees full employment. Within the classical approach, instead, equality between demand and supply does not constitute an analytical condition for determining prices; moreover, their approach does not require general laws of returns connecting demand and supply to prices with stable and continuous functions, monotonically decreasing in the first case and increasing in the second.

Indeed, the theoretical limits of the thesis concerning the self-regulating ability of the market are also recognized by the most rigorous economists within the marginalist tradition; the possibility of externalities and of multiple and unstable equilibriums are well known. In the Cold War climate, however, the majority of economists tended to overlook these analytical results, especially in teaching and in the political debate, considering them to be exceptions to the rule, so as to affirm the absolute superiority of the free market economy. In particular, the issue of stability of full employment equilibriums, which receives so much attention by general equilibrium theoreticians and by the protagonists of the debates on capital theory, is left aside, mistakenly considered as solved or irrelevant. In the United States, between the end of the 1940s and the beginning of the 1960s, even neoclassical synthesis economists (discussed in Chapter 7) are considered as dangerous subversives, since they support anti-cyclical public intervention in the economy; underlying the theoretical debate is a firm belief that any kind of intervention in the economy, hence also active fiscal and monetary policies, would constitute a surrender to socialism and the enemy, the Soviet Union.[2]

We should stress that there are various neo-liberal streams, and that not all of them share such a clear-cut opposition to state intervention in the economy. For this reason as well, the generic etiquette of neo-liberalism is quite difficult to apply. On one hand, within neo-liberalism, there is an adhesion to the traditional marginalist theory of value and distribution, or at least to the results of such theory as far as the tendency to full

---

[2] An example of this literature, which at the time had wide circulation, is a pamphlet by the Veritas Foundation (1960), with seven reprints for a total of 95,000 copies in the short time-span of two years. Veritas, one of the many foundations that – as we shall better see in §8.8 – support and spread conservative economic culture, was founded by a group of Harvard students to oppose the Keynesian drift of their economics department; the pamphlet identifies Keynes with the socialism of the Fabian Society (!), attributing to the latter the responsibility of the diffusion of Keynesism in America (!), attacking its exponents in a rough way.

employment guaranteed by a competitive labour market is concerned. On the other hand, there is also a hostility towards Keynesian theories and policies. In the following pages we shall try to illustrate these points, differences and the connections among the various neo-liberal streams in recent economic (but also philosophical, political and juridical) debate.[3]

We will begin by considering the German-language, European perspectives. In §8.2 we consider ordoliberalism, born in the 1930s, which exerts a strong influence on the post-war German culture and some role in recent European Union policy. As we will see, there are important internal differences between the original ordoliberalism, the theoreticians of the social market economy, and the policies that the German political leadership tries to impose within the European Union.

Then, in §8.3, we will consider the new Austrian school, often considered – with some exaggeration – heterodox with respect to mainstream theory. We will discuss the work of one of its founding fathers, Ludwig von Mises (the other founding father, Hayek, is discussed in Chapter 4), and subsequent developments. We stress in particular the conceptual novelties of this school on the one side, and on the other side its adhesion – impervious to all criticisms – to the theory of value based on the average period of production. In Great Britain, an original version of the Austrian theory in its most abstract form is proposed by John Hicks (§8.4), even if, in this case, it is soon abandoned.

From Europe, we will then turn to the United States, in particular to the Chicago school, developed in the 1950s and 1960s. The Chicago school exerted a noticeable influence on the main policy choices in the 1970s and 1980s. On some accounts, we already dealt with this school in previous chapters; here (§8.5) we focus attention on its main representative, Milton Friedman, and on his monetarism. We will then consider the theory of rational expectations proposed by Robert Lucas and others (§8.6), which dominated the debate in the 1980s and 1990s but now appears to be in decline.

The public choice school, which in many respects takes on ideas from Italian inter-war theoreticians, was born in England with Black and at

---

[3] As we shall see, the same hostility towards state power takes on different forms among ordoliberals and neo-liberals such as Hayek and Mises or the Chicago school. Thus for instance Harvey's thesis, in his critical analysis of the rise of neo-liberism (2005, p. 78) – 'the Gramscian idea of the state as a unit, of political and civil society, gives way to the idea of civil society as a centre of opposition, if not an alternative, to the state' – holds with respect to American and Austrian neo-liberals but not for the ordoliberals, who had in mind a society educated to personal responsibility and to the market order. There are in any case important differences between the classical liberal tradition and that common to the different neo-liberal streams.

Mason University in Virginia with Buchanan. This school of thought developed gradually, and soon became more widely recognized for its relevance; as we will discuss in §8.7, the problems it poses – the processes of selection of political authorities and the motivations driving agents in the public sector – though already considered in the past (for instance by Condorcet and Tocqueville) are now taken up with the traditional tools of economic analysis.

We will then return (in §8.8) to the Mont Pèlerin Society and more generally, the web of foundations and research centres that, though not offering theoretical contributions, have a central role in the diffusion of neo-liberal theses and specifically the so-called Washington consensus.

Finally, in §8.9 we will briefly consider some aspects of the recent debate, accompanying the world financial and economic crisis that began in 2007–8. Here, while traditional theory, with its theses on the automatic tendency of market economies towards optimal equilibriums remains in the background, some applied analyses come to the fore. If the economy does not require the support of expansionary policies, but only needs reforms which improve the functioning of the market (in particular, by increasing competition in the labour market), then even in the presence of a crisis, policy authorities should choose (in opposition to Keynesian ideas) to keep a solid grasp on the public budget. Hence, the so-called expansionary austerity policies emerge: an oxymoron which relies on the examples of some minor countries, such as Denmark, soon contradicted by other analyses but supported nonetheless by the media power of the neo-liberal web.

The different neo-liberal streams differ among them in important respects, as we shall see, both theoretical (the greater or lesser importance attributed to equilibrium analysis: it is in this respect that the Austrian school is sometimes considered heterodox) and political, in particular for its clear-cut opposition between the ordoliberal juridical constructivism and the Austrian thesis of the spontaneous formation of institutions, but also with respect to aspects such as the evaluation of the role of large firms and the anti-trust policy. Each stream, then, evolves over time; for instance, as far as anti-trust policies are concerned, we may notice a shift towards a more accommodating standing both – explicitly – in the generational transition from the first to the second Chicago school, from Simons to Friedman and Aaron Director, and – implicitly – in the transition from the founders to the epigones of ordoliberalism.

In all its versions, however, neo-liberalism maintains the automatic tendency in a competitive market towards an optimal full employment equilibrium as theoretically grounded. As far as the long period is concerned, this tenet is shared with the neoclassical synthesis economists illustrated in Chapter 7, who understand the existence of different frictions as a justification for Keynesian short-period policies. Such policies are instead opposed by all neo-liberal streams, recalling in turn three groups of arguments: existence of strong re-equilibrating tendencies in the short period (in particular, following rational expectations theory), risk that expansionary policies end up by generating inflationary pressures; attributing the same motivations and the same cognitive limits of private economy agents to policy authorities, politicians and state organs (in particular with the public choice school); and finally, politically motivated hostility towards any increased role of the state in the economy as dangerous for individual freedom (a view held by the Austrian school, in particular). Hence, neo-liberals, particularly those involved in policy debates, also hold an anti-trade union stance, favourable to the reduction of the workers' bargaining power. These views correspond not only to the desire to eliminate a non-competitive element in the labour market, but also to an elitist view of government, which occasionally leads to an attitude of acceptance, if not benevolence, towards the worst dictatorships.

8.2   Ordoliberalism: From Eucken and Röpke to Merkel

Ordoliberalism was born in the 1930s with the so-called Freiburg school, and was revitalized after the fall of Nazism and the end of the Second World War. Its founder and main representative was Walter Eucken (1891–1950), son of Rudolf, a well-known neo-Kantian writer and philosopher supporting Christian ethic and social principles in opposition to Nazism. The journal *Ordo*, founded by Eucken together with his colleague, the jurist Franz Böhm (1895–1977), was born in 1937 and after the interval of the war, has been in publication since 1948. 'Ordo' is the society's juridical set-up, oriented to a strong liberal state, so as to guarantee private property, and aiming at equality of initial conditions.

Eucken distinguishes the economic processes of exchange and production on the one side, and the economic order of juridical, political and cultural institutions that orient its working on the other side. Compared to traditional economic research, but with some affinity to the Weberian methodology and that of the German historical school,[4] its attention focuses on the study of institutions, in particular the juridical ones, with

---

[4] In some respects (the thesis of a regulation from above of economic life, the hostility to anarchist individualism, attention to the social issue) also the so-called cathedra socialists collected in the Verein für Sozialpolitik and active in the second half of the nineteenth century constitute an antecedent to ordoliberals.

the aim of determining those better suited to a well-functioning market economy. These should concur to form an 'economic constitution'.[5]

Purposely built institutions ensure competition within the market. Competition is necessary not only for reasons of economic efficiency but also and mainly for a basic political reason: to ensure that private property, a necessary element of the market economy, should not lead to the concentration of power in the hands of the few.[6] Perfect competition is indeed a utopia to which we may tend, but we also must be aware that it continuously re-creates the conditions for its own decay: alongside the efforts to overcome competitors through reduction of costs and qualitative improvements to products, there are efforts aiming to ensure positions of strength in the market that, through various forms of increasing returns, tend to have cumulative effects over time.[7]

Anti-trust policies should aim to break down the 'avoidable monopolies' into various autonomous firms and to regulate the 'unavoidable monopolies' (that is, natural monopolies) so that the regulated monopolistic firm behaves 'as if' it were operating under competitive conditions (Eucken 1949). A strong state is necessary, both as the juridical source of the 'order', that is, of the system of rules presiding to the functioning of a society based on the market economy, and to ensure adequate anti-trust policies against those firms which may have themselves a political strength in addition to an economic strength.

Together with private property and anti-trust policies, the state must ensure a stable currency, coherent and stable policy orientation, and freedom of contract, but within rules addressed to avoid collusive agreements and to consider any externalities.

Eucken thus tries to delineate an organic view of society and the economy, midway between centralism and individualism, with a juridical structure of intermediate bodies (such as the federal system subsequently adopted in Germany with the Lander). Hence, the 'order'

---

[5] According to Foucault (2004, p. 92), 'the Freiburg school developed not simply an economic theory, not even a doctrine. It entirely re-thought the relationship between economics and politics, and the entire art of government.' In Marxian terms (ibid., p. 136), 'according to the ordoliberals, the juridical does not belong to the order of the structure ... The juridical gives form to the economical, which in turn would not be what it is without the juridical.'

[6] In this respect Eucken (1949) speaks of competition as the 'most magnificent and most ingenious instrument of deprivation of power in history'; 'full competition' corresponds to the situation in which no firm has the power to impose on other firms a given behaviour (cf. Ahlburn and Grawe 2006, p. 200).

[7] An analogous distinction, in the context of a classical approach, is that illustrated by Alberto Breglia (1900–1955) in the lectures for 1946–7 posthumously published by Sylos Labini (Breglia 1965, pp. 274–84) between fruitful profits (from cost reduction) and sterile profits (from price increase).

superimposed on society and the market (with an elitist-technocratic view of the government) should direct individual actions within a politically democratic and economically market-based society; the liberal element consists precisely in reaffirming political democracy and the market against centralized planning. This is a doctrine still widely accepted today, and stresses the market as being at the core of the creation of laws and customs, and not the simple result of interrelations among economic agents in a laissez-faire regime.

Thus, the ordoliberals' juridical constructivism or positivism is opposed to the *jus naturalis* tradition and to the Kantian idea of the spontaneous order, re-proposed by Hayek and discussed in §4.5. The ordoliberal view implies a strong state, able to build the institutions of a competitive market and to defend them from the ever-renewing power of private monopolies; Hayek's neo-liberal views, and especially those of the Chicago school, aim instead to a minimal state (anarchic liberalism), even at the cost of rejecting anti-trust policies. Moreover, ordoliberals (especially in post-war developments) maintain that the state should keep into account the social issue, though in ways different from the welfare state, in order to ensure maximum consensus around the market economy. The welfare state is considered damaging in that it domesticates the population, reducing it to a more or less well-nourished flock at the loss of the active principle of individual responsibility. Measures such as universal basic income, consisting in a negative taxation for lower incomes, are instead considered acceptable, and are shared by US neo-liberals.[8]

The institutional system proposed by Eucken relies on an ideology open to the market, to private property and to free entrepreneurial initiative but also to social justice, though it understands the latter term along the lines of religious pietism rather than with socialism. Intervention in support of the poor is considered necessary to fight the ghost of misery and at the same time to ensure sufficient social cohesion, based on meritocracy. Eucken's notion of social justice is near to that of the Catholic tradition of the time, as expressed in the encyclical letters . *Rerum novarum* by Pope Leo XIII (1891) and *Quadragesimo anno* by Pope Pius XI (1931), and should not be confused with the notion of the

---

[8] Neo-liberals such as Hayek or Friedman accept even a dictatorship as a necessary evil (as in the case of Pinochet's Chile) in order to avoid the expansion of public intervention in the economy that accompanies the welfare state. We may recall in this respect Hayek's interview with the Chilean daily *El Mercurio*, 12 January 1981 (quoted in Brennetot 2014, p. 24 n. 9): 'It is possible for a dictator to govern in a liberal way. And it is also possible for a democracy to govern with a total lack of liberalism. Personally I prefer a liberal dictator to democratic government lacking liberalism.' (Brennetot's article also contains information on the geographical distribution of neo-liberalism.)

welfare state, neither in Bismark's version of a concession from above by an aristocratic government aiming at obtaining popular consensus against the growing strength of the bourgeoisie, nor in the Labour Party version of a concrete realization of the conquest of power on the side of the working classes.

A similar, but not identical, position[9] was developed by Wilhelm Röpke (1899–1966), one of the few representatives of ordoliberalism to go into exile after Hitler's ascent to power. Röpke is considered one of the architects of the 'social market economy' (*Soziale Marktwirtschaft*); as adviser to Chancellor Konrad Adenauer (1876–1967) and to the minister Ludwig Erhard (1897–1974), he exerted a strong influence on post-war German economic policy.[10] With him, we should also recall the work of Alfred Müller Armack (1901–78), professor at Cologne, who collaborated with Erhard and was among the negotiators of the Rome Treaty.

As for institutional reforms, the social market economy takes on ordoliberalism's main theses, but strengthens the element concerning the 'social issue' (though always opposing a welfare state expanded to the point of interfering with the functioning of the market). Röpke (1947) speaks of an 'economic humanism' and characterizes it as a third way intermediate between liberalism and socialism (constituting the liberal-socialist etiquette, that should be distinguished from the liberal socialism of Carlo Rosselli ([1930] 1945). The presence of the state in the economy should nonetheless be limited; inflation, which constitutes a serious menace to the social order, depends on the supply of money and of public services; the unbalances in the trade balance have a monetary origin; and interest rates, which are the price of capital, must be freely determined by the market. Differing from the great majority of neo-liberals, however, Röpke (1969, p. 213) maintains that fixed exchange rates are preferable, as they favour international integration.

---

[9] The two views, though present side by side in German policy since the 1950s, may be kept distinct. Cf. Blyth (2013), pp. 135 ff., and Tribe (1995), pp. 203 ff.

[10] On 24 June 1948, on the basis of an opinion by the Economic council he chairs, but without a previous consultation with the Allies' military government, Erhard decrees the end of price controls; a week earlier, on 18 June, a monetary reform introduces the Deutsche Mark. This determines a push not only towards the return of the market economy, but also towards the reconstitution of a German state while ensuring its discontinuity with the 'command economy' of the Nazi state. These are the elements on which Foucault (2004, pp. 77 ff., 108 ff.) relies for his interpretation, according to which the ordoliberal doctrine of the state is driven, in the immediate second post-war period (namely at the time of the Allied occupation of Germany), by the objective of reconstruction of the German state: once market freedom is guaranteed, there will be a 'state under the surveillance of the market': 'there will be a mechanism founding the state and that, controlling it, shall give to all those who have some reason to require it the guarantee that they require'.

The influence of the Freiburg school and of Röpke's social humanism converge in the social market economy stream, concerning more the German political culture of the stage of post-war reconstruction than the economic theory debate.[11] It is not clear whether the term 'social market economy' is coined by Müller Armack or by Ludwig Erhard;[12] it is certain, however, that the latter is responsible for its affirmation in German political life. As Minister of Economics in Konrad Adenauer's governments from 1949 to 1963, and then his successor as chancellor from 1963 to 1966, Erhard is often considered the artificer of the German economic miracle.

Early ordoliberalism, prevailingly Catholic in orientation, constitutes a third way between the planned economy and Manchesterian individualistic liberalism. Later forms of ordoliberalism correspond more closely with Austrian and US neo-liberalism. The contemporary version of the social market economy, as accepted in art. 3.3 of the TEU (Treatise on the European Union),[13] is characterized by a growing fusion with the views of the Washington consensus, hence with the progressive reduction of the space allotted to the social state, notwithstanding the strong tradition it has in German society and culture. The crucial point in this respect is the full adhesion to the mainstream theory of the self-regulating capacity of the market that early ordoliberals and supporters of the social market economy share, though with some caution. We should also note the declining, original Catholic inspiration, gradually replaced by a more Protestant influence.

Thus, confronted with the euro crisis, the fusion of the Washington consensus doctrines with the German ordoliberal and social market economy traditions, with the addition of a persistent neo-mercantilist attitude, has taken on a driving function in European economic policy.[14] This implies a choice of principle in favour of a system of fixed rules and austerity policies, reducing the scope of anti-cyclical policies and engendering unbearable tensions within the euro area, only partly tempered by quantitative easing launched by the European

---

[11] This also holds for the first stages of ordoliberalism: analytical reflection on the theory of value is wholly extraneous to this stream of thought, while criticisms of Keynesism consist in an opposition to its policy orientation motivated by general political considerations, rather than from a critical analytical evaluation of Keynesian theories.

[12] Cf. Hagemann (2013), pp. 45–6.

[13] 'The Union shall establish an internal market. It shall work for the sustainable development of Europe based on balanced economic growth and price stability, a highly competitive social market economy, aiming at full employment and social progress, and a high level of protection and improvement of the quality of the environment. It shall promote scientific and technological advance.'

[14] On the diffusion of a mix between mainstream macroeconomics and ordoliberalism among German economists today, cf. Grimm et al. (2018).

Central Bank (ECB) chairman Mario Draghi. Discontent stemming from unemployment and growing inequalities in income distribution favours the growth of populist and nationalist political movements across Europe.

After the fall of the Berlin Wall (1989), a Franco-German summit between François Mitterrand and Helmut Kohl determined that German unification could be achieved, but only within a European Union reinforced by the institution of a common currency intended as a fly-wheel for strengthening political union. This latter point has been hindered, however, if not halted, by expansion of the Union to Eastern European countries, unavoidable considering the risks of instability that the area would otherwise experience after the disintegration of the Soviet Union. At the same time, construction of the euro is conditioned by conservative economic culture, with the strengthening of the set of rules favourable to austerity policies, rejecting the necessary margins of flexibility in the conduct of national economic policies and the practical abandonment of the symmetry rules that should have driven countries experiencing persistent positive balance of payments such as Germany to adopt expansionary policies. Indeed, part of the German political world appears to aim towards the dismembering of the eurozone, with the creation of a 'strong Euro' area, moving in the direction of the construction of a renewed 'big Reich' in Central Europe. This shift constitutes a betrayal of Kohl's pledges and a menace for the spirit of European appeasement that has presided, after the Second World War and the Holocaust, to the birth of the European Common Market first and the European Union subsequently.

8.3   From the 'Old' to the 'New' Austrian School

As we saw in previous chapters, in the first decades of the post-war period, economics was dominated, at least in the United States, by the reformulation of the theory of general economic equilibrium on the basis of expected utilities, by the diffusion of Marshallian analytical tools for the theory of the firm, by the neoclassical synthesis in the macroeconomics field. The Austrian tradition of Menger and Böhm-Bawerk remains in the shadow, notwithstanding Hayek's recognized authority as the representative of the third generation of this school: first at the London School of Economics then in the United States, with his best-seller *The road to serfdom*. But together with Ludwig von Mises, another representative of the Austrian school (Hayek considers him as his mentor)[15] who also

---

[15] Hayek writes in a number of occasions warm pages of appreciation for Mises (collected in Hayek 1992, pp. 126–59).

transferred to America, the two Austrian economists earned a number of followers, attracted both by their style of research and by their intransigent neo-liberalism.

Hayek has already been discussed. Ludwig von Mises (1881–1973), eighteen years his senior, studied in Vienna, where he attended Böhm-Bawerk's seminars and from 1913 to 1934 was *Privatdozent* (unpaid university lecturer), while working at the Chamber of Commerce and becoming the main economic consultant to the government. Hostile to Nazism, Mises migrated first to Geneva (1934–40), then to Paris and immediately after to New York. With a strong character, not inclined to compromises, Mises was visiting professor at the New York University starting in 1945, where he subsequently gave weekly seminars in economic theory.[16] Together with Hayek, he became one of the founding members of the Mont Pèlerin Society.

His main work, published in German in 1912 and translated in English in 1934, is the *Theory of money and credit*. This is a key contribution to monetary theory within the original Austrian tradition, with focus placed on the conceptual background. In the case of money, Mises's contribution consists of illustrating how the marginal utility of money can be determined, requiring it to be attributed a purchasing power, by going back in time to the moment of the transition from commodity to means of exchange, hence to money, of a specific good. Among other interesting elements of Mises's contribution, there is a critique to the idea of stabilization of the 'price level', an aggregate notion of doubtful solidity, and to the thesis, connected with this notion, of the neutrality of money, which instead prevails in the US neoclassical tradition and is taken up by Friedman's monetarism as well as by the rational expectations theory.

His theory of the trade cycle, worked out in the 1920s, integrates micro and macro elements and may be considered as the immediate precursor of Hayek's theory discussed in §4.3).

Mises also provides an important critical contribution on the possibility of a centrally planned economy, opening a lively debate.[17] Condemnation

---

[16] Mises's arrival in the United States, escaping from Nazi-occupied France, predates Hayek's arrival, who moves to London in 1931 and goes to Chicago in 1950. Mises remains without a tenured job for nearly a decade; then since 1949 the Volker Fund – the same institution that supports the birth of the new Chicago school and of the Mont Pèlerin Society – finances his weekly seminars at New York University, up to 1969. For additional information, cf. the warm portrait by Schulak and Unterköfler (2011), pp. 115–19.

[17] The essay with which Mises opens the debate, originally published in German (Mises 1920), is included in English translation in a volume edited by Hayek, published in 1935, that also includes two wide contributions by Hayek (the opening and the closing essays) and essays by N. G. Pierson and Georg Halm; the book has wide circulation, including an

of public property of the means of production and of economic planning is accompanied by defence of private property and of individual freedom of action, an extreme laissez-faire approach that tentatively limits even anti-trust policies (not to be applied even to cartels and collusive agreements, in homage to the entrepreneurs' freedom of action) and openings to the possibility of entrusting tasks traditionally performed by the state to the market, with an anarchic individualism.[18]

In the post-war years spent in the United States, it is Mises more than Hayek who drew together a group of followers constituting the founding nucleus of the new Austrian school. As Hayek himself states (1994, p. 195): 'Mises ... is the true founder of the American school of Austrian economics.' Hayek adds a hint to the differences existing between them: 'Mises was a rationalist utilitarian, while I am not.' The specific reference to the American Austrian school is important: while many economists of the Austrian school emigrated to the United States (thanks among other things to the support of Karl Pribram, 1859–1942, economic historian and historian of economic thought, responsible for the choice of grantees for the Rockefeller Foundation), only Hans Mayer (1879–1955), a student of Wieser, confirmed in his position after the end of the war notwithstanding being aligned with Nazism (among other things, as president of the Austrian economists society he had decreed expulsion of Jewish members) remained as holder of the economics chair in Wien. Mayer, though proclaiming himself the heir of the Austrian tradition, opposed the return of the emigrates; his successor, Alexander Mahr (1896–1972), nominated in 1950, had remained in Vienna after the Anschluss, though having previously been a recipient of a Rockefeller grant.[19]

Mises's most important book for the birth of the Austrian school in the United States is *Human action* (1947). This work draws on previous research published in German. In it, Mises develops a praxeology, or science of human action (while catallactics is the science of market

---

Italian translation. The well-known essay by Lange (1936–7) that re-proposes a socialist market is in fact an answer to this volume.

[18] Even a liberal such as Henry Simons, exponent of the first Chicago school, feels obliged to distinguish himself from Mises, pointing to him as 'the toughest old liberal or Manchesterite of his time. Arch-enemy of Nazism, communism, socialism, syndicalism, protectionism, and all government interventionism, he is perhaps the worst enemy of his own libertarian cause' (quoted by Caldwell 2011, p. 315 n.). On Mises's hostility to anti-trust policies, cf. Caldwell (2011), p. 319. Assuming a clear-cut dichotomy between the state and the market does not leave room for the analysis of merits and demerits of a mixed society, with variable proportions of market and state, and resolves itself in an ideological choice.

[19] On these vicissitudes see the accurate reconstruction by Schulak and Unterköfler (2011).

phenomena). At the methodological level, Mises contends that a social science based on universal laws and on the notion of human action is possible; perhaps drawing on Robbins (1932), this action is constrained to the pursuit of an attainable target, given available resources, to be reached in the most economical way; the axiom of rational behaviour allows him to consider economics as a deductive, a priori science. His rejection of mathematical formalism, however, implies leaving aside the theoretical debate on the theory of value (for which there is anyhow a clear adhesion to the marginalist approach, in Menger's version, with the explicit assumption of the consumer as sovereign).

Mises appears to contend that the individual's scales of value are not stable over time, which differentiates his theory from that of revealed preferences (Vaughn 1994, pp. 72–3), but deprives the marginalist theory of value of any validity, connected as it is to static comparative analysis. Mises (and after him, nearly all neo-Austrians) stresses that his is a theory of market processes, not of market equilibrium. In the absence of an anchorage to the latter, however, little can be said on the processes of change; in particular, many 'Austrian' analyses, such as Mises's and Hayek's (or Schumpeter's) theories of the trade cycle, presuppose the assumption of full utilization of productive resources, which stems from the traditional marginalist theory of value. According to Mises, indeed, economic crises may be caused only by errors on the side of financial institutions or of policy authorities.

Related to Menger's approach, we should recall the focus on processes of change and the interpretation of the market as transmission mechanism for knowledge, always limited for individual agents; the diffidence towards macroeconomics and aggregate notions (like that of the general price index); the focus on the trade cycle that, as in the case of Hayek, constitutes a decisive challenge for the connection of micro and macro elements and for studying the interrelations between monetary and real phenomena; the importance attributed to entrepreneurship (here possibly under Schumpeter's influence, though rarely recognized in an explicit way); and finally, the importance attributed to time and to limits to knowledge.[20]

The new Austrian school is today a lively reality, with journals (such as the *Review of Austrian Economics*) and research centres (now in decline; up to a few years ago there were lecture courses in Austrian theory in

---

[20] 'All actions must take place in *time*' (O' Driscoll and Rizzo, 2015, p. 20); in this sense, the rate of interest is conceived as stemming from exchange of goods over time (ibid., p. 25). Knowledge is 'localized' or 'private' (ibid., p. 25). Vaughn (1994, p. 134) defines Austrian theory as 'the economics of time and ignorance'.

universities such as New York University and the George Mason University; an institute named after Ludwig von Mises at the Auburn University organizes various activities and edits an internet site rich in materials). Distance from the neoclassical mainstream is noticeable and is frequently stressed by the neo-Austrians, who recently, in some cases show a preference for alliances with other heterodox streams such as the post-Keynesian one, considered as affine for the focus on the theme of uncertainty, notwithstanding the opposition on policy issues,[21] or with the evolutionary and institutionalist streams (to be discussed in Chapter 13).

The foundational moment of the new Austrian school can be attributed to a 1974 conference held at South Royalton in Vermont, financed by the Institute for Humane Studies (among the foundations sponsoring Austrian-oriented research, together with the Rockefeller Foundation and various others).[22] This conference was attended by Israel Kirzner, Ludwig Lachmann and Murray Rothbard. In the years to follow, other conferences were held and the school expanded, enlivened by internal debates among its major protagonists.

At this stage, Mises's dominating influence with his radical individualism may be explained by Hayek's engagement with the Mont Pèlerin Society, which, aiming to coordinate different neo-liberal streams to reinforce their political and cultural impact, tended to relegate the leaders of each stream to a secondary level. As often happens within heterodox streams, the debate internal to the neo-Austrian school is very lively, and occasionally even harsh. Confronted with this internal debate, it is not easy to clearly define the neo-Austrian paradigm. Certainly, it includes methodological individualism, subjectivism, focus on time (both as change/evolution and as space for acquiring knowledge), and the thesis that the market leads to outcomes not directly desired by the agent but nonetheless positive;[23] as for policy, the neo-Austrian school is characterized by an absolute rejection of any element of centralized planning and of Keynesian-type policies of control of demand and total faith in market's

---

[21] A bridge between the two schools is provided by George Shackle (1903–92), student of Hayek at the London School of Economics but then converted to Keynesianism, professor at Leeds and then at Liverpool. Critical of the a-temporal notion of equilibrium, his main contributions are devoted to the analysis of the complex role of expectations in the decisional process. Cf. Shackle (1955).

[22] Vaughn (1994), pp. 104 ff.

[23] This thesis has a long tradition, going back to the Enlightenment; in that case, however, the positive outcome is considered only possible, not necessary (cf. Roncaglia 2005a, pp. 84–7). The thesis that the competitive market guarantees positive outcomes is a direct consequence of adoption of the traditional marginalist theory of value and distribution (and as a matter of fact does not hold even for the versions of such theory that keep into account externalities in production and consumption, or other market failures).

equilibrating mechanisms.[24] The new Austrian school is clearly inserted in the original Austrian variety of marginalism, with an all-out opposition to mainstream macroeconomic models.

The strong ideological characterization of the Austrian school implies that its internal debate often focuses on fidelity to the paradigm. In conformity to the rejection of mathematical models, the debate mainly concerns the conceptual foundations. Fidelity to the Austrian tradition implies, among other things, a-critical acceptance of the results of the marginalist theory of value and distribution, especially in what concerns the equilibrating capacity of the market: results that, as we have repeatedly stressed, have been criticized in a destructive way.[25]

Let us briefly consider the school's main exponents: Kirzner, Lachmann, Rothbard.[26]

Ludwig Lachmann (1906–90) graduated in Berlin but in 1933, with Hitler's rise to power, moved to England. Drawing on the roots of the original Austrian tradition, he tended towards an evolutionary theory and rejected the notion of equilibrium, thus representing a radical position at the theoretical level (Lachmann 1956, 1986).

---

[24] In a 1981 contribution in honour of Mises (recalled by Schulak and Unterköfler 2011, pp. 164–5) Machlup considers the main characteristics of the Austrian school of Mises and followers to be individualism and methodological subjectivism, political individualism, consumer sovereignty and subjective evaluation of tastes and preferences, marginalism and opportunity cost (each choice implies the sacrifice of some alternative).

[25] For a graphical illustration of the neo-Austrian theory of value, distribution, income, employment and money, mainly referred to in writings by Hayek and Mises but also by Rothbard, cf. Garrison (1978). Though noting that 'there is good reason to believe that the problems created by double switching [in fact *reswitching*: cf. §12.6] are confined to the Cambridge paradigm itself' (but without providing any justification of this curious idea), Garrison (1978, p. 16) admits that 'the Austrian model will eventually have to defend against the Cambridge charges'. Unfortunately, 'this task will not be undertaken here' – nor, as far as I know, elsewhere. Less rigorous on the theoretical level, referring to Sraffa's 1932 critique to Hayek illustrated in §4.3, according to which Hayek's theory implies a multiplicity of equilibrium interest rates, Lachmann (1956, p. 76) maintains that the problem would be solved by market mechanisms that in the long run lead to the uniqueness of such rates: which is precisely the thesis that the debates on capital theory deny, as Hayek himself admits in his reply to Sraffa (Hayek 1932). O' Driscoll and Rizzo (2015, p. 203) maintain that 'if the [Austrian capital] theory is interpreted subjectively, the Cambridge challenge misfires', without realizing that, since it refers to a fallacy of composition, the critique based on reswitching has nothing to do with the agent's subjective opinion: whatever the interpretation of technical change, the economy does not necessarily converge to full employment equilibrium, contrary to what O' Driscoll and Rizzo insist in stating ('As long as final output is scarce, versatile resources ought not to be persistently unemployed,' ibid., p. 215; the full employment assumption is also utilized in the theory of the trade cycle, sometimes implicitly, as for instance ibid., p. 219).

[26] On these authors, and more generally on the Austrian school in the United States, cf. Vaughn (1994).

Murray Rothbard (1926–95), US born, the son of Jewish immigrants from Russia and Poland, is a debated personality, especially for his links with Holocaust negationists and his opposition to war with Germany. An ultra-libertarian like Mises (he was among other things vice president of the Mises Institute) but also arch-conservative, he was a strong opponent to feminism as well as to any kind of welfare state or to constraints to the firms even on anti-trust grounds (for instance with reference to collusive agreements, that according to the ordoliberals should be ruled out), he provides contributions to the new Austrian school both on the theoretical level (Rothbard 1962, 1997) and with a wide reconstruction of the pre-Smithian and classical economic thought (Rothbard 1995).[27] Possibly the most aligned to Mises's original teaching, Rothbard represents the most radical position on the plane of political neo-liberalism.

Israel Kirzner (b. 1930), a student of Mises, developed a theory of the entrepreneur that focuses on knowledge issues (Kirzner 1973). Within the Austrian school, he represents a moderate position in theory, nearer to the neoclassical tradition, and averse to denying the importance of the notion of market equilibrium.

8.4   Hicks's Austrian Theory

John Hicks is no doubt one of the main protagonists of the economic debate of the twentieth century. In the 1940s he was the most frequently cited economist, surpassing even Keynes.[28] His best-known contributions pre-date the Second World War, but important works appear after the war as well, and his influence on the development of economic research is strong. On the whole, we might say that his cultural design is similar to the one pursued by Samuelson on the other side of the Atlantic: first, to unify the main streams of the marginalist tradition, the Walrasian stream of general economic equilibrium and the Marshallian stream but also, as we will discuss, the Austrian stream; and second, to insert in the current of the marginalist tradition Keynes's new ideas.

In Chapter 7 we already illustrated Hicks's best-known contribution: the IS-LL model aiming at integrating Keynesian theory within the marginalist tradition of equilibrium analysis (Hicks 1937). In some respects, it is analogous in aim, as it proposes an integration between the Marshallian and the Walrasian general equilibrium streams, in his

---

[27] Following Schumpeter, Rothbard strongly undervalues Smith's contributions, both on the theoretical level and on that of liberalism; thus, strangely without ever naming him, he contradicts the still dominant interpretation by Stigler (1951), who attributes to Smith the thesis of the invisible hand of the market.

[28] Quandt (1976).

wide-ranging book, *Value and capital* (1939): starting with the theory of consumer choices (drawing simultaneously on both Marshall and Pareto) Hicks ends up with accumulation and the trade cycle, in a way that is easy to follow thanks to his use of diagrams rather than mathematics (which, following the example of Marshall's *Principles*, is left to a series of notes at the end of the text). Thus, the book constitutes a basic reference for generations of researchers, in and outside Britain.

Mathematics appears, together with diagrams, in his 1973 book *Capital & time: A neo-Austrian theory*. In it, Hicks sets out to deal with dynamic issues through recourse to the tools of the theory of value developed by the Austrian school, in particular by Böhm-Bawerk, with the average period of production utilized as a measure of the capitalistic intensity of production processes in determining the rate of profits. Hicks even upholds the superiority of this approach in comparison to those he references, in particular, the Leontief-Sraffa and von Neumann models.

Thus, from the Austrians, Hicks draws the analytical technique based on the reduction of the inputs in the production process to a series of dated quantities of labour: if I use looms, wool and labour to produce suits, then I can substitute the looms and the wool with the quantities of labour and means of production necessary for producing them, and again substitute these latter means of production with labour and means of production utilized in their production, and so backward, until the residuum of means of production becomes so small it can be ignored.

This analytical technique is developed and variously utilized by Hicks. Among the developments, there is a step from the *flow-input, point-output* scheme of the Austrian theory (in which a flow of labour obtains, in a given moment in time, a certain quantity of product) to a more general *flow-input, flow-output* scheme, in which the productive process, based on the utilization of durable capital goods, may continue for a period of time. Since it is impossible to exclude that the series of dated quantities of labour have an infinite length, recourse is had to the 'truncation' technique suggested in some papers in those years (Arrow and Levhari 1969; Bhaduri 1970; Nuti 1970): the queue of the eldest elements in the series is eliminated when the value of the residuum of means of production is no longer positive or, in other terms, when the discounted actual value of the productive process is maximum.[29] A 'fundamental theorem' (Hicks 1973, pp. 19–21) ensures an inverse relation between the interest rate and the capital value of the residual process in each moment in time.

---

[29] The problem is that we cannot exclude that this never happens. Burmeister (1974, pp. 419–21) shows that under plausible conditions (as the presence of negative externalities) the 'truncation' is not possible.

Among the applications of the analysis, together with the traditional ones (analysis of full employment equilibrium and of the path of constant full employment growth) we should also note that there are non-conventional analyses of the *traverse*, the transition from one equilibrium to another.

Hicks himself is aware of some limits of his analysis; for instance, in demonstrating his 'fundamental theorem' he excludes by assumption the possibility of *capital reversal*, namely the possibility (already stressed by Wicksell, and holding in general, as it appears from the debates in capital theory of the years immediately preceding publication of Hicks's book) that when the interest rate changes, the value of a set of capital goods varies in the same and not in an opposite direction.[30]

However, the main limit of the analysis of the flows of dated labour is the fact that they are but another way of representing a technology, alternative to the customary one (instantaneous scheme of production) in which given quantities of labour and means of production give rise to given quantities of a product (or of various products, in the case of joint production), which may be represented with a system of equations like the one proposed by Sraffa 1960 (cf. §5.7 and Chapter 5, Appendix).

This point is important, and merits further elaboration. Böhm-Bawerk, in developing his theory of value, aims to show how we may consider time, which is ignored when, in the labour theory of value, we get the value of a commodity simply by summing up the quantities of labour directly or indirectly necessary to its production. In a capitalistic system, in which the service of the factor of production capital is paid according to a rate of interest, the labour utilized in the past has to be weighted according to the period in which it remains immobilized. Hence, this leads us to the idea of identifying capital with the period of time in which labour is immobilized: the so-called average period of production. In any case, we must notice that both in classical economists and in Böhm-Bawerk (and in fact in all theoreticians taking part in the debates on the labour theory of value, from Ricardo and Marx to Jevons and Walras, up to our days) the analysis does not proceed by considering the evolution of production techniques over real time, but on the basis of the technology pertaining to a given moment in time; this also holds true when the technology is represented as labour flows utilized in a purely ideal sequence of time intervals. This means, as Hicks himself remarks, that the vertical (flows of dated quantities of labour over time) and the horizontal (matrix of given quantities of means of production and labour necessary in a given moment in time for the production of the various commodities) representations do not

---

[30] Once again this point is dealt with by Burmeister (1974).

refer to different situations, but are simply different ways of representing the same situation (the same productive technology). The advantage of the one or of the other is to be found in the possibility each of them offers to develop analysis in one direction or another. The results obtained through different representations cannot be contradictory, as they refer to a same basic situation.

The advantages of the presentation in terms of dated quantities of labour adopted by Hicks depend in fact on the simplifying assumptions accompanying them, which Hicks does not sufficiently stress: for example, exclusion of the reswitching of techniques (which as we shall see in §12.6 can be rigorously excluded only for one-commodity worlds) or the assumption that it be always possible, through 'truncation', to limit the series of dated quantities of labour to a finite period of time.

The instantaneous representation is thus equivalent to, if not better than, the Austrian one on the analytical level, as the series of dated quantities of labour have an infinite length as soon as there are in the economy what Sraffa calls 'basic commodities', namely commodities directly or indirectly utilized in every productive process. Recourse to dated quantities of labour of finite length is equivalent to assuming that in the system there are no basic commodities, but in this case all problems in the theory of value disappear: even the old labour theory of value holds. In any case, the results reached with a given representation of the productive process cannot differ from those obtained with an alternative representation, unless the new representation introduces constraints so to exclude analytical difficulties. In particular, Sraffa (1960) and the ensuing theoretical debate show that, owing to the complications arising from a compound rate of interest, the average period of production cannot constitute a valid measure of the quantity of capital employed in production, to be used in determining income distribution, as it itself depends on the rate of interest; moreover, phenomena of capital reversal and reswitching cannot be excluded, and these imply, as we will explore further in §12.6, that the relationship between the rate of interest and capital intensity of productive processes may go in an opposite direction to that required for the validity of the traditional theory (in particular for maintaining the automatic tendency of a competitive market economy to a full employment equilibrium).

Burmeister's (1974) review article immediately points to the various limits in Hicks's analysis.[31] Some of Hicks's epigones insist on his line of

---

[31] Apart from the problems already noticed, Burmeister recalls another basic aspect. In Donzelli's words (1988, p. 85 n.), 'when it is formulated in a consistent way (as ... in Hicks's volume ...), the "Austrian" theory relies on a notion of productive process that

analysis, but demonstrations of instability provided both in the debates in capital theory and in general equilibrium analyses show that analyses of the traverse, namely the transition between two equilibriums, cannot be valid.

8.5   Friedman and the Chicago School

Within the marginalist tradition, a lively debate has taken place, starting in the 1950s, on the plausibility of the assumptions necessary to ensure the efficacy of Keynesian policies aimed at controlling cyclical unemployment. This debate in fact concerns the greater or lesser confidence on the ability of market mechanisms to ensure equilibrium between demand for and supply of labour, and on the efficacy of monetary and fiscal policies.

Among those who trust the market's equilibrating mechanisms and are hostile to public intervention in the economy, the representatives of the Chicago school have played a key role, particularly Milton Friedman, whose contributions are discussed in the text that follows.

The Chicago school has a long history, and has been shaped by a number of important economists, some of whose contributions have already been discussed (George Stigler, Gary Becker in Chapter 6) while others will be considered later in this chapter (Robert Lucas) or in subsequent chapters (Eugene Fama, in §11.4). It is customary by now to distinguish a 'first Chicago school' of the 1930s and 1940s, a 'second Chicago school', commonly identified with Friedman, and a 'third Chicago school' with Becker's developments in the microeconomic field and Lucas's in the macroeconomic one.[32]

In the early twentieth century, private financing was vital to the University of Chicago, so much so that 'critics liked to call [it] Standard Oil University';[33] at that time, however, together with more conservative

---

does not admit the exchangeability of produced capital goods, but only that of original inputs and of final consumption goods. Thus, unless very specific assumptions are introduced (such as the Hicksian one of a "simple profile"), the "Austrian" theory of capital is not able to keep into account, not even implicitly, nor produced and exchanged quantities of capital goods, nor the prices at which the corresponding transactions take place.' Donzelli stresses that Hayek himself is unsuccessful in overcoming this difficulty, 'which in fact is insurmountable', though it appears as decisive for his theory of the cycle.

[32]   Stigler's and Becker's contributions to microeconomics have already been recalled in §6.5: both follow a Marshallian approach (in Viner's version) and both extend the field of application of the marginalist theory in a variety of directions, with what has been called 'economic imperialism', interpreting economics as a unified theoretical structure for the analysis of all aspects of human behaviour (always assuming full rationality). However, as Medema (2011, p. 161) remarks, 'Whereas Stigler had put scarcity at the centre, for Becker "the basis of economics is choice."'

[33]   Peck (2011), p. xxix.

and traditionalist teachers, there was also a strong institutionalist stream (Thorstein Veblen, John Maurice Clark). Founders and protagonists of the first Chicago school were Jacob Viner, Frank Knight and Henry Simons, who contributed the foundations for the scientific consolidation of the university on conservative and neo-liberal lines.[34]

On the origins and development of the 'second' Chicago school, an important reference is the research of a group of historians of economic thought (coordinated by van Horn, Mirowski and Stapleford 2011). The central thesis of the van Horn et al. (2011) book (p. xix) is that 'the early leaders of the post-war Chicago school were not cloistered academics, but empire builders who set up or forged influential relationships with well-funded institutional organizations in order to provide vital support structures for the creation, incubation and propagation of their ideas'; connected with this, there is the aim 'to construct an economics built for policy', in opposition to the Keynesian approaches prominent at Harvard (and MIT).[35]

Another opposition originated from the Cowles Foundation, also initially based in Chicago, with a Walrasian orientation (general economic equilibrium and high-level mathematics, with attention to the new econometric techniques), while at the University of Chicago the Marshallian orientation prevailed. In §6.4 we hinted at the Cowles's attempt to convince Samuelson to move to Chicago, to construct a bridge between Cowles and the university: this attempt was futile, as Samuelson

---

[34] The 'old' Chicago of Frank Knight (1885–1972), Henry Simons (1899–1946) and Jacob Viner (1892–1970) dominates in the period preceding the Second World War. The old Chicago too is liberal, but in a rather different meaning of the term: cf. Tonveronachi (1990) and its bibliography. In particular Simons considers a priority a reform of institutions, where competition is limited because of the market power of big firms and trade unions: cf. Tonveronachi (1982). The 'second' Chicago instead drifts towards positions favourable to limit anti-trust policies, both by extending the notion of competition and because of diffidence towards the ability of rational action on the side of the regulator, and for an issue of principle, the will to guarantee the widest freedom of action to entrepreneurs. On this drift, in particular for what concerns patents, cf. van Horn and Klaes (2011) and van Horn (2011).

[35] External financing is large. See for example the table concerning those obtained not by the whole university but by the Economics Department alone in 1956–7, in Emmet (2011), p. 109. Within the volume, see the essays by Nik-Khah on Stigler's role in the growth of the Chicago school and on his contributions, and by Medema on the Chicago Law School and on the economic analysis of law (concerning which we should recall at least Posner's contribution, 1973). Caldwell illustrates Hayek's complex role in the neo-liberal renaissance in post-war Chicago: initially decisive (in collaboration especially with Simons, focused on the target even more than Hayek), especially in obtaining finance through the Volker Fund; relatively more detached subsequently (Hayek gets an appointment at Chicago only in 1950, four years after Friedman, and not in the economics department). Moreover, Caldwell criticizes on various accounts the interpretation set out by Mirowski et al. (2009).

ultimately remained at MIT. This failed attempt influences successive events, including the transfer of Cowles to Yale University at New Haven, Connecticut.[36]

Milton Friedman (1912–2006, Nobel Prize in 1976) is considered the main proponent of the 'second' Chicago school. We already discussed his contribution to the debate on the meaning to be attributed to the expected utility theory in §6.2. Here, before illustrating briefly his contributions to macroeconomics, we will discuss his methodology.

Before being the theoretician of monetarism, Friedman works in fields of applied economics (income and consumption expenditure, at the National Bureau of Economic Research at Washington) and on statistical and econometric techniques of analysis. This is likely the source of his orientation to establish a strong link between abstract theory and empirical reality. However, differing from the positivist tradition that tries to verify the starting assumptions on which the theoretical reasoning relies, Friedman (1953) instead insists on the correspondence between the facts and the forecasts deduced from the theory: a theory is considered as valid when it is simple and is based on few assumptions, even clearly unrealistic ones.[37]

Friedman appears to predate Popper (1969) in maintaining that what matters are not confirmations but refutations: after arguing that 'the only relevant test of the validity of a hypothesis is comparison of its predictions with experience', he states: 'Factual evidence can never "prove" a hypothesis; it can only fail to disprove it' (Friedman 1953, pp. 8–9).[38]

---

[36] Cowles Foundation and the University of Chicago compete on which institution obtains a greater number of Nobel Prizes. At least for the moment, Cowles leads: among its associates, Tjialling Koopmans, Kenneth Arrow, Gerard Debreu, James Tobin, Franco Modigliani, Herbert Simon, Joseph Stiglitz, Lawrence Klein, Trygve Haavelmo, Leonid Horwicz and Harry Markowitz have received the Nobel.

[37] 'A hypothesis is important if it "explains" much by little, that is, if it abstracts the common and crucial elements from the mass of complex and detailed circumstances surrounding the phenomena to be explained and predicts valid predictions on the basis of them alone. To be important, therefore, a hypothesis must be descriptively false in its assumptions' (Friedman 1953, p. 14). In the same work, Friedman offers as an example the assumption of profit maximization on the side of firms, maintaining that, even if firms behave differently, competition would allow survival only for those who adopt a rational (maximizing) behaviour: a thesis repeatedly taken up, recalling the evolutionary leaning of the old Chicago, but in an approximate way, without specifying the mechanisms that should lead to such a result, far from granted. The thesis is taken up by among others Alchian (1950), and criticized by among others Penrose (1952). On the problems connected to the step from vague evolutionary metaphors to well-structured theories cf. §§13.5 and 13.6.

[38] Samuelson (1963, pp. 232–3), though sharing Friedman's anti-teleological stand and the refusal of the search of ultimate causes, suggests – ironically, and with great caution – that 'Chicagoans use the methodology to explain away every objections to their assertions', after synthesizing as follows what he calls the 'F-Twist': 'A theory is vindicated if (some

In Friedman's analysis, some important questions remain unanswered. First, it is not clear whether a single erroneous forecast is sufficient for abandoning a theory, as it happens in Popper's method of conjectures and refutations, or whether other conditions must be verified, such as a systematic series of erroneous forecasts or the availability of a different theory offering better results.[39]

Second, the argument that the assumptions of a theory are necessarily unrealistic is ambiguous. If we mean that the assumptions are necessarily abstract, namely leaving aside the myriad of details of which empirical reality is rich, then this holds; it is absurd, however, if this line of argument justifies the exclusion of some essential empirical element that impedes getting the desired analytical results: this latter point can be reflected in the case of theories assuming a one-commodity world, or a single representative agent, which is necessary to obtain basic results, such as the existence of an inverse relation between real wage and employment which do not hold in a multi-commodity world.[40]

of) its consequences are empirically valid, to a useful degree of approximation; the (empirical) unrealism of the theory "itself", or of its "assumptions", is quite irrelevant to its validity and worth.' Samuelson concludes (p. 236): 'if the abstract model contains empirical falsities, we must jettison the model, not gloss over their inadequacies': a sentence that recalls Sraffa (1930a, p. 93): if a theory 'cannot be interpreted in a way which makes it logically self-consistent and, at the same time, reconciles it with the facts it sets out to explain ... I think that it is [the] theory that should be discarded'.

[39] This latter thesis is explicitly held by Machlup (1978) and Friedman (1953, pp. 30–31) seems to refer to it, in reply to the 'perennial criticism of "orthodox" economic theory as "unrealistic"': 'criticism of this type is largely beside the point unless supplemented by evidence that a hypothesis differing in one or other of these respects from the theory being criticized yields better predictions for a wider range of phenomena.' This thesis has strongly conservative implications: a new or heterodox theory cannot from its beginning draw on a battery of empirical results as wide as the orthodox theory, as shown by the case of Copernican vs. Ptolemaic theory (Kuhn 1962, p. 92), especially if – as it happens in the case of the comparison between orthodox and heterodox theories – political power is utilized in support of the first ones and, even brutally, to deprive the latter ones of any room for development. Thus, still today mainstream theories dominate, notwithstanding their repeated and clamorous failures in interpreting the dynamic fragility of contemporary economies, for instance with the inability to foresee the crisis of 2007–8 (Lucas 2003 states that crises are simply impossible, as unemployment is always voluntary) while little room is left for Minsky's theories illustrated in §11.6.

Among clamorous forecasting errors we may recall Friedman's one (*Newsweek*, 4 March 1974: in the middle of the oil crisis), based on the assumption of a sufficiently competitive oil market: 'Even if [OPEC] countries] cut their output to zero, they could not for long keep the world price of crude at 10 dollars a barrel. Well before that point the cartel would collapse.' On the role of major oil companies in maintaining prices well above the competitive level, cf. §9.8.

[40] Blaug (1980, p. 103 n.) recalls in this respect the famous story of the economist on a desert island, confronted with a box of food in cans and the failed attempts of his companions, a physicist and a chemist, to open them: 'I know how to do. Let us assume to have a can-opener!'

As for macroeconomics, the first important contributions, on money and consumer theory, were published in the second half of the 1950s (Friedman 1956, 1957). In the second of these works, Friedman criticizes the Keynesian consumption function, according to which consumption depends mainly on current income, maintaining instead the importance of 'permanent income' (long period expected income). Again, in opposition to Keynesian theory, which favours discretionary fiscal and monetary policies (and, within these, fiscal policies compared to monetary ones) for regulating the path of the economy, Friedman developed a series of key contributions in the decades to follow.

In his 1956 book, which contains writings by various authors, Friedman proceeds in two steps. First, he redefines the demand for money (in comparison to the old quantity theory, that connected it directly to income, as transactions demand for money), considering it as a portfolio choice among various assets (money, bonds, shares, fixed capital, human capital). Second, he aims towards a stable demand for money function, connecting it to returns on these different assets and to income. In this way, Friedman aims to sterilize the instability of the speculative demand for money that is instead dominant according to Keynes.

The ponderous *Monetary history of the United States, 1867–1960* (1963), written in collaboration with Anna Schwartz (and followed by another volume in collaboration on the same themes, 1982), brings on various aspects of this approach. The data collected in the volume show that fluctuations in the rate of growth of the stock of money tend to precede the stages of the trade cycle. In this way, the volume provides important, even if controversial, contributions on issues of economic history, such as the interpretation of the Great Crisis, mainly attributed to errors in the conduct of monetary policy (thus opposing Galbraith's 1961 Keynesian interpretation).[41] A new collection of essays (Friedman 1969) further develops this approach, considering the issues as being connected to the supply of money and to the effects of monetary policies.

The results reached in these works led to the formulation of a basic model, illustrated by Friedman in 1974. In this model, the level of prices is endogenously determined, while equilibrium production, employment

---

[41] Friedman stresses the drastic fall in the supply of money; however, as Kaldor (1982, p. 75) notices, while M0, which corresponds to a strict definition of the monetary base and is the variable under the control of the monetary authorities, remains substantially stable, what falls is M2, which includes bank deposits and is thus strongly influenced by the path of monetary income. Therefore, Kaldor remarks, Friedman is simply inverting the cause-and-effect relation: it is not the fall in the money supply that determines the Great Crisis, but on the contrary it is the crisis that provokes the fall in money supply.

and income correspond to the full employment and full resource utilization level and thus depend on technology and on available resources, namely on supply-side factors. This model thus opposes the Keynesian approach that attributes importance to effective demand. Given the technology and the amount of available resources, the price level depends on the supply of money, controlled by the monetary authorities; Friedman thus rearticulates, in a more sophisticated form, the central thesis of the old quantity theory of money.

According to Friedman and the monetarists, the 1974 model differs from that implicit in the Keynesian theory only in relation to the assumption of exogenously determined prices; this interpretation of Keynes (analogous to that adopted by the neoclassical synthesis), however, implies an important twisting of hands to the English economist's original thought. Reducing the basic clash between Keynesian theory and monetarism to differences in the assumptions leads to opposition of the Keynesian assumption of relative stability in the relationship between consumption and income to the monetarist view of a relative stability in the velocity of circulation of money; an empirical debate follows, devoid of effects on the opposed theoretical positions.[42]

The assumption of exogenous money represents a parallel between Friedman and Keynes's *General theory*. For Keynes, however, this is not an assumption necessary to the validity of his theoretical view, but only a simplifying assumption that allows us to focus attention on the notion of liquidity discussed in §3.7 and on the notion of effective demand with its role in determining income and employment.[43] On the contrary, the assumption of exogeous money is essential for the quantity theory of money. Hence, there is a decisive importance of the critique to this assumption, upheld by Kaldor and others: when the definition of money includes not only legal currency but also bank deposits, the cause-and-effect link between money and prices may be turned upside down, with money that varies as a consequence of changing prices.[44]

From the monetarist tradition, represented among others by Simons in pre-war Chicago, Friedman (1960) also develops the thesis according to which monetary authorities should adopt a rule of stable growth rate of the money supply, so as to keep the economy on a stable path of growth.

---

[42] For a wide survey of this debate, cf. Laidler (1985/1997).

[43] As a matter of fact, if we follow Keynes in distinguishing between the notions of money as an instrument for transactions and as liquidity providing flexibility in the presence of uncertainty, the assumption of exogenous money (for instance when money is identified with legal currency) may coexist with endogenous liquidity available in the economy.

[44] Cf. Kaldor (1982); Kaldor repeats this and other critiques to monetarism in various writings; for a survey, see Desai (1989).

These ideas are taken up and developed by many other economists around the world, including Karl Brunner and Alan Meltzer.

Harry Johnson (1972) develops monetarism on an international level: he argues that if monetary authorities avoid sterilizing the effects of the trade balance on the internal supply of money, commercial flows among the various countries would tend automatically towards equilibrium. In a system with perfectly flexible exchange rates (and in the absence of interventions on the side of monetary authorities), the balance of payments (inclusive of capital movements) would tend automatically towards zero. Complete freedom of movement of capitals internationally is a corollary of this approach.

As discussed earlier, Friedman maintains that monetary factors, in particular the money supply determined by the monetary authorities, may affect income and employment only in the short run; in long-run equilibrium (full utilization of available resources), changes in money supply affect only the general price level. In other terms, the Phillips curve turns out to be negatively sloped only in the short run, but becomes vertical in the long run.[45] This can happen in correspondence to a positive unemployment rate, though in equilibrium: the so-called natural rate of unemployment, that depends on the obstacles always present in reality to the perfect functioning of the labour market (frictions in territorial and occupational mobility of workers, missed correspondence between supply and demand of the various kinds of qualified labour, and so on).

Friedman also condemns fiscal and monetary interventions aiming at stabilizing aggregate demand, hence income and employment, which constitute the battle horse of neoclassical synthesis economists: not only the efficacy of such interventions is limited to the short period, but also their short-period effects are uncertain and may turn out to be counter-productive. Indeed, as Friedman argues, policy interventions are subject to three kinds of delays and uncertainties: first, those relative to the evaluation of the situation in which to intervene; second, those relative to the step from such an evaluation to the choice of the tools for intervention and its realization; and finally, those relative to the time required for the intervention to display its effects. As a result of this multiplicity of

---

[45] Cf. Phelps (1967) and Friedman (1968). Both Phelps (who precedes Friedman along this road) and Friedman, in his 1968 article, explain the presence of a short period trade-off with errors in expectations that lead to confound the path of money wages with that of real wages, so that until the error persists – hence not beyond the short period – the economy may found itself out of long period equilibrium. As we shall see in the text that follows, once the problem is framed in this way, it is easy for supporters of rational expectations to show that absent such errors the Phillips curve turns out to be vertical also in the short period.

lags and uncertainties, it may happen, for instance, that interventions exert their foreseen effects in a paradoxical way, even in a situation in which interventions of an opposite sign would have been necessary. Policy interventions may thus have a destabilizing effect, namely one which results in the widening of income fluctuations.

These critiques may hold for the neoclassical synthesis – the theoretical structure of which is substantially analogous to the monetarist one – but do not hold for Keynes's central thesis, concerning the possibility – or even the likelihood – of persistent unemployment, which market mechanisms cannot overcome. Such a thesis, also confirmed by the results of the capital theory debates as well as by the developments of general economic equilibrium theory,[46] imply the need for systematic policies in support of effective demand, including the creation of an adequate international institutional system, and go far beyond the neoclassical synthesis's short-period stabilization fiscal and monetary policies.

Towards the end of the 1970s, inflationary pressures generated first by the Vietnam War, then by increasing militancy of trade unions, and finally by the 1973 and 1979 oil crises, led initially to great instability in the relationship between inflation and the rate of unemployment (the Phillips curve), then to simultaneous increases of inflation and unemployment. In the wake of these events, Friedman launched a political campaign in favour of neo-liberal ideas, with wide resonance (also favoured by his reception of the Nobel Prize in 1976), both in the press with a series of editorials published in *Newsweek* beginning in 1966, and with frequent radio and television interviews, including a BBC series in the 1980s, *Free to choose*. Far more than his theoretical contributions, these activities contribute to reorienting the cultural climate towards abandonment of 'Keynesian' policies (rather stemming from the neoclassical synthesis of MIT economists) and in the direction of neo-liberal views.

8.6   Rational Expectations and Supply-Side Economics

The rational expectations theoreticians, most notably Robert Lucas (b. 1937, Nobel Prize in 1995), developed a thesis even more extreme than that of Friedman. In a 1972 article, Lucas links the assumption of markets in continuous equilibrium with that of rational expectations, originally formulated by Muth (1961).

---

[46] As we repeatedly see in the course of our exposition: cf. e.g. §§ 6.3, 6.4, 12.6. Cf. in particular Hahn (1965) for the demonstration of the non-uniqueness of the Walrasian equilibrium in the presence of money and finance.

According to this hypothesis, 'expectations . . . are essentially the same as the predictions of the relevant economic theory';[47] this corresponds to the assumption of full rationality of the economic agent, who not only deduces from the past what is going to happen in the future (following static expectations, implying a future equal to the past, or extrapolative expectations, foreseeing for the future a prosecution of past tendencies), but also takes into account all we know about the economy, including theoretical explanations of the working of the markets.

As a consequence, as Lucas maintains, economic agents learn to take into consideration public intervention in the economy, discounting its effects as illustrated by economic theory. By way of example, a public expenditure in deficit, which is not financed from a simultaneous increase in taxation, is counterbalanced by a reduction in private consumption which sets aside the savings with which to pay for the increased taxes; these will have to be introduced, sooner or later, in order to meet the costs of public debt with which public expenditure has been financed. Analogously, Kydland and Prescott (1977) suggest, policy authorities must keep into account the reactions of economic agents to their decisions.

The same line of reasoning is pursued by Barro's (1974) article, already discussed in §7.2, which proposes the so-called Ricardian theorem of debt equivalence. Barro's main thesis (his paper also considers some secondary aspects, such as the risk connected to possible sovereign insolvencies and the liquidity services provided by public bills and bonds) is that private debt in the hands of the private sector cannot constitute net wealth, as the flow of coupons and reimbursements of public debt assets is compensated by a corresponding flow of taxes.

As suggested earlier, applying the assumption of rational expectations to customary macroeconomic equilibrium models, and to Friedman's monetarism as well as the neoclassical synthesis, leads us to conclude that the Phillips curve turns out to be vertical in the short term as well: monetary and fiscal interventions only produce increases in the rate of inflation, not in income and employment. Only surprise policies, not foreseen by economic agents, may have some efficacy on real variables, albeit temporarily.

According to Kydland and Prescott's (1977) criticisms, however, discretionary policies of this kind give rise to temporal inconsistency, when policy authorities find it convenient to default on their promises when confronted with a change in situation. This generates instability for the

---

[47] Muth (1961), p. 316. On rational expectations see the anthology edited by Visco (1985) and his wide introduction.

economy and uncertainty for the agents involved; as a consequence, fixed rules in policy are to be preferred over discretionary policies. This critique complements Friedman's critique illustrated earlier, concerning the delays in decision, design and implementation of policy choices, which may lead to opposite results to those desirable in the new situation, and Lucas's (1976) critique illustrated in §9.5, concerning the impossibility of designing a policy through the use – still today quite common – of macroeconomic models characterized by the assumption of parameters that remain unchanged in the wake of policy interventions.

The only kind of policy accepted by rational expectations theoreticians is that which is directed at reducing frictions in the working of the markets: the so-called supply-side policies, consisting for instance in easing workers' mobility from one job to another, or in ensuring that workers' qualifications correspond to the requirements of the economy. Among these policies, there is also a reduction of fiscal pressure, since the increase in income net of taxes is accompanied, in equilibrium, by an increase in the productive sacrifice that agents are willing to make, hence by an increase in production.

In this respect, the so-called Laffer curve is very popular, though it should fall more within anecdotal economics than in economic theory, were it not for the rhetorical influence it exerts on policy authorities. This curve is said to have been drawn on a paper napkin during a lunch with a journalist; it indicates the path of taxes as a share of income when the tax rate increases. The starting point at the origins of the axes is zero, since a zero tax income corresponds to a zero tax rate; but also, for a tax rate equal to 100% the tax income will be nil, as no one would accept to work when the income net of taxes is zero. As a consequence, it seems plausible to assume that the curve initially increases and then decreases. The problem is where we locate the maximum point of the curve, beyond which an increase in the tax rate brings a reduction in tax income. If, as Laffer holds, this point corresponds to a tax rate inferior to that which prevails at a given time, then a policy of tax abatement should be adopted; if instead, as it appears more plausible,[48] the maximum point is decidedly on the right, there is still room for increases in tax rates.

---

[48] Marginal tax rates approaching 90% applied in the second post-war period in various countries coexist with a long and unequalled expansion of income. As for the incentive to evade, we may remark that it is in any case always present; moreover, even if it is plausible that the pressure to evade increases with increasing tax rates, it is also true that tax authorities will find it the more convenient to fight tax evasion the higher is the tax rate. A quite different issue is that of fiscal equity as perceived by the population and the social tensions that high tax rates may generate. In this latter respect the problem depends in a relevant measure on the greater or lesser inequality in the distribution of income gross

The idea that the simultaneous reduction of taxes and public expenditure favours income is a key element in supply-side economics. The validity of this idea depends on its prerequisites, in particular the assumption that the economy tends to be, in the long and short run, in a position of full employment of available resources. In this case, tax rebates incentivize private activity, thereby increasing national income. Alternatively, in conditions of Keynesian involuntary unemployment, Haavelmo's (1945) theorem (also called balanced budget multiplier) shows that a simultaneous reduction of taxes and public expenditure generates an equal reduction in national income, which constitutes the opposite result.

A collateral stream of this debate concerns the idea of the so-called dynamic inconsistency; policy authorities may adopt expansionary policies in order to stimulate income and employment, though remaining aware that this generates inflation, and following this by implementing restrictive policies to counter inflation; but the pressure to adopt expansionary policies persists over time, and restrictive policies are indefinitely postponed (Kydland and Prescott 1977). As a consequence, it is maintained that it is necessary to avoid discretional monetary policy and to pursue fixed rules; in particular, central bank independence needs be ensured: a thesis aimed at hindering monetary financing of public deficits, through the 'divorce' between treasury and central bank. Furthermore, central banks should have inflation control as their unique statutory target (as for the ECB), ruling out objectives such as income and employment, or the correction of territorial inequalities.[49]

The assumption of rational expectations, in the usual context of a one-commodity model, is also the basis of a new theory of the trade cycle, real business-cycle theory.[50] According to this theory, income and employment fluctuations around long-period equilibrium values are determined by unforeseen shocks on the supply side, such as changes in technology, and by the consequent reactions of agents (so that the economy is always in equilibrium, apart from a stochastic element, whatever is the current stage of the cycle).[51]

---

of taxes and on the perceived equity or iniquity of such distribution, on the use of tax income and on the wider or lesser spread of solidarity among the population.

[49] Cf. Rogoff (1985), followed by a wide literature; for a synthetic illustration, cf. Persson and Tabellini (2000), pp. 441–9. For a wide survey of the effects of adoption of an inflation target on the side of central banks, and further bibliographical references on the topic, cf. Almeida and Goodhart (1998).

[50] The seminal contribution is Kydland and Prescott (1982).

[51] In particular, in equilibrium unemployment is always voluntary. Within this approach, stabilization policies appear counterproductive: cyclical fluctuations are considered as optimal responses to the irregular path of technical change. Cf. Lucas (2003).

In passing we may notice that these assumptions presuppose all agents to share the same model of the functioning of the economy and to be endowed with an economic culture and a forecasting ability that it would be a euphemism to define as unrealistic. Indeed, the crucial defect of this theory is not so much the assumption of rational expectations, but mainly, the theoretical model that agents are assumed to adopt as their reference: the mainstream one-commodity model that embodies an inverse relationship between real wage and employment, hence a stable full employment equilibrium under competitive conditions. As already discussed, in a multi-commodity model uniqueness and stability of equilibrium are no longer ensured. The assumption of rational expectations applied to a context in which Keynesian theory is used as a reference would give quite different results. In that context, it would be quite difficult to univocally determine what is meant by rational expectations, aside from the generic statement that at least for the most important decisions agents take into account not only past experience, but also their reasoned interpretation of the situation they are confronting.

After dominating the economic debate in the 1980s, in the following decade rational expectations theory gradually loses ground, even if in the theoretical confrontation with its opponents of the neoclassical synthesis its feeble theoretical foundations – the one-commodity model, also common to their adversaries – go unquestioned. Indeed, on a purely theoretical level, this theory appears as more consistent with the basic views of the marginalist tradition, while the neoclassical synthesis appears as a specific case based on ad hoc assumptions. The real problem concerns its feeble theoretical foundations, which were confirmed by the de facto rejections of these theories, illustrated most recently with the 2008–9 world crisis.

All this notwithstanding, recent years illustrate the emergence, in policy as in teaching, of what is called new consensus macroeconomics (Arestis and Sawyer 2008, Arestis 2009) or new neoclassical synthesis (King 2015, pp. 26–7). This new approach can be synthesized in a simple three-equation model: an aggregate demand curve in which real income is a negative function of the interest rate, a short-period Phillips curve in which inflation is a negative function of the unemployment rate, and an equation representing the so-called Taylor's rule for monetary policy, with the short-period interest rate being a positive function of the inflation rate expected by central banks. With some variants (for instance expanding the model to consider open economies), this approach is adopted by monetary authorities in various countries and in a number of introductory macroeconomics textbooks. These are in fact models combining elements of the neoclassical synthesis, monetarism and rational expectations theory. As the theories from which they originate, they are substantially foreign to the original Keynesian approach, hence ignoring uncertainty and instability, and rely on the erroneous thesis of a systematic tendency of competitive market economies to full employment.

8.7   Public Choice

Public choice theory is defined (Mueller 1989, p. 1) as 'the economic study of nonmarket decision making, or simply the application of economics to political science'. Thus defined, it also includes the wide field of welfare economics, which we will consider separately in §14.4. As seen here, public choice theory is essentially a research stream in which it is assumed that the electorate, politicians and bureaucrats pursue their own self-interest and not an ideal public interest, analogously to what traditional economics assumes for agents in the private sector of the economy. Thus, while traditional welfare theory studies public decisions as concerning the maximization of a social welfare function, or of socially shared objectives, public choice theorists analyse the institutional framework within which the bureaucratic and political classes (or better, the individual bureaucrat or politician) take their choices motivated by their self-interest. While the elector-citizen performs his or her role as consumer-buyer of public services, the various branches of the public sector perform the role of providers-sellers, maximizing their own utility function.

The assumption that all agents, public and private, act in their self-interest, adopted as the foundation by the public choice school, is rather debatable, especially in the context of the issues tackled by this theory. Herein lies a basic difference with the classical – in particular Smithian – view of the agent, motivated by a complex set of passions and interests; both ethics and the smooth functioning of society require that personal interest be different from self-interest, being driven or at least influenced by 'sympathy' towards fellow humans and by the desire for friendly attitudes from others. In other terms, public choice theory studies a society of a-social individuals, as confirmed also by the assumption that individual preferences are independent from the preferences of others, or by the absence of any consideration of the possibility of an argumentative formation of consensus, based on open debate and reciprocal persuasion.[52] Only recourse to such assumptions, however, makes

---

[52] As Sen (1977, p. 99) states, 'The *purely* economic man is indeed close to being a social moron.' According to psychoanalysis, exclusive focus on self-interest is a sign of a deviant personality.

it possible to use the traditional tools of marginalist economic analysis, such as utility maximization (minimization of sacrifice) under the constraint of available resources, and – through game theory – to consider the interrelations among the various decisions (while with the theory of cooperative games, it is also possible to consider the formation of interest groups and coalitions). Politics is seen not as the search for optimal collective choices (society as such cannot have objectives, attributable only to individuals), but as an enquiry into decisional rules, finalized to the resolution of conflicts among individuals.

This line of research is already present in the eighteenth and nineteenth centuries, for instance with Condorcet and his analyses of voting. This is then taken up between the end of the nineteenth and the first half of the twentieth century by a group of Italian public finance scholars (Amilcare Puviani, Antonio De Viti De Marco, etc.).[53] It is then rediscovered in Great Britain by Duncan Black (1908–91) and then by Alan Peacock (1922–2014) and in the United States by James Buchanan (1919–2013, Nobel Prize in 1986).[54]

Public choice theory has a general scope and provides interesting contributions; we consider it here in the context of neo-liberal thought first, because it shares with it recourse to the traditional marginalist theory with all its implications on the invisible hand of the market; and second, because by extending market mechanisms (market for votes in politics, market for favours in the case of the bureaucracy, maximization of self-interest in the case of voters) it leads to the conclusion that the public sector accumulates the possible defects of the market economy with its intrinsic imperfections (in substance, missing the use of prices for transmitting information). As a consequence, this stream of research tends to share with the neo-liberal stream the central political tenet according to which the dimensions of the public sector should be reduced to a minimum and solutions should be found for the issues traditionally attributed to the public sector, mainly aiming at widening the market and increasing its efficiency.

---

[53] For recognition of the role of the Italian school of public finance, cf. Buchanan (1986). For an illustration of this school, cf. Dallera (2013).

[54] Among representative works let us recall Black (1958), Buchanan and Tullock (1962), Downs (1957) and Tullock (1965); a readable illustration of the characteristics of this school is that by Peacock (1992). On Buchanan, cf. Sandmo (1990) and, on a critical line well summarized by the title (*Democracy in chains: The deep history of the radical right's stealth plan for America*), the well documented and lively written book by MacLean (2017).

Among the issues considered by public choice theory, subsequently redefined as political economy,[55] the first concerns the origin of the state, which may consist in the search for efficiency, in the presence of externalities and transaction costs. Research on optimal taxation levels and provision of public services, and on optimal fiscal systems (with in particular the distinction between taxes on capital and on labour incomes), commonly fall within the field of public economics, but here are considered on the basis not of a collective welfare function but of the choices of the various agents and groups of agents involved, including the politicians.

The widest field of research is the choice of voting rules: unanimity, already propounded by Wicksell stressing the nature of the voluntary exchange of collective choices; simple or qualified majority, with related problems, such as the possibility of cyclical outcomes in the case of successive votes with multiple choices; electoral rules for the case of more than two candidates, with a sequence of votes and elimination at each turn of the less voted candidate (Hare's system), of the candidate receiving more votes as the worst candidate (Coombs's rule), of requiring each voter to indicate a ranking of candidates and choosing the one who turns out to be the best placed in the whole set of rankings (Borda counting); or other more complex rules.

Other research considers club theory, defining clubs as voluntary associations providing some public good from the use of which it is possible to exclude third persons: for instance, a bridge or tennis club, or an association for political debate. Freedom of circulation of citizens within the territory of a state makes it possible to consider as a club local institutions too: a citizen discontent with the excessive fiscal charge or on the contrary with the lack of public services may move from one locality to another where the choices are nearer to his or her preferences.[56]

Another field of research concerns the functioning of representative democracy: voting outcomes, behaviour of the elected and behaviour of the electorate.[57] The starting assumption is that 'parties formulate

---

[55] For a wide and accurate survey, from the origins up to the end of the 1980s, cf. Mueller (1989), also providing a number of original hints. For a survey of subsequent developments, under the new name of political economics, cf. Persson and Tabellini (2000).

[56] Obviously we must assume perfect knowledge of the situation in the various localities on the side of the citizens, absence of obstacles to mobility stemming for instance from relocation costs, territorial wage differentials and so on.

[57] As far as voters are concerned, it is considered a 'paradox' the very fact that electors do vote, as each single vote is largely irrelevant while voting implies a loss of time (cf. Downs [1957c] and for an illustration of the debate Mueller [1989], pp. 348–69). Simon (1993, p. 160) comments: 'The voting "paradox" (the fact that people vote) is only a paradox if there is no altruism.' The fact that so many vote constitutes a clamorous empirical

policies in order to win elections, rather than win elections in order to formulate policies':[58] a principle that excludes the element of political passion from the motivations of the leaders. Results depend on these and analogous assumptions, as in the case of the 'theorem of the median voter' (Hotelling [1929], taken up by Downs [1957] and by Black [1958]), according to which the best position for a candidate is at the centre of the political spectrum. Validity of this result requires among other things that there be a single dimension (right–left) along which are located the different political positions. Things get more complex, and results such as cyclical outcomes become possible when the political dimensions relevant for the voters are more than one (for instance, redistributive policies, environmental policy, cultural policies). Additional research explores the distinction between the cases of 'pre-election politics with opportunistic politicians' (see earlier) and those in which elected politicians retain their freedom of action after the election; the cases of 'partisan politicians', in which politicians have well-defined ideological preferences; the cases in which the political power of proposing laws is separate from that of approving or implementing them; the cases where the distinction between parliamentary and presidential regimes is relevant; or the cases where the difference between local and national elections plays a role, and so on. In the deluge of publications dealing with specific issues, in any case, it is very difficult if not impossible to find notes of caution on the foundations common to all such analyses, in particular concerning the basic assumptions of *homo oeconomicus*.

According to the theorists of the Chicago school (e.g. Wittman 1995), electoral competition assumes that the interests of electors and the politicians converge. In the presence of opportunistic politicians (consistently with the basic assumption of the public choice school), however, this result does not have general validity, and depends on a series of somewhat unrealistic assumptions (cf. Persson and Tabellini 2000, pp. 69 ff.).

The presence of interest groups raises further problems, as does the determination of optimal contributions from such groups to political parties, connected to rent seeking through changes in regulations. Rents earned correspond under competitive conditions to the expenditure required for getting them: a well-functioning market should render lobbying useless, while it is useful only in non-perfectly competitive markets and with extended regulatory activity. This results in hostility in principle to regulations. Government is thus seen as 'a malevolent revenue

confutation of the foundations – the *homo oeconomicus* assumption – on which the whole theory of public choice relies.

[58] Downs (1957), p. 28, quoted by Mueller (1989), p. 180.

maximiser rather than a benevolent public good provider' (Mueller 1989, p. 268). Hence, the opportunity of constitutional constraints to government activity, such as those introduced in the European Union with the Maastricht Treaty and subsequently reinforced by the creation of the euro. Ultimately, the thesis of the opportunity of attributing monetary policy not to elected political authorities but to independent central banks (discussed earlier) is possibly limited by statute to the inflation target.

Though public choice theory and political economics mostly refer to microeconomic analysis, considering the results to which they get relatively to macroeconomic issues as micro-founded, such results as a matter of fact decisively depend on recourse to aggregate production functions; this particularly rings true for the inverse relation between 'flexibility in the labour market' (easiness of firings) and unemployment levels.[59]

8.8   Mont Pèlerin Society and the Web of Think Tanks

What is considered as a war in defence of individual freedom of action is waged not only with theoretical arguments, but also and especially with a wide web of well-financed think tanks that contribute to the spread of neo-liberal ideas. In this respect, financial strength and intellectual zeal contribute to bring such theses to hegemony in the economics debate, on many occasions hiding the arguments of approaches different from the mainstream (as it happens for instance with the complex Keynesian notion of uncertainty, assimilated to Knight's simplistic dichotomy between risk and 'total' uncertainty, or for the results of the debate on capital theory which deny the stability of full employment equilibrium).

The Mont Pèlerin Society was founded in 1947, at the outset of the Cold War, by Hayek alongside other prominent US and European economists, such as Frank Knight, Milton Friedman and George Stigler in the

---

[59] For a (rather a-critical) illustration of this thesis cf. Persson and Tabellini (2000), pp. 45–8; notwithstanding the feeble foundations, the inverse relationship is recalled in apodictic terms as one of the most important concrete results of this line of analysis: 'Regulation of the labor market, the generous structure of unemployment insurance, and other labor market programs are certainly major factors behind the widespread unemployment we observe in many parts of the world.' In equally apodictic terms one might uphold the opposite thesis: while high unemployment levels are attributable to neo-liberal austerity policies, the abandonment of institutions supporting wages and the bargaining power of trade unions leads to a slowing down of the dynamics of wages and to an increasing inequality in income and wealth distribution, with negative consequences on demand, hence on employment and, through increasing returns, on productivity and as a consequence on the 'wealth of nations'. Another aspect to be noticed is the attribution to the research stream of political economics of already well-known discoveries, for instance Kalecki's political cycle ('partisan cycle in output', Persson and Tabellini [2000], p. 488).

United States, Walter Eucken and Wilhelm Röpke in Germany (among the founders of ordoliberalism and the social market economy illustrated earlier), Maurice Allais in France, the Austrians Karl Popper and Ludwig von Mises, Salvador de Madariaga (in exile from Franco's dictatorship in Spain) and Luigi Einaudi and Bruno Leoni in Italy.[60]

The organization brought together such thinkers with an interest in the reformulation of classical liberalism, no longer focused on the individual freedom of citizens within the state (as with the stress on the rights of minorities in John Stuart Mill 1859), but rather centred on the freedom of action in the field of economics and in the context of a market economy. Already present at the Colloque Lippmann nine years earlier, differences immediately concerned the opposition between the ordoliberal view of strong institutions necessary to the smooth functioning of the market economy, to be created 'from above' on one hand, and Hayek's views, shared by the Chicago school, of a 'spontaneous order' on the other.

A consequent and fundamental difference concerns competition policies: the ordoliberals advocated for robust active anti-trust policies, aimed also at avoiding power concentrations; alternatively, proponents of the Chicago school called for moderate policies aimed at evaluating advantages and disadvantages of intervention and freely stipulated collusive agreements (at least, in principle) and recognizing entrepreneurial merits.

At the level of pure theory, ordoliberals are more faithful to the traditional marginalist notion of equilibrium, sharing this contention with the Chicago school, while neo-Austrians interpret it – as we saw in §8.3 – in an evolutionary way.[61]

Over time, ordoliberal influence within the Society decreased, while the influence of neo-liberals near the Chicago school grew; a sign of this is Röpke's exit from the Society in the early 1960s.

Supporting a conservative neo-liberalism, the Society constitutes an important pressure group of intellectuals, contributing among other things to the turn from the Bretton Woods system of fixed exchange rates to the system of fluctuating exchange rates prevailing since the 1970s. Many of its members have received the Nobel Prize in economics:

---

[60] The Mont Pèlerin Society has an antecedent in the Colloque Walter Lippmann held in Paris in 1938, in this case as well as an occasion for meeting among exponents of different streams of what precisely in that occasion is christened as neo-liberalism. On the Mont Pèlerin Society see the wide group research coordinated by Mirowski and Plehwe (2009).

[61] Horn and Mirowski's statement (2009, p. 174) according to which 'Among neo-liberals at MPS, the acceptance of neoclassical economic theory as core doctrine took a very long time to become relatively accepted' may be referred to the decline of the neo-Austrian view, not of the basic marginalist structure, on which relies the thesis of the invisible hand of the market, it too shared by 'Austrians' as well as by German ordoliberals.

Maurice Allais, Milton Friedman, Friedrich von Hayek and George Stigler.

While the Mont Pèlerin Society was born from the initiative of a group of academics, though with the financial support of some conservative institutions such as the Volker Fund, various other important research centres (conservative rather than neo-liberal) were born out of the initiative of economic and financial power centres with the support of conservative political forces in the United States and other countries.

By way of example, the American Enterprise Institute, the Hoover Institution, the Cato Society, the Center for International Private Enterprise[62] in the United States and the Fondazione Bruno Leoni in Italy illustrate this trend. The Philadelphia Society, founded in 1964, intends to re-propound within the United States the model of the Mont Pèlerin Society. The Heritage Foundation, instead, is less engaged on the front of theoretical development, and more on that of the diffusion of neo-liberal views.[63] The Institute for International Economics in Washington, more moderate and for some aspects open to the neoclassical synthesis, is known for having organized a 1989 conference which launched the doctrine of the Washington consensus, illustrated in the text that follows. In England, a significant influence is exercised by the Institute for Economic Affairs (IEA), founded by a businessman, Antony Fisher, in 1955, after initial contact with Hayek and a visit to the Foundation for Economic Education.[64] All these centres are active on specific themes of policy,[65] but always from the neo-liberal viewpoint, working in the majority of cases more as centres for pressure and propaganda rather than as centres

---

[62] Founded in 1983 by a group of neo-liberals active in the Reagan administration, 'CIPE developed a "toolkit" that spelled out the tactics to be used: create an advocacy team, identify key issues relevant to the target audience, research the issues, establish a goal, create a message and an advertising campaign, form grassroots advocates, work with the media, and become part of the governmental process' (Blair 2009, p. 398).

[63] On some aspects of the role played by these associations, cf. Blair (2009), who illustrates more generally the transition in the institutional set-up from the stage in which, after Pinochet's coup in Chile (in which an important role is played by ITT), the United Nations gets organized to contain the power of transnational corporations through the launch of the New International Economic Order in 1974, institution of the United Nations Centre on Transnational Corporations (UNCTC) in 1975 and the adoption in 1976 of the Organisation for Economic Co-operation and Development (OECD) Guidelines for Multinational Enterprises, to the stage of dominance of neo-liberal views with widespread adhesion to the Washington consensus and the launch in 1999 of the Global Compact as partnership between UN agencies and transnational corporations.

[64] Cf. Mitchell (2009), who also illustrates the growing influence of neo-liberal views within the World Bank.

[65] For instance, the American Enterprise Institute leads an activity of critical evaluation of federal agencies and their work through the tools of cost–benefit analysis (often with somewhat restrictive evaluations of the benefits).

for research and policy debate, thus obscuring the theoretical element of such work to the advantage of the ideological one.

To better understand the fusion of neo-liberalism and conservatism characterizing these choices, we can refer to the support some of these centres offered to Pinochet's bloody dictatorship in Chile, and the role of the so-called Chicago boys in implementing extreme liberalization measures in collaboration with the Pinochet government. Among these measures, liberalization of the labour market dominates, accompanied by physical persecution of trade unionists, thus ensuring a drastic change in bargaining power between workers and firms.[66]

8.9   The Washington Consensus and Expansionary Austerity

The organized ideological pressure of neo-liberal centres has influenced research departments of the major public institutions of the international economic system since the 1970s, starting with Basel's Bank for International Regulations, the International Monetary Fund (IMF) and the World Bank. With the rise of neo-liberal authority in the United States and in Great Britain (with Ronald Reagan and Margaret Thatcher), since the 1980s these institutions have pushed for neo-liberal reforms, abandoning previous attempts at regulating transnational firms. This implies, among other things, a growing competition among states on the fiscal and regulatory planes, which allows transnational firms to drastically reduce tax payments; competition among states is even utilized to encourage the adoption of neo-liberal policies, such as the reduction of taxes and abolition of regulations in the financial and environmental fields.

Beginning in the 1980s, a doctrine comes to dominate, designed as the Washington Consensus by John Williamson, who indicates its main theses: fiscal discipline (reduction of fiscal deficits); restructuring and reduction of the public expenditure; tax reform to expand the number of contributors through a not 'too' progressive system of tax rates (but without a word on the fiscal elusion made possible by competition of fiscal regimes among different countries); liberalization of interest rates and more generally of national and international financial markets; equilibrium exchange rates (corresponding to equilibrium in balances of

---

[66] On the relationships between neo-liberals and Pinochet's Chile cf. Valdés (1995) and Fischer (2009). We find here a parallel to what happened in Italy with the advent of fascism, when many liberal intellectuals, among them Benedetto Croce, initially did not oppose the nascent dictatorship (in Croce's case, even after the assassination of Matteotti, which was for many a moment of enlightenment), considered useful to contrast the diffusion of socialism.

trade); liberalization of external trade (reduction or abolition of duties, abolition of import contingents); full opening to foreign direct investment; privatization; deregulation; defence of property rights. This set of policies is considered as a set of general rules derived from the best economic doctrine, and is imposed on countries in difficulty as a condition for obtaining loans from the International Monetary Fund or the World Bank (and, after the crisis of sovereign debt in the eurozone, from the so-called *troika*: European Commission, ECB, IMF), without attention to the specific conditions of each country.[67]

As repeatedly indicated, these policies rely on the traditional marginalist doctrine, according to which the invisible hand of the market ensures the automatic tendency towards full resource utilization, so that policy interventions are oriented towards supply-side policies, in particular so-called structural reforms aimed at more efficient markets and at offering incentives to savings and work. Williamson (2004) stresses that in his 1989 presentation, he supports opening to foreign direct investment but not the full liberalization of capital movements; as for the rest, it is difficult to distinguish the policy recipes of the Washington Consensus from neo-liberal propositions.

The 2007–8 crisis casts doubt on various important aspects of the neo-liberal construct (as the series of systemic crises of previous decades should have already done). First, as we shall better see in §11.4, the theory of efficient financial markets that had offered analytical support to the policies of financial liberalization appears lunar, vis-à-vis the Keynesian-derived theory developed by Minsky. The bankruptcy of Lehmann Brothers, hailed on the very day by some neo-liberal economists as a positive sign of adhesion of policy authorities to the rules of a market economy, is immediately followed by a rescue policy with very heavy costs for the public purse, that confirms the thesis 'profits are private, losses are public'. The (Schumpeterian) thesis of the 'creative destruction' (according to which the crisis is useful for long period growth because it frees the field from less efficient firms, freeing resources for more efficient ones) is contradicted by the slowing down of technical progress induced by the fall in production, which in turn constitutes a lasting loss of income. The widespread thesis of the necessity of fiscal consolidation to favour growth (the thesis of expansionary austerity) is based on the analysis of isolated

---

[67] Williamson (1990). Williamson (2004) illustrates the history of the rise of the Washington consensus, inclusive of the role played by the Institute for International Economics, and recalls neo-liberalism, defined (ibid., p. 2) as 'The doctrines espoused by the Mont Pèlerin Society', stressing the differences in comparison to them, apparently identified with monetarism and supply-side economics, namely with the doctrines of the Chicago school.

cases[68] and of low estimates of the multipliers.[69] Reinhart and Rogoff's (2010) thesis according to which gross domestic product (GDP) growth is hindered in countries with a debt/GDP ratio above 90% is criticized by Herndon *et al.* (2013), as based on the exclusion of some countries (Canada, New Zealand, Australia, etc.) that contradict it. As foreseen by Keynes and various Keynesian and neoclassical synthesis economists, while the growth of more efficient firms is certainly not hindered by resource scarcity but by low demand manifested in a low degree of utilization of productive capacity, monetary policies (such as ECB's *quantitative easing*) have partial efficacy: they succeed in avoiding the collapse of the world financial system, then the crisis of the euro; but they do not succeed in re-launching economic growth, if not accompanied by expansionary fiscal policies. This is made clear from the comparison of the timing and pace of US and European recoveries, while over the long run, in the absence of re-regulation of financial markets, expansionary monetary policies risk generating new speculative bubbles.

This notwithstanding, and in spite of the feebleness of their theoretical foundations repeatedly recalled in this chapter, neo-liberal theories and especially neo-liberal policies continue to find support and prevail.[70]

---

[68] Alesina and Ardagna (2009).

[69] The estimates by Barro and Redlick (2011) turn out to be meaningfully inferior to those by Blanchard and Leigh (2013), the fruit of a more accurate analysis.

[70] For an example, in fact a minority one, of interpretation of the 2007–9 crisis through the theory of the trade cycle illustrated in §6; cf. Ohanian (2010), who suggests to find its original causes in a (very strong and sudden) increase in *involuntary* unemployment, due to distorting incentives introduced in the labour market with some fiscal policy measures.

9   Applied Economics and Econometrics

9.1   Theoretical Backgrounds of Applied Economics

Applied economics research always relies on various strata of methodological thinking and theories. Inductivism or pragmatism, logical positivism or subjectivism, marginal or Keynesian theory, concur in often hidden and sometimes contradictory ways to provide the foundations for the different streams of applied economic analysis. While important to consider the theoretical foundations of different streams of applied economic research, this would require an in-depth analysis much wider than is possible here. In the chapter to follow, we will do so by focusing on a few key areas and the example of oil. In doing so, we will explore how the central notion of marginal theory, that of scarcity, reflects itself in the analysis of the energy sources, leading to important misunderstandings.

There are noticeable differences among different research streams in the field of applied economics: input–output tables, systems of national accounts, analyses of the trade cycle and the conjuncture, econometrics and the use of descriptive statistics for interpretative purposes are all considered distinct fields, each with its specialists, who often ignore research conducted in other areas.[1]

In the following pages we will briefly illustrate these various research fields, by focusing on their main characteristics. Once again, we will be unable to follow a rigorous chronological order, but instead aim towards a broad overview of the issues at stake.

Indeed, the idea that economic issues can be solved by looking at the quantitative links between the different variables is as old as the study of economic phenomena. William Petty's political arithmetic in the

---

[1] Let us recall here a stream of holistic research, which tries to look at the issue under consideration from all points of view, with interdisciplinary analyses, re-proposed by the Frankfurt school in the 1950s. An illustrious example of it is Pollock (1956) on automation.

seventeenth century is precisely based on the idea that the structure of the economy is constructed according to mathematical laws, 'in terms of number, weight and measure'. Of course, this is not the view that prevails in subsequent centuries. With Adam Smith, in the eighteenth century, another view prevails: that of political economy as a moral science, an idea in various respects shared by protagonists of economic thought in the nineteenth and twentieth centuries such as Marshall and Keynes, to which we shall return in Chapter 14. The quantitative view is nonetheless dominant, accompanying the development and collection of statistical data (Hacking 1990); we can look to the works by Carl Friedrick Gauss (1777–1855), Karl Pearson (1857–1936) and, on specifically economic themes, by Ernst Engel (1821–96) and Vilfredo Pareto by way of example. A decided recovery of the quantitative approach is undertaken on the theoretical level with Jevons's and Walras's marginalist revolution (while Menger's subjectivism and that of the Austrian school distance noticeably from it).

Let us begin in §9.2 with input–output tables, which have roots in much earlier contributions and that are proposed, in the now accepted form, immediately before the Second World War. Then we shall consider, in §9.3, the gradual development of modern national accounting and, in §§9.4 and 9.5, the birth and developments of econometrics. §9.6 hints at a very wide research field, aimed at defining statistical indicators for complex economic and social phenomena, to be utilized in comparison between countries or geographical areas and for examining the evolution of phenomena over time. Subsequent sections are devoted to some specific fields, recently developed or particularly important in practice, also useful for considering in some concrete instances the relationship between theory and applied economics: the economics of energy sources in §9.7; market regulation, market creation and auctions theory in §9.8; and environmental problems in §9.9.

Some research streams in applied economics have already been discussed in previous chapters or will be explored in following chapters; other fields will be necessarily left aside. Indeed, the field of applied economics is immense and rapidly expanding, favoured by increased availability of computing power and publicly available data.[2] As far as computing power is concerned, we are confronted not only with an (enormous) increase in computing speed and an (enormous) increase in the quantity of data that can be handled, but also with new ways of

---

[2] Let us recall for instance the quarterly and monthly data for macroeconomic variables made available by the Federal Reserve Bank of St Louis (FRED-QD and FRED-MD) and by the Federal Reserve Bank of Philadelphia.

computer use and techniques of analysis, as the so-called machine learning.[3]

More recently, we should note a new source of material: the utilization of new, detailed databases made available thanks to the development of informatics. We have access to databases concerning individual data on public salaries, pensions, tax payments, gas and electricity consumption, balance sheets of banks and financial institutions, supermarket sales and so on, up to 'non-conventional' data such as those produced by satellites, for instance on artificial light intensity in different areas of the world.[4] New frontiers for applied research are thus expanding, already providing interesting results.[5]

9.2   Input–Output Tables

Wassily Leontief (1906–99, Nobel Prize in 1973) refers directly to Walras for his input–output tables. These are a representation of the economy through matrixes, namely squares, of numbers: each column indicates the means of production utilized in a given sector, each distinct by sector of origin; each line indicates the partition of the product of a given sector by sectors of destination (cf. Leontief 1941).

Considering Leontief's formation, the origin of input–output tables can be found in Quesnay's (1758–9) *tableau économique* and in Marx's reproduction schemes in Vol. II of *Capital* (Marx 1867–94; cf. Gilibert 1990).

This twin origin suggests that it is possible to consider Leontief's tables as a technical tool of statistical analysis, in itself open to use within different approaches (for instance, classical or marginalist). At the theoretical level, focusing on the formal elements of analysis of relative prices and produced quantities present in Walrasian or Marxian theories, Leontief's tables constitute a contribution that may be developed within either of the two approaches: either in the direction of a classical theory of prices of production (if, through the assumption of constant returns to scale, we isolate this issue from that of the determination of production levels); or in the direction of modern general equilibrium theory (if we 'close' the model by adding to it consumers' preferences and the choice between alternative techniques of production).

---

[3] On machine learning, cf. Mullainathan and Spiess (2017).
[4] On this, cf. Donaldson and Storeygard (2016).
[5] Big data constitute a recent field of research, at the boundaries between informatics, statistics and econometrics, in very rapid development. For some hints to the works in process, cf. Varian (2014). We consider in §10.3 experimental economics, a field of research at the boundary between behavioural and applied economics.

Input–output tables allow us to compute technical coefficients of production (namely, the quantity of each means of production required for each unit of product). Under the assumption of constant returns to scale in all sectors of the economy, it is possible to determine the quantity of gross production of the different sectors (that include the required means of production) corresponding to a given set of net products available for final uses. On the theoretical level, the system of equations determining gross production levels turns out to be the duality (in the mathematical meaning of the term) of the system of equations determining relative prices on the basis of relative difficulties of production of the various commodities; hence the thesis, advanced by many, of an affinity between Leontief's input–output analysis and Sraffa's analysis of prices discussed in Chapter 5.[6] The connections to linear programming and general equilibrium theory are also quite strong, however. As suggested earlier, Leontief's tables may be inserted, with the necessary cautions, within the one or the other theoretical approach.

The first important use of input–output tables took place within the planning of the US war effort. For instance, within war operations, input–output tables are utilized for locating 'vital' interdependencies for the enemy's armaments production, thus the localities to be chosen as targets for bombing.

In the post-war period the extension to various fields of this kind of use is connected to the development of operational research, in particular linear programming.[7]

Leontief's input–output tables then have wide use in applied economics researches; their construction is by now routine for national statistical institutes and is frequently performed also by private research centres. Apart from the use of individual input–output tables for the analysis of the

[6] The duality between price and quantity systems is at the centre of von Neumann's (1937) equi-proportional growth model, that also points to another correspondence, that between profit rate and rate of growth. Both Leontief's and von Neumann's models, however, are developed on the basis of the assumption of constant returns to scale: an assumption that, as we saw in Chapter 5, is instead extraneous to Sraffa's approach, with the analysis focused on the problem of the relationship connecting relative prices and income distribution.

[7] Originally developed by G. Dantzig in 1947, in a work for the US military aviation, linear programming is connected to the use of the method of the simplex that already at the time allowed obtaining numerical solutions for linear equation systems even with numerous variables. For a systematic exposition, cf. Dorfman, Samuelson and Solow (1958). The limits of applicability of linear programming are stressed by Simon (1997, pp. 66–7): the problem object of analysis must be simplified, without a significant loss of realism, in such a way as to express the quantity to be optimized as a *convex* function of numerical variables; the relations and constraints that together with the target variable define the problem must be expressed as linear equalities or inequalities; the data necessary for the estimates of all parameters in the model must be available.

productive structure of an economy, comparisons between input–output tables relative to different countries or to different years are used for studying differences in national productive structure and technical change. A wide multiregional input–output model of the world economy has been developed within a research program directed by Leontief himself and was sponsored by the United Nations (Leontief et al. 1977).

Another, more recent, use of input–output tables is the so-called TIVA (trade in value added), aimed at measuring how much of the value of each commodity is produced in the different countries that participate in its productive chain; the resulting web of interdependencies has implications for the meanings to be attributed to traditional international trade statistics.

9.3   National Accounting

Another tool of empirical analysis is the national accounting system, elaborated under the stimulus of theoretical developments in the inter-war period, but whose universal use is largely independent of its cultural roots. In this case, the stimulus mainly comes from Keynesian theory and from the macroeconomic categories it uses. At least in the case of the main proponent of this stream of research, Richard Stone (1913–91, Nobel Prize in 1984), however, we should also note the influence of a long tradition of research on the measurement of national income, from William Petty's political arithmetic in the seventeenth century up to the economic historian Colin Clark (1905–89) in England and to Simon Kuznets in the United States.[8]

The system of national accounting offers a set of categories, defined so as to be susceptible to rigorous statistical survey and to respect the principles of double bookkeeping, which represent the functioning of the economy as a web of flows of commodities and money connecting the different sectors of the economy. Alongside the flows (of national income, consumption, investment and so on) necessarily defined in relation to an interval of time, in general the year, also stocks are considered (of private wealth, public debt, etc.) defined in relation to a moment in time, in general 31 December of each year.

---

[8] Stone (1997) provides an accurate reconstruction of the contributions of English arithmeticians and their successors up to 1900. The history of estimates of US and English national incomes in the inter-war period is illustrated by Patinkin (1976).

At the initiative of the United Nations and under Stone's direction, a system of national accounts (SNA) was developed (first in 1953, subsequently revised a number of times) that now constitutes a reference point for the national statistical institutes in different countries.[9]

The tendency towards uniformity of the criteria for statistical surveys among countries, which accelerated after the dissolution of the Soviet system of material accounts, accelerated again, especially within some areas such as the European Union, in tandem with the use of statistical indicators for coordinating economic policies or to verify the respect of some international agreements, such as the so-called Maastricht rules.

National accounting, though developed under the influence of the need to render operational the Keynesian categories of policy, today follows the views typical of the utilitarian–marginalist theory. To understand this point, we can refer to Adam Smith's position according to which only workers employed in the production of material goods are productive (then taken up by Marx, and in its wake by national accounting systems in communist countries) and to Jean-Baptiste Say's critique, according to which any activity generating utility is productive.

Thus, the production of services is also considered as part of the national income. Indeed, it includes whatever goes through the market, including all public sector activities (whose expenditures are an income for the private sector and whose income is an expenditure for the latter). Recently, the frontier has been widened to include the so-called informal and illegal economy (estimated at about 10% of national income). Not considered, however, are costs and advantages not directly evaluable, for instance the environmental costs of economic activity.

In sum, the notion of national income is built as an aggregate (sum) of individual incomes. The definition of these latter also implies various problems that may receive only a conventional solution; after illustrating some of them, Hicks (1939, p. 180) concludes that for the theoretical

[9] The most important restructuring of the national accounts system was made public by the United Nations in 1993, after various years of work; on it relies the European System of Accounts (ESA) published in 1995. For an exposition, cfr. Jackson (2000). SNA 1993 has been newly updated (SNA 2008: details may be found on the website of the United Nations, https://unstats.un.org/unsd/nationalaccount/sna2008. app), but a number of issues remain open. The IMF publishes a *Balance of payments and international investment position manual*, the sixth edition of which was published in 2013 (BPM6, available at www.imf.org/external/pubs/ft/bop/2007/bopman6.htm).

economist, who needs to be rigorous, 'income is a very dangerous term, and it can be avoided', while the notion though an approximate one may be useful in social statistics. In fact, through recourse to the simple aggregation of individual incomes many problems are circumvented. For instance, in the case of externalities, the individual income (product) does not correspond to income (product) from a social point of view; all issues concerning the definition of productive labour are left aside; domestic work (including that concerning care of the old, the young and the ill) is not considered, so that in countries with a larger share of services provided within the family the gross domestic product (GDP) is relatively reduced.

Furthermore, in the history of national accounts, various adjustments take place in order to take into account the changes in the structure of the economy. For instance, the original bipartition dominating at the time of classical economists (agriculture and industry) is followed by a tripartition (agriculture, industry and services); finally, after the share of services surpassed 50% of GDP the distinction between public and private services is added. Analogously, subcategories within industry and services are changed, while some subcategories in agriculture disappear or are reclassified at a lower level of aggregation. On the whole, the field of statistical surveys has enormously increased, and this implies the introduction of new items and the tendency to more and more detailed classification.

Indeed, the magnitudes of national accounts have a relative meaning, to be evaluated each time in relation to the problem under consideration. In various cases, it may be useful to add to national accounting data other information, as the indicators discussed in §9.6.

Importantly, we should emphasize the conventional nature of national accounting categories: an unavoidable fact, if we want to make use of statistical information comparable between countries and through time. This obscures a series of conceptual issues, however, often relegated to a secondary plane relative to more technical issues to be dealt with when trying to reach consensus on operationally efficient definitions and surveying procedures at the international level.

Let us recall, in synthesis, some of these issues. A first aspect concerns the very definition of net national income, which, rigorously speaking, should exclude not only fixed capital amortization, but also the expenditures that would be necessary to reintegrate natural resources used up in production (for instance, exploration expenditures required to locate new mineral reserves, or those for reforestation). The definition of amortization too opens new issues: in general, old machinery is substituted by new machines, making comparisons difficult; further, firms avail themselves of the legal margins of discretion and choose the accounting data for amortisation so as to minimize their tax payments. As for environmental costs, their estimation is also challenging, even more so in the context of climate change. Another theme concerns services provided outside the market, within the family or on a voluntary basis: shifting a share of such services (domestic aid, for instance) to the market may increase national and per capita income without any real change in the quantity of services provided.

Attempts at making the definition of national income more inclusive, like the recent introduction of the informal (or 'submerged') economy and that proposed for the illegal economy, do not take into account the (social, but economic as well) costs of such activities. The missed consideration of the damages caused by natural calamities lends itself to problems of missed coordination between flow and stock accounting, if such damages are considered in stock but not in flow accounting, or of a distance between the data and the real situation, if such damages are not taken into consideration.

Another recently emerged problem concerns financial services, whose share in the GDP has roughly doubled in a majority of countries over the past two to three decades. Insofar as they are services of production, they should be included in gross production but not in income. Unless we want to suggest that the real quantity of financial services, however defined, provided to customers has doubled, we should admit that the growth of such a sector is mainly the result of an important redistribution of income in favour of the financial sector, with a fall of productivity of the resources employed, measured in terms of current values.

All these issues are the subject of debate.[10] They indicate two things: the need to utilize national accounting data with caution, recognizing their enormous informative value but also their enormous limits; the need for keeping alive the scientific debate on such limits, not simply to integrate such data with other information (as the indicators discussed in §9.6), but also for acquiring greater awareness in their use.

Finally, among the analytical developments of national accounting we should include the method of social accounting matrixes, originated by Stone (Stone and Brown 1962) and then developed by Irma Adelman and others. This method is similar to the general computational equilibrium models discussed in §7.6 and to the stock-flow consistent analysis developed by Godley (successor to Stone as director of the Department of

---

[10] As financial services are concerned, cf. Mazzucato (2018), pp. 75 ff.

Applied Economics at Cambridge University) within a Keynesian framework, discussed in §12.5.

9.4   The Naissance of Econometrics

The growing availability of statistical information, sufficiently reliable and collected in categories defined according to sufficiently general criteria, undoubtedly favours the development of applied economics research. Developments in statistical theory, in particular inferential statistics, also play an important role. These elements (and others, such as progress in informatics) help explain the impetuous developments of econometrics (from the Greek *metron*, measure) in recent decades: the discipline that aims to identify quantitative relations among economic variables, as a basis for the interpretation of economic phenomena.[11]

The marginal revolution and the mathematization of economics that followed it played a relatively modest role in the development of econometrics. Attempts to precisely estimate the numerical values to be attributed to economic relations, between the end of the nineteenth and the beginning of the twentieth century, mainly concern aspects external to the nucleus of the theories of value: by way of example, we can refer to the consumption curves studied by Ernst Engel (1821–96)[12] or to Pareto's research on personal income distribution. Moreover, there is a qualitative leap between the simple use of statistical data for descriptive purposes in applied economics and the systematic search of precise quantitative relations among the variables. It is this second aspect, in fact, that marks the birth of econometrics.

The Italian Rodolfo Benini (1862–1956), statistician, demographer and economist, is among the first (cf. Benini 1907) to utilize advanced statistical methods such as multiple regressions in economic analysis. The American Henry Moore (1869–1958) and his pupils (among which let us recall Paul Douglas, 1892–1976, and Henry Schultz, 1893–1938) systematically pursue quantitative analysis through statistical estimates of economic relations.[13]

---

[11] Cliometrics concerns the use of quantitative data in studies in economic history.

[12] 'Engel's law' states that when family income grows, the expenditure for food grows less than proportionally. On the history of this law, cf. Kindleberger (1989, First Lecture). We hinted at 'economic laws' in §7.6.

[13] To Douglas, together with the mathematician Charles Cobb, we owe the construction of the aggregate production function called Cobb–Douglas, very widely utilized not only in statistical analyses but also in theory, notwithstanding the demonstrated erroneousness of its foundations (due to the aggregate notion of capital it employs: cf. §12.6). On the theoretical level, the aggregate production function may be traced back to Wicksell (even if he was aware of its limits: cf. §3.2).

Ambitious methodological foundations for econometrics were developed by the Norwegian Ragnar Frisch (1895–1973),[14] in his editorial to the first issue of the new journal *Econometrica* (Frisch 1933), which he edited until 1955, and conceived as the organ of the Econometric Society, founded in 1930.[15] According to Frisch, econometrics constitutes the unification of statistics, economic theory and mathematics necessary for 'a real understanding of the quantitative relations in modern economic life'.

A stream of research active with important results within the Cowles Commission (then Foundation) is that of the methods of quantitative analysis, alongside that relative to attempts to construct an axiomatic general equilibrium theory. The simultaneous presence of these two research streams corresponds to the idea that theory has direct implications for the interpretation of reality and for policy choices. Even in the case of contributions concerning methods of quantitative analysis we have mainly formalistic developments, on conceptual foundations accepted without an in-depth debate: the subjective approach to probability theory, discussed in §§3.6 and 6.2.

Cowles Commission economists provide crucial contributions to the development of the new econometric techniques: most notably, Jacob Marshak (1898–1977), Tjalling Koopmans (1910–84), Don Patinkin (1922–97), Lawrence Klein (1920–2013, Nobel Prize in 1980).[16] The Norwegian Trygve Haavelmo (1911–99, Nobel Prize in 1989), in an essay published in 1944 as supplement to *Econometrica*, proposes the insertion of econometric relations in a stochastic context. In this way, among other things, Haavelmo defends the econometric approach from some of Keynes's (1973, pp. 295–329) criticisms against Tinbergen's researches on trade cycles and the construction of macroeconomic models.[17]

---

[14] In 1969 Frisch shares with the Dutch Jan Tinbergen (1903–94), another towering figure in the specific field we are dealing with, the first Nobel Prize in economics.

[15] Tsuru (1993, p. 74) quotes a statement by Myrdal, according to whom the Econometric Society 'was planned as a defence organization against the institutionalists'.

[16] For an illustration of the role of the Cowles Commission, cf. Klein (1991); we already hinted in §6.3 about the role of the Cowles Commission for the development of the axiomatic theory of general equilibrium.

[17] There is a mass of writings on the debate between Keynes and Tinbergen; cf. for instance Patinkin (1976) and Hendry (1980). Contrary to a widespread *vulgata*, Keynes's critiques do not stem from a generic hostility to the use of mathematical or statistical tools in the economic field, but from a conscious evaluation of their limits: let us recall that Keynes had authored an important *Treatise on probability* (Keynes 1921). That Keynes's critiques – still actual – are directed to certain kinds of uses of mathematical and statistical tools and not to these tools as such is evident also from his well-known invective in this respect, in the *General theory* (1936, p. 298): 'Too large a proportion of recent

As seen earlier, development of quantitative analysis receives an impulse, particularly in the United States, from its use in support of the war effort during the Second World War. This is especially true for operational research, utilized for solving planning problems in transport and similar fields. Modern econometrics, aimed at construction of large econometric models, sees the light in the immediate post-war period, within the Cowles Commission; the first econometric model of the US economy is authored by Klein.[18] In part due to the growth of public intervention in the economy, the need for macroeconomic forecasts is strongly felt and this favours development of new tools of analysis. Political tensions connected to the Cold War, together with forecasts of an imminent new Great Crisis within market economies with the exhaustion of war expenditure, render the optimistic forecasts of Cowles Commission economists, wholly against the tide, a crucial test in favour of the new analytical techniques, that soon lead to a more widespread diffusion.

Among others, it is important to make note of the FED–MIT–Penn model, starting in 1964 and built under Modigliani's direction. Starting in 1966, he collaborated in the construction of an econometric model at the Bank of Italy. Sylos Labini (1967) also developed an econometric model for the Italian economy: in it, three major economic sectors (industry, agriculture, commerce) are characterized by their attribution to a different market form, with different rules for price formation.

9.5   The Developments of Econometrics

In the golden years of the development of econometrics, many economists were still tentative towards the field. Hendry (1980) recalls the criticisms by Keynes, Worswick, Phelps Brown, Leontief and Hicks; below we will recall Lucas's critique. As Hendry himself stresses, econometrics needs to be utilized with extreme caution in interpreting reality: together with instances

"mathematical" economics are mere concoctions, as imprecise as the initial assumptions they rest on, which allow the author to lose sight of the complexities and interdependencies of the real world in a mess of pretentious and unhelpful symbols.' To Haavelmo's work (who after working at the Cowles Commission goes back to Oslo University in 1947) Morgan (1990) dedicates the closing chapter of her book, in which she illustrates the formative years of econometrics, with particular attention to Frish's method of analysis of historical series and to Tinbergen's schemes.

[18] The model is then developed at the University of Michigan. Klein subsequently heads two other projects aimed at building large macroeconomic models: the so-called 'Brookings model' and the 'project Link', aimed at connecting econometric models built by research centres in different countries, thus producing a world model articulated by large geographical areas and where possible by countries.

of spurious correlation (in Hendry's example, the cumulated fall of rain in the UK 'explains' inflation better than the quantity of money in circulation) and to the many problems already recalled by Keynes (as the frequent omission of relevant variables) we may recall various others, such as the frequent inadequate size of the samples[19] or the distortions introduced with the construction of aggregate variables.[20]

Theoretical work in the econometric field in recent decades has aimed to address these problems. In the meantime, econometrics has spread, thanks to the technological developments in computing, and also to the pressure of academic competition stimulated by the new rules of quantitative evaluation of research output (publish or perish) that generates a mountain of econometric exercises, though often of a quite doubtful validity. Relatedly, the space devoted to econometric teaching in universities has grown, though often limited to introductive courses, with the consequence of a lesser awareness of the limits of the tool (and, still worse, of the limits of the statistical data utilized).

Theoretical work on the construction of new econometric techniques nonetheless continues. Among the most important developments, let us recall those concerning the methods of analysis of time series, with ARMA (autoregressive moving average) models: cf. Box and Jenkins (1970), then ARIMA (where I stands for integrated, concerning non-stationary time series).

Subsequently, the VAR (vector autoregressive) method (cf. Sims, 1980, 1982) is proposed as an alternative to traditional econometrics, radically criticized. In particular Lucas (1976), relying on rational expectations theory (cf. §8.6), recalls that the structural parameters of macroeconomic models are subject to change when confronted with discretionary policy interventions, so that the models cannot be utilized for forecasting the effects of policy measures. This is followed by an avalanche of econometric exercises aimed at verifying or falsifying rational expectations theory (or specific propositions, such as the neutrality of public debt) in opposition to neoclassical synthesis models.

---

[19] A clamorous example is that of models built by the institutions responsible for controlling the financial markets and by many large banks for determining the value at risk utilized for computing their capital requirements: in the majority of cases, series of daily data covering less than a year! When the financial crisis explodes in 2007–8, some influential bankers even maintain, recalling those models in excuse for their own forecasting failures, that the crisis had a probability of one over 10, or 18, times the life of the universe . . . Cf. Roncaglia (2012b).

[20] Though remaining an insignificant fraction of the econometric works published yearly, the critical literature on the theme is expanding and the debate on the validity of econometric studies is lively; cf. for instance Ioannidis *et al.* (2017).

Sims proposes instead an 'a-theoretical econometrics', in which the structure of the model is not predetermined: econometric analysis is responsible for specifying which models are most adequate, rather than for testing pre-assigned hypotheses. The distance between econometrics and economic theory thus widens, as economic theory no longer guides the formation of hypotheses tested within econometrics.

Both theses – the usefulness of econometrics for verifying theories or for locating new theoretical cause-and-effect links – should be treated with caution.[21] On the one hand, it is – or should have been – obvious ab initio that econometric research cannot discriminate between 'right' and 'wrong' theories, as such verification would simultaneously concern the theory itself and the auxiliary hypotheses necessary to translate it into an econometric model.[22] On the other hand, we may recall Hume's scepticism, and of so many others after him, on the possibility of inferring 'laws' from observation of a limited number of data: statistical tests may at most provide working hypotheses that should anyhow be evaluated through theoretical reasoning. In the field of social sciences even more than in the field of natural sciences, it is also quite difficult to utilise econometric tests to falsify a 'law', as its failure in a specific case may be always justified by referring to anomalous circumstances.

9.6 The New Descriptive Statistics: The Search for Indicators

The growing availability of mass data on varied phenomena favours the development of applied analyses on a wide range of issues. In many other cases, however, such research verges on the ridiculous.[23] In other cases, research simply corroborates hypotheses corresponding to common sense; at times, research can be used to support theses with a strong political content but with feeble theoretical foundations. Even in the best cases, in which applied analyses are utilized in search for interpretations of current economic events, references to economic theory are frequently approximate and unaware of the theoretical debates, for instance those concerning the theory of value and distribution. Ultimately, the trend towards specialization has a high cost.

Research fields are very numerous and cover all areas of economics: labour, industry, money and so on. A wide field concerns income

---

[21] For a survey of the analytical innovations that, though not allowing establishment with certainty the existence of cause-and-effect links, contribute to increase favourable or unfavourable circumstantial evidence; cf. Athey and Imbens (2017).

[22] Cf. Cross (1982).

[23] We may look at the list of the IgNobel, at www.improbable.com/ig/.

distribution between and within countries. An imposing dataset on income distribution within the various countries is built by the Luxemburg Income Study (founded and directed by Tim Smeedling from 1983 to 2006); a vast set of studies on various countries, coordinated by Anthony Atkinson and Thomas Piketty, is presented in various writings.[24]

Alongside analyses on income, we should also consider research on the distribution of wealth and on family budgets.[25] We may also consider as a sub-area of research on income distribution that concerning poverty; it is customary in this respect to distinguish between absolute poverty (per capita income inferior to a given limit value – up to a few years ago one dollar per day, now often taken up to two dollars a day) and relative poverty (income inferior to a given percentage of average or median income of the country, for instance 20%).

Another body of research regarding the development of per capita income in different countries and to comparisons between countries at different levels of economic development has also emerged in recent years. By way of example, the development of this work can be exemplified by Angus Maddison's (2007) seminal research, covering, with different levels of detail, an interval of time of more than two millennia and the whole world. Relatedly, van Ark (1997) undertook a three-volume selection of empirical analyses of the various aspects of long-period growth (from models of industrial growth [Chenery 1960], to international comparisons of productivity, [Kravis 1976], or of per capita income [Kravis et al. 1978]).

Data are continuously updated by international organizations, in particular by the World Bank in its important yearly report.[26] Together with statistical updates, each yearly report undertakes an examination of the development process. Following the capability notion proposed by Amartya Sen (discussed in §14.5), the United Nations Development Programme (UNDP), at the initiative of its chairman Ul Haq, developed a human development index (HDI) that synthesizes indicators concerning economic growth (per capita income, in dollars at purchasing power parity), health (life expectation at birth, infant mortality, morbidity), education (reading ability, share of diplomats and university laureates,

---

[24] Cf. the overall presentation by Atkinson et al. (2011) and Piketty's (2013) book, to which we shall return in §14.3. Cf. also Milanovic (2016).

[25] Cf. for instance Deaton (1997). Angus Deaton (b. 1945) receives the Nobel Prize in 2015.

[26] As recalled in §7.6, publication of this important report, always rich in material and analyses, starts in 1978 at the initiative of Hollis Chenery, at the time vice president of the Bank.

etc.). In turn, this indicator is the object of many studies: some dwell on the different aspects of its construction, proposing modifications to the original indicator (some of which were recently accepted by UNDP);[27] others utilize it for interpreting development trends in the economy over time.[28]

The HDI is an example of a synthetic indicator: the best known example of a wide group of indicators developed in order to express in a single quantitative variable a set of aspects considered relevant for the process of economic development, such as the opening to international trade, the degree of competition in internal markets, the degree of democracy or of 'economic freedom', the efficiency of public administration and in particular the efficiency of justice, the extent of corruption, the degree of independence of central banks, the level of financial education of families, up to authoritarian populism and uncertainty.[29]

Various other synthetic indicators aim at measuring gender inequalities. Among the most important, let us recall the GDI (gender-related development index) and the GEM (gender empowerment measure) published by UNDP since 1995.

Other quantitative studies, conducted by some of the main national statistical institutes, aim at constructing indicators of sustainable development, or of society's well-being,[30] a noticeable push in this direction being given by the Commission on the measurement of economic performance and social progress (CMEPSP) instituted by the French government in 2008 and coordinated by Jean-Paul Fitoussi, Amartya Sen and Joseph Stiglitz (Fitoussi et al. 2009).

[27] For instance, Palazzi and Casadio Tarabusi (2004) propose use of a harmonic instead of an arithmetic average for the synthesis of the different basic indicators. For a survey of the debate and an illustration of the changes accepted by the UNDP beginning with the *Human Development Report* for 2010, cf. Klugman et al. (2011); cf. also Casadio Tarabusi and Guarini (2016).

[28] For instance, it is possible to consider the correlation between per capita income and the indicators concerning health and cultural level, and then to analyse the reasons why some countries turn out to be above or below the correlation line. Consider Costa Rica, with an average life expectancy at birth significantly above that 'justified' by its per capita income, and Kuwait in the opposite situation. In explaining these anomalies we may recall education expenditure on which public expenditure focuses in Costa Rica (a country without an army), and segregation of women in Kuwait leading to a significantly higher level of infant mortality. Other studies stress the importance in this context of a greater or lesser inequality in income distribution.

[29] The literature on the theme is abundant. Here we shall limit to two examples. An index of authoritarian populism (Johansson Heinö 2016) is based on electoral results and on a classification of political parties in right-wing authoritarian, centre, left-wing authoritarian. An index concerning policy uncertainties (Economic Policy Uncertainty Index, EPU: Baker et al. 2016), utilized by the Bank of Italy in its *Rapporto sulla stabilità finanziaria* (n.1, 2017, p. 9) is based on 'frequency of references to uncertainty in economic policy present in the articles of the main European newspapers'.

[30] For instance Istat publishes yearly a *Rapporto sul benessere equo e sostenibile* (BES).

Reference to a multiplicity of indicators, rather than to the sole GDP, undoubtedly provides a more complete picture, allowing us to take into account – at least in part – the multidimensionality of human societies. The ways in which these indicators are built, however, leaves much to be desired, both for the subjective choices required for their construction and for the importance of aspects that, not being liable to translation into quantitative terms, are passed over. This notwithstanding, once made available, these indexes are utilized – nearly always without notes of caution or only with some generic reference to their limits – for quantitative research aimed at explaining the more or less rapid development of different countries. In this way, cliometrics ends up by substituting economic history, and the interpretations proposed for the various phenomena appear to acquire a false appearance of objectivity, and hence of superiority in comparison to qualitative analyses in which the importance of the subjective interpretation of the researcher and the need for caution on the results is evident.

9.7 Market Regulation, Market Creation and Auctions

Different microeconomic theories recognize the possibility of situations in which competition does not rule, for reasons that may vary from one case to another: natural monopolies, presence of increasing returns to scale leading to too large size of firms and collusive behaviour of the firms. There are also external economies and diseconomies, when individual choices have collateral effects not taken into consideration when the agents decide on the basis of their own self-interest. As a consequence, even when competition prevails, external diseconomies lead to excessive production (as in the case of pollution) while external economies lead to suboptimal levels of production (as in the case of education).

These aspects, hinted at in §8.7, were already recognized at the end of the nineteenth century, and are for instance discussed in Marshall's *Principles* (1890), to receive subsequently systematic treatment at the hand, for instance, of Pigou (1912). When confronted with natural monopolies, recourse may be had to direct state management or to administrative constraints on prices and product quality, possibly imposed by ad hoc institutions. Confronted with the excessive size of firms, as with collusive policies, beginning at the end of the nineteenth century, an anti-trust legislation (supported by wide popular opposition to concentrations of economic power) gradually takes root and maintains considerable influence, exemplified in the case of dismantling Rockefeller's Standard Oil Trust in 1912, and then again in 1982, when AT&T (American Telephone and Telegraph) was forced to divest itself of local operations. In these cases, in conformity to the traditional paradigm, it is the size of firms (both in absolute terms and as a share of the market of reference) that signals the presence of a non-competitive situation deserving to be sanctioned.

Developments in the period here considered concern various aspects, which we shall briefly discuss. First, we have the thesis that state intervention may constitute a remedy worse than the illness, since (as held by the theory of public choice, discussed in §8.7) regulators are not necessarily *super partes*, but may be induced by their own self-interest to interventions different from those most opportune from the point of view of public interest. This is a thesis parallel to, but going in the opposite direction from, that of the 'regulator's capture' according to which regulators may be persuaded to meet the interests of the firm under their control in pursuing their own self-interest; confronted with this problem, intervening in all cases in which a market power is present rather than waiting for its use against public interest should be reinforced, possibly rendered automatic.

Second, there is the thesis, gradually developing from Schumpeter, and fully developed with the theory of contestable markets by Baumol and others (discussed in §6.6), according to which what matters is not the dimension or the number of firms, but the possibility of entry into and exit from the market at no cost, which renders possible a hit-and-run behaviour whenever there is some opportunity of extra-profits in some sector.

Finally, there is the neo-liberal view, discussed in Chapter 8, according to which defence of the market economy requires not to intervene except in fully exceptional cases, even when confronted with clearly non-competitive situations. In such cases, any behaviour of firms that though enjoying market power conforms to what would happen under competition is considered fair: the notion of 'as if' competition, especially if combined with the notion of effective (adequate, even if not full) competition suggested by Clark (1940), hinders anti-trust proceedings, impeding passing judgements based on the sheer presence of market power. In Italy, as in many other countries, only the demonstrated exploitation of market power on the side of the firm allows for anti-trust intervention.

Anti-trust authorities are a well-established element in the majority of industrialized countries; the importance of their decisions implies important debates between economists and lawyers, concerning both the general orientation and the analysis of the policies followed by major anti-trust authorities (that vary over time and from country to country), and the critical evaluation of the main decisions.

In this respect, a lively debate concerns the air transport sector, where a simple change in regulations introduced in 1978 with the Airline

Deregulation Act in the United States – shifting from the requirement to authorize each route to the authorization to fly *sic et simpliciter* – enormously increases competition between airlines. At the passage of the new millennium, a multibillion-dollar case discussed at the US anti-trust authority concerned Microsoft, accused by Netscape of trying to impose its browser, Internet Explorer, on all Windows users; the proceedings give rise to a wide scientific debate, with involvement on either front of some among the best-known industrial economists.[31] Even more than in other sectors, in the field of informatics, the importance of economies of scale is enormous: fixed costs (required for instance for writing a program and for its launch) may be high, but then marginal costs are nil or nearly so. Network economies (the number of users) are very important for consumers; this is clear for the case of telecommunications, but is still truer for networks such as Facebook, WhatsApp and other similar networks. The provider who initially takes the lead is then favoured in conquering the whole market; entry of a new competitor is very difficult, practically impossible. Thus, a new notion of competition arises, in the rhetorical attempt to avoid anti-trust interventions: from competition 'in' the market we shift to competition 'for' the market.

The customary solution for natural monopolies of a traditional kind, up until recently, was direct public involvement, mainly through nationalized companies, or regulation through independent authorities setting prices and possibly authorizing construction of new plants or a more general expansion of productive capacity. Internal economies and especially diseconomies, for instance pollution, are traditionally dealt with through regulation of the production and consumption activities involved, for instance through the indication of maximum limits to dangerous emissions, but also through systems of incentives and disincentives, following a wide stream of analysis of public finance economists.[32]

---

[31] The reports of two experts, Richard Schmalensee (chair of the MIT Sloan School of Management) for Microsoft and Franklin Fisher (he too professor at MIT, and supervisor of Schmalensee's doctoral dissertation) for the US Department of Justice, available on the web, amount to hundreds of pages and contain original contributions to industrial economics, especially in what concerns the interaction between technological change and evolution of market structure. There is a wide literature on this case (cf. e.g. Sabbatini 2000 and Costa 2004); in general, yearly reports of anti-trust authorities of various countries (and of the European Union), documentation on individual cases and the relative literature amount to tens of thousands of pages.

[32] The debate concerns various aspects, from the possibility of regulator capture on the side of major firms of the sector to the choice of the forms of compensation for nationalized firms. The importance of this latter aspect is shown by the wide debate taking place in Italy at the beginning of the 1960s on whether to compensate the shareholders of the nationalized electric companies or to pay these latter for their plants: the latter way was chosen, favouring the major private economic power centres of the time (grown not for

A key theoretician of regulation in this respect was Alfred Kahn (1917–2010), for decades professor at Cornell University and president of the Civil Aeronautics Board in its crucial years of 1977–8. The two volumes of his *Economics of regulation* (vol. 1, *Economic principles*, 1970; vol. 2, *Institutional issues*, 1971) represent the result of a long series of consulting activities and scientific research, and were groundbreaking at the time of their publication. In the debate on anti-trust and regulation, Kahn focuses attention on the behaviour of firms more than on their market shares; his position is moderately progressive, open to the market but persuaded of the need for corrective interventions in front of monopoly power (rather than ex post interventions against monopolist practices); he is thus opposed to positions more favourable to autonomy of private firms such as those of the Chicago school and their allies.[33]

With the upsurge of neo-liberalism following the 1970s, economists more convinced of the efficiency of the market economy propose solutions consisting in the creation of new markets and in recourse to market mechanisms.

For instance, regarding the problem of pollution, it has been proposed to emit 'permits to pollute' with a market of their own: firms requiring such permits pay for obtaining them, and are authorized to generate a certain quantity of polluting emissions, while firms that succeed in abating their emissions may sell such permits, for a quantity corresponding to abated pollution. In this way, the market allocates the weight of the fight against pollution among firms, each of them choosing the best solution on the basis of their technology. The functioning of the market has a cost; we must also take into consideration the controls by an independent authority, as public authorities cannot limit themselves to register the declarations provided by the firms themselves on the amount of their pollution. Moreover, because of always present imperfection in controls, some firms may dedicate as much effort, if not more, to finding ways to hide their pollution than to searching for more environmentally friendly techniques, considering the gains they may obtain through the sale of permits. Indeed, it is only the assumption of perfect markets customary to traditional theory that renders markets for permits preferable to direct quantitative limits, independently of any case-by-case concrete analysis.

---

their abilities but thanks to their monopoly rents), and this has had in subsequent decades a strong negative influence on Italian political life (and on its morality).

[33] On Kahn's life and contributions cf. Joskow and Noll (2013); on his role in deregulating air transport cf. Button (2015).

The pure theory of regulation has progressed rapidly since the 1970s, on the basis of principal–agent theory (cf. § 6.9). Techniques such as peak-load pricing have been developed, namely the setting of higher prices for the hours characterized by higher demand, utilized for reducing the peak demand for firms (such as in electricity and natural gas) that confront a demand with wide daily, weekly and seasonal variations. This has been exemplified by Laffont and Tirole (1993), two of the main protagonists of this research stream: Tirole (b. 1953) received the Nobel Prize in 2014, and would probably have shared it with Laffont if he had not prematurely died in March of the same year.

To assign concessions (for instance for the use of radio waves, or to explore certain areas at land or sea in search of oil or other minerals), the traditional system based on discretional decisions of the public authorities (a system going back to the Middle Ages and then to absolute monarchies, when nobles and the king conceded privileges to their protégées) is substituted in recent times and in a growing measure in the past few years by recourse to auctions, which by now constitute an important source of revenue for the state.[34] Correspondingly, a theory of auctions has been developed, for evaluating their possible characteristics (the so-called mechanism design), with wide recourse to the tools of game theory. In its more general form, the problem concerns choosing between public auction or auction with offers in sealed envelope, English auction (which starts from a low price and leaves auction participants free to offer more), or Dutch auction (starting from high prices, with offers with price rebates); it is then necessary to specify with precision all auction rules.

Among contributions to this theory, an original starting point is that of Vickrey (1961), which illustrates the convenience, in auctions with sealed envelopes, of the rule that the second rather than the first offer be accepted. Acceptance of the first offer induces participants to the auction to perform strategic behaviour in which each tries to bear in mind what others will do, with the possibility of setting a price immediately above that proposed by the others; with the Vickrey rule, each competitor is induced to declare his or her maximum evaluation. Moreover, this mechanism reduces, among the participants, the fear of the so-called winner's curse: if I offer more than others for the right to explore a certain lot and I win the auction, this depends on the fact that my

---

[34] Still in use are also beauty contests, in which firms submit to public authorities a plan on how they will utilize the resource and the authorities choose the plan most advantageous for the common good; with the first-come-first-served method, attribution takes place on the simple timing of presentation of the demand; with grandfather rights, whoever is already utilizing the resource continues to do so; with lotteries the resource is assigned by drawing a ballot.

evaluation of the foreseeable returns is the most optimistic of all; if, as is likely, the actual return from the lot is closer to the average or median evaluation than to the most optimistic one, this means that the winner of the auction will end up losing.[35]

The number of economists presently engaged in research, in public institutions or in consulting activity in the fields of anti-trust, regulation and auctions is high and growing. We should remark that especially in these fields 'consulting economists are at risk of becoming perceived in the same way as lawyers, namely as hired guns' (Krew and Kleindorfer 2002, p. 16); as in the case of business lawyers, potential earnings are widely superior to those of theoretical economists.

9.8 Between Theory and Applied Economics: The Economics of Energy Sources

Among the fields of application of microeconomic theory, perhaps the most interesting is the field of economics of energy sources, not only for its importance, but also because within it more or less all approaches illustrated in Chapter 6 find some use, from general equilibrium intertemporal theory to the Marshallian theory of the firm and the industry, up to oligopoly theory.

Let us begin with intertemporal general equilibrium theory, more precisely with Hotelling's theorem (1931), concerning all exhaustible natural resources, for each of which the quantity available is considered as given and known.[36] In the case of perfect competition, and considering as given the state of technological knowledge, the price of the exhaustible natural resources (net of extraction costs, that for simplicity we may assume to be constant over time) must grow over time at a rate equal to the rate of interest (that in turn in equilibrium must be equal to the rate of intertemporal preference of the agents present in the market). The increase in price slows down use of the scarce resource, up to the moment of its full exhaustion, when demand too becomes zero. It is thus shown that in the presence of a complete system of spot and future prices competition ensures an optimal allocation of the scarce resource over

---

[35] The collective text edited by Janssen (2004) illustrates in its chapters the various kinds of auctions, some of the main theoretical issues and some case studies and provides further bibliographical information. The winner's curse is the object of many analyses, theoretical, applied and experimental; cf. for instance Kagel and Levin (1986); Thaler (1988, 1992). For a survey of the first and fundamental stage of development of auctions theory cf. McAfee and McMillan (1987).

[36] Harold Hotelling (1898–1973) provides important contributions to statistics and econometrics, and with his model of spatial competition in duopoly anticipates some important aspects of modern game theory (Hotelling 1929).

time.[37] Among the variants of this basic model, Nordhaus (1973) introduces the notion of backstop technology: the price of the scarce resource ceases to increase as soon as it equals the costs required for use of an alternative technology.

The notion of scarcity of natural resources utilized in this theory is fully consonant with the notion of scarcity that plays a central role in the marginalist approach, in all its variants. To understand its implications, we can refer to the Club of Rome report on *The limits to growth* (Meadows *et al.* 1972), which indicates that the exhaustion of all main natural resources is imminent. This view favours the abolition of oil import contingents in the United States: a measure that strongly contributed to the 1973 oil crisis.[38] According to the report, oil should have been exhausted within 17 years (from 1972); indeed, today world oil 'proven' reserves are around forty years of current consumption, while 'ultimate' reserves, of much more uncertain evaluation, are much wider.

Hotelling's theorem has its feeble point in its assumptions: technology and quantity finally available of the resource are considered as given. The definition of 'proven reserves' utilized in statistical data (including those on which the pessimistic elaborations of the Club of Rome rely) indicates the quantity of oil in fields of which localization, width and characteristics are already known, and that may be extracted at economically profitable conditions given the technology in use and at current prices.[39] As happened in the case of Malthusian prophecies of calamity, which do not consider technical progress in agriculture (in Malthus's times about 70% of the population is necessary to produce food sufficient for all, today 4–5% is sufficient), the case of oil improvements in extraction techniques multiply the amount of oil recoverable from already known fields fourfold, between 1972 and today, and enormously reduce the exploration and extraction costs. Such clamorous results relative to an important sector such as that of energy put in doubt the heuristic power of the notion of scarcity itself.

In the case of Hotelling's theorem, when the moment of exhaustion of the natural resource is far into the future, its price net of extraction costs is about nil; the gross price is thus connected to production costs, as that of

---

[37] For a systematic presentation of this theory and its implications, cf. Dasgupta and Heal (1979); for its development, Krautkraemer (1998). For a wide selection of articles on this theme, including Hotelling's original paper, cf. Heal (1993).

[38] Cf. Roncaglia (1983), pp. 127–8. Forecasts of an increase in prices connected to the exhaustion of oil reserves reappear quite often; for instance Benes *et al.* (2015, an IMF study) foresee a doubling of oil prices within a decade. Works of this kind contribute to support prices in strongly speculative markets such as those for oil financial derivatives.

[39] Adelman (1995, pp. 11 ff.) stresses that data on proven reserves should be interpreted more as indicators of industrial inventories than as indicators of scarcity.

any other produced and reproducible commodity.[40] We may then consider three lines of research, which respectively utilize variants of the theory of Ricardian rent, of the Marshallian theory, and of oligopoly theory.

The field of natural resources displays a variety of characteristics, implying differences in unit extraction costs. In the case of the Ricardian theory of rent, the price of corn is determined by production costs on the less fertile among the lands required to obtain an amount of product sufficient to satisfy demand; in our case, the price of oil is determined by extraction costs relative to the most costly among the fields it is necessary to exploit in order to obtain a quantity of crude oil sufficient to meet demand. At any moment in time, technology may be assumed as given; technical progress influences the path of extraction costs, hence of prices, over time. This theory too, as that of Hotelling, assumes competition, which is necessary for ensuring full utilization of the less costly reserves before beginning utilization of more expensive ones: an assumption clearly contradicted in reality, given the underutilization or the missed utilization of very low-cost oilfields, especially in the Middle East.

The idea that competition prevails in the oil sector is justified with a Marshallian model by one of the best-known experts of this subject area, Adelman, who on this basis – and on the basis of an enormous mass of information concerning fields and extraction costs – foresaw (in 1972) a tendency towards falling prices. As in the Marshallian theory of the firm, competition is guaranteed by the presence of increasing costs (decreasing returns). However, the mass of data provided by Adelman in support of this thesis concern the long period and the oil industry as a whole, not the individual firm, and are thus compatible with a non-competitive market.[41]

Sylos Labini's (1956) oligopoly theory, illustrated in §6.6, was in fact born out of a study of the oil sector, for which Frenkel (1946) maintains the presence of strongly increasing returns to scale as a consequence of the high ratio of fixed to variable costs. He thus developed a thesis quite

---

[40] A substantially analogous situation is apparent in the case of other raw materials. Often their prices are analysed jointly, considering them as determined mainly by world demand, hence by the trade cycle, because of the difficulty of supply to adapt rapidly to demand (certainly not a characteristic of oil and natural gas). Cf. for instance Grilli and Yang (1988), who consider the path of the exchange ratio between raw materials and manufactured goods: a central issue in the analysis of developing countries rich in some primary commodity. Obviously the various raw materials differ from each other in many characteristics, in particular in what concerns market structure, and should be the object of separate analyses.

[41] Cf. Adelman (1972) and, for a wider illustration of the critiques, Roncaglia (1983), pp. 31–4. On Adelman's important role for the development of the industrial economics branch at MIT, cf. Garcia Duarte (2014).

different from the one held by Adelman.[42] Applying oligopoly theory to the energy sector, in particular to the oil sector, requires, however, some adaptation. Within the sector, three groups of agents operate: oil companies, producing/exporting countries and consuming/importing countries; within each group market power is noticeably differentiated. We therefore see, for instance, the so-called majors among oil companies, an institution like OPEC among exporting countries, the United States and recently China among consuming countries having a dominant role (while recently the United States also assumed the role of a leading producing country). We can thus speak of a 'trilateral oligopoly', and examine the sector in light of interactions among the main protagonists in each of the three groups of agents.[43]

Changes taking place in the course of time in the structure of power relations within the sector determine a sequence of stages with rather different characteristics, studied in an enormous literature, in which the use of theoretical foundations leaves room to historical reconstruction and to the analysis of organizational details, in particular concerning the methods of price fixing and the role of financial markets.[44]

9.9   The Environment and the Economy

Environmental issues are present in the economic debate since John Stuart Mill's *Principles* (1848). By environment, we mean the natural context in which we live; the environmental problems concern the impact of production and consumption activities on such a natural context (from air and water pollution to deforestation or the creation of hydro-geological risks). According to Mill and many others, these issues – as those concerning the impact of the organization of production on social coexistence, on the dignity of the worker and more generally on the personality of those involved – should be consciously recognized and tackled. In other terms, as the more recent debate clarifies, economic development cannot be identified with simple quantitative growth of total or per capita production. Otherwise we risk ignoring the multiplicity of elements that concur to determine life quality, in particular environmental ones, and losing

---

[42] Think of the high investment costs required for starting the exploitation of a field and the small current costs once production has begun; or, for transport, to the cost of construction in comparison to the cost of use of a pipeline or a crude oil carrier.

[43] For an illustration and application of this ('trilateral oligopoly') theory, cf. Roncaglia (1983).

[44] Cf. Roncaglia (1983, 2015a, 2017), and the bibliography quoted there.

sight of the complexity of the link between economic and civic development.[45]

In some cases, the critiques to the negative impact of productive activities on the environment are more emphatic, critiquing the capitalist mode of production. By way of example, the theories of de-growth point to a change in lifestyles, a more equal distribution of the weight of work, and a reduction in working time for all.[46]

Classical-type ecology should not be confused with the debate on the limits to growth set by the incumbent exhaustion of natural resources.[47] Malthus's conservative pessimism resurfaces in many writings in the course of time, from Jevons's essay on coal (Jevons 1865) to the research on the *Limits to growth* stimulated by the Club of Rome (Meadows *et al.* 1972). Notwithstanding the repeated failures of this kind of forecast, that should raise doubts on the marginalist approach based on the notion of scarcity, their influence on public opinion and on policy choices is substantial. The results may be quite damaging, as discussed earlier in terms of the connection between the Meadows' report and the 1973–4 oil crisis.

As classical-type ecology maintains, the problem to be tackled concerns the whole of interrelations between economic activities and natural environment. The notion of 'sustainable development' set out in a famous report of the World Commission on Environment and Development of the United Nations (Brundtland 1987) proposes a multidimensional view of economic growth, addressing attention towards changes in technology and in the consumption structure driven by ad hoc policies.[48] This is a progressive type of answer to environmental problems (Gro Harlem Brundtland, b. 1939, is repeatedly Norwegian prime minister in labour

---

[45] On the critique of 'growthmania', cf. for instance Mishan (1967) and Fuà (1993); in particular, Fuà shows that the link between GDP growth and qualitative improvements in life (higher life expectancy at birth, lower infant mortality, better and increased education and so on) already noticed by Adam Smith is important in the initial stages of growth, but loses importance when per capita GDP reaches the higher levels now (then, 1995) common to OECD countries.

[46] Cf. for instance Latouche (2006). The origins of this stream of thought may be located (also) in the Marxist tradition, to which we shall return in §13.2, but these are anyhow original developments that shift the focus of the debate from income distribution and public property of means of production to the organization of society and of the productive process, possibly revitalizing the themes of alienation, discussed by Marx in the *Economical-philosophical manuscripts* of 1844 but later abandoned and substituted in *Capital* by the themes of exploitation and commodity fetishism.

[47] Analogously, both classical-type ecology and that based on natural resource scarcity should not be confused with the line of analysis developed by Georgescu-Roegen recalling the second law of thermodynamics: cf. §13.5.

[48] 'Sustainable development is the development that meets the needs of the present without compromising the ability of future generations to meet their own needs' (Brundtland 1987, p. 43).

governments). Alternatively, the theses on the limits to growth, in a world affected by dramatic problems of underdevelopment and poverty, may easily assume a conservative role, analogous to that attributable to the theses concerning the assumed existence of inverse relations between the rate of growth of the economy on one hand, and the defence of workers' rights or development of democracy and political freedoms on the other.[49]

A partly different debate concerns cost–benefit evaluation of environmental policy measures. Such an evaluation is quite difficult, the more so because of different opinions about the social rate of discount to be utilized (costs mainly concern the immediate future; benefits concern a lasting but indeterminate future). The social rate of discount should be relatively low according to Stern (2008, 2009, Chapter 5), somewhat higher according to Nordhaus (2008; William Nordhaus, b. 1941, receives the Nobel Prize in 2018).[50]

Over the past decades, heated debates also concern the theme of global warming. Rejected or discredited by some studies (often financed by oil companies or by conservative research centres),[51] the issue is receiving increasingly wider recognition; the problem leads to a series of international agreements aimed at reducing polluting emissions, such as the Paris Agreement of December 2015. Indeed, the problem is global, and cannot be tackled by any country in isolation; the cost of anti-pollution measures creates a competitive advantage for firms based in countries not adopting such measures.[52]

---

[49] Cf. Roncaglia (2005b), chapter 5.

[50] Attributing to future generations the same importance as present generations may imply a social rate of discount equal to zero in real terms; an alternative theory supports a social rate equal to the average rate of economic growth, or to the growth of per capita income; a third theory, drawing on market fundamentalism (and on the assumption of full employment of resources), points to the agents' rate of intertemporal preference as expressed by prevailing long-run interest rates.

[51] UK's prime minister Thatcher advances in this respect a curious thesis, a new variety of the precaution principle, requiring not adopting costly measures (aimed at hindering global warming) until this trend has not become evident. Confronted with the foreseeable damages stemming from global warming, the precaution principle rather suggests an opposite strategy, to intervene before the problem becomes so evident as to be no longer remediable: even limiting to the sole economic effects, one can show (Roncaglia 1989) that assuming a discount rate equal to the rate of growth of the economy, an even very small probability of an event with very high costs that persist over time renders profitable the investments necessary to avoid it.

[52] Because of this, developing countries require exemptions from or limitations of the measures they are called to adopt, stressing that the global warming derives in the first place from a process begun with industrialization of higher income countries. Such a justification obviously cannot hold for the choice of US president Trump to negate the commitments of the previous Obama administration with adhesion to the Paris Agreements.

A stream of the debate deals with this issue by interpreting it as a problem of negative externalities, to be solved through adoption of apposite taxes (the so-called carbon tax). The idea of exploiting the optimality properties that the neoclassical theory attributes to competitive markets leads then to proposals to create markets for 'permits to pollute' as efficient solution of the problem. The limits of the assumption of perfect competition, however, are quite evident: markets for such permits soon give origin to financial speculation, with price oscillations that certainly do not favour the adoption of less polluting technologies; absence of controls of actual polluting emissions of firms generates a diffuse cheating, significantly reducing the impact of these measures on environment; the low controls in developing countries generate phenomena of environmental dumping.

The notion of sustainable development is extended, in recent years, to include social sustainability, put to a harsh test by rising rates of unemployment, in particular among youth, by poverty, inequalities and concentration of these problems in some regions of each country or some districts in large cities, by persistent low female participation in the labour market, by the difficulties of social integration connected to the rise in migratory flows, often initiated by war events in various areas of the world. Awareness of these problems is increased by a vast amount of regional and urban economics research and by studies on migrations. At the boundaries between economics, demography, sociology and political sciences, such research is often hindered by an excessive rigidity of disciplinary boundaries, adopted for regulating academic careers.

Part IV

The Weakening of the Paradigm

1 0   Behavioural Economics and Bounded Rationality

10.1   Rejecting the Notion of *Homo Oeconomicus*

Mainstream economics, as we saw in previous chapters, draws upon the notion of the *homo oeconomicus* derived from the strictest utilitarian tradition, as an agent maximizing a monodimensional magnitude, utility or income. This notion has been critiqued since its origins in the eighteenth century: the Smithian notion of personal interest does not correspond to that of selfishness, insofar as it also includes a moral dimension within a complex interplay of passions and interests; John Stuart Mill, then, harshly criticizes the simplistic Benthamite version of utilitarianism with its monodimensional felicific calculus.

After the marginalist revolution, and with increasing rigidity in the recent stage of identification of economic theory with the construction of mathematical models, these notes of caution are dropped by mainstream theory. Rational behaviour is interpreted as the choice among a set of alternative actions that maximizes an objective function or, more specifically in the tradition originated with von Neumann and Morgenstern, the value of expected utility. This is true even when we expand the field of economic theory to include the most varied phenomena, from crime to marriage: as seen §6.5 when discussing Stigler's and Becker's contributions, we are always confronted with problems of constrained maximization of a monodimensional utility. However, perplexities towards this conceptualization of rational behaviour and the notion of the *homo oeconomicus* are taken up by various, more or less heterodox research streams, discussed in this chapter.

Let us distinguish between the rejection from above and from below of the monodimensional notion of *homo oeconomicus*. Rejection from below pertains to experimental economics, which aims to see how the typical economic agent makes their decisions, and discovers that quite often the agent's choices diverge from the 'rational' ones, to the point of leading to the search of regularities in the actual behaviour of agents and to notions of bounded rationality. Such notions may be obtained also through research 'from above', adopting as a point of departure the rejection of the postulate of perfect rationality. These approaches exist at the boundary between economics and neurobiology, according to which, among other things long- and short-term decisions appear to be entrusted to two different brain centres; in other words, such approaches stress the uncertainty – of a Keynesian, not probabilistic kind – of human decisions. The main protagonists of these streams of thought often integrate the two points of view, as is the case for the critiques directed at the solipsism usually attributed to economic agents, or towards the assumption that their preferences, though formed in a social context, are not influenced by other people's preferences. Notwithstanding this critical attitude, however, these research approaches try to retain some of the substantive aspects of the marginalist tradition.

Such research thus concerns what we call the conceptualization stage and *in primis* the analysis of the notions of rationality, choice and economic agent. Often, this research takes on an interdisciplinary character, given the importance of other social sciences such as psychology, ethics, ethology and politics to the analysis of these notions. Indeed, the subdivision of reflections on society and the human being into separate compartments is a relatively recent phenomenon, perhaps unavoidable but certainly not positive in all respects.[1]

In what follows, we shall recall first of all the 'paradoxes' proposed immediately after the appearance of expected utility theory. These paradoxes raise doubts about the ability of expected utility theory to describe/ interpret human behaviour as rational choice, as intended by von Neumann and Morgenstern (and by the vast majority of contemporary economists). What remains open, as we will see, is the possibility to attribute a normative meaning to the theory, as an optimal behaviour to be followed compared to which the agents' actual behaviour should be considered as a form of deviancy, even if systematic.

The debate on the paradoxes opens the door to research in experimental economics, including a varied set of approaches (§10.3). On the one side, research corresponding to the mainstream tradition aims to replicate the functioning of simple idealized markets in order to verify their characteristic of efficient allocation mechanisms (and, in the simplified frameworks systematically adopted in experiments of this kind, succeed fairly well in this). On the other side, some research seeks to empirically

---

[1] The connection between the debates on the notion of rationality and on ethics is discussed in §14.2. The difference between the notion of selfishness implicit in the notion of the *homo oeconomicus* and the Smithian notion of self-interest has already been recalled in §2.3.

engage with typical forms of behaviour among agents confronted with problems of choice.

Within this second line of research, some studies have placed importance on locating the direct and indirect (cultural, in a wide sense) forms of interaction among agents or, in other terms, such studies have focused on the social nature of agents, by drawing on comparisons between societies differing by degree of development and cultural traditions.

What the paradoxes ultimately illustrate is not the irrational character of human behaviour, but the fact that the agent chooses in a more complex context than that presupposed by the expected utility theory, in at least two crucial aspects. First, the agent operates under conditions not of certainty or of uncertainty of a probabilistic kind (risk), but of Keynesian-type uncertainty: an uncertainty which, as we saw in §3.6, corresponds to a limited knowledge of the situation at hand (so that Keynes holds that expected probability, when it is possible to give a more or less precise evaluation of it, should be integrated with another element, the degree of confidence that we can have on our probability estimate). This research is characterized by bounded rationality and satisficing behaviour, as proposed by Simon, which we will discuss further in §10.4. Second, the agent does not operate driven by a single motivation, but by a complex set of passions and interests, as stressed by the Enlightenment tradition. Such motivations may be contradictory, they may vary in time and they are socially conditioned, contrary to the solipsism adopted by the marginalist tradition, in coherence with its methodological individualism.

The contention that the agent's behaviour does not follow the precepts of rationality as defined within the paradigm of expected utilities lays the foundation for research at the boundary of economics and psychology, focused on the typical characteristics of human action. The stream of research of prospect theory, inaugurated by Kahneman and Tversky, illustrates this kind of interdisciplinary work. As we shall see in §10.5, this stream of research locates some stylized facts characterizing human choices and draws on them to build interpretative models. What appear as anomalies within the paradigm of expected utilities now appear as normal behaviour, corresponding to a logic that the researcher can understand and represent in a stylized form in his or her analyses.

The dominant strength of the mainstream view based on the paradigm of rational choice in conditions of resource scarcity continues to exert an influence on the behavioural lines of research, keeping them at the boundary between orthodoxy and heterodoxy. In many important cases, mainstream theory remains the stone of comparison for the studies on the actual behaviour of economic agents. Only the separation of research areas – between behavioural economics and the theory of value – makes it possible not to fully perceive, at least in the majority of cases, the weight of the abandonment of the notion of *homo oeconomicus* for the very foundations of mainstream theory.

10.2   Rationality and Behavioural Paradoxes: Behavioural Economics

The debate that follows von Neumann and Morgenstern's 1944 book mainly concerns the definition of the assumption of rationality, underlying the set of axioms of expected utility theory. In this respect, it is possible to distinguish two streams. On the one hand, rationality is understood in a descriptive sense, as a characteristic perhaps not always present in an absolute form in all persons but nonetheless generally valid. The theory relying on this notion of rationality thus aims to contribute to interpreting what happens in reality, while the missed adhesion to rational behaviour is considered as an error on the side of the agent. On the other side, rationality is understood in a normative sense, as the behaviour that agents should stick to, in order to obtain optimal results.[2]

The two interpretations, descriptive and normative, constitute a useful distinctive element among the various positions in the ensuing debate, involving psychologists and economists. The distinction was adopted by Savage (1954, pp. 19–20), after a debate that sees him and Friedman, supporters of the empirical validity of the descriptive interpretation of the postulates, opposed to Allais, Baumol and Samuelson, who tend towards a normative interpretation.[3]

In particular, the French economist Maurice Allais (1911–2010, Nobel Prize in 1988) finds counter-examples in which economists and probability theorists, among them Savage himself, whom we may assume to have a good ability in 'rational' reasoning, make choices not corresponding to

---

[2] Let us notice that this dichotomy differs from the one between the field of positive science and the normative field of ethics proposed by Friedman (1953): even meant in a normative sense, von Neumann and Morgenstern's theory is objective according to Friedman's definition, as it avoids recourse to value assumptions (an assumption of value is instead the imposition to agents to behave rationally, in the specific sense that the notion of rationality takes on in their theory). Von Neumann and Morgenstern, like Savage, consider the axioms at the same time as an abstract but realistic interpretation of human behaviour and as a norm for the adoption of rational decisions. Also Arrow (1951b, p. 406) goes decidedly in this direction. For the story of this debate and more generally of behavioural economics, cf. Heukelom (2014).
[3] On the evolution of Samuelson's, but also Savage's position, in the direction of a prevailingly normative interpretation, cf. Moscati (2016).

those prescribed by the von Neumann–Morgenstern theory.[4] More precisely, Allais proposes two groups of bets, and finds that frequently the choices made within the first group of bets contradict those made within the second group: in one case, aversion to risk appears to dominate, in another case the maximization of expected gains takes precedence. If we interpret expected utility theory as describing the agents' behaviour, Allais's paradox offers an important critique, showing that rational agents violate its postulates.

An analogous critique, aimed at the postulate of independence of preferences utilized by Savage in his version of expected utility theory, was proposed by Daniel Ellsberg in 1961, considering not aversion to risk but aversion to uncertainty (or ambiguity in the definition of the terms of the bet), namely to ignorance on probabilities.[5] In synthesis, the independence postulate (also called the 'sure-thing principle' by Savage) states that if the same event is added to each of the two sets of events among which the agent must choose, the choice should not change; as Ellsberg shows, the postulate, essential for the axiomatic construction of von Neumann–Morgenstern–Savage, is often violated.[6]

As already discussed earlier, the paradoxes contradict expected utility theory in its descriptive version, namely as a theory aiming at interpreting the agents' behaviour. According to the normative interpretation, instead, violations may be simply interpreted as a shift of real agents away from the path of optimal choice.

In the case of the descriptive interpretation, expected utility theory is defended by considering it as a generally valid interpretation, notwithstanding some exceptions found in practice. According to subjective probability theory, proposed by De Finetti and taken up and developed by Savage, each agent has his or her own evaluation (though not

---

[4] For a story of Allais's experiments, conducted by mail (with Savage and others) or at the occasion of conferences such as that held in Paris in May 1952, cf. Heukelom (2014), pp. 44 ff. For an exposition, cf. Allais (1953).

[5] Daniel Ellsberg, b. 1931, is known as the protagonist of the Pentagon Papers case: a secret study of the Pentagon on the US government's decisions on the Vietnam War he makes public in 1971, while he works at the Rand Corporation after a career as military analyst for the government: accused of espionage, with the risk of being sentenced to up to 115 years of prison, is finally absolved in 1973 thanks to an illegal picking of proofs against him on the side of the government. The story is told in a movie (*The Pentagon Papers*, 2003, directed by Rod Holcomb) and in a 2009 documentary, *The most dangerous man in America: Daniel Ellsberg and the Pentagon Papers*, directed by Judith Ehrlich and Rick Goldsmith.

[6] The notion of ambiguity in probability estimates utilized by Ellsberg is quite similar to the more elaborate notion of the degree of confidence utilized by Keynes (1921). However, Ellsberg, who refers to the discussion of probability by Knight (1921), Ramsey, de Finetti and Savage, never quotes Keynes. Ellsberg (1961, p. 260 n.) recalls instead as similar to his notion of ambiguity that of 'credibility' proposed by Georgescu-Roegen (1954).

necessarily correct) of the probabilities and the outcomes (of expected utility) of events, and such an evaluation determines the agent's choices. Errors on the side of the agent may depend on evaluation errors (but this is certainly not the case for Allais's and Ellsber's experiments) but are also attributed to causes such as scarcity of time, decisions taken under conditions of stress and so on. Thus, the debate defers to psychologists' studies on individual decision processes.

These conclusions lead to what is called *behavioural paternalism*: economic agents are sufficiently but not fully rational; the scientist engaged in a program of human engineering, namely in the effort to improve the agents' decisional processes, may better judge and indicate to them what the optimal choices are.[7]

10.3   Experimental Economics

The debate on decisional processes intersects with the parallel developments of mathematical and experimental psychology, concerning both aspects – normative and descriptive – of decision theory. These fields of research are well funded, and are sometimes connected to military research.[8]

Such research can be exemplified by work undertaken on decisional processes at the University of Michigan, within the Institute for Social Research founded in 1947, which includes psychologists; the Mathematical Psychology Group formed in 1949, the Mental Health Research Institute formed in 1955 and the Human Performance Center formed in 1958 also reflect these developments.[9] Ward Edwards (1927–2005), influenced by von Neumann and Morgenstern's work, proposes a fusion of mathematical and experimental psychology, creating the field of behavioural decision theory (the title of his 1961 influential article). The analysis of expected utilities is

---

[7] For further references to this line of thinking cf. Heukelom (2014), pp. 184 ff. On Thaler's and Sunstein's (2003) libertarian paternalism we shall return to later. As already recalled, all these authors presuppose, erroneously, that rational behaviour necessarily leads society to converge towards an optimal equilibrium; this is after all the eighteenth-century faith in the enlightened prince (or benevolent dictator) where the myth of the invisible hand of the market is substituted by that of the omniscient prince.

[8] Mirowski (2002) and Heukelom (2014) offer various examples in this respect.

[9] Heukelom (2014, in particular pp. 149–51) recalls the strong financial support that research programs in experimental economics receive from a variety of foundations. Moscati (2007), who provides a wide reconstruction (and a wealth of bibliographical information) for the period 1930–70, recalls that experimental economics research on consumer demand already began in previous decades, with the aim to reconstruct demand curves, utility functions and indifference maps, but also to verify the transitivity postulate utilized in expected utility theory; Moscati also recalls the numerous anomalies (such as cases of concavity of indifference curves) found in various experiments.

interpreted as a theory of measurement and as the basis for understanding the behaviour of the rational agent under uncertain (or more precisely risk) conditions.[10]

Experimental economics provides contributions both negative and positive, by showing the very numerous cases in which the mainstream notion of rationality is contradicted,[11] and by defining a series of agents' typical behaviours. It is immediately clear that economic agents are influenced, in their choices, by the ways in which the different alternatives are presented (the so-called framing): this therefore produces different answers to the same situation. The framing effect worries experimental economists, as it renders the results of the experiments aleatory. The dependency of results on the way in which the experiment is formulated generates a tendency towards standardized procedures, but this hides the problem rather than solving it. Indeed, we may conclude that experimental economics does not allow for the formulation of general theories.

In a survey of the topic, Conlisk (1996) cites a lengthy series of research which systematically contradicts the assumption of rationality, and points to (p. 670) different types of contradictions emerging from experiments:

People: display intransitivity; misunderstand statistical independence; mistake random data for patterned data and vice versa; ... make errors in updating probabilities on the basis of new information; ...; make false inferences about causality; ignore relevant information; use irrelevant information ...; display overconfidence in judgment relative to evidence; exaggerate confirming over disconfirming evidence relative to initial beliefs; ...; and more.[12]

Notwithstanding the joint attribution of the Nobel Prize to Kahneman and Smith (when Tversky had already died), the stream of experimental economics originated by Vernon Smith (b. 1927, Nobel Prize in 2002) should be kept distinct from the behavioural economics in which Kahneman and Tversky's prospect theory may be included. Prospect theory concerns the behaviour of individuals, while Vernon Smith's

---

[10] These research streams are criticized by Hayek (1952), stressing among other things the missed distinction between the stimuli that the agent receives from the external world and the internal mental states produced by the human nervous system. Cf. Caldwell (2004), pp. 270 ff.

[11] Simon (1997, pp. 6 and 7) recalls how much wider and less constraining is Adam Smith's notion of rationality: 'in his treatment, being rational means having reasons for what you do'; 'The rationality of *The wealth of nations* is the rationality of everyday common sense.'

[12] We should also consider, distanced by a decade, the surveys by Larry Samuelson (2005), illustrating among other things the game theoretical foundations of experimental economics, and by Kao and Velupillai (2015), that together with providing an updated bibliography also suggest a distinction between classical and modern behavioural economics, respectively originating with Herbert Simon and Ward Edwards: the first connected to complexity theory, the second to the subjective notion of probability.

experimental economics concerns the study of the functioning of markets. His experiments and those of his pupils and followers, often conducted on economics students, are designed in such a way as to replicate supply-and-demand mechanisms.

According to Vernon Smith, markets 'work', in the sense that they show convergence towards what mainstream theory foresees. The agents' behaviour may not be rational, but the market operates as a mechanism of natural selection re-establishing dominance of rationality, hence the validity of the theory of rational choice as interpretation of the way of working of a market economy.[13] Apart from the limits repeatedly recalled of such theory, however, we should stress the simplified nature of the experiments by Vernon Smith and collaborators, concerning pure exchange markets, without production and accumulation, in a context in which the data of the problem are sufficiently limited so as to avoid problems of partial or imperfect knowledge.

The techniques of experimental analysis, which over the past years constitute a highly frequented research field, may anyhow be utilized independently from adhesion to Vernon Smith's neo-liberal views.[14]

Finally, more recently, a series of interdisciplinary studies, drawing on collaboration of anthropologists, psychologists and economists, tend to render preference formation endogenous. The important work by Henrich et al., Foundations of human sociality (2004), proposes a series of experiments of ultimatum game conducted by economists and anthropologists in some small social groups in underdeveloped countries.[15] The experiments consisted of questioning pairs of individuals within each society; the first individual in each pair was requested to divide a given sum of money between themselves and their partner; he or she was informed that the second individual would only be asked whether he or

---

[13] Among Vernon Smith's numerous contributions, one among the first is fundamental, Smith (1962). Quite interesting is also the augmented version of his Nobel lecture (Smith 2003) providing a wide critical survey of experimental economics, going back to its cultural roots and connecting its results to an evolutionary view on the emersion of markets.

[14] It is anyhow useful to recall an *ante litteram* critique of experimental economics: Wallis and Friedman (1942) stress that agent's preferences may vary in time and are different from one individual to another; their critiques are addressed to Thurstone's (1931) attempt to estimate an indifference curve, but also hold for a noticeable share of exercises in experimental economics. In Italian, a book edited by Motterlini and Guala (2005) includes together with some of the main works in the field a useful introduction by the editors.

[15] In some cases the ultimatum game is accompanied by other kinds of experiments: dictator game, public goods game, trust game: see the synoptic table in Henrich et al. (2004), p. 9.

she accepts or rejects the proposal; in the case of rejection, both would receive nothing. Rational behaviour prescribes that the first individual proposes an extremely unequal distribution of the sum, as the second individual will find it convenient to accept even a small sum rather than nothing. However, in nearly all experiments the first individual proposes relatively balanced distributions, and if the sum is 'too' unevenly subdivided, the second individual quite often refuses it. Clearly, considerations of equity play a role.

The interest of the experiments lays not only in showing how selfishness is restrained by equity considerations (which is already relevant in itself, since it shows that the Enlightenment notion of a complex of passions and interests driving human actions is to be preferred to the Benthamite-marginalist notion of an economic agent maximizing a monodimensional magnitude). They also point to the role social factors play in illustrating the negotiation between feelings of selfishness and equity.[16] Such researches imply going beyond the original approach of expected utility theory, hence the resistance to including them in the economics field, at least in the field of mainstream economics.

A new field of research, neuroeconomics, enquires into the biological foundations of human behaviour in the economic field, utilizing the advances in neurosciences, which through images of brain activity and other techniques try to explain the working of the brain. Neurosciences have progressed markedly; however, application of their results in the economic field appears as of now rather limited. There are those who foresee revolutionary potentialities for this research stream, which would transform economics into a 'hard science', on the model of natural sciences.[17] Some results, somehow confirming Keynes's ideas on the need to deal separately with issues characterized by different kinds of uncertainty, seem to distinguish areas of thought concerning the long term as more rational, and areas of thought concerning the short period as being more normatively guided (McClure et al. 2004; in the same direction, Kahneman 2011).

---

[16] On altruism and selfishness cf. the previous works by Schelling (1978) and Simon (1993). Schelling stresses the possibility of explaining both altruism and benevolence as strategic behaviour aimed at influencing the behaviour of others in a direction favourable to the agent, with what may be considered as strategic rationality. Simon follows a line of analysis external to traditional microeconomics; he considers the presence of altruistic behaviour as a matter of fact, that may be explained in a context of bounded rationality and/or evolutionary selection and/or group loyalty models; in this way he puts upside down what we have called economic imperialism (cf. §6.5), proposing instead an 'economics based upon the facts of history and political and social life' (Simon 1993, p. 160).

[17] Cf. the wide survey by Camerer et al. (2005).

Most researchers in the field of neuroeconomics (and in that of bioeconomics, which precedes it), appear to base their analyses of agents' behaviour on the assumption of rational behaviour, considered as the result of an evolutionary process of natural selection (cf. e.g. Vromen 2007): a thesis that, as we shall see in discussing evolutionism (§13.5), cannot be taken for granted. Both in this and in the methodological individualism intrinsic to biological explanations of human behaviour that leaves aside social factors, bioeconomics and neuroeconomics show strong elements of continuity with the marginalist tradition and opposition to the classical one (which focuses analysis on the interaction of individuals within society, on the wake of the traditional Aristotelian view of man as a social being).

Within the field of experimental economics, the term cognitive economics is occasionally utilized for pointing to the study of the workings of the human mind in what concerns the economic aspects of life. The basic material for these studies is provided by interviews on hypothetical choices, psychometric data, personal accounts on preferences and expectations or on happiness/unhappiness reactions to events. These analyses focus on the agent, his or her motivations and the operational aspects of choice; in principle, since they circumvent the notion of the *homo oeconomicus*, the developments internal to this research field cannot be referred to the marginalist tradition.[18] However, the approach's subjectivism and the role of introspection present strong affinities with the Austrian tradition, Hayek, and the neo-Austrian school.

Finally, we may recall a kind of theoretical experimental economics, namely research based on the so-called computational models based on computer programs framed in such a way as to re-propose a stylized representation of the phenomenon under consideration, for instance the behaviour of an agent or a group of interacting agents: the so-called agent-based models (hinted at in §13.5). Recourse to such a technique, which underwent a strong expansion in recent years, allows us to obtain experimental results for models too complex to be liable to mathematical solution. The results of such analyses may provide interesting hints, but should be interpreted with great caution, always lending attention to the simplifications necessarily present in any model: sensibility of results to starting assumptions is in such models very high.

---

[18] Cf. for instance Egidi and Rizzello (2004).

10.4   Herbert Simon

As we saw, perplexities already present in Adam Smith and John Stuart Mill on the notion of the perfectly rational agent, subsequently designed as *homo oeconomicus*, reappear in various forms after publication of von Neumann and Morgenstern's book. First, as discussed earlier, we have the distinction between the normative and descriptive notion of rationality. We then have a series of specifications, such as the distinction between rationality meant as internal consistency of the system of choices, or as systematic pursuit of self-interest on the side of the economic agent.[19] Within this latter category we find the notion of substantive rationality, meant as the pursuit of self-interest objectively defined, namely independently from the individual's choices. Instead, instrumental rationality is represented by the agent's pursuit of a given objective, no matter how it is identified.[20]

These specifications, and a series of logical problems connected to them, lead to an emphasis on the distance separating the notion of rationality internal to axiomatic theory of the von Neumann–Morgenstern kind from the actual behaviour of real agents. Yet, the assumption of irrational behaviour also appears as unrealistic. Thus, we need to re-define the notion of rationality.

Herbert Simon (1916–2001, Nobel Prize in 1978; cf. Simon, 1957, 1979a, 1979c) proposes the notion of bounded rationality as a solution to this dilemma.

Simon was a versatile researcher: economist, psychologist and expert in informatics; his chair at Carnegie Mellon University was Psychology and Computer Science. In the field of economics, one of his first contributions, a brief but fundamental note written with Hawkins in 1949, illustrates the necessary and sufficient conditions for positive solutions to an input–output model: the so-called Hawkins–Simon conditions, substantially consisting of the requirement that the economy be able to generate a surplus product, namely that the production of the various commodities exceeds their requirements as means of production.

Another important contribution by Simon concerns the definition of causal ordering and the related distinction between true and spurious correlation (Simon 1953, 1954). Simon (1953) explicitly accepted Hume's criticism, that we cannot perceive necessary connections

---

[19] For a synthetic survey of these aspects and bibliographical information, cf. Sen (1987).
[20] The dichotomy between instrumental and substantive rationality leads once again to the distinction within individual preferences between those expressing the subjective viewpoint of the individual consumer and those based on her objective well-being (between *complacibilitas* and *virtuositas*, according to, Medieval terminology): cf. §14.2.

between events, but only repeat associations. The term 'causation' is therefore to be interpreted, more modestly, as functional relation or interdependency. More precisely, within a model, it is possible to identify a subset of independent variables that directly or indirectly enter into the determination of all variables in the model and that thus are to be considered as the 'cause' of the other variables.[21] This is an operational definition, based on the existence of asymmetric relations among the variables included in the model. We must take into account that the terms 'cause and effect' refer to a model – a system of equations – and not to the real world that the model represents. As Simon (1953) shows, this kind of causation does not imply a temporal sequence, nor does a temporal sequence imply causation.

To identify a genuine correlation in statistical and econometric analyses, we need to extend the basic interpretative model from which the correlation emerges by including in it other explicative variables, to see whether a causal relation as defined earlier appears. For instance, let us consider the negative correlation revealed by statistical analyses between the consumption of sweets and marriage: if we add the relation with age, we discover that both marriage and the consumption of sweets are correlated with age (the first positively, the second negatively), while for any given marriage age there is no correlation between marriage and the consumption of sweets (Simon 1954).

At the disciplinary boundary between economics, psychology and management science is Simon's (1947) analysis of administrative behaviour. This analysis concerns the way in which managerial decisions are taken, not the specification of optimal decisions: what matters is procedural, not substantive, rationality. This work influences the theory of the firm, and led to an experimental stream of economic research. The very definition of the firm focuses on interpersonal relations within the firm, concerning existence of common objectives and an interpersonal web of communications that allows a continuous adaptation of the organization. We are here confronted with a behavioural-evolutionary theory of the firm.

Simon also stresses the informational limits of the entrepreneur, very far from the ideal of the marginalist theory, of an omniscient agent, perfectly rational and concerned only with profit maximization;[22] in a 1956 contribution with Cyert and Trow he stresses the behavioural

---

[21] The analogy with the notions of basic and non-basic commodities independently proposed by Sraffa 1960 (cf. §5.7) is interesting.

[22] This is certainly not a new theme, but Simon deals with it in an original way, drawing innovative conclusions.

dualism between routine decisions and those requiring specific consideration. Complexity of decisional processes leads to the notion of heuristics, a set of rules of thumb adopted for taking decisions whenever a full consideration of all aspects of the issue would in fact be impossible.[23]

Simon also adopts explicitly a notion of the market – as 'a network of communications and transactions' (Simon 1997, p. 35) – analogous to that of classical economists and opposed to that of the traditional marginalist theory (as the place where supply and demand meet: cf. §2.2).

On another important aspect, Simon parallels classical economists more closely, in particular Adam Smith, than the marginalist tradition: in his attention to the multiplicity of passions and interests that jointly drive human action. In this sense we may recall the importance he attributes to 'docility' ('in its sense of teachability or educability, not in its alternative sense of passivity and meekness', Simon 1997, p. 41) and to altruism, concerning which he maintains that 'the combination of bounded rationality with docility provides a powerful mechanism for the maintenance of a substantial level of altruistic behaviour in human society' (p. 42).

Moreover, what he proposes is a theory that focuses on firms: traditional theory represents them as 'small skeletal structures embedded in the network of markets', while it is preferable 'describing markets as threads that link robust firms' (Simon 1997, p. 35).

Starting from these foundations, and drawing on behavioural analyses, Simon (1954, 1955, 1972, 1983) develops his definition of 'bounded rationality'.[24] He suggests we discard the rigid prerequisites of the mainstream notion of rationality: the assumption of a predefined set of alternative lines of action among which to choose, that of full knowledge of the outcomes of the different lines of action (that may admit conditions of probabilistic uncertainty – or risk, in Knight's terminology – but not uncertainty tout court); finally, that of a given utility function (a given objective) to be maximized. Thus, we recognize that most of the time devoted to choosing a line of action is taken by the collection of information, never complete, on the main available lines of action and their outcomes, which remain uncertain. Moreover, confronted with

---

[23] The development of mathematical tools for representing the activity of problem solving constitutes also one of the roots of studies on artificial intelligence. Heuristic leads to the notion of routines adopted by Nelson and Winter (1982) and to that of satisficing behaviour developed by Simon himself.

[24] Simon (1997, p. 16) points to Keynes as 'the true originator of the economics of bounded rationality', recalling his notion of 'animal spirits' that stimulate the agent to take active decisions though in the presence of uncertainty (in the sense of partial knowledge: cf. §3.6).

a multiplicity of objectives it appears reasonable to adopt a 'satisficing' behaviour aimed at reaching an acceptable result for each of the different objectives simultaneously pursued, rather than maximizing a function embodying the different objectives weighted according to their relative importance. Simon (1972) explains that the Scottish term 'satisficing' is adopted (instead of the English 'satisfying') to designate his three-step specific rule: set a target level considered acceptable, then search among the available alternative lines of action until one is found satisfying the target; at that point, stop the search and adopt it. In this sense, 'A theory of bounded rationality is necessarily a theory of procedural rationality', namely 'concerned with *how* the decision maker generates alternatives of action and compares them'.[25]

In these writings Simon tries to provide an operational definition of bounded rationality, utilizing the theory of games and the minimax principle, with the aim to contribute to defining adequate decisional processes for the cases of incomplete information. To better understand this practically oriented approach in writings where mathematical formalization may give the impression of pure (abstract) theory, it is useful to take into account that Simon's studies were initially financed by the Cowles Commission under contract from the Office of Naval Research.

Attempts towards an operational notion of bounded rationality have had a relatively modest impact within the theoretical debate while, though remaining outside of the mainstream approach, such a notion is often referred to, even if only generically, without recognizing its link to Keynes's probability theory and uncertainty: possibly a decisive step to make it fully operational.

10.5   Kahneman and Tversky's Prospect Theory

A different problem tackled in particular by Kahneman and Tversky in the 1970s concerns the fact that agents systematically adopt choices different from those which decision theory considers optimal. Apparently, such choices may be attributed to an insufficient ability to rational reasoning. Their frequency, however, leads to recognizing the need for studies aimed at defining individual decisional criteria differently from rationality defined as the maximization of expected utility.

Work by Amos Tversky (1937–96) towards the end of the 1960s is devoted to verifying the transitivity axiom (if I prefer A to B and B to C, I must also prefer A to C), a necessary condition for the existence of an

---

[25] Simon (1972), p. 19 and p. 18. For a wide survey of the limits of the notion of unbounded rationality cf. Comlisk (1996).

ordinal utility scale. Of course, any violation of the axiom may be attributed to a change in the agent's preferences; but it is clear that this justification cannot recur again and again without becoming ad hoc. Daniel Kahneman (b. 1934, Nobel Prize in 2002) instead studies why agents deviate from a behavioural 'rational' norm, and is convinced that human beings often make cognitive errors. It is then a question of simplifying and reorganizing the decisional process so that even a non-sophisticated agent may tackle and solve it.

Towards the end of the 1960s, this research line sees the beginning of a collaboration between Kahneman and Tversky leading to the so-called prospect theory.[26] This consists in taking as a reference point an S-shaped utility curve, defined by looking at movements away from the status quo: the loss (in terms of disutility) deriving from a negative drift from the status quo is greater than the gain (in terms of utility) deriving from an equal positive drift, due to risk aversion. Kahneman and Tversky conclude that expected utility theory turns out to be disproved as a descriptive theory, while, again on the descriptive level, the theory as reformulated by them holds.

Prospect theory is thus considered as a theory explaining the way in which individuals value risk and choose in the presence of risk. The four main aspects of behaviour as commonly found in agents are, in decreasing order of importance: dependence on a reference situation (in general, the starting position); risk aversion; attribution of a decreasing importance to gains (and of an increasing importance to losses) that may be considered a version of the decreasing marginal utility postulate within the new framework; and the tendency to attribute greater importance to smaller probabilities, and lesser importance to larger probabilities. In this latter respect, Kahneman and Tversky stress that these are not systematic errors in probability estimates, but a transformation of probabilities into something different, which we may call decisional weights. Moreover, emphasis is placed on the framing effect: agents' decisions depend on the way in which the set of possible choices is presented to them.

Kahneman and Tversky's theory differentiates itself from the mainstream less than Herbert Simon's theory discussed in the previous

---

[26] The original version of prospect theory is developed in an article by Kahneman and Tversky (1979). A subsequent version, improving on the 1979 article, is Tversky and Kahneman (1992). In the first of the two articles, the sum of the decisional weights attributed by individuals to the various possible events may be different from 1, thus violating the so-called Kolmogorov axiom, which constitutes the angular stone of the axiomatic theory of probability; the second article offers a solution to this problem, showing how important is for the two authors to remain in the traditional field of axiomatic theory.

section. Indeed, it may be considered as the simple substitution of decisional weights to probabilities in the mathematical theory of choice proposed by expected utility theory, accompanied by the substitution of the
traditional utility function with a function that is first convex and then
(from the point in which the agents find themselves at the moment of
choice) concave.[27] According to the two authors, the traditional theory
remains valid as a normative theory, identifying rational choices in an
objective way.[28]

According to the authors, the problem of operationally determining the
decisional weights does not differ from that of determining probabilities
in expected utility theory, and appears assigned to a mechanism analogous to the one of revealed preferences proposed by Samuelson:
'Decision weights are inferred from choices between prospects much as
subjective probabilities are inferred from preferences in the Ramsey-
Savage approach'.[29] The authors do not dwell on the requirements for
this solution, such as the assumption of stability of decisional weights,
which is indeed even more restrictive than that of stability of preferences,
because as stressed by the very prospect theory such weights vary when
the situation of the agents changes (or more precisely when their initial
endowments of commodities change). Moreover, as in the axiomatic
general equilibrium theory, the space of events is considered as well
defined and closed, in terms of set theory.

Prospect theory gives rise to a long series of empirical studies aimed at
confirming, criticizing or better specifying the behavioural assumptions
recalled earlier. After Tversky's death, Kahneman (2011) moves towards
an at least partly different direction, considering the experimental proofs
in favour of another hypothesis, the distinction between decisions concerning the short and the long run. The two kinds of decisions are to be
attributed to different areas of the brain and involve distinct decisional
processes, the one relative to long-term issues being more rational (the
'slow decisions') and the other more intuitive, relative to decisions taken
in reaction to immediate stimuli. This thesis appears to be confirmed by
a number of experimental tests, as we saw in the previous discussion
relating to the new research area of bioeconomics; compared to prospect
theory, this leads us further away from expected utility theory.

On the wake of prospect theory, but with a somewhat different
approach, Loomes and Sugden (1982) propose regret theory (for precision, regret and rejoice). Presented as an extension of expected utility

[27] Kahneman and Tversky (1979), pp. 278–80.
[28] Cf. Kahneman and Tversky (1979), p. 263.
[29] Kahneman and Tversky (1979), p. 280.

theory and aimed at explaining behavioural anomalies found in reality, this theory as well relies on a modified utility function, which takes into consideration – through a regret and rejoice function – the difference between the utility of 'what it is' and the utility of 'what could have been'. Conceptually analogous but analytically distinct is disappointment theory (Loomes and Sugden 1987). This theory, and other similar ones, reject the basic postulates of expected utility theory, as that of transitivity, but have the advantage of being compatible with (or, as it is held, to explain) anomalies such as Allais's paradox, illustrating the support for regret theory.[30]

Among Kahneman's collaborators and followers, Richard Thaler (b. 1945, Nobel Prize in 2017, professor at Chicago), analyses various aspects connected to prospect theory in a series of articles on the *Journal of Economic Perspectives* (the majority of which as part of a rubric with the title *Anomalies*) and in other contributions.

Anomalies are those experimental results that contradict the paradigm of the *homo oeconomicus* supposedly taking rational choices on a well-defined and relatively stable set of preferences. Among these anomalies we may recall the so-called endowment effect, according to which agents attribute a greater value to things they already possess (if requested to sell, they ask a higher price than that they are willing to pay if they do not already possess these things); the so-called mental accounting, on the basis of which agents, in simplifying their decisions, tend to separately group different expenditure categories (food, dresses, housing, enjoyments and so on); some aspects of irrationality in the working of financial markets and more generally in the field of games, as the tendency to bet on whoever is winning (extrapolative expectations, which may lead to speculative bubbles and sooner or later are contradicted) or the tendency to sell titles that have grown in value in the previous period in preference to those that have experienced losses (the so-called disposition effect), or again the tendency to estimate risks separately for the different assets without taking into account their interrelations (the so-called narrow framing).[31]

Thaler considers behavioural economics as a development, not an alternative, to the marginalist mainstream tradition. In this direction, in his best-known work (Thaler and Sunstein 2008), he maintains that we

---

[30] Bleichrodt and Wakker (2015), pp. 500 ff.; the paper also provides a useful survey of the developments briefly recalled above.

[31] A clear and synthetic presentation of prospect theory that stresses Thaler's contributions, in particular those in the field of finance, is Barberis (2013). Anomalies include, among other things, the experimental results contradicting the theory of the life cycle discussed in §7.2: cf. Thaler (1990).

should rely on market forces while public authorities should limit themselves to exerting a gentle push (*nudge*) for addressing agents to overcome the deviations from fully rational behaviour theorized by mainstream economics, with what may be considered as a compromise between paternalism and liberalism (Thaler and Sunstein 2003).

Ultimately, the many examples/anecdotes provided by Thaler and Sunstein in their book illustrate how easy it is to influence humans and their behaviour. In this sense, they confirm the limits of human rationality, something which is well known to all marketing operators, whose work consists in influencing consumers' preferences, though leaving them full freedom of choice. In fact, a nudge may be used in the interests of society but, as the case of advertising shows, it is utilized mainly in the interests of those practising it. The doubt that constitutes one of the strong points of liberal philosophy (expressed by Adam Smith 1759, p. 219), on the ability of anyone else to take care of us better than we ourselves can do, retains its full validity. Thaler's work may be considered as a subtle but devastating attack on the notion of the rational *homo oeconomicus*, but remains founded on a solipsistic notion of the agent, focused on the pursuit of their own selfish interests, and especially on an absolute faith in the optimizing powers of the market, that in fact constitutes a characteristic sign of the Chicago school.[32]

---

[32] On the wake of Stigler and Becker, Thaler and Sunstein (2008) are favourable to what has been called the imperialism of economics, in particular to extending markets to fields such as social security, even to a market of human organs.

11 From Efficient Financial Markets to the Theory of Crises

11.1 Introduction

Money and the financial markets have already come under our attention at various points, and in particular in Chapter 7, when we considered the evolution of macroeconomics and the neoclassical synthesis. Here we shall consider in greater depth some aspects only briefly mentioned: the broad stream of monetarist theory; the transition of policy from positions nearer, even if not equal, to Keynes's to a substantial affinity with monetarist tenets; the theory of efficient financial markets, which constitutes the theoretical foundations for the process of liberalization of financial markets that began in the 1970s; some aspects of the wide debate on financial markets and institutions; Keynesian-type instability and crisis theory as developed by Minsky towards the end of the 1960s; and, finally, Minsky's notion of a new stage of development of capitalism dominated by finance, namely money manager capitalism.

The opposition between monetarism and Minskyan analysis is clear-cut. On the plane of the overall working of the economy, on the one hand we have the monetarist (and neo-liberal) idea according to which markets generate order; on the other hand we have the thesis (which Minsky took up from Keynes) of an intrinsic instability of capitalism, permeated by uncertainty, particularly in the financial markets. On the theoretical level, on the one hand, according to monetarism, money vicissitudes influence only monetary variables, and so the general price level, but not activity and employment levels, nor even relative prices; on the other hand we have a theory of crises, more than a theory of the trade cycle, with the tenet of a decisive influence of money and financial markets on the real variables of the economy. On the practical level, we have a twofold opposition. First, as far as policies of control of short-period fluctuations of the economy are concerned, the monetarists support fixed rules for monetary policy; Minsky, on the other hand, proposes discretional interventions in support of liquidity in periods of crisis, or in the opposite direction when speculative bubbles take shape. Second, and most importantly, we have on the one hand the neo-liberal thesis that financial institutions should be left free to pursue their own interests, trusting in the invisible hand of the market; on the other hand, Minsky develops an interventionist position that maintains the need for constraints on the financial markets and operators in order to prevent the structural fragility of these markets from translating into widespread crises (indeed, of repeated crises of ever greater impact).

In an area intermediate between these opposed positions we have analyses of the actual modus operandi of the financial markets, as of the composition of financing to firms or the techniques for evaluating risk: aspects – very important in practice – that provide a large share of the economists active today with jobs, but to which we will refer only briefly, so as to focus attention on the theoretical debate.

11.2   Monetarism

Modern monetarism, associated with the name of Milton Friedman,[1] takes up (and, on the analytical level, takes ahead) a centuries-old tradition, namely the idea of a close link between money supply and prices, which had gained ground with the inflationary crises that took place in Europe, particularly in Spain, after the discovery of gold and silver mines in the Spanish colonies in America at the beginning of the sixteenth century. In the modern period, the nexus between quick rise in monetary circulation and dramatic inflationary push reappears with German hyperinflation in the 1920s.

On the analytical level, the immediate reference is to Fisher's equation of exchanges: $M\,V = P\,Q$, where M is the money supply, V the velocity of circulation, P an index of prices and Q the quantity of product. If we exclude asset purchases and sales (concerning financial assets, houses, jewels, art, etc.), the equation may be interpreted ex post as an accounting identity: the value of commodities passing from one hand to another is equal to the money flow going in the opposite direction in payment for the commodities (where by money we mean any means of exchange). To derive a theory from this equation, we need to introduce a few assumptions. Original monetarist theory relies on three fundamental assumptions: supply of money determined by monetary authorities; velocity of circulation given by the operational habits of economic agents, hence relatively stable; quantity of product set at the full employment

---

[1] On Friedman's contributions cf. §8.5. An extensive collection of contributions to the naissance and development of monetarism edited by Chrystal came out in 1990.

level, which according to the marginalist theory of value and distribution constitutes an equilibrium position for the economy. In this situation, changes in money supply cannot but translate into price changes.

What the theory thus formulated does not explain is how – through which transmission mechanisms – changes in money supply impact on prices. In dealing with this issue, Friedman develops a theoretical scheme more complex than Fisher's simple equation of exchanges. We already illustrated this theoretical framework in §8.5; here we briefly recall the elements more directly relevant to monetary theory.

In Friedman's model, the money supply is considered as exogenous, determined by the monetary authorities. Demand for money depends on the volume of exchanges (or on national income, which constitutes a proxy for it); on the share of income and/or wealth that agents desire to keep in money form; and on the opportunity cost of keeping money rather than other assets generating an income (bonds and bills, shares, houses, human capital …). The function connecting the demand for money to these elements is considered stable, in clear-cut opposition to the neoclassical synthesis economists' theses of marked instability in the speculative demand for money, which constitutes the dominant share of the demand for money and especially of its variations in the short and very short run. According to both Friedman and the supporters of the neo-classical synthesis, it is the return on real capital that determines the real rate of interest in the long run, while according to Keynes the rate of interest, aggregate demand and activity levels are determined by the interaction among liquidity preference, available liquidity, and expecta-tions of financial agents and entrepreneurs.

The central nucleus of monetarist theory concerns the long run. Together with a traditional model for determination of employment and income (for instance, Pigou's model illustrated in Chapter 7, Appendix), which implies an automatic tendency to a full employment equilibrium under perfectly competitive conditions, this theory leads to the conclusions recalled earlier: nil, or limited to the short period, rele-vance of monetary and financial events over real variables (income, employment, relative prices, including the equilibrium values for the distributive variables wage rate and rate of profits); preference for a monetary policy based on fixed rules rather than discretionary choices by the monetary authorities; and preference for laissez-faire vis-à-vis financial agents and markets.

Friedman's 'new' monetary theory was proclaimed in direct opposition to Keynes's; critique of the latter is an integral part of the monetarist theoretical edifice. The critiques are partly empirical (in conformity to Friedman's tenet (1974, p. 61) 'that the basic differences among economists are empirical, not theoretical', and partly theoretical. These latter are limited to recalling the traditional marginalist theory of full employment equilibrium,[2] and the real wealth (or Pigou) effect that ensures convergence to full employment equilibrium even in the presence of downward rigidity of the money wage.[3] As for the empirical critiques, the main point is the stability of the demand for money function. In support of this thesis, which he sees as definitively established, Friedman refers to Friedman and Schwartz (1963).[4]

In relation to the assumption of an exogenous money supply, we may recall that the supply of money is a difficult magnitude to define and keep under control; as subsequently indicated by 'Goodhart's law',[5] when one tries to keep the supply of money according to any definition under control, the flexibility typical of private finance regularly finds ways to circumvent the constraints by creating new kinds of financial assets (for instance, introducing time banking accounts connected to current bank accounts and so on).

In the wake of Friedman's monetarist theory, a monetary theory of the balance of payments was then developed (Johnson 1972; Frenkel and Johnson 1976). This theory follows a tradition originated by David Hume, with his essay on the adjustment process of the balance of payments in a gold-based international monetary system (Hume 1752): when the balance of payments of any country is negative, gold flows out of the country and, since gold constitutes the basis of any country's

---

[2] 'There is a well-developed economic theory, summarized in the Walrasian equations of general equilibrium, that explains what determines the level of output' (Friedman 1974, p. 44).

[3] 'Keynes's error consisted in neglecting the role of wealth in the consumption function' (the so-called Pigou effect illustrated in the Appendix to Chapter 7); thanks to this mechanism, 'there is no fundamental flaw in the price system' that leads to full employment (Friedman 1974, p. 16). The assumption of downward wage rigidity is attributed to Keynes (ibid., p. 18), considering it essential for his analysis, while in fact Keynes (1936, chapter 19) explicitly maintains that it is not so.

[4] In reaffirming the Keynesian thesis according to which changes in money supply are associated with changes in the velocity of circulation, Kaldor (1970) stresses that, to obtain his empirical results, Friedman needs to adopt definitions of the money supply that include elements, such as bank money, not under direct control of monetary authorities; 'thus, the explanation ... for all the empirical findings on the "stable money function" is that the "money supply" is "endogenous", not "exogenous"' (ibid., p. 269). Cf. also Kaldor (1982).

[5] Cf. Goodhart (1997). Charles Goodhart, b. 1936, has been a member of the Monetary Policy Committee of the Bank of England and professor at the London School of Economics. Originally formulated with reference to monetary theories, Goodhart's law subsequently assumes a more general scope: whenever any variable is chosen as policy target, and so necessarily defined in such a way as to be the object of regular statistical surveys, it becomes the object of manipulations and ceases to be a good indicator (as has happened in recent years for bibliometric indicators utilized in research evaluation).

monetary system, the money supply falls, engendering a decrease in prices that increases the international competitiveness of national products, thus leading to an adjustment in the balance of trade. In very simplified terms, something similar takes place according to the monetary theory of the balance of payments in an inconvertible currency world: the equilibrating effect in this case comes from changes in exchange ratios, which fall for the countries with negative balance of payments (improve for the countries with a positive balance), thus improving (worsening) the competitiveness of national products; the price effect is strengthened by an income effect, consisting in a fall of internal demand in countries whose exchange rate worsens, due to a loss of internal purchasing power.

Post-Keynesian critiques concern alternatively, but separately, both the monetarist theory and the underlying marginalist-neoclassical theory of real equilibrium; together, the two kinds of criticism should have a destructive impact on monetarism. Yet, the many debates in applied economics on this or that aspect of monetary theory do not seem to lead to final conclusions (correlations that cannot establish the direction of causal links, stability of functions that depends on the precise definition of the variables involved and so on). On the other hand, the thesis that the unemployment appearing in statistics is voluntary, or wholly due to frictions of various kinds and/or to policy errors seems more the object of apodictic statements than of serious applied research work (while other social sciences, from psychology to sociology and political sciences, are rich in studies on the implications of involuntary unemployment, considered as a systematic element, on the existence – and importance – of which no doubt is possible).

11.3   Economic Policy: From Keynesianism to Monetarism

The Keynesian tradition, including the neoclassical synthesis, favours a monetary policy based on control of interest rates with the aim of regulating the trade cycle: thus with an eye to production and employment levels, but also to inflation and exchange rates, with the aim to avoid through the latter excessive imported inflation and the formation of disequilibria in the balance of current payments. With respect to this latter element, Keynes's proposals at the Bretton Woods 1944 conference aimed to institutionalize disincentives to the accumulation over time of active balances in the balance of payments. However, his proposals were not accepted, and the result was asymmetry in interventions: necessitated in the case of persistent negative balances that risk exhausting currency reserves, but optional in the case of active balances that simply imply an increase in reserves (possibly utilized for financial investments in foreign countries). In Keynes's view, structural interventions in support of the economy – public investment, adequate rules for the international game – count much more than fine tuning of the trade cycle on which the neoclassical synthesis economists focus; at the international level, Keynes is favourable to a balanced opening of international trade but decidedly opposed to international short-term flows of financial capital, as favoured, instead, by the monetarists.[6]

In any case, the stability of exchange rates, guaranteed by the Bretton Woods agreements and supported by International Monetary Fund (IMF) interventions, together with the gradual abandonment of protectionist policies on the part of major countries, favoured relatively rapid economic development in the first quarter of century after the end of the war and – together with US aid – very rapid reconstruction in the defeated countries – Germany, Japan and Italy. Exchange rate stability also hampered international financial speculation, notwithstanding the defeat of Keynes's proposals specifically aimed at preventing very short run capital flows and financial speculation on exchange rates.

Towards the end of the 1960s this model entered into crisis. The neoclassical synthesis at the theoretical level and the Bretton Woods rules at the political level both constitute a hybrid compromise between Keynes's original vision and the tradition; in both cases, these are unstable compromises, in which the strength of the tradition is destined to prevail, with rational expectations theory at the theoretical level and with the rise of neo-liberalism (in particular, liberalization of financial flows) at the level of international economic institutions. The Vietnam War led the United States to cumulate passive balances of payments that in the course of time exceeded their gold reserves (which, according to the Bretton Woods agreements, should have been available to the central banks of other countries cumulating active balances of payments in exchange for their dollar surpluses). On 15 August 1971 the then president of the United Sates, Richard Nixon, unilaterally declared the end of the convertibility of the dollar into gold, and thus abandonment of the parity of 35 dollars per ounce of gold that had constituted anchorage for the exchange rate system in the previous quarter of a century. Shortly after, in a few months the 1973 oil crisis quadrupled oil prices, determining colossal active positions in the balances of payments of the oil exporting countries and colossal passive positions for importing countries. The solution to the problem of recycling the 'petrodollars' – which should return from the exporting countries to the oil importers, so as to allow for

---

[6] Cf. Keynes (1980) and Skidelsky (2000), pp. 179–263, 300–453.

continuing exchange flows and prevent collapse in the world economy – was largely entrusted to the major international banks, which acted as a bridge between countries with active and passive balances of trade, with extremely rapid growth of the eurodollar market and global finance.[7] Together with increasing currency speculation ensuing on abandonment of fixed exchange rates, these choices favoured an increasing financialization of the international economy and financial globalization.

The oil crisis also determined an inflationary upsurge, with a wage–price spiral driven by the distributional clash on whether real wages or profits should bear the increased energy costs. Simultaneous growth in inflation and unemployment – stagflation, as it is called – gave rise to a great debate in economic theory, followed by a redirection of policy.

Critics of Keynesian policies immediately stressed the breakdown of the Phillips curve, i.e. of the inverse relation between rate of unemployment and rate of growth of money wages, and so of prices, which represents a central element of the neoclassical synthesis. Simultaneous growth of inflation and unemployment was hailed as demonstrating the erroneousness of Keynesian theses. In the cultural and political climate of the time, foreshadowing the rise of conservative neo-liberalism (with President Reagan in the United States and Prime Minister Thatcher in Great Britain), the role of the distributive tensions arising from the oil crisis was undervalued, and the possibility of inflation caused by increased production costs rather than increased money supply failed to receive due attention. As we saw in Chapter 8, this leads to the notion of a vertical Phillips curve, thus denying the role of monetary and fiscal policies in fighting unemployment.

The reaction to Keynesian policies ran along various lines. First, the policy of control over interest rates gave way (in the United States on the initiative of Volcker, authoritative president of the Federal Reserve from 1979 to 1987)[8] to a policy of control of the money supply, as prescribed by monetarist theory for keeping inflation under control. The result was increasing instability in interest rates, and hence in exchange rates. This instability in turn reinforced the role of speculative finance and favoured

---

[7] The proposals of alternative solutions discussed at the time mostly imply IMF (and in some cases World Bank) intervention, both as intermediary between countries with active and passive balance of trade and through the creation of international liquidity (in particular through emission of Special Drawing Rights) and/or mobilization of gold reserves, together with an acceleration of flows of goods and services from oil-importing to oil-exporting countries. Cf. for instance Triffin (1974).

[8] Paul Volcker, b. 1927, was under-secretary at the Treasury in 1971 when dollar convertibility into gold was suspended.

the development of derivatives, utilized in both covering and speculative operations.

In response to the thesis that monetary policy should have as the sole target control of inflation through control of the money supply, the call arose for the central banks to be independent of the political powers, so as to avoid being obliged – through subscription of the public debt – to finance public deficits, considered useless as a stimulus to employment and counter-productive since – it was maintained – expansion of the public sector reduces global economic efficiency.[9] In some central banks, the norms that guaranteed independence were accompanied by focus on inflation as the main if not the sole policy objective. These choices stemmed from theoretical views relying on full employment equilibrium and the inefficacy of monetary policy vis-à-vis the real variables.[10]

Relying on the principle that all markets, including currency markets, automatically tend to an optimal equilibrium, free fluctuation of exchange rates was preferred to a system of fixed exchange rates such as instituted at Bretton Woods.[11] The situation created after the 1971 and 1973–4 crises was thus considered not optimal only because of active interventions by the central banks in the currency markets.

The development of the eurodollar market stimulated by petrodollar recycling also came in for positive evaluation, as did the markets for derivatives on exchange ratios and interest rates. Even the financialization of the economy was considered positive, with growing importance for financial intermediation and speculation, as measured by the share of financial services in gross domestic product (GDP), over the most recent

---

[9] The lesser efficiency of the public sector is considered so obvious as to discourage studying its causes, which among other things determine marked differences between countries and historical periods. Moreover, the lesser efficiency of the private sector in pursuing public objectives, such as environmental control, is overlooked: the (certainly not unfounded) assumption of questionable morality among public sector operators appears to be accompanied by the decidedly unwarranted assumption of a perfect morality among private sector operators, who are assumed to pursue their own interests in perfect respect of the rules (on, say, pollution).

[10] The debate on central bank independence (mentioned in §8.6) is obviously much more complex, involving among other things the question of the expediency of separate surveillance over credit institutions from monetary policy, or that of creating a system of weights and counter-weights between techno-structure and elected political authorities. The point we wish to stress here is the monetarist thesis on the expediency of focusing central banks on the target of inflation control, thus excluding from their tasks that of controlling unemployment and the trade cycle, even if in collaboration with other policy authorities.

[11] Cf. for instance Friedman (1953), pp. 157–72. Originally written in 1950, the essay is entitled 'The case for flexible exchange rates'.

period;[12] indeed, greater liquidity favoured investment financing and credit to consumption, as well as the financing of public deficits and passive balances of payments.

We should, however, compare advantages to costs, both in terms of resources absorbed by production of financial services and in terms of greater financial fragility for the economy. In some respects doubt may be cast on the very utility of financial services: as a service offered to savers, for instance, we may observe that the returns of the funds utilized for investing pension savings are generally lower, even before deducting intermediation commissions, than the average market return (the so-called benchmarks: cf. e.g. Fama and French 2010). The power shift towards private financial institutions is at the same time favoured by neo-liberal pressures and favours them, in a cumulative spiral in which cultural and political hegemony is consolidated by greater availability of financial means.

11.4   The Theory of Efficient Financial Markets: From Modigliani–Miller to Fama

Both the classical and neoclassical pre-Keynesian traditions tend to consider money as a veil, important only in determining monetary variables, as the general price level, but not in determining real variables. The marginalist tradition includes among these latter also the interest rate, determined by the demand for and supply of loanable funds, namely saving and investment. Opposing this tradition, Keynes holds that monetary events play a relevant role in determining the path of real variables, and that the set of interest rates is determined within the financial markets.

Within the neoclassical synthesis, once again it is Modigliani who intervenes (with the so-called Modigliani–Miller theorem, 1958) to show the neutrality of financial choices, from the specific point of view of decisions on how to finance investments. According to this theorem, under conditions of perfect competition, together with regulatory and fiscal neutrality, perfect foresight on the part of entrepreneurs, and the assumption that managers act in the interest of shareholders, for the firms it is a matter of indifference whether to finance investment with internal funds (retained profits) or with external funds (bank loans, bonds, shares).[13]

---

[12] Cf. Greenwood and Scharfstein (2013). For a critical evaluation of this trend, cf. Mazzucato (2018).
[13] The article by Modigliani and Miller is extensive and deals with various issues, from the capitalization of uncertain income flows to the implications of financial leverage (variously defined as the ratio of total debt to total assets, or the ratio of total debt to own

The theorem may also be interpreted as an indication of the very rigid conditions outside of which managers do not see the choices concerning investment financing as neutral, preferring internal to external funds. Even under this interpretation, in any case, the theorem falls fully within the marginalist tradition, considering the influence of monetary events limited to situations in which competitive conditions (on which pure theory focuses) are violated.

The Modigliani–Miller theorem shows, among other things, that maximizing the value of shares is equivalent to profit maximization: a result holding under the usual conditions of perfect competition and perfect knowledge (or probabilistic risk).[14] The result is important for many reasons, including the fact that it justifies the attribution of stock options to firm managers, as a tool for ensuring correspondence of their interests to those of the owners of the firm (the shareholders), thus overcoming the so-called principal–agent problem referred to in §7.4. Moreover, this should guarantee that the drive to technical progress offered by the search for profits is not hindered by the financialization of the economy, which, as we shall see, attributes direct relevance to maximizing the value of shares in the very short run.

Portfolio choice among assets endowed with different risks sees a role for financial mathematics, a field that has developed over time. Risk is initially identified in the simplest way, as variability of the price of the financial asset within a chosen time span: a greater risk, identified by variance (in the statistical meaning of the term) of the price series, must correspond to greater returns, with the difference in comparison to less risky assets that constitutes a premium for risk. This is the so-called average-variance model by Markowitz (1952), followed by the capital asset pricing model (CAPM, originally developed by Sharpe, 1964), which also takes into account the covariance of the prices of the financial assets included in a portfolio, namely the tendency of the prices of the different assets to change in the same direction (thus increasing risk) or in opposite directions (thus reducing risk). We may also recall the formula proposed by Fisher Black and Myron Scholes (1973) for determining

---

capital) or of company taxation, including an interesting applied analysis of the cost of capital for electricity and oil companies.

[14] In perfect markets, the value of share capital of a firm corresponds to the discounted flow of expected profits; obviously, with expectations differing from one person to another, the value attributed to the shares differs from one agent to another and the market price of shares corresponds to an average of these evaluations. Tobin's q (mentioned in §7.2), which corresponds to the ratio between the market value of the share capital of a firm and the accounting value of its assets as registered in the balance sheet of the firm, indicates whether the prospects of the firm are positive ($q > 1$) or negative ($q < 1$), at least according to current market evaluation.

option prices, which favoured the rapid development of activity in this field of financial derivatives.

Tending in the same direction as the theory of Modigliani and Miller is the theory of efficient financial markets proposed by Eugene Fama (b. 1939, professor at the University of Chicago, Nobel Prize in 2013). According to this theory (Fama 1970), the prices of financial assets fully and continuously reflect the underlying situation of the real economy.[15] Once again, perfect competition and perfect knowledge (or probabilistic risk) are assumed. Under these conditions, speculative activity does not make sense or (in the case of normally distributed causal deviations from the 'true value') favours a rapid convergence to equilibrium.[16]

In principle, arbitrage operations eliminate the influence of any element of knowledge on the path of financial asset prices, and in particular of share prices in the stock exchange, which should thus follow a random path: an agent tossing up what assets to buy or sell (or a monkey inserting orders in the system by turning a lever up or down) should have the same chances of success or failure as an expert agent operating on the basis of an extensive knowledge of the situation and of sophisticated argumentations; the only systematic gains may come from insider trading.

Arbitrage operations taking place in the real world do not respect the ideal conditions (absolute absence of risk, no capital requirement) often attributed to them in university textbooks: they are mostly performed by a limited number of professional, highly specialized agents who do not operate with their own capital and assume high risks. Under these conditions, arbitrage may not succeed in eliminating the

---

[15] 'A market in which prices always "fully reflect" the available information is called "efficient"' (Fama, 1970, p. 383). This is a specific meaning of the term 'efficiency', which does not correspond, for instance, to the usual meaning for a productive activity, namely providing a service at the minimum cost. We may note, in general, that informational efficiency is a necessary but not sufficient condition for allocational efficiency.

[16] This research line has been rewarded with various Nobel Prizes: apart from Modigliani, who gave important contributions in many fields, and Tobin, others who received the prize were Harry Markowitz (b. 1927), Merton Miller (b. 1923) and William Sharpe (b. 1934) in 1990; Robert Merton (1910–2003) and Myron Scholes (b. 1941) in 1997; and Eugene Fama (b. 1939), Lars Peter Hansen (b. 1952) and Robert Shiller (b. 1946) in 2013. Fisher Black (1938–1995) would probably have shared the prize with Merton and Scholes in 1997, had he not died two years earlier. Together with John Meriwether, Merton and Scholes are also known as the co-founders of the hedge fund Long Term Capital Management (LTCM), which, after some years of high profits, crashed resoundingly in 1998, the year following award of the Nobel Prize. It is also worth noting that among the winners for 2013, together with the original proponent of the theory of efficient financial markets (Fama) we find an exponent of the quite different research line of behavioural finance (Shiller) and an econometrician known for his empirical studies on the prices of financial assets (Hansen).

anomalies that continuously appear in financial markets.[17] Behavioural finance economists are well aware of these aspects; they illustrate how the actual behaviour of financial agents differs from the ideal one of a perfectly rational *homo oeconomicus* endowed with all the necessary information.[18]

The theory of efficient financial markets implies the impossibility of speculative bubbles involving the prices of financial or real estate assets (apart from the case of strong rigidities severely hindering the functioning of such markets). Alan Greenspan, chairman of the Federal Reserve in the years preceding the financial crisis, defending his choice not to intervene to halt what many economists (Kindleberger, Sylos Labini and others) considered speculative bubbles jeopardizing the stability of the financial system, maintains precisely that within efficient financial markets prices are determined by underlying conditions and that in any case the information available to the monetary authorities is no better than that of the agents in the market, so that the existence of a speculative bubble can be verified only ex post.[19]

The theory of efficient financial markets leads to the same laissez-faire conclusions as monetarism as far as policy orientation is concerned, reinforcing them with respect to the uselessness of regulatory constraints on financial institutions. In this direction, it provides cultural support to the triumphant march of financial deregulation, although its limits as interpretation of the real world are widely recognized.[20]

Since the outbreak of the financial crisis in 2007–8, the theory of efficient financial markets has apparently fallen into oblivion in policy debate, though retaining an important place in university lecture courses in monetary and financial economics, and although the reasons for its failure once again appear to be sought in violations of the perfect competition and perfect knowledge assumptions rather than in basic defects of the underlying theory.

---

[17] Cf. Shleifer and Vishny (1997).

[18] Apart from Shiller, already cited, another Nobel laureate who contributed to the development of behavioural finance is Thaler, recalled in §10.5); cf. Thaler and Sunstein (2008).

[19] Cf. Greenspan (2009), Kindleberger (1995, 2002) and Sylos Labini (2003).

[20] For a brief survey, rich in bibliographical references, of the many incongruities cf. Conlisk (1996), p. 673: 'stock prices display: slow mean reversion . . .; predictable end-of-week, end-of-year, seasonal, and holiday effects . . .; excess fluctuations in prices relative to fluctuations in fundamentals . . .; dramatic bubbles unexplained by changes in fundamental values . . .; excess risk premia relative to bonds . . .; systematic deviation of mutual fund prices from the values of the component securities . . .; excess trading volume on shares that have risen in price relative to volume on shares that have fallen in price.'

11.5   Financial Markets and Institutions

Here, having no hope of surveying the vast mass of works concerning the functioning of financial markets and institutions, we will simply offer a brief review of some research streams.

A complex debate has arisen over the nature of the money supply: exogenous or endogenous? This debate is connected to the question of what is meant by 'money', from legal currency to including all instruments of payment (current bank accounts, time deposits, treasury bills and bonds, etc.). Clearly, while the supply of legal currency depends on the choices of the monetary authorities and can thus be considered as exogenous, for bank deposits the answer depends on more or less rigid reserve requirements (as with the theory of the multiplier of bank deposits, equal to the inverse of the reserve coefficient) or on attributing to banks more or less wide margins of manoeuvre. These debates go back to the clash between the banking school and currency school at the beginning of the nineteenth century, but have continued, as for instance with the monetarist assumption of exogenous money supply and the critiques this assumption raised on the part of various economists.

The notion of deposit multiplier is typical of the traditional view of banks, attributing them with the role of savings management. An active view of the role of banks (typical of Keynesian theory but also of Wicksell and Schumpeter among others), on the other hand, focuses attention on the process of deposit creation as a tool for credit provision. With innovations in banking techniques of management of active and passive items in their balance sheets it is possible to circumvent reserve constraints, which with the Basel Agreements tend to be substituted by minimum capital requirements as tools for limiting the growth of bank actives and contain their risk.

As for the demand for money, the tradition established since Petty and Locke in the seventeenth to early eighteenth centuries only takes into consideration the transactions demand for money related to the volume of exchanges, and so to income, and the precautionary demand, connected to the volume of wealth. Keynes, with his *General theory*, added the speculative demand for money (or, more precisely, the preference for liquidity) attributing it with a central role for the economy. Widespread debate then arose over this element.

As we saw in §3.6, Keynes's theory is closely connected with his views on uncertainty. Unlike Knight's rigid dichotomy between risk and uncertainty, the Keynesian notion of uncertainty does not correspond to the borderline case of absolute ignorance, the opposite limit being that of certainty or of probabilistic risk. According to Keynes, we are always faced with uncertainty, but with different degrees of confidence in our evaluation of the situation. As a consequence, the theories concerning phenomena characterized by different degrees of confidence should be considered separately. We thus have, in succession: theory of financial markets, based on a very short-period perspective and speculation, which determines interest rates and the liquidity conditions of the system; investment theory, in which interest rates (and/or the conditions of liquidity) enter as causal factors together with expected returns, based on evaluations concerning periods of time that are very long but that precisely for this reason may change quite rapidly; and theory of output (and employment) levels, concerning decisions that may be quickly adapted to changes in the situation and that as a consequence are less uncertain. Obviously, the succession of these three theoretical blocks indicates the causal relations that the theoretician considers dominant, but does not exclude the presence of dynamic feedbacks, which may enrich the picture at lesser abstraction levels, adapting it to situations differing in time and between countries.

As part of his neoclassical synthesis, Hicks collects these different theoretical levels into a single general equilibrium system, putting the three kinds of decisions on the same level. Friedman does the same when grouping demand for money, financial assets, housing and human capital into one and the same problem of portfolio choice.[21] The sequential nature of the Keynesian theory thus disappears, and with it the active role of the financial markets in determining the path of the economy, so that real factors take the lead in determining equilibrium, which, with competitive labour markets (downward wage flexibility), turns out to be full-employment equilibrium. The debate on money and finance is thus connected to the macroeconomic debate.

Within the macro schemes of general equilibrium, wide-ranging debate has arisen over the transmission mechanisms for the different stimuli, with different degrees of specification for the financial markets and the institutions. Differences among the various theories concern analytical issues, such as the different assumptions on the kind and role of expectations, and applied issues, such as the values of some key parameters like the responsiveness (elasticity) of interest rates to variations in money supply. The structure of interest rates, too, has been the object of theoretical and applied researches: the monetary authorities influence short-period rates, while investment decisions are influenced by long-period rates. The link between the two kind of rates may be addressed with deterministic models if we assume that differences between long and

---

[21] Cf. for instance Friedman (1974).

short rates depend solely or mainly on the greater risks of long-term financial investments, since their market prices vary more in response to changes in interest rates; it may also be addressed with stochastic models, or with less rigidly structured theories, if financial agents' expectations regarding the evolution of the markets over time enter into the picture.

Debate on the role of banks and financial markets is connected to debate on basic macroeconomic theory. On the one hand, those who, in the light of traditional theory, consider the economy as relatively stable around a full employment equilibrium see it as useless, indeed counter-productive, to set limits to the financial institutions. Thus, with the dominance of neo-liberalism as from the end of the 1970s, the separation between the commercial banks that collect deposits from savers and whose activities are limited to the short period, and investment banks that operate over the long term and on more speculative financial markets, is abolished; at the same time, the growth of financial derivatives is unconstrained. These facts had heavy repercussions on the crisis that broke out in 2007–8. On the other hand, those who follow Keynes's original theory, and even more Minsky's ideas on financial fragility as the cause of more and more serious crises, argue the need for re-regulation of the financial markets and institutions.

11.6   The Keynesian Theory of Financial Markets: Hyman Minsky

The Modigliani–Miller theory, showing the irrelevance of the financial structure to the real economy, and the theory of efficient financial markets, which sees the prices of financial assets as dependent on real variables, dominated economic teaching and culture for over half a century. It was only after the 2007–8 financial crisis that a quite different view came to the fore, taking up Keynes's views on uncertainty and the active role of the financial markets – a view that had, in fact, been proposed as early as the mid-1960s by an American economist (Minsky 1964) and developed in various writings.[22]

Hyman Minsky (1919–96) offered an important scientific contribution by analysing the working of a capitalist economy and bringing to light its intrinsic instability and the tendency to repeated crises. He was thus able to indicate policy lines to avoid crises and achieve full employment, which he saw as a major objective. Indeed, it is on full employment that his proposals to consider the government as 'employer of last resort' rest,

---

[22] In this and the following section I draw on Roncaglia (2013).

alongside the role commonly attributed to the central bank as lender of last resort.[23]

Minsky's contribution may be summed up in three points: uncertainty, financial fragility, money manager capitalism. Let us begin with the first two, which combine in a theory of financial crises.

In his first book, *John Maynard Keynes* (1975), Minsky proposes an interpretation of Keynes that differs not only from that of Hicks's and Samuelson's neoclassical synthesis, but also from the interpretation prevailing among the post-Keynesians who studied at Cambridge with Keynes, including Kahn and Joan Robinson (discussed in the next chapter). Minsky attributes a basic role to uncertainty, discussed by Keynes in his 1921 *Treatise on probability*. Uncertainty is not considered as a generic notion opposed to probabilistic risk, but the general case in a range that has as extremes absolute certainty and total uncertainty. As we have already seen (§§3.6 and 3.7), this notion of uncertainty underlies Keynes's theory, and in particular his notions of effective demand and liquidity preference.

On this basis, and making innovative use of the analysis of flows of funds in the tradition of Irving Fisher, Minsky builds his theory of endogenous financial fragility, opposed to the mainstream view of the invisible hand of the market – the tenet of a strong self-regulating capacity of market economies. With respect to this theory we may refer to *Stabilizing an unstable economy* (1986) and to the essays collected in *Can 'It' happen again?*, 1982. The reference in the title, 'It', is to the 1929 Great Crisis; Minsky's prophecy was that a crisis of that magnitude may happen again, as in fact did come about.

Minsky describes the economy as a system of active and passive flows to and from the various agents. More precisely, the position of each agent may be expressed as a sequence of expected incoming and outgoing money flows; discounted at the interest rate prevailing in the market, these flows may be expressed in a single value, the actual (expected) value of the position of the agent (who can be for instance an entrepreneur financing his investments with debt, or a financial operator with active and passive items in titles with different degrees of risk, so that determination of the expected value of the position is in both cases accompanied by a higher or lower degree of confidence in the evaluation).

In this scheme of analysis Minsky introduces the distinction between (1) covered positions, in which the decisions of the agent lead, with a sufficient degree of confidence, to foreseeing for all future periods incoming flows greater than payments on interest and debt amortization;

---

[23] Some of his contributions on this theme are collected in Minsky (2013).

(2) speculative positions, in which for some periods the position may be 'not covered' and the agent knows that he or she will be obliged to resort to the financial market in order to refinance his or her position; and finally (3) Ponzi positions, in which the debt of the agent increases over time due to the impossibility of meeting the outflows for interest and debt amortization payments with current earnings. This is the case, for instance, when the agent speculates on the price of a house or financial asset, resorting to new loans to cover current payments in the hope that gains in the capital account to be realized when selling the asset will allow for reimbursement of all the accumulated debts, including interest on loans, plus some profits.

In a world subject to continuous change, agents continuously modify their structure of active and passive items. When refinancing their positions, they are confronted with an evolving state of liquidity of the economy. Here the financial institutions come into play, with their ability to provide flexibility to the financial management of firms and families, supplying credit also for the medium to average term though relying on short- or very short-period funding. Thus the financial institutions operate in a speculative position. This implies two kinds of risk: liquidity and solvency.[24] Refinancing long-term positions may turn out to be difficult and/or more costly than expected, thus creating a liquidity problem; in this situation, agents may be compelled to liquidate some assets, driving their prices downward, and this in turn may create solvency problems. Increases in interest rates themselves determine changes in the value of discounted flows of payments and takings, which may also generate solvency problems. The fragility of a financial institution largely depends on the degree of financial fragility of its counterparts: a bank loan, even short term, going to finance fixed capital investments entails for the bank the liquidity and solvency risks discussed above.

Minsky observes that when the economy is flourishing and the general climate of opinion improves, the share of speculative and Ponzi positions tends to increase, making the financial state of the economy more fragile. Indeed, as optimistic expectations are validated by facts, the agents' optimism increases in evaluating expected

---

[24] The solvency (or credit) risk concerns the probability of debtor bankruptcy; in this case, the creditors will undergo loss of part of their credit, the extent of loss depending on the results of bankruptcy procedures. The liquidity risk concerns the possibility of finding oneself with too few liquid funds to meet payments coming to date, though owning assets (houses, shares of firms not quoted on the stock exchange, and so on) of a value more than sufficient to cover the payments, but difficult to sell quickly and on adequate conditions.

incoming and outgoing flows. Moreover, in a calmer phase (less variability) the agents' degree of confidence in their evaluations tends to increase and the margins of guarantee required by financial institutions for loans provision are correspondingly reduced. However, when, after a long period of asset price increases, they stabilize or even decrease – suffice it to recall the case of the US housing market around 2007 – the climate of opinion abruptly changes, the required margins of guarantee are increased and agents no longer succeed in refinancing their uncovered positions, thus leading to liquidation of assets, entailing a plunge in their prices, and to a crisis that is both financial and real (what is called debt deflation). This is the case in particular with Ponzi operations, based on acquisition, financed with debt, of an asset for which price increases at a rate higher than the interest rate are expected.

We thus have the financial fragility hypothesis: financial crises are an unavoidable consequence of the temporary stability that generates an evolution of the financial structure of the economy with the role of speculative and Ponzi positions growing in importance. But this is not all: episode after episode, these crises may turn out to be ever more frequent and violent as, on the basis of previous experience, agents fall back on the conviction that the state will step in to save the situation, implying that they can take on ever greater risks.

With the crisis that began in 2007–8, references to Minsky's theory multiplied. We may debate whether the crisis follows the precise path indicated by Minsky's theory and what is new about it, but it is certain that Minsky's theory provides fundamental elements for understanding the situation and for intervening in it, not only in the immediate circumstances, in support of the financial structure and with stimuli for recovery of economic activity, but also on a wider scale with regulatory measures for the financial markets to prevent continual increase in financial fragility. Moreover, contrary to the tenets of efficient financial markets theory, policy should pay attention not only to income and inflation but also to asset prices, as maintained in the years before the crisis by, among others, Charles Kindleberger, who utilizes Minsky's theory for his celebrated history of crises.[25]

---

[25] Charles Kindleberger, 1910–2003, an economic historian and professor of international economics at MIT, was among the designers of the Marshall Plan for aid to European reconstruction after the Second World War. His fascinating book on the history of financial crises (Kindleberger 1978) explicitly relies on Minsky's theory. For his contributions on the need to lend attention to asset prices and on the forecast of a crisis as a consequence of speculative bubbles, cf. Kindleberger (1995, 2002).

11.7   Money Manager Capitalism

To understand the present we should also take into account the evolution of the very nature of capitalism over time. In this respect we may refer to another contribution by Minsky, published in 1990 in a collection of essays in honour of Paolo Sylos Labini, 'Schumpeter and finance' (Minsky, like Sylos, was a pupil of Schumpeter). In this work, and earlier on in some lectures in the 1980s at the Trieste International Summer School for Advanced Economic Studies, Minsky remarked that the stages of commercial, financial and managerial capitalism are followed by a stage of money manager capitalism.

Economic growth in the 1950s and 1960s generated an increase in wealth, and within it in the share of financial assets. Thus the role of professional fund managers was growing, having previously been limited to managing the wealth of the richest. Further development of their role was also favoured by privatization of part of public welfare (pension funds, health insurance, etc.) and the increased complexity of financial portfolio management (financial innovations like money market funds, development of mathematical-statistical models and derivatives).

We thus arrive at a stage in which the financial markets dominate the real economy: financial managers, who manage enormous stocks of wealth by continuously buying and selling assets so as to earn even on minimal price variations, have a very short temporal horizon. Moreover, by substantially operating on derivative financial markets with a high leverage (ratio between overall passives and own capital) they increase both their own risk, the financial fragility of the system and market volatility. The previous conditions of managerial capitalism no longer apply, for the managers of big corporations can no longer rely on sub-stantive power vis-à-vis many small shareholders, but must deal with financial operators like hedge fund managers who are able to put together (or sell) substantial share packages, sufficient to escalate even big cor-porations. Development of this stage has proceeded in parallel with the liberalization of financial markets in the 1980s and 1990s.[26]

According to the theoreticians of the managerial economy (for instance Marris 1964), the managers who control a firm try to make profits on the difference between earnings and costs along the whole lifespan of an industrial plant, and in particular try to maximize their controlling power over the long run; financial managers, Minsky remarks, aim,

---

[26] On the growth of the financial sector of the economy in its various components and the positive and especially negative implications of this trend, cf. Greenwood and Scharfstein (2013). On the link between financialization, asset inflation and fragility of the economy cf. Toporowski (2000).

rather, to make profits on price differences in an asset between now and tomorrow, or in an hour or a few minutes' time. Thus even firm managers must focus attention on their firms' share prices or, as is commonly said, on value creation for their shareholders in the immediate run, even over-looking important elements for a sustainable growth of their firms over time, such as good industrial relations within the plant or consolidation of confidential relations with providers and customers. In other terms, while corporate managers' investment choices are validated or not validated by the ensuing income flows, money managers' choices are validated or not validated by the variations in financial asset prices. All this renders the economy less efficacious in terms of productivity growth or ecological and social sustainability issues, given the reduced attention paid to long-period issues such as pursuit of technological progress – more unstable in relation to changes in the climate of opinion, more difficult to control through the traditional policy tools. The economy turns out to be more unstable: the income flows that, stemming from productivity increases, validate investment choices are permanent; on the contrary, financial decisions that increase liquidity and thus the prices of financial assets are easily followed by decisions of an opposite sign when expectations change.

An aspect of money manager capitalism stressed by Minsky concerns high managerial retributions, commonly assimilated to wages while they should be considered jointly with profits. The form these retributions assume (bonuses on the annual performance of firms, or on the value of the managed portfolios of financial assets) constitutes an important incentive to choices looking to the short or very short period. Moreover, they amount to a by no means irrelevant element in the growth of distributive inequalities that has been taking place over the past decades, of such a magnitude as also to determine a growing polarization of power relations and, indeed, of the social structure.[27]

Keynes remarks, in the *General theory*, that it would be a very difficult situation if the tail of finance were to wag the dog of the real economy; this is now precisely what is happening, not occasionally but systematically, in the money manager capitalism described by Minsky.

Minsky's analyses illustrated in the preceding pages indicate that the main problem policy should tackle is not capitalism's cyclical instability, but its systemic instability, namely the predisposition to crises. This has various important implications; let us consider the main ones.

First, we cannot allow the morphology of financial systems to be driven by their spontaneous evolution, or in other words by the decisions of

---

[27] Cf. Milanovic (2016).

private financial operators, with the state retreating to the role of arbiter on the basis of rules substantially dictated by the markets. This calls for a change in cultural orientations, but also in bargaining powers, inverting the tendency manifest since the internationalization of finance that sees national jurisdictions losing ground relatively to international finance.

Second, it is clear that the scope of policy interventions cannot be limited to short-period control of aggregate demand through monetary and fiscal policy tools. It is also and above all necessary to keep the financial fragility of the economy under control, as far as possible, so as to limit the extent and frequency of financial crises and their impact on the real economy. This implies getting down to finance regulation, for instance with constraints on the leverage and dimensions of financial firms, so as to prevent systemic risks arising from their eventual bankruptcy (the 'too big to fail' issue), or with rules constraining speculative activities (for instance with a tax on derivatives or constraints on high-frequency trading). Preventive interventions are better than ex post measures, due to moral hazard; moreover, any rescue of financial institutions should be conducted in such a way that their costs fall on the managers and shareholders.[28]

Third, support for effective demand must be systematic. In this respect, Minsky (1975, p. 148) recalls Keynes's proposal of 'socializing investments', integrating direct interventions on income distribution and decentralized market mechanisms;[29] moreover, as mentioned earlier, he suggests that the policy authorities should pursue full employment as their main objective, acting as 'employer of last resort'.[30]

Fourth, monetary policy should attribute importance to changes in the price of assets, so as to prevent the formation of speculative bubbles or, more generally, any situation in which Ponzi schemes would appear attractive (i.e. situation that sees a continuous rise in asset prices occurring at a rate higher than the relevant interest rate).[31]

---

[28] 'We have to establish and enforce a "good financial society" in which the tendency by business and bankers to engage in speculative finance is constrained' (Minsky, 1982, p. 69). For some proposals in this direction cf. for instance Montanaro and Tonveronachi (2012).

[29] As Keynes (1931, p. 311, quoted by Minsky 1975, p. 147) maintains, the political problem of human societies is 'to combine three things: economic efficiency, social justice, and individual liberty'.

[30] Cf. Minsky (2013). Minsky (1982, p. 5) also stresses that 'the federal government not only stabilizes income but the associated increase in the federal debt, by forcing changes in the mix of financial instruments owned by the public, makes the financial system more stable'.

[31] We should recall that 'in a capitalist economy there are two "price levels", one of current output and the second of capital assets' (Minsky, 1982, p. 79). Obviously, given the

Fifth, the earnings of financial operators should be kept under control, also considering that the financial sector is characterized by oligopolistic market forms such that extra-profits easily translate into managerial retributions higher than those prevailing under competitive conditions.[32] This acts as a disincentive both to investments and to human capital formation in the manufacturing sector, thus hindering productive efficiency and technical progress.

Finally, we should aim at reducing uncertainty which increases liquidity preference and the scope for financial speculation and thus increases interest rates and their instability, constituting a disincentive for real investments. This implies adequate – national, international and supranational – institutions (for instance, such as to favour exchange rate stability).

interrelations among different monetary policy targets, we need to intervene in a coordinated way on the entire range of monetary, fiscal and regulatory policies.

[32] On transformation of extra-profits into higher retributions under oligopoly, cf. Sylos Labini (1984).

Part V

Is a New Paradigm Possible?

12 Post-Keynesian Macroeconomics

12.1 The Cambridge Tradition

For more than half a century, between the end of the nineteenth and the beginning of the twentieth century, the English University of Cambridge constituted the main centre for the elaboration and diffusion of economic culture: initially, thanks to the intellectual and academic force of Marshall (among other things, founder of both the Royal Economic Society and the *Economic Journal*) and to the fact that there the first degree course in economics had been established, favouring the concentration of a group of leading economists and economic historians; subsequently, thanks also to the happy combination of a persistent important position within the marginalist tradition (with Arthur Pigou, 1877–1959, Marshall's successor, and Dennis Robertson, 1890–1963) and the innovative contribution of extraordinary importance that Keynes had to offer.

The post-war period saw Cambridge economics orphaned when Keynes died in 1946, to be revitalized, however, with new blood. On the neoclassical front, James Meade (1907–99, who subsequently moved to Oxford to win the Nobel Prize in 1977) developed the welfare economics started by Pigou; on the applied economics front, Richard Stone (1913–91, Nobel Prize in 1984) developed the system of national accounts – two important innovative contributions. Robertson and, in the first stage, Pigou continued to defend the Marshallian tradition (the former with the accent on the evolutionary aspect, the latter focusing on comparative static analysis).

On the opposite front, that of classical economics, one of the major protagonists was Piero Sraffa, who had been at Cambridge since 1927, invited there by Keynes. He was already known for his 1925 and 1926 articles critical of the Marshallian approach, later acclaimed for his edition of Ricardo's works, and finally author of *Production of commodities by means of commodities*, published in 1960. Then there were Maurice Dobb (1900–76), a Marxist, historian of economic thought and theoretician of

289

economic planning and, later on, Richard Goodwin (1913–96), who arrived there from the United States, a student of Schumpeter and a brilliant mathematician.[1]

Closer to this group than to the opposite front were Keynes's main pupils, his collaborators in the stage preceding publication of the *General theory*: Richard Kahn (1905–88), whose analysis of the Marshallian short period (cf. Kahn 1929/1983) and income multiplier were utilized by Keynes in constructing his theory; and Joan Robinson (1903–83), a passionate polemist, who, after the theory of imperfect competition developed at the beginning of the 1930s within the Marshallian framework, set about extending the Keynesian theory to the long run. They were joined by the brilliant Hungarian Nicholas Kaldor (1908–86), who moved to Cambridge from the London School of Economics, being fascinated by Keynes but endowed with an autonomous personality that kept him apart from the group of Keynes's pupils and interested in utilizing elements of the classical tradition, such as the major role attributed to the division of labour and increasing returns, with which to build a bridge between theory, policy strategies and applied economics, including contributions to the policies of developing countries and the post-war policies of international institutions.

Kaldor, Kahn and Joan Robinson, together with their circle of pupils, constituted the Keynesian current and, together with Sraffa, a centre of attraction for economists from near and far, especially Indians and Italians, such as Amartya Sen (b. 1933, Nobel Prize in 1998), Ajit Singh (1940–2015), Luigi Pasinetti (b. 1930), Pierangelo Garegnani (1930–2011), Luigi Spaventa (1934–2013) and many others generally included under the label of 'the Cambridge school'.

---

[1] Dobb, Sraffa's collaborator in the final stages of the work on the Ricardo edition, is the author of some important studies of Marxist orientation on the borderline between theory, economic history and history of economic thought, including a volume on the Soviet Union (1928 and successive editions), a volume titled *Studies in the development of capitalism* (1947) in which he discusses among other things the theme of the transition from feudalism to capitalism and a volume on the history of economic thought (Dobb 1973). For Goodwin (whose papers are kept at Siena University, where he taught after his retirement from Cambridge) we may recall the works on the multiplier and the trade cycle; in particular, Goodwin (1967) presents a model of the trade cycle based on the evolutionary prey–predator scheme originally studied by the mathematician Vito Volterra (1860–1940); this approach is then developed in a theory of chaotic economic dynamics in Goodwin (1990). We may consider as a compendium of his views a volume with the ironic title *Elementary economics from the higher standpoint* (1970), which utilizes elegant graphical representations (Goodwin was also a refined painter); see also the collection of essays in Goodwin (1982a); for an autobiographical interview and a biography, cf. Goodwin (1982b).

As from the post-war period, however, the force of attraction of US economics waxed strong: big traditional universities like Chicago and the more liberal ones on the Atlantic coast, from Harvard to Yale and the Massachusetts Institute of Technology (MIT), plus research centres such as the Cowles Foundation and the Rand Corporation together with the universities that developed and applied the new econometric techniques, as did Lawrence Klein's (Nobel Prize in 1980) Pennsylvania University. It was these centres, better endowed than English universities, hence with a particular force of attraction for the younger economists, that reaped a major crop of Nobel Prizes: due not only and not so much to the undoubted excellence of their economists as especially – we may suspect – to the political and economic primacy that the US acquired after the end of the war, together with the influence of political evaluations, important for a prize founded and funded by the Swedish central bank. It is indeed a shame that among the winners we do not find such major economists as Sraffa, Kahn, Joan Robinson, Kalecki, Kaldor, Luigi Pasinetti; even in the United States heterodox economists like Hyman Minsky, whose importance has generally been recognized since the recent financial crisis, do not feature in the list of winners.

The economic gap certainly plays a part in Cambridge's gradual decline (as in that of Oxford, though high-ranking economists like Hicks teach there) with respect to major US universities. The flow of grants financed by the United States attracts students from around the world, while on the English front students coming from (and financed by) other countries replenish university coffers with growing registration fees. Also important – though probably to a lesser extent – is the salary gap between US and British universities, and the difficulty of career deriving from the lower number of full professorships that English universities are able to finance (Kaldor and Joan Robinson were over sixty by the time they became professors). But also strategical and tactical errors matter, to some extent deriving from a certain animosity between the various streams of heterodox theory vis-à-vis the less divided internal front of major US universities, although in competition among themselves.[2]

---

[2] For instance, in the period I spent at Cambridge, the appointment to professor of an applied economist such as Robert Neild (b. 1924) on the post-Keynesian side (rather than, for instance, Pasinetti) while the neoclassical side appointed one of the top general equilibrium theoreticians, Frank Hahn (1925–2013), certainly contributed to modifying the balance between the two groups (notwithstanding Hahn's sympathy for post-Keynesian distribution theories and the respect he showed for Kaldor in the policy field). The construction of a rigid policy doctrine based on among other things protectionism (compatible with Keynesian theory, but certainly not logically implicit in it), warmly supported by members of the post-Keynesian side to the point of making it a distinctive character of the Cambridge school, contributed to a growing isolation.

It is a fact that the defeat of Cambridge (UK) in the clash with the US mainstream did not take place on the terrain of theory – in this, in the famous debate on capital theory in the 1960s even a Samuelson had to admit defeat – but on that of cultural influence: the Gramscian hegemony, for which the strength of the arguments matter, but also, and indeed very much, the ability to spread and support one's views. Thus, the increasing influence of what is called the mainstream allows economists to ignore the adversary's arguments,[3] resorting to 'that's what everybody does': the majority rule, certainly valid in politics (and, even in this case, provided minority rights are ensured), but in principle inapplicable to the field of theoretical debates.

It is not easy to find an order in illustrating the array of doctrines formulated by the Cambridge economists and the many debates within the group. We may begin with a survey of the major protagonists of the new Cambridge school, like Richard Kahn and Joan Robinson. We then consider two atypical personages: the Polish economist Kalecki, who developed the theory of effective demand at the same time as Keynes, and was thus considered – albeit with some wringing of hands – as close to the Cambridge school; and the Hungarian, naturalized British, Nicholas Kaldor, well integrated in Cambridge but with an autonomous personality. We then go on to consider some of the main subjects of debate: interpretation of Keynes's theory, the Cambridge (or post-Keynesian) theory of distribution, the debate with Cambridge (US) on the theory of capital, the various 'Sraffian schools' and the attempts at a synthesis between the Keynesian and Sraffian approaches.

12.2   The New Cambridge School

As one might expect, the impact of Keynes's *General theory* was particularly strong in Cambridge. It was not a total conquest: at least initially, together with Arthur Cecil Pigou, there was a defender of Marshallian orthodoxy of the level of Dennis Robertson, who moved to London in 1939 but returned in 1944 as successor to Pigou in the economics chair, held up to retirement in 1957. However, the role of Keynes's pupils and their allies gradually grew. The new Cambridge school (as distinct from the old Cambridge school, of Marshall and his pupils) flourished in the 1950s and 1960s, including protagonists like Kahn and Joan Robinson, or

---

[3] Typical is the annoyance commonly shown by mainstream macroeconomists faced with reminders of the shaky foundations of the aggregate notion of capital (a point also stressed by general equilibrium economists, also increasingly seen as espousing a fastidious form of excessive purity) or the impossibility of proving an automatic tendency to full employment.

Piero Sraffa, closer to Keynes than some interpreters think but following an autonomous path (illustrated in Chapter 5), and others like Nicholas Kaldor, who arrived there after the end of the war, Dobb and Goodwin. Richard Kahn was Keynes's closest collaborator, his pupil and then his literary executor. A student and then teacher in Cambridge, at the beginning of the 1930s Kahn animated the Circus that accompanied Keynes's transition from the *Treatise on money* to the *General theory*.[4] To the analytical apparatus of the latter Kahn contributed an important element, namely the theory of the multiplier, which connects changes in employment to changes in autonomous expenditure (investments, public expenditure, exports) and the savings propensity: a connection that presupposes the existence of unemployed workers (Kahn 1931). For economists living at the time of the Great Crisis, this was a fact; but it was also an element, as already recalled more than once, that contradicted a central tenet of the dominant theory, namely the automatic tendency to full employment equilibrium in a competitive economy.

Kahn began a path of gradual distancing from this theory through his research on 'the economics of the short period' (the title of his 1930 fellowship dissertation, to remain unpublished for more than fifty years: Kahn 1983), developing the theme of market imperfections already present in Marshall's work but relegated to a secondary level in Pigou's Marshallian vulgate. Author of a few but well meditated pages,[5] Kahn also gave an important contribution to monetary theory, both with some studies of his own (like the article *Some notes on liquidity preference*, 1954) and with his collaboration on the influential *Radcliffe Report* (1959), which developed a Keynesian view of the working of financial markets and of the role of monetary policy tools. Kahn's influence also made itself felt in Joan Robinson's researches on imperfect competition.

Joan Violet Maurice Robinson (wife of Austin Robinson, 1897–1993, also a convinced Keynesian and an influential economics professor at Cambridge, but more interested in applied economics issues) was the flag-bearer of Keynesian theory: a lively and prolific writer, passionate and brilliant lecturer and vigorous polemist, she had a notable impact in universities all the world over. Among her contributions, together with writings divulging Keynes's views, we may recall *The economics of imperfect competition* (1933). With this text Joan Robinson originated what is called

---

[4] Organized on Keynes's initiative, the Circus was constituted by a group of young Cambridge economists, including Meade, Sraffa and Joan and Austin Robinson, who met to discuss Keynes's *Treatise on money* (1930); Kahn acted as 'messenger angel', referring to Keynes the content of the discussions. On the Circus cf. Keynes (1973), vol. 13, pp. 337 ff.

[5] The main contributions are collected in Kahn (1972).

the 'imperfect competition revolution', perhaps with some exaggeration as the work substantially remains within a Marshallian framework,[6] so much so in fact as to bring Robinson herself to take a distance from it in the Preface to a new 1969 edition. We may then recall her attempt to extend Keynes's analysis to the long period, in particular with *The accumulation of capital*, 1956. The book is best known for the taxonomy of growth models (the age of gold, iron, platinum and so on) while the analysis of the interrelation between changes in effective demand and in productive capacity, which is the focus of Robinson's work as it was in Harrod's (1939) model, remains more in the shade.

The Cambridge school also included, in subsequent stages, many Italian economists attracted there by the Keynesian tradition but also by Sraffa's fame: from Luigi Pasinetti to Pierangelo Garegnani, from Luigi Spaventa to Mario Nuti (b. 1937, an expert in socialist planning, subsequently professor in Siena and in Rome), protagonists of the debate on capital theory which saw the English Cambridge opposed to its US sister in the 1960s: a debate mainly stemming from Sraffa's contribution, as we saw in §5.8 and as we shall see in §12.6.

12.3   Michał Kalecki

When Keynes published the *General theory*, a young Polish economist, Michał Kalecki (1899–1970),[7] bought the book and realized that his celebrated English colleague had rediscovered a theory of employment and the trade cycle he had already published, in Polish, a few years earlier. This interpretation of the events, related by Joan Robinson,[8] certainly includes a grain of truth, but obscures substantial differences in approach between the two great theoreticians.

Kalecki, who matured within the Marxian tradition, was influenced by the growth schemes in the second book of Marx's *Capital*, taken up by Tugan-Baranowskji (1905), and by Rosa Luxemburg's (1913) underconsumption theories. It was thus easier for him than for Keynes to evade the grasp of the traditional marginalist approach that relies on the notion of equilibrium between supply and demand and the tenet of an automatic tendency to full employment under perfect competition. The scheme of the relations between income, consumption, savings and employment proposed by Kalecki offers a theory of income and

---

[6] Chamberlin's contemporaneous work on monopolistic competition (1933) has instead general equilibrium theory as cultural background, thus leaving aside the notion of industry.

[7] On his formation and the first stage of his activity cf. Toporowski (2013).

[8] Cf. for instance Robinson (1977).

employment quite similar to Keynes's, both in considering full employment as a limit rather than the general case, and in attributing the role of prime mover of the economy to autonomous expenditures and in particular to investment decisions.

There are, however, notable differences. The role of uncertainty and expectations, basic in Keynes, is practically absent in Kalecki, and a theory of the financial markets is also missing.[9] On the other hand Kalecki, though (especially in his first writings) open to Marshall's influence, embodies in his analyses mechanisms such as the full cost principle, which characterizes the behaviour of firms endowed with market power. This latter situation was implicitly taken by Kalecki as the general case, with perfect competition and monopoly as the extreme poles. According to the full cost principle, firms set prices in relation to variable costs, increasing them by a proportional margin (mark-up) that covers general and fixed costs corresponding to the normal degree of capacity utilization and allows for the rate of profit usual for the sector. In this way the mark-up is connected to the market power of firms and the sector (the degree of monopoly), and so to a theory of distribution, though, as we shall now see, in a way mediated by his theory of income.[10]

Kalecki thus extends his analysis to deal with problems of cycle and development, and connects these theories with analysis of income distribution between social classes.[11] In his theoretical system, capitalists' expenditure decisions (for investments and consumption) determine profits; in a few words, as a well-known approximate but expressive motto has it, 'capitalists get what they spend, workers spend what they get'. This means that an increase in the mark-up, stemming from an increase in the degree of monopoly, and so in the firms' market power,

---

[9] Kalecki proposes a 'principle of increasing risk' as an explanation of the limits to the possibility of financing investments on the side of each firm. This theme is taken up and developed by Kalecki's collaborator, the Austrian Josef Steindl (1912–93), in his theory of the firm: cf. Steindl (1945) and the writings collected in Steindl (1990, pp. 1–73). Steindl develops Kaleckian themes also in his best known work, *Maturity and stagnation in American capitalism* (1952; II edit. 1976), where he upholds the thesis of a tendency to stagnation in capitalist economies due to the gradual rise of oligopolistic market forms. A similar thesis (the transmission of the effects of technical progress generates development in a competitive economy, but not in an oligopolistic one) is proposed by Sylos Labini (1956). A similar tendency to stagnation is proposed also by the US economist Alvin Hansen (1887–1975) on more direct Keynesian grounds (Hansen 1938); Hansen played an important role in the diffusion of Keynesian ideas in the United States, both in teaching and within policy institutions. The principle of increasing risk was also taken up by Minsky, as already mentioned in §11.6.

[10] Cf. e.g. Kalecki (1943). Studied by Philip Andrews (1914–71; see the writings collected in Andrews [1993]), the full cost principle was then integrated within the theory of oligopoly by Sylos Labini (1956).

[11] Of particular interest is his theory of the political trade cycle (Kalecki 1971, pp. 138–45).

cannot modify the overall level of profits but implies a decrease in real wages, and hence in the demand for wage goods, in production and employment. In other words, redistributing income from workers to capitalists implies a fall in national income: a thesis unlike the post-Keynesian theory of distribution.

Many of Kalecki's major contributions concern planned and mixed economies.[12] A moving spirit in Warsaw of the liveliest research and teaching centre in Eastern European countries, in the final years of his life Kalecki was marginalized by the authorities of his country. Comparison with Keynes shows how much country, birth conditions and the political environment count in determining the impact of an economist's ideas and analyses.

12.4   Nicholas Kaldor

A convert to Keynesianism, Nicholas Kaldor was born in Budapest in the Austro-Hungarian empire to then become a British citizen and Lord for merits acquired as economic adviser to Labour governments. Before Keynes published the *General theory*, the young Kaldor already had in his curriculum some important articles in theory of capital and the firm (with an original synthesis of Hayek's and Marshall's ideas). UN Commission expert on Europe immediately after the end of the Second World War, consultant to many developing countries and, repeatedly, to the British government, Kaldor contributed to the theoretical corpus of the Cambridge school a theory of income distribution in which distribution between wages and profits depends on the saving propensity of capitalists and the rate of growth of the economy.[13]

Added to this theory of distribution in successive versions of a growth model (Kaldor 1957, 1961) were theories of accumulation of Keynesian and classical (Ricardian) inspiration where the implications of the main

---

[12] A selection of Kalecki's main writings, edited by the author himself but published posthumously, is subdivided into two slim volumes, one on capitalist economies (Kalecki 1971, including the three articles in Polish of 1933, 1934 and 1935 that anticipate important aspects of Keynesian theory), and one on socialist and mixed economies (Kalecki 1972). These volumes drew attention to Kalecki's contribution in Western economic culture. There is an extensive literature on Kalecki and his relations with Keynes; cf. for instance Chilosi (1979), the works cited there and subsequently the essays collected in Sebastiani (1989, 1994).

[13] Originally presented in a 1956 article, this theory was taken up and developed by Pasinetti (1962); in the course of subsequent debates with Samuelson and Modigliani, Kaldor (1966) connected it with the financial strategies of the firm, and hence to the new stream of managerial capitalism. For a survey of the debate and other aspects of Kaldor's thought and a bibliography of his writings, cf. Thirlwall (1987) and Targetti (1988).

'stylized facts' of developed capitalist economies are analysed.[14] Among these stylized facts, which have held sufficiently well for more than fifty years (at least up to the micro-informatics revolution), there is the constancy of the capital-income ratio, as a consequence of which the rate of growth of per capita income depends more or less exclusively on the rate of growth of productivity per worker. In Kaldorian growth models, increasing returns dominate, both in the static and in the dynamic form (learning by doing, especially what is known as Verdoorn's law – Verdoorn [1949] – connecting the rate of growth of productivity to the rate of growth of the product). Increasing returns are embodied in a 'technical progress function' connecting the rate of growth of labour productivity to the rate of growth of capital per worker, thus making technical progress endogenous, as largely embodied in new capital goods. An important implication of this is that the growth of per capita income (Smith's wealth of nations) depends on the path of the product: situations of underemployment, in particular crises, imply a loss, not only transitory but also lasting, of productivity and income (of well-being).

Kaldor stresses that Verdoorn's law holds for the manufacturing sector, but not for agriculture and the services; hence his thesis, at least partially accepted in the United Kingdom, that taxes are better concentrated in services, especially those not subject to international trade. Manufactures are for Kaldor the driving sector of the economy. However, this does not justify construction of monosector models: given the different characteristics and different role in the growth process of the main sectors (manufactures, services, agriculture) it is necessary to build multisector models.[15]

Kaldor also contributed to the development of Keynesian monetary theory (beginning with the 1959 *Radcliffe Report*, up to a long series of

[14] The method of 'stylized facts' as basic assumptions for theory construction recalls the Weberian method of 'ideal types' (cf. §3.4). In economics this method does not seem to find widespread acceptance, notwithstanding its use in the field of social sciences in general; in any case, it appears preferable to Friedman's method (cf. §8.5), according to which the realism of the assumptions is wholly irrelevant.

The methodology developed by another Cambridge don, Tony Lawson, in various writings (cf. in particular Lawson [1994, 1997]), taking up some ideas of the philosopher Bhaskar (1978), appears compatible with Kaldor's. In a nutshell, Lawson's 'critical realism' holds that (1) the world is 'structured', namely not reducible to events of sensorial experience; (2) these structures (or stratifications) are 'intransitive', namely exist independently of their identification; (3) the 'deep' social stratifications are irreducible to those underlying them and are not directly observable, but it is possible to infer them through 'retroduction' procedures. In conformity with these ideas, Lawson (1997, p. 208) criticizes Kaldor's terminology stressing that the 'stylized facts' must themselves be explained.

[15] The same logic, independently developed, underlies the construction of Sylos Labini's 1967 econometric model.

contributions criticizing Friedman's monetarism and its Thatcherite vulgate). In contrast with Friedman's position, according to Kaldor it is not the money supply that influences the general price level, but the latter that influences the transaction demand for money and hence also the money supply, which depends on the choices of banks and financial institutions and is therefore responsive to changes in demand, so that it may be considered largely if not fully endogenous (Kaldor 1982).[16]

Finally, his policy suggestions had great influence: from an unbalanced taxation system focused on services, as seen earlier, to institution of stabilization funds at the international level to stabilize raw material prices. This latter proposal, also shared by other exponents of the Cambridge school including Richard Kahn, stems from rejection of the quantity theory of money as an explanation of inflation, the causes of which are rather to be found in the dynamics of labour costs and of raw material prices, influenced not only by supply and demand but also by speculation.[17]

12.5   The Debate on Interpretation of Keynes

Confronted with the reinterpretation of Keynes's theory proposed by the neoclassical synthesis and with the monetarist critiques, there has been a decided reaction on the part of post-Keynesian economists, from exponents of the new Cambridge school like Richard Kahn, Nicholas Kaldor and Joan Robinson to some US economists like Sidney Weintraub (1914–83), Hyman Minsky (1920–96) and Jan Kregel (b. 1944).

These economists stress that the IS-LL schema proposed by Hicks ('hydraulic Keynesianism') and expanded by Modigliani to include the labour market relegates to a secondary level the most characteristic element of the Keynesian approach, namely the uncertainty of the future that dominates the decisions of economic agents.[18] In the case of the investment function, far more important than the rate of interest are entrepreneurs' expectations of returns on the various investment projects.

---

[16] Taken to the extreme, this thesis leads to a horizontal money supply curve, opposed to the vertical curve attributed to monetarism; hence an interpretation of the opposition between monetarists and Keynesians as between 'verticalists' and 'horizontalists' (cf. Moore 1988).

[17] In this respect various Keynesian economists developed proposals with the aim of moderating the dynamics of money wages; the best known is probably TIP (tax-based incomes policy) by Wallich and Weintraub (1971), proposing a tax on firms which grant salary increases above a predetermined norm.

[18] Cf. in particular Kahn (1984), focused on the preparatory stage of the *General theory* and on the critique of Hicks's IS-LL model, and especially Minsky (1975) and Kregel (1976, 1980b).

These expectations, according to Keynes, may remain pessimistic for a long time, generating stagnation; may self-fuel in both positive and negative directions; and are volatile, likely to change frequently, for instance according to the political climate or general economic conditions. In the case of the demand for money, Keynes considers expectations (to be precise, of the future path of interest rates, essential in determining the speculative demand for money) also to be extremely volatile, even more than expectations of returns on investment projects. Moreover, the speculative demand for money connected to the Keynesian notion of liquidity (cf. §3.7) is considered the main component of the demand for money – on account of both its size and its instability – as connected to the choice, constantly subject to revision by economic agents, on the form in which to keep the accumulated stock of wealth, while the transaction demand for money is related to the flow of income.

Given the importance of uncertainty, of the volatility of expectations and the consequent variability of the relations that (in different ways in the two cases) connect investments and speculative demand for money to the interest rate, post-Keynesian economists consider it misleading to represent markets as in simultaneous equilibrium, for commodities as for money, based on well-defined and sufficiently stable demand and supply functions, namely the view on which the scheme IS-LL relies.

In the place of the simultaneous equilibrium of the different markets, typical of the marginalist tradition and taken up in the IS-LL scheme, post-Keynesian economists propose a view of the economy as based on a sequence of cause-and-effect links: the speculative demand for money, or better liquidity preference, affects the rate of interest; in turn this, together with expectations, affects the investment level; investments then, through the multiplier, determine income and employment levels.[19] In this way unemployment, even persistent, turns out to be a normal situation for what Keynes calls the monetary production economy.

The thesis of consumer sovereignty that characterizes the marginalist tradition is also overturned: the decisions that matter are those of the financial operators and entrepreneurs; in particular, investments (together with exports and public expenditure in the expanded model) determine savings, income, employment (and imports and taxes). The influence of events in the monetary and financial markets on income and employment is also stressed, in opposition to the classical and marginalist traditional tenet of the neutrality of money. Furthermore, a number of post-Keynesian economists (like Kaldor, as recalled earlier) also maintain

---

[19] Cf. for instance Pasinetti (1974), chapter 2.

that the money supply is endogenous: namely, that the quantity of money in circulation (in particular bank money) is not controlled rigidly by the monetary authorities, but depends at least in part on other agents' decisions. As a consequence, monetary policy should assume as an immediate target control of the interest rate and not of the money supply, as held in various versions of the quantity theory of money.[20]

Abandonment of the tenet of consumer sovereignty, the importance of expectations and the central role of monetary and financial variables, all appear to concur towards building macroeconomic foundations for microeconomics, or at least rejecting general models intended to provide macroeconomics with microeconomic foundations (models that, as we saw, often imply unacceptable simplifications or errors in the theory of value).

Criticisms were then raised, in particular by Joan Robinson (for instance in Robinson 1974), of the static notion of equilibrium and the extraneousness to neoclassical theory of historical time (irreversible by its very nature: see the catchword of non-ergodicity, used especially by Paul Davidson, who makes of it the foundation for his interpretation of Keynes).[21] She also maintains that this criticism applies not only to the models of the neoclassical synthesis but also to Sraffa's analysis of prices.

Debate on this point raises complex issues over the kinds of abstraction necessary for developing economic theory and their limits; from this viewpoint Robinson's critiques appear less disruptive than the purely logical ones developed in the course of the debates in the field of capital

---

[20] Within post-Keynesian theories and in the context of open economies, control of the interest rate is often viewed as a tool for influencing the exchange rate (even more than investments, which, when expectations are negative, may not respond, or respond too little, to reductions in the cost of loans), and through it exports and effective demand. Thus, while Keynes was favourable to fixed exchange rates (useful for reducing uncertainty, as well as preventing competitive devaluations such as those that occurred after the 1929 Great Crisis), various post-Keynesian economists were hostile to the construction of currency areas characterized by a single currency (like the euro) or irrevocably fixed exchange rates in the presence of freedom of movements of capital also in the short and very short run, as this makes it impossible to conduct an autonomous monetary policy aimed at supporting employment. On the other hand, fixed exchange rate systems integrated with efficacious controls on short- and very short-term capital movements appear acceptable.

[21] Cf. for instance Davidson (2007); see, then, the recent controversy within the post-Keynesian school between Davidson and others, in particular O'Donnell (2014–15). O'Donnell (ibid, p. 188) distinguishes between 'ontological uncertainty' and 'epistemological uncertainty': the former, attributed to Davidson, 'relates to uncertainty deriving (ultimately) from the ontological characteristics of the investigated world', while the latter 'relates to uncertainty deriving (ultimately) from the limited abilities of agents to know about the investigated world'. The distinction is useful, but both kinds of uncertainty are co-present in Keynes.

theory.[22] Debate on the relative importance of the two kinds of critiques even led to spirited clashes between the two branches of heterodox Cambridge, the 'Marshallian' branch of Keynes's direct pupils (in particular Joan Robinson) and the 'Sraffian' branch (in particular Garegnani). This mutual opposition led in some cases to extending criticism to the adversary's constructive contributions: as if Sraffian analysis proposed a self-contained theoretical construct, incompatible with recognition of historical evolution and uncertainty; or as if Keynesian analysis were inextricably linked to the Marshallian short period.[23]

An important element in defending Keynes's thought against the misunderstandings it came up against is the critical edition of his writings, the *Collected writings of John Maynard Keynes*, originally planned in twenty-four volumes and then published in thirty volumes in a relatively short time span, between 1971 and 1989, under the auspices of the Royal Economic Society. This was a major enterprise; the time it took for Sraffa to complete his edition of Ricardo's writings (from 1930 to 1973) must have been present to the Society's directorate, suggesting they should retain direct control over the work, with a committee in which together with Keynes's literary executor Richard Kahn we find Roy Harrod, author of a biography of Keynes (Harrod [1951], much criticized by successive biographers) and Austin Robinson, successor to Keynes as general secretary of the Society. The books published by Keynes in his lifetime were reprinted with very short introductions. The volumes including correspondence and unpublished documents were entrusted

---

[22] Any theory concerns logical, not historical time; the real problem lies in evaluating whether the various assumptions adopted in building the theory render it useless for interpreting reality (as happens in the case of results only holding in one-commodity worlds). The very distinction between the short and the long period, which Keynes and his pupils Kahn and Joan Robinson inherited from Marshall, is in fact a logical distinction, between partial adjustment (within which the endowment of fixed capital, hence productive capacity, is given and unchangeable) and total adjustment (within which fixed capital endowments and productive capacity may vary): in 'historical' time, fixed capital and productive capacity vary continuously, even if as a consequence of decisions taken in earlier periods.

[23] The harsh controversy on this issue between Robinson and Garegnani is an example of those tensions within the post-Keynesian field that weighed down on its cultural impact. Among other things, both sides proposed substantially the same interpretation of Sraffa's analysis, considered as referring to 'long period positions': an interpretation external to the classical approach, which, rather, takes on the Marshallian temporal scansion and is opposed to that proposed in §5.7. Something analogous holds for the interpretation of Keynes: the assumption of a given productive capacity in the *General theory* concerns the way one reads the expectations on which entrepreneurs rely for their decisions on production and employment levels but also for the distinct decisions concerning investments; this is thus a different context from the Marshallian short period, which concerns one of the models for determining equilibrium prices and quantities for the firm and the industry (cf. Kregel 1976, 1980b; Tonveronachi 1983).

to Elizabeth Johnson and Donald Moggridge. Except for some volumes, in particular 13, 14 and 29 (*The general theory and after*) and the volumes on *Activities* that illustrate Keynes's work at the Treasury during the two wars, the volumes were published with little analytical apparatus; we may say that the edition is helpful for researchers engaged in the difficult task of interpreting Keynes, but does not provide an interpretation of its own able to assert itself on the basis of its philological rigour, as happened with Sraffa's Ricardo edition. Skidelsky's monumental biography (1983, 1992, 2000), and the abridged single-volume version (2010) are from this viewpoint much more useful, but cannot substitute a better-structured edition of Keynes's writings. It is certainly not a missed opportunity, but an opportunity only partially exploited.

In any case, as far as interpretation of Keynes's theory is concerned, the debate brought to light some limits of the theses of certain post-Keynesians. In particular, authors like Joan Robinson (1974) or Shackle (1955) presented a diametrical opposition between the notion of uncertainty and that of certainty or probabilistic risk, without connecting them to Keynes's subtler analysis in the *Treatise on probability* (1921) and overlooking the distance separating Keynes's notion of uncertainty from that of Knight (1921). In fact, we have an opposition between two views of the world, a Keynesian and a marginalist one, without the Keynesian side succeeding in fully illustrating its own viewpoint with a philological rigour comparable to that of Sraffa's re-proposal of the classical viewpoint in his Ricardo edition.

The debate on interpretation of Keynes grew quite vigorous in Italy; here we have, on partly different lines, some of the most philologically accurate contributions. Vicarelli (1977), focusing attention on the first stage in Keynes's research, brings to light in particular the Keynesian thesis of instability in the capitalist economies; Tonveronachi (1983), focusing attention on the *General theory* (Keynes 1936) and on its gradual elaboration starting from the *Treatise on money* (Keynes 1930), stresses 'underemployment equilibriums' (cf. §3.7).

In various fields the Keynesian approach led to original contributions. We may recall, in particular, Thirlwall's model (1979) connecting differences in growth rates in the various countries to different propensities to import and export, thereby stressing the role of effective demand, and Biasco's (1987, 1988) contributions, which attribute a dominant role to the speculative motive in determining exchange rates; these, in turn, influence (and interact with) the productive structure of the various countries, thus stressing a causal link running from financial events to events in the real economy.

Another research line drawing on Keynes is that of the consistent stock-flow models developed by Godley and Lavoie (2007), recalled in §9.3. The structure of stock and flow relations, monetary and real, is expressed by a set of equations, varying in extensiveness according to the disaggregation level adopted, that represent accounting identities; the model is then closed with Keynesian hypotheses on the behaviour of agents that do not imply full employment (which constitutes a possible neoclassical closure). These models are utilized for interpreting the economy and for designing macroeconomic policies.[24] At least partly different, and more difficult to classify, is the 'theory of the monetary circuit', which interprets money as credit (bank money) and stresses its endogenous nature.[25]

12.6 The Debate on the Theory of Capital and Critique of the Marginalist Theory of Value

The opening salvo in the modern debate on capital theory, also known as the Cambridge (UK) versus Cambridge (US, MIT) debate, was fired with an article by Joan Robinson (1953) criticizing the neoclassical aggregate production function. This article appears to have foreshadowed some of the arguments subsequently developed in Sraffa's 1960 book; however, the 1953 critiques focused on the aggregate notion of capital utilized in the aggregate production function and did not dwell on the 'reswitching of techniques' which, as we shall now see, played a central role in Sraffa's argument and the ensuing debate.[26] The 1953 article is thus a tactical error: in the ensuing debate in the 1960s and 1970s many marginalist authors focused on Robinson's critiques,[27] as if the object of the

---

[24] On the basis of this analysis, Godley is among those who foresaw the 2007–8 crisis: cf. Godley and Izurieta (2004). Moreover, the requirement of consistency between flows and stocks brings out certain contradictions in some neo-liberal policy tenets, such as the imposition of reduction of public and private debt on various countries while wide active trade balances are tolerated in the case of strong countries.

[25] For an organic exposition, rich in references to previous contributions, cf. Graziani (2003).

[26] Robinson (1970, p. 145) recalled as a source of inspiration Sraffa's introduction to the Ricardo edition, but it is likely that the theme had been suggested to her in direct oral communication. For a different opinion, cf. Marcuzzo (2005).

[27] Cf. for instance Samuelson (1947), new 1983 ed., p. 568 (already recalled in §6.3). Solow (1963, quoted by Joan Robinson 1970, p. 144) stated that 'everybody except Joan Robinson agrees about capital theory', thus leaving aside the more general criticisms deriving from Sraffa (1960) and leaving room for Pasinetti's (1969) criticisms. Ferguson (1969), aware of Sraffa's criticisms, states 'that belief in neoclassical theory is a matter of faith' (quoted by Robinson 1970, p. 145). In recent times the Cambridge–Cambridge debate has continued to be interpreted as concerning the conditions of aggregation and the Cobb–Douglas function and centred on Joan Robinson's clash with Samuelson and Solow (Hodgson 1999, p. 46; Backhouse 2014b).

'Sraffian' critique were solely the aggregate notion of capital, and not the notion of capital and labour as factors of production whose prices – respectively, wage and rate of profits – would be determined by well-behaved demand-and-supply functions, such as to generate a decrease in the capital/labour ratio when the wage decreased, as is necessary to ensure stability in full employment equilibrium.

The true premise to the debate came with publication, in 1960, of *Production of commodities by means of commodities*. Here Sraffa immediately stresses its role as a prelude to a critique of the marginalist theory of value and distribution; apart from contributing to reconstruction of the classical approach (as shown in Chapter 5), it also provides the analytical elements necessary for a critique from within the marginalist approach.

Sraffa's criticisms concern two aspects: first, the Austrian theory's attempt to obtain an aggregate measure of capital with the average period of production; second, the monotonic inverse relation between real wage and capital intensity of production processes. This relation plays a central role in the traditional marginalist theory of value and distribution and in the macroeconomics of the neoclassical synthesis, being utilized to obtain an inverse relation between real wage and employment. Thanks to it, it is possible to hold that in a competitive labour market the equilibrium wage is equal to the marginal productivity of labour in full employment; moreover, in the presence of unemployment (which corresponds to a disequilibrium situation), wage flexibility is sufficient to ensure a tendency towards the full employment equilibrium.

As for the first aspect, Sraffa (1960, chapter 6) remarks that the weighted arithmetic average of the periods of production of the various sectors, originally utilized by Bohm–Bawerk, does not take into account compound interest rates, the presence of which may lead to results that violate the monotonic relation between wage and the capital intensity of production processes, necessary to obtain a tendency to full employment. This difficulty had already been noticed by Wicksell (1901–6), but modern representatives of the Austrian school again came to rely on the average period of production (Hayek 1931: cf. §4.3). Harrod, too, in a review of *Production of commodities by means of commodities* (Harrod 1961), insisted on defending the Austrian theory of value, but a short reply by Sraffa (1962) sufficed to clarify the issue once and for all. Harrod remarked that it is in any case possible to define univocally an average period of production for a given rate of interest, even in the presence of compound interest rates; Sraffa replied that this was not the point, but rather the fact that the period of production does not turn out to be independent of the rate of profit itself, as would, however, be necessary in order to use it as a measure of capital in explaining the rate of profit.

As for the second aspect, Sraffa's (1960, chapter 13) criticism, based on the reswitching of techniques, is essentially general: it is possible for the economy to shift from technique A to technique B when the rate of profit increases, and subsequently return to technique A. However the capital is measured, this means that if in one of the two cases the economy moves in the direction foreseen by marginalist theory, in the other case it moves in the opposite direction.

These criticisms gave rise to extensive debate. Simultaneously with publication of Sraffa's book, Garegnani (1960) directly criticized some of the main theoretical contributions of the marginalist tradition, showing among other things that the problems in capital theory are also present in Walras's original general equilibrium theory. Publication of Sraffa's book was followed by lively debate. An opening skirmish (Harrod 1961; Sraffa 1962) has already been illustrated. A second clash arose over Samuelson's 1962 attempt to present the aggregate production function as a 'parable' that does not betray the essential characteristics of a productive system, and indeed Levhari's 1965 thesis that the problems raised by Sraffa concern only the individual industry but not the economy as a whole. These theses were immediately rejected: Samuelson's by Spaventa (1968) and Garegnani (1970); Levhari's by Pasinetti (1966), followed by others; Samuelson (1966) and Levhari with Samuelson (1966) recognized their theses to be erroneous. Nevertheless, in subsequent years some further skirmishes occurred, without, however, adding anything substantial to the previous debate: for instance, between Gallaway and Shukla (1974) and Garegnani (1976), and between Burmeister (1977, 1979) and Pasinetti (1979a, 1979b). It is also worth recalling that Pasinetti (1969) criticized the resort on the part of Solow (1963, 1967) to the Fisherian notion of the rate of return, considered by Solow himself (1963, p. 16) as 'the central concept in capital theory', since it is assumed as an index of the quantity of capital definable independently of the profit rate and thus utilizable to explain the latter. For the discussion following on Pasinetti's criticisms, cf. in particular Solow (1970), Pasinetti (1970), Dougherty (1972) and Pasinetti (1972).[28]

The crucial issue of the import of the criticism based on the reswitching of techniques remained more in the shade. Contrary to what many appear to believe, it does not only apply to the aggregate production function, notwithstanding its defects still used in various versions of mainstream macroeconomics, as in real cycle theory (cf. §8.6). Sraffa's criticism also applies to all cases in which, though recognizing that capital is in fact

---

[28] For surveys of these debates, cf. Harcourt (1972) and Kurz and Salvadori (1995); a collection of the main articles is edited by Harcourt and Laing (1971).

a heterogeneous set of means of production, the rate of profit (or of interest: the terminology may vary, but the substance remains the same) is considered a supply-and-demand determined price of a factor of production 'capital' however defined (aggregate of value, waiting, abstinence, average period of production and rate of return). This result undermines not only the traditional marginalist theory of value and distribution but also practically the whole of contemporary mainstream macroeconomics, based as it is on the assumption of an inverse relation between real wage and employment, necessary for ensuring a stable full employment equilibrium.[29]

In subsequent decades, debate no longer dwelt on the aggregate production function, the defects of which were widely recognized,[30] but in particular on the thesis that the Sraffian criticisms of the notion of capital and the marginalist theory of value and distribution do not hold for the axiomatic (Arrow–Debreu) model of general economic equilibrium. In this respect, we should distinguish two aspects: the validity of the traditional marginalist theory of value and distribution, and the validity of the

---

[29] In reply to these critiques, various authors have tried to demonstrate that the 'reswitching of techniques' is a rare event. These attempts are often conducted through numerical simulations, obviously based on a very limited number of basic commodities. However, the number of points of encounter of the wage–profit curves relative to two techniques depends on the degree of the two equations; in general, as Krishna Bharadwaj (1970) shows, the maximum number of switch points between techniques depends on the number of basic commodities in the economy. Since the two curves may meet not only in the positive quadrant but also in the quadrants corresponding to negative values of the wage or the profit rate, when the number of basic commodities is limited it is quite unlikely for there to be intersections in the positive quadrant; however, the probability increases when the number of commodities increases.

[30] As mentioned earlier, the aggregate production function is utilized in Solow's (1956, 1957) growth model; since then, notwithstanding the disruptive criticism to which this analytical tool is subjected, nothing seems to have changed in the framing and in the foundations of mainstream growth theory, that on the contrary undergoes wide-ranging developments (as recalled in §7.3). Among the critiques, we should recall Shaikh's (1974) and Simon's (1979b) on the tautological nature of the empirical results obtained through estimates of the Cobb–Douglas function; Sylos Labini (1995) also stresses the unrealism of the constant returns assumption, necessary for ensuring (through Euler's theorem) that the sum of profits and wages be equal to income: empirical analyses show the systematic prevalence of increasing returns to scale. After extensive survey of the different aspects of this issue, Felipe and McCombie (2013, p. 411) ask: 'why have criticisms of the aggregate production function generally been ignored?' and go on to quote Samuelson's (1966, p. 583) conclusions: 'if all this [the shaky analytical foundations of the aggregate notion of capital] causes headaches for those nostalgic for the old time parables of neoclassical writings, we must remind ourselves that scholars are not born to live an easy existence. We must respect and appraise the facts of life.' In other words, persisting in the use of an aggregate production function is a demonstration of scant scientific seriousness: confronted with a basic unsolved difficulty, mainstream economists choose quite simply to ignore it.

general equilibrium model as a representation of the working of the economy.

As for the first aspect, the results arrived at in Sraffa's book are also replicable in a general equilibrium model: it is impossible to hold as a general law the existence of an inverse relation between real wage and employment, necessary to show a tendency to full employment equilibrium (that is, the existence of the invisible hand of the market). Indeed, as noted in §6.3, research within general equilibrium theory on the existence and stability of equilibrium leads to overall negative results: equilibriums are in general multiple and demonstration of stability requires quite restrictive ad hoc assumptions.

As for the second aspect, on the plane of internal logical consistency the axiomatic model of general equilibrium, as developed over time by authors such as Arrow and Debreu, is unassailable. The issue is whether it helps us more or less than other approaches, and in particular the classical and Keynesian approaches, to understand the world we live in.

From this point of view, the theory of general economic equilibrium presents clear limits. Within it, as we have seen, the existence of solutions can be demonstrated, but not their uniqueness or stability. Furthermore, the assumptions on which it relies are significantly constraining: in particular, there is the assumption of convexity of production sets, which excludes increasing returns, so important in reality; but also the idea that price formation is based on the equality of quantities demanded and supplied, acceptable only for non-reproducible goods and in the world of financial markets, and even in this case only in part. Besides, the criticism of the aggregate notion of capital, or Sraffa's criticism of the Marshallian theory of partial equilibriums, applies to all attempts to utilize simplified versions of the general equilibrium model, which, apart from the nominal claim, are in fact partial equilibrium models with a single basic commodity and/or 'representative' agent. Such, for instance, is the case of the so-called overlapping generations general equilibrium models in macroeconomics, which consider a single commodity, or the 'new-Keynesian' models, which are in fact framed as partial equilibrium models.[31] On the whole, general equilibrium theory,

---

[31] Here and elsewhere, by one-commodity models we mean models with a single basic commodity, namely a commodity that directly or indirectly enters as means of production in all production processes. Models with a multiplicity of non-basic commodities (namely commodities not used as means of production, or used only in their own production process or in that of other non-basic commodities) but a single basic commodity (or none at all) are 'well-behaved', displaying stability and uniqueness of equilibrium.

both in its pure axiomatic version or in versions derived from it, does not provide an adequate representation of a capitalist economy.

Mainstream theory takes advantage of this confusion (between models endowed with internal consistency but with scant heuristic value and simplified models with desperately fragile analytical foundations) to keep on utilizing one-commodity models and the inverse relation between real wage and employment used in support of the thesis of the invisible hand, i.e. the automatic tendency in a competitive economy towards full employment. Criticisms of this tenet receive no answer: they are simply ignored.[32] Thus the Cambridge school may boast victory in the theoretical clash, but at the same time lament losing hegemony over research and policy orientations. How this could have come about is a question that concerns not so much the history of economic analysis as, rather, the sociology of academic life and reconstruction of power relations within academies.

12.7   The Cambridge Theory of Distribution

The Cambridge theory of distribution considers two social classes, capitalists and workers, and two income categories, profits and wages; as we shall see, we need to be careful in distinguishing the two dichotomies. Also, this theory assumes as points of departure equality between income (the sum of savings and consumption) and aggregate demand (which, under the simplifying assumption of an economy with no state and no foreign trade, is equal to the sum of consumption and investments). Finally, two different saving propensities are assumed for the two social classes (obviously, higher for the capitalists, lower for the workers).

The first model was Kaldor's (1956). The equilibrium condition between aggregate demand and supply implies equality of savings and investments; it is obtained considering savings variable, while investments are assumed to be equal to the level corresponding through the multiplier to full employment. Given the different savings propensities of workers and capitalists, it is variations in income distribution between the two classes that bring savings equal to investments. If we then assume the savings propensity of workers to be nil, the solution is simplified and the rate of growth of the economy (equal, under the assumption of

---

[32] Nor can the criticisms of the notion of the representative agent be ignored: it, too, is an aggregate notion that presents problems analogous to those of the aggregate notion of capital: cf. Kirman (1992) and Forni and Lippi (1997). As Kirman (2006, p. 257) notes, mainstream macroeconomics requires uniqueness and stability of equilibrium, and in order to obtain this result the assumption of representative agent is essential; it is a pity that it is an indefensible assumption!

constant technical coefficients, to the ratio between investments and capital) turns out to be equal to the rate of profits multiplied by the capitalists' savings propensity.[33] In this way, income distribution depends on investment decisions: while the workers' expenditure depends on consumption, in the case of the capitalists it is their income that depends on expenditure (a point Kalecki also insists on).

The second model was devised by Pasinetti (1962). He stresses that if the workers save, they, too, end up by possessing some capital. We therefore need to distinguish between the savings propensity of workers and that on wages, and between the savings propensity of capitalists and that on profits. Pasinetti shows that, in any case, under sufficiently general simplifying assumptions the results remain substantially unchanged.

A controversy with Samuelson and Modigliani (1966) then followed. They sought to construct a dual situation in which the rate of growth depends on the savings propensity of workers. The ensuing debate, with numerous contributions, shows that the dual theorem only holds under clearly unrealistic assumptions.

In the course of this debate, Kaldor (1966) introduced a further element, drawing on the theory of managerial capitalism expounded by Berle and Means (1932) as taken up and developed by Robin Marris (1964), namely the distinction between profits distributed as dividends and profits set aside by firms. These latter constitute a favoured fund for investment financing, to the extent, indeed, that subsequently a number of post-Keynesian economists (Wood 1975; Eichner 1976) connected the pricing policy of large firms to their investment decisions. In this case, too, the distinctive nature of the post-Keynesian theory of distribution is that of considering investments as given, so that they appear as the *primum mobile* with regard not only to production levels but also to income distribution.

However, the problem that Kaldor's theory leaves open is precisely which of the two variables, production levels or income distribution, is determined by the level of investments. As noted earlier, Kaldor takes production levels as given and focuses on determining income distribution; he thus earned the nickname Jean-Baptiste Kaldor, with an implicit allusion to Say's law (that is, the assumption of persisting full employment) that should be anathema to a Keynesian. Once again it is Pasinetti (1981) who provides a solution to the dilemma, interpreting the model in which investments determine income distribution as a normative, not

---

[33] Let us denote with $g = \Delta Y/Y$ the rate of growth of income Y, with I/K the investment/ capital ratio, with r the rate of profits and with s_c the savings propensity of capitalists; we then have $g = I/K = r\, s_c$.

a descriptive, model, developing it – as we shall see – in a dynamic context with a multiplicity of commodities.

12.8   The Sraffian Schools

For reasons of space, it is not possible to illustrate here the work done by many economists in the wake of Sraffa's contribution.[34] We can only recall that initially this work proceeded along three distinct lines, corresponding to the three main research streams in Sraffa's work. We have first a number of researches into the history of economic thought, contributing to a reconstruction of the precise nature of the classical approach and its differences to the marginalist approach.[35] Second, we have the debates concerning the marginalist theory of value and capital, illustrated in §12.6, including the critiques of the marginalist approach in the different fields of economic research, such as the pure theory of international trade.[36] Finally, we have analytical development and transposition into rigorous mathematical terms of Sraffa's analysis of prices of production,[37] and the treatment of specific issues, such as the theory of non-reproducible commodities.[38]

Sraffa's work also, directly or indirectly, prompted various contributions to the reconstruction of political economy. We may distinguish three main orientations that, for ease of exposition, we will associate with the names of the three leading representatives of the classical approach: Smith, Ricardo, Marx.

12.8.1   Pasinetti's 'Ricardian' Reconstruction

We can see the first wide-ranging development of Sraffa's analysis in the contributions made in particular by Luigi Pasinetti (b. 1930) in a number of writings, culminating in his 1981 volume on *Structural change and economic growth*.

Pasinetti's main reference is to Ricardian analysis. On methodological grounds, Pasinetti followed the principles of logical deduction, leaving a purely illustrative role to historical references, like Ricardo, and in direct

---

[34] For a survey, cf. Roncaglia (1990), from which material for this section has been drawn.
[35] Cf. e.g. Dobb (1973), Roncaglia (1977, 2005a), Bharadwaj (1978) and Quadrio Curzio and Scazzieri (1984).
[36] Parrinello (1970); Steedman (1979).
[37] Lippi (1979); Schefold (1989); Kurz and Salvadori (1995).
[38] Cf. e.g. Quadrio Curzio (1967) and Quadrio Curzio and Pellizzari (1996). The issue is important for clarifying the different role of scarcity within Sraffa's approach and within the marginalist one.

opposition to Smith's predilection for historical generalizations as opposed to analysis through models. Moreover, Ricardo's 'model' was the subject of a 1960 article that may be considered the ideal starting point for the development of his growth model (Pasinetti 1965). This latter also incorporated Pasinetti's 1962 formulation of the post-Keynesian theory of distribution illustrated earlier. Subsequently, the development of the theory of vertically integrated sectors (Pasinetti 1973) constituted a decisive analytical step to move on from Sraffa's analysis of the relationship between relative prices and income distribution to analysis of economic growth. The text of *Lectures on the theories of production* (Pasinetti 1975) can, then, also be seen as a reinterpretation of the history of economic thought, especially the recent history (Sraffa, Leontief, von Neumann). This set of writings contributed to providing the basis for a specific view of the nature and role of economic science: a view which cannot be considered as opposed to that implicit in Sraffa's writings, but which neither can be identified with, nor logically deduced from, the latter.

Pasinetti's (1981, p. 19) purpose is 'to build a unifying theory behind all the new contributions to economics': Keynes and Kalecki, theories of the firm, Leontief and Sraffa, theories of the cycle, the Harrod–Domar model and the post-Keynesian theories of income distribution. Such a unifying theory has its main pillar 'not in the caprice and scarcity of Nature, but in the progress and ingenuity of Man', namely in the classical approach interpreted as the reproducibility view (p. 23).[39]

Proceeding on this basis Pasinetti (1981, p. 28) aims to develop 'a theory which remains neutral with respect to the institutional organization of society', focusing attention on 'the "primary and natural" features'. By this he means 'the conditions under which it may grow and take advantage of exploiting all its potential possibilities'. A model of non-proportional growth based on the full employment assumption is utilized to identify these conditions, interpreted as 'necessary requirements for equilibrium growth' (p. 25). Specifically, in any vertically integrated sector the 'natural' rate of profits – which differs from sector to sector – must be such as to ensure an amount of profits equal to the 'equilibrium' value of investments, that is, to the amount of investments required to expand productive capacity at a rate equal to 'the rate of population growth' plus 'the rate of increase of per capita demand for each consumption good' (p. 130). To explain the changes over time in the structure of demand, Pasinetti draws on 'Engel's law', thus avoiding any reference to

---

[39] On the limits of this interpretation of the marginalist and classical approaches, cf. Roncaglia (1975), pp. 5–7 and 124–6.

subjective elements such as utility maps and consumers' preferences. In equilibrium the increase in per capita income and demand corresponds to the increase in per capita product due to technical progress (which can proceed at different rates in different sectors).

In this context the notion of equilibrium assumes a normative meaning, connected as it is to the assumption of full employment of the available labour force and of productive capacity (cf. also Pasinetti 1981, pp. 96–7, where the 'dynamic' equilibrium corresponds to the conditions allowing for continuous full employment over time). Pasinetti's analysis focuses on what should happen to ensure full employment, not on the actual behaviour of an economic system necessarily bound up with specific institutions.

From this viewpoint the issue of the relationship between the short and the long period is discussed: 'the *very nature* of the process of long run growth requires a structural dynamics which leads to difficulties in the short run'. Hence the methodological suggestion 'of singling out first the fundamental structural dynamics which must take place and then of trying to facilitate them' (Pasinetti 1981, pp. 243–4), a suggestion that tends to affirm the priority of the normative analysis.

Obviously all this is not meant to deny the possibility and usefulness of a direct analysis of short-period issues, and more generally of the – certainly not optimal – way of functioning of concrete economies. In fact, various elements in Pasinetti (1981, especially the four closing chapters) point in this direction. But there is no doubt that, compared to the long-run normative analysis discussed earlier, such elements are far less developed: they appear to constitute for Pasinetti a second stage of analysis, subsequent to that decisive first stage which is the object of systematic formal analysis in his work.[40]

12.8.2   Garegnani's 'Marxian' Reconstruction

Some economists are convinced that the potentially most fruitful way to pursue reconstruction of classical political economy along the line started by Sraffa consists in bringing to the fore Marx's vision. As Pierangelo Garegnani (1930–2011) states, 'a revival of the Classical economists' theoretical approach cannot ... take place but starting from the highest

---

[40] On the limits of this approach (the normative character of the analysis, the exogenous nature of technical progress, the exclusion from the analysis of the role of market forms and of monetary and financial factors, as well as on the role of short-period elements in long-period evolution) cf. Roncaglia (1990a), pp. 207–9.

point of development which such an approach received in the past: the point which was reached with Marx' (Garegnani 1981, p. 113).

Naturally the Marx thus re-proposed is a specific Marx: not necessarily a travesty, as many orthodox Marxists maintain (for instance Medio 1972), but certainly a Marx in which some elements are given emphasis, while others – though undoubtedly present in his writings, such as materialistic dialectic – are played down. Also, Sraffa's own analytical contribution cannot leave Marx's vision untouched (in the broader sense of the term).[41]

The analytical core common to the classical economists, to Marx and Sraffa, is located by Garegnani (cf. in particular Garegnani 1981, 1984) in the set of relations concerning production prices and distributive variables analysed in Sraffa (1960). More precisely, 'the surplus theories have ... a *core* which is isolated from the rest of the analysis because the wage, the social product and the technical conditions of production appear there as already determined. It is in this "core" that we find the determination of the shares other than the wage as a residual: a determination which ... will also entail the determination of the relative values of the commodities. Further, as a natural extension of this, we shall find in the "core" an analysis of the relations between, on the one hand, the real wage, the social product and the technical conditions of production (the independent variables) and, on the other hand, the shares other than wages constituting the surplus, and the relative prices (the dependent variables).'[42]

This analytical core is then taken as the foundation on which to develop the analysis in different directions, corresponding to the elements

---

[41] For instance, the use of Sraffian analytical tools shows that the Marxian 'law of the tendency of the falling rate of profits' is devoid of general validity (cf. Steedman 1977, chapter 9; the issue is debated in various articles collected in Screpanti and Zenezini 1978). Furthermore, contrary to what various authors maintain (Meek 1961; Medio 1972; Eatwell 1975b), the standard commodity does not constitute the analytical tool capable of connecting the world of labour values to the world of prices of production (cf. Roncaglia 1975, pp. 76–9); the widely debated issue of the 'transformation of labour values into prices of production' (for a history of which cf. for instance Vicarelli [1975]) is solved, in light of Sraffa's analytical results, by concluding that in general the results arrived at in terms of labour values cannot be confirmed by an analysis conducted in terms of prices of production (cf. in particular Steedman [1977]).

[42] Garegnani (1981), pp. 13–14. Two notes of caution are to be stressed. First, side by side with the relations considered internal to the core, the variables under consideration (both dependent and independent) can also be connected by other relations, which 'were left to be studied outside the "core"' (Garegnani 1984, p. 297). Second, the notion of a core of the surplus theories remains substantially unchanged when the profit rate replaces the wage as the independent distributive variable determined exogenously, that is, outside the core (Garegnani 1984, pp. 321–2); the importance of this modification is stressed in Roncaglia (1975, 1990a).

considered as exogenous data in Sraffa's book (income distribution, production and employment levels, technology).

The analysis of the relations internal to the core and of those external to it constitute, according to this interpretation, 'distinct logical stages' (Garegnani 1984, p. 297), and the nature of the analysis is substantially different in the two cases. Garegnani provides a clear-cut illustration of this difference. He points to a 'distinction between two fields of analysis': only within the first, corresponding to the core, 'general quantitative relations of sufficiently definite form can be postulated'; in the second field of analysis, instead, 'relations in the economy are so complex and variable according to circumstances, as not to allow for general quantitative relations of sufficiently definite form'.[43]

12.8.3   Sylos Labini's 'Smithian' Reconstruction

A 'Smithian' interpretation of the central aspects of classical political economy was developed in a long series of writings by Paolo Sylos Labini (1920–2005; see, in particular, Sylos Labini 1954, 1956, 1972, 1974, 1976, 1983, 1984, 2000). In these writings Sylos Labini brought to the centre of the program for reconstruction of classical political economy initiated by Sraffa the role of market forms in their interaction with the division of labour and the process of accumulation. This meant bringing to the centre of the analysis a causal chain owing more to Smith than to Ricardo or Marx – the causal chain that runs from changes in the division of labour (or, more specifically, from technological changes) to changes over time in market forms and hence in the rate of accumulation. Developments in income distribution are then made to depend on these elements, together with aspects concerning public policy and the politico-institutional setting.

More generally, Smith's vision of a development process characterized by both positive and negative elements, but fundamentally positive, and conditioned by institutional reforms (from the elimination of custom barriers to free elementary education) was re-proposed by Sylos Labini as an alternative, if not in opposition to, the traditional Marxian view of a progressive deterioration of capitalism (law of increasing misery, proletarization, tendency to a falling rate of profits) up to the inevitable breakdown and the unavoidable revolutionary outcome.[44]

---

[43] Garegnani (1990), pp. 123–4; the expressions used are more cautious in form, but not in substance, than those used in the original text distributed on the occasion of the Florence conference in 1985. For a critique of this distinction, cf. Roncaglia (1990a, pp. 209–11 and 1990b).

[44] This opposition is particularly clear in Sylos Labini's writings on social classes (1974) and on under-development (1983).

In dealing with such issues, it is clear that the problem of the relationship between production prices and income distribution, which is at the centre of Sraffa's analysis, constitutes a crucial knot – in fact, *the* crucial one – for the construction of a theoretical system based on the notion of the surplus. However, it did not constitute for classical economists, and should not constitute today, the main objective of economic enquiry. The objective should, rather, be located in the 'wealth of nations' and the factors determining its development over time and in different countries – especially the distribution of income and wealth among different groups of economic agents. In other words, in order to re-propose a classical interpretation of the development of the economic systems in which we live it is not sufficient to build on the analysis developed by Sraffa in *Production of commodities by means of commodities*: neither in the sense of gradually extending a basic formal model, nor in the sense of gradually extending a restricted analytical nucleus of causal relations.

The connection between the different lines of research contributing to the reconstruction of classical political economy (and in particular the connection between two lines of enquiry such as investigation into the relationship between relative prices and income distribution, and into market forms) is to be found in the reference to a common conceptual framework: the representation of the economy as a circular process, centred on the causes which allow for the production of the surplus and determine its distribution among the different social classes and the different sectors of the economy, as well as its utilization. Within this common conceptual framework, however, it is possible to distinguish a whole series of analytical issues, obviously connected but best dealt with through separate analysis (though without losing sight – 'at the back of our minds', as Keynes put it – of their interconnections). The analytical separability of the different issues (propounded in Roncaglia 1975, chapter 7, as a possible interpretation of the method implicit in Sraffa 1960) thus opens the way to the use of different analytical areas to address different analytical issues.

For instance, Sylos Labini (1956) revives the classical conception of market forms, based on the difficulty of entry of new firms into a sector rather than on the number of firms present in that sector, and analyses the factors determining the barriers to entry facing new firms. Such factors are viewed as determining a deviation of the sectoral profit rate from the basic profit rate that would prevail under free competition, i.e. in the case of unrestrained freedom of entry. This analysis of market forms is clearly compatible with the idea of a tendency to a uniform rate of profits in the case of free competition in all sectors of the economy, and is thus compatible with Sraffa's analysis: in comparison to the assumption of a uniform rate of profits, the introduction of non-competitive market forms can be considered as a second approximation. However, the objective of the analysis (to locate the factors determining the size of the barriers to entry into the different sectors of the economy) can be pursued independently of an analysis of the type presented in Sraffa (1960). Among other things, too direct a link between the two lines of analysis could limit the horizon of the study of the barriers to entry to the determination of sectoral profit rate differentials, as these represent the formal link connecting the analysis of market forms to the analysis of the relationship between natural prices and income distribution. On the other hand, side by side with sectoral profit rate differentials, and possibly more importantly, the analysis of market forms casts light on issues such as the influence of barriers to entry on the rate of technological change, on the rhythm of accumulation and on income distribution (especially when the nature of the barriers to entry and their size differ in the different sectors of the economy: cf. Sylos Labini 1956, 1972, 1984).

12.9   Towards a Keynesian–Sraffian Synthesis?

As we saw earlier, referring to the interpretative controversies concerning the Keynesian and subsequently Sraffian theories, there are keen internal tensions in the two streams we may consider foremost in heterodox theory today. On the one hand we have the rejection of the Marshallian notion of short-period equilibrium, a notion utilized, albeit in a modified form, in the construction of Keynes's theory and considered essential – and not a simple superstructure – by some Sraffians. On the other hand, we have the rejection of the notion of long-period equilibrium implicit, according to some post-Keynesians, in the Sraffian analysis of prices.[45]

Such tensions make it difficult, but not impossible, to synthesize Sraffa's and Keynes's contributions in such a way as to constitute a reference ground for the different streams of heterodox theory. The

---

[45] Garegnani (1979) includes both a critique of the Keynesian short period (pp. 110 ff.) and, in the Appendix (pp. 119–43), his contributions and those of Joan Robinson, essentially concerning the nature of the criticisms to be made of neoclassical theory: those arising with the debate on capital theory according to Garegnani and those concerning the essential role of uncertainty and historical time, absent from the marginalist notion of equilibrium, according to Joan Robinson. Various post-Keynesians oppose a reconstruction of economic theory based on Sraffa's analysis by attributing his analysis with a notion of long-period equilibrium between supply and demand that Sraffa clearly rejected, as we saw in §5.7. Confusion on this point is favoured by the equally erroneous attribution to Sraffa of the notion of 'gravitation of market prices towards natural prices' and of these latter as part of a 'long period position' (Vianello 1985; Garegnani 1990b; for a critique, cf. Roncaglia 2009, pp. 49–51, 157–61).

reciprocal hardening of positions on the two sides, the Sraffians and the Keynesians, clashes with what we know of the reciprocal esteem and collaboration between the leaders of the two approaches. As for Sraffa, the fact that he took Keynes's side in the controversy with Hayek is well known.[46] And as for Keynes himself, his remark – for which Sraffa himself (1960, p. vi) was grateful – on the need to explicitly indicate the absence of assumptions on returns to scale – is well-known: it implies a separation between analysis of prices (and of their relation to distributive variables) and analysis of production levels, hence the idea that the traditional neoclassical notion of equilibrium can be dispensed with. Moreover, by choosing the rate of profits as exogenous, as determined by the interest rate, Sraffa (1960, p. 43) opened the way to recognizing the influence of monetary and financial variables on real ones.[47] Finally, in his discussions with Wittgenstein, Sraffa rejected a theory 'closed' in a single formal construction and opened the way to Wittgenstein's thesis of the multiplicity of 'word games', or in other words the opportunity to construct different interpretative models to deal with different issues, even if within a unitary conceptual frame.[48] Thus the search for a synthesis between the Keynesian and the Sraffian analyses should not proceed by trying to bring them both to one and the same analytical plane, not to speak of including one within the other. We should, rather, explicitly recognize the need for a flexible methodology, with distinct theoretical analyses for different problems, but within a common view that allows us to understand their relation. In this way it becomes possible to recognize the points of strength of each of the two approaches – the Keynesian one for an understanding of the working of a monetary production economy and the Sraffian one for analysing the conditions of reproduction of a capitalist economy based on the division of labour – and to connect them with other theoretical contributions, such as the analysis of oligopoly based on the barriers to entry.

Keynes's analysis, as seen in §§3.6 and 3.7, begins with a notion of uncertainty developed at length, which brings to light the existence of degrees of knowledge qualitatively different for agents operating in different contexts. Hence we have a ranking of decisional frameworks that can be analysed sequentially: those concerning financial decisions, those

---

[46] Cf. Sraffa's contributions in Keynes (1973, 1979: vols. 13, 14 and 29 of Keynes's *Collected writings*) and Sraffa 1932; cf. §§4.3 and 5.4.

[47] Panico (1988) tries to insert the financial sector in the Sraffian analysis of prices of production and so determine the rate of profits. Roncaglia (2012a), on the other hand, considers it preferable to separate the two issues and, following Sylos Labini (1972, 1984), perform a dynamic treatment of income distribution.

[48] Cf. Roncaglia (2009), pp. 25–8 and 126–31.

concerning investment decisions and those concerning decisions on production (and consequently employment) levels. Within this kind of analysis, the issue of relative prices and its relationship to income distribution is secondary; on the other hand, it has a central role, with a critical function, in the case of attempts to insert the Keynesian analysis within a marginalist theory of value and distribution, to deny the automatic tendency of a competitive economy towards full employment.

In sum, there is no obstacle to considering the Keynesian analysis of financial markets, investment decisions, income and employment determination as compatible with determination of production prices based on the difficulty of producing the various commodities, and their relation with income distribution for given levels of production. Similarly, there is no obstacle to considering the Sraffian analysis of prices of production and their relation with income distribution between wages and profits as concerning given levels of production and a given distribution of income, taken as problems to be dealt with separately: the first through the Keynesian approach, the second through an analysis of power relations among social classes that also takes into account the role of finance.[49]

---

[49] Cf. Roncaglia and Tonveronachi (2014).

13   Marxism, Evolutionism, Institutionalism

13.1   Introduction

The -isms we are considering in this chapter – Marxism, evolutionism, institutionalism – are in various respects interconnected, especially the last two. All three continue heterodox but widely accepted traditions, flourishing from the middle of the nineteenth to the middle of the twentieth centuries; all three tend to favour development and change rather than static analysis of prices and consumer equilibrium, and deny the role of the consumer as sovereign in the market. However, there are considerable differences among and within them, and in particular there is an important neo-institutional stream that presents itself as a development of mainstream microeconomics.

In the aftermath of the Second World War, Marxism (discussed in §13.2) was conditioned by the Cold War: as the official doctrine of the Soviet Union, it was characterized by heavy Stalinist dogmatism which drastically obstructed the streams not conforming to the official doctrine, and was focused mainly on pursuit of a compromise between market and state ownership of the means of production (for instance, already embarked on before the war, with Oskar Lange). Marxism flourished again, in at least partly innovative forms, in the season of student and worker protests in 1968, which extended to the Soviet Bloc with the Prague Spring. After the fall of the Berlin Wall and the dissolution of the Soviet Union, Western Marxism sought outlets in the direction of environmentalism, feminism, critical analyses of the work process or of the growing inequalities in income distribution and radical critique of neo-liberalism.

Sometimes considered as close to the Marxist tradition, Karl Polanyi studied the major historical processes of transformation of institutions, contrasting the market, where economic life subordinates to itself all other aspects of social life, with the societies where it is the economy that is *embedded* in society, with non-market distributive mechanisms.

Together with him, in §12.3 we shall be considering John Kenneth Galbraith, looked upon as a crypto-communist in the climate of the McCarthy witch-hunt,[1] but in fact a liberal, advisor to Kennedy, an object of fierce hostility on the part of the neo-liberals, also due to the success of his works, in which he asserts the similarity between the power structures in capitalist and communist societies, both dominated by a military-industrial techno-structure.

In a few words, institutions consist in the sets of formal and informal rules that regulate the interaction among agents. The institutional streams, which attribute central importance to the institutions and their evolution, have deep roots in the German historical school and in Max Weber. In the cultural framework of the time, opposition to these streams as well as to positivism came from new streams of thought, such as Diltey's intuitionism, according to which only introspection (more precisely, the method of internal comprehension, or *Verstehen*) can provide the foundations for a scientific construct.[2] It is to this latter view that the marginalist theory is connected (in particular, with greater awareness, the Austrian stream of Menger and Hayek), deducing from the axioms of rational choice a theoretical building brought into relation with reality only a posteriori. Hence the so-called imperialism of economic science, which claims to include within itself all aspects of life – not only economic life. Along the same line we find neo-institutionalism, considered in §13.4; it utilizes the traditional tools of marginalist analysis to explain the origins of and change in institutions, and occasionally to define optimal institutions, based on the myth of the invisible hand of the market.

Institutionalism – heterodox with respect to mainstream economic culture – is closer to the original historic-Weberian tradition (and, in the United States, to the charismatic personality of Veblen). It rests on an integration between history of culture, as of political and juridical institutions, and economic analysis, sociology and anthropology; we shall be looking more closely into it in §13.5. Of the more recent lines of enquiry that may have exerted an influence on modern institutionalism, we may recall the Frankfurt school with its interdisciplinary research, on the borderline between sociology, psychology and economics, of which Pollock's (1956) work on automation is a good example.

Institutionalism is rich in contributions on various different themes: from the structure of society as a whole to the organization of firms or of

---

[1] A lively account of an incident of this nature is provided by Galbraith himself, in the Preface to *The Great crash* (1955).
[2] Cf. Stuart Hughes (1958), pp. 186 ff.

financial markets, and from the world of work to the processes of scientific research and innovation. Indeed, we may consider as institutionalist analyses works such as those by Berle and Means on managerial economics, or by Minsky on money manager capitalism, already discussed in §§6.6 and 11.7.

The developments of institutionalism intersect with those of evolutionism, which, in studying processes of change, recall with varying degrees of rigorousness the Darwinian (or, occasionally, Lamarckian) theories. Attention is devoted to the field of technological change, on the borderline between institutionalism and evolutionism (§13.6). Connected to evolutionism in some respects we have the economics of development, focusing on the interactions with cultural evolution; in §13.7 we shall be taking a look at Hirschman's contributions. Finally, in §13.8 we will go on to address the theme of competition among different institutional systems.

13.2 Criticism of the Labour Theory of Value and Developments in Marxism

Marx's influence in the decades following publication of the first book of *Capital* and up to a recent times has been enormous. His thought inspired vast, well-organized communist movements in Western industrialized countries, and regimes which long dominated in major developing countries from the Soviet Union from the 1917 revolution to China after the Second World War. This accounts for the great mass of Marxist literature and its importance in the cultural debate. Here we will briefly recall the history of the period preceding the Second World War, going on to focus on the subsequent period.

Marx's immediate successors – his friend Friedrich Engels and his pupil Karl Kautsky (1854–1938) – edited some of the master's major works, published posthumously: the second and third volumes of *Capital* (1885, 1894) by Engels and the *Theories of surplus value* (Marx 1905–10) by Kautsky. In the first volume of *Capital*, Marx promised for the following volumes a solution to the difficulties, already recognized at the time, involved in the labour theory of value as an explanation of relative prices.[3] Engels, in the preface to the third volume, declared that it contained the solution to what was known as the problem of transformation of labour values into prices of production; however, first Böhm-Bawerk and then Bortkievicz demonstrated its erroneousness. Their criticisms were

---

[3] These difficulties were already known at the time of Ricardo's *Principles* (1817), and indeed explicitly recalled in the very first chapter of that work.

subsequently borne out by Sraffa (1960) and extended to other aspects of Marx's thought by Steedman (1977).

In any case, the debate internal to Marxism was not confined to the *vexata quaestio* of the theory of value, but also concerned issues in political strategy, in particular the choice between revolution and gradualism, between the dictatorship of the proletariat and democracy, between central planning and the market. Kautsky was also, in his political activity, one of the first 'revisionists', stressing the importance of the market (and, consequently, of money) for social and political progress, preferring a long period of transition from capitalism to socialism to a sudden revolutionary leap towards a fully centralized system based on state property of means of production, as had happened in the Soviet Union after the 1917 Bolshevik Revolution.[4]

Eduard Bernstein (1850–1932) took much the same line, but more explicitly and clearly; his best-known work, *The prerequisites of socialism and the task of social democracy* (1899), develops an evolutionary view of the building of socialism (significantly, the title of the English translation of the book is *Evolutionary socialism*), stressing the central importance of democratic institutions for political and social progress, in contrast with the Marxian tenet of the need for a proletarian dictatorship in the socialist stage of transition towards communism.

Bernstein proposes to expunge the Hegelian dialectic from Marx's analysis; also, he takes a somewhat diffident view of the most theoretical aspects of Marxian economic thought, from the theory of labour value to the 'laws' of the falling rate of profit and the increasing poverty of workers, attributing importance to what empirical data may tell us about them.

A rather similar line of thought was followed by the socialists of the Fabian Society, founded in 1884 by a group of English intellectuals including the playwright George Bernard Shaw (1856–1950) and the economic historians Sidney Webb (1859–1947) and his wife Beatrice (1858–1943).[5] Shaw, Webb and others brought out a collective work, *Fabian essays in socialism* (Shaw 1889), departing quite sharply from

---

[4] On Kautsky and more generally on the debate at the time among the various currents of Marxian socialism, cf. Salvadori (1976).

[5] The Webbs support, among other things, universal social security schemes financed through taxes, as proposed in the Beveridge Report (1942), introduced in Great Britain after the Second World War, hence with important redistributive implications, substantially different from the system adopted by Bismarck, insurance-based and financed through contributions. In 1895 they also founded the London School of Economics, designed to favour the development of a progressive economic culture deeply rooted in empirical research and not conditioned by the conservative ideology prevailing in traditional universities. (On the subsequent radical changes of the London School, cf. Robbins [1971].)

Marxism to support an evolutionary socialism even less radical than Bernstein's. The very name of the group is indicative of this program, recalling the Roman consul Fabius Maximus, dubbed the 'cunctator' (literally 'delayer') for his victorious war tactic based on small steps rather than great battles.

On the level of economic theory, the *Fabian essays* were influenced by the controversy following an article by Philip Wicksteed, '*Das Kapital*: a criticism', published in the review *To-Day* in October 1884. Wicksteed's criticisms of the labour theory of value and the Marxian theory of exploitation that rests on it found favour with the Fabians, and in particular George Bernard Shaw. Wicksteed, reviewing the *Fabian essays*, was able to assert that 'the "Fabians" had been at work on political economy, and the result is the distinct and definitive abandonment of the system of Karl Marx'.[6] With the Fabians, evolutionary socialism, a direct offspring of Marxism, broke sharply away from it.

Also heterodox in relation to the original 'brand' of Marxism were the currents of thought that, mainly on the basis of their political success, came to be labelled Marxian orthodoxy. The core of this orthodoxy was represented by 'Marxism–Leninism' (to which the notion of the proletarian dictatorship is connected), which, as from the end of the 1920s, had been imposed as official doctrine within the Soviet Union and in European communist parties under the political leadership of Josif Stalin (1879–1953).[7] His choices of accelerated industrialization and economic statalism dominated, for better and for worse, the development of the Soviet Union.[8] As for economic theory, a relevant aspect is the

---

[6] *The Inquirer*, 16 August 1890, quoted by Steedman (1989, p. 131), who also provides an account of the debate (ibid., pp. 117–44).

[7] Indeed, considering the theses he had already proposed before the Soviet revolution, Vladimir Il'ič Ul'janov (1870–1924), known under the pseudonym of Lenin, should be considered heterodox in relation to Marx's analysis, both for his theses on the revolutionary potential of a backward country such as Russia (Lenin 1898), and for his recognizing, in the short essay, 'Imperialism, the highest stage of capitalism' (1916), an element contradicting Marx's analysis, namely the identification of workers and socialist parties in each country with the national interests in the context of the war.

[8] The idea that forced accumulation, after favouring industrialization, would lead the Soviet Union to reach and possibly even to surpass the economic power of the United States was widespread among Marxist economists, in communist as in Western countries, after the end of the Second World War. This idea was also favoured by the thesis that the Great Crisis of the 1930s was only interrupted but not ended by the war: a thesis apparently shared by Stalin himself, and also accepted by many Western economists. As recalled in §9.5, the optimistic forecasts of the first econometric models were at the time considered with scepticism, so much so that their unforeseen success contributed to overcoming the diffidence towards the new techniques of applied analysis. The Korean War and especially Japanese and European reconstruction, supported by US aid, together with the recovery of international trade favoured by the reconstruction of the international monetary system on the lines agreed on at the Bretton Woods conference (1944) with

thesis of the 'validity of the law of value within the socialist economy', stated with increasing determination in the period following the Second World War, having earlier been denied. This thesis, presented in a cryptic form, is interpreted as attributing greater relevance to the price mechanism within socialist economies.

The debate internal to Marxism in the post-war period made continual reference to the themes mentioned earlier in this section; even the opponents to Marxism (as in the case of the different neo-liberal streams discussed in Chapter 8) developed their analyses in opposition to these theses, including such heterodox theses as those of the Fabians, which is why we consider them here although they relate to a period preceding the war.

After the end of Stalinism, in a less suffocating intellectual climate although respect for orthodoxy was still compulsory, the debate on the law of value within socialist economies saw the development of some courageous heterodoxies, especially in the 'Warsaw school' dominated by the personality of Michał Kalecki (cf. §12.3); Oskar Lange (1904–65) and Włodzimierz Brus (1921–2007), among others, proposed theses favouring the development of a socialist market.[9]

In China, after the victory of Mao Tse-tung (or Mao Zedong, 1893–1976) over the Chiang Kai-shek nationalists in 1949, another form of Marxist orthodoxy arose – Maoism. This was quite different from Marx's original thought, adapted to a peasant society without an industrial proletariat and with a very different cultural tradition from the Western ones.[10] The Maoist strategy went through great changes: from the Great Leap Forward (1958–1961), based on forced collectivization of agriculture and aiming to provide the means for a diffused industrialization, but with a tragic cost in terms of repression and famine (between 14 and 30 million deaths) and the alliance with Stalin, to confrontation with the Soviet Union, and the Cultural Revolution (1966–9) aimed against the intellectual middle class and also the source of serious economic crisis

Keynes's decisive contribution, however, guaranteed the Western block sustained growth rates of production and income. After the end of the Second World War, instead, Russia remained a largely underdeveloped country: political totalitarianism (and Stalinist terror), apart from the damage they generated in terms of civic growth, did not pay even in terms of economic growth.

[9] Lange's (1936–7) article was recalled in Chapter 4, illustrating Hayek's critiques of his views. We may also include in this stream the analyses of social conflict within the centrally planned economies and of the role of the politico-bureaucratic apparatus as those of the Pole Bronislav Minc (1913–2004) or the Czech Ota Šik (1919–2004).

[10] The official edition of Mao's writings, in five volumes, originally published in Chinese in 1960, was immediately made available in French and English translation: Mao Tse-tung (1960). For a didactic version of the dogmatic Chinese Marxism, widely utilized as a manual in China in the 1960s and 1970s and also available in Italian, cf. Xu He (1963).

and social instability, together with widespread violence, taking an unknown but very heavy toll of victims. The subsequent stabilization gradually led, after Mao's death and up to the present day, to a situation based on persistent political dictatorship and strong centralized power with openings to the market economy that, accompanied by widespread corruption, favour an increasingly unequal distribution of income, wealth and power.[11]

Of the original contributions by Western Marxist economists, we may recall those by Paul Baran (1910–64) and Paul Sweezy (1910–2004) in the United States. The former is the author of *The political economy of growth* (1957), an analysis of capitalist development processes based on the notion of potential surplus and study of the factors – political and institutional, in particular – that in various different countries and periods hinder full use of productive capacity. As well as the aforementioned *The theory of capitalist development* (1942) – still the best illustration of Marx's economic theory – Sweezy, a pupil of Schumpeter, was also, together with the historian Leo Huberman, the founder of the *Monthly Review* in 1949.[12] In 1966, Baran and Sweezy together published *Monopoly capital*, a book that, like the writings of the philosopher Herbert Marcuse (in particular *One-dimensional man*, 1956), became a reference point for the student revolts that spread from California to Paris and then all the world over in 1967–8.[13]

A great debate arose over the transition from feudalism to capitalism. While Maurice Dobb (1946) focused on the conflict between nobles and peasants for the appropriation of the surplus of agricultural production, Paul Sweezy stressed the expansion of commerce and cities. Theses analogous to Dobb's were proposed by Robert Brenner in the 1970s, with a follow-up of critiques and counter-critiques that constituted the 'Brenner debate', as it came to be known (Aston and Philpin 1976).

After the fall of the Berlin Wall in 1989 and fragmentation of the Soviet Union, Marxism faced a crisis – political and cultural – though retaining a vast cultural influence, especially in Eastern Asia, Africa and Latin

---

[11] Another experience arousing interest and debate within Marxist culture, but more relevant to the field of politics than to economics, was to be seen in Cuba, illustrated, for instance, in Tutino (1968).

[12] On Sweezy's life and work, cf. Howard and King (2004).

[13] In this brief survey we leave aside the Marxist thought more directly pertaining to the philosophical field, with such important figures as Louis Althusser in France, or Galvano Della Volpe and Lucio Colletti in Italy (Colletti [1968, p. 431], who complained that 'Sraffa has made a bonfire of Marx's analysis' and subsequently joined Forza Italia, the political conservative movement founded by Berlusconi). Also, as far as Italy is concerned, we should recall the anti-fascist occupation of Rome University in 1966, which antedated the student revolts in other European countries by two years.

America. However, the debate on Marxism fell into the background, while the dominant role of Soviet Marxism came to an end, fossilized in orthodoxy and the principle of authority, with an opening up to issues and streams of thought such as ecology or utopian visions of the end of compulsory labour.[14] These developments, however, appear to have had relatively little to do with the basic Marxian tenets, from exploitation to commodity fetishism, from historical materialism to the necessary transition from capitalism to socialism and then communism.

Here we will confine our attention to three of the many streams. One is the tradition of the New School in New York, internally diversified and Marxist only in a general way, influenced from the period following its foundation in 1919 by the influx of German and Austrian scholars escaping from Nazism; it retains a strong link with European culture and its developments such as Keynes's thought and Sraffa's contributions (Foley 1986; Nell 1998; Shaikh 2016). Then we have the Marxian analysis of the cooperative economy, which rejects both private ownership of means of production and central planning, proposing as a model the self-management of firms by their workers (Jossa 2010). Lastly, we have the analytical Marxism of John Roemer and others, based on methodological individualism (hence, essentially, on a marginalist approach) to propose a socialist market and reformulation of the notion of exploitation (Roemer 1994).

13.3   Analyses of Change in the Economic and Social Structure: Polanyi and Galbraith

Like many studying change in the social and economic structure, Karl Polanyi (1886–1964, born in Vienna but of Hungarian origin) was a social scientist working on the borderline between economics, sociology, anthropology and philosophy. Having graduated in law in 1909, he fought in the Austro-Hungarian army during the First World War and was wounded. Among the founders of the Hungarian radical party, of which he was also secretary, he migrated to Vienna after the communists took power. Here he worked as a journalist and took an interest in economics, with a critical attitude towards Menger's Austrian school. An opponent of Nazism, in 1933 he migrated again, this time to London and from there in 1940 to the United States, where he taught at Columbia University from 1947.

---

[14] An author of Marxist origins dealing with the environmental issue with a radical proposal of transformation of society is the French writer Serge Latouche, with his thesis of 'sereine décroissance'. Cf. for instance Latouche (2006).

The notes of the evening lectures in economics held during his stay in London constitute the basis for his main work, *The great transformation* (1944); the notes of the seminars at Columbia University became the basis of another important work (in collaboration with C. Arensberg and A. Pearson), *Trade and markets in the early empires* (1957). Another work with A. Rotstein, published posthumously in 1966, on the Dahomey slave trade in the eighteenth century, some articles and some collections of essays (of which the one edited by Dalton in 1968 is particularly useful) combine to constitute the corpus of his writings.

Human beings depend for their survival on nature and other human beings, but the form in which this happens varies from one social system to another. In studying different social arrangements, Polanyi's research concerns in particular the working of societies preceding the market economy, the origins of the markets and the complex – political, social and cultural – conditions of their survival. A collateral aspect of his research consists in his critique of the thesis, characteristic of the Austrian school, according to which *homo oeconomicus*, comparing resources and desires in making rational (maximizing) choices, represents the archetype of the human being. Polanyi shows that *homo oeconomicus* was born later, together with the system that embodies/subordinates society in/to the economy; the market economy cannot be considered the natural epilogue of the history of human civilizations.[15]

Polanyi also rejects the individualism and formalism characterizing economic theory, from Ricardo to the marginalists. Confining their analyses to the working of the price mechanism in a market economy, theoretical economists lose sight of the issues concerning the very structure of societies embedded in the market.[16] Institutions like the gold system and the equilibrium of powers in the international arena, the market and liberal regimes in the national contexts, generate contradictions: the market has a disruptive effect on the system of reciprocity, and so on the social nature of humans, as well as generating distributional conflicts that unavoidably lead to an extension of social control (dictatorships, but also the New Deal and the welfare state).

In his writings, Polanyi contrasts with the social integration realized through market exchanges and the connected dominance of the economy over all other aspects of social life (namely, the system in which the

---

[15] After recalling that, as Aristotle says, man is a social animal, Polanyi (1968, p. 65) states: 'Man's economy is, as a rule, submerged in his social relations. The change from this to a society which was, on the contrary, submerged in the economic system was an entirely novel development.'

[16] 'The "economistic fallacy" ... consisted in an artificial identification of the economy with its market form' (Polanyi 1968, p. 142 n.).

economy embeds into itself the social life) two other modalities of organization of economic life: the systems in which it is not exchange, but
redistribution by the centre, or reciprocity, that regulates economic life,
permitting integration of the economy into society.

The importance attributed to the study of primitive societies stems
from the fact that, according to Polanyi, the analysis of modern societies,
too, means comparing different economic and social systems. Within
primitive societies, the mechanisms of social integration are based on
the reciprocity of gifts (within families, groups of kinsmen, tribes) and
on forms of redistribution ensured by the central powers, realized through
compulsory tributes to political and religious authorities (mainly in the
form of transfers of goods or provision of services). On the contrary,
within market societies, in which income depends on selling one's labour
or, for the capitalists, on obtaining profits,[17] social relations are
embedded in economic relations. The degradation of the workers does
not derive from exploitation, as Marx held, but from the disintegration of
the culture based on social relations of reciprocity.[18]

Polanyi's analysis was taken up by Immanuel Wallerstein (b. 1930),
a sociologist, economist and historian of civilizations, who also recognizes
the influence of Fernand Braudel, the founder of the French school of the
Annales and theoretician of long-view history. Wallerstein distinguishes
two kinds of world systems: the empire world, characterized by
a centralized management of economic resources and in which the economy is, as Polanyi puts it, embedded in society, and the economy world,
that of the capitalist market, in which it is society that is embedded in the
economy. His main work is *The modern world system* (in three volumes,
1974, 1980, 1989). Close to 'third world' scholars such as Samir Amin,
Giovanni Arrighi and André Gunder Frank, together with them he
upholds the thesis that underdevelopment is closely connected to (caused
by) capitalist development in industrialized countries: a 'theory of dependency' opposed to mainstream 'theories of modernization' that study the

---

[17] 'The notion of gain was specific to merchants, as was valor to the knight, piety to the
priest, and pride to the craftsman' (Polanyi 1968, p. 67). Commerce – exchange – was
something different from the market, with stable prices set by habit or by the political
power: exchange was an exchange of benefits, with advantages for both parties to it
(Polanyi 1968, pp. 109–10), a 'fluxus et refluxus gratiarum' (a giving and receiving of
graces), as Albert the Great neatly put it (Roncaglia 2005a, p. 38).

[18] 'Not economic exploitation, as often assumed, but the disintegration of the actual
environment of the victim is then the cause of degradation' (Polanyi 1968, p. 46). One
of Polanyi's main contributions to the comparative study of economic and social systems
lies in showing how money and foreign trade, present in all kinds of societies, operate in
different ways and take on a different social role in market economies and in economies
based on reciprocity and centralized redistribution.

issue of development in countries in the South of the world without taking into account the influence that the richest and strongest countries have on them.[19]

The best-known exponent of institutionalism is John Kenneth Galbraith (1908–2006);[20] some of his works, such as *American capitalism* (1952), the lively account/interpretation of the 1929 Great Crisis (*The great crash*, 1955),[21] *The affluent society* (1958) and *The new industrial state* (1967), have enjoyed very wide circulation.

In the first of these books, Galbraith illustrates the role of big corporations in the American economy and society, noting their efficiency, which allows for continuous expansion of production and consumption, but at the same time stressing the high concentration of power and the need for countervailing powers. In *The affluent society* (1958) these themes are taken up again, stressing the ability of the big corporations to address the consumption choices of citizens and the formation, in the face of private opulence, of largely unsatisfied requirements of culture (schools, but also museums), public infrastructure (roads, public transport), security services and interventions to prevent environmental decline.

The last of the four books is devoted to a counter-current analysis of the economic and political structure of modern capitalist societies, of which the United States constitutes the paradigmatic case. According to Galbraith, the paradigm of perfectly competitive equilibriums is a pathetically inappropriate means to interpret contemporary economies. Their evolution is in fact largely determined by the interaction between big and powerful protagonists, such as governments, the major corporations and the trade unions, which together constitute the 'technostructure'. 'So far from being the controlling power in the economy, markets were ever more accommodated to the needs and convenience of business organizations, (Galbraith 1967, p. 9). 'The accepted sequence', running from consumer's choices to the market and from it to the producer, is substituted by a 'revised sequence' running from the choices of the large firm to the control of consumer's attitudes and to market regulation (p. 216). In other words, also consumers and the public sector adapt (or perhaps better, are driven to

---

[19] In his last book, *Adam Smith in Beijing* (2007), Giovanni Arrighi (1937–2009) stressed the shift from North America to Eastern Asia of the barycentre of the world economy and the naissance of a world market; he also criticized the neoclassical theory of economic development and the distortions it creates in the interpretation of Adam Smith.

[20] According to Tsuru's (1993, p. 78) acute observation, Galbraith 'marries, so to speak, Veblen and Keynes'.

[21] This 'Keynesian' interpretation was fiercely opposed by Friedman, with far less success with the public; cf. Friedman and Schwartz (1963). For a frontal attack on Galbraith, cf. Friedman (1977) ('I do not know of any serious scholar who has validated his conception', ibid., p. 13).

adapt) to the exigencies of the corporations; even trade union power has been facing a decline (p. 15). While the role of the market decreases, the role of planning increases: not centralized planning of the Soviet type, but multipolar planning realized by the state–military apparatus and the big corporations, each in its specific field of activity and, interconnecting among themselves and with the government, for the economy as a whole. Education also takes on greater importance, both strictly technical and, in the broadest sense, cultural; here we have a decisive element of social stratification (and of persistence of the social stratification inherited from the past).

Together with the role of large corporations and of state apparatuses, Galbraith stresses at least for the United States that of military expenditure, also as an engine for research.[22]

As for policy, the big corporation is less in need of a form of control of demand realized through monetary and fiscal policy, such as that obtaining in the first two decades after the conclusion of the war: the system of firms may respond to changes in demand through changes in labour inputs (Galbraith 1967, p. 229).

In the wake of Schumpeter, but coming to the opposite conclusion,[23] Galbraith perceives a possibility of salvation: 'The industrial system, in contrast with its economic antecedents, is intellectually demanding. It brings into existence, to serve its intellectual and scientific needs, the community that, hopefully, will reject its monopoly of social purpose' (p. 400).[24]

With Galbraith, who was also personal counsellor to President Kennedy, institutionalism intersects with post-Keynesianism. It is also worth recalling in this respect that Galbraith played a decisive role, together with Sidney Weintraub and Paul Davidson, in the founding of the *Journal of Post Keynesian Economics*.

The paradox of opulent consumption that favours the segmentation of society, already illustrated by Veblen (cf. §3.3), is taken up by Fred Hirsch (1931–78). In his main work (*Social limits to growth*, 1976) Hirsch utilizes

---

[22] This theme was subsequently treated in depth by other authors. Cf. for instance Mirowski (2009), pp. 153–231.

[23] According to Schumpeter, the intellectuals would corrode capitalism from inside with their critical activity, thus leading to socialism (a direction opposite to the one he himself would like to see: cf. §3.5).

[24] At the same time, Galbraith appears to foresee the advent of populist movements: 'suspicion or resentment is no longer directed to the capitalists or the merely rich. It is the intellectuals who are eyed with misgivings and alarm. . . . Nor should it be a matter for surprise when semi-literate millionaires turn up leading or financing the ignorant in struggle against the intellectually privileged and content. This reflects the relevant class distinction in our time' (ibid., p. 250).

the notion of positional goods that contribute to determining the social placement of the individual and that are desired and demanded for this reason, even at the cost of objectively more useful goods and services, with negative consequences for the civil development of society. Specifically, material consumption is privileged, sacrificing education and time devoted to others and engendering social malaise (alienation, deterioration of conditions of urban life, inflation and unemployment, loss of humanity in the relations with others).

Recently, in his book *The predator state* (2008), James Galbraith (b. 1952, Kenneth's son) has returned to the Veblean notion of 'predator' to hold that contemporary capitalism, far from being competitive, as marginalist theory would have it, undergoes a shift from a system built for the middle classes to a system in which the middle classes are systematically preyed upon in favour of a predator class that controls the economy and politics: a state managed as a corporation, following the interests represented by managers, in a system of (pharmaceutical, oil, financial, military) lobbies that drive its action.[25]

On the whole, these authors follow a methodological approach based on analysis of the institutions and their historical evolution, stressing the interrelations between economic and non-economic aspects of social life. We thus have a 'classical', intrinsically dynamic, vision of capitalism, opposed to the marginalist one, intrinsically static or at most stationary (homothetic quantitative growth), of a competitive market economy driven by the consumer's rational choices as the sole paradigm for modern society and even for societies of any historical epoch and place.

13.4   Neo-institutionalism

In §6.6 we referred to Coase's 1937 contribution that sought to account for the existence of the firm on the basis of transaction costs. This article is commonly considered as marking the birth of neo-institutionalism, which may be viewed as an nth operation to extend the marginalist approach: the issue of institutions, traditionally dealt with through historical-sociological analyses, is brought into the field of the theory of rational behaviour of maximizing agents that leads to spontaneous self-adjustment processes with outcomes often considered as optimal (to some extent in parallel to Hayek's views). The institutions are seen as rules of the game (also in the technical sense of the term, given the

---

[25] A curious fact: in the weeks following its publication this book was heading the US sale rankings for contemporary essays, while the book by his father on the Great Crash was heading the rankings for non-contemporary essays.

widespread use of the theory of games) that derive spontaneously from the behaviour of rational agents aiming to reduce transaction costs, and thus depending on the characteristics of the transaction costs themselves.

More generally, both neo-institutionalism and the institutionalism of the original tradition consider institutions as 'the set of socially learned and shared values, norms, beliefs, meanings, symbols, customs and standards that delineate the range of expected and accepted behaviour in a particular context' (Nelson 1995, p. 80). What distinguishes neo-institutionalism, as pointed out earlier in this section, is resort to the conceptual tools of the marginalist approach, beginning with the notion of *homo oeconomicus*.

Actually, Ronald Coase (1910–2013, Nobel Prize in 1991), though considered the founder of neo-institutionalism, is in some respects atypical with respect to the neo-institutionalist vulgate, as he himself repeatedly stressed. English by birth, a student and subsequently teacher at the London School of Economics from 1935 to 1951, he moved to the United States and from 1964 was a professor at the Law School of the University of Chicago, director of the *Journal of Law and Economics* from 1964 to 1982 and a convinced neo-liberal, having been a socialist when young. With his Marshallian background, he remained hostile to mathematical formalization and to simplifying assumptions that distort reality. Hence the importance attributed to transaction costs (which may also be considered as 'a cost of using the price mechanism', Coase [1937], p. 38), not only for explaining the origin of the firm, but more generally for rejecting a-critical use of theorems valid only for a perfect market. He criticizes the notions of utility ('a non-existent entity which plays a part similar, I suspect, to that of ether in the old physics', Coase [1988], p. 2), of rational maximizer, of market without transaction costs: 'We have consumers without humanity, firms without organization, and even exchange without markets' (p. 3).

Coase attributes great importance to the definition of property rights; in his view, it is they, and not physical commodities, that are the object of exchange. On them he grounds his analysis of the divergence between private and social costs (or private and social product) due to the presence of external effects. According to welfare economics as developed by Pigou, these should be offset by taxes (negative externalities) or subsidies (positive externalities). Coase stresses that this would require a more complete analysis, which should also take into account the repercussions of taxes and subsidies and, most importantly, the transaction costs involved; the best solution would be to avoid interventions from above, like taxes and subsidies, but resorting to appropriate markets, the development of which must be made possible with a well-specified allocation of property rights; it is thus possible to resort to direct bargaining between the producer of externalities and the persons affected by them.[26]

In this respect, the Coase theorem states that, in the absence of transaction costs, the result that can be arrived at by this route is independent of the original attribution of the property right (to pollute or to not being polluted, for instance). However, unlike those who (like Stigler) appear to hold that resort to the market solves the problem of externalities, Coase himself remarks that this is no longer the case in the presence of high transaction costs, for example when the pollution produced by a plant affects too large a number of persons, so that the transaction costs are too high. The road indicated by Coase is in fact that of case-by-case analysis (in which, contrary to their habits, judges should take into account the economic consequences of their sentences, rather than deciding on the basis of a priori arguments) which should take into account non-nil transaction costs.[27]

Among the main representatives of neo-institutionalism we may recall Douglass North (1920–2015, Nobel Prize in 1993) and Oliver Williamson (b. 1932, Nobel Prize in 2009).[28] The latter, a student of Coase and Simon, studies the relationship between decisions internal and external to the market, between market and hierarchy, and hence the borderlines between the firm and the market, and the state and the market, proposing a more realistic theory of the organization of the firm than the traditional one, as it takes into account the internal management problem associated with transaction costs.[29]

---

[26] 'Most externalities should be allowed to continue if the value of production is to be maximized. . . . the gain from [eliminating them] would be offset by what would be lost' (Coase 1937, pp. 26–7). The law should assign the property rights with precision: 'without the establishment of this initial delimitation of rights there can be no market transactions to transfer and recombine them' (Coase 1960, p. 104).

[27] 'The world of zero transaction costs to which the Coase Theorem applies, is the world of modern economic analysis', while 'What my argument does suggest is the need to introduce positive transaction costs explicitly into economic analysis so that we can study the world that exists' (Coase 1988, p. 15). In passing we may observe that the same reasoning should hold for the absence of perfect certainty or probabilistic risk, or of a one-commodity world.

[28] Cf. for instance North (1990), Williamson (1975, 1986, 2000) and Eggertsson's (1990) extensive survey. A monumental collection of neo-institutionalist contributions has been edited in seven hefty volumes by Ménard (2004).

[29] According to Alchian and Woodward (1988, pp. 71–2), Williamson's work implicitly confutes 'the myth that firms are owned, controlled and administered by "capital" rather than "labor"', while in fact 'the leader of the team (management) is the member with the comparative advantage in deciding what the team and its members should do', where the term 'team' indicates the firm, understood as (p. 70) 'a coalition among owners of separately owned resources whose value as a team exceeds the sum of the market values each could get separately'.

North is also known for his contributions to the so-called new economic history, cited in the motivation for his Nobel Prize, received together with the economic historian Robert William Fogel: an approach that largely utilizes quantitative and econometric methods (what is known as cliometrics) and counterfactual reasoning based on neoclassical theory.

Both Williamson and North attribute massive importance to transaction costs (about 50% of GDP, according to Wallis and North [1986]), referring to them for the naissance and development of institutions; in this respect Williamson distinguishes the case of isolated contracts and the case of repeated contracts, for which reputation acquires importance.

From the world of the firm and production (to which the issue of externalities mainly refers), neo-institutional analyses extend to other fields, such as political institutions (democracy and dictatorship), the rules of international trade and natural resources. In some of these fields transaction costs are considered to be important, while in others they are disregarded; what remains, as a common characteristic, is the theoretical derivation of optimal institutions in the marginalist context of methodological individualism (which, however, turns out to be a matter of begging the question when utilizing the notion of the representative agent or the aggregate notion of capital).

Explicitly devoted to the factors determining political institutions that drive the decisional processes of communities is the study by Acemoglu and Robinson (2006), who put together brief historical references (anecdotes more than systematic reconstructions) and a basic theoretical structure founded on simplified game-theoretic models that, in the tradition of the public choice school, derive political events from individual interests.[30]

An essentially empirical finding (the theoretical foundation consists in an aggregate production function, with decreasing returns to scale!)[31] to be found in Alesina *et al.* (2000) is of 'a strong positive correlation from 1870 to today, between the number of countries in the world and a measure of trade openness' (p. 1276).

Considered on the borderline between institutionalism and neo-institutionalism,[32] Elinor Ostrom (1933–2012, Nobel Prize in economics

---

[30] Cf. also Acemoglu (2008) and Acemoglu *et al.* (2011).

[31] However, the hypothesis of spurious correlation also fails to receive serious consideration, notwithstanding the importance of the thesis proposed: that 'trade openness and political separation go hand in hand: economic integration leads to political "disintegration"' (ibid., p. 1277).

[32] Closer to the former than to the latter, as her arguments imply rejection of the axiom of *homo oeconomicus*, closer to the latter because of her adhesion to methodological individualism.

in 2009, the first and so far only woman to receive it) studies the development of a variety of institutions destined to tackle the problems of sustainable management of natural resources, such as air or water, denominated commons since they are not (or at least, not commonly) private property or state direct property. The so-called tragedy of the commons consists in the tendency to exhaust them, since each individual user draws benefits from their use, while the costs of intensive exploitation fall on society. On the basis of numerous field studies conducted by herself or by her collaborators, Ostrom notes the multiplicity of possible institutional solutions to the problem, apparently preferring those that develop from below, in the ambit of small communities of users, based on cultural norms of confidence and reciprocal control.

13.5   Evolutionism and Institutionalism

Neo-institutionalism is thus opposed to the institutional school that, under Thorstein Veblen's influence (already considered in §3.3), had a wide following in the United States at the beginning of the twentieth century, inspiring among other things the foundation of the American Economic Association in 1885. Veblen's institutionalism and that of his immediate followers nevertheless retains some influence on contemporary debate, with hints occasionally emerging in heterodox research streams, as in the case of Galbraith's analysis of the affluent society.

Opposing the static nature of mainstream economics based on the notion of equilibrium between supply and demand, in the wake of the institutionalism of Veblen and Commons, Polanyi and Galbraith and many others, two lines of research developed, external to mainstream economic culture, one evolutionary, the other institutional (to be kept distinct from the neo-institutional line mentioned earlier). In many respects these two lines of research are reciprocally connected: Veblen himself was the author, in 1898, of an article proposing economics as an evolutionary science; evolutionism and institutionalism are presented as included in one another (and vice versa) by their exponents in surveys on the developments of the two streams (cf. Nelson [1995] and Hodgson [1988, 1998]).[33]

---

[33] The proximity of the two research streams calls for some compromises: the difficulty of choosing between the two labels – institutions, evolution – led to adopting for the journal founded in 1967 as the scientific organ of the two approaches the anodyne title of *Journal of Economic Issues* (Hodgson 1999, p. 110). This journal, at present edited by the Association for Evolutionary Economics, was joined in 1991 by the *Journal of Evolutionary Economics*, the organ of the International Joseph Schumpeter Association;

Both research lines tend to assert dynamic analysis: the field of the institutionalist-evolutionary approach, against equilibrium analysis, and the field of the traditional theory of value.[34] In this way both marginalist and classical-Sraffian analyses are rejected. However, this is a mistake: lacking a choice between the two approaches, in research as in teaching economists are led to consider the two fields – static and dynamic analyses – as independent, much as happens in the case of micro- and macroeconomics. This opens the way to re-appropriation of the institutional-evolutionary field on the part of the dominant marginalist theory of value, as happens with the growing success of the neo-institutional school, as no economics approach can do without a theory of value. Also, while there are good reasons to see static equilibrium analysis and dynamic-evolutionary analyses as opposed within the marginalist theories of value and distribution, within the classical-Sraffian approach production prices are not determined by the equilibrium between supply and demand but only by the conditions of reproduction of the economy, and it is thus possible to consider analysis of them as concerning a 'photograph' of an economy in continuous evolution, as indicated in Chapters 2 and 5.

The influence of subterranean reference to the marginalist tradition within the evolutionary and institutional research streams is often apparent, for instance, in the notion of 'creative destruction' proposed by Schumpeter and taken up by various authors within the evolutionary approach. The closure of firms adopting traditional techniques is necessary to free resources for innovative firms only because, in the wake of traditional marginalist theory, it is assumed that the invisible hand of the market leads the economy towards full employment equilibrium. In the case of the Keynesian–Sraffian theory instead – which admits as possible, indeed likely, the presence of unused resources – the 'destruction' is not a prerequisite for making room for firms adopting the new techniques: these latter firms may develop precisely by utilizing the unused resources.

Together with the reference to Schumpeter, we should also stress the references to the Marshallian tradition, frequent even if not unanimous among evolutionary theorists – the exoteric one of oral tradition and footnotes to the text of the *Principles*, rather than the static one of

there is also the European Association for Evolutionary Political Economy (Hodgson 1999, pp. 127–8; in this volume see also the extensive bibliography).

[34] According to Tsuru (1993, p. 73), institutionalism is characterized by four elements: the open system nature of the activities of production and consumption, emphasis (common to evolutionism) on dynamic processes of technological change and of circular-cumulative causation, recognition of the need for some form of social management (planning) and the normative nature of economic science which is entrusted with the task of formulating social objectives.

U-shaped cost curves. Marshall derived his evolutionary views from the sociologist Herbert Spencer, who in turn drew more on Lamarck than on Darwin. The distinction is essential in relation to the use of evolutionism in the economics field: Lamarck admits hereditariness of characteristics acquired during the life of the organism, while Darwin focuses attention on random variation of genetic characteristics between one generation and the next, and on the natural selection of characteristics more conducive to survival. Also, the 'minimal concept' of a Darwinian population, which justifies recalling the Darwinian evolutionary method, 'implies recalling three ingredients . . .: variation in individual character, which affects reproductive output, and which is heritable' (Godfrey Smith 2009, p. 6).[35] If we take these elements into account, it is clear that much of what is considered evolutionism in economics has little to do with Darwin.

Indeed, reference to (Darwinian or Lamarckian) evolutionism may be considered a metaphor, rather than a precise methodological rule. This is the line followed by Armen Alchian (1914–2013), with a 1950 article pointing to competition as the process of selecting the best firms: a neo-liberal version of evolutionism widely referred to but more as a tool of political rhetoric than as a new theoretical approach.[36] An answer to Alchian came from Edith Penrose (1952), who criticized the evolutionary metaphor also recalling the Marshallian 'life cycle' of firms; Penrose specifically stressed the intentional nature of economic decisions, which is absent in the evolutionary processes studied by biologists.

Nearly fifty years later the theme of biological metaphors was reproposed by Geoffrey Hodgson (1999, pp. 73 ff.), who considers them useful, affirming evolutionary metaphors against the mechanistic ones that characterize the development of marginalist theory. In much the same direction we have Simon's (1983, p. 37) definition according to which 'Evolutionary theories explain the way things are, by showing that this is the way they have to be in order for the organism to survive'.[37] On this basis we might distinguish an evolutionism in the strict sense (be it

---

[35] Simon (1983, p. 40) stresses 'the variation-selection mechanism of the Darwinian theory', and then (p. 49) the element of hereditariness that distinguishes Darwin from Lamarck, to conclude that (p. 70) 'Evolution, at least in a complex world, specifies means (the process of variation and selection) that do not lead to any predictable end', which implies leaving aside the notion of equilibrium, central in all variants of mainstream economics.

[36] Mirowski (2011b, p. 247) identifies in Alchian's paper the starting point of the 'saga of evolution at Chicago', which is critically reviewed.

[37] Simon stresses that evolutionary processes take on central importance also for their policy implications when they may lead to different equilibriums.

Lamarckian or Darwinian) from an evolutionism *latu sensu* that, as Hodgson himself remarks, ends up by joining institutionalism.

Nicholas Georgescu-Roegen (1906–94) may be considered an evolutionist *latu sensu*. He came up with important contributions in different fields of economics, starting with the pure theory of consumer behaviour (Georgescu-Roegen 1936). In this field, distinguishing between ordinal and measurable preferences, he proposes what he calls a lexicographic ordering, rejecting the monodimensional view of utility systematically adopted by mainstream microeconomics. More generally, Georgescu-Roegen rejects the 'aritmomorphic' view of economics: a mechanistic view based on the attempt to construct economics on the model of Newtonian physics, requiring the variables under study to be definable with precision and measurable, while in the field of human beings and society there can be no getting away from notions surrounded by a 'dialectic penumbra' that makes it impossible to satisfy these requirements. Hence the proposal of an evolutionary view of economics, recalling the second principle of thermodynamics according to which entropy is in continuous increase over time (in simplistic terms, this means a flattening out of the state of nature): the human being, in exploiting nature's powers, uses precisely the differences in potential existing in nature and by using them annihilates them. Thus Georgescu-Roegen develops an original version of environmentalism, aware of the interaction between productive activities and state of nature. Some of Georgescu-Roegen's contributions concern the theory of production, for which he proposes an innovative view that considers the temporal structure of the productive process and stresses the importance of increasing returns to scale, incompatible with the traditional theory of competition.[38]

The evolutionary metaphor prompts us to stress the need to pay attention to processes of change, in opposition to the static nature of the marginalist approach. Obviously, evolutionary theory cannot be limited to describing/interpreting change as an economic historian might do, but has to develop theoretical analysis of dynamic processes, taking into consideration mechanisms capable of performing systematic selection among the characteristics of the population under study, possibly utilizing the mathematical tools of analysis of stochastic processes.[39]

---

[38] On these aspects cf. Georgescu-Roegen (1966, 1971, 1972, 1976). His fascinating autobiography, sadly uncompleted, is in Georgescu-Roegen (1988, 1993); in it he recalls among other things the vicissitudes connected to the rise to power of the Communist Party in Romania and his consequent personal misfortunes, up to his adventurous escape to the West.

[39] Nelson himself (1995, p. 90) stresses that these mechanisms may correspond to Lamarckian evolutionism, which admits inheritability of acquired characteristics, more than to the Darwinian version.

Within the evolutionary approach, important contributions – such as Nelson and Winter 1982, already discussed in §6.6 – concern the behaviour of firms and industries in the process of technological change.[40]

Within an evolutionary approach, the theory of repeated games (in the absence of coalitions) is utilized in studying a more complex notion of rationality than that of traditional theory: a notion that takes into account strategic interactions and evolution in strategies, frequently with computer tournaments – a tool utilized because of the difficulty of directly solving problems with more than two players.[41] In these tournaments each player is represented by a program, which can be equal to, or different from, that chosen by other players; the computer then has such programs interacting according to pre-set rules of the game. In what is by now a classic (Axelrod 1984), players meet in a series of direct encounters; as in the prisoner's dilemma, the choice not to cooperate gives a better pay-off than the choice to cooperate, but if both players decide not to cooperate the outcome is worse than if both decide to cooperate. In the case of non-repeated games, the equilibrium solution is the choice not to cooperate. In the case of repeated games, instead, if any player recalls how the other behaved in previous encounters, openness to cooperate may emerge. Indeed, the tournament experiments studied by Axelrod show that in the spectrum between altruism and asocial selfishness the mechanism of repeated interactions rewards an intermediate position, the so-called strategy of tit for tat, in which the agent is ready to cooperate but then punishes whoever answers with a non-cooperative attitude, though ready to pardon whoever returns to a cooperative behaviour.

This line of analysis developed widely with agent-based models, recourse to which had already been proposed by Nelson and Winter (1982), and of which Axelrod's model is an example. These are models

---

[40] With reference to Nelson and Winter's theory, Simon (1983, p. 41) remarks that the process of change 'is adaptive, but not necessarily optimizing'. As we shall see in §13.6, the same thing holds for the cumulative mechanisms analysed by Brian Arthur and David. Moreover, Simon (1981, p. 56) classifies Nelson and Winter's model as Lamarckian, not Darwinian. Hodgson (1999, p. 162) sees in Penrose (1959) a forerunner of the notion of routines, and recalls (p. 167) that Nelson and Winter do not consider their theory as opposed to the neoclassical mainstream, from which they draw analytical tools such as the aggregate production function, but as an analysis that embodies neoclassical theory as a special case.

[41] A series of developments such as use of the notion of reputation in the theory of industrial organization and for some macroeconomic problems remain within the traditional theory: if non-cooperative behaviour can be punished, but punishment has an immediate cost for whoever inflicts it greater than pardon, it may nevertheless be opportune to choose it within a repeated game, since the reputation of non-compliance thus acquired will induce others to be more cooperative.

also used in biology and in other social sciences, built by isolating a specific, well-delimited issue in which a multiplicity of agents (homogeneous in the initial stages of development of this technique, subsequently also heterogeneous), each characterized by a set of target and instrumental variables, interact among themselves, each able to recall what they learn from the behaviour of other agents and the results of the interaction. The model is then translated into a program allowing for computer simulation of a finite series of interactions among agents; in a number of cases (such as in Axelrod's) the series of simulations converges towards a structure of behaviours and interaction outcomes that may be considered as an 'emerging property', utilizable for interpreting reality.[42] In some cases simulations may be performed on the sole basis of a priori assumptions (as in Axelrod's model); in other cases the parameters of the model are calibrated with econometric tests. This line of research has led to a great many studies and widespread enthusiasm; the results, however, should be taken gingerly, as indicating possible but not necessary outcomes.[43]

13.6   Evolutionism, Institutionalism and Analysis of Technical Change

We have already recalled Nelson and Winter's theory of the firm based on routines. Analyses of technological change are then extended from the firm to the economy as a whole, with the notion of technological paradigm proposed by Dosi (1984; cf. also Dosi et al. 1988): a stage of progressive refining of a consolidated technology – a technological paradigm – is followed by a stage of radical change induced by an innovation that has a profound impact on the whole economy (as in the 'long waves' analysed by Schumpeter), hence the transition to a new technological paradigm.

Various researches in this field utilize the tool of stochastic analysis; others focus on the history of technology. This latter kind is exemplified by Sabel and Piore (1984), who distinguish between flexible production, typical of the first stage of industrial development, and standardized production typical of the Fordist–Taylorist stage; the second takes the lead thanks to economies of scale, but according to Sabel and Piore a return to the first would be possible and opportune for reasons of social sustainability. In the essays collected in his volume, Rosenberg (1982)

---

[42] For instance, a cyclical path of the economy may emerge from the agents' interaction: cf. Delli Gatti et al. (2008).

[43] For a general overview and some bibliographical information, cf. Hanappi (2017). The Italian Economic Journal devotes a special issue to 'Agent-based models in economics' (vol. 3 n. 3, November 2017) with articles by Dosi and Rovantini (2017) and others.

discusses interrelations between technical change and economic theory within a classical (Smithian–Marxian) approach.

An extensive comparative group research (Nelson 1993) illustrates the different national 'systems of innovation', taking into account the role of the public and the private sectors in research processes and technological development in countries at different levels of development, as well as the role of leader and follower sectors and countries.

The strength of institutional research lies, in fact, in empirical studies covering a wide range of topics: large firms, banks and financial systems, trade unions and so on. Here there is an intersection with the work of economic historians, such as Chandler (1990) on the history of big manufacturing firms.

Within institutionalism but also on the borderline between Marxism and post-Keynesianism we have the French *régulation* school, which studies long-period transformations of capitalist economies, taking into account the various institutional aspects of an economy (wage relations, market forms, kinds of public intervention, placement in the international division of labour, and so on) as interacting among themselves with reciprocal adaptation processes. The main representatives of this school are Michel Aglietta and Robert Boyer.[44]

Like games theory, also the mathematical tool of stochastic processes is utilized within the framework of both the mainstream approach (for instance in macroeconomics, within real trade cycle theories) and of heterodox, specifically evolutionary, theories. In this latter case, the outcome depends on the causal path followed initially (path dependence). In the oft-cited example of the typewriter (Paul David 1985) as in Brian Arthur's (1994) analysis, learning by doing or increasing returns to scale – essentially, the presence of cumulative phenomena – generates outcomes that depend on historical vicissitudes. Thus, a new technique that for causal reasons is chosen more often than another in an initial stage – one keyboard or another, the petrol or electric engine – progressively takes the lead, up to the point in which phenomena of lock-in arise, namely extreme difficulty if not impossibility to change the technological paradigm: an initial small advantage becomes insurmountable due to the presence of cumulative processes.[45]

---

[44] Boyer (1990) provides a presentation of the school and bibliographical references. The *Revue de la régulation*, founded in 2008, is available online (https://regulation.revues.org); in the previous decade an annual issue of the *L'année de la régulation* is published, also edited by the Association Recherche & Régulation.

[45] An important case is that of the so-called web externalities, for which the addition of any new user increases the value of the services for all user, as happens with the social networks, such as Facebook, Twitter, Whatsapp and Skype.

This kind of phenomena, utilized in the field of researches on techno-logical change, also lies behind the new economic geography (Krugman 1990), which aims to account for the phenomena of territorial concentra-tion of specific productive activities.[46] A causal initial distribution of firms over a territory may evolve over time, driven by cumulative mechanisms connected to the presence in the different productive sectors of increasing returns of localization; the result is that the productive structures of different countries and localities progressively differentiate, generating lock-in phenomena in the geographical division of labour and in the flows of international trade. In all these cases, we are confronted with stochastic processes of the non-ergodic type – that is, in which the arrow of time cannot be inverted, as instead is possible in the case of ergodic processes.[47]

Chaos theory, too, is utilized within both mainstream theories and the evolutionary views attributing a central role to uncertainty and the impor-tant part played by history. Chaos theory is, in substance, a mathematical theory in which the path followed by a variable (or by a set of variables) is determined by non-linear differential equations. It is a theory utilized in different fields of research within the natural sciences: for instance, in meteorology (and it is in this context that the theory of fractals emerged, a fascinating theory for the beauty of the geometrical objects it generates, in which the space dimensions vary continuously rather than by integers. The theory still has few applications to economic issues, but it might prove useful, for instance, in criticizing the deterministic theories in the macroeconomics field). Chaos theories show the great sensitivity of the temporal path of the variables considered to starting conditions, so that even a slight difference in such conditions leads to highly diverging paths (in a famous example, the flapping of a butterfly's wings in Peking may cause a storm in New York). In the macroeconomics field, use of chaos mathematics shows how easy it is to obtain non-regular cyclical paths for the economy. With this analytical tool it is possible to criticize results obtained by models based on linear equations, but it is of little use in explaining the actual paths of production, prices, or other phenomena.[48]

---

[46] Paul Krugman, b. 1953, Nobel Prize in 2008, repeatedly declares he does not consider himself a heterodox economist. In policy, his critiques mainly concern the ultra-liberals, supply-side theoreticians and monetarists, but are certainly not incompatible with the neoclassical synthesis. His attention to increasing returns to scale may within limits remain compatible with the microeconomic foundations of traditional theory through recourse to monopolistic competition.

[47] As seen in §12.5, this distinction is utilized by Davidson (misleadingly, according to some critics) within the macroeconomic debate to distinguish the role played by time in post-Keynesian and mainstream theories.

[48] See, in any case, Goodwin (1990).

13.7   Development Economics and Interactions
with Cultural Evolution

As we have already had occasion to point out more than once, the influence of Weber and the German historical school can be seen to underlie many analyses that connect the processes of economic development with the cultural traditions of the different societies and the evolution of these traditions over time. The interrelation between culture, productive system and degree of economic development has long been an object of research in economic history; the *Annales* school founded by Braudel, with its accent on the 'long duration', has exerted a strong influence in this respect. The importance of institutions is stressed, for instance, in studies on the borderline between economics and economic history, such as Rosenberg and Birdzell (1986), who stress the differences among the various areas of the world to explain the more rapid development of the Western economies.

An original position, connecting development economics, economic history and history of economic thought, is to be seen in the work of Albert Otto Hirschman (1915–2012).

Hirschman was one of the great protagonists of economic culture in the second half of the twentieth century. An opponent of fascism and Nazism from the outset, his clandestine activity in occupied France to favour the escape of Jewish people destined to die in the lagers remains legendary.[49] For long years at Princeton's Institute for Advanced Studies, an author of influential books and articles with a wide circulation and many translations, Hirschman contributed to development economics and history of culture, as well as studies on the ethical and cultural roots of the market economy and on the motivations of human agents.

In the field of development economics, Hirschman (1958) proposes the thesis of unequal development. Confronted with the difficulties in starting an industrialization process in countries lagging behind, and in opposition to the models of proportional growth (from the schemes in the second book of Marx's capital to von Neumann's growth model, up to the positions implicit in input–output theory and linear programming), Hirschman maintains the need to focus efforts on some specific sectors of the economy; he also insists on the need to eradicate the cultural barriers that hinder development with the assumption that disorganization, backwardness and the presence of parasitic forces enjoying positions of rent are unavoidable. His theses have met with widespread response in many

---

[49] See on this (as for the full story of his life) the fascinating biography by Adelman (2013).

countries in Latin America, where he worked as a consultant of the local governments and international organizations.

On the motivations and modalities of human action, his well-known tri-partition exit–voice–loyalty (Hirschman 1970) is useful in studying the choices of shareholders in a large firm as citizens' choices, as well as many analogous issues. Confronted with decisions they do not share, share-holders or citizens have three possibilities: loyalty, namely the sense of belonging to the institution, leading to accepting, even unwillingly, the choice of the managers or the political authorities; voice, with open manifestation of dissent and possibly pursuit of alliances to exert pressure on those responsible for the decisions or to have them replaced; and finally exit, i.e. abandonment of the institution (sale of shares, migration). Hirschman discusses the cases in which one or the other of the three possibilities is chosen and the likely evolution over time of the situation with shifts from one to the other. Among other things, this kind of analysis may bring light to bear in the study of democratic processes or of social malaise and its consequences (and it is clear that Hirschman's personal experience as a refugee from Nazi Germany, but also sometimes in tacit, sometimes in open disagreement with the policies of his country of adoption, the United States, helps him identify the different aspects of his tri-partition).

His analysis of the dichotomy between passions and interests casts light on various aspects: their simultaneous presence among the motivations of human action, their varied nature (both passions and interests are to be declined in the plural), the changing weights (from the former to the latter) in the transition from feudalism to capitalism, and the persistent role of the former also within the market economy (which helps us under-stand the difference between the Smithian notion of personal interest, mitigated by ethical sensibility and by the desire to be loved, and the marginalist monodimensional, perfectly selfish, notion of the *homo oeconomicus*).

Like Hirschman, various other economists play an active role in ela-borating economic policy strategies for the development of African, Eastern–South Asian and Latin American countries. In many instances these economists take into account social and cultural aspects that appear decisive for the development process to take off. We may recall, for instance, the fortunate experiences of Irma Adelman and Bela Balassa in South Korea; of Paul Streeten (n. 1917),[50] consultant to India and Malta and author of various theoretical contributions; of Nicholas Kaldor

---

[50] In exile from Austria after its annexation to Nazi Germany, a soldier in the English army during the Second World War, his autobiography (Streeten 1986) is fascinating. (Like

(on whom see §12.4) and Thomas Balogh, both Hungarians and naturalized UK citizens, both consultants to UK prime ministers or chancellors and then Lords, both consultants to international organizations and to various African countries; of the Swedish Gunnar Myrdal, who studied problems of Asian economic development (Myrdal 1968); and of Thandika Mkandawire, with his notion of the concrete possibility of 'developmental states' combining both aspirations and economic performance (Mkandawire 2001).

One aspect considered only by some of these scholars but explored in depth by others – the Third World scholars recalled in §13.3 – is the importance of the colonial inheritance, so strong as to induce some to speak of neo-colonialism. In countries in the South of the world the transition to capitalism, in the second half of the twentieth century, took place in forms differing from those that characterize countries in the North of the world, given the presence of strong international influences and opaque links between economic and political powers that often hinder the realization of even imperfect forms of democracy.

13.8   Competition among Institutions

Among the most promising research lines, we may recall those on the 'varieties of capitalism' that analyse the different institutions of the developed countries: the presence or absence of the welfare state, the relative importance of banks (Rhine capitalism) or of financial markets (US model), the role of the markets and flexibility of the labour market (conflict, neo-corporatist, competitive models), the role of the public sector for the evolution of the productive system (industrial policies, policies in support of basic and applied research), and so on: a varied set of issues, dealt with in preference by making use of historical-sociological-empirical analyses and avoiding mainstream models.[51]

One aspect of research on institutions concerns the competition between different institutions, adopted in the various nation-states or in different areas of the world. Before separately examining the issues of welfare, the labour market and the financial structure (and analogous

the autobiography, various of his articles have been published in the *BNL Quarterly Review*.)

[51] See, for instance, the essays collected in Hall and Soskice (2001) and the extensive bibliography presented there. Hall and Soskice distinguish among liberal market economies, market coordinated economies and mixed cases. Amable (2003) associates the first with 'majoritarian democracies', the second with 'coordinated economies'; Ljippart (1999) associates the latter with 'consensual democracies' as opposed to 'majoritarian democracies'. Cf. also Trigilia (2016). On the importance of an active research policy, see Mazzucato (2011).

researches may concern other aspects, from the educational and professional training system to the political system), we must recall Hayek's position (already illustrated in §4.6), which favours competition among institutions so as to stimulate adoption of the more market-friendly systems, in particular such as to ensure a lighter fiscal burden on the shoulders of economic agents. This position also underlies the favourable attitude shown in general by neo-liberal economists towards free trade areas not accompanied by convergence in institutions and in economic sovereignty, as in the case of the common European market and then the euro, and hostility towards any form of control of even short- or very short-run capital movements.[52]

The history of public welfare is long and varied. Take, for instance, the poor laws in Elizabethan England, when the policy of enclosures deprived masses of serfs of their means of subsistence, driven away from the lands they had traditionally cultivated for decades; take the debates in the eighteenth century between Turgot and Necker on the utility of orphanages (defended by the former and denied by the latter, with arguments that foreshadow the Malthusian theory of population);[53] or take, for instance, Bismarck's policy in the nineteenth century as a precursor of the welfare state in the framework of a conservative policy designed to ensure the support of the masses for the monarchy and the aristocratic government.[54] In the post-war period, the history of the welfare state began with the Beveridge Report (1942) in Great Britain and continued with the adoption of pension and health assistance programs in many European countries.

In the United States, health assistance and pensions remain mainly entrusted to the private sector, and specifically to insurance companies that provide life policies and health insurance both to individuals and to firms and their employees; the development of the financial sector then provides pension funds and management of mutual health funds for firms or trade categories.

The economic debate on the different, private and public, forms of management of health insurance and the pension system concerns various aspects: incentives or disincentives to private savings, effects on economic growth (disincentives to savings hinder growth according to marginalist theories based on the automatic tendency to full employment, but may produce the opposite result according to Keynesian theories that have

---

[52] This resistance is taken to the point of favouring not only fiscal evasion but also dirty money recycling and the financing of international terrorism through export of funds to foreign countries adopting particularly lax forms of bank regulation.

[53] Cf. Roncaglia (2005a), pp. 158–61 and 169–72.   [54] Cf. Maddison (1984).

production and employment depending on effective demand), the relative efficiency of private and public systems (with neo-liberal economists maintaining the greater efficiency of private systems, and opposite results of various applied analyses stressing the greater administrative and management costs of private assistance in comparison to universal assistance, apart from spending on advertising and the higher pay level in the private as compared to public health sector), and the possibility of their coexistence.[55]

In Europe, the debate on the relation between the institutions and social structure has recently re-arisen over the increasing difficulties of financing the welfare state (essentially education, health assistance and public pension system) with taxes due to competition from countries with lower taxes. In this case as well the debate proceeds on the borderline between economics, sociology and political sciences; for concise but rich illustration of the different issues we may refer to Dahrendorf (1995), who in this respect speaks of 'squaring the circle'.

The debate on the institutional aspects of the labour market mostly concerns the opposition between two theses and their variants. On the one hand the marginalist tradition, supporting the tenet of the invisible hand of the market, maintains the need to bring the labour market as near as possible to perfect competition: in the presence of unemployment, it is competition that drives down the real wage, and with it unemployment. Moreover, a competitive market ensures the greatest efficiency of the workers and flexibility in their use by employers. On the other hand, the classical and Keynesian traditions suggest that unemployment may rise with the reduction of real wages and that the unequal bargaining power of workers and employers characterizing a fully competitive labour market is conducive to the growing inequalities in income distribution; in turn, this, they hold, generates tensions and social conflicts, with a negative impact on the overall efficiency of the economy and especially on the democratic institutions.

Since the end of the 1970s debate on financial systems has once again concerned comparison among different institutions: the Japanese system of the *keiretsu*, the German system of the universal bank, the Anglo-Saxon system based on markets.[56] In this respect the post-Keynesian theory of finance constitutes fecund mediation between the anti-theoretical leaning of the institutionalists and Keynes's theories.[57]

---

[55] See the extensive comparative analysis by Lindert (2004).

[56] Considering the origins of this debate, we should also recall Hilferding's (1910) work, written from a Marxist perspective; Hilferding discusses the dominance exerted by financial over the industrial capital.

[57] Cf. for instance Davidson (1972), Minsky (1982), Tonveronachi (1989) and Kregel (1996).

In all these cases, the protagonists of the various debates tend to consider their respective problems as closed in themselves, with minimal references to debate in the field of pure theory. However, as we have frequently remarked, to evaluate the opposed positions it is often necessary to consider whether the automatic market adjustment mechanisms really do hold, as maintained by the traditional marginalist theory of value and distribution and denied by the Keynesian and Sraffian approaches.

14 Ethics and the Problem of Power

14.1 Introduction

The societies in which we live have three foundational characteristics: they are based on the division of labour, they are market economies and the presence of the state is strong. These three elements are connected. As Adam Smith teaches us, the division of labour allows for high and increasing productivity. However, when each produces, or contributes to producing, a specific commodity, it is then necessary to pass it on to others to obtain the means of production and subsistence necessary to continue activity. This is possible either through changes regulated from the centre or through market exchanges, the latter being the way that prevailed. As a matter of fact, however, the state won, or found itself necessarily playing, an active role of coordination and intervention regarding various different aspects. First, it intervenes to guarantee the sound functioning of the market: not only defence and administration of justice, but also surveillance against fraud in commerce, imposition of minimal standards of quality for products (for instance, but not only, for medicines), bank surveillance and so on. The state also intervenes to tackle market failures: macroeconomic ones, for instance, with monetary and fiscal policy to counter inflation and/or in defence of employment, when confronted with severe crises or with prolonged periods of stagnation; microeconomic ones, for instance with anti-trust policies to check the tendency to the formation of concentrations of economic power, or with specific taxes and subsidies to counterbalance positive and negative externalities. Finally, it intervenes in various ways for redistributive purposes or for ensuring for all citizens services such as basic education and a social safety net, which with the welfare state in various countries extends to health assistance and pensions.

The economic system thus presents a complex picture, with marked differences in income, wealth and power between different individuals and social groups. Thus, together with the problems of market failures

349

and of coordination mentioned and discussed in previous chapters, we are confronted with major ethical issues. These in turn imply problems of evaluating both the situation confronting us and the possible means of intervention.

The first stream of research we shall briefly consider concerns ethics in relation to the economy and society, and more precisely the choice of judgement criteria. As we shall see in §14.2, opposition between deontological and consequential ethics has deep historical roots, specifically in the Age of Enlightenment, but also has a direct link with debate on the theory of value, distribution and employment. Utilitarianism, which finds relatively easy acceptance within the marginalist approach, has come to show its limits in recent debate; this appears to prompt endeavour to construct an ethic open to the complexity of evaluations and subsequent choices.

The existence of power derives from a differential between the situation of some (individuals, social strata and classes, countries) and of other members of a population – a differential difficult to measure, as it concerns a variety of dimensions (income and wealth, social placement and network of relations, gender, nationality, technical abilities and natural qualities, and so on). In the economic field, this differential is commonly related to differences in income and wealth. The other aspects mentioned above are, however, also important: the role of each person in the economy (in other words, belonging, to some extent or another, to a certain class or social stratum) cannot be reduced solely to inequalities in income and wealth. In the relations between states, differences in economic power (in different respects, both national product and per capita income count) intersect with differences in political and military power, but also with religious identity and the set of institutions influencing education, scientific research and the diffusion of culture. The various dimensions of power are not independent but interact among themselves. As a consequence, the dynamic processes of evolution of the power relationships are extremely complex; the task of reconstructing them is commonly entrusted to historical analysis.

In the economic field, the most highly developed research field is in income distribution (and, to a lesser extent, in wealth), to be considered in §14.3. Studies on income and wealth distribution are a continuous flow; they involve synthetic measures of inequality, and investigation into its origins, its relations with economic growth, ethical evaluations and possible forms of public intervention.

Economic theory enters directly into discussion of distributive equity and efficiency. There is in fact a contrast between the marginalist and the classical approaches. Within the former, distributive variables – wage, rate of profits, rent – are simply the prices of the factors of production, the optimal values of which are determined under competition by their relative productivities and scarcities. Within the latter, we need, rather, to consider the power relationships between social classes, while the connection among income distribution, employment and growth is determined by a set of elements. In the first case, inequalities are the inevitable corollary of the pursuit of efficiency in the allocation of factors of production through the market. Redistributive interventions may be entrusted to taxes, taking care not to hit the incentives to production. The trickle-down thesis – or rain-like diffusion of the advantages of an increase in production even if accompanied by more unequal distribution – stresses that greater efficiency translates (at least potentially) into higher production, employment and productivity levels and hence into advantages for all. It is a different case with the classical approach. An important role here may be played, both in stimulating growth and in improving income distribution, by direct interventions aiming at modifying the power relations between social classes: from the abolition of duties on corn imports, as called for by Ricardo in opposition to landowners and their rents, up to legislative interventions in the field of industrial relations, as was the case in Italy with the Workers' Statute.

Problems of equity, we shall see, concern not only the distribution of wealth and income, which is the object of attention in welfare economics, discussed in §14.4, together with the problems deriving from positive and negative externalities. The quest for equity, if not equality, concerns various fields of human activity; the very definition of equality leads to the question, raised by Amartya Sen: equality of what? As we shall see, this question may be met with different answers, each with some justification. Sen's answer, which in turn is the origin of an extensive and expanding field of research, is connected to the notion of capabilities, illustrated in §14.5.

On addressing power differentials, various issues open up. Obviously, the scholar has as a first objective that of locating the tendencies underway, then going on to interpret the causes that determine and modify the distribution of power, and finally evaluating the possibilities and modalities of intervention with the aim of reducing power inequalities within society. These themes are dealt with in §14.6.

However, the scholar is also part of the society he or she studies. This may influence his or her analysis and evaluation of the situation; the scholar is objective (which is commonly considered an ethical value in the research field) when he or she succeeds in rendering this influence minimal, though it is never possible to annihilate it completely, and to keep it under control.[1] In the ethical evaluation both of the situation and

---

[1] On this cf. specifically Weber (1919).

of the trends he or she is faced with, and of the possible and opportune interventions, the researcher is driven by the economic theories he or she shares (as we saw, for instance, with the opposition between equity and efficiency in the case of income distribution). For this reason, to the complexity of choice among ethical criteria of judgement we must add that of the choice between different theoretical approaches. As we have seen in previous chapters, the variety of theoretical approaches is considerable; the objectivity of the researcher, and hence his or her work ethics, requires full awareness of the existence of different approaches, and thus openness to the critical debate in the theoretical field.

Far from being a 'dismal science', economics is a warm science, animated by passions – including the hope of improving the lot of human beings – that motivate economists in their research work; such passions – as is the case of so many passions widespread among humankind – constitute most useful stimuli to engage in research, but need to be kept under control by the researcher's ethics.

14.2   Utilitarianism and the Ethics of Consequences

Reflection on ethical issues dates back to the ancient world. To simplify a long and complex history, we may say that for a long period ethics followed a deontological approach, according to which what is good and what is bad is decided by some authority: religion (as with the Ten Commandments), state law, *pater familias*. Prevailing public opinion accepts the principles established by such authorities; dissenters are automatically in the wrong. Even science had to bow to the truths of faith: Giordano Bruno burnt at the stake and Galileo's abjuration are but the best-known examples of events that in different forms systematically recur over time.

Beginning in the seventeenth century, reaction to this state of affairs matured with the Enlightenment in the eighteenth century, in particular with Bentham's utilitarianism. Good and bad were no longer a priori characteristics of actions, according to an evaluation deriving from some authority; in Bentham's hands, utilitarianism was a tool for upholding a consequential ethic, according to which human actions are to be judged in terms of their consequences for society as a whole. Such consequences can, at least in principle, be evaluated precisely with the felicific calculus: namely the sum of the utility and disutility caused by each action to each human being (with positive algebraic value for utility and negative for disutility), under the assumption of equal value of each individual (i.e. attributing the same weight to the utility/disutility of each).

Obviously, the felicific calculus requires all outcomes of an action to be evaluable on a monodimensional scale. It matters little whether felicific calculus proves extremely difficult in practice: it provides a direction along which to look for an answer to the ethical issues, to systematically pursue, even if in many cases it will be difficult if not impossible to get a clear answer. Some elements are, however, evident: punishments should be proportional to offences; in deciding them, we should take into account the incentive or disincentive effects they have. For instance, in the case of stealing or robbery without anyone being killed the punishment should be lesser than when accompanied by homicide, otherwise the criminals would find it in their interest to kill to limit the risk of being discovered.

We may thus distinguish within classical utilitarianism two steps in sequence: choices should be based on an evaluation of their consequences (and not on their intrinsic value, however established); and consequences are to be evaluated in terms of the utility they imply for individuals belonging to the society in question. The first stage constitutes what is known as consequentialism. In the second stage variations of the criteria are in principle possible, and have in fact occurred. For instance, according to Rawls's (1971) 'principle of difference', consequences are to be evaluated by observing the well-being of the least advantaged individual – a maximin principle (maximizing the minimum) that Sen (1992, p. 146) considers too extreme, and which, for instance, would not register any improvement in the situation obtaining even with a great shift of income or wealth from the rich to the poor within a society of millions of individuals that, however, leaves the conditions of the poorest individual unchanged.

More generally Rawls, drawing in some respects on Kant and the deontological tradition, holds that the principles of justice are those that rational agents would choose in an initial situation of equality, in which nobody knows the position he or she will occupy in society. Rawls's rationality is not that of the monodimensional *homo oeconomicus* maximizing his utility, but that of an agent able to focus attention on some 'primary goods', namely 'things that every rational man is presumed to want' (Rawls 1971, p. 60), which include wealth and income, basic freedoms, freedom of movement and of choice of employment, a working and social position adequately endowed with powers and responsibilities – in short, the social foundations of self-respect. Primary goods are a vast notion, including both what Rawls calls 'basic liberties' and 'the worth of liberty', which refers to the availability of means to exercise such freedoms. This distinction is analogous only in some respects to the one proposed by Isaiah Berlin (1958; cf. also 2002) between negative freedoms (freedom from constraints, absence of interferences) and positive freedoms (to do, to achieve self-fulfilment).

Utilitarianism may be considered the foundation of evaluations concerning both individual ethics and public choices. The two elements are simultaneously present in some representatives of this philosophical stream, like John Stuart Mill; in Bentham the issue of government choices dominates. Thus in his case the idea of the felicific calculus is accompanied by the thesis of the enlightened prince to whom the formulation of a rational code of law on utilitarian bases can be entrusted.

As for the Scottish Enlightenment, both David Hume and Adam Smith were sceptical about the ideas of the felicific calculus and of the enlightened prince. In their view, each individual has a right to choose for him- or herself, as he or she can evaluate his or her own situation better than anybody else; as we saw in §2.3, however, pursuit of self-interest must be accompanied by respect for the analogous right of others, favoured by the natural human sociability that leads to desiring approval of the others. Ethical rules, like adhesion to a society organized into a state and to its laws, are grounded on a common consent that, unlike Rousseau's idea of a social contract, cannot and should not concern all aspects of life, but constitutes a sufficient common ground for the survival of a society in which individuals differing in various respects, from consumption habits to religious practices, coexist.[2] A somewhat similar line, but more decidedly characterized in the direction of a deontological ethic, is followed by Kant with his a priori principles.

A compromise between Bentham's utilitarian consequentialism and the view, proposed by the Scottish Enlightenment as by others, including Voltaire, of a society with sufficient internal cohesion but diversified, was proposed by John Stuart Mill, with his distinction between different kinds of pleasures and pains, considered incommensurable. Poetry and music on the one hand, like children's games or the pleasures of the table on the other, cannot be directly compared with a monodimensional felicific calculus.[3] Some differences in evaluation may depend on different levels of education, and 'it is better to be a human being dissatisfied than a pig satisfied; better to be Socrates dissatisfied than a fool satisfied. And if the

---

[2] Cf. Roncaglia (2005b), chapter 7.

[3] As Mill (1859, p. 224) observes, 'I regard utility as the ultimate appeal on all ethical questions; but it must be utility in the largest sense, grounded on the permanent interests of man as a progressive being.' Classifying pleasures in one category or the other, higher or common, itself implies a prior value judgement of a deontological kind. On the other hand, choosing a simple dichotomy rather than an *n*-ple of categories simply concerns a choice of higher or lower level of abstraction; in Mill's case, the dichotomy is sufficient to clarify and motivate his criticism of Bentham.

fool, or the pig, are of a different opinion, it is because they only know their own side of the question' (Mill 1861, p. 281). Other differences lie in the fact that strong and contradictory passions and interests may be simultaneously present as, for example, in Greek tragedies, the structure of which is dictated by conflicts of this kind, between values such as love of one's country or of family. All this does not mean, however, that we should abandon consequentialism: compared to deontological ethics, imposed from above, the new ethics is not always able to provide univocal answers, as it reflects the complexity of humans moved by a multiplicity of motivations, but it nonetheless indicates a path opening the way to rationally motivated ethical judgements and, at the same time, to accepting the possibility of different judgements and – through open discussion– to understanding their motivations, thus enabling recognition and acceptance, at least within certain limits, of the individual's freedom of self-determination.[4]

Marginalist theory, with Jevons, adopts utilitarian calculus as a basis for the theory of individual choices. As we know, however, Jevons rejects the interpersonal comparability of utility and hence utilitarianism as ethics. A positive evaluation of the competitive market economy arises, rather, with 'demonstration' of its optimal nature: according to Pareto's principles, each perfectly competitive system leads to an equilibrium that is a Pareto optimum, i.e. such that each deviation from it reduces the utility of one at least among the agents in the economy; in a dual way, each Pareto optimum corresponds to a competitive equilibrium. This solution has well-known limits, to which we shall return in §14.4 dealing with welfare economics. In another respect, the equilibrium values of distributive variables, interpreted as prices of factors of production established in competitive markets, are considered 'just' because they correspond to marginal productivities and thus to the productive contribution of each factor of production. However, this thesis falls down as soon as we recognize the need to abandon the marginalist theory of distribution because of its logical faults.

In any case, the post-war period saw a reprise of utilitarian ethics in the wake of the contributions to microeconomics by von Neumann and Morgenstern (1944), who re-proposed the cardinal utility viewpoint. It was possible for the principle of interpersonal comparability of utility to

---

[4] Generalizing this point, Rawls (1982, p. 160) stresses, 'The presupposition of liberalism (as a philosophical doctrine), as represented by Locke, Kant and J. S. Mill, is that there are many conflicting and incommensurable conceptions of the good, each compatible with the full autonomy and rationality of human persons.'

be introduced into their expected utility theory in a normative interpretation on the basis of the principle for which 'each one counts for one': individuals differ among themselves, but on the ethical plane these differences can, and should, be disregarded.

From here begins the story of modern utilitarianism, characterized by a great debate. Within this debate, one reference point was the book *Utilitarianism and beyond*, edited by Amartya Sen and Bernard Williams (1982), in which the different positions are represented by their major exponents.

First in the debate came the evaluation of individuals' well-being through a monodimensional magnitude (utility). As Sen and Williams (1982, p. 8) observe, '*Reduction* is the device of regarding all interests, ideals, aspirations, and desires as on the same level, and all representable as preferences, of different degrees of intensity, perhaps, but otherwise to be treated alike'. This is necessarily the position of those who, like Harsanyi (cf. e.g. Harsanyi 1988), try to build utilitarianism as an axiomatic system, based on the general theory of rational behaviour proposed by von Neumann and Morgenstern.

In the wake of John Stuart Mill, various authors (including Sen and Williams) have considered this requisite too restrictive and thus prefer to accept the non-uniqueness of the answers to problems of individual ethics or of public choice; the answers may possibly be made more precise with the help of open and rational debate.[5] Atkinson (2009, p. 796) stresses that the non-uniqueness of the answers stems from the presence of 'plurality and diversity in the welfare criteria' where '*plurality* refers ... to the fact that a single person may bring to bear more than one set of welfare criteria' (like 'greatest happiness' or 'personal liberty'), while '*diversity* refers to the fact that different people hold different sets of values.'

We then come to the problem raised by irrational preferences, concerning both the possibility that the individual desires something contrary to his or her real well-being (as in the case of drug or alcohol addiction), and the paucity of information relevant to a rational choice, as well as possible antisocial proclivities (envy, malice).[6] Looking to utilitarianism

---

[5] Cf. in particular Sen (2009).

[6] Envy is here meant in the usual sense, i.e. discontent accompanied by malevolence or rancour towards whomsoever is in some respects in a better position. In the theoretical debate on the themes we are considering, the term is used in a specific technical sense: the preference for the basket of goods possessed by another compared to the basket of goods we possess. In this sense a notion of equity as absence of envy has been proposed (Foley 1967; Varian 1974). Varian shows in his contribution that, understood in this sense, equity is not in contradiction with efficiency. De Clippel (2008), however, shows that the introduction of informational asymmetries suffices to reject this result.

as the criterion for individual ethical evaluations or for public choices means assuming that these problems can be overcome.[7]

We then have the distinction between act utilitarianism and rule utilitarianism, or in other words between an ethical evaluation of individual actions based on the felicific calculus and the adoption of general rules. With his proposal of a rational penal code, and aiming at a role as counsellor of the prince, Bentham looks to the latter category. The individualistic ethical tradition, which in the wake of the marginalist approach considers as optimal the outcomes of a competitive market economy, also looks to the second category, pursuing a positive evaluation of the market economy more on the level of principles than an actual ethical evaluation of individual actions. In fact, the concrete examples of ethical evaluation referring to individual acts are rare and rather simple; rule utilitarianism, operating on large aggregates, is necessarily more approximate but allows for actual evaluations based on good-sense assumptions. Occasionally, this distinction tends to overlap, at least partially, on the distinction between utilitarianism as individual ethics and as a rule for public choices.

Theories such as expounded in Rawls (1971) are to be kept distinct from rule utilitarianism: Rawls's theory, in fact, focuses on institutions regulating the collective decision process, but considers them from an a priori viewpoint, derivable from a hypothetical contract obtainable between agents in their 'original position', namely in ignorance of (or, perhaps better, leaving aside) the fate of each. Thanks to the artifice of the 'original position', a situation of general equality is established, thus

---

[7] Cf. Harsanyi (1988), chapter 3; he explicitly notes that exclusion of antisocial prefer-ences is necessary to prevent paradoxical consequences, and distinguishes 'personal preferences' (those driving the agent in his or her daily behaviour and that are expressed in his or her utility function) from 'moral preferences', which assign the same value to the interests of any individual and are expressed by the social welfare function, though without discussing the problems that may arise when, as happens in general, the two functions do not coincide. Mirrlees (1982, p. 83) refers in much the same way to 'considered preferences' (and notes, p. 68, that they must be 'immutable'). Sen repeat-edly utilizes the clause 'objectives we have reason to value' (e.g. Sen 1992, p. xi), adding (p. 56 n.): 'The need for reflection, or for having reasons for one's goals and objectives, is a qualification that can be quite exacting.' For instance, we may add, it implies the abandonment of revealed preferences. The distinction between the two aspects is far from new: it had already been stressed in the Middle Ages, with the terms *complacibilitas* and *virtuositas*, i.e. utility from the subjective point of view of the individual agent (as the preference for drugs) and utility from the objective point of view of his or her well-being (as in the need for healthy nutrition); cf. Roncaglia (2005a), p. 40n. We should also recall John Stuart Mill's reference to utility 'in the largest sense', quoted earlier. This notwithstanding, no word of caution ever appears in mainstream illustrations of con-sumer theory.

guaranteeing the equity of the contract, which should therefore, according to Rawls, be generally accepted.[8]

Returning to utilitarianism, another aspect cropping up in debate is the
presence of deontological a priori elements even within a utilitarian ethic
and public choice theory. For instance, Hare (1982) maintains the importance of children's education in learning some general moral principles,
constituting a first level of individual ethics, on which a second level of
utilitarian reasoning then grows in adults.

There is, then, the problem of the incompleteness of evaluations (or, in
other words, of the field over which the function to be maximized is
defined). Some objectives may not prove qualitatively comparable,
which may lead to apparent inconsistency in evaluations. In fact, as
John Stuart Mill remarked, this leads to a multidimensional ethical theory
or theory of public choice (the 'multisidedness' that Mill 1873, p. 98,
attributes to Goethe). The principles of consequentialism and welfarism
(ethical evaluation based on consequences, in turn evaluated on the basis
of individuals' well-being or utility) may continue to be accepted; what
falls is the compact axiomatic construction built on the basis of von
Neumann and Morgenstern's expected utility theory (in any case subject
to criticisms in other respects).

A use of utilitarianism that takes into account these limits opens the way
to compromises with deontological ethics; thus, for instance, it is possible
to recognize the role of customs and social conventions as corresponding
not only to the strength of tradition in determining ethical rules, but also to
the evaluation of uncertain elements on the basis of popular experience.

Finally, as we shall see in the next pages, there are the issues raised by
the distinction between the benefits obtainable by a given choice, and
those stemming from the very freedom to choose.

On the whole, consequentialism, even if widespread (thanks also to the
dominance of the marginalist–utilitarian tradition in the theory of individual
choices), comes up against problems precisely because of the connection – in
principle not necessitated – with maximization of individual utility.[9]

The theories we have concisely summarized are to be kept distinct from
those (as for example Layard 2005) that propose the notion of 'happiness', as a substitute for or supplement to that of utility, or of that of well-
being based on per capita income. As a matter of fact, the notion of
happiness often turns out to be a modified version of the traditional

---

[8] Critical discussion of these issues extends on a vast scale; cf. e.g. Sen (2009), in particular
pp. 52–74.
[9] Hausman and McPherson (1996, pp. 9–21) provide some examples of contradictions
between the prescriptions of consequentialism and common sense.

notion of utility (Layard [2005] repeatedly recalls Bentham, with the difference that, like Jevons, he stresses the non-comparability of individual utilities). Happiness is in any case considered a monodimensional magnitude, objective (as corresponding to differentiated neurological states) and measurable through questionnaires (Layard 2005), to the extent that we might speak of a theory of 'revealed happiness'. Altruistic motivations that contribute to determining the state of satisfaction (or happiness) of the individual bring externality problems – destructive for the marginalist theory of the consumer – into the determination of equilibrium. Although this aspect tends to be overlooked, it is precisely this – namely recognition of the presence of important social factors in the agent's choices that imply externalities – that constitutes the main contribution of this line of research, stressing the limits of the egocentric objectives traditionally attributed to the economic agent.

A different approach is proposed by Scitovsky (1976): critical of utilitarianism and the associated *homo oeconomicus* notion, he does not aim to build a positive theory of happiness, but tries to analyse (and criticize) the 'American way of life' which, relegating to a secondary role the elements of sociality and solidarity, leads to a 'joyless economy' (the title of his book). The notion of happiness is in this case non-quantifiable; Scitovsky aims to distinguish (oppose) it from (to) the notion of material well-being, to show that, while in principle the two should be correlated, this is not true of a politico-cultural system such as US capitalism.

Intermediate between these two approaches we have the research stream developed by some Italian authors (cf. for instance Bruni and Zamagni 2004), who contrast the solidarity motivation with that of the pursuit of profit in their analyses, thus coming to distinguish three sectors in the economy: the private sector, the public sector and a third sector corresponding to the world of non-profit and voluntary service associations. Strongly supported by the Roman Catholic world (even mentioned in some papal encyclicals), this approach seeks to obtain for third-sector associations a privileged status, also for fiscal purposes. However, the clear-cut opposition between different motivations for human action (typical of the neoclassical theory, which isolates selfishness as the motivation of *homo oeconomicus*) was already being considered too simplistic in the classical tradition (including authors such as Genovesi, Verri or Beccaria, misleadingly quoted by Bruni and Zamagni), which, rather, proposed a varied simultaneous presence of interests and passions as drivers of human action.[10]

---

[10] Solidarity is present, to a greater or lesser extent, in the vast majority of human actions; were it not so, the market economy could not survive. Yet, very strong elements of solidarity constitute the foundation of criminal associations such as the mafia,

Various authors stress the presence of altruistic motivations in human action. Simon (1993) stresses that if altruism is defined as behaviour that, at the economic level, reduces individual well-being, while increasing that of others, then a society in which altruistic behaviour is widespread may turn out to be better geared for survival than a society in which selfishness is more widespread. Loyalty (in the sense of readiness to show altruistic behaviour towards other members of one's own community, for instance one's country, ethnic type or religious confession) in general constitutes an element of strength for the organization.

Analogous theses are proposed by a research stream developed among others by Putnam (1993, 2000), who considers civic traditions and 'social capital' as essential requisites for socially sustainable growth. Putnam's (2000) notion of social capital concerns relations among individuals, social connections, and the reciprocity and trust norms deriving from them. Putnam also distinguishes between 'bridging' and 'bonding' social capital: the former constitutes a civic virtue, while the latter may characterize closed communities (such as the family in amoral familism or the mafia). In his 1993 book, the fruit of two decades of research on the field, Putnam shows that the effects of the presence or absence of the civic virtues persist at length, to the extent of accounting for the different efficacy of regional governments in centre-north and southern Italy.

14.3   Income Inequalities as an Ethical Issue

In the preceding chapters we have often had occasion to consider theories of income distribution between the social classes of workers, capitalists and landlords. We touched on classical, marginalist and post-Keynesian theories. Here we will briefly consider some more recent works concerning income distribution between individuals, which intersect with the ethical debate on equality.[11]

First we have a series of researches on the construction of inequality indexes. The most famous index is still the one devised by Gini (1912), built in such a way as to vary continuously between 0 (absolute equality) and 1 (maximum inequality: all income or wealth are concentrated in a single individual). Other indexes are more rudimentary, but can readily

---

ndrangheta and camorra, and so-called amoral familism, which causes so much damage to the Italian economy. We may add that third-sector associations are not exempt from being involved in criminal actions.

[11] Among previous works, let us once again recall 'Pareto's law' concerning individual income distribution, originally (Pareto 1896) presented as corresponding to the distribution of individuals' original abilities, and subsequently interpreted as the result of stochastic processes (cf. the works collected in Corsi 1995).

be understood (share of income or wealth of the richest (or poorest) 1%, or 10%, or 0.1% of the population, and suchlike). Yet others focus attention on measuring poverty (defined in an absolute sense, as share of population subsisting with less than 1 dollar per day, or – more recently – 2 dollars per day; or in a relative sense, as share of the population with an income below 20%, or 25% or 10% of the average or median income).[12]

Major researches (it is worth specifically mentioning Deaton 1980) concern income and wealth distribution and their influences on consumption.[13]

Researches on inequality and poverty have been showing renewed vigour in recent years. Many researches bring to light a significant inversion in a trend: a period of gradual reduction of inequalities, in the first decades after the conclusion of the Second World War, has been followed by a decided change. Starting in the 1980s, with the neo-liberal shift in policy, we have an increase in the share of income and wealth of the richest 1% (and the 0.1%) and a decrease in the share not only of the poorest (with an increase in the area of poverty, in both the developing and developed countries), but also of the middle classes, such as to provoke a perceptible political reaction on the part of the latter.

A recent, massive book by Piketty (2013) has enjoyed vast circulation. Exploiting the results of a series of empirical researches (some of which recalled in §9.6), the book illustrates the historical evolution of distributive inequalities within the main countries and groups of countries, and proposes a theory of distribution based on the joint use of elements that, to tell the truth, appear incompatible: a post-Keynesian theory, the neo-classical aggregate production function, and a definition of capital (for the economy as a whole) that includes not only the value of machinery but also financial assets. Appreciated for its rich empirical information, Piketty's work prompts perplexities and criticisms at the theoretical level.[14]

We may consider as an aspect of the problem of distribution also the distance between countries, commonly attributed to development economics. Thanks to the availability of statistical data it is possible to

[12] The statistical debate on inequality indexes (currently utilized also for variables other than income and wealth) is on a vast scale, and also stresses the limits of the Gini index; variously detailed illustrations of this debate and bibliographical references are available in the main introductory statistics textbooks. Among other inequality indexes we may also recall the one proposed by Atkinson (1970), which measures the loss of social welfare compared to the level in a situation of income equality.
[13] For these researches Angus Deaton (b. 1945) won the Nobel Prize in 2015.
[14] Cf. for instance Rowthorn (2014).

analyse within the various countries the influence of income and wealth inequality – considering this element separately from average per capita income – on indicators of human development such as life expectancy at birth, infant mortality, illiteracy and educational levels, morbility, etc.[15]

The issue of income and wealth inequalities is a source of perennial controversies. The ideal of perfect equality, occasionally realized within small religious communities, is utilized in justification of dictatorial measures that lead to heavy suffering, as in the case of the China of the Cultural Revolution or the Cambodia of the Red Khmer. Contemplating the social differences of feudal times and the widespread idea, then as in classical antiquity, of innate differences in human beings that determine their social ranking and economic situation, Adam Smith (1776) maintains that human abilities are largely acquired. He also maintains that in a market economy the wages are reduced to a minimum due to the greater bargaining power of the capitalists and are differentiated according to five causes: 'first, the agreeableness or disagreeableness of the employments themselves, secondly, the easiness and cheapness, or the difficulty and expense of learning them; thirdly, the constancy or inconstancy of employment in them; fourthly, the small or great trust which must be reposed in those who exercise them; and, fifthly, the probability or improbability of success in them' (Smith 1776, p. 116). Within marginalist theory, the distributive variables correspond to the prices of factors of production reflecting their contribution to production and thus have optimal equilibrium values in competitive markets. On the other hand, heterodox theories of distribution tend to stress the role of unequal bargaining power between the social classes, or more generally social and cultural factors.[16]

Associated with the marginalist tradition, we have a widespread tendency to justify income inequalities as due to greater ability and/or diligence, and so to differences innate or acquired through investments in human capital. Criticisms of proposals of redistributive policies (mostly based on taxes and subsidies) rely on these theses, stressing that they imply a reduction of incentives to acquire new and better abilities and to increase the work effort, with the consequence of a possible loss in social production and wealth. Equality, which constitutes a principle endowed with strong attraction on the ethical plane, should rather have to do with conditions at the outset, and be realized as far as possible but always

---

[15] On these themes we may refer readers to the yearly reports of the World Bank and the yearly reports on human development of the UNDP (United Nations Development Programme).

[16] For instance, Sylos Labini (1972) stresses the importance of a politico-cultural element such as trade union combativeness.

taking into account the individual rights of freedom, which include defence of private property and hence the right of freely availing oneself of it, for instance leaving it as inheritance to one's relatives or friends (Nozik 1974). Obviously, in this way the descendants of the rich are advantaged in comparison with the descendants of the poor: equality of starting points is sacrificed to the safeguarding of property rights. As Sen (1992) remarks, income inequalities are often justified by resort to the principle of equality, but in different dimensions (individual rights, opportunities, etc.).[17] Choice of a single dimension within which to pursue equality, which distinguishes different approaches to the ethical issue, is bound to come into conflict with pursuit of equality in other dimensions.[18]

14.4 Welfare Economics

Welfare economics seeks to establish, within the framework of the marginalist theories of value and distribution, the optimum conditions for society as a whole. In this way, identifying what is good with the pursuit of the maximum possible collective well-being, ethics becomes an organic part of the theory of rational behaviour.

Obviously, as a first step it is necessary to establish what is meant by optimum: not the sum of individual utilities, as individual utilities are held not to be comparable. Pigou (1912) recalls the notion of net social product but develops it in a (Marshallian) context of partial equilibrium theory, which implies logical contradictions in the context of general equilibrium (cf. §5.3).

For the same reason, the attempt to aggregate consumer's surplus of individual agents into a collective consumer surplus is also to be rejected. In any case this measure, like any other aggregate measure of product or income, leaves open the problem of distribution among the individuals belonging to the society. In sum, the search for an aggregate measure

---

[17] Side by side with the '"wrong space"' argument', Sen (1992, p. 138) recalls 'the "incentive" argument' (which concerns the conflict between equality and efficiency) and the '"operational asymmetry" argument' (the opportuneness of an asymmetric treatment of individuals in relation to their different qualifications and abilities, but also to the assumed need for some persons to have more authority and power than others for the sound functioning of the social structure.

[18] 'For example, to demand equal entitlements to an extensive set of libertarian rights as a basic requirement of social organization (as is done by Nozik [1974]) has the consequence of undermining any insistence on the equality of income, wealth, or utility as well. Similarly, if equal incomes are to be achieved, then we could not insist also on equality in utilities, or rights, or freedoms' (Sen 1992, p. 131).

maximization of which should constitute the definition of a social optimum cannot lead to an acceptable result.

The social welfare function (proposed by Bergson [1938] and developed by Samuelson [1947], chapter 8) has as its arguments the individual welfare functions; the need to compare individual gains and losses to find the point of social optimum implies a cardinal notion of utility and the possibility of interpersonal comparisons.[19] Arrow rejects the cardinality assumption, probably because of the risk that the measures of individuals' cardinal utilities effected by some bureaucratic organism be taken as the basis for social choices. However, this rejection opens the way to Arrow's (1951a) theorem on the impossibility of a decisional procedure that respects some obvious conditions of consistency: a point to which we shall return later in this section.

If we abandon the road of the social welfare function, welfare economics must limit itself to searching out the conditions of Pareto optimum: a situation with respect to which improvement in the conditions of one or more individuals necessarily implies a worsening of the conditions of one or more others. The first fundamental theorem of welfare economics (Lerner 1934; Lange 1942; Arrow 1951a) demonstrates that each competitive equilibrium is a Pareto optimum.

To arrive at this result, the usual assumptions of general equilibrium marginalist theory are needed, and in particular that each individual only cares for his or her own well-being, basically identified with his or her own consumption. In other words, an egocentric economic agent is assumed, wholly indifferent to the conditions of others. This assumption, though systematically present in the whole of the marginalist tradition, appears all the more incongruous when dealing with social welfare.

Another problem is that multiple Pareto optima are possible. From the outset, welfare economics has recognized that each initial endowment of resources gives a different Pareto optimum. Furthermore, general equilibrium theory (as we saw in §6.3) also tells us that for a given original allocation of resources equilibriums are generally multiple. This means that in the absence of criteria for comparing the various equilibriums it is not possible to consider any Pareto optimum as optimal for society. Take, for example, a mountain range like the Dolomites: the peak of the lowest of the Five Towers (now alas only four) constitutes a point of local maximum, moving even ten metres from which the level decreases (quite rapidly in that case); but the Marmolada glacier, much lower than the peak of that mountain, is also higher than even the highest of the Five Towers.

---

[19] For an illustration of the debate on this topic, cf. Mueller (1989), pp. 373 ff.

Two other problems concern the assumption of the absence of externalities in production as in consumption, and the absence of public goods. This second aspect is generally considered in the framework of public choice theory, discussed in §8.7; here we will only recall the reference text on this subject, Samuelson (1958b), who analyses the determination of the optimal level of provision of a public good, namely a good the consumption of which is open to all (such as national defence).[20]

Externalities are involved in those cases in which decisions on production or consumption levels taken by the individual firm or consumer have positive or negative effects on others: for instance, pollution generated by a plant, which is all the greater the larger is its production, or the loss of sleep I might cause for my neighbours playing the piano (badly, alas) in my house (negative externalities). In the presence of positive effects external to the individual producer or consumer, the activity of production or consumption tends to come to a halt before reaching the socially optimal level; it is then opportune for the state to intervene with a subsidy, which will be all the greater the greater are the externalities. On the other hand, should negative effects external to the individual producer or consumer be present, production or consumption activity tends to be greater than the socially optimal level; it is therefore opportune to intervene with ad hoc taxes, which will be all the greater the greater are the external diseconomies.

The solution to the externality problem consisting in subsidies and taxes, proposed by Pigou (1912), was later on followed by Coase's (1960) proposal to define property rights appropriately, then leaving economic agents free to bargain and agree on contracts among themselves; in conditions of perfect competition this leads to the optimal solution. For instance, if we state the right for each citizen to the property of clean air, the polluting firm will have to acquire from the citizens damaged by the pollution the right to produce; on the other hand, if production is free to proceed with no concern for the consequences of pollution, it will be the damaged citizens who will have to pay the polluting firm for inducing it to limit pollution. Compared to the solution based on taxes and subsidies, this solution has the advantage of determining the degree of damage through the market, rather than relying on the evaluation of the public authorities. There is, however, an important limit, signalled by Coase himself: transaction costs may be high while,

---

[20] With respect to welfare economics, after producing various contributions also in this field, Samuelson ended up by considering it a cul-de-sac: cf. Hammond (2015) for a reconstruction of his trajectory.

moreover, in various cases the number of agents concerned may be too small to guarantee competitive conditions.[21]

In any case, the main problem lies in income distribution (which, in a competitive economy, depends on the original distribution of endowments among individuals). In fact, to any possible original distribution of resources there corresponds at least one Pareto equilibrium. This means, however, that any system of transfers through taxes and subsidies not affecting individuals' incentives to produce may attain a desired income distribution to which a Pareto optimum corresponds in a competitive economy. This, in essence, is the content of the 'second fundamental theorem of welfare economics'.

Let us recall that this theorem also holds under the customary restrictive hypotheses (selfish individuals, convexity of production and consumer's preference sets). The main problem is how to choose among different income distributions on the basis of objective criteria.

The first of such criteria, proposed by Kaldor (1939), consists in what is known as the compensation principle: one income distribution is preferable to another when anyone whose position is worsened may receive compensation from the individual who sees his or her situation improving, and who is still better off even after paying the compensation, to such an extent as to leave him or her indifferent between the old and the new situation. The compensation may be virtual: the fact that it is possible is sufficient to define which situation is better.

As a matter of fact, this principle avoids any ethical evaluation of the distribution: as Little (1950) remarks, an increase in income by a billion pounds for the richest person in the country accompanied by a loss of income of 900 pounds of the poorest million of the country's citizens, who thus are thrown into the streets, passes the compensation test (which, let us recall, may be virtual).

We may then think of seeking an evaluation on which, if not everyone, at least the majority of citizens may agree. However, the 'Condorcet paradox' (1785) had already indicated that even with only three individuals and three alternatives we may arrive at incoherent sequence (cyclical) results, with the first alternative preferred to the second, the second to the third and the third to the first. Arrow (1951a) generalizes Condorcet's reasoning, bringing it into the context of a general equilibrium marginalist theory: it is impossible to find a criterion for voting enabling us to select

---

[21] Cf. Arrow (quoted by Duffie and Sonnenschein 1989, p. 581): 'Markets for externalities usually involve small numbers of beggars and sellers ... Even if competitive equilibrium could be defined, there would be no force driving the system to it: we are in the realm of imperfect competition.'

a situation that respects some wholly reasonable conditions: universality (the chosen criterion must be applicable independently of individual preferences), Pareto consistency (if all prefer a given situation, it must turn out to be the preferred one also by applying the chosen criterion), independence from irrelevant alternatives, and exclusion of dictatorial choices in which the preferences of one agent systematically dominate those of the others.

Proceeding along this road, Sen (1970) proposes his thesis of 'the impossibility of the Paretian liberal'. In the example proposed by Sen, two individuals with opposite preferences attribute more importance to what the other does than to their own action: the maximum of social utility obtains if each of the two can impose his or her preferences on the other, but in such a case a basic liberal principle, namely that each may decide by him- or herself what he or she prefers, is violated.

Welfare economics thus reaches a substantially negative situation: notwithstanding the repeated references to the two fundamental theorems, there is no objective criterion allowing us to prefer one situation to another. The problem of aggregating individual preferences into a social welfare function remains unsolved, at the theoretical level. This outcome shows the limits of the marginalist approach, while it appears wholly consistent with the classical approach, which avoids the pretence of general theoretical constructions and leaves to the rhetoric of persuasion the choice among different policies affecting income distribution in different ways. Among other things, as we shall see more in detail in §14.5, together with income distribution other elements must be taken into account, such as the distribution of wealth, power and capabilities.

14.5   Equality of What? The Capabilities

Amartya Sen (b. 1933, Nobel Prize in 1998) was born to a well-off family in the part of India that was to become Pakistan soon after his birth (among his first reminiscences there is the violence of the period when the separation of the two nations occurred); he studied at Cambridge (UK) and subsequently in the United States, to become professor in India and at Harvard (where he held an economics and philosophy chair), master of Trinity College in Cambridge and engaged in various civic and social battles.

His research path touches various themes, on the borderline between the foundations of economics, development economics and ethics.[22] To

---

[22] Sen is the author of many texts, and has brought out a number of collections of his essays. See, for instance, Sen (1982, 1984, 2002a).

the first group belong his works on Arrow's impossibility theorem, i.e. the impossibility of deducing from individual preference rankings a social ranking according to 'democratic' criteria.[23] Within the second group we have his theory of famines, attributed – at least since the end of the Second World War – not to the scarcity of food but to its mal-distribution (or to a mal-distribution of the purchasing power to obtain it).[24] The third group includes writings considered in this section.

Sen (1991) proposes a moderate variant of consequentialism, noting that, even within it, elements of deontological evaluation are unavoidable. We can thus speak of a 'new consequentialism', developed between the end of the 1970s and the beginning of the 1980s, which breaks the rigid link with utilitarianism, stressing the distinction between rights, functions and capabilities.

In subsequent decades a wide-ranging view, richer and more complex than the one inherited from the classical or the marginalist traditions, has prevailed in the debate on the notion of rationality as in ethics. *The idea of justice* (Sen 2009) is a (provisional) point of arrival on a long research path.

Here we focus attention on the distinction between rights, functions, abilities and specifically the notion of capabilities, developed gradually and applied to a long series of issues. The notion is difficult to define: it concerns the field of action open to the individual or, in the negative case, the constraints that limit his or her freedom of action.[25] First among these constraints is undoubtedly income, or in the terms of traditional theory the budget constraint. However, together with it we find a varied set of elements that constrain the individual from acting freely in satisfying his or her needs and desires: from belonging to a disadvantaged gender, or race, or caste, or religious minority, or social stratum, to educational deficiencies and physical handicaps.

For all these and similar aspects we compare basic differences among individuals and hence in their needs. Any attempt to move towards equality, and even to define it, must take this fact into account. From it originates the notion of 'capabilities to function', which represents 'the various combinations of functioning (beings and doings) that the person can achieve. Capability is, thus, a set of vectors of functionings, reflecting the person's freedom to lead one type of life or another.'[26] Sen insists

---

[23] Some of these writings (including the one mentioned here on the theorem of the impossibility of the Pareto liberal) are collected in Sen (1982).

[24] Cf. Sen and Dréze (1990).

[25] 'The capability approach points to the need to examine freedom to achieve in general and capabilities to function in particular' (Sen 1992, p. 129).

[26] Sen (1992), p. 41. Sen adds in a footnote that it is quite difficult to define and concretely evaluate the vectors representing the capabilities. This does not stand in the way of an

repeatedly on the distinction between functionings and capabilities; for instance, 'functionings are constitutive of well-being, capability represents a person's freedom to achieve well-being' (Sen 1992, p. 45); 'In the space of functionings, any point represents an *n* tuple of functionings. Capability is a *set* of such functionings *n* tuples, representing the various alternative combinations of functionings from which the person can choose one combination' (Sen 1992, p. 50).

Compared with acquired abilities, which are important, as human capital theory stresses, the notion of capability concerns a prior aspect, including the ability to acquire and develop new abilities, to be kept distinct from abilities as such.

In the same way, we should distinguish between achieving something and the freedom to achieve (Sen 1992, pp. 8, 31, 39): for instance, to be able to walk in the mountains is positive in itself, even more than actually having the walk. On an analogous plane, Sen differentiates between '"*realized* agency success" and "*instrumental* agency success" ... distinguishing between "the occurrence of A" and "the occurrence of A through our own efforts"' (Sen 1992, p. 58), thus stressing the importance of active participation, together with that of obtaining a certain result.

The notion of capabilities influences the notion of equity in the distribution of income and wealth: a disadvantaged person, for instance because of a physical handicap, needs more resources for reducing his or her disadvantage in terms of freedom of action than a non-handicapped person. Judging equality within the space of primary goods, Sen (1992, p. 8) recalls, means assigning priority to the '*means* of freedom' over '*extents* of freedom'.

The development of this notion has various important implications. For instance, the aforementioned human development index (developed on the basis of the notion by Ul Haq at UNDP) is widely utilized for studying conditions in less developed countries and the nature of development processes in a more comprehensive way than traditionally done on the basis of the sole economic indicator of per capita income. The multidimensionality of the human development index impacts on development studies, making it increasingly difficult to limit analysis to strictly economic factors alone.

In some research fields, such as that of gender, the notion of capabilities needs to be supplemented with the distinction between 'heterogeneity' and 'difference'[27] – exogenous the former, endogenous the latter – in

---

extensive series of exercises of application of this notion: cf. for instance the essays collected in Comim *et al.* (2008).

[27] Cf. D'Ippoliti (2011).

relation to the variables usually considered in social and economic analyses. Obviously, in the context of an analysis of gender issues opposed to the neoclassical tradition, what is stressed is not aspects of innate gender differences (such as having or not having to go through pregnancy to have progeny), but diversities stemming from the law, social customs, culture and prejudices. In the opposition between innate heterogeneity and differences created by a society's culture and institutions lies the opposition between marginalist and classical-Smithian frameworks for the analysis of gender issues.[28] The importance of innate differences is, on the other hand, stressed by radical feminists such as Luce Irigaway, although they focus attention on the psychoanalytic aspects of the gender issue, leaving aside the economic and social ones. Nussbaum (1999) proposes reading gender issues with the key of Sen's capability approach. Of the many writings on the topic of gender we may mention a collection of essays by Bina Agarwal (2016). Attesting to the vitality of this research field, a continuous stream of articles has been appearing in the journal *Feminist Economics*.

In specific fields such as gender or race or caste issues, the notion of capabilities opens the way to consideration of what we might define intersecting inequalities, namely interrelation among various areas of inequality (income, wealth, power, health, education, social relations, etc.) and the cumulative processes that might stem from this. Hence the importance of active equilibrating policies, such as resort to quotas for university admissions or for management or political councils.

More generally, recognizing a plurality of objectives (or values) and of capabilities for each individual implies the need for rational and open debate on the choices to be made. Also, more than defining a perfectly just world and trying to achieve it (both impossible tasks), pursuit of justice implies the 'prevention of manifest injustice in the world'.[29]

On this count, the sustainability of economic development, which requires a sufficient degree of social cohesion, relies on containing inequalities (both in income and wealth and in the various elements mentioned earlier and included in the notion of capabilities)[30] and on a well-functioning political democracy that, through open comparison of the various interests and worldviews, guarantees a – continuously revised – choice of road in the interest of the common weal.[31]

---

[28] Cf. Roncaglia (2005b), chapter 4.
[29] Sen (2012), p. 106; cf. Sen (2009) for full argumentation of this thesis.
[30] The progressive extension of rights proposed by Bobbio (1994, pp. 152–3) runs in much the same direction.
[31] Cf. Sen (1999).

14.6   Conservation, Revolution or Reforms

In this chapter even more than in previous ones, other areas of research commonly separated from economics, such as moral philosophy, have been encroached upon. Indeed, subdividing the study of society and humans into separate fields is a relatively recent phenomenon (suffice it to recall that Adam Smith was in fact a professor of moral philosophy): perhaps unavoidable, but certainly not positive in all respects. Inevitably, borders are also crossed when we turn our attention to contributions concerning the themes of power and social structure.

Debate on these themes follows different streams. In studying the dualism between developed and developing countries, after a mass of works supporting the most varied theses, it is clear that neither inequalities in income distribution nor authoritarian political systems constitute prerequisites for sustainable economic growth; on the other hand, we may maintain that progress in conditions of civil life (education, hygienic-sanitary conditions, honesty and efficiency in public administration, public order and an efficient administration of justice, up to active participation of citizens in political life in a context of democratic freedoms) all constitute basic prerequisites for a socially sustainable process of economic development.[32]

There has been lively debate, especially within the countries concerned, on the conditions of the transition to the market economy of ex-planned economies in the 1990s. In this field there is an opposition between the thesis of 'big-bang' liberalization and the thesis of a gradual transition, relying on the previous construction of the institutional preconditions for the sound working of the markets (including, for instance, efficient surveillance and anti-trust authorities), accompanied by policies aiming at reducing the social costs of change. The substantive victory of neo-liberal views favours a 'primitive accumulation' based on privatization of public assets in conditions that come short of transparency and a level playing field, thus creating a new oligarchy closely connected to political power and the sudden shift from a markedly egalitarian to a markedly unequal distribution of income and wealth; simultaneously, the crisis of the state institutions implies a worsening of the services provided by the welfare state. The middle to low social strata are damaged, which favours the rise of populist political movements.

---

[32] As already recalled, an enormous mass of data, together with interesting analyses, is provided in the World Bank yearly reports and in the yearly *Human Development Report* of the United Nations Development Programme (UNDP). On the connection between civil and economic development, cf. Sylos Labini (2000).

In debate on the industrialized countries, analyses of the internal power structure (including studies on property and governance of firms: see e.g. Barca [1994]) are accompanied by analyses of social conflict (among which we may recall Dahrendorf [1959]). Then we have the (only apparently utopian) proposals concerning democracy within the firm: a particularly rich stream in Europe (for a survey see Tarantelli 1986), where we find debate on self-managed firms (Vanek 1970; Jossa 2010), profit-sharing (Meade 1972), trade union participation in the management of firms (Tarantelli 1978) and on the so-called labour army. This latter foreshadows among other things the participation of all citizens for a short span of their life in less qualified and most unpleasant jobs, a drastic reduction of the share of life devoted to work and a small guaranteed income for all citizens – all this with the aim of a drastic reduction of compulsory labour, to be equally distributed among all (Rossi 1946). Actual experiments of joint management of firms by workers and shareholders, with the participation of workers' representatives in the firm's surveillance council, have found widespread application in Germany, together with a system of publicly owned regional banks.

The difficulties encountered with these proposals concern not so much the possibility of activating them within a market economy as, rather, their incompatibility with maintaining competitiveness in the international markets in an increasingly integrated world economy. This takes us to the problem of globalization. Enormous progress in the transmission of information made possible by telecommunications, information and communication technology (ICT) developments and lower transport costs, with the growing integration of the financial markets and the essentially uncontrollable migratory flows – all this means that each country has increasingly to match up with the rest of the world. In a regime of imperfect but ever easier technological transfers, competition from low-wage economies exerts an increasing pressure on workers in more developed countries; initially mainly on low-qualification workers, but increasingly also on more highly qualified workers, with a general loss of ground on the part of the middle classes. The same holds for environmental and safety regulations, and indeed for taxes on firms: international competition implies in all these respects a downward realignment.

Here we find economic problems intersecting with demographic, political, social and cultural ones, confronting us with choices that have rather little to do with university economics textbooks but concern, among other things, the institutional set-up of the different countries and more generally the different forms that social coexistence assumes in cultural traditions as diverse as the European, American, Japanese, Arab, Indian and Chinese ones.[33]

The debate on the problems raised by the simultaneous presence of different cultural traditions and ethnic groups has a long history, which has seen gradual retrogression from the initial dominance of segregationist positions, justified with the need to defend the 'national spirit' if not with simple racism, in favour, at least in an initial stage, of integration policies. Subsequently the liberal thesis of 'multiculturalism' has prevailed, with acceptance of different traditions in one and the same area; their rights, in particular in the field of religious practices, are gradually being recognized. However, major contradictions emerge, especially when confronted with practices (from more or less rigid female segregation to infibulation of young girls) that are commonly felt to be contrary to fundamental human rights.[34]

A new boost to segregationist, if not explicitly racist, theses in the political debate has been favoured, in the recent period, by apparently unstoppable migratory flows (especially with the lack of coordination among the countries affected), far greater in dimension and impact – lacking adequate integration policies – than the sustainable migratory flows proposed as objective by Collier (2013). Confronted with the risks of a 'clash of civilizations' such as foreshadowed by Huntington (1996) referring mainly, but not only, to Islamic fundamentalism, the theses of cultural integration appear (unfortunately) to be losing ground, though based among other things on a fact of life, namely the simultaneous sense of belonging to many different, intersecting spheres (what Sen [2002b, p. 52] calls 'the unavoidable plurality of our freedoms'): from religion to political orientation, from sentiments to support for football teams.[35]

In the case of migratory flows, the religious, social and political tensions leading in various countries to the collapse of state institutions are accelerating a phenomenon that requires the ability to integrate economic with demographic, political, social and ethical analyses: a challenge that

---

[33] Dahrendorf (1995, p. 14) tellingly stresses, 'The task facing the First World in the coming next decade is that of squaring the circle connecting wealth creation, social cohesion, political freedom.' The neo-liberal solution, substantially adopted in the decade following publication of Dahrendorf's work, sacrifices the element of social cohesion (which Dahrendorf himself associates with the welfare state, together with a sufficiently egalitarian income distribution), leading to a political and social (but also economic) crisis of world dimensions, accompanied by the spread of populist movements; the problem thus remains unsolved.

[34] To have an idea of the complexity of the dilemma – being liberal implies not reacting to cannibals? – cf. Lukes (2003).

[35] A basic difference between policies based on multiculturalism and those based on integration is that between leaving ample room to confessional schools or, on the other hand, decidedly favouring (with adequate financing) public schools.

appears to find economic culture unprepared, and that also appears largely ineffective in face of the world economic crisis of the past years, let alone the crisis of the European Union. Some serious thinking about the basic characteristics of the different streams of economic research and their vicissitudes in our cultural history is, in this situation, an ethical priority.

In tackling this task, we need to take into account two difficulties that we hope are apparent in our reconstruction of the recent economics debate: the influence of economic and political power on the course of the debate, and the difficulties of open exchange of views among radically different approaches.

14.7   The Economists' Ethics

The physicist who studies the structure of matter, and in general his or her colleagues engaged in the various areas of physical and natural sciences, may nourish a passion for the subject of their studies and for the theories they or their masters and pupils formulate; however, in choosing the initial line of research their class or social stratum interests are not directly involved. In the economic and social field, instead, the researcher's vision is inevitably affected by his or her position in society.

As we have seen, different approaches exist: classical, marginalist and Keynesian, not reducible to a common denominator, with the same notions taking on different meanings in each of them. Each approach leads to interpreting reality from a different viewpoint, stressing some elements rather than others; for instance, supporting or criticizing the tenet of a re-equilibrating role of the market, or of the existence of an optimal income distribution. The results of economic research are not neutral with respect to the economic interests of class and social strata.

Thus we have seen the role of some foundations in financing research groups oriented in one direction rather than another (as with the naissance of the monetarist school in Chicago). In general, in the economic field as in the wider field of the social sciences, the choices to finance this or that research stream often do not correspond to a scientific evaluation but, rather, to a politico-cultural evaluation. Thus, what should be a level-playing field for scientific debate among the various approaches turns out to be unbalanced by the choices of those with more financial means.

This is apparent in the studies on global warming: the amount of financing going to critics of this thesis (also by major oil companies) is decidedly greater than the financing going to its supporters (thus favouring some delay in response to fight the phenomenon). Something analogous seems to be happening in the case of neo-liberalism: an orientation whose theses appear on the whole less solid than might be suggested by their diffusion or awards of Nobel Prizes. The foundation of this success is to be found more in dominance than in cultural hegemony: a dominance stemming from connections with economic powers that in various ways influence research and university life. In Western Europe this latter aspect is reinforced by research evaluation criteria imposed from above, which penalize both heterodox theories and the history of economic thought, essential for an understanding of the existence of different approaches and thus of the erroneousness of reducing all traditions to the currently dominant one. These are not insurmountable barriers: as in oligopoly theory, we are confronted with barriers to entry of different heights (for academic careers as for research funds) for those in the orthodox or the heterodox field. This height changes over time; in the recent stage it has been increasing.

Differences in theoretical approach accompany differences in politico-cultural orientation (even if the two are better kept distinct). It is rather difficult to specify them quite distinctly, with a range of positions going from the right to the left; however, some elements appear sufficiently clear. A basic point of reference concerns the notions of equality and inequality, though – as we have seen – these are multidimensional notions, and although absolute equality turns out to be a very dangerous utopia. As summarized by Bobbio (1994, p. 132) in a book in which he insists on the lasting usefulness of the distinction between right and left, 'Egalitarian are those who tend to attenuate the differences, un-egalitarian those who tend to accentuate them'. 'The pressure towards ever greater equality among humans is ... irresistible', Bobbio (1994, p. 152) adds, while leaving economic inequalities to a secondary role and stressing those concerning social class, race and gender. Bobbio identifies the 'process of civilization' with this tendency to a reduction of inequalities; he stresses that this tendency is not necessitated, but only possible, thereby admitting both the possibility of stages of regression, and the need for active engagement for its realization.

As in the case of the debate on ethics, once we have accepted that the various elements in play do not allow for univocal evaluations, we have to recognize the need for open exchange among the various positions: a rational exchange, according to rules of rhetorical exchange such as those holding in the debate between prosecutor and defence in tribunals. The researcher's ethic concerns not only aspects such as plagiarism, 'adjusted' data or, more recently, 'citation rings' to improve bibliometric indicators; it also concerns openness to a debate on a footing of parity with those holding different views.

Notwithstanding the widespread geo-centrism (in the sense of a tendency to reduce all cultures to one's own), open debate among supporters of different approaches is possible provided that each be able to put him- or herself in the other's clothes. We may say that 'the economist is useful when ethically engaged in the pursuit of the common weal' (Roncaglia 2016b, p. 8), but the problem remains of how to define the 'common weal', it too a multidimensional notion that must take into account the existence of conflicts of interests within society.[36] Economists have an active role in society, and each of us interprets it according to our own convictions, reached on the basis of an arduous pursuit of logical rigour and realism; each of us has the duty to state our results in the clearest possible way, without compromising with fashions or the powers that be; at the same time each of us has the duty to be open to debate and criticism. For this reason, the study of the other economists' thought – the study of the history of thought, ancient and recent – must remain a central aspect of our activity.

[36] On the notion of common weal cf. Roncaglia (2015b).

References

[The year after the author's name indicates the original date of publication. The original date of writing is occasionally indicated in square brackets. Page references in the text refer to the last of the editions cited below not in brackets. When this is not an English edition, the translation of the passages cited in the text is mine.]

Abramovitz, M. 1989. *Thinking about growth and other essays*. Cambridge: Cambridge University Press.

Acemoglu, D. 2008. 'Oligarchic versus democratic societies'. *Journal of the European Economic Association* 6: 1–44.

Acemoglu, D., Cantoni, D. and Johnson, J. A. 2011. 'The consequences of radical reform: the French Revolution'. *American Economic Review* 101: 3286–307.

Acemoglu, D. and Robinson, J. A. 2006. *Economic origins of dictatorship and democracy*. Cambridge: Cambridge University Press.

Adelman, I. 1961. *Theories of economic growth and development*. Stanford, CA: Stanford University Press.

Adelman, I. 1988. 'Confessions of an incurable romantic'. *BNL Quarterly Review* 41 (164): 391–411.

Adelman, J. 2013. *Worldly philosopher: the odyssey of Albert O. Hirschman*. Princeton, NJ: Princeton University Press.

Adelman, M. A. 1972. *The world petroleum market*. Baltimore, MD: Johns Hopkins University Press.

Adelman, M. A. 1995. *The genie out of the bottle: world oil since 1970*. Cambridge, MA: MIT Press.

Aftalion, A. 1913. *Les crises périodiques de surproduction*. Paris: Rivière.

Agarwal, B. 2016. *Gender challenges*. 3 vols. Oxford: Oxford University Press.

Aghion, P. and Howitt, P. 1992. 'A model of growth through creative destruction'. *Econometrica* 60: 323–51.

Aghion, P. and Howitt, P. 1998. *Endogenous growth theory*. Cambridge, MA: MIT Press.

Ahlborn, C. and Grave, C. 2006. 'Walter Eucken and ordoliberalism: an introduction from a consumer welfare perspective'. *Competition Policy International* 2 (2): 197–217.

Akerlof, G. 1970. 'The market for lemons'. *Quarterly Journal of Economics* 84: 488–500.

Akerlof, G. 1980. 'A theory of social custom, of which unemployment might be a consequence'. *Quarterly Journal of Economics* 94: 749–75.

377

Akerlof, G. 2007. 'The missing motivation in macroeconomics'. *American Economic Review* 97: 3–36.

Akerlof, G. and Kranton, R. 2000. 'Economics and identity'. *Quarterly Journal of Economics* 115: 715–53.

Alchian, A. 1950. 'Uncertainty, evolution and economic theory'. *Journal of Political Economy* 58: 211–22.

Alchian, A. and Woodward, S. 1988. 'The firm is dead; long live the firm: a review of Oliver E. Williamson's *The economic institutions of capitalism*'. *Journal of Economic Literature* 26: 65–79.

Alesina, A. and Ardagna, S. 2009. 'Large changes in fiscal policy: taxes versus spending'. NBER Working Paper 15438. Cambridge, MA: National Bureau of Economic Research.

Alesina, A., Spolaore, E. and Wacziarg, R. 2000. 'Economic integration and political disintegration'. *American Economic Review* 90: 1276–96.

Allais, M. 1947. *Economie et intérêt*. 2 vols. Paris: Imprimerie Nationale.

Allais, M. 1953. 'Le comportement de l'homme rationnel devant de le risque: critique des postulats et axiomes de l'école americaine'. *Econometrica* 21: 503–46.

Almeida, A. and Goodhart, C. 1998. 'Does adoption of inflation targets affect central bank behavior?' *BNL Quarterly Review*, Supplement to n. 204, *Globalization and stability of financial markets*, 19–107.

Amable, B. 2003. *The diversity of modern capitalism*. Oxford: Oxford University Press.

Amin, S. 1974. *The accumulation of capital on a world scale*. New York: Monthly Review Press.

Amin, S. 1994. *Unequal development: an essay on the social formations of peripheral capitalism*. New York: Monthly Review Press.

Andrews, P. W. S. 1993. *The economics of competitive enterprise: selected essays*. Ed. by F. S. Lee and P. E. Earl. Aldershot: Edward Elgar.

Arestis, P. 2009. 'New consensus macroeconomics: a critical appraisal'. *Working Paper* 564. Annandale-on-Hudson: Levy Economics Institute.

Arestis, P. and Sawyer, M. 2008. 'A critical reconsideration of the foundations of monetary policy in the new consensus macroeconomics framework'. *Cambridge Journal of Economics* 32: 761–79.

Ark, B. van, ed. 1997. *Economic growth in the long run: a history of empirical evidence*. 3 vols. Cheltenham: Edward Elgar.

Arrighi, G. 1978. *The geometry of imperialism*. New York: Verso.

Arrighi, G. 2007. *Adam Smith in Beijing: lineages of the twenty-first century*. New York: Verso.

Arrow, K. J. 1951a. *Social choice and individual values*. New York: John Wiley & Sons.

Arrow, K. J. 1951b. 'Alternative approaches to the theory of choice in risk-taking situations'. *Econometrica* 19: 404–37.

Arrow, K. J. 1962. 'The economic implications of learning by doing'. *Review of Economic Studies* 26: 155–73.

Arrow, K. J. 1983–5. *Collected papers*. 6 vols. Boston: Belknap Press of Harvard University Press (vol. 1, *Social choice and justice*; vol. 2, *General equilibrium*; vol.

3, *Individual choice under certainty and uncertainty*; vol. 4, *The economics of information*; vol. 5, *Production and capital*; vol. 6, *Applied economics*).

Arrow, K. J. and Debreu, G. 1954. 'Existence of an equilibrium for a competitive economy'. *Econometrica* 22: 265–90.

Arrow, K. J. and Hahn, F. H. 1971. *General competitive analysis*. San Francisco: Holden-Day.

Arrow, K. J. and Levhari, D. 1969. 'Uniqueness of the internal rate of return with variable life of investment'. *Economic Journal* 79: 560–66.

Arthur, B. 1994. *Increasing returns and path dependence in the economy*. Ann Arbor: University of Michigan Press.

Asimakopulos, T. 1986. 'Harrod and Domar on dynamic economics'. *BNL Quarterly Review* 39(158): 275–90.

Asimakopulos, T. 1991. *Keynes's general theory and accumulation*. Cambridge: Cambridge University Press.

Aspromourgos, T. 1986. 'On the origins of the term "neoclassical"'. *Cambridge Journal of Economics* 10: 265–70.

Aspromourgos, T. 2009. *The science of wealth: Adam Smith and the framing of political economy*. Abington: Routledge.

Aston, T. H. and Philpin, C. H. E., eds. 1976. *The Brenner debate: agrarian class struggle and economic development in pre-industrial Europe*. Cambridge: Cambridge University Press.

Athey, S. and Imbens, J. W. 2017. 'The state of applied econometrics: causality and policy evaluations'. *Journal of Economic Perspectives* 31: 3–32.

Atkinson, A. 1970. 'On the measurement of inequality'. *Journal of Economic Theory* 2: 244–63.

Atkinson, A. 2009. 'Economics as a moral science'. *Economica* 76: 791–804.

Atkinson, A., Piketty, T. and Saez, E. 2011. 'Top incomes in the long run of history'. *Journal of Economic Literature* 49: 3–71.

Aumann, R. 1966. 'Existence of competitive equilibria in markets with a continuum of traders'. *Econometrica* 34: 1–17.

Axelrod, R. 1984. *The evolution of cooperation*. New York: Basic Books.

Babbage, C. 1832. *On the economy of machinery and manufactures*. London: Charles Knight; reprint of the IV ed. (1835), New York: M. Kelley, 1963.

Backhouse, R. E. 2014a. 'Paul A. Samuelson's move to MIT'. *History of Political Economy* 46 (Supplement): 60–77.

Backhouse, R. E. 2014b. 'MIT and the other Cambridge'. *History of Political Economy* 46 (Supplement): 252–70.

Backhouse, R. E. 2017. *Founder of modern economics: Paul A. Samuelson, vol. 1, Becoming Samuelson, 1945–1948*. Oxford: Oxford University Press.

Bain, J. S. 1956. *Barriers to new competition*. Cambridge, MA: Harvard University Press.

Bair, J. 2009. 'Taking aim at the New International Economic Order'. In Mirowski and Plehve, pp. 347–85.

Baker, S.R., Bloom, N. and Davis, S.J. 2016. 'Measuring economic policy uncertainty'. *Quarterly Journal of Economics* 131: 1593–1636.

Banerjee, A. and Duflo, E. 2011. *Poor economics*. New York: Public Affairs.

Baran, P. A. 1957. *The political economy of growth.* New York: Monthly Review Press.

Baran, P. A. and Sweezy, P. M. 1966. *Monopoly capital: an essay on the American economic and social order.* New York: Monthly Review Press.

Baranzini, M. 2005. 'Modigliani's life-cycle theory of savings fifty years later'. *BNL Quarterly Review* 58 (233–4): 109–72.

Barberis, N.C. 2013. 'Thirty years of prospect theory in economics: a review and assessment'. *Journal of Economic Perspectives* 27: 173–96.

Barca, F. 1994. *Imprese in cerca di padrone: proprietà e controllo nel capitalismo italiano.* Rome and Bari: Laterza.

Barone, E. 1908. 'Il ministro della produzione nello stato collettivista'. *Giornale degli economisti* 2: 267–93 and 391–414.

Barro, R. J. 1974. 'Are government bonds net wealth?'. *Journal of Political Economy* 82: 1095–117.

Barro, R. J. and Grossman, H. I. 1971. 'A general disequilibrium model of income and employment'. *American Economic Review* 61: 82–93.

Barro, R. J. and Redlick, C. J. 2011. 'Macroeconomic effects from government purchases and taxes'. *Quarterly Journal of Economics* 126: 51–102.

Baumol, W. J. 1959. *Business behaviour, value and growth.* New York: Harcourt & C.

Baumol, W. J. and Bowen, W. 1966. *Performing arts, the economic dilemma: a study of problems common to theater, opera, music, and dance.* New York: Twentieth Century Fund.

Baumol, W. J., Panzar, J. C. and Willig, R. D. 1982. *Contestable markets and the theory of industry structure.* San Diego: Harcourt Brace Jovanovich.

Becker, G. 1974. 'A theory of social interactions'. *Journal of Political Economy* 81: 813–46.

Becker, G. 1996. *Accounting for tastes.* Cambridge, MA: Harvard University Press.

Becker, G. 1998. *L'approccio economico al comportamento umano.* Ed. by A. Cigno. Bologna: il Mulino.

Benes, J., Chauvet, M., Kamenik, D., Kumhof, M., Laxton, D., Mursula, S. and Sebody, J. 2015. 'The future of oil: geology versus technology'. *International Journal of Forecasting* 31(1): 207–21.

Benini, R. 1907. 'Sull'uso delle formule empiriche nell'economia applicata'. *Giornale degli economisti*, II series, 35: 1053–63.

Bergson, A. 1938. 'A reformulation of certain aspects of welfare economics'. *Quarterly Journal of Economics* 52: 310–34.

Berle, A. A. and Means, G. 1932. *The modern corporation and private property.* New York: The Commerce Clearing House.

Berlin, I. 1958. *Two concepts of liberty.* Oxford: Oxford University Press.

Berlin, I. 2002. *Liberty.* Ed. by H. Hardy. Oxford: Oxford University Press.

Bernstein, E. 1899. *Die Voraussetzungen des Sozialismus und die Aufgaben der Sozialdemokratie.* Stuttgart: Dietz. Italian transl., *Socialismo e socialdemocrazia.* Bari: Laterza, 1968.

Beveridge, W. H. 1942. *Social insurance and allied services: the Beveridge Report in brief.* London: HMSO.

Beveridge, W. H. 1944. *Full employment in a free society: a report.* London: Allen & Unwin.

Bhaduri, A. 1970. 'A physical analogue to the reswitching problem'. *Oxford Economic Papers* 22: 148–55.

Bharadwaj, K. 1970. 'On the maximum number of switches between two production systems'. *Schweizerische Zeitschrift für Volkswirtschaft und Statistik* 106: 409–29.

Bharadwaj, K. 1978. *Classical political economy and rise to dominance of supply and demand theories.* Calcutta: Orient Longman.

Bhaskar, R. 1978. *A realist theory of science.* Hemel Hempstead: Harvester Press.

Biasco, S. 1987. 'Currency cycles and the international economy'. *BNL Quarterly Review* 40(160): 31–60.

Biasco, S. 1988. 'Dynamic and incapsulating processes in the generation of the world demand'. *BNL Quarterly Review* 41(165): 179–215.

Binmore, K. 1987. 'Modeling rational players: Part I'. *Economics and Philosophy* 3: 179–214.

Black, D. 1958. *The theory of committees and elections.* Cambridge: Cambridge University Press.

Black, F. and Scholes, M. 1973. 'The pricing of options and corporate liabilities'. *Journal of Political Economy* 81: 637–54.

Blair, J. 2009. 'Taking aim at the new international economic order'. In Mirowski and Plehwe, 2009, pp. 347–85.

Blanchard, O. and Leigh, D. 2013. *Growth forecast errors and fiscal multipliers.* Washington: IMF Working Paper.

Blaug, M. 1980. *The methodology of economics.* Cambridge: Cambridge University Press.

Bleichrodt, H. and Wakker, P. P. 2015. 'Regret theory: a bold alternative to the alternatives'. *Economic Journal* 125: 493–512.

Blyth, M. 2013. *Austerity: the history of a dangerous idea.* Oxford: Oxford University Press.

Bobbio, N. 1994. *Destra e sinistra: ragioni e significati di una distinzione politica.* Rome: Donzelli; IV ed., 2004.

Boggio, L. and Seravalli, G. 2003. *Lo sviluppo economico: fatti, teorie, politiche.* Bologna: il Mulino.

Böhm-Bawerk, E. von. 1889. *Kapital und Kapitalzins. zweite Abteilung: Positive Theorie des Kapitales.* Innsbruck: Verlag der Wagner'schen Universitäts-Buchhandlung. Italian transl., *La teoria positiva del capitale.* Turin: Utet, 1968.

Böhme, R., Christin, N., Edelman, B. and Moore, T. 2015. 'Bitcoin: economics, technology, and governance'. *Journal of Economic Perspectives* 29: 213–38.

Boianovsky, M. and Hoover, K. D. 2014. 'In the kingdom of Solovia: the rise of growth economics at MIT, 1956–70'. *History of Political Economy* 46 (Supplement): 198–228.

Box, G. E. P. and Jenkins, J. M. 1970. *Time series analysis: forecasting and control.* San Francisco: Holden-Day.

Boyer, R. 1990. *The regulation school: a critical introduction.* New York: Columbia University Press.

Breglia, A. 1965. *Reddito sociale.* Rome: Edizioni dell'Ateneo.

Brenner, R. 1978. 'Dobb on the transition from feudalism to capitalism'. *Cambridge Journal of Economics* 2: 121–40.

Brennetot, A. 2014. 'Geohistory of neoliberalism'. *Cybergeo: European Journal of Geography*, art. 677. www.cybergeo.revues.org/26324.

Brundtland, G. H., ed. 1987. *Our common future* (Brundtland Report, World Commission on Environment and Development). Oxford: Oxford University Press.

Bruni, L. and Zamagni, S. 2004. *Economia civile: efficienza, equità e pubblica felicità*. Bologna: il Mulino.

Buchanan, J. M. 1986. 'Better than plowing'. *BNL Quarterly Review* 39(159): 359–75.

Buchanan, J. M. 1989. *Stato, mercato e libertà*. Bologna: il Mulino.

Buchanan, J. M. and Tullock, G. 1962. *The calculus of consent: logical foundations of constitutional democracy*. Ann Arbor: University of Michigan Press.

Burmeister, E. 1974. 'Synthesizing the neo-Austrian and alternative approaches to capital theory: a survey'. *Journal of Economic Literature* 12: 413–56.

Burmeister, E. 1977. 'On the social significance of the reswitching controversy'. *Revue d'économie politique* 87: 330–50.

Burmeister, E. 1979. 'Professor Pasinetti's "unobtrusive postulate", regular economies, and the existence of a well-behaved production function'. *Revue d'économie politique* 89: 644–52.

Button, K. 2015. 'A book, the application, and the outcomes: how right was Alfred Kahn in 'The economics of regulation' about the effects of the deregulation of the US domestic airline market?'. *History of Political Economy* 47: 1–39.

Caldwell, B. J. 2004. *Hayek's challenge: an intellectual biography of F. A. Hayek*. Chicago: University of Chicago Press.

Caldwell, B. J. 2011. 'The Chicago school, Hayek, and neoliberalism'. In van Horn *et al.*, pp. 301–34.

Camerer, C., Loewenstein, G. and Prelec, D. 2005. 'Neuroeconomics: how neuroscience can inform economics'. *Journal of Economic Literature* 43: 9–64.

Cantillon, R. 1755. *Essai sur la nature du commerce en general*. London: Fletcher Gyles. Repr. with an English transl. ed. by H. Higgs. London: Macmillan 1931; repr. New York: M. Kelley 1964.

Carlin, W. and Soskice, D. 1990. *Macroeconomics and the wage bargain*. Oxford: Oxford University Press.

Casadio Tarabusi, E. and Guarini, G. 2016. 'Level dependence of the adjustment for unbalance and inequality for the Human Development Index'. *Social Indicators Research* 126: 527–53.

Cassel, G. 1918. *Theoretische Sozialökonomie*. Leipzig: C. F. Winter, English transl., *Theory of social economy*. London: T. F. Unwin 1923.

Chafuen, A. A. 1986. *Christians for freedom: Late-Scholastic economics*. San Francisco: Ignatius Press.

Chamberlin, E. 1933. *The theory of monopolistic competition*. Cambridge, MA: Harvard University Press.

Chandler, A. D. 1990. *Scale and scope: the dynamics of industrial capitalism*. Cambridge, MA: Harvard University Press.

Chenery, H. B. 1955. 'The role of industrialization in development programs'. *American Economic Review* 45: 40–57.

Chenery, H. B. 1960. 'Patterns of industrial growth'. *American Economic Review* 50: 624–54.

Cherrier, B. 2014. 'Towards a history of economics at MIT, 1940–72'. *History of Political Economy* 46 (Supplement): 15–44.

Chilosi, A., ed. 1979. *Kalecki*. Bologna: il Mulino.

Chrystal, K. A., ed. 1990. *Monetarism*. 2 vols. Aldershot: Edward Elgar.

Ciocca, P. and Rinaldi, R. 1997. 'L'inflazione in Italia, 1914–20. Considerazioni a margine della tesi di laurea di Piero Sraffa'. *Rivista di storia economica* 13: 3–40.

Cipolletta, I. 1992. *Congiuntura economica e previsione*. Bologna: il Mulino.

Clapham, J. A. 1922. 'Of empty economic boxes'. *Economic Journal* 32: 305–14.

Clark, J. M. 1940. 'Toward a concept of workable competition'. *American Economic Review* 30: 241–56.

Clower, R. W. 1965. 'The Keynesian counter-revolution: a theoretical appraisal'. In F. H. Hahn and F. P. R. Brechling (eds.), *The theory of interest rates*. London: Macmillan, pp. 103–25.

Coase, R. H. 1937. 'The nature of the firm'. *Economica* 4; repr. in Coase 1988, pp. 33–55.

Coase, R. H. 1960. 'The problem of social cost'. *Journal of Law and Economics* 3: 1–44; repr. in Coase 1988, pp. 95–156.

Coase, R. H. 1988. *The firm, the market and the law*. Chicago: University of Chicago Press.

Coddington, A. 1983. *Keynesian economics: the search for first principles*. London: Allen & Unwin.

Colletti, L. 1968. *Il marxismo ed Hegel*. Bari: Laterza.

Collier, P. 2013. *Exodus: how migration is changing our world*. Oxford: Oxford University Press.

Comim, F., Qizilbash, M. and Alkire, S., eds. 2008. *The capability approach: concepts, measures and applications*. Cambridge: Cambridge University Press.

Condorcet, J.-A.-N., marquis de Caritat 1785. *Essai sur l'application de l'analyse à la probabilité des decisions rendues à la pluralité des voix*. Paris: Imprimerie Royale.

Conlisk, J. 1996. 'Why bounded rationality?'. *Journal of Economic Literature* 34: 669–700.

Corsi, M., ed. 1995. *Le diseguaglianze economiche*. Turin: Giappichelli.

Costa, S. 2004. *Antitrust e software: il caso Microsoft*. Rome: Carocci.

Crew, M.A. and Kleindorfer P.R. 2002. 'Regulatory economics: twenty years of progress?'. *Journal of Regulatory Economics* 21: 5–22.

Croce, B. and Einaudi, L. 1957. *Liberismo e liberalismo*. Ed. by P. Solari. Milan and Naples: Riccardo Ricciardi.

Cross, R. 1982. 'The Duhem-Quine thesis, Lakatos and the appraisal of theories in macroeconomics'. *Economic Journal* 92: 320–40.

Cyert, R., Simon, H. and Trow, D. B. 1956. 'Observation of a business decision'. *Journal of Business* 29: 237–48.

Dahrendorf, R. 1959. *Class and class conflict in industrial society*. London: Routledge & Kegan Paul.

Dahrendorf, R. 1995. *Quadrare il cerchio*. Rome and Bari: Laterza.

Dallera, G. 2013. 'La "scuola" italiana di scienza delle finanze'. *Moneta e Credito* 66(161): 45–93.

Darwin, C. 1859. *On the origin of species by means of natural selection.* London: Murray.

Darwin, C. 1871. *The descent of man, and selection in relation to sex.* London: Murray.

Dasgupta, P. S. and Heal, G. M. 1979. *Economic theory and exhaustible resources.* Cambridge: Cambridge University Press.

David, P. 1985. 'Clio and the economics of QWERTY'. *American Economic Review, Papers and Proceedings* 75: 332–7.

Davidson, P. 1972. *Money and the real world.* London: Macmillan.

Davidson, P. 2007. *John Maynard Keynes.* Houndmills: Palgrave Macmillan.

Deaton, A. 1980. *Economics and consumer behavior.* New York: Cambridge University Press.

Deaton, A. 1997. *The analysis of household surveys: a microeconometric approach to development policy.* Baltimore, MD: Johns Hopkins University Press.

Debreu, G. 1959. *Theory of value: an axiomatic analysis of economic equilibrium.* Cowles Foundation Monograph n. 17. New Haven, CT: Yale University Press.

Debreu, G. 1974. 'Excess demand functions'. *Journal of Mathematical Economics* 1: 15–23.

de Cecco, M. 1993. 'Piero Sraffa's "Monetary inflation in Italy during and after the war": an introduction'. *Cambridge Journal of Economics* 17: 1–5.

De Clippel, J. 2008. 'Equity, envy and efficiency under asymmetric information'. *Economics Letters* 99: 265–7.

de Finetti, B. 1930. 'Fondamenti logici del ragionamento probabilistico'. *Bollettino dell'Unione matematica italiana* 9: 258–61.

de Finetti, B. 1931. *Probabilismo: saggio critico sulla teoria delle probabilità e sul valore della scienza.* Napoli: Perrella.

de Finetti, B. 1937. 'La prévision, ses lois logiques, ses sources subjectives'. *Annales de l'Institut Henri Poincaré* 7: 1–68.

de Finetti, B. 1974. 'The value of studying subjective evaluations of probability'. In C.-A. S. von Holstein (ed.), *The concept of probability in psychological experiments.* Dordrecht-Boston: Reidel.

Delli Gatti, D., Gaffeo, E., Gallegati, M., Giulioni, G. and Palestrini, A. 2008. *Emergent macroeconomics: an agent-based approach to business fluctuations.* New York: Springer Science+Business Media.

Denison, E. F. 1967. *Why growth rates differ: post-war experience in nine Western countries.* Washington, DC: Brookings Institution.

Desai, M. 1989. 'The scourge of monetarism: Kaldor on monetarism and on money'. In Lawson *et al.*, pp. 171–82.

De Vivo, G. 2017. *Nella bufera del Novecento: Antonio Gramsci e Piero Sraffa tra lotta politica e teoria critica.* Rome: Castelvecchi.

Diggins, J. P. 1999. *Thorstein Veblen, theorist of the leisure class.* Princeton, NJ: Princeton University Press.

D'Ippoliti, C. 2011. *Economics and diversity.* Abingdon: Routledge.

Dobb, M. 1928. *Russian economic development since the revolution.* London: Routledge.

Dobb, M. 1946. *Studies in the development of capitalism.* London: Routledge.

Dobb, M. 1955. *On economic theories and socialism*. London: Routledge.

Dobb, M. 1973. *Theories of value and distribution since Adam Smith*. Cambridge: Cambridge University Press.

Dobb, M., Sweezy, P., Takabashi, H., Hilton, R. and Hill, C. 1954. *The transition from feudalism to capitalism: a symposium*. New York: Arena Publications.

Domar, E. D. 1946. 'Capital expansion, rate of growth and employment'. *Econometrica* 14: 137–47.

Donaldson B. and Storeygard, A. 2016. 'The view from above: applications of satellite data in economics'. *Journal of Economic Perspectives* 30: 171–98.

Donzelli, F. 1986. *Il concetto di equilibrio nella teoria economica neoclassica*. Rome: NIS.

Donzelli, F. 1988. 'Introduzione'. In F.A. von Hayek, *Conoscenza, mercato, pianificazione*. Bologna: il Mulino, pp. 7–91.

Dorfman, R. 1991. 'Review article: economic development from the beginning to Rostow'. *Journal of Economic Literature* 29: 573–91.

Dorfman, R., Samuelson, P. and Solow, R. 1958. *Linear programming and economic analysis*. New York: McGraw-Hill.

Dosi, G. 1984. *Technical change and industrial transformation*. London: Macmillan.

Dosi, G., Freeman, C., Nelson, R., Silverberg, G. and Soete, L., eds. 1988. *Technical change and economic theory*. London: Pinter.

Dosi, G. and Roventini, A. 2017. 'Agent-based macroeconomics and classical political economy: some Italian roots'. *Italian Economic Journal* 3: 261–83.

Dougherty, C. R. S. 1972. 'On the rate of return and the rate of profit'. *Economic Journal* 82: 1324–50.

Downs, A. 1957. *An economic theory of democracy*. New York: Harper and Row.

Downs, A. 1967. *Inside bureaucracy*. Boston: Little, Brown.

Drèze, J. and Sen, A., eds. 1990. *The political economy of hunger*. 3 vols. Oxford: Clarendon Press.

Duffie, D. and Sonnenschein, H. 1989. 'Arrow and general equilibrium theory'. *Journal of Economic Literature* 27: 565–98.

Dunlop, J. T. 1938. 'The movement of real and money wage rates'. *Economic Journal* 48: 413–34.

Eatwell, J. 1975. 'Mr. Sraffa's standard commodity and the rate of exploitation'. *Quarterly Journal of Economics* 89: 543–55.

Eatwell, J., Milgate M. and Newman P., eds. 1987. *The new Palgrave: a dictionary of economics*. 4 vols. London: Macmillan.

Edwards, W. 1961. 'Behavioral decision theory'. *Annual Review of Psychology* 12: 473–98.

Eggertsson, T. 1990. *Economic behavior and institutions*. Cambridge: Cambridge University Press.

Egidi, M. and Rizzello, S., eds. 2004. *Cognitive economics*. 2 vols. Cheltenham: Elgar.

Eichner, A. S. 1976. *The megacorp and oligopoly*. Cambridge: Cambridge University Press.

Ellsberg, D. 1961. 'Risk, ambiguity and the Savage axioms'. *Quarterly Journal of Economics* 75: 643–69; repr. in Gärdenfors and Sahlin 1988, pp. 245–69.

Emmet, R.B. 2011. 'Sharpening tools in the workshop'. In van Horn *et al.*, pp. 93–115.

Eucken, W. 1949. 'Die Wettbewerbsordnung und ihre Vertwirklichung'. *ORDO* 2: 1–99. English transl. *The competitive order and its implementation*, 2006, http://cpi.esapience.org.

Fama, E. 1970. 'Efficient capital markets: a review of theory and empirical work'. *Journal of Finance* 25: 383–417.

Fama, E. and French, K. 2010. 'Luck versus skill in the cross-section of mutual funds returns'. *Journal of Finance* 65: 1915–47.

Fanon, F. 1961. *Les damnés de la terre*. Paris: François Maspero; Italian transl., *I dannati della terra*. Milan: Edizioni di Comunità, 2000.

Faucci, R. 1986. *Einaudi*. Turin: Utet.

Felipe, J. and McCombie, J. 2013. *The aggregate production function and the measurement of technical change*. Cheltenham: Edward Elgar.

Ferguson, C. E. 1969. *The neoclassical theory of production and distribution*. Cambridge: Cambridge University Press.

Fischer, R. 2009. 'The influence of neoliberals in Chile before, during and after Pinochet'. In Mirowski and Plehwe, pp. 305–46.

Fischer, S. 1977. 'Long-term contracts, rational expectations and the optimal money supply rule'. *Journal of Political Economy* 85: 191–205.

Fitoussi, J.-P., Sen, A. and Stiglitz, J. 2009. *Report by the Commission on the measurement of economic performance and social progress*. Paris. www.stiglitz-sen-fitoussi.fr/en/index.htm.

Fleming, J. M. 1962. 'Domestic financial policies under fixed and floating exchange rates'. *IMF Staff Papers* 9: 369–79.

Flux, A. W. 1894. 'Review: K. Wicksell, *Über Wert, Kapital und Rente*; P. H. Wicksteed, *An essay on the coordination of the laws of distribution*'. *Economic Journal* 4: 305–13.

Foley, D. 1967. 'Resource allocation and the public sector'. *Yale Economic Essays* 7: 45–98.

Foley, D. 1986. *Understanding capital*. Cambridge, MA: Harvard University Press.

Forni, M. and Lippi, M. 1997. *Aggregation and the microfoundations of dynamic macroeconomics*. Oxford: Clarendon Press.

Foucault, M. 2004. *Naissance de la biopolitique: cours au Collège de France 1978–1979*. Paris: Seuil-Gallimard. Italian transl., *Nascita della biopolitica*. Milan: Feltrinelli, 2005; UE Feltrinelli, III ed., 2017.

Frankel, P. H. 1946. *Essentials of petroleum*. II ed. London: Frank Cass 1969.

Frenkel, J. and Johnson, H. G., eds. 1976. *The monetary approach to the balance of payments*. Toronto: University of Toronto Press.

Friedman, M. 1953. *Essays in positive economics*. Chicago: University of Chicago Press.

Friedman, M. 1956a. 'The quantity theory of money: a restatement'. In Friedman 1956b, pp. 3–21.

Friedman, M., ed. 1956b. *Studies in the quantity theory of money*. Chicago: University of Chicago Press.

Friedman, M. 1957. *A theory of the consumption function*. Princeton, NJ: Princeton University Press.

Friedman, M. 1960. *A program for monetary stability*. New York: Fordham University Press.

Friedman, M. 1962. *Price theory*. Chicago: Aldine; repr. 2007.

Friedman, M. 1968. 'The role of monetary policy'. *American Economic Review* 58: 1–17.

Friedman, M. 1969. *The optimum quantity of money and other essays*. Chicago: Aldine.

Friedman, M. 1974. *Milton Friedman's monetary framework: a debate with his critics*. Ed. by R. J. Gordon. Chicago: University of Chicago Press.

Friedman, M. 1977. *From Galbraith to economic freedom*. Occasional Paper 49. London: Institute of Economic Affairs.

Friedman, M. and Schwartz, A. 1963. *A monetary history of the United States, 1867–1960*. Princeton, NJ: Princeton University Press.

Friedman, M. and Schwartz, A. 1982. *Monetary trends in the United States and the United Kingdom*. Chicago: University of Chicago Press.

Frisch, R. 1933. 'Editorial'. *Econometrica* 1: 1–4.

Fuà, G., ed. 1976. *Il 'Modellaccio': modello dell'economia italiana elaborato dal gruppo di Ancona*. 4 vols. Milan: Franco Angeli.

Fuà, G. 1993. *Crescita economica: le insidie delle cifre*. Bologna: il Mulino.

Fudenberg, D. and Tirole, J. 1991. *Game theory*. Cambridge, MA: MIT Press.

Furtado, C. 1964. *Development and underdevelopment*. Berkeley: University of California Press.

Furtado, C. 1970. *Théorie du développement économique*. Paris: Presses Universitaires de France. Italian transl., *Teoria dello sviluppo economico*. Bari: Laterza, 1972.

Galavotti, M. C. 2005. *Philosophical introduction to probability*. Stanford: CSLI Publications.

Galbraith, John K. 1952. *American capitalism: the concept of countervailing power*. Boston: Houghton Mifflin.

Galbraith, John K. 1955. *The great crash*. Boston: Houghton Mifflin.

Galbraith, John K. 1958. *The affluent society*. Boston: Houghton Mifflin.

Galbraith, John K. 1967. *The new industrial state*. Boston: Houghton Mifflin; repr. Harmondsworth: Penguin 1967.

Galbraith, James K. 2008. *The predator state*. New York: Free Press.

Galilei, G. 1623. *Il Saggiatore*. Rome: Accademici dei Lincei; repr. in *Opere*. Milan and Naples: Ricciardi 1953, pp. 89–352.

Gallaway, L. and Shukla, V. 1974. 'The neoclassical production function'. *American Economic Review* 64: 348–58.

Garcia Duarte, P. 2014. 'The early years of the MIT PhD program in industrial economics'. *History of Political Economy* 65 (Supplement): 81–108.

Gärdenfors, P. and Sahlin, N. E. 1982. 'Unreliable probabilities, risk taking, and decision making'. *Synthese* 53: 361–86; repr. in Gärdenfors and Sahlin 1988, pp. 313–34.

Gärdenfors, P. and Sahlin, N. E., eds. 1988. *Decision, probability and utility*. Cambridge: Cambridge University Press.

Gårdlund, T. 1956. *Knut Wicksell, rebell l det nya riket*. Stockholm: Bonniers. English transl., *The life of Knut Wicksell*. Cheltenham: Edward Elgar, 1996.

Garegnani, P. 1960. *Il capitale nelle teorie della distribuzione*. Milan: Giuffrè.

Garegnani, P. 1970. 'Heterogeneous capital, the production function and the theory of distribution'. *Review of Economic Studies* 37: 407–36.

Garegnani, P. 1976. 'The neoclassical production function: comment'. *American Economic Review* 66: 424–7.

Garegnani, P. 1979. *Valore e domanda effettiva*. Turin: Einaudi.

Garegnani, P. 1981. *Marx e gli economisti classici*. Turin: Einaudi.

Garegnani, P. 1984. 'Value and distribution in the classical economists and Marx'. *Oxford Economic Papers* 36: 291–325.

Garegnani, P. 1990a. Sraffa: 'Classical versus Marginalist analysis'. Bharadwaj, K. and Schefold, B. (eds.). *Essays on Sraffa*. London: Unwin Hyman 1990, pp. 112–41.

Garegnani, P. 1990b. 'On some supposed obstacles to the tendency of market prices towards natural prices'. *Political Economy* 6: 329–59.

Garrison, R. W. 1978. *Austrian macroeconomics: a diagrammatic exposition*. Menlo Park, CA: Institute for Humane Studies.

Georgescu-Roegen, N. 1936. 'The pure theory of consumer's behavior'. *Quarterly Journal of Economics* 50: 545–93.

Georgescu-Roegen, N. 1954. 'Choice, expectation and measurability'. *Quarterly Journal of Economics* 68: 503–34.

Georgescu-Roegen, N. 1966. *Analytical economics: issues and problems*. Cambridge, MA: Harvard University Press.

Georgescu-Roegen, N. 1971. *The entropy law and the economic process*. Cambridge, MA: Harvard University Press.

Georgescu-Roegen, N. 1972. 'Process analysis and the neoclassical theory of production'. *American Journal of Agricultural Economics* 54: 279–94.

Georgescu-Roegen, N. 1976. *Energy and economic myths*. New York: Pergamon.

Georgescu-Roegen, N. 1988. 'An emigrant from a developing country: autobiographical notes – I'. *BNL Quarterly Review* 41 (164): 3–32; repr. in J. Kregel ed. *Recollections of eminent economists*, vol. 2. London: Macmillan, 1989, pp. 99–127.

Georgescu-Roegen, N. 1993. 'An emigrant from a developing country: autobiographical notes– II'. *BNL Quarterly Review* 46 (184): 3–30.

Geroski, P. A. and Schwalbach, J., eds. 1991. *Entry and market contestability*. Oxford: Blackwell.

Gilibert, G. 1990. 'La scuola russo-tedesca di economia matematica e la dottrina del flusso circolare'. In G. Becattini (ed.), *Il pensiero economico: temi, problemi e scuole*. Turin: Utet, pp. 387–403.

Gilibert, G. 1998. 'Mani visibili, invisibili, nascoste'. In Sissa-Laboratorio interdisciplinare, Laboratorio dell'immaginario scientifico, *Adam Smith e dintorni*. Naples: Cuen, pp. 137–56.

Gini, C. 1912. *Variabilità e mutabilità: contributo allo studio delle distribuzioni e delle relazioni statistiche*, Bologna: Paolo Cuppin; repr. in Biblioteca dell'economista, series V, vol. 13, pp. 1–151.

Giraud, Y. 2014. 'Negotiating the "middle-of-the-road" position: Paul Samuelson, MIT and the politics of textbook writing, 1945–55'. *History of Political Economy* 65 (Supplement): 135–52.

Godfrey-Smith, P. 2009. *Darwinian populations and natural selections*. Oxford: Oxford University Press.

Godley, W. and Izurieta, A. 2004. 'The US economy: weaknesses of the "strong" recovery'. *BNL Quarterly Review* 57(229): 131–9.

Godley, W. and Lavoie, M. 2007. *Monetary economics: an integrated approach to credit, money, income, production and wealth*. London: Palgrave Macmillan.

Goodfriend, M. and King, R. G. 1997. 'The new neoclassical synthesis and the role of monetary policy'. In B. S. Bernanke and J. J. Rotenberg (eds.), *NBER macroeconomics annal : 1997*. Cambridge, MA: MIT Press.

Goodhart, C. A. E. 1997. 'Whither now?'. *BNL Quarterly Review* 50(203): 385–430.

Goodwin, R. M. 1967. 'A growth cycle'. In C. H. Feinstein (ed.), *Socialism, capitalism and economic growth: essays presented to Maurice Dobb*. Cambridge: Cambridge University Press, pp. 54–8.

Goodwin, R. M. 1970. *Elementary economics from the higher standpoint*. Cambridge: Cambridge University Press.

Goodwin, R. M. 1982a. *Essays in economic dynamics*. London: Macmillan.

Goodwin, R. M. 1982b. *Intervista a un economista*. Ed. by M. Palazzi. Biblioteca Walter Bigiavi della Facoltà di economia e commercio dell'Università di Bologna.

Goodwin, R. M. 1990. *Chaotic economic dynamics*. Oxford: Clarendon Press.

Gordon, R. J. 2011. 'The history of the Phillips curve: consensus and bifurcation'. *Economica* 78: 10–50.

Gramsci, A. 1975. *Quaderni del carcere*. Critical ed., Ed. by V. Gerratana, 4 vols. Turin: Einaudi. English ed., *Prison notebooks*, 3 vols. New York: Columbia University Press, 2011.

Gramsci, A. and Sraffa, P. 1924. 'Problemi di oggi e di domani'. *Ordine nuovo*, 1: 4.

Gray, J. 1984. *Hayek on liberty*. Oxford: Blackwell; repr. 1986.

Graziani, A. 2003. *The monetary theory of production*. Cambridge: Cambridge University Press.

Greenspan, A. 2009. 'We need a better cushion against risk'. *Financial Times. Supplement on The future of capitalism: the big debate*, 12 May.

Greenwood, R. and Scharfstein, D. 2013. 'The growth of finance'. *Journal of Economic Perspectives* 27: 3–28.

Grilli, E. 2005. *Crescita e sviluppo delle nazioni*. Turin: UTET.

Grilli, E. and Yang, M.C. 1988. 'Primary commodity prices, manufactured good prices, and the terms of trade in developing countries: what the long run shows'. *World Bank Economic Review* 2: 1–47.

Grimm, C., Püringer, S. and Kapeller, J. 2018. 'Paradigms and policies: the state of economics in German-speaking countries'. *ICAE Working Paper Series* 77, Linz: Johannes Kepler University.

Haavelmo, T. 1944. 'The probability approach in econometrics'. *Econometrica* 12 (Supplement): 1–118.

Haavelmo, T. 1945. 'Multiplier effect of a balanced budget'. *Econometrica* 13: 311–18.

Hacking, I. 1990. *The taming of chance*. Cambridge: Cambridge University Press.

Hagemann, H. 2013. 'Germany after World War II: ordoliberalism, the social market economy and Keynesianism'. *History of Economic Theory and Policy* 1: 37–51.

Hahn, F. 1965. 'On some problems of proving the existence of equilibrium in a monetary economy'. In F. Hahn and F. Brechling (eds.), *The theory of interest rates*. London: Macmillan, pp. 126–35.

Hahn, F. 1973. *On the notion of equilibrium in economics*. Cambridge: Cambridge University Press.

Hahn, F. 1982. 'Stability'. In K. Arrow and M. Intriligator (eds.), *Handbook of mathematical economics*. Amsterdam: North Holland, vol. 2, chapter 16.

Hahn, F. and Matthews R. C. O. 1964. 'The theory of economic growth: a survey'. *Economic Journal* 74: 779–902.

Hall, P. and Soskice, D., eds. 2001. *Varieties of capitalism*. Oxford: Oxford University Press.

Hammond, J. D. 2015. 'Paul Samuelson on public goods: the road to nihilism'. *History of Political Economy* 47 (Supplement): 147–73.

Hanappi, G. 2017. 'Agent-based modeling: history, essence, future'. *PSL Quarterly Review* 70 (283): 449–72.

Hansen, A. 1938. *Full recovery or stagnation?* New York: Norton.

Hansen, A. 1949. *Monetary theory and fiscal policy*. New York: McGraw-Hill.

Hansen, A. 1953. *A guide to Keynes*. New York: McGraw-Hill.

Harcourt, G. C. 1972. *Some Cambridge controversies in the theory of capital*. Cambridge: Cambridge University Press.

Harcourt, G. C. and Laing, N. F., eds. 1971. *Capital and growth*. Harmondsworth: Penguin.

Hare, R. M. 1982. 'Ethical theory and utilitarianism'. In Sen and Williams (eds.), pp. 23–38.

Harrod, R. 1939. 'An essay in dynamic theory'. *Economic Journal* 49: 14–33.

Harrod, R. 1951. *The life of John Maynard Keynes*. London: Macmillan.

Harrod, R. 1961. 'Review of P. Sraffa, *Production of commodities by means of commodities*'. *Economic Journal* 71: 783–87.

Harsanyi, J. C. 1977. 'Morality and the theory of rational behavior'. *Social Research* 44: 623–56.

Harsanyi, J. C. 1988. *L'utilitarismo*. Milan: Il Saggiatore; II ed., 1994.

Harsanyi, J. C. and Selten, R. 1988. *A general theory of equilibrium selection in genes*. Cambridge, MA: MIT Press.

Harvey, D. 2005. *A brief history of neoliberalism*. Oxford: Oxford University Press.

Hausman, D. M. and McPherson, M. S. 1996. *Economic analysis and moral philosophy*. Cambridge: Cambridge University Press.

Hawkins, D. and Simon, H. 1949. 'Note: some conditions of macroeconomic stability'. *Econometrica* 17: 245–8.

Hayek, F. von. 1926. 'Friedrich Freiherr von Wieser'. *Jahrbücher für Nationalökonomie und Statistik* 125: 513–30. English transl. in F. Hayek, *The fortunes of liberalism. The collected works of F. A. Hayek*, vol. 4. Chicago: University of Chicago Press, 1992, pp. 108–25.

Hayek, F. von. 1931. *Prices and production*. London: Routledge.

Hayek, F. von. 1931–32. 'Reflections on the pure theory of money of Mr. J. M. Keynes'. *Economica* 11 (1931): 270–95 and 12 (1932) 22–44; repr. in F. Hayek, *Contra Keynes and Cambridge*, B. Caldwell (ed.), *The collected works of F. A. Hayek*, vol. 9. Chicago: University of Chicago Press, 1995, pp. 121–46 and 174–97.

Hayek, F. von. 1932. 'Money and capital: a reply'. *Economic Journal* 42: 237–49.

Hayek, F. von. 1933. 'Uber "Neutrales Geld"'. *Zeitschrift für Nationalökonomie* 4 (5): 655–61. English transl., 'On "neutral" money'. In Hayek 1999a, pp. 228–31.

Hayek, F. von. 1935. 'The nature and history of the problem' and 'The state of the debate'. In F. Hayek (ed.), *Collectivist economic planning*, London: Routledge; repr. in Hayek 1948, pp. 119–47 and 148–80.

Hayek, F. von. 1937. 'Economics and knowledge'. *Economica* 4(13): 33–54.

Hayek, F. von. 1940. 'Socialist calculation: the competitive "solution"'. *Economica* 7: 125–49; repr. in Hayek 1948, pp. 181–208.

Hayek, F. von 1941. *The pure theory of capital*. London: Routledge and Kegan Paul.

Hayek, F. von. 1942. 'The Ricardo effect'. *Economica* 9(34): 127–52; repr. in Hayek 1948, pp. 220–54.

Hayek, F. von. 1942–4. 'Scientism and the study of society'. *Economica*, Part 1 (1942), 9(35): 34–63; Part 2 (1943), 10 (37): 34–63; Part 3 (1944), 11 (41): 27–39.

Hayek, F. von. 1943. 'A commodity reserve currency'. *Economic Journal* 53: 176–84; repr. in Hayek 1999b, pp. 106–14.

Hayek, F. von. 1944. *The road to serfdom*. Chicago: University of Chicago Press; repr. 1994.

Hayek, F. von. 1945. 'The use of knowledge in society'. *American Economic Review* 35: 519–30.

Hayek, F. von. 1948. *Individualism and economic order*. Chicago: University of Chicago Press.

Hayek, F. von. 1952. *The sensory order: an inquiry into the foundations of theoretical psychology*. London: Routledge & Kegan Paul.

Hayek, F. von. 1960. *The constitution of liberty*. Chicago: University of Chicago Press.

Hayek, F. von. 1973. *Law, legislation and liberty*, vol. 1: *Rules and order*. London: Routledge and Kegan Paul.

Hayek, F. von. 1974. *Nobel lecture*, 11 December. www.nobelprize.org/nobel-prizes/economic_sciences/laureate/1974/hayek_lecture.html.

Hayek, F. von. 1976. *Denationalisation of money*. London: Institute of economic affairs; II ed., 1978; repr. in Hayek 1999b, pp. 128–229.

Hayek, F. von. 1988. *Conoscenza, mercato, pianificazione*. Ed. by F. Donzelli. Bologna: il Mulino.

Hayek, F. von. 1991. *The trend of economic thinking: essays on political economists and economic history*. W. W. Bartley III and S. Kresge (eds.), *The collected works of F. A. Hayek*, vol. 3. Chicago: University of Chicago Press.

Hayek, F. von. 1992. *The fortunes of liberalism*. In P. G. Klein (ed.), *The Collected Works of F. A. Hayek*, vol. 4. Chicago: University of Chicago Press.

Hayek, F. von. 1994. *Hayek on Hayek*. Ed. by S. Kresge and L. Wenar. Chicago: University of Chicago Press.

Hayek, F. von. 1999a. *Good money. Part I. The new world*. In S. Kresge (ed.), *The collected works of F. A. Hayek*, vol. 5. Chicago: University of Chicago Press.

Hayek, F. von. 1999b. *Good money. Part II. The standard*. In S. Kresge (ed.), *The collected works of F. A. Hayek*, vol. 6. Chicago: University of Chicago Press.

Hayek, F. von. 2011. *Autobiografia*. Soveria Mannelli: Rubbettino 2011.

Hayek, F. von. 2015. *Hayek on Mill: the Mill-Taylor friendship and related writings*. In S. Peart (ed.), *The collected works of F. A. Hayek*, vol. 16. London: Routledge.

Heal, G., ed. 1993. *The economics of exhaustible resources*. Aldershot: Edward Elgar.

Hendry, D. F. 1980. 'Econometrics: alchemy or science?'. *Economica* 47: 387–406.

Hennings, K. H. 1997. *The Austrian theory of value and capital*. Cheltenham: Edward Elgar.

Henrich, J., Boyd, R., Bowles, S., Camerer, C., Fehr, E. and Gintis, H., eds. 2004. *Foundations of human sociality*. Oxford: Oxford University Press.

Herndon, T., Ash, M. and Pollin, R. 2013. *Does high public debt consistently stifle economic growth? A critique of Reinhart and Rogoff*. PERI Working Paper 322.

Heukelom, F. 2014. *Behavioral economics: a history*. Cambridge: Cambridge University Press.

Hicks, J. 1937. 'Mr. Keynes and the classics: a suggested interpretation'. *Econometrica* 5: 147–59.

Hicks, J. 1939. *Value and capital*. Oxford: Clarendon Press; II ed., 1946.

Hicks, J. 1973. *Capital and time: a neo-Austrian theory*. Oxford: Clarendon Press.

Hilferding, R. 1910. *Das Finanzkapital*. Vienna: Wiener Volksbuchhandlung Ignaz Brand. English transl., *Finance capital: a study of the latest phase of capitalist development*. London: Routledge & Kegan Paul, 1981.

Hirsch, F. 1976. *Social limits to growth*. Cambridge, MA: Harvard University Press.

Hirschman, A. O. 1958. *The strategy of economic development*. New Haven, CT: Yale University Press.

Hirschman, A. O. 1970. *Exit, voice, and loyalty*. Cambridge, MA: Harvard University Press.

Hirschman, A. O. 1977. *The passions and the interests*. Princeton, NJ: Princeton University Press.

Hirschman, A. O. 1982. 'Rival interpretations of market society: civilizing, destructive, or feeble?'. *Journal of Economic Literature* 20: 1463–84.

Hobbes, T. 1651. *Leviathan*. London: Andrew Crooke. Italian transl., *Leviatano*. Rome and Bari: Laterza, 1974.

Hobbes, T. 1658. *De homine*. London: Andrew Crooke. Italian transl., *De homine*. Rome and Bari: Laterza, 1984.

Hobsbawm, E. 1994. *Age of extremes: the short twentieth century, 1914–1991*. New York: Random House.

Hodgson, G. M. 1988. *Economics and institutions*. Cambridge: Polity Press.

Hodgson, G. M. 1998. 'The approach of institutional economics'. *Journal of Economic Literature* 36: 166–92.

Hodgson, G. M. 1999. *Evolution and institutions*. Cheltenham: Edward Elgar.

Hollander, J. 1904. 'The development of Ricardo's theory of value'. *Quarterly Journal of Economics* 18: 455–91.

Hollander, J. 1910. *David Ricardo: a centenary estimate*. Baltimore; repr. New York: McKelley, 1968.

Hotelling, H. 1929. 'Stability in competition'. *Economic Journal* 39: 41–57.

Hotelling, H. 1931. 'The economics of exhaustible resources'. *Journal of Political Economy* 39: 137–75.

Howard, M. C. and King, J. E. 2004. 'The economic contributions of Paul Sweezy'. *Review of Political Economy* 16: 411–56.

Hume, D. 1752. 'Of the balance of trade'. In *Political discourses*. Edinburgh: A. Kincaid and A. Donaldson; repr. in E. F. Miller (ed.), *Essays: moral, political, and literary*. Indianapolis: Liberty Press 1987, pp. 308–26.

Huntington, S. P. 1996. *The clash of civilizations and the remaking of the world order*. New York: Simon & Schuster.

Ioannidis, J. P., Stanley, T. D. and Doucouliagos, H. 2017. 'The power of bias in economic research'. *Economic Journal* 127: F256–F265.

Jackson, D. 2000. *The new national accounts*. Cheltenham: Edward Elgar.

Janssen, M. C. W., ed. 2004. *Auctioning public assets*. Cambridge: Cambridge University Press.

Jeffrey, K. C. 1965. *The logic of decision*. New York: McGraw-Hill; II ed., Chicago: University of Chicago Press, 1983.

Jevons, W. S. 1865. *The coal question*. London: Macmillan; repr., New York: Augustus M. Kelley, 1965.

Jevons, W. S. 1871. *The theory of political economy*. London: Macmillan; II ed. 1879; repr. Harmondsworth: Penguin Books, 1970.

Johansson Heinö, A. 2016. *Timbro authoritarian populism index*. Stockholm: Timbro.

Johnson, H. G. 1972. *The monetary approach to balance of payments theory*. In H. G. Johnson, ed., *Further essays on monetary economics*. London: Macmillan.

Joskow, P. L. and Noll, R. G. 2013. 'Alfred Kahn, 1917–2010'. *Review of Industrial Organization* 42: 107–26.

Jossa, B. 2010. *Esiste un'alternativa al capitalismo? L'impresa democratica e l'attualità del marxismo*. Rome: Manifestolibri.

Kagel, J. and Levin, D. 1986. 'The winner's curse and public information in common value actions'. *American Economic Review* 76: 894–920.

Kahn, A. 1970–71. *The economics of regulation* (vol. 1, *Economic principles*, 1970; vol. 2, *Institutional issues*, 1971). New York: John Wiley & Sons.

Kahn, R. F. 1931. 'The relation of home investment to unemployment'. *Economic Journal* 41: 173–98; repr. in Kahn 1972, pp. 1–27.

Kahn, R. F. 1954. 'Some notes on liquidity preference'. *Manchester School* 22: 229–57; repr. in Kahn 1972, pp. 72–96.

Kahn, R. F. 1972. *Selected essays on employment and growth*. Cambridge: Cambridge University Press.

Kahn, R. F. [1929] 1983. *L'economia del breve periodo*. Ed. by M. Dardi. Turin: Boringhieri. English ed., *The economics of the short period*. New York: St. Martin's Press, 1989.

Kahn, R. F. 1984. *The making of Keynes's 'General theory'*. Cambridge: Cambridge University Press.

Kahneman, D. 2011. *Thinking, fast and slow*. New York: Farrar, Straus and Giroux.

Kahneman, D. and Tversky, A. 1979. 'Prospect theory: an analysis of decision under risk'. *Econometrica* 47: 263–91.

Kaldor, N. 1939. 'Welfare propositions of economics and interpersonal comparisons of utility'. *Economic Journal* 49: 549–52.

Kaldor, N. 1942. 'Professor Hayek and the concertina effect'. *Economica* 9: 359–82.

Kaldor, N. 1956. 'Alternative theories of distribution'. *Review of Economic Studies* 23: 94–100.

Kaldor, N. 1957. 'A model of economic growth'. *Economic Journal* 67: 591–624.

Kaldor, N. 1961. 'Capital accumulation and economic growth'. In F. A. Lutz (ed.), *The theory of capital*. London: Macmillan, pp. 177–220.

Kaldor, N. 1966. 'Marginal productivity and the macro-economic theories of distribution: comment on Samuelson and Modigliani'. *Review of Economic Studies* 33: 309–19.

Kaldor, N. 1970. 'The new monetarism'. *Lloyds Bank Review*, July, pp. 1–17; repr. in A. A. Walters (ed.), *Money and banking*. Harmondsworth: Penguin, 1973, pp. 261–78.

Kaldor, N. 1982. *The scourge of monetarism*. Oxford: Oxford University Press; II ed., 1985.

Kalecki, M. 1943. *Studies in economic dynamics*. London: George Allen and Unwin.

Kalecki, M. 1971. *Selected essays on the dynamics of the capitalist economy*. Cambridge: Cambridge University Press.

Kalecki, M. 1972. *Selected essays on the economic growth of the socialist and the mixed economy*. Cambridge: Cambridge University Press.

Kao, Y.-F. and Velupillai, V. 2015. 'Behavioural economics: classical and modern'. *European Journal of the History of Economic Thought* 22: 236–71.

Keynes, J. M. 1913. *Indian currency and finance*. London: Macmillan; repr. in J. M. Keynes, *Collected writings*, vol. 1. London: Macmillan, 1971.

Keynes, J. M. 1921. *A treatise on probability*. London: Macmillan; repr. in J. M. Keynes, *Collected writings*, vol. 8. London: Macmillan, 1973.

Keynes, J. M. 1923. *A tract on monetary reform*. London: Macmillan; repr. in J. M. Keynes, *Collected writings*, vol. 4. London: Macmillan, 1971.

Keynes, J. M. 1930. *A treatise on money*. 2 vols., London: Macmillan; repr. in J. M. Keynes, *Collected writings*, vols. 5 and 6. London: Macmillan, 1971.

Keynes, J. M. 1931. *Essays in persuasion*. London: Macmillan; repr. in J. M. Keynes, *Collected writings*, vol. 9. London: Macmillan, 1972.

Keynes, J. M. 1936. *The general theory of employment, interest and money*. London: Macmillan; repr. in J. M. Keynes, *Collected writings*, vol. 7. London: Macmillan, 1973.

Keynes, J. M. 1937. 'Some economic consequences of a declining population'. *Eugenics Review* 29: 13–17; repr. in Keynes 1973, vol. 14, pp. 124–33.

Keynes, J. M. 1973. *The General Theory and after*. In *Collected writings*, vols. 13 (Part I: *preparation*) and 14 (Part II: *defence and development*). Ed. by D. Moggridge. London: Macmillan.

Keynes, J. M. 1979. *The General Theory and after: a supplement*. In *Collected writings*, vol. 29. Ed. by D. Moggridge. London: Macmillan.

Keynes, J. M. 1980. *Activities 1941–1946: shaping the post-war world, Bretton Woods and reparations*. In *Collected writings*, vol. 26. Ed. by D. Moggridge. London: Macmillan.

Kindleberger, C. P. 1978. *Manias, panics and crashes: a history of financial crises*. New York: Basic Books.

Kindleberger, C. P. 1989. *Economic laws and economic history*. Cambridge: Cambridge University Press.

Kindleberger, C. P. 1995. 'Asset inflation and monetary policy'. *BNL Quarterly Review* 48(192): 17–37.

Kindleberger, C. P. 2002. 'The price level of monetary policy'. *BNL Quarterly Review* 55(220): 3–12.

King, J. E. 2015. *Post Keynesian economics*. Cheltenham: Edward Elgar.

Kirman, A. 1992. 'What or whom does the representative individual represent?'. *Journal of Economic Perspectives* 6: 117–36.

Kirman, A. 2006. 'Demand theory and general equilibrium: from explanation to introspection, a journey down the wrong road'. *History of Political Economy* 38 (Supplement): 246–80.

Kirzner, I. 1973. *Competition and entrepreneurship*. Chicago: University of Chicago Press.

Klein, L. R. 1991. 'Econometric contributions of the Cowles Commission, 1944–1947: a retrospective view'. *BNL Quarterly Review* 44(177): 107–17.

Klugman, J., Rodríguez, F. and Choi, H.-J. 2011. 'The HDI 2010: new controversies, old critiques'. *Journal of Economic Inequalities* 9: 249–88.

Knight, F. H. 1921. *Risk, uncertainty and profit*. Boston: Hart, Schaffner & Marx; repr. Boston: Houghton Mifflin, 1940.

Kosnik, L.-R. 2015. 'What have economists being doing for the last 50 years? A text analysis of published academic research from 1960–2010'. *Economics. The open-access, open-assessment e-journal* 9(13): 1–37.

Krautkraemer, J. A. 1998. 'Nonrenewable resource scarcity'. *Journal of Economic Literature* 36: 2065–107.

Kravis, J. B. 1976. 'A survey of international comparisons of productivity'. *Economic Journal* 86: 1–44.

Kravis, J. B., Heston, A. W. and Summers, R. 1978. 'Real GDP per capita of more than one hundred countries'. *Economic Journal* 88: 215–42.

Kregel, J. A. 1976. 'Economic methodology in the face of uncertainty: the modelling methods of Keynes and the post-Keynesians'. *Economic Journal* 86: 209–25.

Kregel, J. A. 1980a. 'Economic dynamics and the theory of steady growth: an historical essay on Harrod's "knife edge"'. *History of Political Economy* 12: 97–123.

Kregel, J. A. 1980b. 'Markets and institutions as features of a capitalistic production system'. *Journal of Post Keynesian Economics* 3: 32–48.

Kregel, J. A. 1996. *Origini e sviluppo dei mercati finanziari*. Arezzo: Banca popolare dell'Etruria e del Lazio.

Kreps, D. M. 1990. *Game theory and economic modelling*. Oxford: Oxford University Press.

Krouse, C. G. 1990. *Theory of industrial economics*. Oxford: Blackwell.

Krugman, P. R. 1990. *Rethinking international trade*. Cambridge, MA: MIT Press.

Kuhn, T. S. 1962. *The structure of scientific revolutions*. Princeton, NJ: Princeton University Press; II ed. 1970.

Kula, W. 1958. *Rozwazania o historii*. Warszawa: Państwowe Wydawnictwo Naukowe. Italian transl., *Riflessioni sulla storia*. Venezia: Marsilio, 1990.

Kurz, H. and Salvadori, N. 1995. *Theory of production: a long period analysis*. Cambridge: Cambridge University Press.

Kuznets, S. 1955. 'Economic growth and income inequality'. *American Economic Review, Papers and Proceedings* 45: 1–28.

Kuznets, S. 1965. *Towards a theory of economic growth*. New York: W. W. Norton & Co.; repr. 1968.

Kydland, F. E. and Prescott, E. C. 1977. 'Rules rather than discretion: the inconsistency of optimal plans'. *Journal of Political Economy* 85: 473–92.

Kydland, F. E. and Prescott, E. C. 1982. 'Time to build and aggregate fluctuations'. *Economica* 50: 1345–70.

Lachmann, L. 1956. *Capital and its structures*. London: Bell & Sons; new ed., Institute for Humane Studies, Menlo Park, and Cato Institute, San Francisco, 1978.

Lachmann, L. 1986. *The market as an economic process*. Oxford: Basil Blackwell.

Laffont, J.-J. and Tirole, J. 1993. *A theory of incentives in procurement and regulation*. Cambridge, MA: MIT Press.

Laidler, D. 1985. *The demand for money: theories, evidence and problems*. New York: Harper Collins; new ed., London: Pearson, 1997.

Lakatos, I. 1978. *The methodology of scientific research programmes. Philosophical papers*. Cambridge: Cambridge University Press.

Lancaster, K. 1966. 'A new approach to consumer theory'. *Journal of Political Economy* 74: 132–57.

Lancaster, K. 1971. *Consumer demand: a new approach*. New York: Columbia University Press.

Landes, D.S. 1986. 'What do bosses really do?'. *Journal of Economic History* 46: 585–623.

Lange, O. 1936–7. 'On the economic theory of socialism'. *Review of Economic Studies* 4: 53–71 and 123–42.

Lange, O. 1942. 'The foundations of welfare economics'. *Econometrica* 10: 215–28.

Latouche, S. 2006. *Le pari de la décroissance*. Paris: Librairie Arthème Fayard. Italian transl., *La scommessa della decrescita*. Milan: Feltrinelli, 2007.

Lawson, T. 1994. 'The nature of Post Keynesianism and its links to other traditions'. *Journal of Post Keynesian Economics* 16: 503–38.

Lawson, T. 1997. *Economics & reality*. London: Routledge.

Lawson, T., Palma, J. G. and Sender, J., eds. 1989. *Kaldor's political economy*. London: Academic Press.

Layard, R. 2005. *Happiness*. Harmondsworth: Penguin. Italian transl., *Felicità*. Milan: Rizzoli, 2005.

Leibenstein, H. 1966. 'Allocative efficiency vs. "X-efficiency"'. *American Economic Review* 56: 392–415.

Leijonhufvud, A. 1968. *On Keynesian economics and the economics of Keynes*. London: Oxford University Press.

Lenin (Vladimir Ilyich Ulianov). 1898. Italian transl., *Lo sviluppo del capitalismo in Russia*. Rome: Editori Riuniti, 1955.

Lenin (Vladimir Ilyich Ulianov). 1916. Italian transl., *L'imperialismo fase suprema del capitalism*. Rome: Edizioni Rinascita, 1956.

Leontief, W. 1941. *The structure of the American economy, 1919–1939*. New York: Oxford University Press; II ed., 1951.

Leontief, W., Carter, A. P. and Petri, P. A. 1977. *The future of the world economy: a United Nations study*. New York: Oxford University Press.

Lerner, A. 1934. 'The concept of monopoly and the measurement of monopoly power'. *Review of Economic Studies* 1: 157–75.

Lerner, A. and Colander, D. 1980. *MAP, a market anti-inflation plan*. New York: Harcourt, Brace and Jovanovich.

Levhari, D. 1965. 'A nonsubstitution theorem and switching of techniques'. *Quarterly Journal of Economics* 79: 98–105.

Levhari, D. and Samuelson, P. 1966. 'The nonswitching theorem is false'. *Quarterly Journal of Economics* 80: 518–19.

Lewis, W. A. 1954. 'Economic development with unlimited supplies of labour'. *Manchester School of Economic and Social Studies* 22: 139–91.

Lijphart, A. 1999. *Patterns of democracy: government forms and performance in thirty-six countries*. New Haven, CT: Yale University Press; II ed., 2014.

Lindahl, E. R. 1939. *Studies in the theory of money and capital*. London: Allen & Unwin.

Lindbeck, A. and Snower, D. J. 1988. *The insider-outsider theory of employment and unemployment*. Cambridge, MA: MIT Press.

Lindert, P. H. 2004. *Growing public*. 2 vols. Cambridge: Cambridge University Press.

Lippi, M. 1979. *I prezzi di produzione*. Bologna: il Mulino.

Lipsey, R. G. 1960. 'The relation between unemployment and the rate of change of money wage rates: a further analysis'. *Economica* 27: 1–31.

Little, I. M. D. 1950. *A critique of welfare economics*. Oxford: Clarendon Press.

Loomes, G. and Sugden, R. 1982. 'Regret theory: an alternative theory of rational choice under uncertainty'. *Economic Journal* 92: 805–24.

Loomes, G. and Sugden, R. 1987. 'Testing for regret and disappointment in choice under uncertainty'. *Economic Journal* 97 (Supplement): 118–29.

Lucas, R. E. 1972. 'Expectations and the neutrality of money'. *Journal of Economic Theory* 4: 103–24.

Lucas, R. E. 1976. 'Econometric policy evaluation: a critique'. In K. Brenner and A. M. Meltzer (eds.), *The Phillips curve and labor markets*. Amsterdam: North Holland, pp. 19–46.

Lucas, R. E. 1988. 'On the mechanics of economic development'. *Journal of Monetary Economics* 22: 3–42.

Lucas, R. E. 2003. 'Macroeconomic priorities'. *American Economic Review* 93: 1–14.

Lukes, S. 2003. *Liberals & cannibals: the implications of diversity*. London: Verso.

Lutz, V. 1958. 'The growth process in a "dual" economic system'. *BNL Quarterly Review* 11(46): 279–325.

Luxemburg, R. 1913. *Die Akkumulation des Kapitals: ein Beitrag zur ökonomischen Erklärung Des Imperialismus*. Berlin: Paul Singer. Italian transl., *L'accumulazione del capitale*. Turin: Einaudi, 1960; repr., 1968.

Maas, H. 2014. 'Making things technical: Samuelson at MIT'. *History of Political Economy* 46 (Supplenement): 272–94.

Machina, M. 1983. 'Generalized expected utility analysis and the nature of observed violations of the independence axiom'. In B. P. Stigum and F. Wenstøp (eds.), *Foundations of utility and risk theory with applications*. Dordrecht: D. Reidel, pp. 263–93; repr. in Gärdenfors and Sahlin 1982, pp. 215–43.

Machlup, F. 1976. 'Hayek's contribution to economics'. In *Essays on Hayek*. Ed. by F. Machlup. Hillsdale, MI: Hillsdale College Press, pp. 13–59.

Machlup, F. 1978. *Methodology of economics and other social sciences*. New York: Academic Press.

MacLean, N. 2017. *Democracy in chains: the deep history of the radical right's stealth plan for America*. New York: Viking.

Maddison, A. 1984. 'Origins and impact of the welfare state, 1883–1983'. *BNL Quarterly Review* 37(148): 55–87.

Maddison, A. 2007. *Contours of the world economy, 1–2030 AD*. Oxford: Oxford University Press.

Malcolm, N. 1958. *Ludwig Wittgenstein: a memoir*. Oxford: Oxford University Press.

Malinvaud, E. 1977. *The theory of unemployment reconsidered*. Oxford: Blackwell.

Malinvaud, E. 1987. 'The overlapping generations model in 1947'. *Journal of Economic Literature* 25: 103–5.

Mankiw, N. G. 1985. 'Small menu costs and hedge business cycles: a macroeconomic model of monopoly'. *Quarterly Journal of Economics* 100: 529–39.

Mantel, R. 1974. 'On the characterisation of aggregate excess demand'. *Journal of Economic Theory* 7: 348–53.

Mao Tse-tung. 1960. *Selected works*. 5 vols. Peking: Foreign Languages Press.

Marcuse, H. 1956. *One-dimensional man*. Boston: Beacon Press.

Marcuzzo, M. C. 2005. 'Robinson and Sraffa'. In D. Gibson (ed.), *The economic legacy of Joan Robinson*. Cheltenham: Elgar, pp. 29–42.

Marglin, S. A. 1974. 'What do bosses do?'. *Review of Radical Political Economy* 6: 60–112.

Markowitz, H. 1952. 'Portfolio selection'. *Journal of Finance* 7: 77–91.

Marris, R. 1964. *The economic theory of 'managerial' capitalism*. London: Macmillan.

Marshall, A. 1890. *Principles of economics*. London: Macmillan; VIII ed., 1920; critical ed., C. W. Guillebaud ed., 2 vols. London: Macmillan, 1961.

Marx, K. [1844] 1932. *Ökonomisch-philosophische Manuskripte aus dem Jahre 1844*. In *Karl Marx – Friedrich Engels Historisc-kritische Gesamtausgabe*. Ed. by V. Adoratskij. Berlin: Marx-Engels Gesamtausgabe (MEGA). Italian transl., *Manoscritti economico-filosofici del 1844*. Turin: Einaudi, 1949, II ed., 1968.

Marx, K. 1867–94. *Das Kapital*. 3 vols. Hamburg: O. Meissner. Italian transl., *Il capitale*. Rome: Editori Riuniti, 1968.

Marx, K. 1905–10. *Theorien über den Mehrwert*. Ed. by K. Kautsky. Stuttgart: Dietz. English transl., *Theories of surplus-value*. Moscow: Foreign Languages Publishing House and London: Lawrence and Wishart, Part 1, 1963; Part 2, 1969; Part 3, 1972.

Mas-Colell, A. 1985. *The theory of general economic equilibrium: a differentiable approach*. Cambridge: Cambridge University Press.

Mas-Colell, A., Whinston, M. D. and Green, J. R. 1995. *Microeconomic theory*. New York: Oxford University Press.

Mazzucato, M. C. 2011. *The entrepreneurial state*. London: Anthem Press.

Mazzucato, M. C. 2018. *The value of everything*. London: Penguin Books.

McAfee, R. P. and McMillar, J. 1987. 'Auctions and biddings'. *Journal of Economic Literature* 25: 699–738.

McClure, S. M., Laibson, D. I., Loewenstein, G. and Cohen, J. D. 2004. 'Separate neural systems value immediate and delayed monetary rewards'. *Science* 306: 503–7.

McKenzie, L. 1954. 'On equilibrium in Graham's model of world trade and other competitive systems'. *Econometrica* 22: 147–61.

Meade, J. 1972. 'The theory of labour-managed firms and of profit sharing'. *Economic Journal* 82: 402–28.

Meadows, D. H., Meadows, D. L., Randers, D. L. and Beherens, W. W. III 1972. *The limits to growth*. New York: New American Library.

Meagher, K. 2019. 'Reflections of an engaged economist: an interview with Thandika Mkandawire'. *Development and Change*, in press.

Medema, S. G. 2011. 'Chicago price theory and Chicago law and economics'. In van Horn *et al.*, pp. 151–79.

Medio, A. 1972. 'Profits and surplus value: appearance and reality in capitalist production'. In E. K. Hunt and J. G. Schwartz (eds.), *A critique of economic theory*. Harmondsworth: Penguin, pp. 312–46.

Meek, R. 1961. 'Mr. Sraffa's rehabilitation of classical economics'. *Scottish Journal of Political Economy* 8: 119–36. Repr. in Meek 1967.

Meek, R. 1967. *Economics and ideology and other essays*. London: Chapman and Hall.

Ménard, C., ed. 2004. *The international library of the new institutional economics*. 7 vols. Abingdon: Edward Elgar.

Menger, C. 1871. *Grundsätze der Volkswirtschaftslehre*. Vienna: Braumuller; II ed. Ed. by K. Menger, 1923. Italian transl., *Principi di economia politica*. Turin: Utet, 1976.

Michael, R. and Becker, G. S. 1973. 'On the new theory of consumer behaviour'. *Swedish Journal of Economics* 75: 378–96.

Milanovic, B. 2016. *Global inequality*. Cambridge, MA: Belknap Press of Harvard University Press.

Mill, J. S. 1848. *Principles of political economy.* London: John W. Parker.

Mill, J. S. 1859. *On liberty.* London: John W. Parker; repr. in *Essays on politics and society.* Part I, vol. 18, *Collected works of John Stuart Mill.* Ed. by J. M. Robson. Toronto: University of Toronto Press, 1977, pp. 213–310.

Mill, J. S. 1861. 'Utilitarianism'. *Fraser's Magazine* 64: 383–4; repr. in J. S. Mill and J. Bentham, *Utilitarianism and other essays.* Ed. by A. Ryan. London: Penguin Books, 1987, pp. 272–338.

Mill, J. S. 1873. *Autobiography.* London: Longmans, Green Read and Dyer; repr., London: Oxford University Press, 1971.

Minsky, H. P. 1964. 'Financial crisis, financial systems and the performance of the economy'. In *Commission on money and credit: private capital markets.* Englewood Cliffs, NJ: Prentice-Hall.

Minsky, H. P. 1975. *John Maynard Keynes.* New York: Columbia University Press.

Minsky, H. P., 1982. *Can 'it' happen again? Essays on instability and finance.* Armonk, NY: Sharpe.

Minsky, H. P. 1986. *Stabilizing an unstable economy.* New Haven, CT: Yale University Press; new ed., New York: McGraw-Hill,2008.

Minsky, H. P. 1990. 'Schumpeter and finance'. In S. Biasco, A. Roncaglia and M. Salvati (eds.), *Market and institutions in economic development.* Houndmills: Macmillan, pp. 103–15.

Minsky, H. P. 2013. *Ending poverty: jobs, not welfare.* Ed. by D. Papadimitriou. Annandale-on-Hudson: Levy Economics Institute.

Mirowski, P. 2002. *Machine dreams: economics becomes a cyborg science.* Cambridge: Cambridge University Press.

Mirowski, P. 2006. 'Twelve theses concerning the history of postwar neoclassical price theory'. *History of Political Economy* 38: 343–79.

Mirowski, P. 2011. 'On the origins (at Chicago) of some species of neoliberal evolutionary economics'. In van Horn *et al.*, pp. 237–75.

Mirowski, P. and Plehwe, D., eds. 2009. *The road from Mont Pèlerin: the making of the neoliberal thought collective.* Cambridge, MA: Harvard University Press.

Mirrlees, J. A. 1982. 'The economic uses of utilitarianism'. In Sen and Williams 1982, pp. 63–84.

Mises, L. von. 1912. *Theorie des Geldes und der Umlaufsmittel.* Munich: Dunker & Humblot; II ed., 1924.

Mises, L. von. 1920. 'Die Wirtschaftsrechnung im Sozialistischen Gemeinwesen'. *Arkiv für Sozialwissenschaft und Sozialpolitik* 47: 86–121. Italian transl., 'Il calcolo economico nello Stato socialista'. In F. von Hayek *et al., Pianificazione economica collettivista.* Turin: Einaudi, 1946, pp. 85–124.

Mises, L. von. 1949. *Human action: a treatise on economics.* New Haven, CT: Yale University Press; II ed., 1963; III ed. Washington, DC: Henry Regnery, 1966.

Mishan, E. J. 1967. *The costs of economic growth.* London: Staples Press.

Mitchell, T. 2009. 'How neoliberalism makes its world'. In Mirowski and Plehwe, pp. 386–416.

Mkandawire, T. 2001. 'Thinking about developmental states in Africa'. *Cambridge Journal of Economics* 25: 289–313.

Modigliani, F. 1944. 'Liquidity preference and the theory of interest and money'. *Econometrica* 12: 45–88.

Modigliani, F. 1958. 'New developments on the oligopoly front'. *Journal of Political Economy* 66: 215–32.

Modigliani, F. 1963. 'The monetary mechanism and its interaction with real phenomena'. *Review of Economics and Statistics* 45 (Supplement): 79–107.

Modigliani, F. 1977. 'The monetarist controversy or, should we forsake stabilization policies?'. *American Economic Review* 67: 1–19.

Modigliani, F. and Brumberg, R. 1954. 'Utility analysis and the consumption function: an interpretation of cross-section data'. In K. K. Kurihara (ed.), *Post Keynesian economics*. New Brunswick: Rutgers University Press.

Modigliani, F. and Miller, M. 1958. 'The cost of capital, corporation finance and the theory of investment'. *American Economic Review* 48: 161–97.

Modigliani, F. and Tarantelli, E. 1976. 'Market forces, trade union action, and the Phillips curve in Italy'. *PSL Quarterly Review* 30(120): 165–98.

Montanaro, E. and Tonveronachi, M. 2012. 'Financial re-regulation at a crossroad: how the European experience strengthens the case for a radical reform built on Minsky's approach'. *PSL Quarterly Review* 65(163): 335–83.

Montesano, A. 2005. 'La nozione di razionalità in economia'. *Rivista Italiana degli Economisti* 10: 23–42.

Moore, B. 1988. *Horizontalists and verticalists: the macroeconomics of credit money*. Cambridge: Cambridge University Press.

Morgan, M. S. 1990. *The history of econometric ideas*. Cambridge: Cambridge University Press.

Moscati, I. 2007. 'Early experiments in consumer demand theory: 1930–1970'. *History of Political Economy* 39: 359–401.

Moscati, I. 2016. 'How economists came to accept expected utility theory: the case of Samuelson and Savage'. *Journal of Economic Perspectives* 30: 219–36.

Motterlini, M. and Guala, F., eds. 2005. *Economia cognitiva e sperimentale*. Milan: Egea-Università Bocconi.

Mueller, D. C. 1989. *Public choice II*. Cambridge: Cambridge University Press.

Mullainathan, S. and Spiess, J. 2017. 'Machine learning: an applied econometric approach'. *Journal of Economic Perspectives* 31: 87–106.

Mundell, R. 1961. 'A theory of optimum currency areas'. *American Economic Review* 51: 657–65.

Mundell, R. 1963. 'Capital mobility and stabilization policy under flexible exchange rates'. *Canadian Journal of Economic and Political Science* 29: 475–85.

Muth, J. F. 1961. 'Rational expectations and the theory of price movements'. *Econometrica* 29: 315–35.

Myrdal, G. 1968. *Asian drama: an inquiry into the poverty of nations*. New York: Pantheon.

Naldi, N. 1998. 'Dicembre 1922: Piero Sraffa e Benito Mussolini'. *Rivista italiana degli economisti* 3: 271–99.

Nash, J. F. 1950. 'Equilibrium points in N-person games'. *Proceedings of the National Academy of Sciences of the USA* 36: 48–9.

Nash, J. F. 1996. *Essays on game theory*. Aldershot: Edward Elgar.

Nash, J. F. 2002. *The essential John Nash*. Ed. by H. W. Kuhn and S. Nasar. Princeton, NJ: Princeton University Press.

Nell, E. J. 1998. *The general theory of transformational growth*. Cambridge: Cambridge University Press.

Nelson, R., ed. 1993. *National innovation systems: a comparative analysis*. Oxford: Oxford University Press.

Nelson, R. 1995. 'Recent evolutionary theorizing about economic change'. *Journal of Economic Literature* 33: 48–90.

Nelson, R. and Winter, S. 1982. *An evolutionary theory of economic change*. Cambridge, MA: Harvard University Press.

Neumann, J. von. 1937. 'Über ein ökonomisches Gleichungssystem und eine Verallgemeinerung des Brouwerschen Fixpunktsatzes'. In K. Menger (ed.), *Ergebrisse eines mathematischen Kolloquiums, 1935–36*, vol. 8, pp. 73–83. Vienna: Deuticke. English transl., 'A model of general economic equilibrium'. *Review of Economic Studies* 13 (1945): 1–9.

Neumann, J. von and Morgenstern, O. 1944. *Theory of games and economic behavior*. Princeton, NJ: Princeton University Press; II ed., 1947; III ed., 1953.

Nik-Khah, E. 2011. 'George Stigler, the Graduate School of Business, and the pillars of the Chicago School'. In van Horn *et al.*, pp. 116–47.

Nordhaus, W. D. 1973. 'The allocation of energy resources'. *Brookings Papers on Economic Activity* 3: 529–70.

Nordhaus, W. D. 2008. *A question of balance*. New Haven, CT: Yale University Press.

North, D. C. 1990. *Institutions, institutional change and economic performance*. Cambridge: Cambridge University Press.

Nozick, R. 1974. *Anarchy, state and utopia*. Oxford: Blackwell.

Nurkse, R. 1953. *Problems of capital formation in developing countries*. Oxford: Oxford University Press.

Nussbaum, M. 1999. *Women and human development: the capabilities approach*. Cambridge: Cambridge University Press.

Nuti, D. M. 1970. 'Capitalism, socialism and steady growth'. *Economic Journal* 80: 32–57.

O'Donnell, R. 2014–15. 'A critique of the ergodic/nonergodic approach to uncertainty'. *Journal of Post Keynesian Economics* 37: 187–209.

O'Driscoll, G. P. and Rizzo, M. J. 2015. *Austrian economics re-examined*. Abington: Routledge.

Ohanian, L. E. 2010. 'The economic crisis from a neoclassical perspective'. *Journal of Economic Perspectives* 24: 45–66.

Palazzi, P. and Casadio-Tarabusi, E. 2004. 'An index for sustainable development'. *BNL Quarterly Review* 57(229): 185–206.

Panico, C. 1988. *Interest and profit in the theories of value and distribution*. London: Macmillan.

Panzieri, R. 1976. *Lotte operaie nello sviluppo capitalistico*. Ed. by S. Mancini. Turin: Einaudi.

Pareto, V. 1896. 'La courbe de la répartition de la richesse'. In *Recueil publié par la Faculté de Droit de l'Université de Lausanne à l'occasion de l'Exposition nationale de 1896*, pp. 373–87. Italian transl., 'La curva di ripartizione della ricchezza'. In Corsi 1995, pp. 51–70.

Pareto, V. 1896–7. *Cours d'économie politique*. 2 vols., Lausanne: F. Rouge.

Pareto, V. 1906. *Manuale di economia politica*. Milan: Società editrice libraria; repr., Rome: Bizzarri, 1965.

Pareto, V. 1916. *Trattato di sociologia generale*. 2 vols. Florence: Barbera; repr., Rome: Bizzarri, 1964.

Parrinello, S. 1970. 'Introduzione a una teoria neoricardiana del commercio internazionale'. *Studi economici* 25: 267–321.

Pasinetti, L. 1960. 'A mathematical formulation of the Ricardian system'. *Review of Economic Studies* 27: 78–98.

Pasinetti, L. 1962. 'Rate of profit and income distribution in relation to the rate of economic growth'. *Review of Economic Studies* 29: 267–79.

Pasinetti, L. 1965. 'A new theoretical approach to the problems of economic growth'. *Academiae Pontificiae Scientiarum Scripta Varia* 28: 571–696.

Pasinetti, L. 1966. 'Changes in the rate of profits and switches of techniques'. *Quarterly Journal of Economics* 80: 503–17.

Pasinetti, L. 1969. 'Switches of technique and the "rate of return" in capital theory'. *Economic Journal* 79: 508–31.

Pasinetti, L. 1970. 'Again on capital theory and Solow's "rate of return"'. *Economic Journal* 80: 428–31.

Pasinetti, L. 1972. 'Reply to Mr. Dougherty'. *Economic Journal* 82: 1351–2.

Pasinetti, L. 1973. 'The notion of vertical integration in economic analysis'. *Metroeconomica* 25: 1–29.

Pasinetti, L. 1974. *Growth and income distribution: essays in economic theory*. Cambridge: Cambridge University Press.

Pasinetti, L. 1975. *Lezioni di teoria della produzione*. Bologna: il Mulino.

Pasinetti, L. 1979a. 'The unpalatability of the reswitching of techniques'. *Revue d'économie politique* 89: 637–42.

Pasinetti, L. 1979b. 'The "unobtrusive postulate" of neoclassical economic theory'. *Revue d'économie politique* 89: 654–6.

Pasinetti, L. 1981. *Structural change and economic growth*. Cambridge: Cambridge University Press.

Pasinetti, L. 2000. 'Critique of the neoclassical theory of growth and distribution'. *BNL Quarterly Review* 53(215): 383–431.

Patinkin, D. 1956. *Money, interest and prices*. Evanston, IL: Row Peterson; III ed., Cambridge, MA: MIT Press, 1989.

Patinkin, D. 1974. 'The role of the "liquidity trap" in Keynesian economics'. *BNL Quarterly Review* 27(108): 3–11.

Patinkin, D. 1976. 'Keynes and econometrics: on the interaction between the macroeconomic revolutions of the interwar period'. *Econometrica* 44: 1091–123.

Peacock, A. 1992. *Public choice analysis in historical perspective*. Cambridge: Cambridge University Press.

Peck, J. 2011. 'Orientation'. In van Horn *et al.*, pp. xxv–lii.

Penrose, E. 1952. 'Biological analogies in the theory of the firm'. *American Economic Review* 42: 804–19.

Penrose, E. 1959. *The theory of the growth of the firm*. Oxford: Basil Blackwell.

Persson, T. and Tabellini, G. 2000. *Political economics: explaining economic policy*. Cambridge, MA: MIT Press.

Petty, W. 1690. *Political arithmetick*. London: Robert Clavel and Henry Mortlock; repr. in W. Petty, *Economic writings*. Ed. by C. H. Hull, 2 vols. Cambridge: Cambridge University Press, 1899, vol. 1, pp. 233–313.

Phelps, E. S. 1967. 'Phillips curves, expectations of inflation and optimal unemployment over time'. *Economica* 34: 254–81.

Phelps, E. S., ed. 1970. *Microeconomic foundations of employment and inflation theory*. New York: W. W. Norton.

Phelps, E. S. 1990. *Seven schools of macroeconomic thought*. Oxford: Oxford University Press.

Phelps, E. S. and Taylor, J. B. 1977. 'Stabilising powers of monetary policy under rational expectations'. *Journal of Political Economy* 85: 163–90.

Phillips, A. W. 1958. 'The relationship between unemployment and the rate of change of money wage rates in the United Kingdom, 1861–1957'. *Economica* 25: 283–99.

Pigou, A. C. 1912. *Wealth and welfare*. London: Macmillan; new ed., *The Economics of welfare*. London: Macmillan, 1920.

Pigou, A. C. 1933. *The theory of unemployment*. London: Macmillan.

Pigou, A. C. 1950. *Keynes's General Theory: a retrospective view*. London: Macmillan.

Piketty, T. 2013. *Le capital au XXIe siècle*. Paris: Editions du Seuil. English transl., *Capital in the twenty-first century*. Cambridge, MA: Harvard University Press, 2014.

Piore, M. and Sabel C. 1984. *The second industrial divide*. New York: Basic Books.

Pissarides, C. 1985. 'Short-term equilibrium dynamics of unemployment, vacancies and real wages'. *American Economic Review* 75: 676–90.

Polanyi, K. 1944. *The great transformation*. New York: Rinehart.

Polanyi, K. 1966. *Dahomey and the slave trade*. Seattle: University of Washington Press.

Polanyi, K. 1968. *Primitive, archaic and modern economies: essays of Karl Polanyi*. Ed. by G. Dalton. New York: Doubleday; repr. Boston: Beacon Press, 1971.

Polanyi, K., Arensberg, C. M. and Pearson, H. W., eds. 1957. *Trade and market in the early empires*. Glencoe, IL: The Free Press.

Pollock, F. 1956. *Automation: Materialien zur Beurteilung der ökonomischen und sozialen Folgen*. Frankfurt am Main: Europäische Verlagsanstalt; II ed., 1964.

Popper, K. R. 1945. *The open society and its enemies*. 2 vols. London: Routledge and Kegan Paul.

Popper, K. R. 1969. *Conjectures and refutations*. London: Routledge and Kegan Paul.

Posner, R. 1973. *Economic analysis of law*. Boston: Little, Brown and Co.

Prebish, R. 1950. *The economic development of Latin America and its principal problems*. New York: United Nations.

Putnam, R. D. 1993. *Making democracy work: civic traditions in modern Italy*. Princeton, NJ: Princeton University Press.

Putnam, R. D. 2000. *Bowling alone: the collapse and revival of American communities*. New York: Touchstone – Simon & Schuster.

Quadrio Curzio, A. 1967. *Rendita e distribuzione in un modello economico plurisettoriale*. Milan: Giuffré.

Quadrio Curzio, A. and Pellizzari, F. 1996. *Risorse, tecnologia, rendita*. Bologna: il Mulino.

Quadrio Curzio, A. and Scazzieri, R. 1984. 'Sui momenti costitutivi dell'economia politica'. *Giornale degli economisti* 43: 37–76.

Quandt, R. E. 1976. 'Some quantitative aspects of the economic literature'. *Journal of Political Economy* 84: 741–55.

Quesnay, F. 1758–9. *Tableau économique*, Paris (I, 1758; II, 1759; III, 1759); repr. with English transl. in M. Kuczynski and R. L. Meek (eds.), *Quesnay's tableau économique*. London: Macmillan and Kelley, 1972; anastatic reprint ed. by G. De Vivo. Milan: Fondazione Raffaele Mattioli per la storia del pensiero economico, 2009.

Quinton, A. 1968. 'The later philosophy of Wittgenstein'. In G. Pitcher (ed.), *Wittgenstein, a collection of critical essays*. London: Macmillan, pp. 8–21.

Radcliffe Report. 1959. Committee on the working of the monetary system. London: HMSO.

Radner, R. 1968. 'Equilibrium under uncertainty'. *Econometrica* 36: 31–58.

Ramsey, F. P. 1931. *The foundations of mathematics*. London: Routledge and Kegan Paul.

Rawls, J. 1971. *A theory of justice*. Cambridge, MA: Harvard University Press.

Rawls, J. 1982. 'Social unity and primary goods'. In Sen and Williams 1982, pp. 159–86.

Reinhart, C. M. and Rogoff, K. S. 2010. 'Growth in a time of debt'. NBER *Working Paper* 15639.

Ricardo, D. 1951–5. *Works and correspondence*. Ed. by P. Sraffa. 10 vols. Cambridge: Cambridge University Press (vol. 11, *Indexes*, 1973).

Robbins, L. 1932. *An essay on the nature and significance of economic science*. London: Macmillan.

Robbins, L. 1971. *Autobiography of an economist*. London: Macmillan.

Robertson, D. 1924. 'Those empty boxes'. *Economic Journal* 34: 16–30.

Robertson, D. 1930. 'The trees of the forest'. *Economic Journal* 40: 80–89.

Robinson, J. 1933. *The economics of imperfect competition*. London: Macmillan; II ed., 1969.

Robinson, J. 1953. 'The production function and the theory of capital'. *Review of Economic Studies* 21: 81–106.

Robinson, J. 1956. *The accumulation of capital*. London: Macmillan; III ed., 1969.

Robinson, J. 1970. 'Capital theory up-to-date: a review of C. E. Ferguson, *The neoclassical theory of production and distribution*'. *Canadian Journal of Economics* 3: 309–17; repr. in *Collected economic papers*, vol. 4. Oxford: Basil Blackwell, 1973, pp. 144–54.

Robinson, J. 1974. *Time in economics*. London: Thames Polytechnic.

Robinson, J. 1977. 'Michal Kalecki on the economics of capitalism'. *Oxford Bulletin of Economics and Statistics* 33: 7–17.

Roemer, J. 1994. *Egalitarian perspectives*. Cambridge: Cambridge University Press.

Rogoff, K.S. 1985. 'The optimal degree of commitment to an immediate monetary target'. *Quarterly Journal of Economics* 100: 1169–90.

Romer, P. 1986. 'Increasing returns and long-run growth'. *Journal of Political Economy* 94: 1002–37.

Roncaglia, A. 1975. *Sraffa e la teoria dei prezzi*. Rome and Bari: Laterza; II ed., 1981. English transl. *Sraffa and the theory of prices*. Chichester: John Wiley & Sons, 1977.

Roncaglia, A. 1977. *Petty: la nascita dell'economia politica*. Milan: Etas Libri; English transl., *Petty. The origins of political economy*. Armonk, NY: M. E. Sharpe 1985.

Roncaglia, A. 1983. *L'economia del petrolio*. Rome and Bari: Laterza. English transl., *The international oil market*. London: Macmillan, 1985.

Roncaglia, A. 1984. 'Sraffa e le banche'. *Rivista milanese di economia* 10: 104–2.

Roncaglia, A. 1989. 'Research in fusion as investment'. *Giornale degli economisti* 48: 293–307.

Roncaglia, A. 1990a. 'Le scuole sraffiane'. In G. Becattini (ed.), *Il pensiero economico: temi, problemi e scuole*. Turin: Utet, pp. 233–74. English transl., 'The Sraffian schools'. *Review of Political Economy* 1991, 3: 187–219.

Roncaglia, A. 1990b. 'Is the notion of long-period positions compatible with classical political economy?'. *Political Economy* 6: 103–11.

Roncaglia, A. 2005a. *The wealth of ideas*. Cambridge: Cambridge University Press.

Roncaglia, A. 2005b. *Il mito della mano invisibile*. Rome and Bari: Laterza.

Roncaglia, A. 2009a. 'Keynes and probability: an assessment'. *European Journal of the History of Economic Thought* 16: 485–510.

Roncaglia, A. 2009b. *Piero Sraffa*. Houndmills: Palgrave Macmillan.

Roncaglia, A. 2012a. 'A patchwork post-Keynesian/evolutionary approach to income distribution'. In C. Gehrke, N. Salvadori, I. Steedman and M. Sturm (eds.), *Classical political economy and modern theory: essays in honour of Heinz Kurz*. Abingdon: Routledge, pp. 207–18.

Roncaglia, A. 2012b. 'Keynesian uncertainty and the shaky foundations of statistical risk assessment models'. *PSL Quarterly Review* 65(263): 437–54.

Roncaglia, A. 2013. 'Hyman Minsky's monetary production economy'. *PSL Quarterly Review* 66(265): 79–96.

Roncaglia, A. 2015a. 'Oil and its markets'. *PSL Quarterly Review* 68(273): 151–75.

Roncaglia, A. 2015b. 'Institutions, resources and the common weal'. In M. Baranzini, C. Rotondi and R. Scazzieri (eds.), *Resources, production and structural dynamics*. Cambridge: Cambridge University Press, pp. 259–78.

Roncaglia, A. 2016a. *Breve storia del pensiero economico*. Bari and Rome: Laterza. English transl., *A brief history of economic thought*. Cambridge: Cambridge University Press, 2017.

Roncaglia, A. 2016b. 'L'etica dell'economista'. *Moneta e Credito* 69(273): 7–19.

Roncaglia, A. 2017. 'La rivoluzione dello shale oil e i mercati finanziari'. *Moneta e Credito* 70(278): 173–93.

Roncaglia, A. and Tonveronachi, M. 1985. 'The pre-Keynesian roots of the neoclassical synthesis'. *Cahiers d'économie politique* 10: 51–65.

Roncaglia, A. and Tonveronachi, M. 2014. 'Post-Keynesian, post-Sraffian economics: an outline'. In D. Papadimitriou (ed.), *Contributions to economic theory, policy, development and finance: essays in honor of Jan A. Kregel*. Houndmills: Palgrave Macmillan, pp. 40–64.

Röpke, W. 1947. *Civitas humana*. Edinburgh: William Hodge.

Röpke, W. 1969. *Against the tide*. Chicago: Henry Regnery.

Rosenberg, N. 1982. *Inside the black box: technology and economics*. Cambridge: Cambridge University Press.

Rosenberg, N. and Birdzell, L. E. 1986. *How the West grew rich*. New York: Basic Books.

Ross, S. 1973. 'The economic theory of agency: the principal's problem'. *American Economic Review* 63: 134–9.

Rosselli, C. [1930] 1945. *Socialismo liberale*. Ed. by A. Garosci. Rome/Florence/Milan:Edizioni U; new ed. Turin: Einaudi 1973; repr. Turin: Einaudi Tascabili, 1997.

Rossi, E. 1946. *Abolire la miseria: la fiaccola*; repr. ed. by P. Sylos Labini. Rome and Bari: Laterza, 1977.

Rossi, P. 2007. *Max Weber: una idea di Occidente*. Rome: Donzelli.

Rostow, W. W. 1960. *The stages of economic growth*. London: Cambridge University Press.

Rothbard, M. 1962. *Man, economy, and state*. New York: D. van Nostrand.

Rothbard, M. 1995. *An Austrian perspective on the history of economic thought* (vol. 1, *Economic thought before Adam Smith*; vol. 2, *Classical economics*). Aldershot: Edward Elgar.

Rothbard, M. 1997. *The logic of action*. 2 vols. Aldershot: Edward Elgar.

Rothschild, E. 1994. 'Adam Smith and the invisible hand'. *American Economic Review. Papers and Proceedings* 84: 319–22.

Rowthorn, R. 1977. 'Conflict, inflation and money'. *Cambridge Journal of Economics* 1: 215–39.

Rowthorn, R. 2014. 'A note on Piketty's *Capital in the twenty-first century*'. *Cambridge Journal of Economics* 38: 1275–84.

Russell, B. and Whitehead, A. N. 1910–13. *Principia mathematica*. 3 vols. Cambridge: Cambridge University Press.

Sabbatini, P. 2000. *La concorrenza come bene pubblico. Il caso Microsoft*. Rome and Bari: Laterza.

Sabel, C. and Piore, M. 1984. *The second industrial divide*. New York: Basic Books.

Salvadori, M. L. 1976. *Kautsky e la rivoluzione socialista, 1880–1938*. Milan: Feltrinelli.

Samuelson, L. 2005. 'Economic theory and experimental economics'. *Journal of Economic Literature* 43: 65–107.

Samuelson, P. A. 1938. 'A note on the pure theory of consumer's behavior' and 'An addendum'. *Economica* ns 5: 61–71 and 353–4.

Samuelson, P. A. 1947. *Foundations of economic analysis*. Cambridge, MA: Harvard University Press; expanded ed., 1983.

Samuelson, P. A. 1948a. *Economics*. New York: McGraw-Hill.

Samuelson, P. A. 1948b. 'International trade and the equalization of factor prices'. *Economic Journal* 58: 163–84.

Samuelson, P. A. 1958a. 'An exact consumption-loan model of interest with or without the social contrivance of money'. *Journal of Political Economy* 66: 467–82.

Samuelson, P. A. 1958b. 'The pure theory of public expenditure'. *Review of Economics and Statistics* 36: 387–9.

Samuelson, P. A. 1962. 'Parable and realism in capital theory: the surrogate production function'. *Review of Economic Studies* 29: 193–206.

Samuelson, P. A. 1963. 'Problems of methodology: discussion'. *American Economic Review* 53: 231–6.

Samuelson, P. A. 1966. 'A summing up'. *Quarterly Journal of Economics* 80: 568–83.

Samuelson, P. A. 1966–2011. *The collected scientific papers of Paul Samuelson*. 7 vols. Cambridge, MA: MIT Press.

Samuelson, P. A. and Modigliani, F. 1966. 'The Pasinetti paradox in neo-classical and more general models'. *Review of Economic Studies* 33: 269–301.

Samuelson, P. A. and Solow, R. 1960. 'Analytical aspects of anti-inflation policy'. *American Economic Review, Papers and Proceedings* 50: 177–94.

Sandmo, A. 1990. 'Buchanan on political economy. A review article'. *Journal of Economic Literature* 28: 50–65.

Savage, L. J. 1954. *The foundation of statistics*. New York: John Wiley & Sons.

Schefold, B. 1989. *Mr Sraffa on joint production and other essays*. London: Unwin & Hyman.

Schelling, T. 1960. *The strategy of conflict*. Cambridge, MA: Harvard University Press.

Schelling, T. 1978. 'Altruism, meanness, and other potentially strategic behaviors'. *American Economic Review* 68: 229–30.

Schmalensee, R. and Willig, R. D., eds. 1989. *Handbook of industrial organization*. 2 vols. Amsterdam: North Holland.

Schulak, M. E. and Unterköfler, H. 2011. *The Austrian school of economics*. Auburn, AL: Ludwig von Mises Institute.

Schumpeter, J. 1908. *Das Wesen und der Hauptinhalt der theoretischen Nationalökonomie*. Munich and Leipzig: Duncker & Humblot. Italian transl., *L'essenza e i principi dell'economia teorica*. Rome and Bari: Laterza, 1982.

Schumpeter, J. 1912. *Theorie der wirtschaftlichen Entwicklung*. Munich and Leipzig: Duncker & Humblot; II ed. 1926; III ed. 1931; IV ed. 1935. English edn., *The theory of economic development*. Cambridge, MA: Harvard University Press, 1934; repr., New York: Oxford University Press, 1961.

Schumpeter, J. A. 1928. 'The instability of capitalism'. *Economic Journal* 38: 361–86.

Schumpeter, J. 1939. *Business cycles: a theoretical, historical and statistical analysis of the capitalist process*. 2 vols. New York: McGraw-Hill; repr., Philadelphia: Porcupine Press 1982. (Partial repr., R. Fels ed., New York and London: McGraw-Hill, 1964).

Schumpeter, J. 1942. *Capitalism, socialism and democracy*. New York: Harper & Bros.; II ed. 1947; III ed. 1950.

Schumpeter, J. 1946. 'L'avenir de l'entreprise privée devant les tendences socialistes modernes'. In *Comment sauvegarder l'entreprise privée*. Canada: Editions Association Professionelle des Industriels, pp. 103–8.

Schumpeter, J. 1954. *History of economic analysis*. Ed. by E. Boody Schumpeter. New York: Oxford University Press.

Scitovsky, T. 1976. *The joyless economy*. Oxford: Oxford University Press.

Screpanti, E. and Zenezini, M., eds. 1978. *Accumulazione del capitale e progresso tecnico*. Milan: Feltrinelli.

Sebastiani, M., ed. 1989. *Kalecki's relevance today*. London: Macmillan.

Sebastiani, M. 1994. *Kalecki and unemployment equilibrium*. London: Macmillan.

Selten, R. 1975. 'Reexamination of the perfectness concept for equilibrium points in extensive games'. *International Journal of Game Theory* 4: 25–55.

Sen, A. 1970. 'The impossibility of a Paretian liberal'. *Journal of Political Economy* 78: 279–86.

Sen, A. 1973. 'Behaviour and the concept of preference'. *Economica* 40: 241–59; repr. in Sen 1982, pp. 54–73.

Sen, A. 1977. 'Rational fools: a critique of the behavioural foundations of economic theory'. *Philosophy and public affairs* 6: 317–44; repr. in Sen 1982, pp. 84–106.

Sen, A. 1982. *Choice, welfare and measurement*. Oxford: Blackwell.

Sen, A. 1984. *Resources, values and development*. Oxford: Blackwell.

Sen, A. 1987. 'Rational behaviour'. In Eatwell *et al.* 1987, vol. 4, pp. 68–76.

Sen, A. 1991. *Money and value: on the ethics and economics of finance*. Rome: Edizioni dell'Elefante.

Sen, A. 1992. *Inequality reexamined*. Oxford: Clarendon Press.

Sen, A. 1999. *Development as freedom*. New York: Alfred A. Knopf.

Sen, A. 2002a. *Rationality and freedom*. Cambridge, MA: Harvard University Press.

Sen, A. 2002b. *Globalizzazione e libertà*. Milan: Mondadori.

Sen, A. 2003. 'Sraffa, Wittgenstein, Gramsci'. *Journal of Economic Literature* 41: 1240–55.

Sen, A. 2009. *The idea of justice*. London: Allen Lane.

Sen, A. 2012. 'Values and justice'. *Journal of Economic Methodology* 19: 101–8.

Sen, A. and Drèze, J., eds. 1990 *The political economy of hunger*. 3 vols. Oxford: Clarendon Press.

Sen, A. and Williams, B., eds. 1982. *Utilitarianism and beyond*. Cambridge: Cambridge University Press.

Shackle, G. L. S. 1955. *Uncertainty in economics and other reflections*. Cambridge: Cambridge University Press.

Shaikh, A. 1974. 'Laws of production and laws of algebra: the humbug production function'. *Review of Economics and Statistics* 61: 115–20.

Shaikh, A. 2016. *Capitalism*. Oxford: Oxford University Press.

Shapiro, C. and Stiglitz, J. 1984. 'Equilibrium unemployment as a worker discipline device'. *American Economic Review* 74: 433–44.

Sharpe W. F. 1964. 'Capital asset prices: a theory of market equilibrium under conditions of risk'. *Journal of Finance* 19: 425–42.

Shaw, G. B., ed. 1889. *Fabian essays in socialism*. London: Walter Scott; repr. Gloucester, MA: Peter Smith, 1967.

Shleifer, A. and Vishny, R. W. 1997. 'A survey of corporate governance'. *Journal of Finance* 52: 737–83.

Simon, H. A. 1953. 'Causal ordering and identifiability'. In W. C. Hood and T. C. Koopmans (eds.), *Studies in econometric method*. New Haven, CT: Yale University Press.

Simon, H. A. 1954. 'Spurious correlations: a causal interpretation'. *Journal of the American Statistical Association* 49: 467–79.

Simon, H. A. 1955. 'A behavioral model of rational choice'. *Quarterly Journal of Economics* 69: 99–118.

Simon, H. A. 1957. *Models of man*. New York: John Wiley & Sons.

Simon, H. A. 1972. 'Theories of bounded rationality'. In C. B. McGuire and C. Radner (eds.), *Decision and organization*. Amsterdam: North Holland, pp. 161–76.

Simon, H. A. 1979a. *Models of thought*. New Haven, CT: Yale University Press.

Simon, H. A. 1979b. 'On parsimonious explanations of production relations'. *Scandinavian Journal of Economics* 81: 459–74.

Simon, H. A. 1979c. 'Rational decision making in business organizations'. *American Economic Review* 69: 493–512.

Simon, H. 1981. *The sciences of the artificial*, II ed. Cambridge, MA: MIT Press.

Simon, H. A. 1983. *Reason in human affairs*. Stanford, CA: Stanford University Press,.

Simon, H. A. 1993. 'Altruism and economics'. *American Economic Review* 83: 156–61.

Simon, H. A. 1997. *An empirically based microeconomics*. Cambridge: Cambridge University Press.

Sims, C. A. 1980. 'Macroeconomics and reality'. *Econometrica* 48: 1–48.

Sims, C. A. 1982. 'Policy analysis with econometric models'. *Brookings Papers on Economic Activity* 1: 107–64.

Singer, H. 1950. 'The distribution of gains between investing and borrowing countries'. *American Economic Review, Papers and Proceedings* 40: 473–85.

Skidelsky, R. 1983. *John Maynard Keynes: hopes betrayed, 1883–1920*. London: Macmillan.

Skidelsky, R. 1992. *John Maynard Keynes: the economist as saviour, 1920–1937*. London: Macmillan.

Skidelsky, R. 2000. *John Maynard Keynes: fighting for Britain, 1937–1946*. London: Macmillan.

Skidelsky, R. 2010. *Keynes: a very short introduction*. Oxford: Oxford University Press.

Smith, A. 1759. *The theory of moral sentiments*. London: A. Millar; critical ed. ed. by D. D. Raphael and A. L. Macfie. Oxford: Oxford University Press, 1976.

Smith, A. 1776. *An inquiry into the nature and causes of the wealth of nations*. London: W. Strahan and T. Cadell; critical ed. ed. by R. H. Campbell and A. S. Skinner. Oxford: Oxford University Press, 1976.

Smith, A. 1795. *Essays on philosophical subjects*. London: T. Cadell and W. Davies; critical ed. ed. by W. P. D. Wightman and J. C. Bryce. Oxford: Oxford University Press, 1980.

Smith, V. 1962. 'An experimental study of competitive market behavior'. *Journal of Political Economy* 70: 111–37.

Smith, V. 2003. 'Constructivist and ecological rationality in economics'. *American Economic Review* 93: 465–508.

Solow, R. M. 1956. 'A contribution to the theory of economic growth'. *Quarterly Journal of Economics* 79: 65–94.

Solow, R. M. 1957. 'Technical change and the aggregate production function'. *Review of Economics and Statistics* 39: 312–20.

Solow, R. M. 1963. *Capital theory and the rate of return*. Amsterdam: North Holland.

Solow, R. M. 1967. 'The interest rate and transition between techniques'. In C. H. Feinstein (ed.), *Socialism, capitalism and economic growth: essays presented to Maurice Dobb*. Cambridge: Cambridge University Press, pp. 30–39.

Solow, R. M. 1970. 'On the rate of return: reply to Pasinetti'. *Economic Journal* 80: 423–8.

Solow, R. M. 1988. 'Growth theory and after'. *American Economic Review* 78: 307–17.

Solow, R. M. 2000. 'The neoclassical theory of growth and distribution'. *BNL Quartertly Review* 53(215): 349–81.

Sonnenschein, H. 1972. 'Market excess demand functions'. *Econometrica* 40: 549–56.

Soros, G. 2008 *The new paradigm for financial markets*. New York: Public Affairs.

Spaventa, L. 1959. 'Dualism in economic growth'. *BNL Quarterly Review* 12(51): 199–250.

Spaventa, L. 1968. 'Realism without parables in capital theory'. In *Récherches récentes sur la fonction de production*. Centre d'études et de récherches universitaire de Namur, pp. 15–45.

Sraffa, P. 1920. *L'inflazione monetaria in Italia durante e dopo la guerra*, Milan: Scuola tipografica salesiana; repr. in *Economia politica*, 1994: 163–96.

Sraffa, P. 1922a. 'The bank crisis in Italy'. *Economic Journal* 32: 178–97.

Sraffa, P. 1922b. 'Italian banks today'. *Manchester Guardian Commercial. The reconstruction of Europe* 11: 694–95; repr. (in Italian) in Sraffa 1986, pp. 239–44.

Sraffa, P. 1925. 'Sulle relazioni fra costo e quantità prodotta'. *Annali di economia* 2: 277–328.

Sraffa, P. 1926. 'The laws of returns under competitive conditions'. *Economic Journal* 36: 535–50.

Sraffa, P. 1930. 'A criticism' and 'A rejoinder', in 'Symposium on increasing returns and the representative firm'. *Economic Journal* 40: 89–93.

Sraffa, P. 1932. 'Dr. Hayek on money and capital' and 'A rejoinder'. *Economic Journal* 42: 42–53 and 249–51.

Sraffa, P. 1951. 'Introduction'. In Ricardo, vol. I, pp. xiii–lxii.

Sraffa, P. 1960. *Production of commodities by means of commodities*. Cambridge: Cambridge University Press.

Sraffa, P. 1962. 'Production of commodities: a comment'. *Economic Journal* 72: 477–9.

Sraffa, P. 1986. *Saggi*. Bologna: il Mulino.

Sraffa, P. 1991. *Lettere a Tania per Gramsci*. Ed. by V. Gerratana. Rome: Editori riuniti.

Steedman, I. 1977. *Marx after Sraffa*. London: New Left Books.

Steedman, I. 1979. *Trade amongst growing economies*. Cambridge: Cambridge University Press.

Steedman, I. 1989. *From exploitation to altruism*. Cambridge: Polity Press.

Steindl, J. 1945. *Small and big business: economic problems of the size of firms*. Oxford: Basil Blackwell.

Steindl, J. 1952. *Maturity and stagnation in American capitalism*. Oxford: Basil Blackwell; repr., New York: Monthly Review Press, 1976.

Steindl, J. 1990. *Economic papers, 1941–88*. London: Macmillan.

Stern, N. 2008. *The economics of climate change: the Stern Review*. Cambridge: Cambridge University Press.

Stern, N. 2009. *A blueprint for a safer planet: how to manage climate change and create a new era of progress and prosperity*. London: Bodley Head.

Stigler, G. J. 1941. *Production and distribution theories: the formative period*. New York: Macmillan.

Stigler, G. J. 1946. *The theory of price*. New York: Macmillan.

Stigler, G. J. 1951. 'The division of labor is limited by the extent of the market'. *Journal of Political Economy* 59: 185–93.

Stigler, G. J. 1961. 'The economics of information'. *Journal of Political Economy* 69: 213–25.

Stigler, G. J. 1971. 'A theory of regulation'. *Bell Journal of Economics and Management Science* 2: 3–21.

Stigler, G. J. 1994. *Mercato, informazione, regolamentazione*. Ed. by G. Fiorentini. Bologna: il Mulino.

Stigler, G. J. and Becker, G. 1977. 'De gustibus non est disputandum'. *American Economic Review* 67: 76–90.

Stiglitz, J. 2002. *Informazione, economia pubblica e macroeconomia*. Ed. by A. Boitani and A. Petretto. Bologna: il Mulino.

Stockhammer, E. 2008. 'Is the NAIRU theory a monetarist, new Keynesian, post Keynesian or Marxist theory?'. *Metroeconomica* 59: 479–51.

Stone, R. 1997. *Some British empiricists in the social sciences, 1650–1900*. Cambridge: Cambridge University Press.

Stone, R. and Brown, A. 1962. *A computable model of economic growth*. London: Chapman and Hall.

Streeten, P. 1972. *The frontiers of development studies*. New York: John Wiley & Sons.

Streeten, P. 1986. 'Aerial roots'. *BNL Quarterly Review* 39(157): 135–59.

Stuart Hughes, H. 1958. *Consciousness and society*. New York: Alfred A. Knopf.

Sugden, R. 1991. 'Rational choice: a survey of contributions from economics and philosophy'. *Economic Journal* 101: 751–85.

Sugden, R. 2001. 'The evolutionary turn in game theory'. *Journal of Economic Methodology* 8: 113–30.

Svorenčík, A. 2014. 'MIT's rise to prominence: outline of a collective biography'. *History of Political Economy* 46 (Supplement): 109–33.

Swan, T. W. 1956. 'Economic growth and capital accumulation'. *Economic Record* 32: 334–61.

Sweezy, P. 1942. *The theory of capitalist development.* NewYork: Monthly Review Press, repr. 1968.

Sylos Labini, P. 1954. 'Il problema dello sviluppo economico in Marx ed in Schumpeter'. In G. U. Papi (ed.), *Teoria dello sviluppo economico.* Milan: Giuffrè; repr. in P. Sylos Labini, *Problemi dello sviluppo economico.* Bari: Laterza, 1970, pp. 19–73.

Sylos Labini, P. 1956. *Oligopolio e progresso tecnico.* Milan: Giuffrè; IV ed., Turin: Einaudi, 1967. English transl., *Oligopoly and technical progress.* Cambridge, MA: Harvard University Press, 1962; II ed., 1969.

Sylos Labini, P. 1967. 'Prices, distribution and investment in Italy 1951–1966: an interpretation'. *BNL Quarterly Review* 20(83): 316–75.

Sylos Labini, P. 1972. *Sindacati, inflazione e produttività.* Rome and Bari: Laterza.

Sylos Labini, P., ed. 1973. *Prezzi relativi e distribuzione del reddito.* Turin: Boringhieri.

Sylos Labini, P. 1974. *Saggio sulle classi sociali.* Rome and Bari: Laterza.

Sylos Labini, P. 1976. 'Competition: the product markets'. In Wilson and Skinner 1976, pp. 200–32.

Sylos Labini, P. 1983. *Il sottosviluppo e l'economia contemporanea.* Rome and Bari: Laterza.

Sylos Labini, P. 1984. *Le forze dello sviluppo e del declino.* Rome and Bari: Laterza.

Sylos Labini, P. 1987. 'The theory of unemployment, too, is historically conditioned'. *BNL Quarterly Review* 40(163): 379–435.

Sylos Labini, P. 1995. 'Why the interpretation of the Cobb-Douglas production function must be radically changed'. *Structural Change and Economic Dynamics* 6: 485–504.

Sylos Labini, P. 2000. *Sottosviluppo: una strategia di riforme.* Rome and Bari: Laterza.

Sylos Labini, P. 2003. 'Prospects for the world economy'. *BNL Quarterly Review* 56(226): 179–206.

Syrquin, M. 2018. 'Quantifying economic development: Kuznets, Chenery, and the quantitative approach to development economics'. *History of Political Economy*, 50 (Supplement): 211–30.

Tarantelli, E. 1978. *Il ruolo economico del sindacato.* Rome and Bari: Laterza.

Tarantelli, E. 1986. *Economia politica del lavoro.* Turin: Utet.

Targetti, F. 1988. *Nicholas Kaldor.* Bologna: il Mulino.

Tarshis, L. 1939. 'Changes in real and money wages'. *Economic Journal* 49: 150–54.

Tawney, R. H. 1926. *Religion and the rise of capitalism.* London: Murray; repr., Harmondsworth: Penguin Books, 1975.

Taylor, J. 1980. 'Aggregate dynamics and staggered contracts'. *Journal of Political Economy* 88: 1–23.

Thaler, R. 1988. 'Anomalies: the winner's curse'. *Journal of Economic Perspectives* 2: 191–202.

Thaler, R. 1990. 'Saving, fungibility, and mental accounts'. *Journal of Economic Perspectives* 4: 193–205.

Thaler, R. 1992. *The winner's curse: paradoxes and anomalies of economic life.* New York: Free Press; new ed., Princeton, NJ: Princeton University Press, 1994.

Thaler, R. and Sunstein, C. 2003. 'Libertarian paternalism'. *American Economic Review* 93: 175–9.

Thaler, R. and Sunstein, C. 2008. *Nudge: improving decisions about health, wealth, and happiness.* New Haven, CT: Yale University Press.

Thirlwall, A. P. 1979. 'The balance of payments constraint as an explanation of international growth rate differences'. *BNL Quarterly Review* 32(128): 45–53.

Thirlwall, A. P. 1987. *Nicholas Kaldor.* Brighton: Wheatsheaf.

Thirlwall, A. P. 2018. 'Reflections of an economist'. *BNL Quarterly Review* 71 (284): 9–39.

Thirlwall, A. P. and Leon-Ledesma, M. 2000. 'Is the natural rate of growth endogenous?'. *BNL Quarterly Review* 53(215): 433–45.

Thomas, W. 2014. 'Decisions and dynamics: postwar theoretical problems and the MIT style of economics'. *History of Political Economy* 46 (Supplement): 295–314.

Thornton, H. 1802. *Enquiry into the nature and effects of the paper credit of Great Britain.* London: Hatchard; repr., ed. by F. Hayek, London: London School of Economics, 1939.

Thünen, J. H. von. 1826–50. *Der isolierte Staat in Beziehung auf Landwirtschaft und Nationalökonomie.* Rostock: Leopold.

Thurstone, L. L. 1931. 'The indifference function'. *Journal of Social Psychology* 2: 139–67.

Tirole, J. 1988. *The theory of industrial organization.* Cambridge, MA: MIT Press.

Tobin, J. 1958. 'Liquidity preference as behavior towards risk'. *Review of Economic Studies* 25: 65–86.

Tobin, J. 1969. 'A general equilibrium approach to monetary theory'. *Journal of Money, Credit and Banking* 1: 15–29.

Tobin, J. 1971–85. *Essays in Economics.* 3 vols. (vol. 1, 1971; vol. 2, 1975; vol. 3, 1985), Amsterdam: North Holland.

Togliatti, P., ed. 1962. *La formazione del gruppo dirigente del Partito comunista italiano.* Rome: Editori Riuniti.

Tonveronachi, M. 1982. 'Monetarismo e regole fisse in H.C. Simons'. *Moneta e Credito* 35: 309–30.

Tonveronachi, M. 1983. *J. M. Keynes. Dall'instabilità ciclica all'equilibrio di sottoccupazione.* Rome: NIS.

Tonveronachi, M. 1989. *Struttura ed evoluzione dei sistemi finanziari.* Arezzo: Banca Popolare dell'Etruria e del Lazio.

Tonveronachi, M. 1990. 'Teorie monetarie a Chicago'. In G. Becattini (ed.), *Il pensiero economico: temi, problemi e scuole.* Turin: Utet, pp. 349–85.

Tonveronachi, M. 1992. 'Keynes and equilibrium: a note'. In M. Sebastiani (ed.), *The notion of equilibrium in the Keynesian theory*. Houndmills: Macmillan, pp. 18–31.

Toporowski, J. 2000. *The end of finance: capital market inflation, financial derivatives and pension fund capitalism*. London: Routledge.

Toporowski, J. 2013. *Michał Kalecki: an intellectual biography*, vol. 1: *Rendez-vous in Cambridge, 1899–1939*. Houndmills: Palgrave Macmillan.

Tribe, K. 1995. *Strategies of economic order. German economic discourse 1750–1950*. Cambridge: Cambridge University Press.

Triffin, R. 1974. 'Crisi del petrolio e problemi internazionali e comunitari'. *Moneta e Credito* 27(106): 148–61.

Trigilia, C. 2016. 'Tipi di democrazia e modelli di capitalismo: un'agenda di ricerca'. *Stato e Mercato* 36: 183–213.

Tsuru, S. 1993. *Institutional economics revisited*. Cambridge: Cambridge University Press.

Tugan-Baranowskij, M. J. 1905. *Theoretische Grundlagen des Marxismus*. Leipzig: Dunker & Humblot.

Tullock, G. 1965. *The politics of bureaucracy*. Washington, DC: Public Affairs Press.

Turgot, A.-R.-J. [1766]. 'Réflexions sur la formation et la distribution des richesses'; publ. in 1769–70 in the *Ephémérides du citoyen*; repr. in Ravix and Romani (eds.), Turgot. *Formation et distribution des richesses*. Paris: Flammarion, pp. 157–226.

Tutino, S. 1968. *L'ottobre cubano*. Turin: Einaudi.

Tversky, A. and Kahnemann, D. 1992. 'Advances in prospect theory: cumulative representation of uncertainty'. *Journal of Risk and Uncertainty* 5: 297–323.

Valdés, J. G. 1995. *Pinochet's economists: the Chicago school in Chile*. Cambridge: Cambridge University Press.

Vanek, J. 1970. *The general theory of labor managed market economies*. Ithaca, NY: Cornell University Press.

Van Horn, R. 2011. 'Jacob Viner's critique of Chicago neoliberalism'. In Van Horn et al., pp. 279–300.

Van Horn, R. 2014. 'Henry Simon's death'. *History of Political Economy* 46: 525–35.

Van Horn, R. and Klaes, M. 2011. 'Intervening in laissez-faire liberalism: Chicago shift on patents'. In Van Horn et al., pp. 180–207.

Van Horn, R. and Mirowski, P. 2009. 'The rise of the Chicago school of economics and the birth of neoliberalism'. In Mirowski and Plehwe, pp. 139–78.

Van Horn, R., Mirowski, P. and Stapleford, T. A., eds. 2011. *Building Chicago economics*. Cambridge: Cambridge University Press.

Varian, H. R. 1974. 'Equity, envy and efficiency'. *Journal of Economic Theory* 9: 63–91.

Varian, H. R. 2014. 'Big data: new tricks for econometrics'. *Journal of Economic Perspectives* 28: 3–28.

Vaughn, K. I. 1994. *Austrian economics in America: the migration of a tradition*. Cambridge: Cambridge University Press.

Veblen, T. 1898. 'Why is economics not an evolutionary science?'. *Quarterly Journal of Economics* 12: 373–97.

Veblen, T. 1899. *The theory of the leisure class.* New York: Macmillan.

Veblen, T. 1904. *The theory of business enterprise.* New York: Charles Scribner's Sons.

Veblen, T. 1919. *The place of science in modern civilization and other essays.* New York: B. W. Huebsch.

Verdoorn, P. 1949. 'Fattori che regolano lo sviluppo della produttività del lavoro'. *L'industria* 1: 3–10.

Veritas Foundation. 1960. *Keynes at Harvard: economic deception as a political credo.* New York: Veritas Foundation.

Vianello, F. 1985. 'The pace of accumulation'. *Political Economy: Studies in the Surplus Approach* 1: 69–87.

Vicarelli, F. 1977. *Keynes: L'instabilità del capitalismo.* Milan: Etas libri.

Vicarelli, S. 1975. 'Il "problema della trasformazione": fine di una controversia'. *Note economiche* 8: 91–138.

Vickrey, W. 1961. 'Counterspeculation, auctions and competitive sealed tenders'. *Journal of Finance* 16: 8–37.

Viner, J. 1927. 'Adam Smith and laissez-faire'. *Journal of Political Economy* 35: 198–232; repr. in Viner 1991, pp. 85–113.

Viner, J. 1931. 'Cost curves and supply curves'. *Zeitschrift für Nationalökonomie* 3: 23–46.

Viner, J. 1978. 'Religious thought and economic society: four chapters of an unfinished work'. J. Melitz and D. Winch, eds. *History of Political Economy* 10: 1–192.

Viner, J. 1991. *Essays on the intellectual history of economics.* Ed. by D. A. Irwin. Princeton, NJ: Princeton University Press.

Visco, I., ed. 1985. *Le aspettative nell'analisi economica.* Bologna: il Mulino.

Vromen, J. J. 2007. 'Neuroeconomics as a natural extension of bioeconomics: the shifting scope of standard economic theory'. *Journal of Bioeconomics* 9: 145–67.

Wald, A. 1936. 'Über einige Gleichungssysteme der Mathematischen Ökonomie'. *Zeitschrift für Nationalökonomie* 7: 637–70. English transl., 'On some systems of equations of mathematical economics'. *Econometrica* 19 (1951): 368–403.

Wallerstein, I. 1974, 1980, 1989. *The modern world-system.* 3 vols. New York: Academic Press.

Wallich, H. C. and Weintraub, S. 1971. 'A tax-based incomes policy'. *Journal of Economic Issues* 5: 1–19; repr. in Weintraub 1978, pp. 259–80.

Wallis, J. J. and North, D. C. 1986. 'Measuring the transaction sector in the American economy, 1870–1970'. In S. L. Engerman and R. E. Gallman (eds.), *Long-term factors in American economic growth.* Chicago: University of Chicago Press, pp. 95–162.

Wallis, W. A. and Friedman, M. 1942. 'The empirical derivation of indifference functions'. In O. Lange, F. M. Intyre and T. O. Yntema (eds.), *Studies in mathematical economics and econometrics, in memory of Henry Schultz.* New York: Books for Libraries Press, pp. 175–89.

Walras, L. 1874. *Eléments d'économie politique pure.* Lausanne: Corbaz; English transl., ed. by W. Jaffé. *Elements of pure economics.* London: Irwin, 1954; repr., London: Allen & Unwin, 1965.

Weber, M. 1904–5. 'Die protestantische Ethik und der Geist des Kapitalismus'. *Archiv für Sozialwissenschaft und Sozialpolitik* 20–21; II ed. In *Gesammelte Aufsätze zur Religionssoziologie.* Tübingen: Mohr 1922; Italian transl., *L'etica protestante e lo spirito del capitalismo.* Florence: Sansoni, 1965.

Weber, M. 1919. *Politik als Beruf, Wissenschaft als Beruf.* Berlin: Duncker & Humblot; Italian transl., *Il lavoro intellettuale come professione.* Turin: Einaudi 1948; repr. 1976.

Weber, M. 1920–21. *Gesammelte Aufsätze zur Religionssoziologie.* Tübingen: J. C. B. Mohr. Italian transl., *Sociologia della religione,* ed. by P. Rossi. Milan: Edizioni di Comunità 1982; II ed., 4 vols. Turin: Edizioni di Comunità, 2002.

Weber, M. 1922a. *Gesammelte Aufsätze zur Wissenschaftslehre.* Tübingen: Mohr; Italian transl., *Il metodo delle scienze storico-sociali.* Turin: Einaudi 1958; repr. Milan: Oscar Mondadori, 1980.

Weber, M. 1922b. *Wirtschaft und Gesellschaft.* 2 vol. Tübingen: Mohr. Italian transl., *Economia e società.* 2 vols. Milan: Edizioni di Comunità, 1962.

Weintraub, R. 1977. 'The microfoundations of macroeconomics: a critical survey'. *Journal of Economic Literature* 15: 1–23.

Weintraub, R. 2014. 'MIT's openness to Jewish economists'. *History of Political Economy* 46 (Supplement): 45–59.

Weintraub, S. 1978. *Keynes, Keynesians, and monetarists.* Philadelphia: University of Pennsylvania Press.

Wicksell, K. 1893. *Über Wert, Kapital, und Rente.* Jena: G. Fischer; English transl., *Value, capital and rent.* London: Allen & Unwin, 1954.

Wicksell, K. 1898. *Geldzins und Güterpreise bestimmenden Ursachen.* Jena: G. Fischer; English transl., *Interest and prices.* London: Macmillan, 1936.

Wicksell, K. 1900. 'Om gränsproduktivitaten såsom grundval för den nationale-konomiska fördelningen'. *Ekonomisk Tidskrift* 2: 305–37; English transl., 'Marginal productivity as the basis for distribution in economics'. In K. Wicksell, *Selected papers on economic theory.* London: Allen & Unwin, 1958, pp. 93–121.

Wicksell, K. 1901–6. *Forelasningar i nationalekonomi.* 2 vols. Stockholm and Lund: Fritzes-Berlingska. English transl., *Lectures on political economy.* 2 vols. London: Routledge and Kegan Paul, 1934–5.

Wicksteed, P. H. 1884. '*Das Kapital:* a criticism'. *To-day* 2: 388–409; repr. in P. H. Wicksteed, *The common sense of political economy and selected papers and reviews on economic theory.* Ed. by L. Robbins. London: Routledge, 1934, vol. 2, pp. 705–24.

Williamson, J. 1990. *Latin American adjustment: how much has happened?* Washington, DC: Institute for International Economics.

Williamson, J. 2004. *A short history of the Washington consensus.* Washington, DC: Institute for International Economics. https://piie.com/publications/papers/wil liamson0904-2.pdf.

Williamson, O. 1975. *Markets and hierarchies: analysis and antitrust implications.* New York: Free Press.

Williamson, O. 1986. *Economic organization*. Brighton: Wheatsheaf Books.

Williamson, O. 2000. 'The new institutional economics: taking stock, looking ahead'. *Journal of Economic Literature* 38: 595–613.

Wittgenstein, L. 1921. 'Logisch-philosophische Abhandlung'. *Annalen der Naturphilosophie* 14, 185–262. Revised English ed., *Tractatus logico-philosophicus*. London: Kegan Paul, 1922.

Wittgenstein, L. 1953. *Philosophische Untersuchungen*. Oxford: Basil Blackwell.

Wittman, D. 1995. *The myth of democratic failure: why political institutions are efficient*. Chicago: University of Chicago Press.

Wood, A. 1975. *A theory of profits*. Cambridge: Cambridge University Press.

Xu He 1963. Italian transl., *Trattato di economia politica*. 2 vols. Milano: Mazzotta 1975.

Young, A. 1928. 'Increasing returns and economic progress'. *Economic Journal* 38: 527–42.

Index

Note: This Index contains names of sources substantively discussed or quoted in the text. A full list of names of all sources may be found in the Bibliography.

Abramowitz, Moses, 170
Accumulation in classical approach, 20
The accumulation of capital (Robinson), 293–4
Acemoglu, Daron, 334
Act utilitarianism, 357–8
Adam Smith in Beijing (Arrighi), 329
Adelman, Irma, 170, 344–5
Adelman, Morris, 225–6, 239, 240–1
Adenauer, Konrad, 184, 185
The affluent society (Galbraith), 329
Agarwal, Bina, 370
Agent-based models, 256, 339–40
Aggregate demand, 55, 148, 149–50, 159–60, 207, 285, 308–9
Aggregate production function, 128–9, 305–6, 334
Aghion, Philippe, 163–4
Aglietta, Michel, 341
Agriculture, technical progress in, 239
Akerlof, George, 132–3, 144, 159
Alchian, Armen, 198, 333, 337
Alesina, Alberto, 334
Allais, Maurice, 118, 119, 120, 158, 212–14, 250–2
Allais paradox, 119
Althusser, Louis, 325
Altruism, 210–11, 255, 360
Amable, Bruno, 345
American capitalism (Galbraith), 329
American Economic Association, 35, 36, 335
American Enterprise Institute, 214–15
American Telegraph and Telephone Company (AT&T), 233–4
Amin, Samir, 328–9
Andrews, Philip, 295
Annales School, 328–9, 343
Anomalies, 263

Antitrust legislation, 61, 182, 188, 234–5
Apostles (secret society), 48–9
Applied economics
 generally, 218–20
 auctions, 237–8
 descriptive statistics, 230–3
 econometrics (*See Econometrics*)
 energy sources and,238–41 (*See also Energy sources*)
 environment and, 241–4
 gender empowerment measure (GEM), 232
 gender-related development index (GDI), 232
 human development index (HDI), 231–2
 indicators, 230–3
 input-output tables, 8, 24, 120, 220–2
 market creation and, 235–8
 market regulation and, 233–8
 national accounting, 222–6
 pure theory of regulation, 237
 theoretical background, 218–20
Approaches, connections between, 2–4
Arbitrage, 275–6
Aristotle, 24, 59, 130, 327
Arrighi, Giovanni, 328–9
Arrow, Kenneth
 generally, 72, 198
 behavioural economics and, 250
 on economic development, 169
 general equilibrium theory and, 121, 122, 125, 307
 growth theory and, 163–4
 impossibility theorem, 125, 367–8
 welfare economics and, 364, 366–7
Arthur, Brian, 339, 341
Asimakopulos, Athanasios, 160
Association for Evolutionary Economics, 335–6

Atkinson, Anthony, 230–1, 356, 361
Auburn University, 189–90
Auctions, 237–8
Austrian Institute for Economic Research,
    64
Austrian School
    experimental economics and, 256
    Hayek in, 179
    Hicks and, 192–6
    marginalist approach and, 26
    New Austrian school, 8, 179, 186–92
    Polanyi versus, 327
    Stigler and, 132
Authoritarian populism, 232
Authors, treatment of, 3
Autobiography (Hayek), 72, 74
Average period of production, 33, 67, 107,
    193
Average-variance model, 274
Axelrod, Robert, 339–40
Axiomatic analysis, 121–3
Ayers, Clarence, 36

Babbage, Charles, 18, 20
Bacon, Francis, 14
Bain, Joe, 80–1, 114–15, 136–7, 139
Balance of payments, 268–9
Balassa, Bela, 344–5
Balogh, Thomas, 344–5
Banca Commerciale Italiana, 90, 100
Banca di Roma, 90
Banca Italiana di Sconto, 90
Banerjee, Abhijit, 170
Bank for International Regulations, 215
Banking
    central banks, 272
    financial markets, role in, 277, 279
Bank of Italy, 228, 232
Baran, Paul, 325
Baranzini, Mauro, 151
Barone, Enrico, 76
Barro, Robert J., 157, 204, 217
Bartley, W.W. III, 66
Baumol, William, 135, 137–8, 168, 234,
    250
Baumol's Law, 168
A beautiful mind (film), 141
Beccaria, Cesare, 359
Becker, Gary, 131–2, 196, 247
Behavioural economics, 250–2
    generally, 9
    Arrow and, 250
    behavioural paternalism, 252
    expected utility theory and, 251–2
    Friedman and, 250

    Morgenstern and, 250–1
    Samuelson and, 250
    von Neumann and, 250–1
Benes, Jaromir, 239
Benini, Rodolfo, 226
Bentham, Jeremy
    generally, 67
    felicific calculus and, 13, 21–2, 247,
        352–3, 354
    Hayek and, 77–8
    Jevons and, 26–7
    Mill and, 22
    utilitarianism and, 352–3, 354, 357,
        358–9
Bergson, Abram, 364
Berle, Adolf, 80–1, 135–6, 309, 320–1
Berlin, Isaiah, 353–4
Berlin Wall, 319
Berlusconi, Silvio, 325
Bernoulli, Daniel, 49
Bernstein, Eduard, 322
Bertrand, J.L.F., 118
Besicovitch, Abram S., 100
Beveridge, William, 64–5
Beveridge Report, 64–5, 322, 346
Bhaduri, Amit, 193
Bharadwaj, Krisha, 306
Bhaskar, Roy, 297
Biasco, Salvatore, 302
Binmore, Kenneth, 143
Bioeconomics, 256
Birdzell, L.E., Jr., 343
von Bismarck, Otto, 183–4, 322, 346
Bitcoins, 83, 87
Black, Duncan, 179–80, 209, 211
Black, Fisher, 274, 275
Blanchard, Olivier, 217
Blaug, Mark, 199
Bloomsbury Circle, 48–9
BNL Quarterly Review, 10
Bobbio, Norberto, 375
Böhm, Franz, 181
von Böhm-Bawerk, Eugen
    generally, 186, 187
    average period of production and, 33, 67,
        107, 193
    on interest, 26, 43–4
    Marxism and, 321–2
    theory of capital, 69, 304
    theory of value and, 194–5
Bordiga, Amadeo, 92
Bortkiewicz, Ladislaus, 17, 321–2
Bounded rationality, 257–60
    generally, 138, 249
    administrative behaviour and, 258

causal ordering and, 257–8
correlation and, 257–8
entrepreneurs and, 258–9
game theory and, 260
heuristics and, 258–9
Keynes and, 259
market and, 259
prospect theory compared, 261–2
satisficing behaviour and, 249, 259–60
Simon and, 138, 249, 257–60
theory of the firm and, 259
Bourbaki, Nicholas, 121
Boyer, Robert, 341
Braudel, Fernand, 328–9, 343
Breglia, Alberto, 182
Brenner, Robert, 325
Bretton Woods, 7–8, 48–9, 56, 84, 213–14, 269–71, 272, 323–4
Brief history of economic thought (Roncaglia), 10
British Economic Association, 29
Brumberg, Richard, 150–1
Brundtland, Gro Harlem, 242–3
Bruni, Luigino, 359
Brunner, Karl, 201–2
Bruno, Giordano, 352
Brus, Wlodzmierz, 324
Buchanan, James, 179–80, 209
Burmeister, Edwin, 193, 195–6, 305
Business cycle. *See Trade cycle theory*
Business cycles (Schumpeter), 46

Caldwell, Bruce, 63, 66, 77, 197
Cambodia, income inequality and, 362
Cambridge University
decline of, 291–2
Keynes at, 97–100, 289–90
New Cambridge School, 292–4
tradition of, 9–10, 289–90
Wittgenstein at, 97–100
Can 'It' happen again? (Minsky), 280
Cantillon, Richard, 15
Capabilities theory, 6–7, 10, 170–1, 231–2, 351, 368–70
Capital, theory of, 61–2, 69, 71–5, 87, 303–8
Capital and time (Hicks), 75, 193
Capital asset pricing model (CAPM), 274
Capitalism, socialism and democracy (Schumpeter), 46
Capital (Marx), 24, 220, 242, 294, 321–2
Casadio Tarabusi, Enrico, 232
Cassel, Gustav, 33, 120
Cato Society, 214–15
Causal ordering, 257–8

Center for International Private Enterprise (CIPE), 214–15
Central banks, 152, 211–12, 217, 272
Chamberlin, Edward, 47–8, 94, 96, 294
Chandler, Alfred D., 136, 341
Change in social and economic structure, 326–8
Chaos theory, 342
Chenery, Hollis, 170, 231
'Chicago boys', 215
Chicago School
generally, 50–1, 117, 179, 187
evolution of, 196–7
financing of, 197
fiscal policy and, 196
Friedman and, 50–1, 117, 130–1, 179, 196, 197, 198
'invisible hand' and, 131
Knight and, 50–1, 196–7
microeconomics in, 129–33
monetary policy in, 196
Mont Pèlerin Society and, 213
Samuelson and, 197–8
'second' Chicago School, 197, 198
Stigler and, 196, 197
Veblen and, 196–7
Child labor legislation, 82
Chile, dictatorship in, 60, 183, 214, 215
China
Cultural Revolution, 324–5, 362
Great Leap Forward, 324–5
income inequality and, 362
Marxism in, 324–5
Circus, 293
Clapham, John H., 93–4
Clark, Colin, 222
Clark, John Bates, 120, 128–9
Clark, John Maurice, 36, 120, 196–7, 234
Classical approach
generally, 5, 13
accumulation in, 20
cyclical nature of economics in, 16, 19
division of labour in, 16, 18, 19–20
ethics and, 350–1
felicific calculus in, 13, 21–2
labour theory of value in, 15, 17
marginalist approach versus, 13–14, 24–6
Marx and, 22–4
natural prices in, 14–15, 17–18, 19
nature of market in, 19
objectivism of, 15
overview, 20
Political Anatomy, 14–15
Political Arithmetic, 14–15
production costs in, 16–17

Classical approach (cont.)
  profits in, 17–20
  self-interest in, 13, 21
  self-regulating mechanism in, 178
  surplus in, 15–16
  wealth of nations in, 18, 19–20
Classical probability theory, 49–50
Clower, Robert, 157
Club of Rome, 239, 242
Club theory, 210
Coase, Ronald, 134, 331–3, 365–6
Coase Theorem, 333
Cobb, Charles, 226
Cobb-Douglas function, 128–9, 226, 306
Cognitive economics, 256
Cold War, 113, 165
The collected works of F.A. Hayek (Bartley
  and Caldwell, eds.), 66
Collected writings of John Maynard Keynes,
  301–2
Colletti, Lucio, 325
Colloque Walter Lippmann, 213
Commission on the Measurement of
  Economic Performance and Social
  Progress (CMEPSP), 232
Commodities, 104–5
Commons, John, 36, 335
Comparative static analysis, 43, 127–8, 153
Compensation principle, 366
Competitive capitalism, 135–6
de Condorcet, Marquis, 179–80, 209
Condorcet paradox, 366–7
Conlisk, John, 253
Consequentialism, 358, 368
Conspicuous consumption, 35–6
The constitution of liberty (Hayek), 60
Constructive rationalism, 78
Consumer behaviour, 133, 338
Contingent goods, 123
Contingent markets, 124
Correlation, 257–8
Cosmo, Umberto, 91
Costa Rica, per capita income in, 232
Cournot, Augustin, 118
Cowles, Alfred, 120
Cowles Foundation
  generally, 7, 113, 291
  bounded rationality and, 260
  Chicago School and, 197–8
  econometrics and, 227–8
  general equilibrium theory and, 120–2,
    126
Creative destruction, 47, 69, 216
Credito Italiano, 90
Crises

Minsky and, 216, 279–82
  oil crisis, 270–1
  2007–2008 crisis, 152, 180, 216–17, 279,
    282
Croce, Benedetto, 88–9, 215
Crypto-currencies, 83, 87
Cultural evolution, 321, 343–5
Cultural traditions, 372–3
Cyert, Richard, 136, 258–9

Dahrendorf, Ralf, 347, 373
Dantzig, George, 221
Darwin, Charles, 35, 336–7, 338, 339
Darwinism, 29–30
Das Kapital: a criticism (Wicksteed), 323
David, Paul, 339, 341
Davidson, Paul, 300, 330, 342
Deaton, Angus, 361
Debreu, Gerard
  generally, 72, 198
  general equilibrium theory and, 120, 121,
    122, 123, 125, 307
Debt equivalence theorem, 204
Decision analysis, 113–14
Decision theory, 117
de Clippel, Geoffrey, 356
de Finetti, Bruno, 51–2, 116, 118, 251–2
Definition of economics, 2
De gustibus non est disputandum (Stigler and
  Becker), 132
Della Volpe, Galvano, 325
Democratic socialism, 322
Denationalization of money, 83–7
Denison, Edward Fulton, 163
Deontological ethics, 352, 354, 358
Dependency theory, 166
Developing countries, economic develop-
  ment in, 165–7
Development economics, 321, 343–5,
  361–2
de Viti de Marco, Antonio, 209
Dictatorship, 60, 183, 214, 215
Dilthey, Wilhelm, 320
D'Ippoliti, Carlo, 369
Director, Aaron, 180
Disequilibrium, 157
Distribution, theory of, 296, 308–10, 311
Division of labour
  in classical approach, 16, 18, 19–20
  Marx on, 20
  Smith on, 19–20, 135, 349
  Sraffa on, 102–3
  technical progress and, 18
  theories of the firm and, 135
Dmitriev, Vladimir K., 17

Dobb, Maurice, 76, 289–90, 292–3, 325
Domar, Evsey, 160, 311
Donzelli, Franco, 72, 73, 76, 195–6
Dosi, Giovanni, 340
Douglas, Paul, 226
Downs, Anthony, 209, 211
Draghi, Mario, 185–6
Drèze, Jean, 169
Duflo, Esther, 170
Dunlop, John T., 54–5
Dynamic analysis, 336
Dynamic stochastic general equilibrium
  (DSGE), 152

Econometrica, 227
Econometrics
  generally, 8
  a-theoretical econometrics, 230
  autoregressive integrated moving average
    (ARIMA) model, 229
  autoregressive moving average (ARMA)
    model, 229
  developments in, 228–30
  evolution of, 226–8
  Hicks and, 228–9
  Keynes and, 228–9
  Leontief and, 228–9
  Lucas and, 228–9
  Modigliani and, 228
  neoclassical synthesis and, 152
  Pareto and, 226
  Sylos Labini and, 228, 297
  vector autoregressive (VAR) method, 229
Econometric Society, 8, 122, 227
Economica, 65
Economic agent. *See* Homo oeconomicus
Economical-philosophical manuscripts
  (Marx), 242
Economic Commission for Latin America
  and the Caribbean (CEPAL), 166–7
Economic development theories, 164–71
  capabilities and, 170–1
  dependency theory and, 166
  developing countries and, 165–7
  economic dualism and, 167
  integrated theory, 168–9
  multinationals and, 167
  productivity growth and, 169
  technical progress and, 164–5
Economic dualism, 167
Economic geography, 342
Economic Journal, 29, 48–9, 93–4, 95, 96,
  97, 289
Economic liberalism
  Hayek and, 59–61, 77, 81

Schumpeter and, 42
The economics of imperfect competition
  (Robinson), 293–4
Economics of regulation (Kahn), 236
Economics (Samuelson), 126
Economies of scale. *See Returns to scale*
Economists, ethics of, 351–2, 374–6
Economy and society (Weber), 37
Edgeworth, Francis, 95
Edwards, Ward, 252–3
Effective demand, principle of, 54–5
Efficient financial markets, theory of, 273–6
Eichner, Alfred, 137
Einaudi, Luigi, 88–9, 212–13
Einstein, Albert, 115
*Elementary economics from the higher stand-
  point* (Goodwin), 290
Elements of pure economics (Walras), 25
Ellsberg, Daniel, 118, 251–2
Ely, Richard, 36
Employment. *See Unemployment*
Energy sources
  applied economics and, 238–41
  competition and, 240
  oligopoly and, 240–1
  rent and, 240
Engel, Ernst, 168, 219, 226
Engels, Friedrich, 321–2
Engel's Law, 168, 226
England, public welfare in, 346
Enlightenment, 21, 249, 255, 352, 354–5
Entrepreneurs, bounded rationality and,
  258–9
Environment
  applied economics and, 241–4
  cost-benefit analysis and, 243
  global warming, 243–4
  social sustainability, 244
  sustainable development, 242–3, 244
Envy, 356
Equilibrium
  general equilibrium (*See General equili-
    brium theory*)
  intertemporal equilibrium, 71, 124
  temporary equilibrium, 71, 124
Erhard, Ludwig, 184, 185
Essays (Tobin), 151
Ethics
  generally, 10, 349–52
  capabilities theory and, 368–70
  classical versus marginalist approach,
    350–1
  cultural traditions and, 372–3
  deontological ethics, 352, 354, 358
  of economists, 351–2, 374–6

Ethics (cont.)
  ethnic groups and, 372–3
  globalization and, 372
  income inequality and, 360–3 (*See also* *Income inequality*)
  migration and, 373–4
  multi-culturalism and, 373
  power, problem of, 350, 371–4
  welfare economics and, 363–7 (*See also* *Welfare economics*)
Ethnic groups, 372–3
Eucken, Rudolf, 181
Eucken, Walter, 181–4, 212–13
Euro, 185–6, 217
Eurodollars, 270–1, 272–3
European Association for Evolutionary Political Economy, 335–6
European Central Bank (ECB), 152, 216
European Commission, 216
European System of Accounts (ESA), 223
Evolutionism, 335–40
  generally, 6–7, 321
  agent-based models and, 339–40
  dynamic analysis in, 336
  game theory and, 339
  institutionalism and, 335–40
  Keynes and, 336
  Marshall and, 336–7
  Schumpeter and, 336
  Simon and, 337–8, 339
  Sraffa and, 336
  technological change and, 340–2
  Veblen and, 335
Exit-voice-loyalty, 344
Exogenous money, 201
Expansionary austerity, 215–17
Expectations, 7–8, 203–8
Expected utility theory, 115–19
  generally, 7, 114–15
  behavioural economics and, 251–2
  game theory and, 7, 116, 117–18
  Morgenstern and, 115–19, 247, 248
  paradoxes of, 248–9
  rationality and, 118
  von Neumann and, 115–19, 247, 248
Experimental economics, 252–6
  generally, 248–9
  agent-based models, 256
  bioeconomics, 256
  cognitive economics, 256
  neuroeconomics, 255–6
  preference formation and, 254–5
  prospect theory compared, 253–4
  rationality and, 253
  selfishness and, 255

Exploitation, 23, 323, 328
Externalities, 365–6

Fabian essays in socialism (Shaw), 322–3
Fabian Society, 178, 322–3
Fabius Maximus, 322–3
Facebook, 235
Fama, Eugene, 196, 275
FED-MIT-Penn model, 228
Felicific calculus, 13, 21–2, 247, 352–3, 354
Felipe, Jesus, 306
Feminist economics, 370
Ferguson, Charles E., 76, 303
Financial markets
  generally, 265–6
  banks, role of, 277, 279
  demand for money and, 277
  fragility and, 280–2
  interest and, 278–9
  Keynesian theory of, 216, 279–82
  money manager capitalism, 283–6
  money supply and, 277
  state, role of, 284–6
  theory of efficient financial markets, 273–6
  uncertainty and, 280
Firm, theories of, 133–8
  generally, 311
  barriers to entry and, 137–8
  bounded rationality and, 259
  Coase on, 134
  competitive capitalism, 135–6
  division of labour and, 135
  evolutionary theories, 138
  law and economics and, 138
  managerial capitalism, 135–6
  market power and, 136–7
  Modigliani and, 137
  post-Keynesian theories, 137
  profits and, 136–8
  radical theories, 134–5
  Simon and, 134, 136, 259
  transaction costs and, 134
  x-inefficiency and, 136
Fiscal policy
  central banks and, 152
  Chicago school and, 196
  in Keynesianism, 54, 150–1, 154, 217
  neoclassical synthesis and, 203
  unemployment and, 155, 271
Fisher, Anthony, 214–15
Fisher, Franklin, 235
Fisher, Irving, 120, 266–7, 280
Fitoussi, Jean-Paul, 232

Fixed exchange rates, 270
Flow-input, flow-output scheme, 193
Fluctuating exchange rates, 272
Fogel, Robert W., 334
Fondazione Bruno Leoni, 214–15
Forced savings, 45, 67–8, 70
Fordism, 340–1
Foreign trade, 56, 101, 129, 166–7, 269–70, 328
Foucault, Michel, 182, 184
Foundation for Economic Education, 214–15
Foundations of economic analysis (Samuelson), 125, 126, 127–8
Foundations of human sociality (Henrich), 254
Foundations of statistics (Savage), 118
Frank, André G., 328–9
Frankel, Paul H., 240–1
Frankfurt School, 218, 320
Free to choose (Friedman), 203
Freiburg School, 181, 182, 185
Frequentist theory, 50, 116
Friedman, Milton
    generally, 6, 126, 131–2, 180, 213–14
    behavioural economics and, 250
    Chicago School and, 50–1, 117, 130–1, 179, 196, 197, 198
    on dictatorship, 183
    exogenous money and, 201
    experimental economics and, 254
    on fiscal policy, 200
    Galbraith and, 329
    on hypotheses, 198–9
    Kaldor and, 200, 297–8
    Keynesianism versus, 200–1, 203
    life of, 198
    monetarism and, 266, 267–8
    on monetary policy, 187, 200–3
    Mont Pèlerin Society and, 212–13
    on neoclassical synthesis, 150–1, 154, 203
    neo-liberalism and, 203
    Phillips curve and, 202
    portfolio choice and, 200, 278
    price theory and, 130–1
    rational expectations theory and, 203–8
    Sraffa and, 130
    on unemployment, 155
    on wages, 202
Frisch, Ragnar, 227
Fuà, Giorgio, 242
Full employment in a free society (Beveridge), 64–5
Functional finance, 150

Galavotti, Maria Carla, 51
Galbraith, James, 331
Galbraith, John Kenneth
    generally, 10, 36, 80–1, 320, 329, 335
    on corporations, 330
    on fiscal policy, 285
    Friedman and, 329
    institutionalism and, 329–30
    on military expenditures, 330
    on monetary policy, 330
    on populism, 330
    Schumpeter and, 330
Galileo, 14, 15, 352
Gallaway, Lowell E., 305
Game theory, 139–44
    generally, 114–15
    backward induction and, 142
    bounded rationality and, 260
    evolutionary turn in, 143
    evolutionism and, 339
    expected utility theory and, 7, 116, 117–18
    extended form, 141–2
    homo oeconomicus and, 142–3
    industrial organization theory and, 140
    as methodological revolution, 140–1
    Modigliani and, 139
    monopoly and, 139–40
    Morgenstern and, 140–1
    normal form, 141
    oligopoly and, 139–40
    Pareto and, 141
    prisoner's game, 142
    repeated games, 142–3, 339
    rules in, 143
    strategic form, 141
    utilitarianism and, 142
    von Neumann and, 140–1
Garegnani, Pierangelo
    generally, 313–14
    aggregate production function and, 305
    at Cambridge, 290
    'Marxian' reconstruction, 312–14
    in New Cambridge School, 294
    Robinson and, 301, 316
Garrison, Roger W., 191
Gauss, Carl Friedrick, 219
Gender, capabilities theory and, 369–70
Gender empowerment measure (GEM), 232
Gender-related development index (GDI), 232
General equilibrium theory
    generally, 114–15
    Arrow and, 121, 122, 125, 307

General equilibrium theory (cont.)
    assumptions in, 123
    axiomatic formulation of, 121, 123
    contingent goods in, 123
    contingent markets in, 124
    dated goods in, 123
    Debreu and, 120, 121, 122, 123, 125,
        307
    dynamic stochastic general equilibrium
        (DSGE), 152
    evolution of, 120–1
    Hicks and, 278
    impossibility theorem and, 125
    individual versus society in, 125
    marginalist approach and, 27–8
    Marshall and, 120, 122
    Morgenstern and, 125
    Pareto and, 28, 73, 97–8, 120, 121
    postulates in, 124–5
    Samuelson and, 121–2, 125, 126–9
    science, economics as, 127
    stability and, 127–9
    stream of research, 144–5
    theory of capital and, 306–8
    von Neumann and, 125
    Walras and, 119–25, 305
    welfare economics and, 363, 364
General theory (Keynes), 49, 53, 71, 100,
    159–60, 172–3, 201, 227–8, 277, 284,
    292, 293, 302
Genovesi, Antonio, 359
George Mason University, 179–80, 189–90
Georgescu-Roegen, Nicholas, 242, 338
Germany, public welfare in, 346
Geroski, Paul, 140
Gini, Corrado, 360–1
Global Compact, 214
Globalization, 372
Global warming, 243–4
Gobetti, Piero, 88–9, 90–1
Godley, Wynne, 225–6, 303
von Goethe, Johann Wolfgang, 358
Gold standard, 84
Goodhart, Charles, 268
Goodhart's Law, 268
Goodwin, Richard, 41, 289–90, 292–3
Gramsci, Antonio, 10, 88, 91–3, 98
Graziani, Augusto, 303
The great crash (Galbraith), 329
The great transformation (Polanyi), 327
Greenspan, Alan, 276
Gresham's Law, 85, 144
Grilli, Enzo, 240
Grossman, Herschel I., 157
Growth theory, 159–64

    Arrow and, 163–4
    equilibrating mechanisms and, 161–2
    Harrod and, 24, 147, 159–60, 162, 164,
        174–5
    Kaldor and, 161–2
    knife-edge problem, 160–1
    Lucas and, 163
    monopoly and, 163–4
    neoclassical theory, 162–4
    Pasinetti and, 164
    population and, 161–2
    savings and, 160, 162
    Solow and, 121–2, 128–9, 147, 162–4,
        175–6
    Sraffa and, 162
    stability and, 160–1
    technical progress and, 163–4
    wages and, 161–2
Guala, Francesco, 254

Haavelmo, Trygve, 198, 206, 227–8
Hahn, Frank, 121–2, 125, 153, 161, 291
Hall, Peter A., 345
Halm, Georg, 187–8
Handbook of industrial organization
    (Schmalensee and Willig, eds.), 140
Hansen, Alvin, 46, 295
Hansen, Lars Peter, 275
Happiness, utilitarianism versus, 358–9
Hare, Jan, 358
Harrod, Roy
    generally, 94, 294, 311
    growth theory and, 24, 147, 159–60, 162,
        164, 174–5
    on Keynes, 301–2
    theory of capital and, 304
Harsanyi, John C., 356, 357
Hart, Oliver, 144
Harvard University, 291
Harvey, David, 179
Hawkins-Simon conditions, 109
von Hayek, Friedrich A.
    generally, 5–6, 26, 27, 32, 34, 62, 187–8,
        190, 213–15
    Bentham and, 77–8
    on child labour legislation, 82
    constructive rationalism and, 78
    criticism of, 69–71
    on currency, 82
    denationalization of money and, 83–7
    on dictatorship, 183
    economic liberalism and, 59–61, 77, 81
    employment theory and, 61
    equilibrium and, 71, 73, 191
    experimental economics and, 253, 256

on fiscal policy, 84
on gold standard, 84
Hicks and, 75
institutionalism and, 10, 320
on interest, 67–8, 69
Kaldor, debate with, 62, 71–5, 80–1
Keynes and, 65, 66–7, 69, 70, 71, 84,
    86–7
knowledge diffusion and, 76–8, 80
life of, 63–6
limitations of, 83
market adjustment mechanisms and,
    80–1
Menger and, 66, 69, 77–9, 80
methodological individualism and, 42
Mises and, 64, 77, 188
on monetary policy, 82, 84, 85
Mont Pèlerin Society and, 8, 62, 66, 83,
    186–7, 190, 212–13
movement of capital and goods and, 81–3
neo-liberalism and, 60–1
in New Austrian school, 179
New Austrian school and, 8
on ordoliberalism, 183
political liberalism and, 59–61, 81
'Ricardo effect' and, 68, 74–5
scientism and, 78
spontaneous order and, 76–8
Sraffa and, 61, 65, 69–71, 74, 80–1, 88,
    91, 100–1
on stability, 117
state power and, 179
on taxation, 82
theory of capital and, 61–2, 71–5, 87
trade cycle theory and, 45, 61, 66–71,
    189
on wages, 73–5
Wicksell and, 67, 69, 73
Health care, 346–7
Heckscher, Eli, 129
Hegel, G.W.F., 59
Hendry, David F., 228–9
Henrich, Joseph, 254
Heritage Foundation, 214–15
Herndon, Thomas, 217
Heukelom, Floris, 252
Heuristics, 258–9
Hicks, John
    generally, 6, 27, 34, 122, 146, 280, 291
    Austrian school and, 192–6
    capital reversal and, 194
    dated quantities of labour and, 193,
        194–5
    econometrics and, 228–9
    equilibrium and, 71, 72, 73

flow-input, flow-output scheme and, 193
general equilibrium theory and, 278
Hayek and, 75
on interest, 53
IS-LL model and, 148–9, 153–4, 192–3,
    298–9
Keynes and, 149
national accounting and, 223–4
neoclassical synthesis and, 148–9, 153–4
traverse and, 194
Hildebrand, Bruno, 37
Hilferding, Rudolf, 347
Hirsch, Fred, 330–1
Hirschman, Albert O., 170, 321, 343–4
Hobbes, Thomas, 14
Hobsbawn, Eric, 6
Hodgson, Geoffrey, 337–8, 339
Hollander, Jacob, 101
Holmstrom, Bengt, 144
Homo oeconomicus
    anomalies and, 263
    game theory and, 142–3
    marginalist approach and, 26–7
    Polanyi on, 327
    rejection of, 247–50
    utilitarianism and, 127, 359
Hoover Institution, 214–15
Horizontalists, 298
Horwicz, Leonid, 198
HOS theorem, 129
Hotelling, Harold, 118, 211, 238–40
Howitt, Peter, 163–4
Huberman, Leo, 325
Human action (Mises), 188–9
Human development index (HDI), 231–2
Human Performance Center, 252–3
Hume, David, 50, 78, 84, 257–8, 268–9,
    354
'Hydraulic Keynesianism', 152–3, 298
Hypotheses, 198–9

The idea of justice (Sen), 368
Imperfect competition, 95–7
Imperialism, the highest stage of capitalism
    (Lenin), 323
Impossibility theorem, 125, 367–8
Income inequality, 360–3
    generally, 350
    development economics and, 361–2
    increase in, 361
    indexes of, 360–1
    marginalist approach and, 362
    Pareto and, 360
    Sen and, 363
    Smith and, 362

428   Index

Income inequality (cont.)
  Sylos Labini and, 362
Increasing risk, principle of, 295
Indian currency and finance (Keynes), 89–90
Industrial organization theory, 140
Inflation
  non-accelerating inflation rate of unemployment (NAIRU), 156–7
  Phillips Curve and, 155–7
  Sraffa on, 88–9
  unemployment, relation to, 155–7
Informatics, 220
Input-output tables, 8, 24, 120, 220–2
Insider-outsider models, 159
Institute for Advanced Study, 115
Institute for Economic Affairs, 214–15
Institute for Humane Studies, 190
Institute for International Economics, 214–15
Institute for Social Research, 252–3
Institute of Economic Affairs, 83
Institutionalism
  generally, 6–7, 10, 31, 320–1
  competition among institutions, 321, 345–8
  corporations and, 330
  elements of, 336
  evolutionism and,335–40 (*See also Evolutionism*)
  Galbraith and, 329–30
  Hayek and, 10, 320
  Menger and, 320
  military expenditures and, 330
  neo-institutionalism, 331–5 (*See also Neo-institutionalism*)
  Polanyi and, 326–328
  technological change and, 340–2
  Veblen and, 35–7, 320, 330–1
  Weber and, 320
Interest
  Böhm-Bawerk on, 26, 43–4
  financial markets and, 278–9
  Hayek on, 67–8, 69
  Hicks on, 53
  Keynes on, 52–4, 55
  monetary policy and, 271–2
  post-Keynesianism and, 300
  Schumpeter on, 43–4
  Sraffa on, 195
  Wicksell on, 34
Interest and prices (Wicksell), 33
International Development Association (IDA), 165
International Joseph Schumpeter Association, 335–6

International Monetary Fund, 56, 165, 215, 216, 270, 271
International trade. *See Foreign trade*
Internet Explorer, 235
Intertemporal equilibrium, 71, 124, 238–9
Intrinsic instability of market economics, 9
Investment, Keynes on, 52–4, 55
'Invisible hand', 131, 177, 192
IS-LL model, 148–9, 153–4, 192–3, 298–9
Italian Economic Journal, 340
Italy
  Communist Party, 91
  economic dualism in, 167
  Forza Italia, 325
  Workers' Statute, 351

Janssen, Maarten C.W., 238
Jeffrey, Richard, 117
Jevons, William Stanley
  generally, 5, 14
  environment and, 242
  marginalist approach and, 24, 25, 26–7
  quantitative view of economics and, 219
  on Ricardo, 101
  Schumpeter and, 42–3
  Sraffa and, 88
  utilitarianism and, 355, 358–9
John Maynard Keynes (Minsky), 280
Johnson, Elizabeth, 301–2
Johnson, Harry, 202
Journal of Economic Issues, 335–6
Journal of Evolutionary Economics, 335–6
Journal of Law and Economics, 332
Journal of Political Economy, 35
Journal of Posy Keynesian Economics, 330
'Joyless economy', 359

Kahn, Alfred, 236, 280
Kahn, Richard, 53
  generally, 9–10, 298
  at Cambridge, 290, 291, 292
  debate on interpretation of Keynes, 298
  on Keynes, 301–2
  in New Cambridge school, 292–3
  short versus long period, 301
Kahneman, Daniel, 9, 249, 253–4, 260–2
Kaldor, Nicholas
  generally, 9–10, 147, 151–2, 291, 292
  at Cambridge, 290, 291
  debate on interpretation of Keynes, 298
  development economics and, 344–5
  on economic development, 169
  Friedman and, 200, 297–8
  growth theory and, 161–2
  Hayek, debate with, 62, 71–5, 80–1

knowledge diffusion and, 62
monetarism and, 268
in New Cambridge school, 292–3
as post-Keynesian, 296–8
spontaneous order and, 62
stylized facts and, 167–8, 169, 296–7
technical progress and, 297
theory of distribution and, 296, 308–10
welfare economics and, 366
Kalecki, Michał, 9–10, 291, 292, 294–6,
    324
Kant, Immanuel, 353, 354
Kao, Ying-Fang, 253
Kautsky, Karl, 321–2
Kennedy, John F., 320, 330
Keynes, John Maynard
generally, 5, 13, 29, 31–2, 46, 62, 95,
    101–2, 147, 217, 251, 285, 311
analytical blocks and, 52–4
on banking, 277
bounded rationality and, 259
Bretton Woods and, 7, 323–4
at Cambridge, 97–100, 289–90
Circus and, 293
classical probability theory and, 49–50
debate on interpretation of, 298–303
demand, policies supporting, 55–6
econometrics and, 228–9
on economics as science, 219
evolutionism and, 336
on exchange rates and prices, 84
frequentist theory and, 50
Hayek and, 65, 66–7, 69, 70, 71, 84, 86–7
Hicks and, 149
on income, 55
on interest, 52–4, 55
on investment, 52–4, 55
life of, 48–9
on liquidity, 54
Marxism and, 326
on monetary policy, 55–6, 269–70
neoclassical synthesis and (*See
    Neoclassical synthesis*)
neo-liberalism and, 60
political liberalism and, 59–60, 81
principle of effective demand and, 54–5
on probability, 49–52, 116
on savings, 55
Schumpeter and, 41–2
short versus long period, 301
socializing investments and, 285
Sraffa and, 70, 89–90, 91, 96, 97, 98,
    100, 116
theory of finance, 86–7
Tinbergen and, 227–8

on uncertainty, 50–1, 52–4, 277–8
on unemployment, 55–6, 196
on wages, 55
on wealth, 53–4
Wicksell and, 34–5
Keynesianism
crisis in, 269–73
fiscal policy in, 54, 150–1, 154, 217
Friedman versus, 200–1, 203
'hydraulic Keynesianism', 152–3, 298
Keynesian-Sraffian synthesis, 316–18
monetarism versus, 267–8, 298
monetary policy in, 54, 150, 154,
    299–300
theory of financial markets, 216, 279–82
Kindleberger, Charles, 276, 282
Kirman, Alan, 308
Kirzner, Irving, 190, 192
Klein, Lawrence, 152, 198, 227–8, 291
Knies, Karl, 37, 38
Knife-edge problem, 160–1
Knight, Frank
generally, 94, 131, 251, 259
Chicago school and, 50–1, 196–7
Mont Pèlerin Society and, 212–13
on risk and uncertainty, 50–1, 116, 277,
    302
Knowledge diffusion, 62, 76–8, 80
Kohl, Helmut, 186
Koopmans, Tjalling, 198, 227
Kranton, Rachel, 132–3
Kregel, Jan A., 9–10, 160, 298
Kreps, David M., 142–3
Kresge, Stephen, 83
Krouse, Clement G., 140
Krugman, Paul, 342
Kuhn, Thomas S., 114
Kula, Witold, 4
Kuwait, per capita income in, 232
Kuznets, Simon, 168, 170, 222
Kuznets's Law, 168
Kydland, Finn E., 204–5

Labour theory of value
in classical approach, 15, 17
Marxism and, 321–2
Marx on, 15, 23
Ricardo on, 15, 17
Lachmann, Ludwig, 190, 191
Laffer Curve, 205–6
Laffont, Jean-Jacques, 237
Lamark, Jean-Baptiste, 30, 336–7, 338, 339
Lancaster, Kelvin, 132
Landes, David, 135
Lange, Oskar, 76, 187–8, 319, 324

Laplace, Pierre-Simon, 49
Latouche, Serge, 242, 326
Lausanne school, 27–8
Lavoie, Marc, 303
Law and economics, 138
Laws of returns, 93–5
Lawson, Tony, 297
Layard, Richard, 358–9
Learning by doing, 163–4, 169, 297, 341
Lectures on political economy (Wicksell), 33, 34, 61
Lectures on the theory of production (Pasinetti), 311
Lehman Brothers, 216
Leibenstein, Harvey, 136
Leigh, Daniel, 217
Leijonhufvud, Axel, 157
Lenin, 323
Leoni, Bruno, 212–13
Leontief, Wassily
    generally, 41, 128, 193, 311
    econometrics and, 228–9
    input-output tables and, 8, 24, 120, 220–2
Leo XIII (Pope), 183–4
Lerner, Abba, 150
Levhari, David, 305
Lewis, W. Arthur, 167
The limits to growth (Club of Rome), 239, 242
Lindhal, Erik, 34, 71, 73
Linear programming, 221
L'inflazione monetaria in Italia durante e dopo la guerra (Sraffa), 88–9
Liquidity, 54
Little, Ian M.D., 366
Ljippart, Ared, 345
Locke, John, 277
London School of Economics, 64–5, 67, 90, 322, 332
Long Term Capital Management, 275
Loomes, Graham, 262–3
L'ordine nuovo, 91–2
Lorenz, Konrad, 66
Lucas, Robert
    generally, 196
    econometrics and, 228–9
    growth theory and, 163
    on neoclassical synthesis, 152
    rational expectation theory and, 179, 203–5
Luxembourg Income Study, 230–1
Luxemburg, Rosa, 294

Machlup, Fritz, 63, 191
MacLean, Nancy, 209

de Madariaga, Salvador, 212–13
Maddison, Angus, 231
Mahr, Alexander, 188
Malcolm, Norman, 99
Malinvaud, Edmond, 157, 158
Malthus, Thomas Robert, 67, 239, 242
Managerial capitalism, 135–6
Mantel, Rolf, 125, 153
Maoism, 324–5
Mao Tse-tung, 324–5
Marcuse, Herbert, 325
Marginalist approach
    generally, 5, 13
    Austrian school and, 26
    classical approach versus, 13–14, 24–6
    Darwinism and, 29–30
    ethics and, 350–1
    general equilibrium theory and, 27–8
    homo oeconomicus and, 26–7
    income inequality and, 362
    Jevons and, 24, 25, 26–7
    Lausanne school and, 27–8
    Marshall and, 28–30
    Menger and, 24, 25, 26
    neoclassical synthesis and (See Neoclassical synthesis)
    'Robinson Crusoe' analogy, 27
    scarcity and utility in, 24, 25
    self-regulating mechanism in, 178
    Sraffa, criticism by, 106–8
    supply and demand in, 24, 25
    theory of capital and, 303–8
    utilitarianism and, 355
    Walras and, 24, 25, 27–8
Marglin, Stephen, 134–5
Market creation, 235–8
Market power, 136–7
Market regulation, 233–8
Markowitz, Henry, 198, 274, 275
Marris, Robin, 80–1, 135–6, 138, 283–4, 309
Marshak, Jacob, 227
Marshall, Alfred
    generally, 52, 69, 114
    Cambridge and, 289–90
    competition and, 240
    criticism by Sraffa, 93–5, 96–7
    on economics as science, 219
    equilibrium and, 73
    evolutionism and, 336–7
    general equilibrium theory and, 120, 122
    laws of returns and, 93–5
    marginalist approach and, 28–30
    neoclassical synthesis and, 157–9
    New Cambridge school and, 292–4

on Ricardo, 101
short versus long period, 301
Sraffa and, 88
Marshall Plan, 165, 282
Marx, Karl
  generally, 5, 13, 15, 18, 59
  classical approach and, 22–4
  development economics and, 343–4
  on distribution of income, 23
  on division of labour, 20
  on labour theory of value, 15, 23
  national accounting and, 223
  Polanyi and, 328
  political ideas of, 23–4
  Rostow and, 168–9
  Schumpeter and, 41, 46
  Sraffa and, 88, 106
  on surplus, 16
  theory of value and, 8–9
  trade cycle theory and, 46
  on unemployment, 155
  Weber and, 39, 40
'Marxian' reconstruction, 312–14
Marxism, 321–6
  generally, 6–7, 319
  Böhm-Bawerk and, 321–2
  democratic socialism, 322
  Keynes and, 326
  labour theory of value and, 321–2
  Maoism, 324–5
  Marxism-Leninism, 323–4
  Sraffa and, 321–2, 326
Mas-Colell, Andreu, 122, 144
Massachusetts Institute of Technology
  (MIT), 7, 126, 291
Mathematical Psychology Group, 252–3
Matteotti, Giacomo, 215
Matthews, Robert C.O., 161
Mattioli, Raffaele, 100
*Maturity and stagnation in American capital-
  ism* (Steindl), 295
Mayer, Hans, 188
Mazzucato, Mariana, 225, 273, 345
McCombie, John, 306
McKenzie, Lionel, 122
Meade, James, 289, 293
Meadows, Dennis L., 242
Meadows, Donella H., 242
Means, Gardiner, 80–1, 135–6, 309, 320–1
Medema, Steven G., 196, 197
Meltzer, Alan, 201–2
Menger, Carl
  generally, 5, 14, 32, 42, 186, 189
  Hayek and, 66, 69, 77–9, 80
  institutionalism and, 320

marginalist approach and, 24, 25, 26
quantitative view of economics and, 219
Schmoller and, 38
Sraffa and, 88
Mental Health Research Institute, 252–3
Meriwether, John, 275
Merton, Robert, 275
Methodological individualism, 42, 78–80
Methodological liberalism, 41–2
Michael, Robert T., 132
Microsoft, 235
Migration, 373–4
Mill, John Stuart
  generally, 4, 65, 213, 247
  Bentham and, 22
  environment and, 241–2
  on felicific calculus, 22
  on freedom, 81
  Jevons and, 27
  Marshall and, 28–9
  on rationality, 257
  utilitarianism and, 354–5, 356, 357, 358
Miller, Merton, 137, 273–5
Minc, Bronisław, 324
Minsky, Hyman
  generally, 9–10, 41, 265–6, 279–80, 291
  debate on interpretation of Keynes, 298
  on fiscal policy, 285
  fragility and, 280–2
  on instability, 9
  Keynesian theory of financial markets
    and, 216, 279–82
  monetarism versus, 265–6
  on monetary policy, 285
  money manager capitalism and, 283–6,
    320–1
  neoclassical synthesis and, 280
  uncertainty and, 280
Mirowski, Philip, 114, 213, 337
Mirrlees, James, 357
von Mises, Ludwig
  generally, 26, 187–8
  on antitrust legislation, 188
  on central planning, 187–8
  forced savings and, 67
  Hayek and, 64, 77, 188
  life of, 186–7
  market process and, 189
  Mont Pèlerin Society and, 186–7,
    212–13
  in New Austrian school, 179, 188–9
  on planned economy, 76
  on stability, 189
  state power and, 179
  trade cycle theory and, 46, 189

Mises Institute, 192
Mitchell, Wesley, 35, 36, 66
Mitterand, François, 186
Mkandawire, Thandika, 170, 344–5
The modern world system (Wallerstein),
    328–9
Modigliani, Franco
    generally, 7, 146, 198, 275, 298
    econometrics and, 228
    game theory and, 139
    on neoclassical synthesis, 149–51, 154,
        159, 173–4
    theories of the firm and, 137
    theory of distribution and, 296, 309
    theory of efficient financial markets and,
        273–5
Modigliani-Miller theorem, 137, 273–5,
    279
Moggridge, Donald, 301–2
Moneta e Credito, 10
Monetarism, 266–9
    generally, 265–6
    analytical level, 266–7
    balance of payments and, 268–9
    evolution of, 266
    Friedman and, 266, 267–8
    Kaldor and, 268
    Keynesianism versus, 267–8, 298
    Minsky versus, 265–6
    money supply and, 266–7, 268, 271–2
    Pigou and, 267
    Post-Keynesian critiques of, 269
*Monetary history of the United States,
    1867–1960* (Friedman and Schwartz),
    200
Monetary policy
    central banks and, 152, 211–12, 217, 272
    in Chicago school, 196
    in Keynesianism, 54, 150, 154, 299–300
    neoclassical synthesis and, 203
    unemployment and, 55–6, 150, 155, 271
Money manager capitalism, 283–6, 320–1
Money supply
    financial markets and, 277
    monetarism and, 266–7, 268, 271–2
    post-Keynesianism and, 299–300
Monopoly
    antitrust legislation and, 182
    game theory and, 139–40
    growth theory and, 163–4
    Kalecki and, 295–6
    market regulation and, 235, 236
    natural monopoly, 233, 235
    oligopoly and, 136–7
    ordoliberalism and, 183

Monthly Review, 325
Mont Pèlerin Society, 212–15
    generally, 180, 187, 216
    Chicago school and, 213
    founding of, 212–13
    Friedman and, 212–13
    Hayek and, 8, 62, 66, 83, 187, 190,
        212–13
    Knight and, 212–13
    Mises and, 187, 212–13
    ordoliberalism and, 213
    Stigler and, 212–14
Moore, George, 48–9, 51
Moore, Henry, 226
Morgan, Mary S., 227–8
Morgenstern, Oskar
    generally, 115
    behavioural economics and, 250–1
    expected utility theory and, 115–19, 247,
        248
    experimental economics and, 252–3
    game theory and, 140–1
    general equilibrium theory and, 125
    on rationality, 257
    utilitarianism and, 355–6, 358
Moscati, Ivan, 252
*The most dangerous man in America: Daniel
    Ellsberg and the Pentagon Papers* (docu-
    mentary), 251
Motterlini, Matteo, 254
Müller Armack, Alfred, 184, 185
Multi-culturalism, 373
Multinationals, economic development
    and, 167
Mundell, Robert, 154
Mundell-Fleming model, 153–4
Mussolini, Benito, 90, 215
Muth, John F., 203
Myrdal, Gunnar, 34, 36, 101–2, 170, 227,
    344–5

Nash, John, 119, 141
Nash equilibrium, 141
National accounting, 222–6
National Bureau of Economic Research
    (NBER), 35, 64, 66, 198
Natural monopoly, 233, 235
Natural prices in classical approach, 14–15,
    17–18, 19
Nature and significance of economic science
    (Robbins), 64
Necker, Jacques, 346
Negative freedoms, 353–4
Neild, Robert, 291
Nelson, Richard, 138, 259, 338, 339–40

Neoclassical economics, 29, 329
Neoclassical synthesis, 147–55
  behavioural norms and, 159
  disequilibrium and, 157
  dynamic stochastic general equilibrium (DSGE) and, 152
  econometrics and, 152
  economic development theories, 164–71 (*See also Economic development theories*)
  fiscal policy and, 203
  Friedman on, 150–1, 154, 203
  functional finance and, 150
  goods, market for, 148
  growth theory, 159–64 (*See also Growth theory*)
  Hicks and, 148–9, 153–4
  'hydraulic Keynesianism' and, 152–3
  insider-outsider models, 159
  IS-LL model and, 148–9, 153–4
  labour, market for, 149–50
  Lucas on, 152
  Marshall and, 157–9
  Minsky and, 280
  Modigliani on, 149–51, 154, 159, 173–4
  monetary policy and, 203
  monetary theory and, 151–2
  money, market for, 148–9
  Mundell-Fleming model and, 153–4
  'new Keynesian economics', 158
  overlapping generations models, 158
  Phillips curve, 155–7, 202, 204, 207, 271
  price rigidity and, 159
  Samuelson and, 158
  savings in, 148, 150–1, 158
  search models, 159
  tax-augmented incomes policy (TIP) and, 150
  unemployment and, 150
  varieties of, 157–9
  wage rigidity and, 158
  wages in, 150, 158–9
  wealth in, 148–9, 150–1
Neo-colonialism, 165–6
Neo-institutionalism, 331–5
  aggregate production function and, 334
  property rights and, 332–3
  transaction costs and, 331–2, 333, 334
Neo-liberalism
  generally, 5–6, 178–81
  Austrian school (*See Austrian school*)
  Chicago school (*See Chicago school*)
  expansionary austerity, 215–17
  former planned economies and, 371
  Friedman and, 203

  Hayek and, 60–1
  Keynes and, 60
  market creation and, 236
  market regulation and, 234
  Mont Pèlerin Society (*See Mont Pèlerin Society*)
  ordoliberalism, 181–6 (*See also Ordoliberalism*)
  public choice theory, 208–12 (*See also Public choice theory*)
  rational expectations theory, 7–8, 203–8
  streams of, 177–81
  Washington Consensus, 180, 185–6, 214, 215–17
Netscape, 235
Neuroeconomics, 255–6
New Austrian school, 8, 179, 186–92
New Cambridge school, 292–4
New Deal, 77
New historical school, 37
The new industrial state (Galbraith), 329–30
New International Economic Order, 166–7, 214
'New Keynesian economics', 158
New School, 326
New School for Social Research, 36
New York University, 187, 189–90
Nik-Khah, Edward, 197
Nixon, Richard, 270
Nobel Prize, 66, 126, 144, 198, 213–14, 227, 237, 253–4, 275, 291, 334
Non-accelerating inflation rate of unemployment (NAIRU), 156–7
Nordhaus, William, 239, 243
North, Douglass, 333–4
Nozick, Robert, 362–3
Nurske, Ragnar, 170
Nussbaum, Martha, 370
Nuti, Mario, 294

Obama, Barack, 243
O'Donnell, Rod, 300
O'Driscoll, Gerald P., 191
Office of Naval Research, 260
Ohanian, Lee E., 217
Ohlin, Bertil, 34, 129
Oil crisis, 270–1
Oil markets. *See Energy sources*
Old historical school, 37
Oligopoly, 96, 114–15, 139–40, 240–1
One-dimensional man (Marcuse), 325
The open society (Popper), 59
Ordo, 181
Ordoliberalism, 181–6
  generally, 179

Ordoliberalism (cont.)
  antitrust legislation and, 182
  competition in, 182
  economic humanism and, 184
  Hayek on, 183
  institutions in, 181–6
  monopoly and, 183
  Mont Pèlerin Society and, 213
  social market economy and, 184
  Washington Consensus and, 185–6
Organisation for Economic Co-operation
    and Development (OECD), 214
Organization of Petroleum Exporting
    Countries (OPEC), 241
Österreichische
    Konjunkturforschungsinstitut, 64
Ostrom, Elinor, 334–5
Overlapping generations models, 158
Oxford University, 291

Palazzi, Paolo, 232
Panico, Carlo, 317
Pareto, Vilfredo
  generally, 192–3
  econometrics and, 226
  game theory and, 141
  general equilibrium theory and, 28, 73,
    97–8, 120, 121
  income inequality and, 360
  quantitative view of economics and, 219
  utilitarianism and, 355
Pareto optimum, 364, 366
Pareto's Law, 360
Parrinello, Sergio, 310
Pasinetti, Luigi
  aggregate production function and, 305
  at Cambridge, 290, 291
  growth theory and, 164
  in New Cambridge school, 294
  on profits, 311–12
  'Ricardian' reconstruction, 310–12
  theory of capital and, 303
  theory of distribution and, 296, 309–10
Paternalism, 263–4
Patinkin, Don, 152–3, 222, 227
Peacock, Alan, 209
Pearson, Karl, 219
Penrose, Edith, 198, 337, 339
Pensions, 346–7
Pentagon Papers, 251
The Pentagon Papers (film), 251
Persson, Torsten, 212
Petrodollars, 270–1, 272–3
Petty, William
  generally, 18, 277

national accounting and, 222
  Political Arithmetic and, 14–15, 218–19
  surplus and, 16
Phelps, Edmund, 156, 158, 202
Phelps Brown, Henry, 228–9
Philadelphia Society, 214–15
Phillips, A.W., 155
Phillips Curve, 155–7, 202, 204, 207,
    271
Philosophical investigations (Wittgenstein),
    98–9
Pierson, Nicolaas G., 187–8
Pigou, Arthur Cecil
  generally, 29, 30, 151, 172–3
  at Cambridge, 289
  Marshall and, 93–4, 96–7, 233
  monetarism and, 267
  in New Cambridge school, 292–3
  welfare economics and, 363, 365
Pigou effect, 149–50, 267–8
Piketty, Thomas, 230–1, 361
Pinochet, Augusto, 60, 183, 214,
    215
Piore, Michael, 340–1
Pius XI (Pope), 183–4
The place of science in modern civilization
    (Veblen), 35
Planning, 60, 76, 77, 329–30
Plato, 59
Polanyi, Karl
  generally, 10, 319–20, 327, 328, 335
  Austrian school versus, 327
  on change in social and economic struc-
    ture, 326–8
  on formalism, 327
  on homo oeconomicus, 327
  on individualism, 327
  institutionalism and, 326–328
  life of, 326
  Marx and, 328
Polanyi, Michael, 77
The political economy of growth (Baran), 325
Political liberalism
  Hayek and, 59–61, 81
  Schumpeter and, 42
Pollock, Friedrich, 320
Pollution, 236
Ponzi schemes, 281–2, 285
Popper, Karl, 59, 60, 79, 198–9, 212–13
Population
  growth theory and, 161–2
  Malthus on, 239
  overlapping generations models and, 158
  Smith on, 16, 19–20
Populism, 330

Portfolio choice, 200, 274, 278
Positive freedoms, 353–4
Post-Keynesianism
  generally, 6–7, 9–10
  Cambridge tradition, 289–90
  causality and, 299
  consumer sovereignty and, 299–300
  debate on interpretation of Keynes, 298–303
  interest and, 300
  Kaldor and, 296–8
  Kalecki and, 294–6
  Keynesian-Sraffian synthesis, 316–18
  macroeconomics, 146–7
  'Marxian' reconstruction, 312–14
  monetarism, critiques of, 269
  monetary policy in, 299–300
  money supply and, 299–300
  New Cambridge school, 292–4
  'Ricardian' reconstruction, 310–12
  'Smithian' reconstruction, 314–16
  theories of the firm, 137
  theory of capital, 303–8
  theory of distribution, 308–10
Post-utilitarianism, 6–7
Power relations, 7
Prague Spring, 319
Prebish, Raúl, 166–7
Precaution principle, 243
The predator state (Galbraith), 331
The prerequisites of socialism and the task of social democracy (Bernstein), 322
Prescott, Edward C., 204–5
Pribram, Karl, 188
Prices and production (Hayek), 61, 65, 67, 69, 71, 72–3
Principal-agent problem, 144–5, 237
Principle of effective demand, 54–5
Principle of increasing risk, 295
Principles (Mill), 241–2
Principles of economics (Marshall), 28, 29–30, 93, 94, 129–30, 192–3, 233, 336–7
Principles of political economy (Menger), 25, 63
Principles (Ricardo), 101, 102, 321
Prisoner's game, 142
Prison notebooks (Gramsci), 92–3
Privatseminar, 64
Probability
  classical probability theory, 49–50
  Keynes on, 49–52, 116
  Wittgenstein on, 116
Production costs in classical approach, 16–17

Production of commodities by means of commodities (Sraffa), 88, 96, 98, 100, 101, 102–6, 289–90, 304, 315
Productivity growth, 169
Professionalization of economics, 114
Profits
  in classical approach, 17–20
  Kalecki on, 295–6
  in Keynesian-Sraffian synthesis, 316–18
  money manager capitalism and, 283–6
  Pasinetti on, 311–12
  Sraffa on, 104–6, 107–10
  Sylos Labini on, 315–16
  theories of the firm and, 136–8
  theory of distribution and, 308–10
Property rights, 332–3
Prospect theory, 260–4
  generally, 249
  bounded rationality compared, 261–2
  experimental economics compared, 253–4
  risk in, 261
  status quo and, 261
'Prospect theory', 9
Protestant ethic and the spirit of capitalism (Weber), 37
Protestantism, 40, 185
PSL Quarterly Review, 10
Public choice theory, 208–12
  generally, 179–80
  club theory and, 210
  democracy and, 210–11
  interest groups and, 211–12
  neo-liberalism and, 209
  self-interest and, 208–9
  Sen and, 208
  state and, 210
  voting and, 210–11
Public debt, 204, 272
Public finance, 33
Public welfare, 346
The pure theory of capital (Hayek), 71, 74
Pure theory of regulation, 237
Putnam, Robert D., 360
Puviani, Amilcare, 209

Quadragesimo anno (Pius XI), 183–4
Quadrio Curzio, Alberto, 310
Quesnay, François, 18, 220

Radcliffe Report, 293, 297–8
Radner, Roy, 124
Ramsey, Frank P., 51–2, 100, 116, 118–19, 251
Rand Corporation, 7, 113, 291

Rational expectations theory, 7–8, 203–8
Rationality
  bounded rationality (*See Bounded rationality*)
  expected utility theory and, 118
  experimental economics and, 253
Rawls, John, 353–4, 355, 357–8
Reagan, Ronald, 7–8, 214, 215, 271
Redlick, Charles J., 217
Regret theory, 262–3
Régulation School, 341
Reinhart, Carmen M., 217
Rent, energy sources and, 240
Representative firm, 95–7
Rerum novarum (Leo XIII), 183–4
Research, treatment of, 3
Reswitching of techniques, 107–8, 191, 195, 303–4, 305, 306
Returns to scale
  economic development theories and, 164–5, 169
  growth theory and, 163
  input-output tables and, 220–1
  oligopoly and, 240–1
  Samuelson and, 127, 128
  Sraffa and, 103–4, 106–7
  theories of the firm and, 29, 97
Revealed preferences, 118–19, 127, 262, 357
Review of Austrian Economics, 189–90
'Ricardian' reconstruction, 310–12
Ricardo, David
  generally, 5, 13–14, 15, 18, 22–3, 97–8, 327, 351
  critical edition by Sraffa, 88, 100–2, 301–2
  Jevons on, 101
  on labour theory of value, 15, 17
  Marshall on, 101
  Pasinetti and, 310–11
  rent and, 240
  on Say's Law, 20
  Sraffa and, 88, 102
'Ricardo effect', 68, 74–5
Risk
  Knight on, 50–1, 116, 277, 302
  principle of increasing risk, 295
  in prospect theory, 261
  uncertainty versus, 50–1, 116, 277–8, 302
Rivoluzione liberale (Gobetti), 90–1
Rizzo, Mario J., 191
The road to serfdom (Hayek), 60, 65, 186
Robbins, Lionel, 33, 61, 64, 65, 94, 131

Robertson, Dennis, 71, 94, 96–7, 100–1, 130, 289, 292–3
Robinson, Austin, 293, 301–2
Robinson, James A., 334
Robinson, Joan
  generally, 9–10, 280, 294, 303
  aggregate production function and, 128–9
  at Cambridge, 290, 291, 292
  Circus and, 293
  debate on interpretation of Keynes, 298, 300–1, 302
  Garegnani and, 301, 316
  on imperfect competition, 96
  in New Cambridge School, 292–4
  short versus long period, 301
  theory of capital and, 303–4
'Robinson Crusoe' analogy, 27
Rockefeller, John D., 233–4
Rockefeller Foundation, 64, 190
Rogoff, Kenneth, 217
Roman Catholicism, 183–4, 185, 359
Romer, Paul, 163
Rome Treaty, 184
Roncaglia, Alessandro, 291, 315, 317, 376
Roosevelt, Franklin D., 77
Röpke, Wilhelm, 184–5, 212–13
Roscher, Wilhelm, 37, 38
Rosenberg, Nathan, 340–1, 343
Rosenstein-Rodan, Paul, 170
Ross, Stephen, 144
Rosselli, Carlo, 81, 88–9, 184
Rosselli, Nello, 88–9
Rostow, Walt, 168–9
Rothbard, Murray, 190, 192
Rotstein, Abraham, 327
Rousseau, Jean-Jacques, 354
Royal Economic Society, 98, 289, 301–2
Rule utilitarianism, 357–8
Russell, Bertrand, 48–9, 98

Sabel, Charles, 340–1
Samuelson, Larry, 253, 262
Samuelson, Paul
  generally, 6, 7, 41, 114–15, 153, 280, 292
  aggregate production function and, 305, 306
  behavioural economics and, 250
  Chicago school and, 197–8
  general equilibrium theory and, 121–2, 125, 126–9
  neoclassical synthesis and, 158
  Phillips curve and, 156
  returns to scale and, 127, 128
  Sraffa and, 128–9

on stability, 43
theory of capital and, 303
theory of distribution and, 296, 309
welfare economics and, 364, 365
Satisficing behaviour, 249, 259–60
Savage, Leonard J., 51–2, 116, 118–19, 250–2
Savings
forced savings, 45, 67–8, 70
growth theory and, 160, 162
Keynes on, 55
in neoclassical synthesis, 148, 150–1, 158
theory of distribution and, 308–10
Say, Jean-Baptiste, 223
Say's Law, 20, 309–10
Scarcity, 24, 25
Schelling, Thomas, 143, 255
Schlick, Moritz, 63
Schmalensee, Richard, 140, 235
von Schmoller, Gustav, 37, 38, 42
Scholes, Myron, 274, 275
Schrödinger, Erwin, 66
Schultz, Henry, 226
Schumpeter, Joseph A.
generally, 1, 4, 5, 13, 31, 32, 72, 126, 153, 192, 283, 289–90, 325
on banking, 44–5, 277
on bureaucratization, 47
creative destruction and, 47, 69, 216
on decline of capitalism, 46–7
dynamic versus static approach, 43–4
economic liberalism and, 42
on entrepreneurs, 44–5
evolutionism and, 336
forced savings and, 67
Galbraith and, 330
on interest, 43–4
Jevons and, 42–3
Keynes and, 41–2
laws of returns and, 94
life of, 41
on market regulation, 234
Marx and, 41, 46
methodological individualism and, 42
methodological liberalism and, 41–2
political liberalism and, 42
on prices, 43
social change and, 48
on stability, 43
theory of market forms, 47–8
trade cycle theory and, 45–6, 189
Weber and, 46, 47
Schwalbach, Joachim, 140
Schwartz, Anna, 200, 268, 329
Science, economics as, 127

Scientism, 78
Scitovsky, Tibor, 359
Search models, 159
'Second' Chicago school, 197, 198
Self-interest, 13, 21, 208–9, 247, 354
Selfishness, 255
Sen, Amartya
generally, 98, 126–7
at Cambridge, 290
capabilities theory and, 10, 170–1, 231–2, 351, 368–70
consequentialism and, 368
on economic development, 169
income inequality and, 363
indicators and, 231–2
life of, 367
public choice theory and, 208
utilitarianism and, 353, 356, 357
welfare economics and, 367
Seneca, 130
Shackle, George, 190, 302
Shaikh, Anwar, 306
Sharpe, William, 274, 275
Shaw, George Bernard, 322–3
Shiller, Robert, 275, 276
'Short century', 5–6
Shove, Gerald, 94
Shukla, Vishwa, 305
Šik, Ota, 324
Simon, Herbert
generally, 130, 198, 333
on administrative behaviour, 258
aggregate production function and, 306
on altruism, 210–11, 255, 360
bounded rationality and, 138, 249, 257–60
causal ordering and, 257–8
correlation and, 257–8
on entrepreneurs, 258–9
evolutionism and, 337–8, 339
experimental economics and, 253
heuristics and, 258–9
life of, 257
on market, 259
on rationality, 253
Smith and, 259
theories of the firm and, 134, 136, 259
Simons, Henry, 180, 188, 196–7, 201–2
Sims, Christopher A., 230
Singer, Hans, 166
Singh, Ajit, 290
Skidelsky, Robert, 301–2
Smeedling, Tim, 230–1
Smith, Adam
generally, 5, 14, 15, 130, 155

Smith, Adam (cont.)
  on division of labour, 19–20, 135, 349
  on economics as science, 219
  income inequality and, 362
  'invisible hand' and, 130, 177, 192
  Jevons and, 27
  national accounting and, 223
  on natural prices, 14
  objectivism and, 15
  on population, 16, 19–20
  on rationality, 253, 257
  on Say's Law, 20
  on self-interest, 13, 21, 247, 354
  Simon and, 259
  spontaneous order and, 76
  Sraffa and, 88
  on surplus, 16
  on wages, 362
Smith, Vernon, 253–4
'Smithian' reconstruction, 314–16
Social capital, 360
Social choice and individual values (Arrow),
  125
Socializing investments, 285
Social limits to growth (Hirsch), 330–1
Social sustainability, 244
Social welfare function, 364, 367
Solidarity, 359–60
Solow, Robert
  generally, 7
  aggregate production function and, 305,
    306
  growth theory and, 121–2, 128–9, 147,
    162–4, 175–6
  Phillips curve and, 156
  theory of capital and, 303
Sonnenschein, Hugo, 125
Soskice, David, 345
Soviet Union
  collapse of, 319, 325–6
  economy in, 323–4
  Marxism in, 322, 323–4
Spann, Othmar, 63
Spaventa, Luigi, 290, 294, 305
Spencer, Herbert, 30, 336–7
Spontaneous order, 62, 76–8
Sraffa, Angelo, 90
Sraffa, Piero
  generally, 5–6, 9–10, 24, 26, 29, 32, 130,
    193, 194, 291, 303
  average period of production and, 107
  at Cambridge, 97–100, 289–90
  choice of techniques and, 107–8
  Circus and, 293
  on commodities, 104–5

on constant returns, 103–4, 106–7
critical edition of Ricardo, 88, 100–2,
  301–2
criticism of Marshall, 93–5, 96–7
on division of labour, 102–3
evolutionism and, 336
on exchange rates and prices, 84, 89–90
Friedman and, 130
Gramsci and, 88, 91–3, 98
growth theory and, 162
Hayek and, 61, 65, 69–71, 74, 80–1, 88,
  91, 100–1
imperfect competition and, 95–7
on inflation, 88–9
input-output tables and, 221
on interest, 195
Jevons and, 88
Keynes and, 70, 89–90, 91, 96, 97, 98,
  100, 116
Keynesian-Sraffian synthesis, 316–18
laws of returns and, 93–5
marginalist approach, criticism of, 106–8
Marshall and, 88
Marx and, 88, 106
Marxism and, 321–2, 326
Menger and, 88
on monetary policy, 90–1
on natural prices, 17–18
in New Cambridge school, 292–3, 294
overview, 108
price equations, 108–10
on profits, 104–6, 107–10
on representative firm, 95–7
returns to scale and, 103–4, 106–7
Ricardo and, 88, 102
Samuelson and, 128–9
short versus long period, 301
Smith and, 88
standard commodity and, 105
Stigler and, 130
theory of capital and, 303–8
on value, 103
on wages, 104–5
Walras and, 88
Wittgenstein and, 88, 98–100, 119
Sraffian schools
  generally, 292, 310
  'Marxian' reconstruction, 312–14
  'Ricardian' reconstruction, 310–12
  'Smithian' reconstruction, 314–16
Stability
  general equilibrium theory and, 127–9
  growth theory and, 160–1
  Hayek on, 117
  Mises on, 189

Samuelson on, 43
Schumpeter on, 43
Stigler on, 117, 131–2
Stabilizing an unstable economy (Minsky), 280
Stagflation, 271
Stalin, Josif, 323–5
Stalinism, 319, 323–4
Standard commodity, 105
Standard Oil Trust, 233–4
Static analysis, 43, 127–8, 153
Stato operaio (Tasca), 90–1
Steedman, Ian, 321–2
Steindl, Josef, 137, 295
Stern, Nicholas, 243
Stewart, Dugald, 155
Stigler, George
  generally, 126, 247
  Austrian school and, 132
  Chicago school and, 196, 197
  on 'invisible hand', 130, 177, 192
  life of, 131
  Mont Pèlerin Society and, 212–14
  price theory and, 130–1
  Sraffa and, 130
  on stability, 117, 131–2
Stiglitz, Joseph, 158, 198, 232
Stochastic analysis, 340–1
Stock exchanges, 19, 24, 151–2, 275
Stone, Richard, 222, 223, 225–6, 289
Strachey, Lytton, 48–9
Streeten, Paul, 170, 344–5
Structural change and economic growth (Pasinetti), 310
Studies in the development of capitalism (Dobb), 290
Stylized facts, 167–8, 169, 296–7
Sugden, Robert, 143, 262–3
Sunstein, Cass, 252, 263–4
Supply and demand in marginalist approach, 24, 25
Supply-side economics, 205–6
Sure-thing principle, 119
Surplus in classical approach, 15–16
Sustainable development, 242–3, 244
Swan, Trevor, 162
Swedish Academy of Sciences, 101–2
Swedish School, 31, 32–4
Sweezy, Paul, 325
Sylos Labini, Paolo
  generally, 41, 80–1, 182, 276, 283, 295
  aggregate production function and, 306
  econometrics and, 228, 297
  income inequality and, 362

on oligopoly, 96, 114–15, 136–7, 139, 240–1
on Phillips curve, 156
on profits, 315–16
'Smithian' reconstruction, 314–16
theory of distribution and, 317
Sympathy, 21, 208
Syrquin, Moshe, 170

Tabellini, Guido, 212
Tableau économique (Quesnay), 18, 220
Tarantelli, Ezio, 156, 372
Tarshis, Lorie, 54–5
Tasca, Angelo, 90–1
Tawney, Richard H., 40
Taxation, 82
Tax-based incomes policy (TIP), 150, 298
Taylor, Elisabeth, 65
Taylor, John B., 158
Taylorism, 340–1
Taylor's Rule, 207
Technical progress
  in agriculture, 239
  division of labour and, 18
  economic development theories and, 164–5
  growth theory and, 163–4
  Kaldor and, 297
  oligopoly and, 240–1
Technological change, 340–2
  generally, 321
  chaos theory and, 342
  economic geography and, 342
  Régulation school and, 341
  stochastic analysis and, 340–1
  systems of innovation and, 341
Temporary equilibrium, 71, 124
Thaler, Richard, 252, 263–4, 276
Thatcher, Margaret, 7–8, 215, 243, 271
Theories of surplus value (Marx), 321–2
The theory of business enterprise (Veblen), 35
Theory of capital (Hayek), 75
The theory of capitalist development (Sweezy), 325
Theory of economic development (Schumpeter), 44
Theory of games and economic behaviour (von Neumann and Morgenstern), 115
Theory of money and credit (Mises), 187
Theory of moral sentiments (Smith), 21
Theory of political economy (Jevons), 25
Theory of social economy (Cassel), 33
The theory of the leisure class (Veblen), 35
Thirlwall, Anthony, 160, 164, 302
Thomas Aquinas, 24

Thornton, Henry, 67
Thurstone, Louis L., 254
Tinbergen, Jan, 227–8
Tirole, Jean, 140, 237
Tobin, James, 151–2, 198, 274, 275
Tobin Tax, 151–2
de Tocqueville, Alexis, 179–80
Tonveronachi, Mario, 197, 302
Tractatus logico-philosophicus, 98
Tract on monetary reform (Keynes), 84, 89–90
Trade and markets in the early empires (Polanyi), 327
Trade cycle theory
    Hayek and, 45, 61, 66–71, 189
    Marx and, 46
    Mises and, 187, 189
    Schumpeter and, 45–6, 189
Tragedy of the commons, 334–5
Transaction costs
    neo-institutionalism and, 331–2, 333, 334
    theories of the firm and, 134
Treatise on money (Keynes), 53, 84, 89, 100, 293, 302
Treatise on probability (Keynes), 49, 52, 65, 71, 227–8, 280, 302
Treaty on the European Union (TEU), 185
Trow, Donald B., 258–9
Trump, Donald, 243
Tsuru, Shigeto, 35, 36, 41, 227, 329, 336
Tugan-Baranowskji, Mikhail, 294
Tullock, Gordon, 209
Turgot, Anne-Robert-Jacques, 346
Tversky, Amos, 9, 249, 253–4, 260–2

ul Haq, Mahbub, 231–2, 369
Uncertainty
    financial markets and, 280
    index of, 232
    Keynes on, 50–1, 52–4, 277–8
    Knight on, 50–1, 116, 277, 302
    risk versus, 50–1, 116, 277–8, 302
Unemployment
    fiscal policy and, 155, 271
    Friedman on, 155
    inflation, relation to, 155–7
    Keynes on, 55–6, 196
    Marx on, 155
    monetary policy and, 55–6, 150, 155, 271
    neoclassical synthesis and, 150
    non-accelerating inflation rate of unemployment (NAIRU), 156–7
    Phillips curve and, 155–7

United Nations
    generally, 165
    Center on Transnational Corporations (UNCTC), 166–7, 214
    Conference on Trade and Development (UNCTAD), 166–7
    Development Programme (UNDP), 231–2, 369, 371
    national accounting and, 223
    World Commission on Environment and Development, 242–3
United States
    Airline Deregulation Act, 234–5
    Civil Aeronautics Board, 236
    convertibility of gold in, 270
    Federal Reserve Bank, 219
    Federal Reserve Board, 271–2, 276
    health care in, 346–7
    Justice Department, 235
    McCarthyism, 320
    pensions in, 346–7
    shift of centre of economics to, 113
University of Chicago, 291, 332. *See also Chicago school*
University of Michigan, 252–3
University of Pennsylvania, 291
Utilitarianism
    generally, 350
    act utilitarianism, 357–8
    altruism and, 360
    Bentham and, 352–3, 354, 357, 358–9
    evaluation of choices versus evaluation of consequences, 353
    felicific calculus and, 352–3, 354
    game theory and, 142
    happiness versus, 358–9
    homo oeconomicus and, 127, 359
    incomplete evaluations, 358
    irrational preferences and, 356–7
    Jevons and, 355, 358–9
    'joyless economy' and, 359
    marginalist approach and, 355
    Mill and, 354–5, 356, 357, 358
    Morgenstern and, 355–6, 358
    Pareto and, 355
    post-utilitarianism, 6–7
    a priori elements, 358
    rule utilitarianism, 357–8
    self-interest and, 354
    Sen and, 353, 356, 357
    social capital and, 360
    solidarity and, 359–60
    utility and, 356
    von Neumann and, 355–6, 358

Utilitarianism and beyond (Sen and Williams, eds.), 356
Utilitarianism (Mill), 22
Utility
    expected utility theory, 115–19 (*See also Expected utility theory*)
    scarcity and, 24, 25
    utilitarianism and, 356

Value, capital and rent (Wicksell), 33
Value, theory of
    Böhm-Bawerk and, 194–5
    labour theory of value (*See Labour theory of value*)
    Marx and, 8–9
Value and capital (Hicks), 27, 192–3
van Ark, Bart, 231
van Horn, Robert, 213
Vaughn, Karen, 70
Veblen, Thorstein
    generally, 5, 13, 31
    Chicago school and, 196–7
    conspicuous consumption and, 35–6
    evolutionism and, 335
    institutionalism and, 35–7, 320, 330–1
    on leisure, 35–6
Velocity of circulation, 171–3, 201, 266–7
Velupillai, Vela, 253
Verdoorn, Petrus Johannes, 297
Verdoorn's Law, 163–4, 169, 297
Verein für Socialpolitik, 37
Veritas Foundation, 178
Verri, Pietro, 359
Verticalists, 298
Vicarelli, Fausto, 302, 313
Vickrey, William S., 237–8
Vickrey Rule, 237–8
Vietnam War, 270
Viner, Jacob, 29, 30, 40, 50–1, 120, 129–30, 196–7
Volcker, Paul, 271–2
Volker Fund, 187, 197, 214
Voltaire, 354
Volterra, Vito, 290
von Neumann, John
    generally, 7, 193, 221
    behavioural economics and, 250–1
    development economics and, 343–4
    expected utility theory and, 115–19, 247, 248
    experimental economics and, 252–3
    game theory and, 140–1
    general equilibrium theory and, 125
    on rationality, 257
    utilitarianism and, 355–6, 358

Wages
    Friedman on, 202
    growth theory and, 161–2
    Hayek on, 73–5
    Keynes on, 55
    in neoclassical synthesis, 150, 158–9
    Phillips curve and, 155–7, 271
    Smith on, 362
    Sraffa on, 104–5
    theory of distribution and, 308–10
Wagner, Adolph, 168
Wagner's Law, 168
Wallerstein, Immanuel, 328–9
Wallich, Henry, 150, 298
Wallis, W. Allen, 254
Walras, Léon
    generally, 5, 14, 73, 97–8
    general equilibrium theory and, 119–25, 305
    marginalist approach and, 24, 25, 27–8
    on natural prices, 17
    quantitative view of economics and, 219
    Sraffa and, 88
Washington Consensus, 180, 185–6, 214, 215–17
Watson, Alister, 100
Wealth
    classical approach, wealth of nations in, 18, 19–20
    Keynes on, 53–4
    in neoclassical synthesis, 148–9, 150–1
The wealth of ideas (Roncaglia), 10
The wealth of nations (Smith), 14, 21
Webb, Beatrice, 64–5, 322–3
Webb, Sidney, 64–5, 322–3
Weber, Max
    generally, 4, 5, 13, 31, 63–4
    on capitalism, 39–40
    development economics and, 343
    ideal types and, 167–8
    institutionalism and, 320
    Marx and, 39, 40
    methodology and, 38–9
    politics and, 40–1
    Schumpeter and, 46, 47
    sociology and, 40
    theory and history and, 37–41
Weintraub, Roy, 153
Weintraub, Sidney, 9–10, 150, 298, 330
Welfare economics, 363–7
    generally, 351
    Arrow and, 364, 366–7
    compensation principle and, 366
    externalities and, 365–6
    general equilibrium theory and, 363, 364

Welfare economics (cont.)
  Kaldor and, 366
  Pareto optimum, 364, 366
  Pigou and, 363, 365
  Samuelson and, 364, 365
  Sen and, 367
  social welfare function, 364,
    367
Welfare state, 183–4, 346
WhatsApp, 235
Wicksell, Knut
  generally, 5, 13, 31, 74, 210
  on banking, 277
  equilibrium and, 73
  forced savings and, 67
  Hayek and, 67, 69, 73
  on interest, 34
  Keynes and, 34–5
  Swedish school and, 32–4
  theory of capital and, 61, 304
  theory of distribution, 33
Wicksteed, Philip, 323
von Wieser, Friedrich, 64
Williams, Bernard, 356
Williamson, John, 215–16
Williamson, Oliver, 333–4

Willig, Robert D., 140
Windows, 235
Winter, Sidney, 138, 259, 339–40
Wisconsin School, 36
Wittgenstein, Ludwig
  generally, 51–2, 66, 99, 124–5
  at Cambridge, 97–100
  on probability, 116
  Sraffa and, 88, 98–100, 119
Wood, Adrian, 137
Woodward, Susan, 333
Woolf, Virginia, 48–9
Works and correspondence of David Ricardo
    (Sraffa, ed.), 101–2, 105
World Bank, 56, 165, 170, 215, 216, 231,
    271, 371
Worswick, G.D.N., 228–9
von Wright, Georg Henrik, 99

X-inefficiency, 136

Yale University, 291
Yang, Maw Cheng, 240
Young, Allyn, 94

Zamagni, Stefano, 359